# FoxTrot

## Assembled with Care

## Other FoxTrot Books by Bill Amend

FoxTrot
Pass the Loot
Black Bart Says Draw
Eight Yards, Down and Out
Bury My Heart at Fun-Fun Mountain
Say Hello to Cactus Flats
May the Force Be with Us, Please
Take Us to Your Mall
The Return of the Lone Iguana
At Least This Place Sells T-shirts
Come Closer, Roger, There's a Mosquito on Your Nose
Welcome to Jasorassic Park
I'm Flying, Jack . . . I Mean, Roger
Think iFruity
Death by Field Trip
Encyclopedias Brown and White
His Code Name Was The Fox

Anthologies

FoxTrot: The Works
FoxTrot *en masse*
Enormously FoxTrot
Wildly FoxTrot
FoxTrot Beyond a Doubt
Camp FoxTrot
Assorted FoxTrot

# FoxTrot

## Assembled with Care

## by Bill Amend

**Andrews McMeel
Publishing**

Kansas City

**FoxTrot** is distributed internationally by Universal Press Syndicate.

05 06  BAM  10 9 8 7 6 5 4

ISBN 13: 978-0-7407-2664-4
ISBN 10: 0-7407-2664-1

Library of Congress Control Number: 2002102327

**To my real family.**

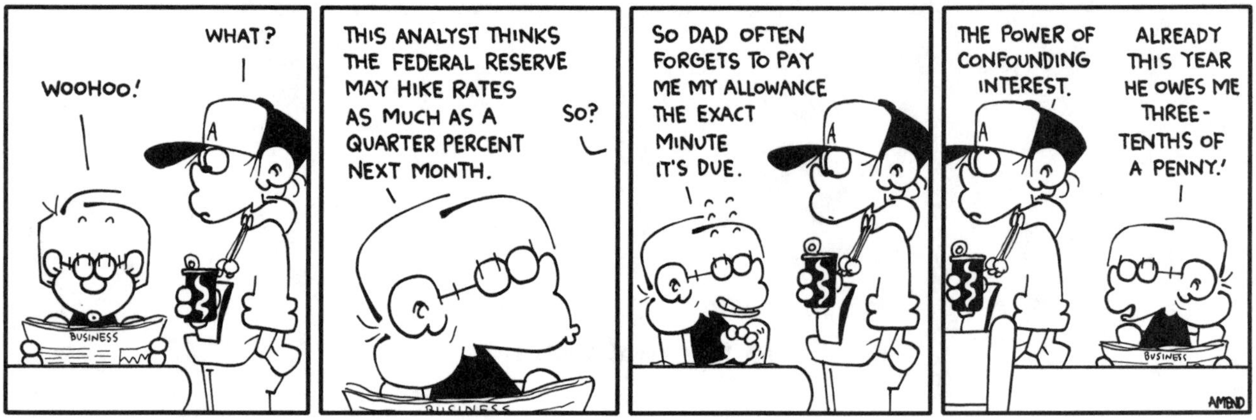
WOOHOO!
WHAT?
THIS ANALYST THINKS THE FEDERAL RESERVE MAY HIKE RATES AS MUCH AS A QUARTER PERCENT NEXT MONTH.
SO?
SO DAD OFTEN FORGETS TO PAY ME MY ALLOWANCE THE EXACT MINUTE IT'S DUE.
THE POWER OF CONFOUNDING INTEREST.
ALREADY THIS YEAR HE OWES ME THREE-TENTHS OF A PENNY!
BUSINESS
AMEND

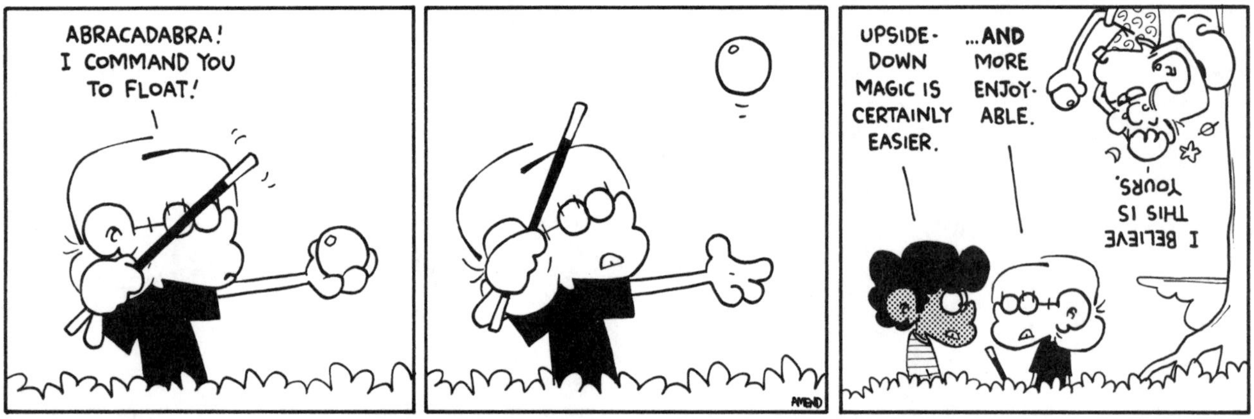
ABRACADABRA! I COMMAND YOU TO FLOAT!
UPSIDE-DOWN MAGIC IS CERTAINLY EASIER.
...AND MORE ENJOY-ABLE.
I BELIEVE THIS IS YOURS.
AMEND

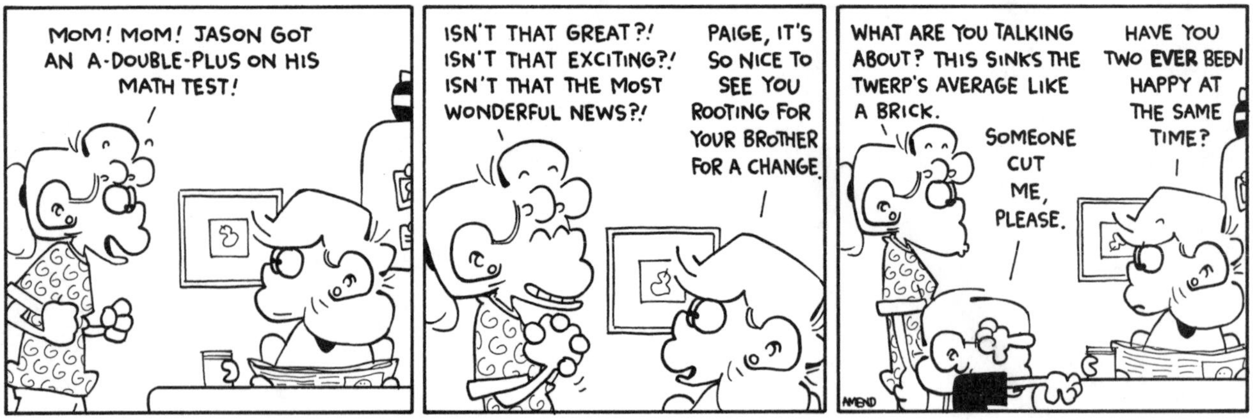
MOM! MOM! JASON GOT AN A-DOUBLE-PLUS ON HIS MATH TEST!
ISN'T THAT GREAT?! ISN'T THAT EXCITING?! ISN'T THAT THE MOST WONDERFUL NEWS?!
PAIGE, IT'S SO NICE TO SEE YOU ROOTING FOR YOUR BROTHER FOR A CHANGE.
WHAT ARE YOU TALKING ABOUT? THIS SINKS THE TWERP'S AVERAGE LIKE A BRICK.
SOMEONE CUT ME, PLEASE.
HAVE YOU TWO EVER BEEN HAPPY AT THE SAME TIME?
AMEND

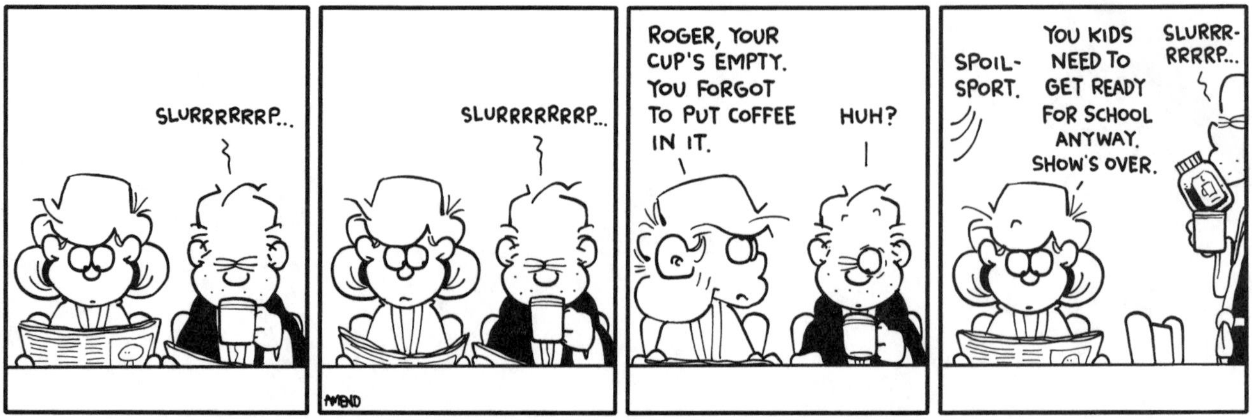
SLURRRRRRP...
SLURRRRRRRP...
ROGER, YOUR CUP'S EMPTY. YOU FORGOT TO PUT COFFEE IN IT.
HUH?
SPOIL-SPORT.
YOU KIDS NEED TO GET READY FOR SCHOOL ANYWAY. SHOW'S OVER.
SLURRR-RRRRP...
AMEND

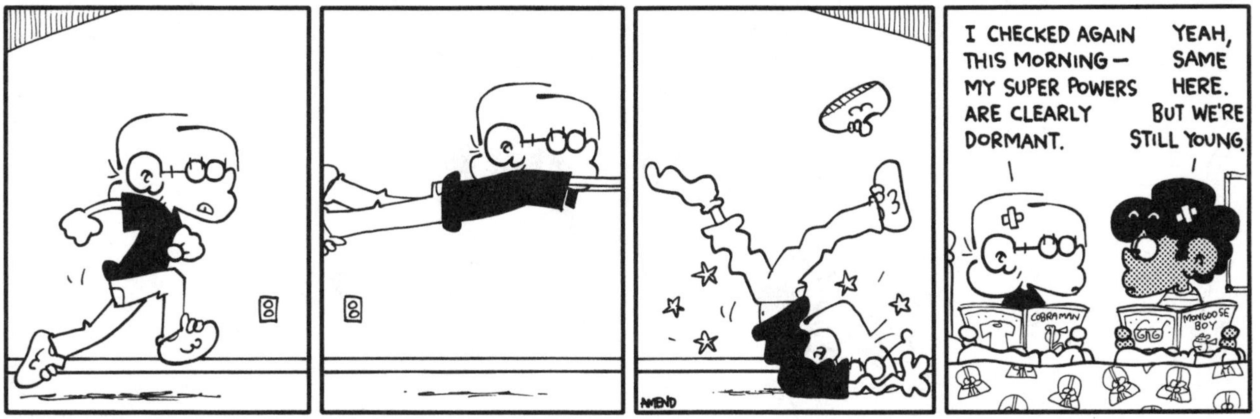
I CHECKED AGAIN THIS MORNING — MY SUPER POWERS ARE CLEARLY DORMANT.
YEAH, SAME HERE. BUT WE'RE STILL YOUNG.
COBRAMAN
MONGOOSE BOY
AMEND

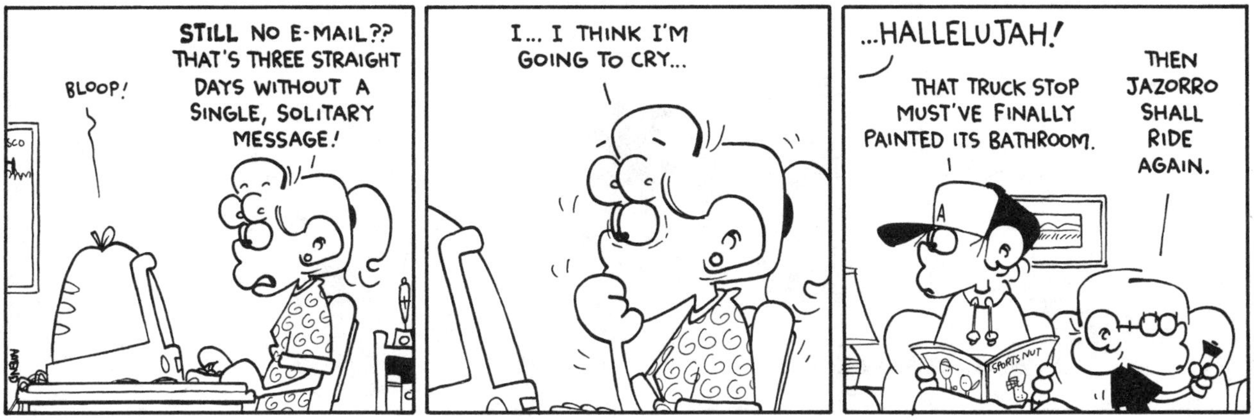
BLOOP!
STILL NO E-MAIL?? THAT'S THREE STRAIGHT DAYS WITHOUT A SINGLE, SOLITARY MESSAGE!
I... I THINK I'M GOING TO CRY...
...HALLELUJAH!
THAT TRUCK STOP MUST'VE FINALLY PAINTED ITS BATHROOM.
THEN JAZORRO SHALL RIDE AGAIN.
SPORTS NUT

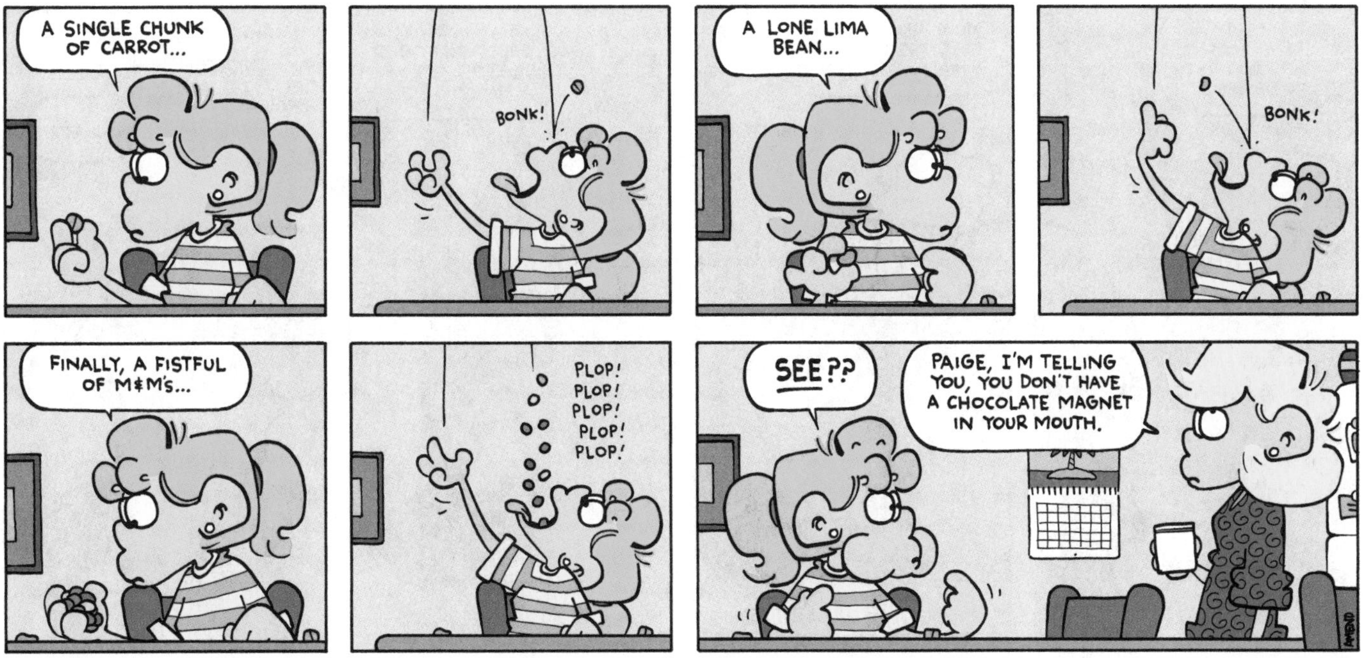
A SINGLE CHUNK OF CARROT...
BONK!
A LONE LIMA BEAN...
BONK!
FINALLY, A FISTFUL OF M&M's...
PLOP! PLOP! PLOP! PLOP! PLOP!
SEE??
PAIGE, I'M TELLING YOU, YOU DON'T HAVE A CHOCOLATE MAGNET IN YOUR MOUTH.
AMEND

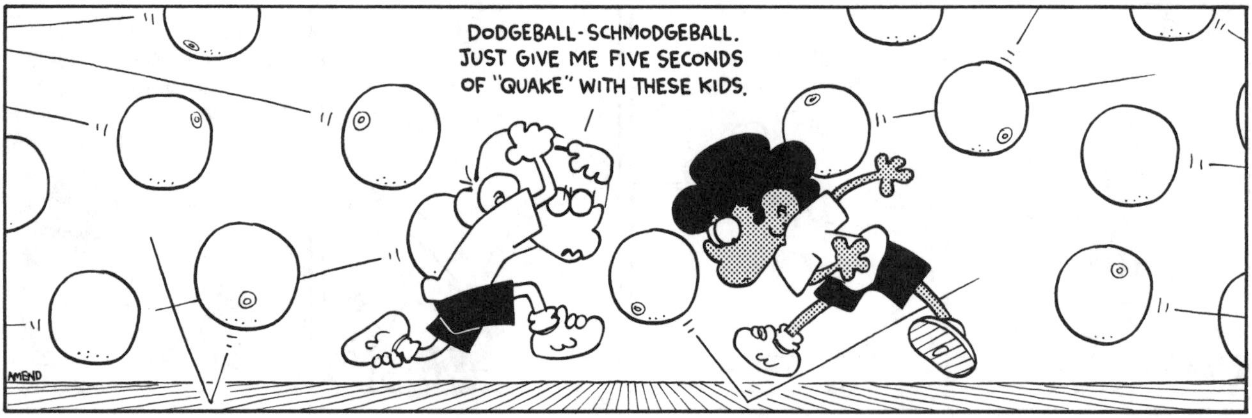
DODGEBALL-SCHMODGEBALL. JUST GIVE ME FIVE SECONDS OF "QUAKE" WITH THESE KIDS.
AMEND

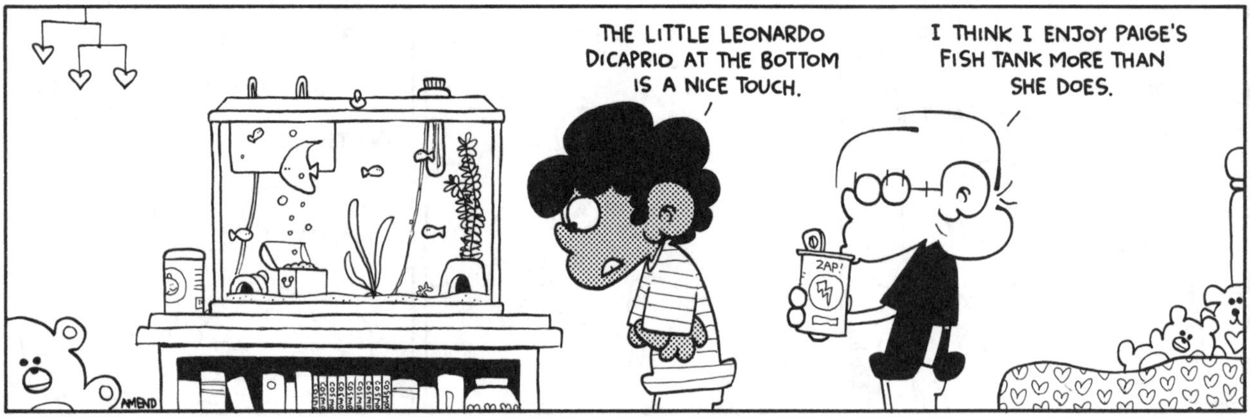
THE LITTLE LEONARDO DICAPRIO AT THE BOTTOM IS A NICE TOUCH.
I THINK I ENJOY PAIGE'S FISH TANK MORE THAN SHE DOES.
ZAP!
AMEND

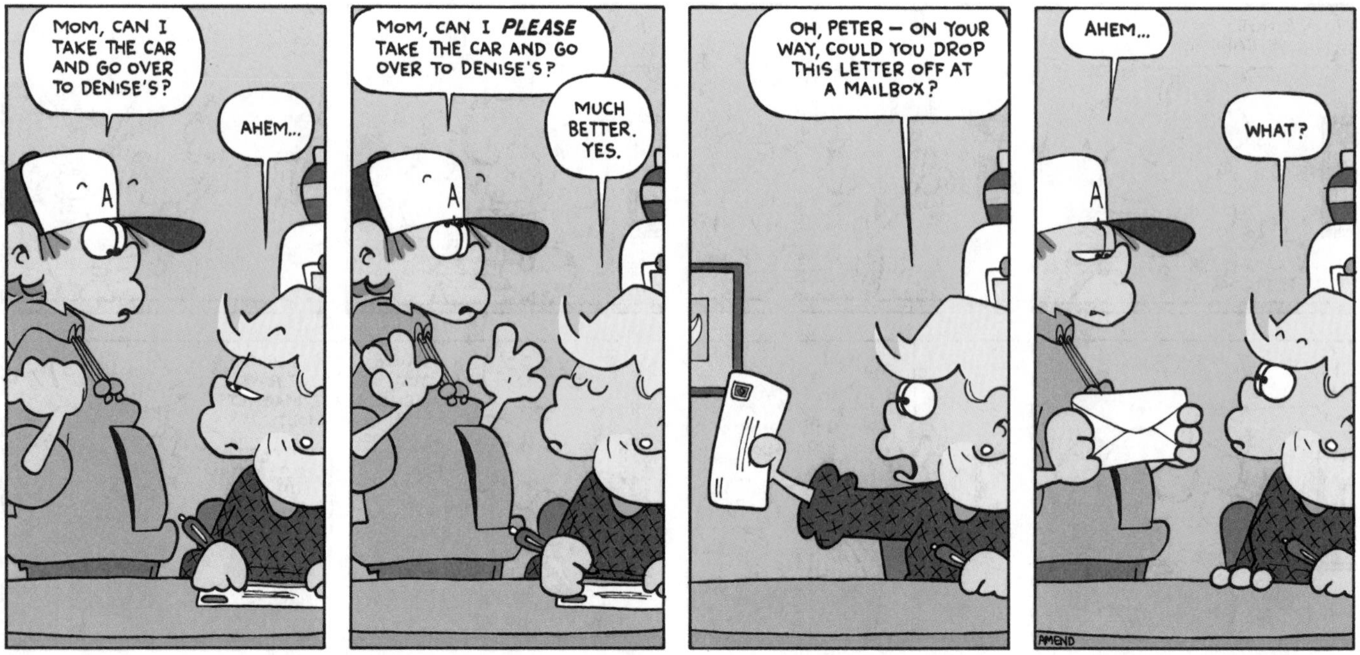
MOM, CAN I TAKE THE CAR AND GO OVER TO DENISE'S?
AHEM...
MOM, CAN I *PLEASE* TAKE THE CAR AND GO OVER TO DENISE'S?
MUCH BETTER. YES.
OH, PETER – ON YOUR WAY, COULD YOU DROP THIS LETTER OFF AT A MAILBOX?
AHEM...
WHAT?
AMEND

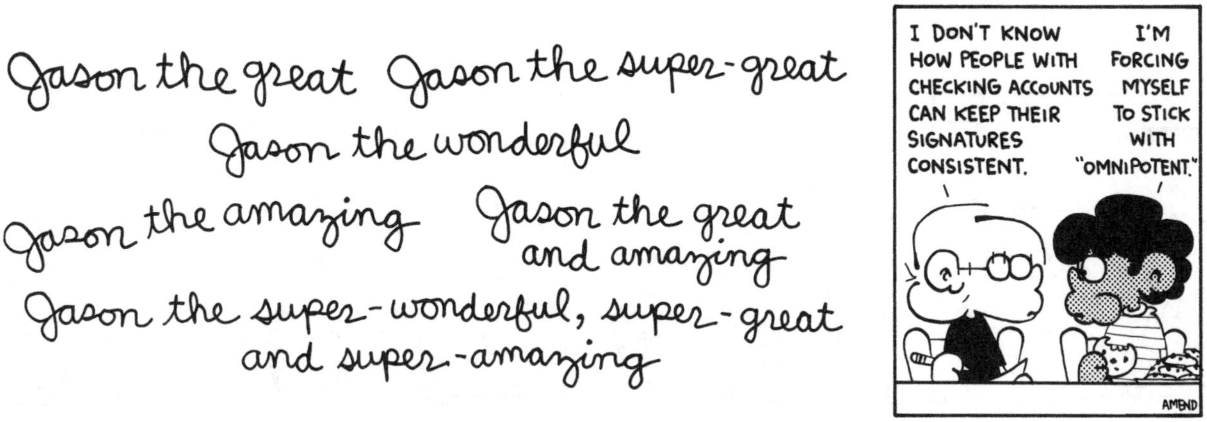
Jason the great Jason the super-great
Jason the wonderful
Jason the amazing Jason the great and amazing
Jason the super-wonderful, super-great and super-amazing
I DON'T KNOW HOW PEOPLE WITH CHECKING ACCOUNTS CAN KEEP THEIR SIGNATURES CONSISTENT.
I'M FORCING MYSELF TO STICK WITH "OMNIPOTENT."
AMEND

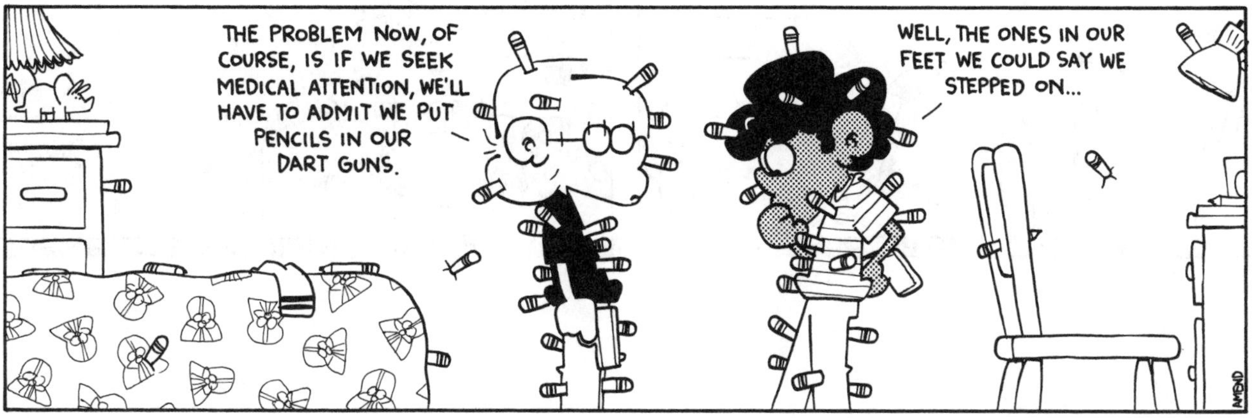
THE PROBLEM NOW, OF COURSE, IS IF WE SEEK MEDICAL ATTENTION, WE'LL HAVE TO ADMIT WE PUT PENCILS IN OUR DART GUNS.
WELL, THE ONES IN OUR FEET WE COULD SAY WE STEPPED ON...
AMEND

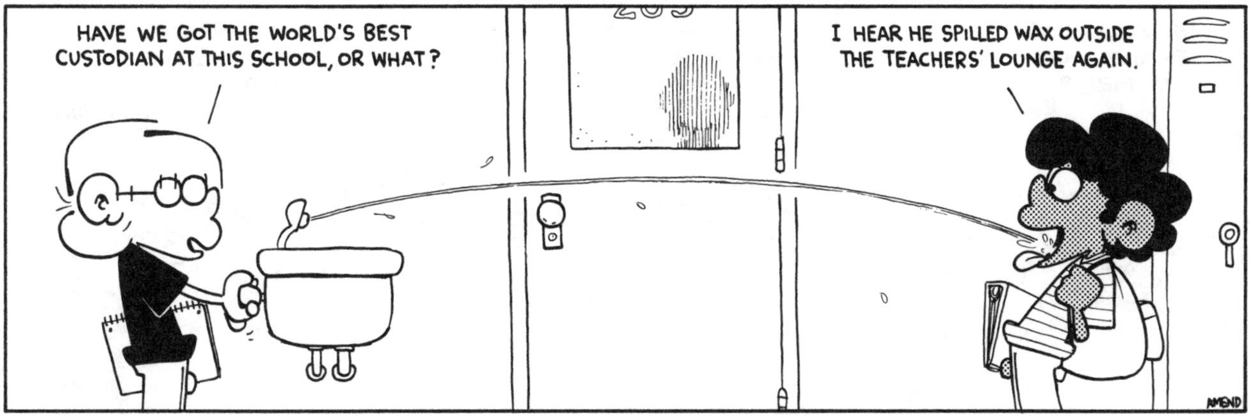
HAVE WE GOT THE WORLD'S BEST CUSTODIAN AT THIS SCHOOL, OR WHAT?
I HEAR HE SPILLED WAX OUTSIDE THE TEACHERS' LOUNGE AGAIN.
AMEND

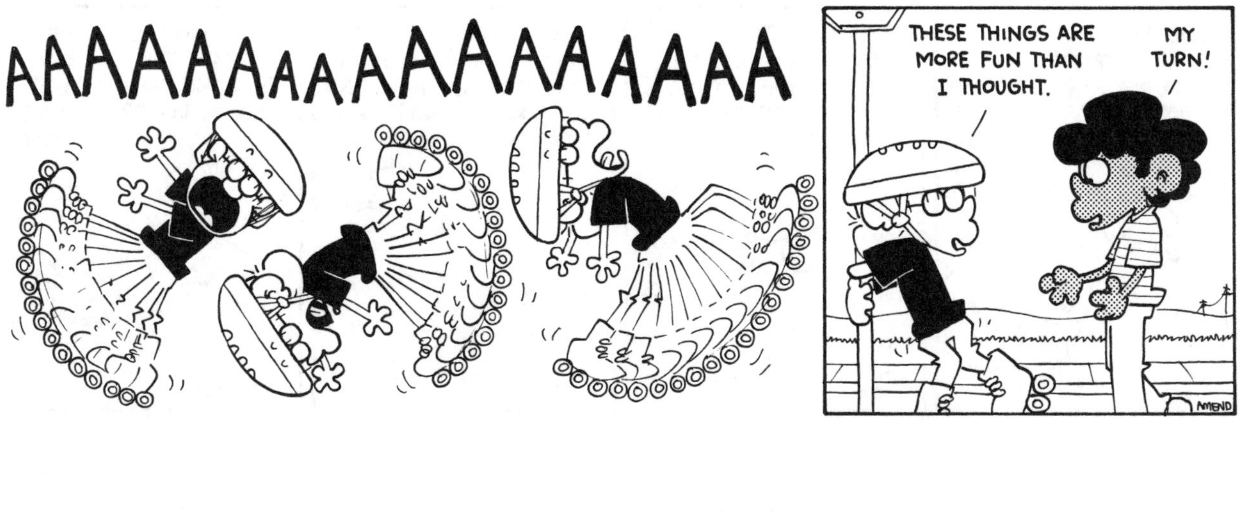
AAAAAAAAAAAAAAAAA
THESE THINGS ARE MORE FUN THAN I THOUGHT.
MY TURN!
AMEND

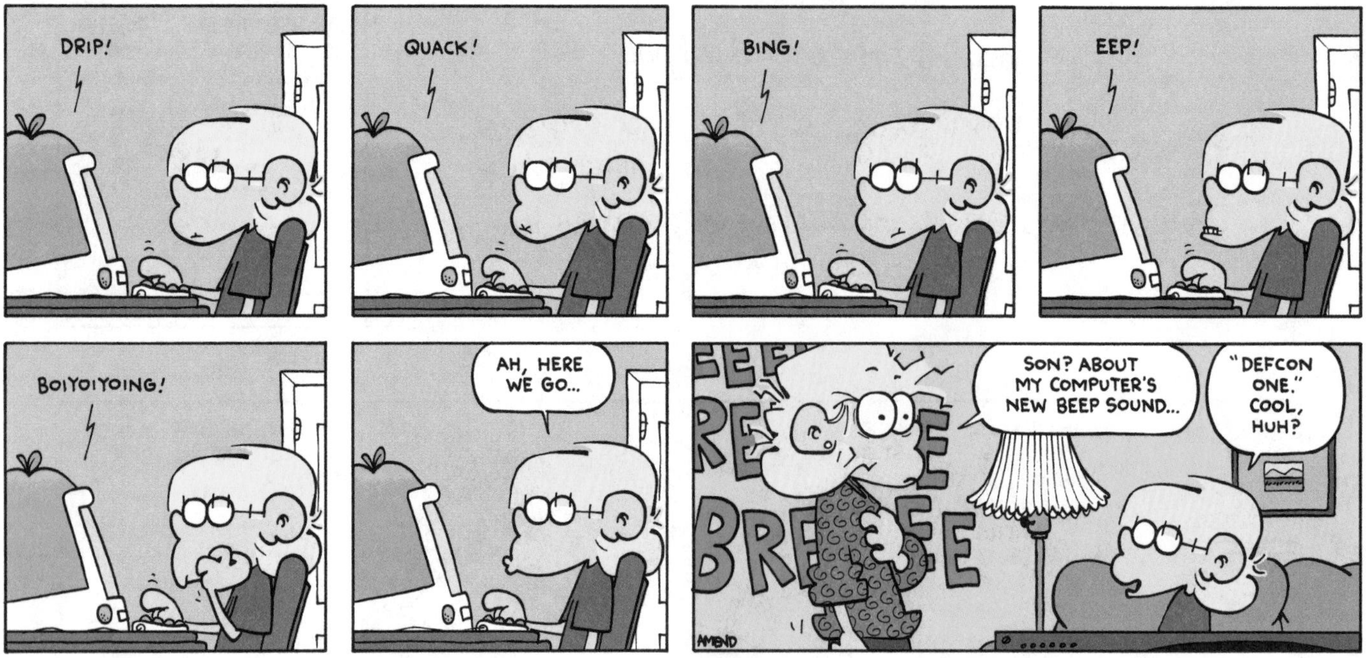
DRIP!
QUACK!
BING!
EEP!
BOIYOIYOING!
AH, HERE WE GO...
SON? ABOUT MY COMPUTER'S NEW BEEP SOUND...
"DEFCON ONE." COOL, HUH?
AMEND

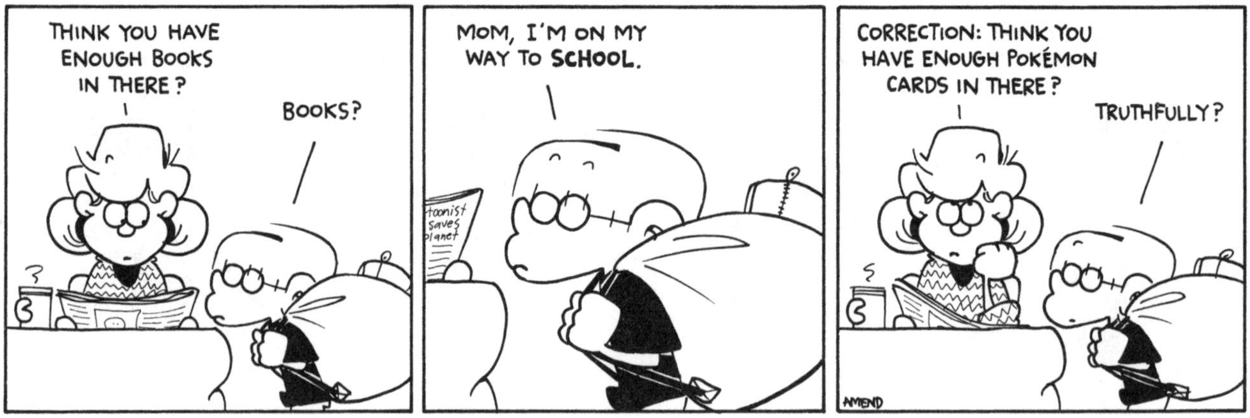
THINK YOU HAVE ENOUGH BOOKS IN THERE?
BOOKS?
MOM, I'M ON MY WAY TO SCHOOL.
CORRECTION: THINK YOU HAVE ENOUGH POKÉMON CARDS IN THERE?
TRUTHFULLY?
AMEND

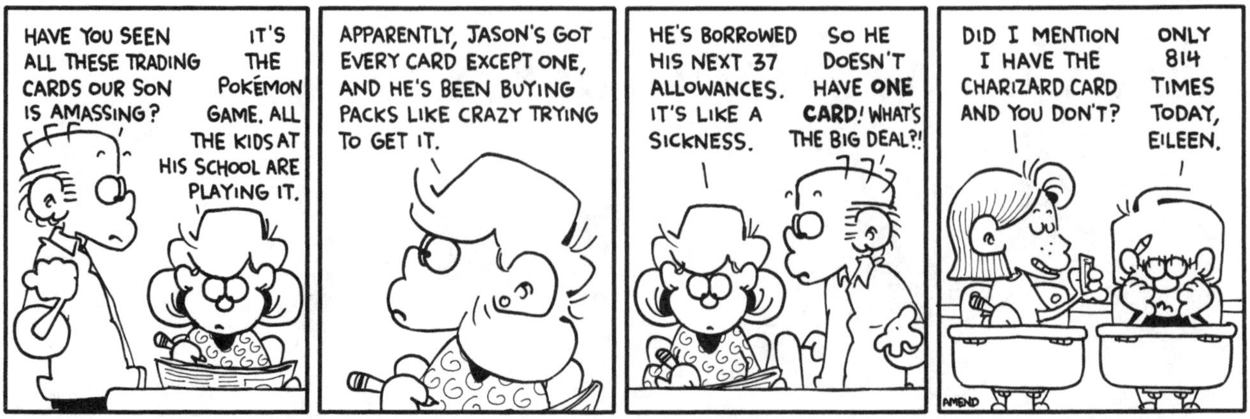
HAVE YOU SEEN ALL THESE TRADING CARDS OUR SON IS AMASSING?
IT'S THE POKÉMON GAME. ALL THE KIDS AT HIS SCHOOL ARE PLAYING IT.
APPARENTLY, JASON'S GOT EVERY CARD EXCEPT ONE, AND HE'S BEEN BUYING PACKS LIKE CRAZY TRYING TO GET IT.
HE'S BORROWED HIS NEXT 37 ALLOWANCES. IT'S LIKE A SICKNESS.
SO HE DOESN'T HAVE ONE CARD! WHAT'S THE BIG DEAL?!
DID I MENTION I HAVE THE CHARIZARD CARD AND YOU DON'T?
ONLY 814 TIMES TODAY, EILEEN.
AMEND

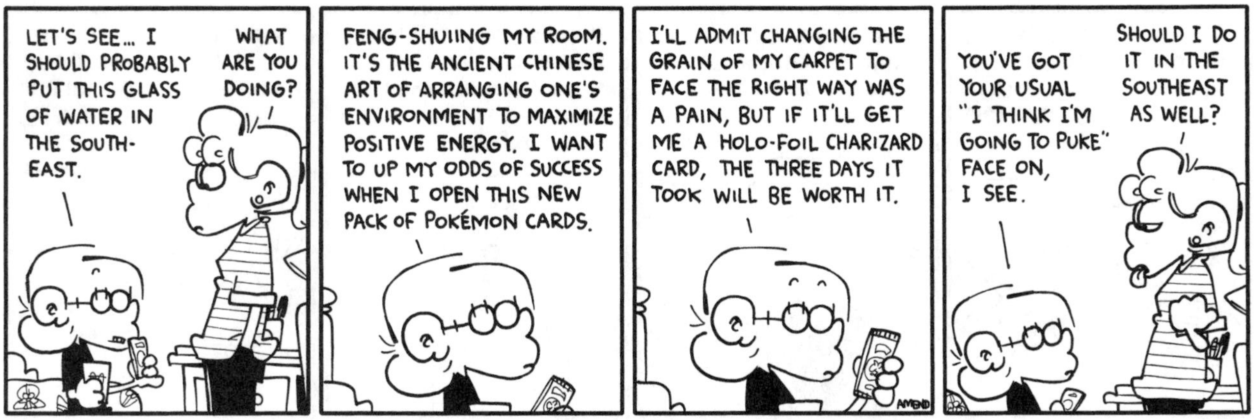
LET'S SEE... I SHOULD PROBABLY PUT THIS GLASS OF WATER IN THE SOUTH-EAST.
WHAT ARE YOU DOING?
FENG-SHUIING MY ROOM. IT'S THE ANCIENT CHINESE ART OF ARRANGING ONE'S ENVIRONMENT TO MAXIMIZE POSITIVE ENERGY. I WANT TO UP MY ODDS OF SUCCESS WHEN I OPEN THIS NEW PACK OF POKÉMON CARDS.
I'LL ADMIT CHANGING THE GRAIN OF MY CARPET TO FACE THE RIGHT WAY WAS A PAIN, BUT IF IT'LL GET ME A HOLO-FOIL CHARIZARD CARD, THE THREE DAYS IT TOOK WILL BE WORTH IT.
AMEND
YOU'VE GOT YOUR USUAL "I THINK I'M GOING TO PUKE" FACE ON, I SEE.
SHOULD I DO IT IN THE SOUTHEAST AS WELL?

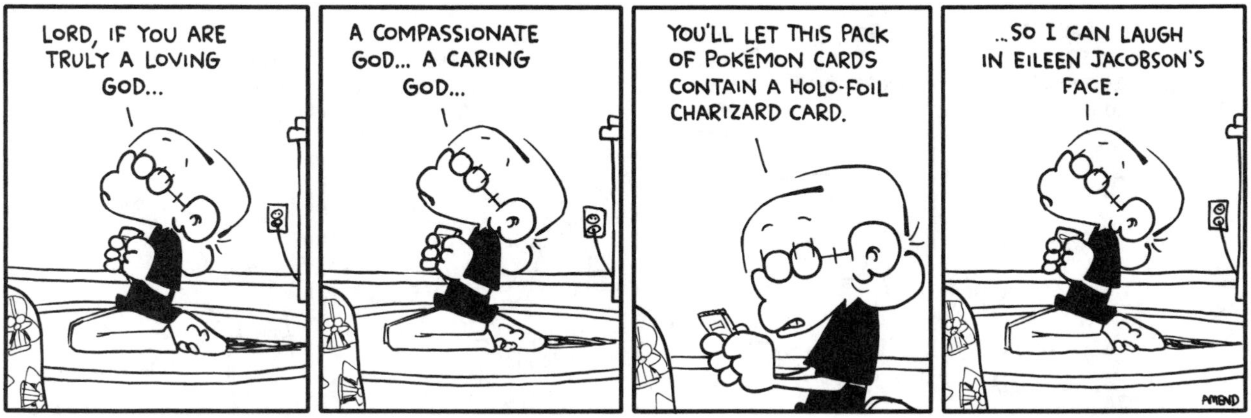
LORD, IF YOU ARE TRULY A LOVING GOD...
A COMPASSIONATE GOD... A CARING GOD...
YOU'LL LET THIS PACK OF POKÉMON CARDS CONTAIN A HOLO-FOIL CHARIZARD CARD.
...SO I CAN LAUGH IN EILEEN JACOBSON'S FACE.
AMEND

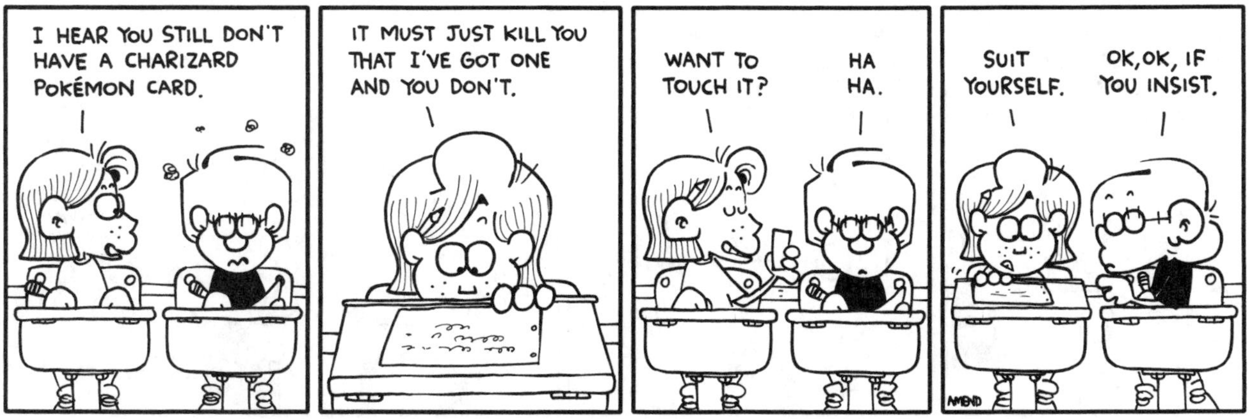
I HEAR YOU STILL DON'T HAVE A CHARIZARD POKÉMON CARD.
IT MUST JUST KILL YOU THAT I'VE GOT ONE AND YOU DON'T.
WANT TO TOUCH IT?
HA HA.
SUIT YOURSELF.
OK, OK, IF YOU INSIST.
AMEND

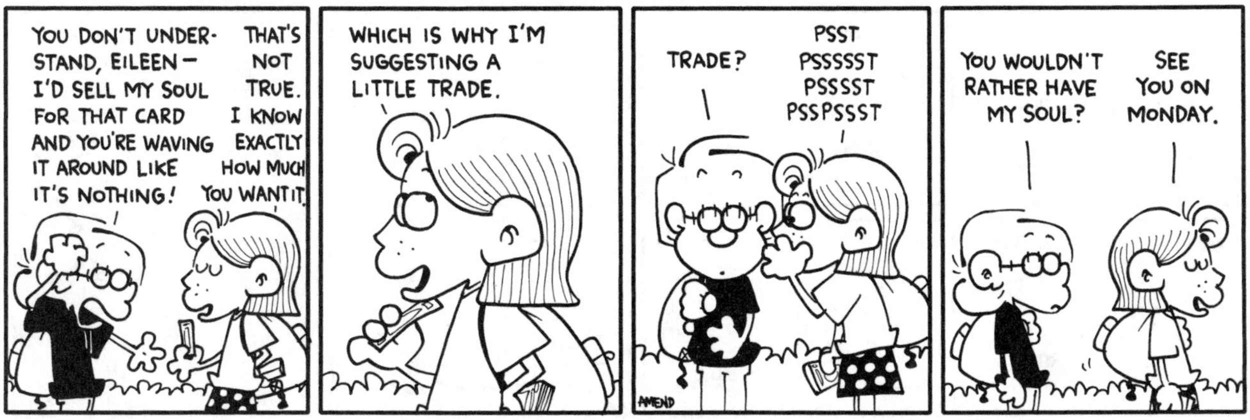
YOU DON'T UNDER-STAND, EILEEN — I'D SELL MY SOUL FOR THAT CARD AND YOU'RE WAVING IT AROUND LIKE IT'S NOTHING!
THAT'S NOT TRUE. I KNOW EXACTLY HOW MUCH YOU WANT IT.
WHICH IS WHY I'M SUGGESTING A LITTLE TRADE.
TRADE?
PSST PSSSSST PSSSST PSSPSSST
AMEND
YOU WOULDN'T RATHER HAVE MY SOUL?
SEE YOU ON MONDAY.

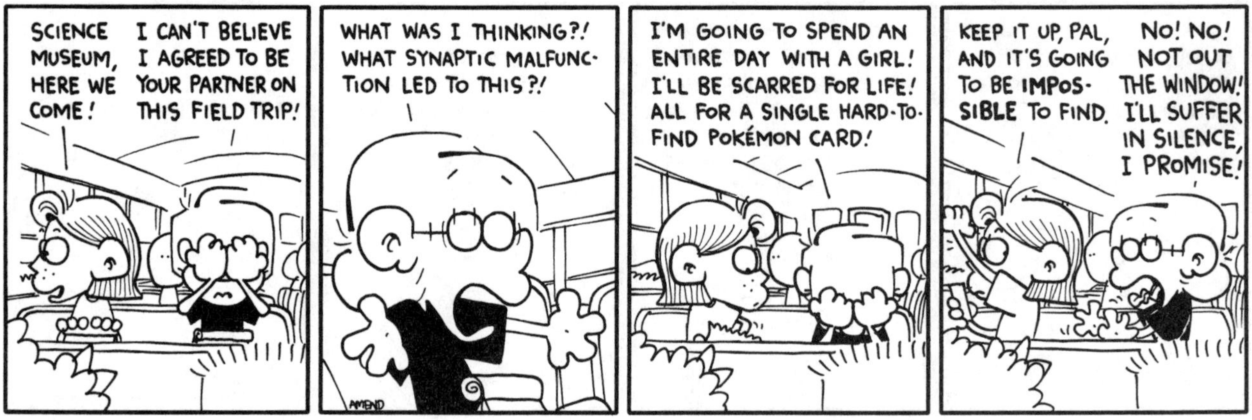
SCIENCE MUSEUM, HERE WE COME!
I CAN'T BELIEVE I AGREED TO BE YOUR PARTNER ON THIS FIELD TRIP!
WHAT WAS I THINKING?! WHAT SYNAPTIC MALFUNCTION LED TO THIS?!
AMEND
I'M GOING TO SPEND AN ENTIRE DAY WITH A GIRL! I'LL BE SCARRED FOR LIFE! ALL FOR A SINGLE HARD-TO-FIND POKÉMON CARD!
KEEP IT UP, PAL, AND IT'S GOING TO BE IMPOSSIBLE TO FIND.
NO! NO! NOT OUT THE WINDOW! I'LL SUFFER IN SILENCE, I PROMISE!

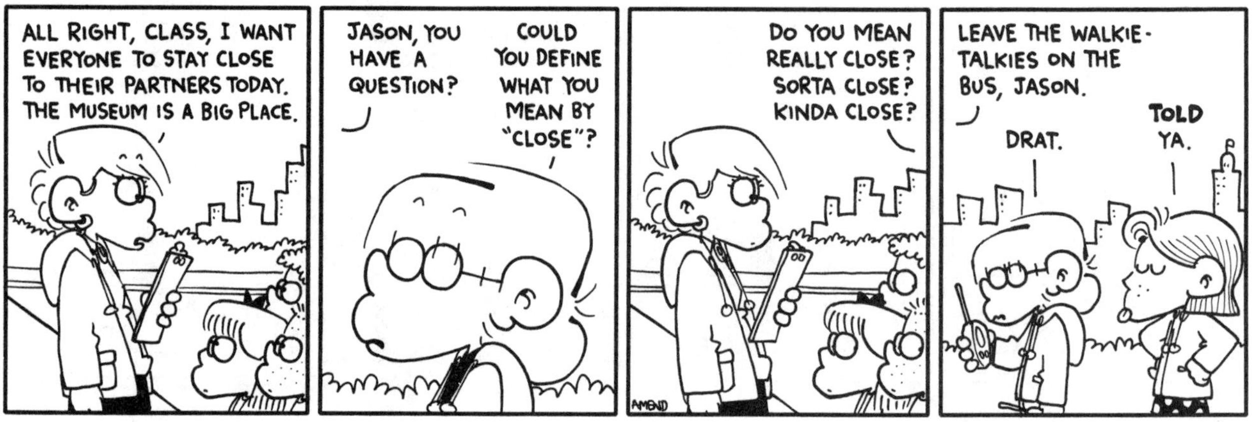
ALL RIGHT, CLASS, I WANT EVERYONE TO STAY CLOSE TO THEIR PARTNERS TODAY. THE MUSEUM IS A BIG PLACE.
JASON, YOU HAVE A QUESTION?
COULD YOU DEFINE WHAT YOU MEAN BY "CLOSE"?
DO YOU MEAN REALLY CLOSE? SORTA CLOSE? KINDA CLOSE?
AMEND
LEAVE THE WALKIE-TALKIES ON THE BUS, JASON.
DRAT.
TOLD YA.

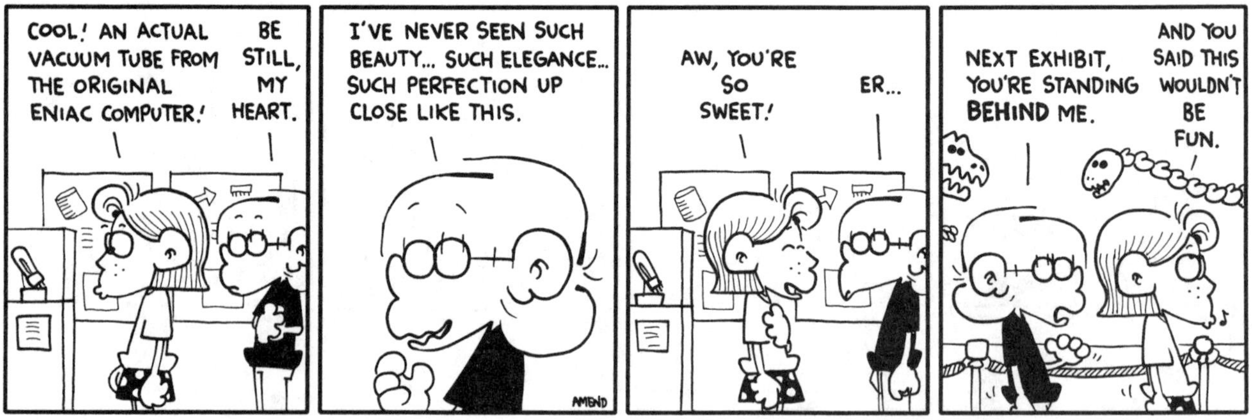
COOL! AN ACTUAL VACUUM TUBE FROM THE ORIGINAL ENIAC COMPUTER!
BE STILL, MY HEART.
I'VE NEVER SEEN SUCH BEAUTY... SUCH ELEGANCE... SUCH PERFECTION UP CLOSE LIKE THIS.
AMEND
AW, YOU'RE SO SWEET!
ER...
NEXT EXHIBIT, YOU'RE STANDING BEHIND ME.
AND YOU SAID THIS WOULDN'T BE FUN.

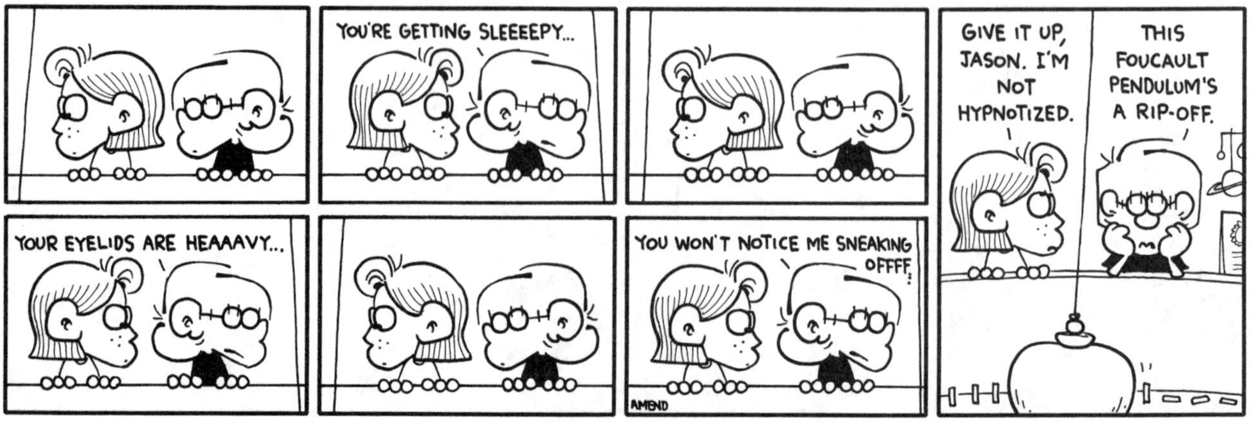
YOU'RE GETTING SLEEEEPY...
YOUR EYELIDS ARE HEAAAVY...
YOU WON'T NOTICE ME SNEAKING OFFFF!
AMEND
GIVE IT UP, JASON. I'M NOT HYPNOTIZED.
THIS FOUCAULT PENDULUM'S A RIP-OFF.

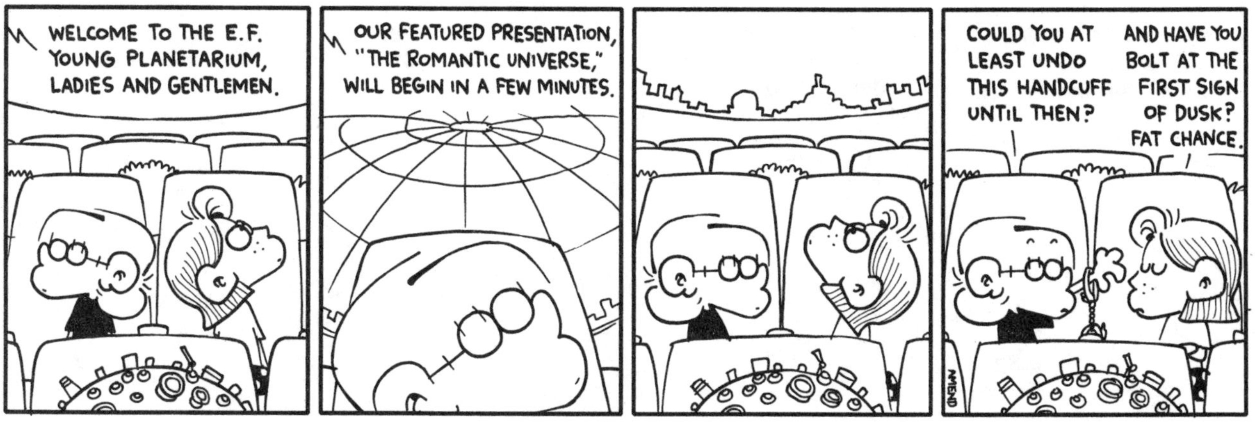
WELCOME TO THE E.F. YOUNG PLANETARIUM, LADIES AND GENTLEMEN.
OUR FEATURED PRESENTATION, "THE ROMANTIC UNIVERSE," WILL BEGIN IN A FEW MINUTES.
COULD YOU AT LEAST UNDO THIS HANDCUFF UNTIL THEN?
AND HAVE YOU BOLT AT THE FIRST SIGN OF DUSK? FAT CHANCE.
AMEND

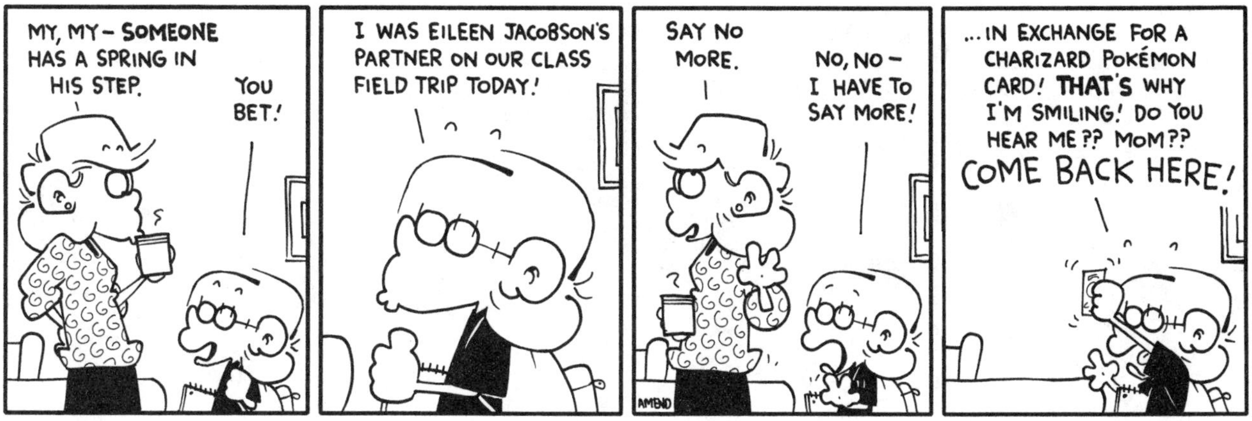
MY, MY – SOMEONE HAS A SPRING IN HIS STEP.
YOU BET!
I WAS EILEEN JACOBSON'S PARTNER ON OUR CLASS FIELD TRIP TODAY!
SAY NO MORE.
NO, NO – I HAVE TO SAY MORE!
AMEND
...IN EXCHANGE FOR A CHARIZARD POKÉMON CARD! THAT'S WHY I'M SMILING! DO YOU HEAR ME?? MOM??
COME BACK HERE!

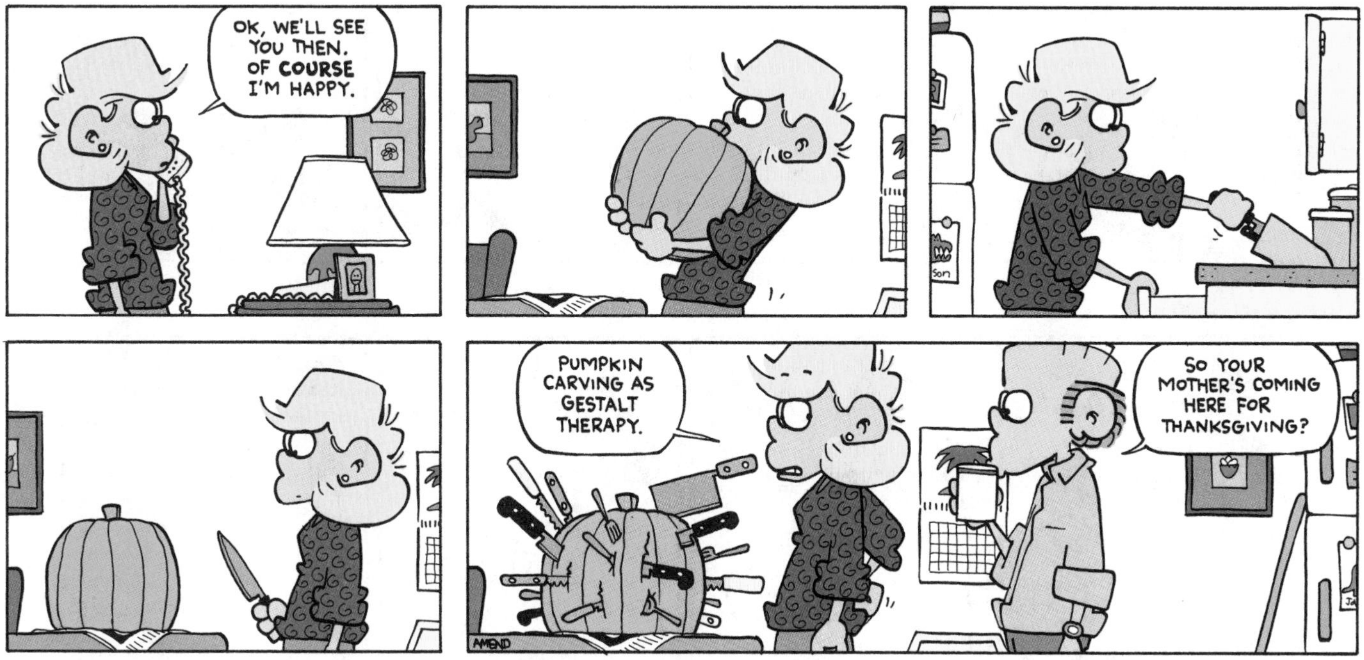
OK, WE'LL SEE YOU THEN. OF COURSE I'M HAPPY.
PUMPKIN CARVING AS GESTALT THERAPY.
SO YOUR MOTHER'S COMING HERE FOR THANKSGIVING?
AMEND

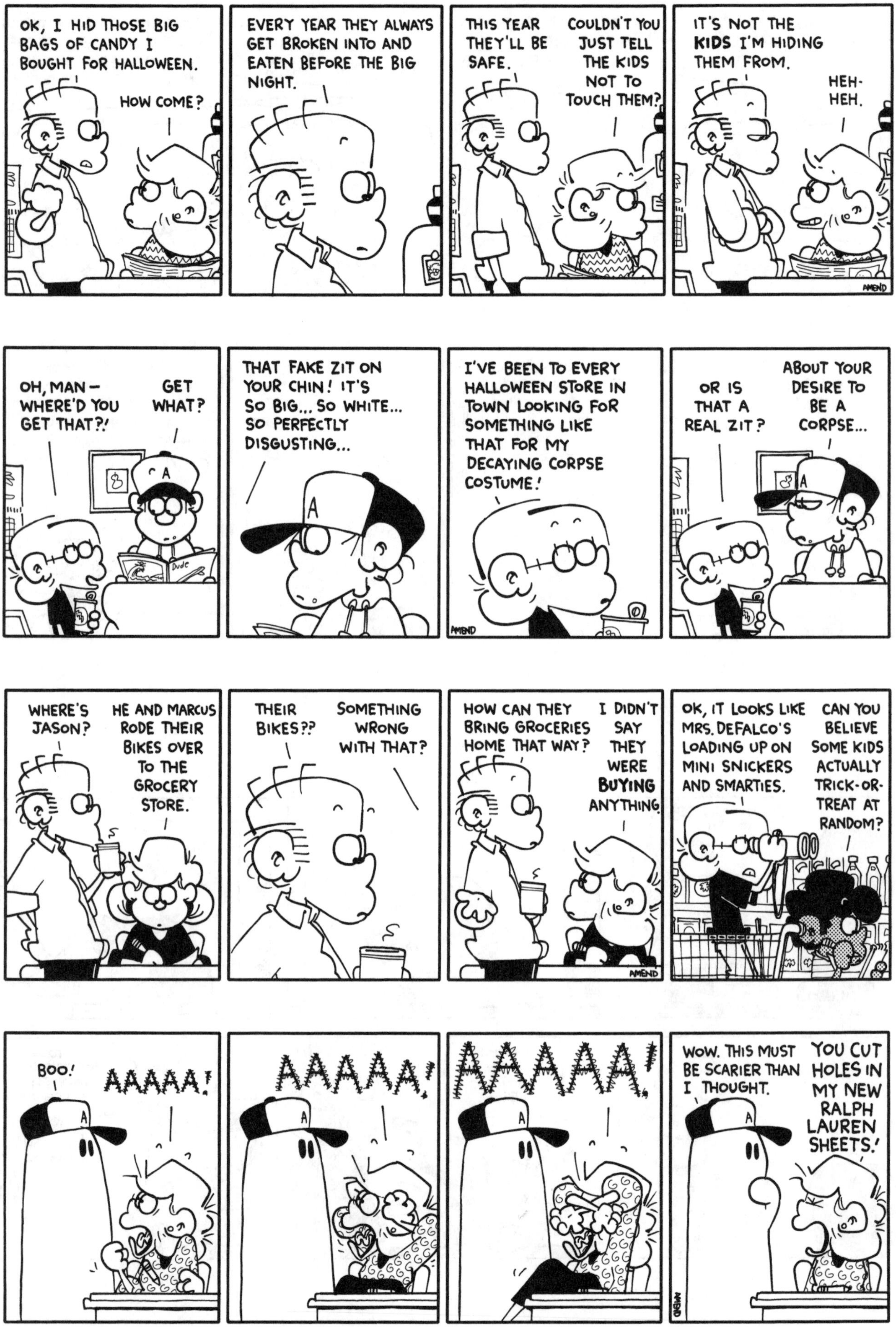
OK, I HID THOSE BIG BAGS OF CANDY I BOUGHT FOR HALLOWEEN.
HOW COME?
EVERY YEAR THEY ALWAYS GET BROKEN INTO AND EATEN BEFORE THE BIG NIGHT.
THIS YEAR THEY'LL BE SAFE.
COULDN'T YOU JUST TELL THE KIDS NOT TO TOUCH THEM?
IT'S NOT THE **KIDS** I'M HIDING THEM FROM.
HEH-HEH.
AMEND
OH, MAN— WHERE'D YOU GET THAT?!
GET WHAT?
THAT FAKE ZIT ON YOUR CHIN! IT'S SO BIG... SO WHITE... SO PERFECTLY DISGUSTING...
I'VE BEEN TO EVERY HALLOWEEN STORE IN TOWN LOOKING FOR SOMETHING LIKE THAT FOR MY DECAYING CORPSE COSTUME!
AMEND
OR IS THAT A REAL ZIT?
ABOUT YOUR DESIRE TO BE A CORPSE...
WHERE'S JASON?
HE AND MARCUS RODE THEIR BIKES OVER TO THE GROCERY STORE.
THEIR BIKES??
SOMETHING WRONG WITH THAT?
HOW CAN THEY BRING GROCERIES HOME THAT WAY?
I DIDN'T SAY THEY WERE **BUYING** ANYTHING.
AMEND
OK, IT LOOKS LIKE MRS. DEFALCO'S LOADING UP ON MINI SNICKERS AND SMARTIES.
CAN YOU BELIEVE SOME KIDS ACTUALLY TRICK-OR-TREAT AT RANDOM?
BOO!
AAAAA!
AAAAA!
AAAAA!
WOW. THIS MUST BE SCARIER THAN I THOUGHT.
YOU CUT HOLES IN MY NEW RALPH LAUREN SHEETS!

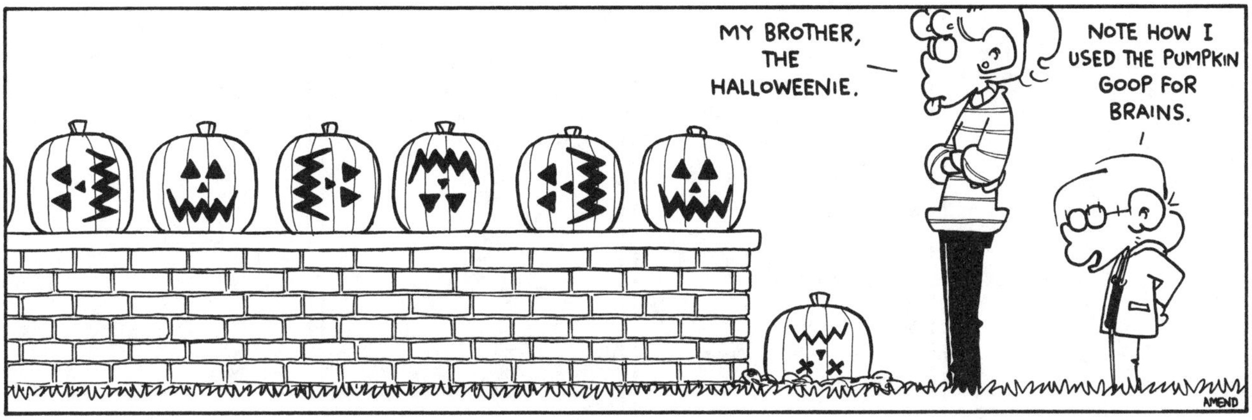
MY BROTHER, THE HALLOWEENIE.
NOTE HOW I USED THE PUMPKIN GOOP FOR BRAINS.
AMEND

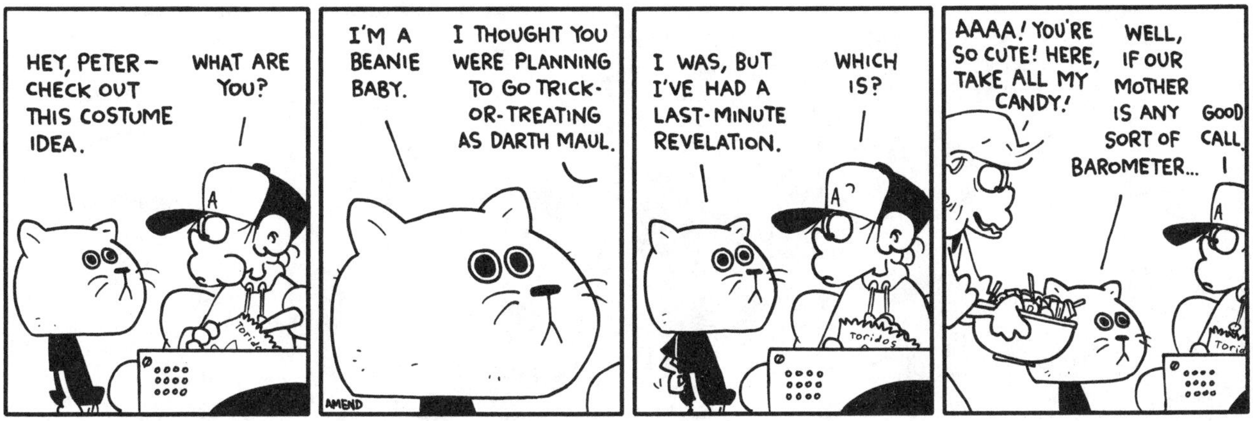
HEY, PETER— CHECK OUT THIS COSTUME IDEA.
WHAT ARE YOU?
I'M A BEANIE BABY.
I THOUGHT YOU WERE PLANNING TO GO TRICK-OR-TREATING AS DARTH MAUL.
I WAS, BUT I'VE HAD A LAST-MINUTE REVELATION.
WHICH IS?
AAAA! YOU'RE SO CUTE! HERE, TAKE ALL MY CANDY!
WELL, IF OUR MOTHER IS ANY SORT OF BAROMETER...
GOOD CALL.
AMEND

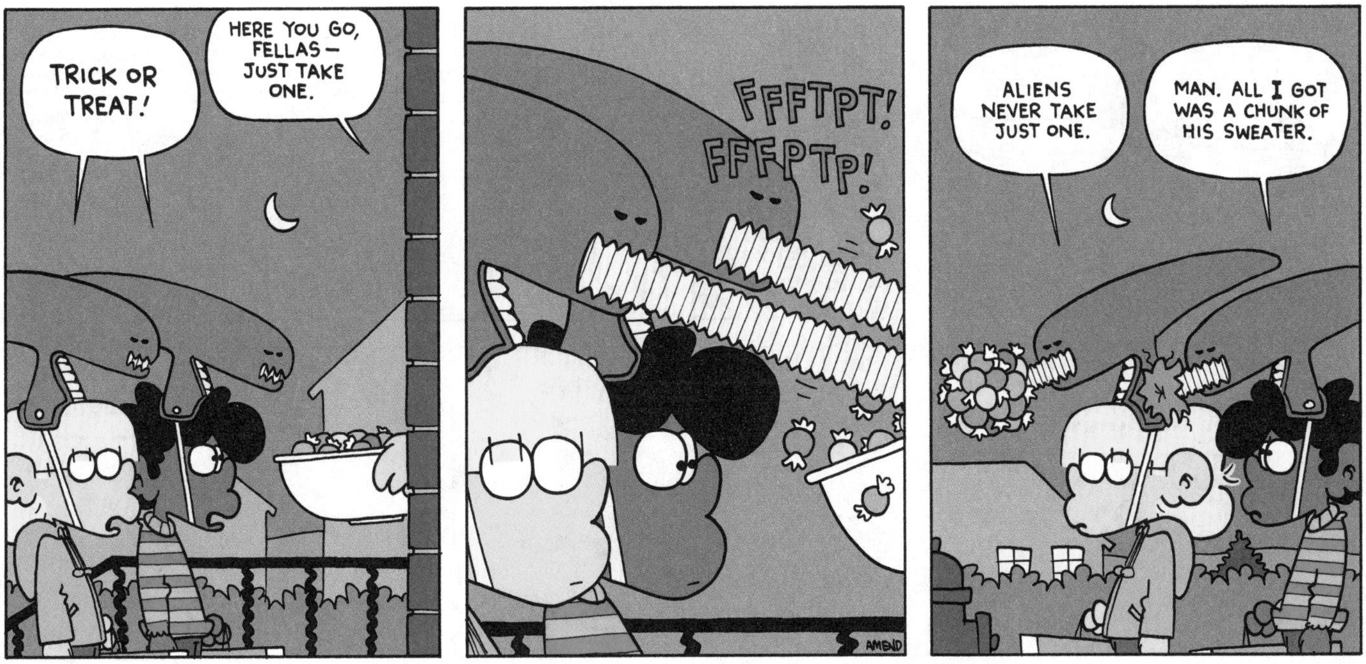
TRICK OR TREAT!
HERE YOU GO, FELLAS— JUST TAKE ONE.
FFFTPT!
FFFPTP!
ALIENS NEVER TAKE JUST ONE.
MAN. ALL I GOT WAS A CHUNK OF HIS SWEATER.
AMEND

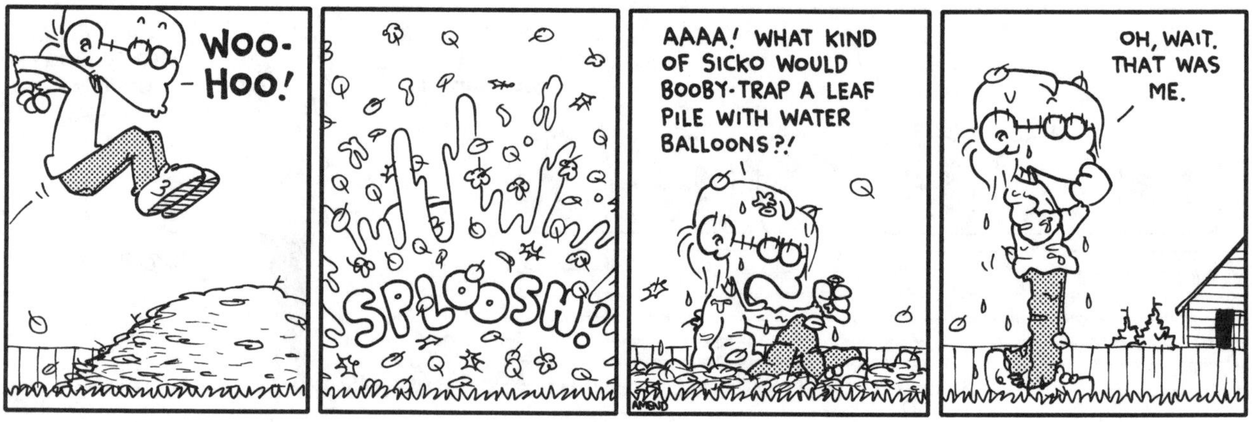
WOO-HOO!
SPLOOSH!
AAAA! WHAT KIND OF SICKO WOULD BOOBY-TRAP A LEAF PILE WITH WATER BALLOONS?!
OH, WAIT. THAT WAS ME.
AMEND

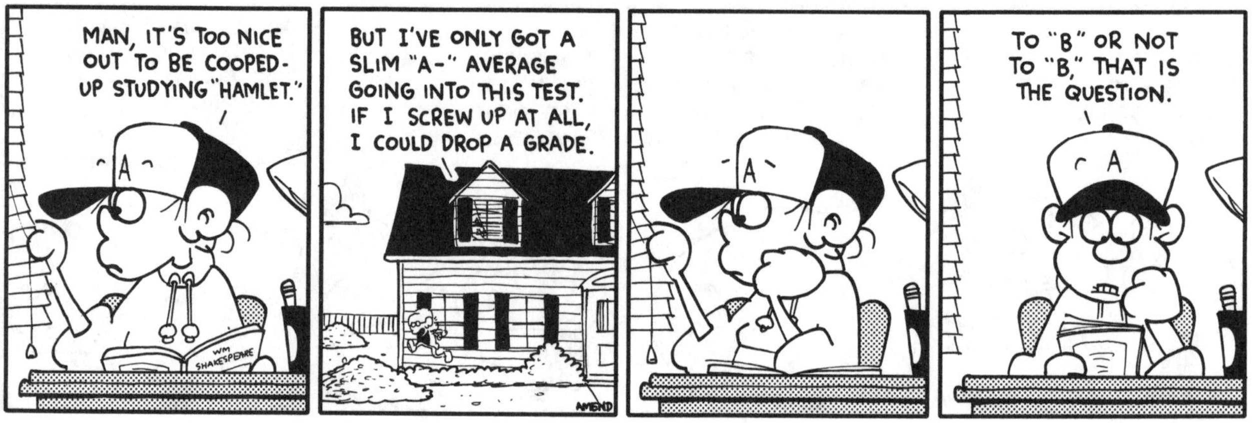
MAN, IT'S TOO NICE OUT TO BE COOPED-UP STUDYING "HAMLET."
WM SHAKESPEARE
BUT I'VE ONLY GOT A SLIM "A-" AVERAGE GOING INTO THIS TEST. IF I SCREW UP AT ALL, I COULD DROP A GRADE.
AMEND
TO "B" OR NOT TO "B," THAT IS THE QUESTION.

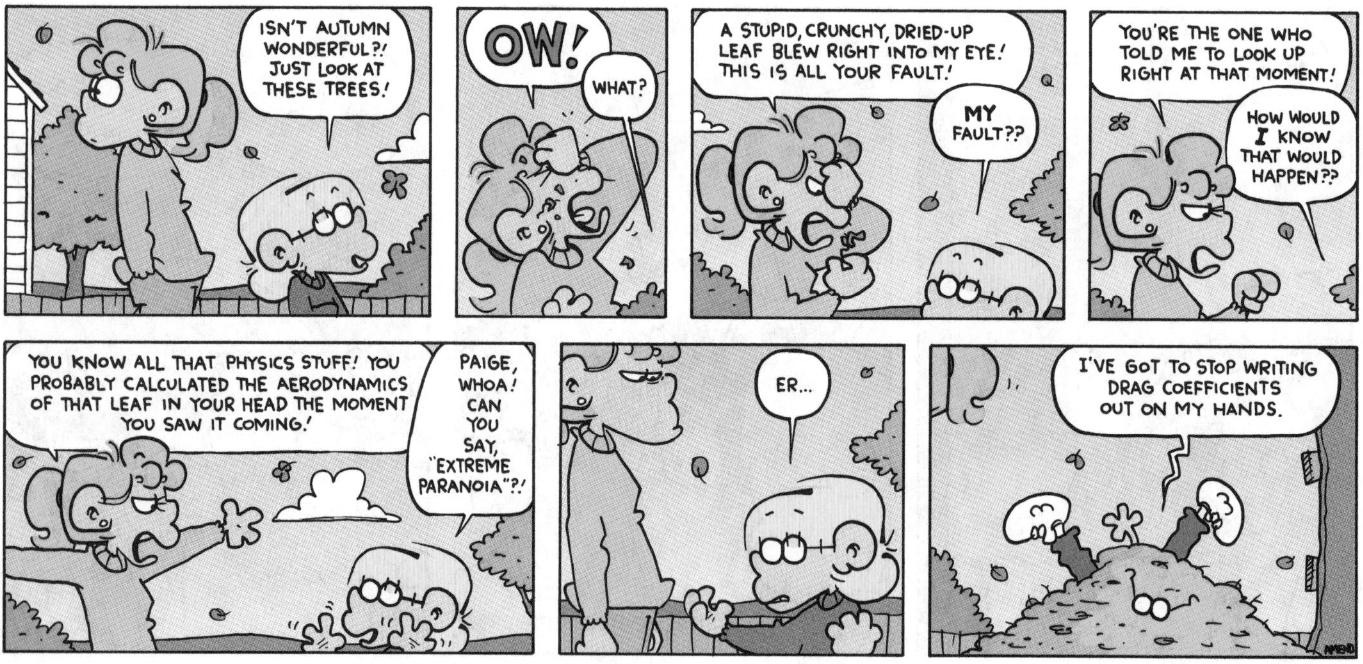
ISN'T AUTUMN WONDERFUL?! JUST LOOK AT THESE TREES!
OW!
WHAT?
A STUPID, CRUNCHY, DRIED-UP LEAF BLEW RIGHT INTO MY EYE! THIS IS ALL YOUR FAULT!
MY FAULT??
YOU'RE THE ONE WHO TOLD ME TO LOOK UP RIGHT AT THAT MOMENT!
HOW WOULD I KNOW THAT WOULD HAPPEN??
YOU KNOW ALL THAT PHYSICS STUFF! YOU PROBABLY CALCULATED THE AERODYNAMICS OF THAT LEAF IN YOUR HEAD THE MOMENT YOU SAW IT COMING!
PAIGE, WHOA! CAN YOU SAY, "EXTREME PARANOIA"?!
ER...
I'VE GOT TO STOP WRITING DRAG COEFFICIENTS OUT ON MY HANDS.
AMEND

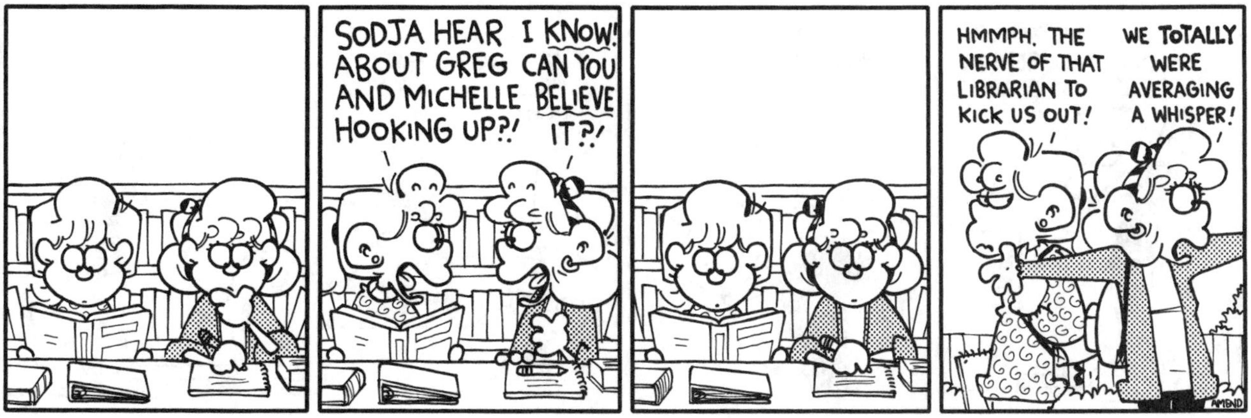
SODJA HEAR ABOUT GREG AND MICHELLE HOOKING UP?!
I KNOW! CAN YOU BELIEVE IT?!
HMMPH. THE NERVE OF THAT LIBRARIAN TO KICK US OUT!
WE TOTALLY WERE AVERAGING A WHISPER!

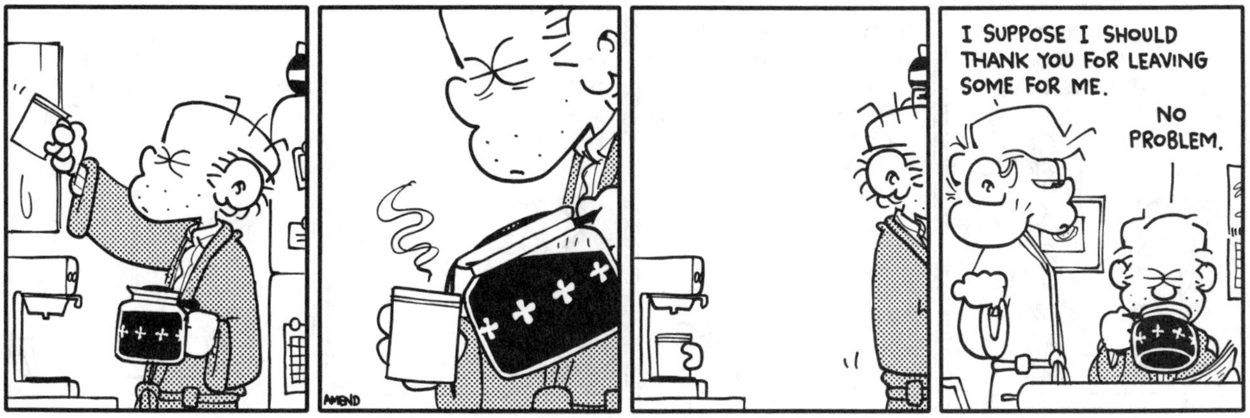
I SUPPOSE I SHOULD THANK YOU FOR LEAVING SOME FOR ME.
NO PROBLEM.

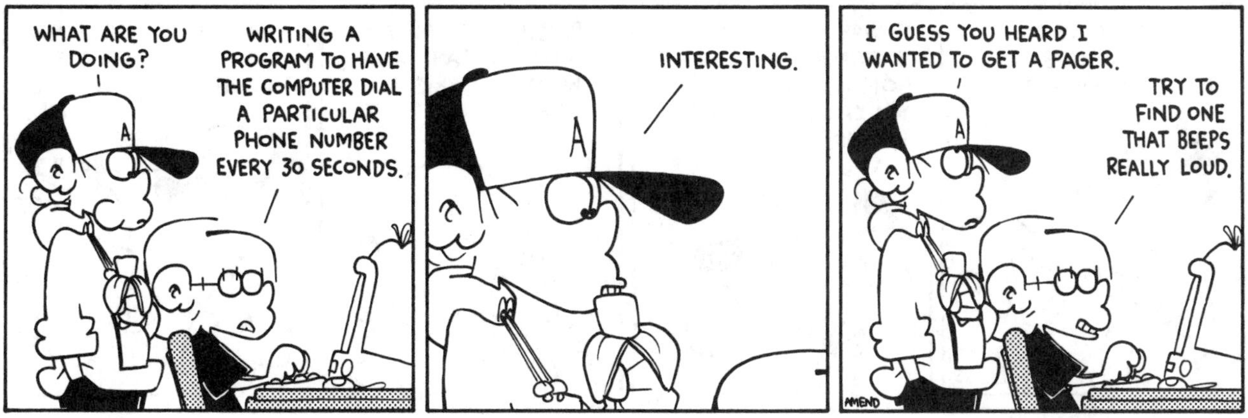
WHAT ARE YOU DOING?
WRITING A PROGRAM TO HAVE THE COMPUTER DIAL A PARTICULAR PHONE NUMBER EVERY 30 SECONDS.
INTERESTING.
I GUESS YOU HEARD I WANTED TO GET A PAGER.
TRY TO FIND ONE THAT BEEPS REALLY LOUD.

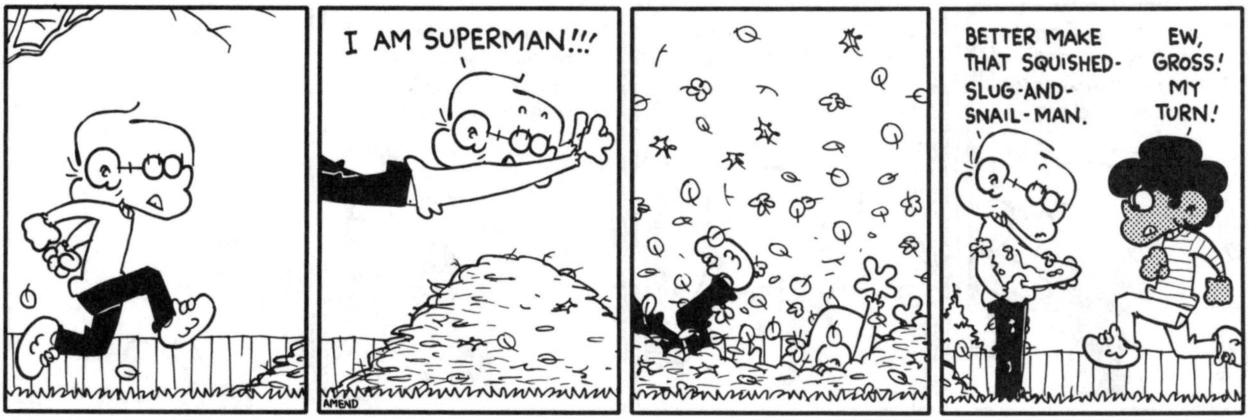
I AM SUPERMAN!!!
BETTER MAKE THAT SQUISHED-SLUG-AND-SNAIL-MAN.
EW, GROSS! MY TURN!

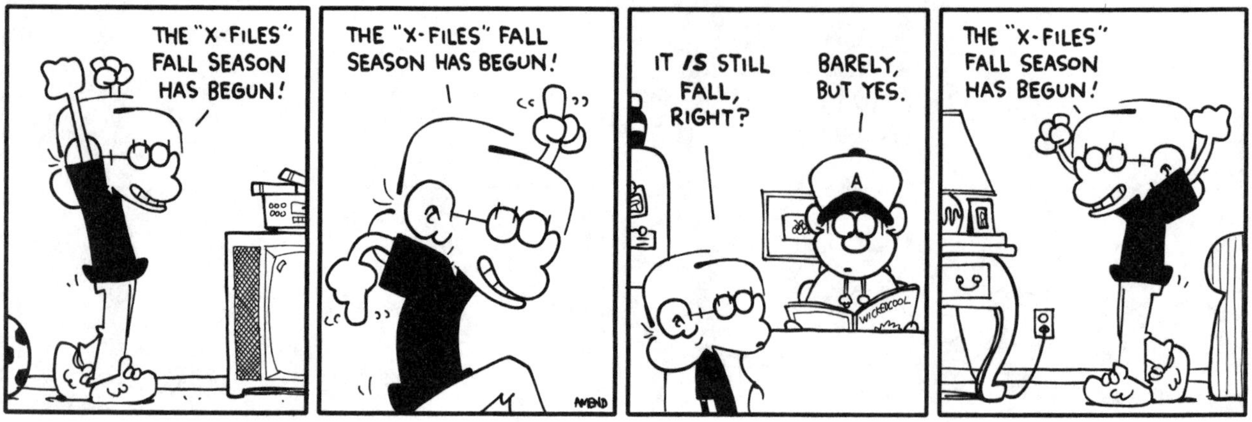
THE "X-FILES" FALL SEASON HAS BEGUN!
THE "X-FILES" FALL SEASON HAS BEGUN!
IT IS STILL FALL, RIGHT?
BARELY, BUT YES.
THE "X-FILES" FALL SEASON HAS BEGUN!

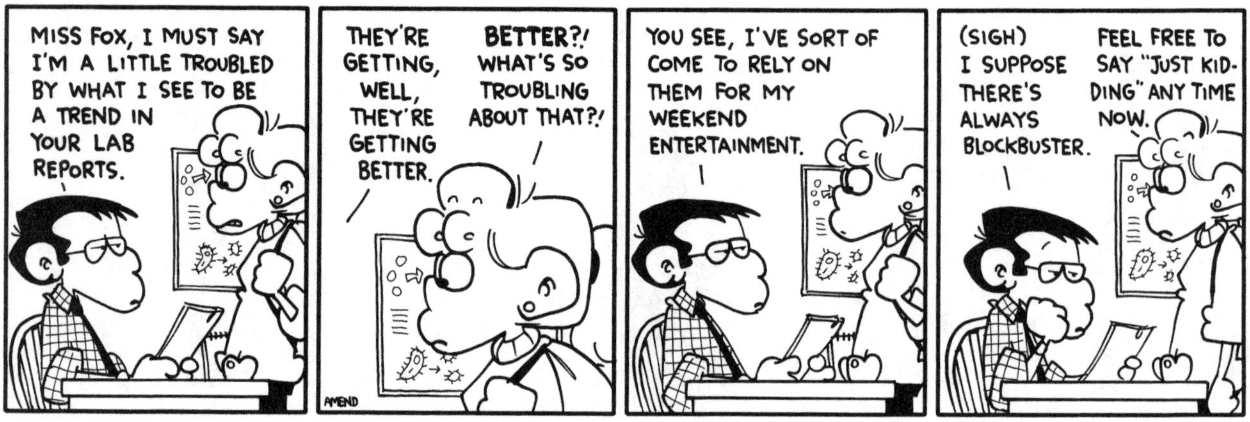
MISS FOX, I MUST SAY I'M A LITTLE TROUBLED BY WHAT I SEE TO BE A TREND IN YOUR LAB REPORTS.
THEY'RE GETTING, WELL, THEY'RE GETTING BETTER.
BETTER?! WHAT'S SO TROUBLING ABOUT THAT?!
YOU SEE, I'VE SORT OF COME TO RELY ON THEM FOR MY WEEKEND ENTERTAINMENT.
(SIGH) I SUPPOSE THERE'S ALWAYS BLOCKBUSTER.
FEEL FREE TO SAY "JUST KIDDING" ANY TIME NOW.

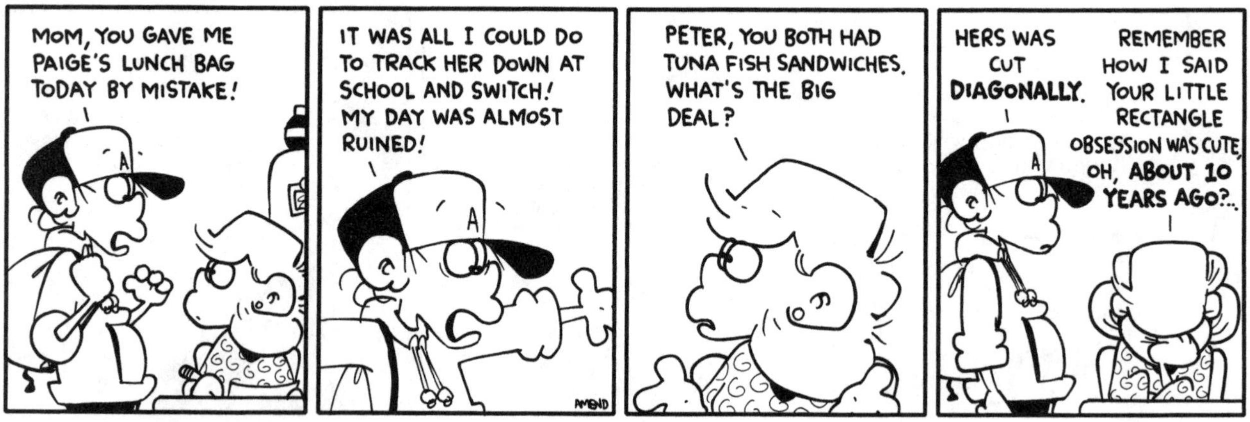
MOM, YOU GAVE ME PAIGE'S LUNCH BAG TODAY BY MISTAKE!
IT WAS ALL I COULD DO TO TRACK HER DOWN AT SCHOOL AND SWITCH! MY DAY WAS ALMOST RUINED!
PETER, YOU BOTH HAD TUNA FISH SANDWICHES. WHAT'S THE BIG DEAL?
HERS WAS CUT DIAGONALLY.
REMEMBER HOW I SAID YOUR LITTLE RECTANGLE OBSESSION WAS CUTE, OH, ABOUT 10 YEARS AGO?..

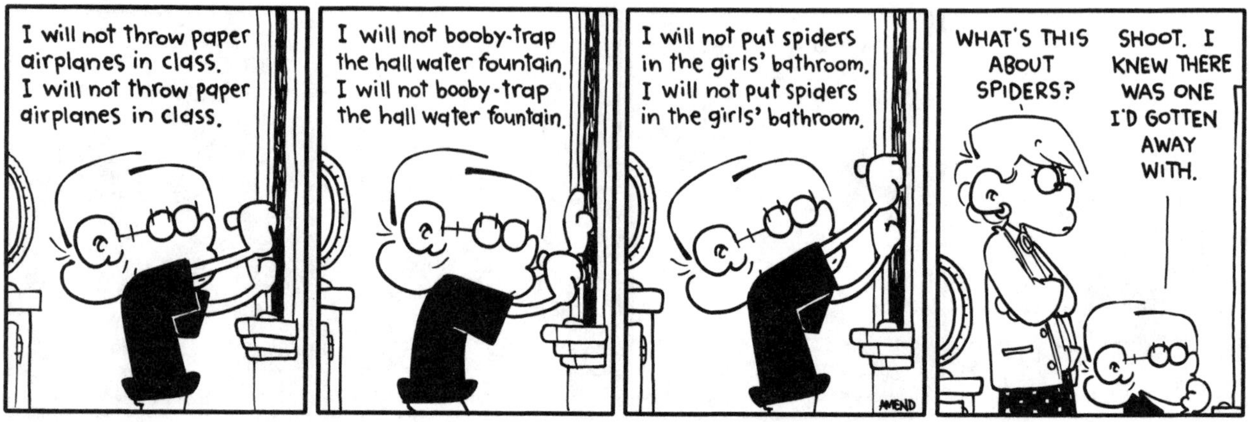
I will not throw paper airplanes in class. I will not throw paper airplanes in class.
I will not booby-trap the hall water fountain. I will not booby-trap the hall water fountain.
I will not put spiders in the girls' bathroom. I will not put spiders in the girls' bathroom.
WHAT'S THIS ABOUT SPIDERS?
SHOOT. I KNEW THERE WAS ONE I'D GOTTEN AWAY WITH.

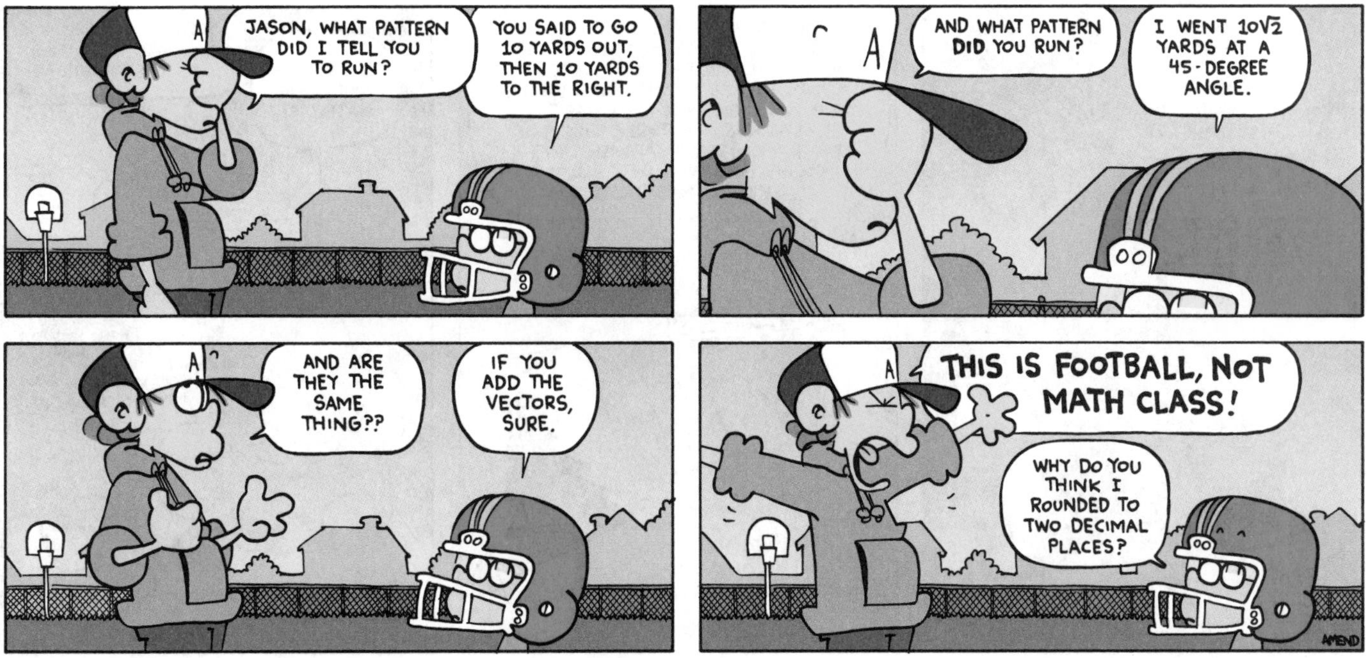
JASON, WHAT PATTERN DID I TELL YOU TO RUN?
YOU SAID TO GO 10 YARDS OUT, THEN 10 YARDS TO THE RIGHT.
AND WHAT PATTERN DID YOU RUN?
I WENT 10√2 YARDS AT A 45-DEGREE ANGLE.
AND ARE THEY THE SAME THING??
IF YOU ADD THE VECTORS, SURE.
THIS IS FOOTBALL, NOT MATH CLASS!
WHY DO YOU THINK I ROUNDED TO TWO DECIMAL PLACES?
AMEND

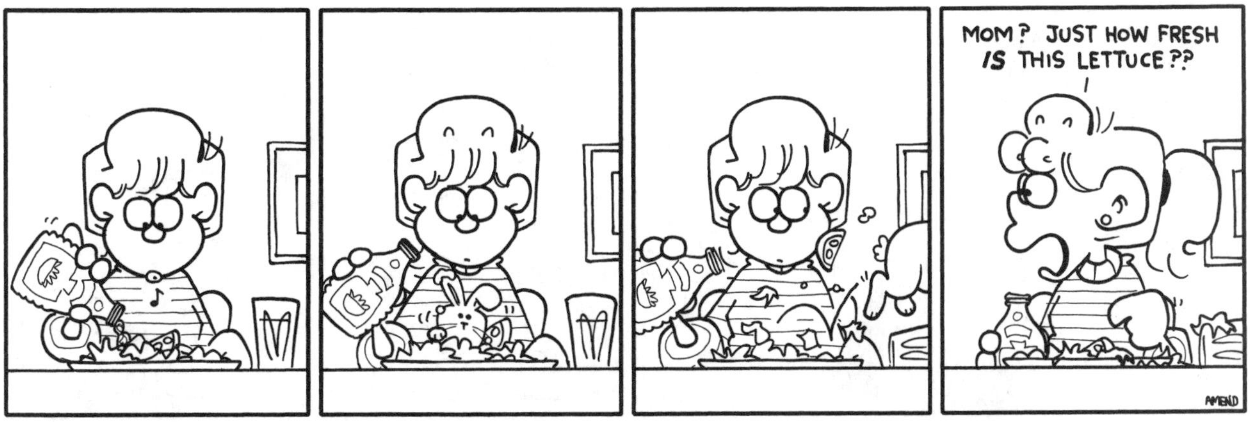
MOM? JUST HOW FRESH IS THIS LETTUCE??
AMEND

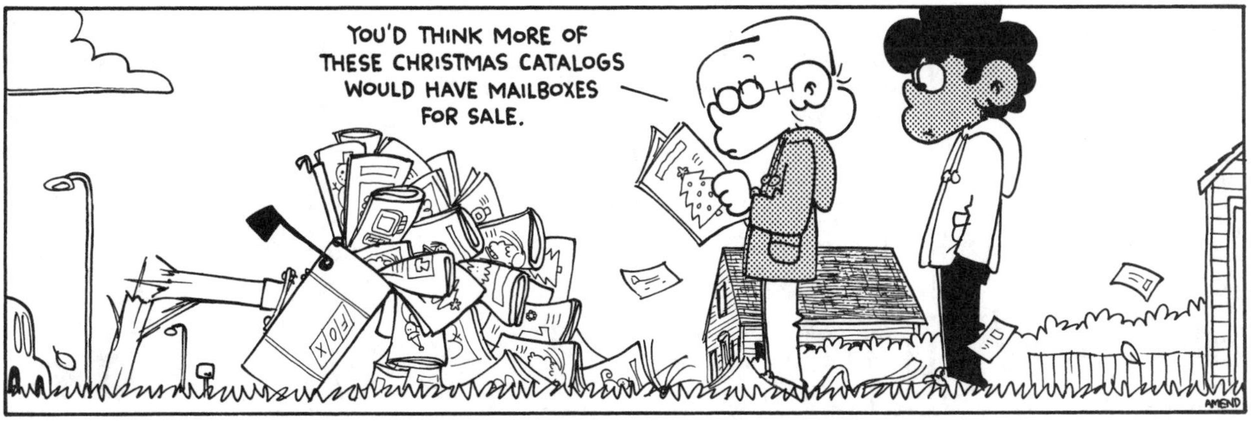
YOU'D THINK MORE OF THESE CHRISTMAS CATALOGS WOULD HAVE MAILBOXES FOR SALE.
FOX
AMEND

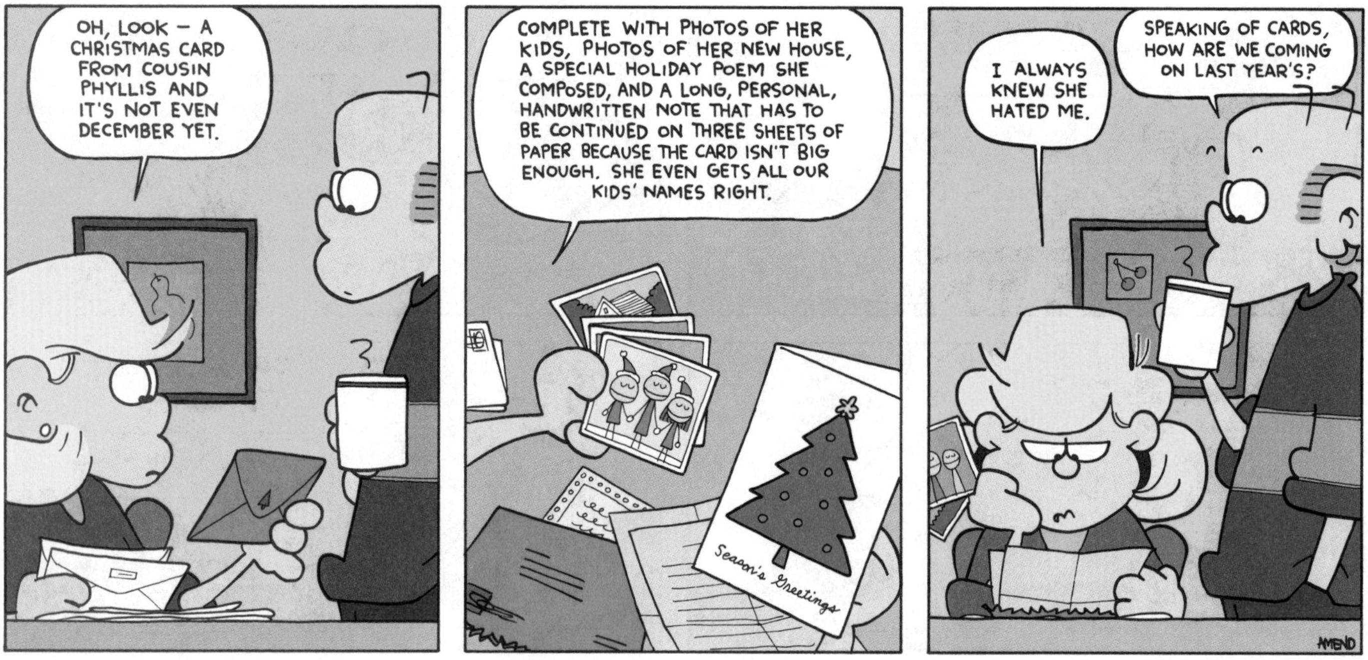
OH, LOOK — A CHRISTMAS CARD FROM COUSIN PHYLLIS AND IT'S NOT EVEN DECEMBER YET.
COMPLETE WITH PHOTOS OF HER KIDS, PHOTOS OF HER NEW HOUSE, A SPECIAL HOLIDAY POEM SHE COMPOSED, AND A LONG, PERSONAL, HANDWRITTEN NOTE THAT HAS TO BE CONTINUED ON THREE SHEETS OF PAPER BECAUSE THE CARD ISN'T BIG ENOUGH. SHE EVEN GETS ALL OUR KIDS' NAMES RIGHT.
Season's Greetings
I ALWAYS KNEW SHE HATED ME.
SPEAKING OF CARDS, HOW ARE WE COMING ON LAST YEAR'S?
AMEND

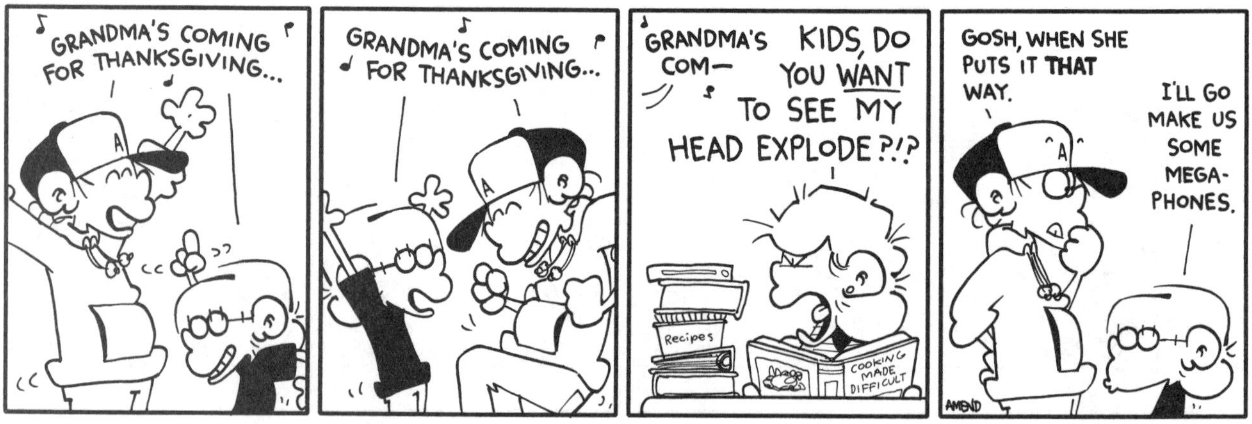
GRANDMA'S COMING FOR THANKSGIVING...
GRANDMA'S COMING FOR THANKSGIVING...
GRANDMA'S COM—
KIDS, DO YOU WANT TO SEE MY HEAD EXPLODE?!?
Recipes
COOKING MADE DIFFICULT
GOSH, WHEN SHE PUTS IT THAT WAY.
I'LL GO MAKE US SOME MEGA-PHONES.
AMEND

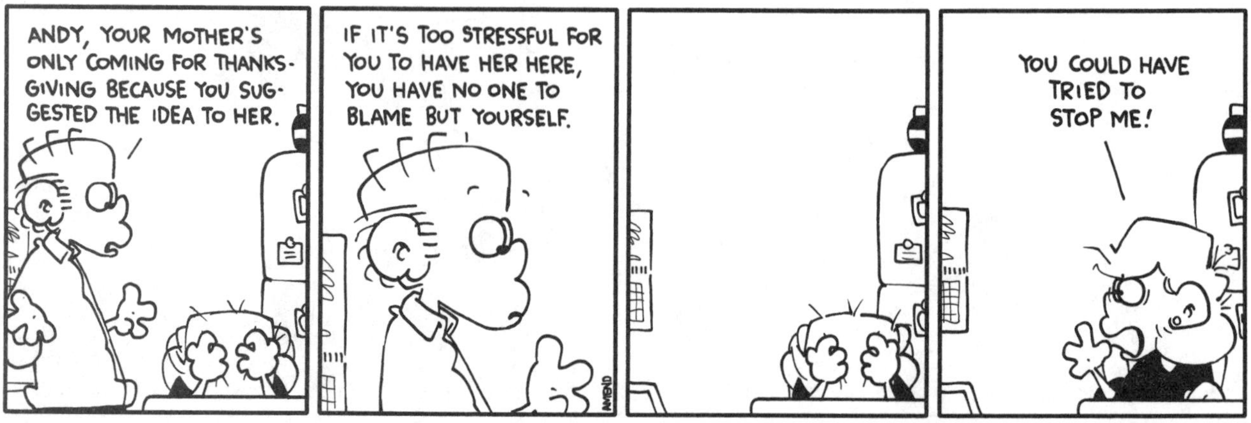
ANDY, YOUR MOTHER'S ONLY COMING FOR THANKS-GIVING BECAUSE YOU SUG-GESTED THE IDEA TO HER.
IF IT'S TOO STRESSFUL FOR YOU TO HAVE HER HERE, YOU HAVE NO ONE TO BLAME BUT YOURSELF.
AMEND
YOU COULD HAVE TRIED TO STOP ME!

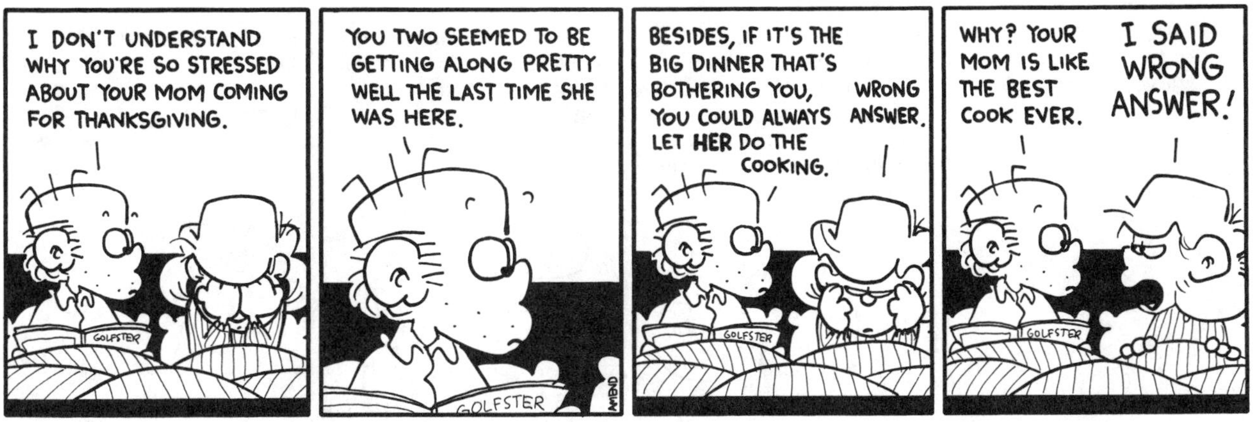
I DON'T UNDERSTAND WHY YOU'RE SO STRESSED ABOUT YOUR MOM COMING FOR THANKSGIVING.
GOLFSTER
YOU TWO SEEMED TO BE GETTING ALONG PRETTY WELL THE LAST TIME SHE WAS HERE.
GOLFSTER
AMEND
BESIDES, IF IT'S THE BIG DINNER THAT'S BOTHERING YOU, YOU COULD ALWAYS LET HER DO THE COOKING.
WRONG ANSWER.
GOLFSTER
WHY? YOUR MOM IS LIKE THE BEST COOK EVER.
I SAID WRONG ANSWER!
GOLFSTER

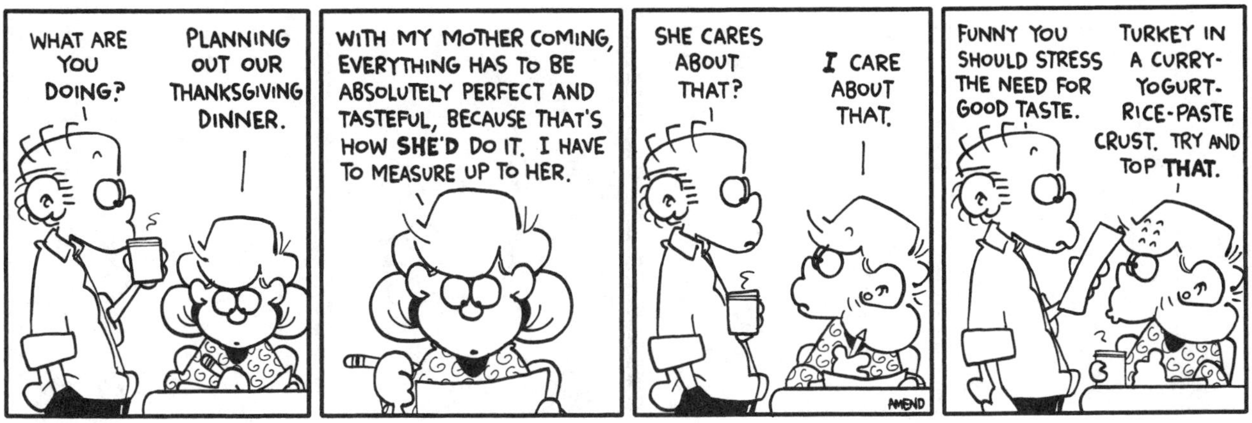
WHAT ARE YOU DOING?
PLANNING OUT OUR THANKSGIVING DINNER.
WITH MY MOTHER COMING, EVERYTHING HAS TO BE ABSOLUTELY PERFECT AND TASTEFUL, BECAUSE THAT'S HOW SHE'D DO IT. I HAVE TO MEASURE UP TO HER.
SHE CARES ABOUT THAT?
I CARE ABOUT THAT.
AMEND
FUNNY YOU SHOULD STRESS THE NEED FOR GOOD TASTE.
TURKEY IN A CURRY-YOGURT-RICE-PASTE CRUST. TRY AND TOP THAT.

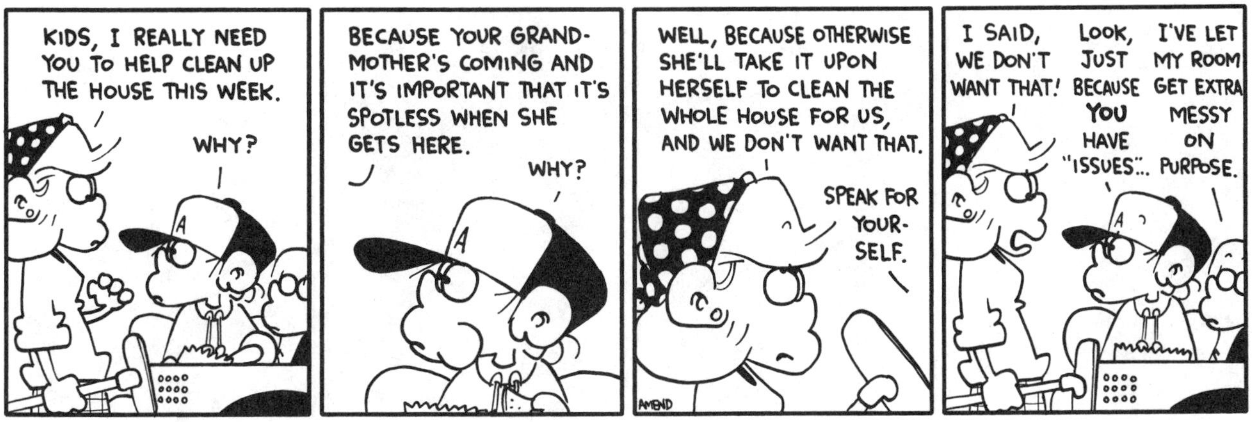
KIDS, I REALLY NEED YOU TO HELP CLEAN UP THE HOUSE THIS WEEK.
WHY?
BECAUSE YOUR GRAND-MOTHER'S COMING AND IT'S IMPORTANT THAT IT'S SPOTLESS WHEN SHE GETS HERE.
WHY?
WELL, BECAUSE OTHERWISE SHE'LL TAKE IT UPON HERSELF TO CLEAN THE WHOLE HOUSE FOR US, AND WE DON'T WANT THAT.
SPEAK FOR YOUR-SELF.
AMEND
I SAID, WE DON'T WANT THAT!
LOOK, JUST BECAUSE YOU HAVE "ISSUES"...
I'VE LET MY ROOM GET EXTRA MESSY ON PURPOSE.

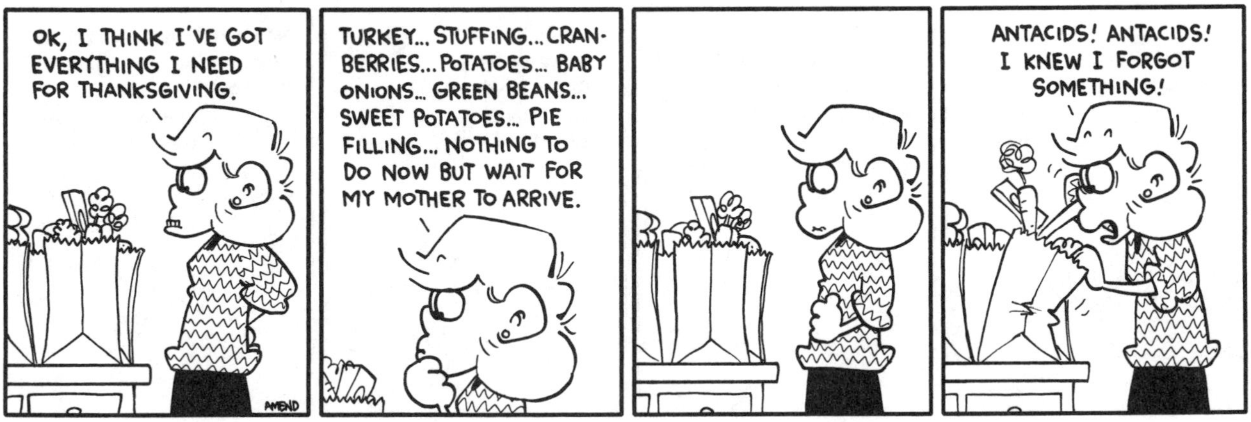
OK, I THINK I'VE GOT EVERYTHING I NEED FOR THANKSGIVING.
AMEND
TURKEY... STUFFING... CRAN-BERRIES... POTATOES... BABY ONIONS... GREEN BEANS... SWEET POTATOES... PIE FILLING... NOTHING TO DO NOW BUT WAIT FOR MY MOTHER TO ARRIVE.
ANTACIDS! ANTACIDS! I KNEW I FORGOT SOMETHING!

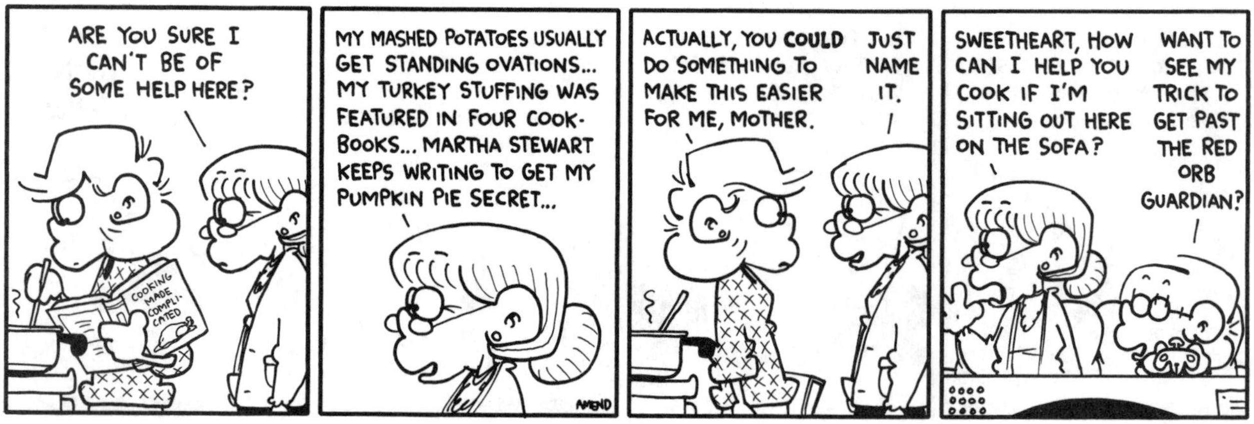
ARE YOU SURE I CAN'T BE OF SOME HELP HERE?
COOKING MADE COMPLI-CATED
MY MASHED POTATOES USUALLY GET STANDING OVATIONS... MY TURKEY STUFFING WAS FEATURED IN FOUR COOK-BOOKS... MARTHA STEWART KEEPS WRITING TO GET MY PUMPKIN PIE SECRET...
AMEND
ACTUALLY, YOU COULD DO SOMETHING TO MAKE THIS EASIER FOR ME, MOTHER.
JUST NAME IT.
SWEETHEART, HOW CAN I HELP YOU COOK IF I'M SITTING OUT HERE ON THE SOFA?
WANT TO SEE MY TRICK TO GET PAST THE RED ORB GUARDIAN?

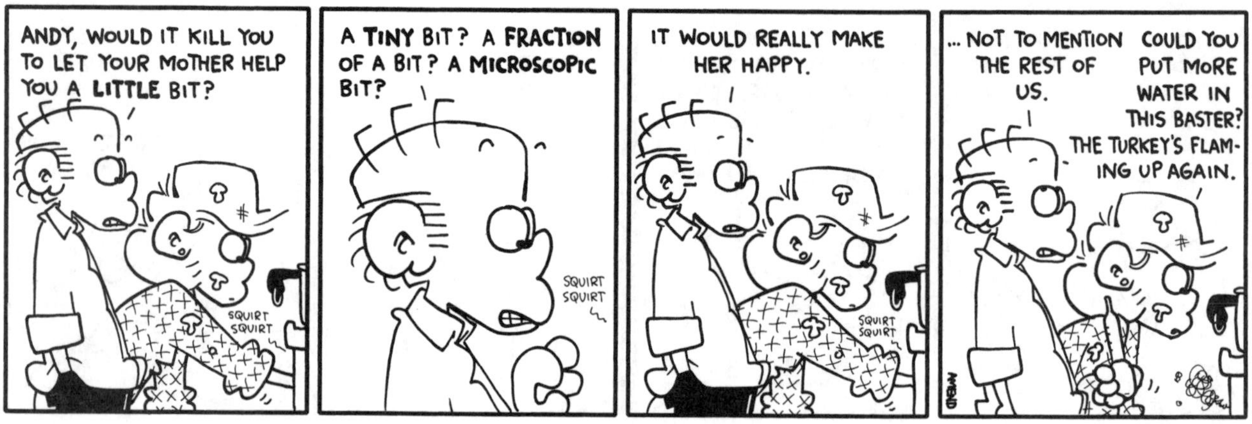
ANDY, WOULD IT KILL YOU TO LET YOUR MOTHER HELP YOU A LITTLE BIT?
SQUIRT SQUIRT
A TINY BIT? A FRACTION OF A BIT? A MICROSCOPIC BIT?
SQUIRT SQUIRT
IT WOULD REALLY MAKE HER HAPPY.
SQUIRT SQUIRT
... NOT TO MENTION THE REST OF US.
COULD YOU PUT MORE WATER IN THIS BASTER? THE TURKEY'S FLAM-ING UP AGAIN.
AMEND

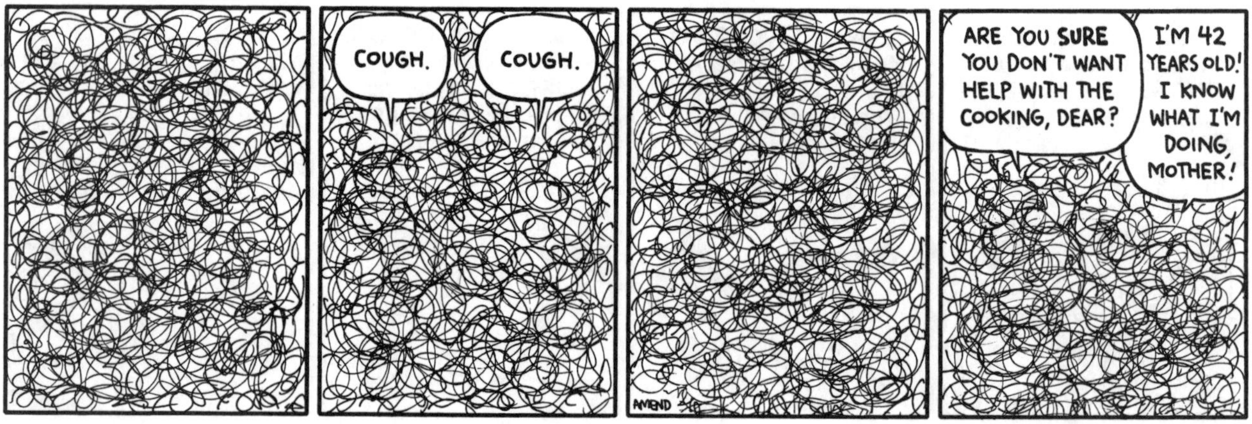
COUGH.
COUGH.
AMEND
ARE YOU SURE YOU DON'T WANT HELP WITH THE COOKING, DEAR?
I'M 42 YEARS OLD! I KNOW WHAT I'M DOING, MOTHER!

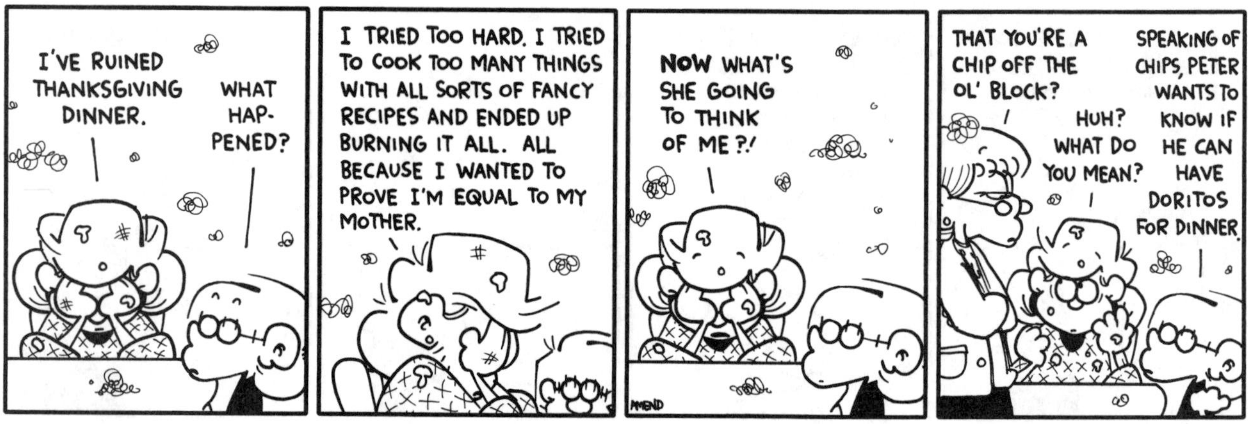
I'VE RUINED THANKSGIVING DINNER.
WHAT HAP-PENED?
I TRIED TOO HARD. I TRIED TO COOK TOO MANY THINGS WITH ALL SORTS OF FANCY RECIPES AND ENDED UP BURNING IT ALL. ALL BECAUSE I WANTED TO PROVE I'M EQUAL TO MY MOTHER.
NOW WHAT'S SHE GOING TO THINK OF ME?!
AMEND
THAT YOU'RE A CHIP OFF THE OL' BLOCK?
HUH? WHAT DO YOU MEAN?
SPEAKING OF CHIPS, PETER WANTS TO KNOW IF HE CAN HAVE DORITOS FOR DINNER.

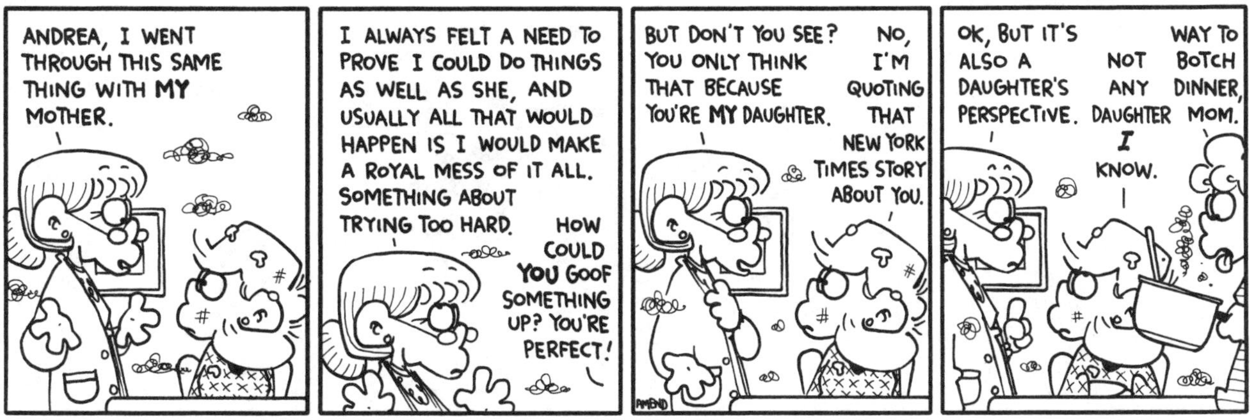
ANDREA, I WENT THROUGH THIS SAME THING WITH MY MOTHER.
I ALWAYS FELT A NEED TO PROVE I COULD DO THINGS AS WELL AS SHE, AND USUALLY ALL THAT WOULD HAPPEN IS I WOULD MAKE A ROYAL MESS OF IT ALL. SOMETHING ABOUT TRYING TOO HARD.
HOW COULD YOU GOOF SOMETHING UP? YOU'RE PERFECT!
BUT DON'T YOU SEE? YOU ONLY THINK THAT BECAUSE YOU'RE MY DAUGHTER.
NO, I'M QUOTING THAT NEW YORK TIMES STORY ABOUT YOU.
OK, BUT IT'S ALSO A DAUGHTER'S PERSPECTIVE.
NOT ANY DAUGHTER. I KNOW.
WAY TO BOTCH DINNER, MOM.
AMEND

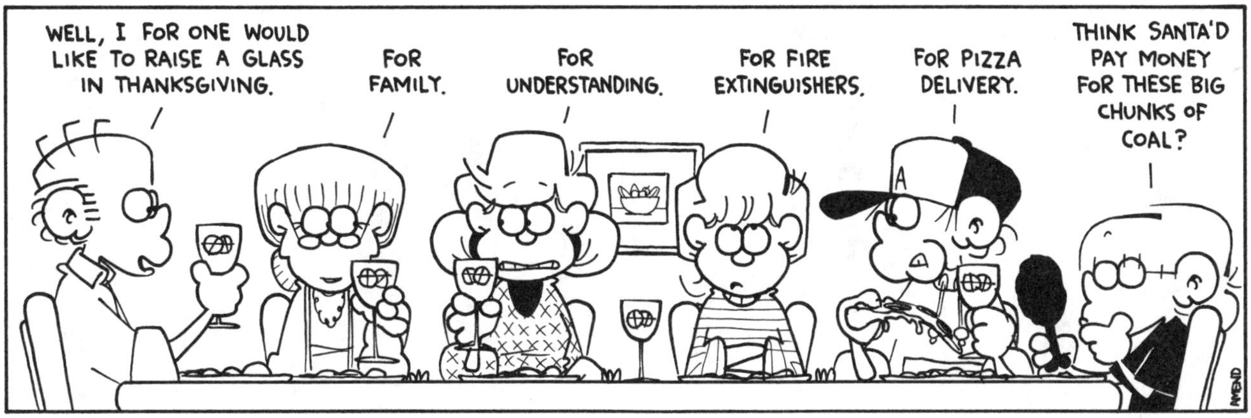
WELL, I FOR ONE WOULD LIKE TO RAISE A GLASS IN THANKSGIVING.
FOR FAMILY.
FOR UNDERSTANDING.
FOR FIRE EXTINGUISHERS.
FOR PIZZA DELIVERY.
THINK SANTA'D PAY MONEY FOR THESE BIG CHUNKS OF COAL?
AMEND

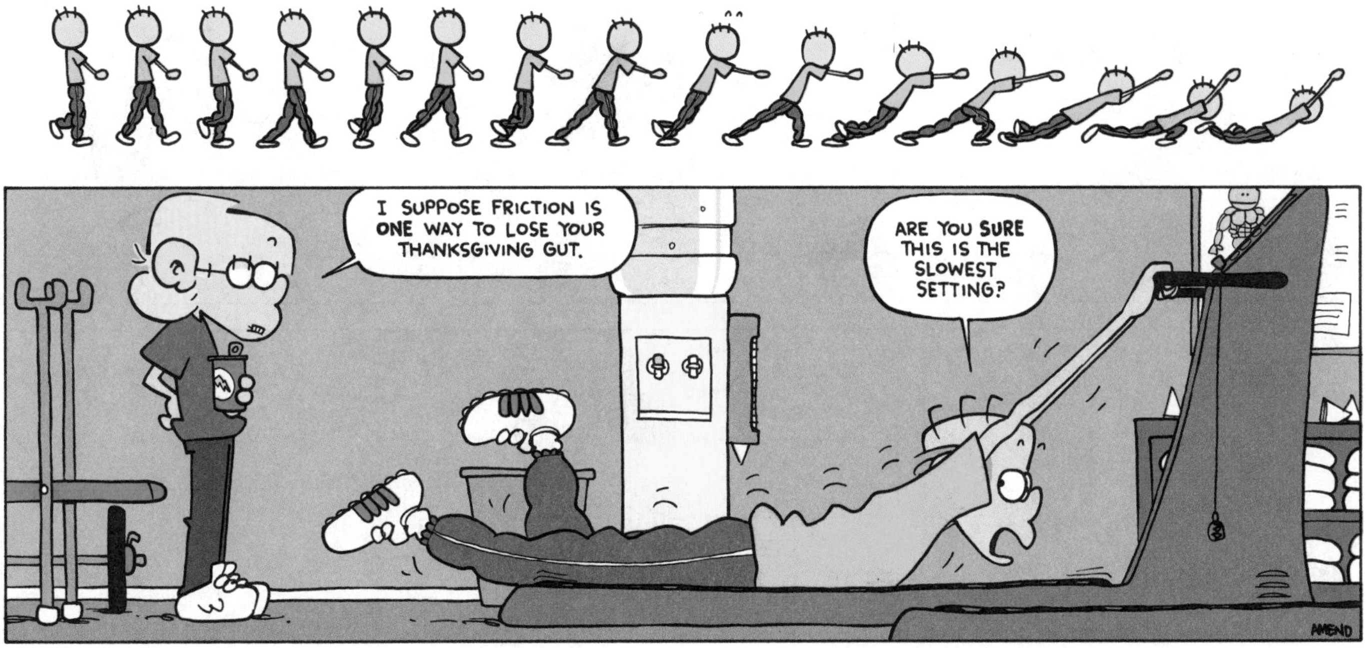
I SUPPOSE FRICTION IS ONE WAY TO LOSE YOUR THANKSGIVING GUT.
ARE YOU SURE THIS IS THE SLOWEST SETTING?
AMEND

WOOHOO! IT'S THE WEEK AFTER THANKSGIVING!
TIME TO PUT ON A SCARF... HAT... MITTENS...
... AND LET THE SLEDDING SEASON BEGIN!
SOME-THING'S NOT RIGHT.
SON, LOOK OUT- I'M PRACTICING MY CHIPPING.
AMEND

IN MY 10 YEARS OF EXISTENCE, I'VE NEVER SEEN SUCH MISERABLE NOVEMBER WEATHER!
IT'S **NEVER** BEEN LIKE THIS BEFORE!
I DON'T EVEN KNOW WHY I CAME OUTSIDE, IT'S SO BAD!
CURSE YOU, LA NIÑA!
WHEN YOU'RE THROUGH RANTING, COULD YOU SMEAR SOME SUNTAN LOTION ON MY BACK?
AMEND

PIFF!
PIFF!
PIFF!
PIFF!
GIVE IT UP, GUYS.
PIFF!
OUR STYROBALL BARRAGE SEEMS TO LEAVE SOMETHING TO BE DESIRED.
I SWEAR, IF IT DOESN'T SNOW SOON, I'M MOVING TO ALASKA.
AMEND

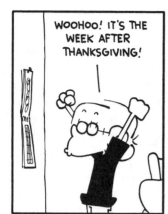

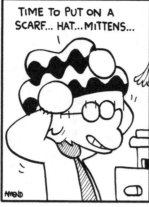

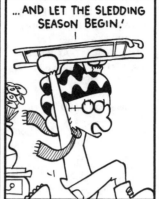

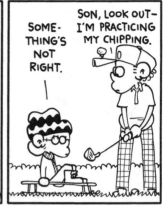

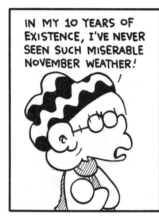

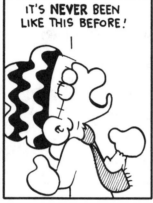

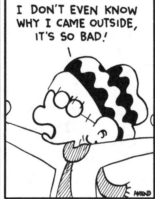

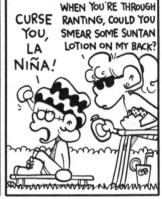

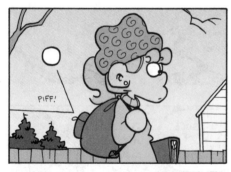

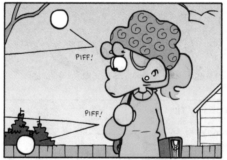

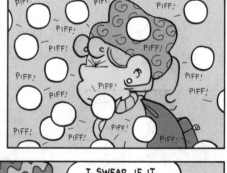

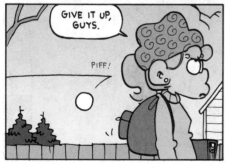

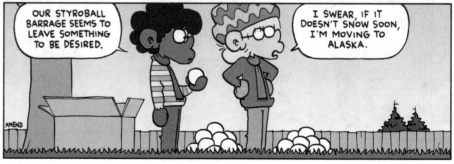

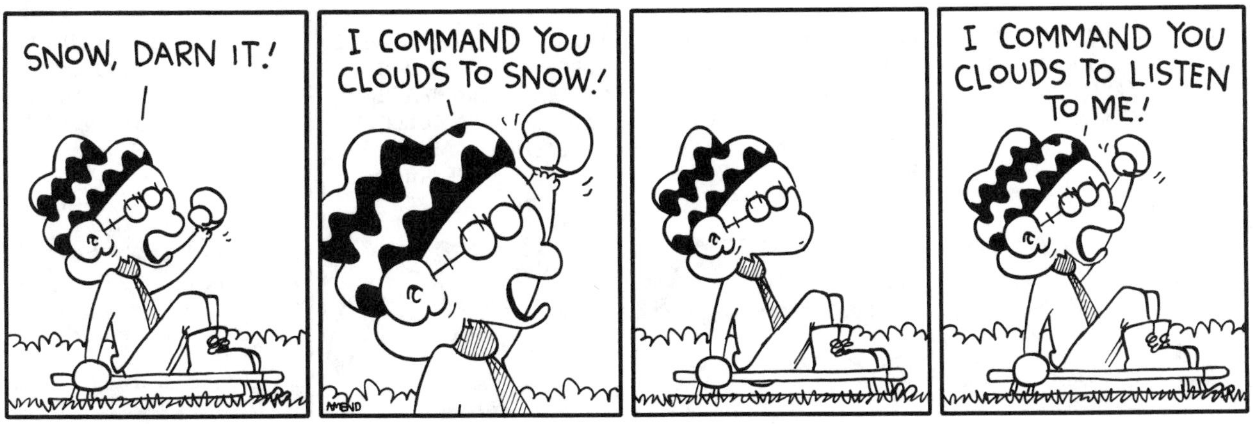
SNOW, DARN IT!
I COMMAND YOU CLOUDS TO SNOW!
I COMMAND YOU CLOUDS TO LISTEN TO ME!
AMEND

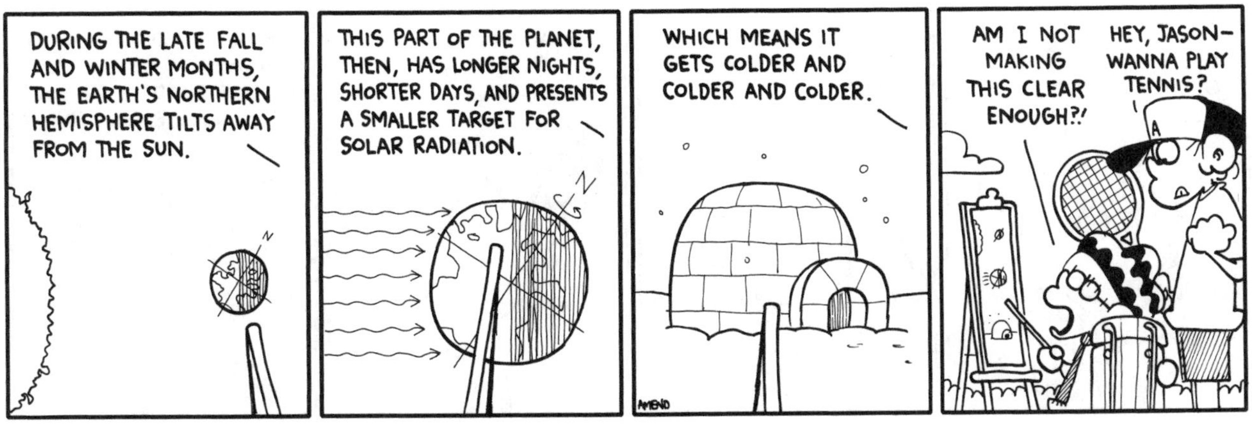
DURING THE LATE FALL AND WINTER MONTHS, THE EARTH'S NORTHERN HEMISPHERE TILTS AWAY FROM THE SUN.
THIS PART OF THE PLANET, THEN, HAS LONGER NIGHTS, SHORTER DAYS, AND PRESENTS A SMALLER TARGET FOR SOLAR RADIATION.
WHICH MEANS IT GETS COLDER AND COLDER AND COLDER.
AM I NOT MAKING THIS CLEAR ENOUGH?!
HEY, JASON— WANNA PLAY TENNIS?
AMEND

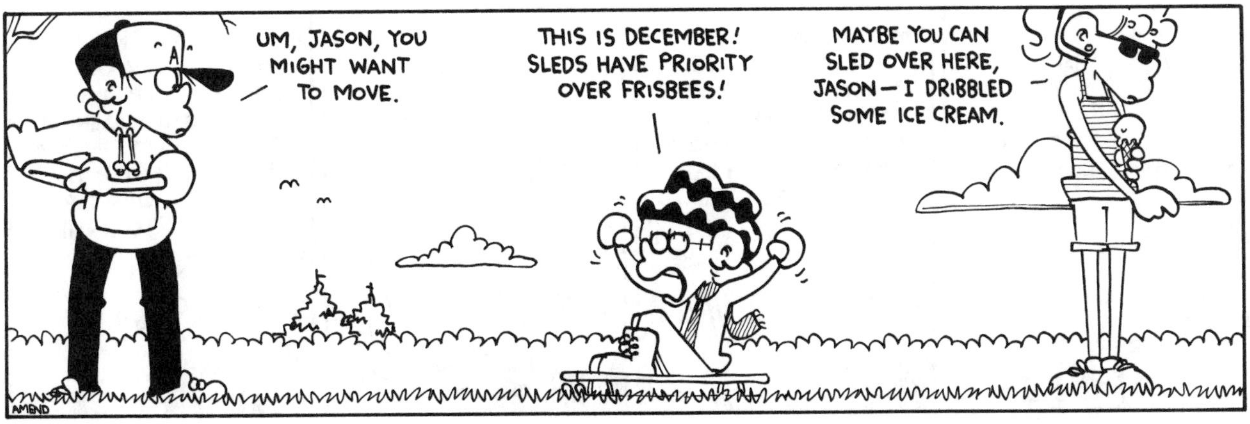
UM, JASON, YOU MIGHT WANT TO MOVE.
THIS IS DECEMBER! SLEDS HAVE PRIORITY OVER FRISBEES!
MAYBE YOU CAN SLED OVER HERE, JASON—I DRIBBLED SOME ICE CREAM.
AMEND

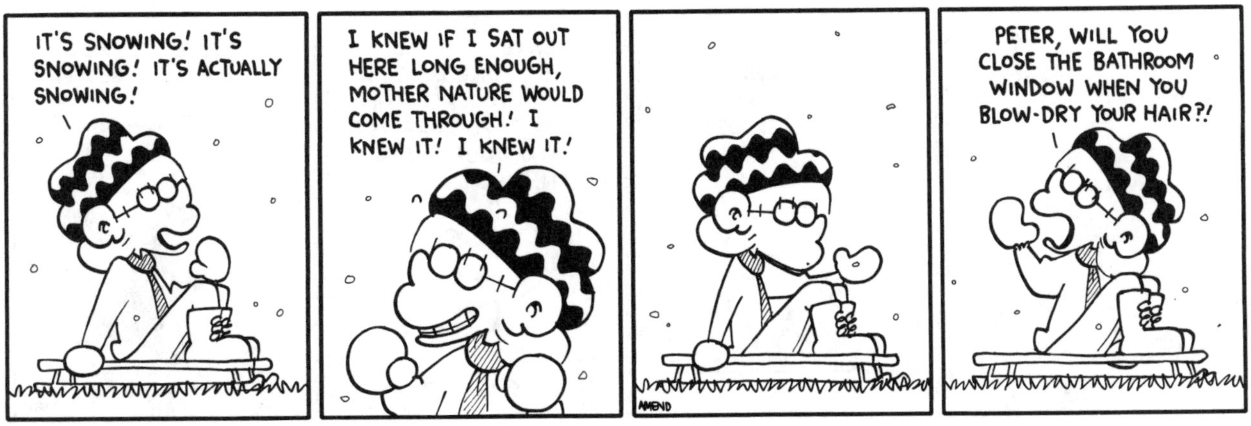
IT'S SNOWING! IT'S SNOWING! IT'S ACTUALLY SNOWING!
I KNEW IF I SAT OUT HERE LONG ENOUGH, MOTHER NATURE WOULD COME THROUGH! I KNEW IT! I KNEW IT!
PETER, WILL YOU CLOSE THE BATHROOM WINDOW WHEN YOU BLOW-DRY YOUR HAIR?!
AMEND

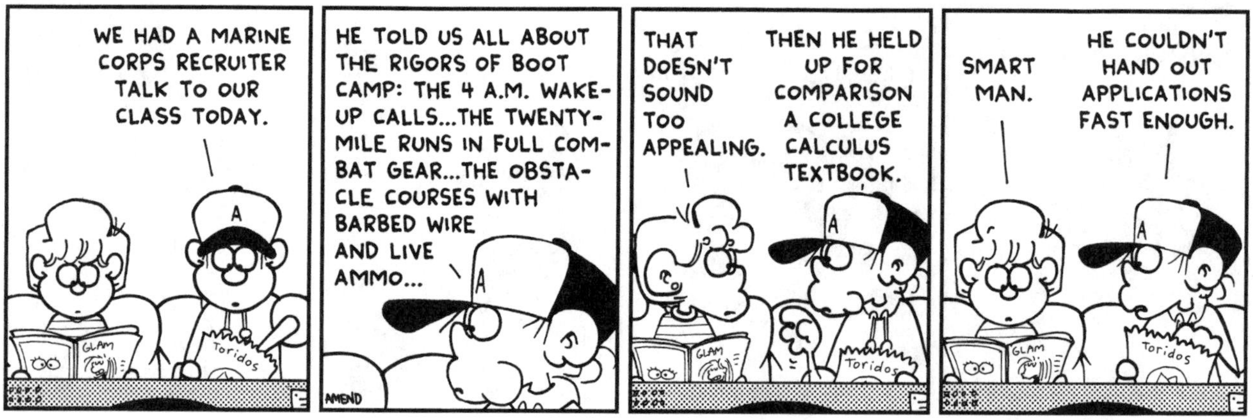
WE HAD A MARINE CORPS RECRUITER TALK TO OUR CLASS TODAY.
HE TOLD US ALL ABOUT THE RIGORS OF BOOT CAMP: THE 4 A.M. WAKE-UP CALLS...THE TWENTY-MILE RUNS IN FULL COMBAT GEAR...THE OBSTACLE COURSES WITH BARBED WIRE AND LIVE AMMO...
THAT DOESN'T SOUND TOO APPEALING.
THEN HE HELD UP FOR COMPARISON A COLLEGE CALCULUS TEXTBOOK.
SMART MAN.
HE COULDN'T HAND OUT APPLICATIONS FAST ENOUGH.
AMEND

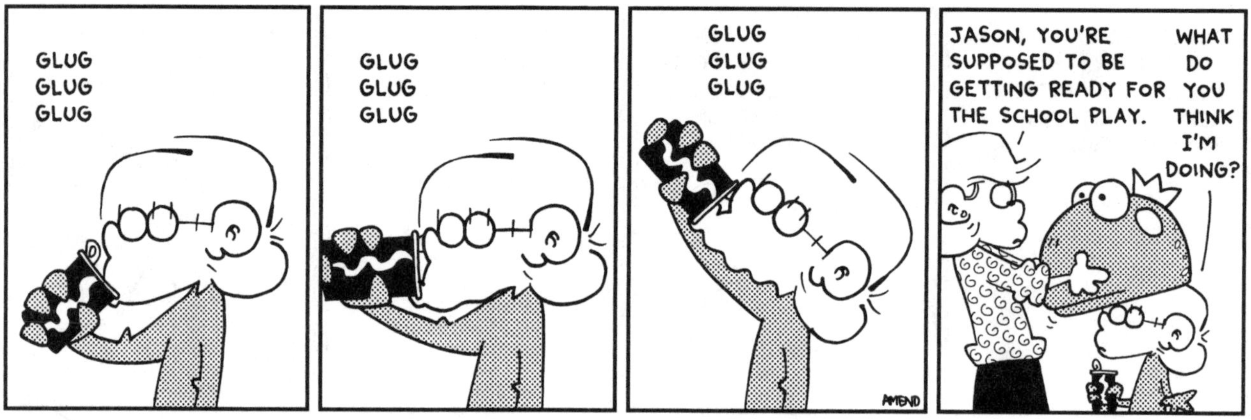
GLUG GLUG GLUG
GLUG GLUG GLUG
GLUG GLUG GLUG
JASON, YOU'RE SUPPOSED TO BE GETTING READY FOR THE SCHOOL PLAY.
WHAT DO YOU THINK I'M DOING?
AMEND

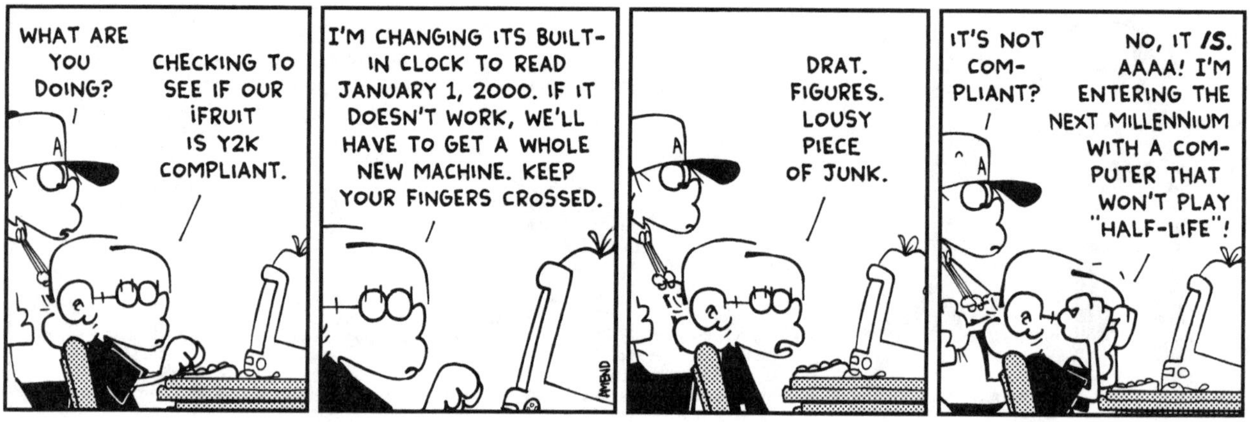
WHAT ARE YOU DOING?
CHECKING TO SEE IF OUR iFRUIT IS Y2K COMPLIANT.
I'M CHANGING ITS BUILT-IN CLOCK TO READ JANUARY 1, 2000. IF IT DOESN'T WORK, WE'LL HAVE TO GET A WHOLE NEW MACHINE. KEEP YOUR FINGERS CROSSED.
AMEND
DRAT. FIGURES. LOUSY PIECE OF JUNK.
IT'S NOT COMPLIANT?
NO, IT IS. AAAA! I'M ENTERING THE NEXT MILLENNIUM WITH A COMPUTER THAT WON'T PLAY "HALF-LIFE"!

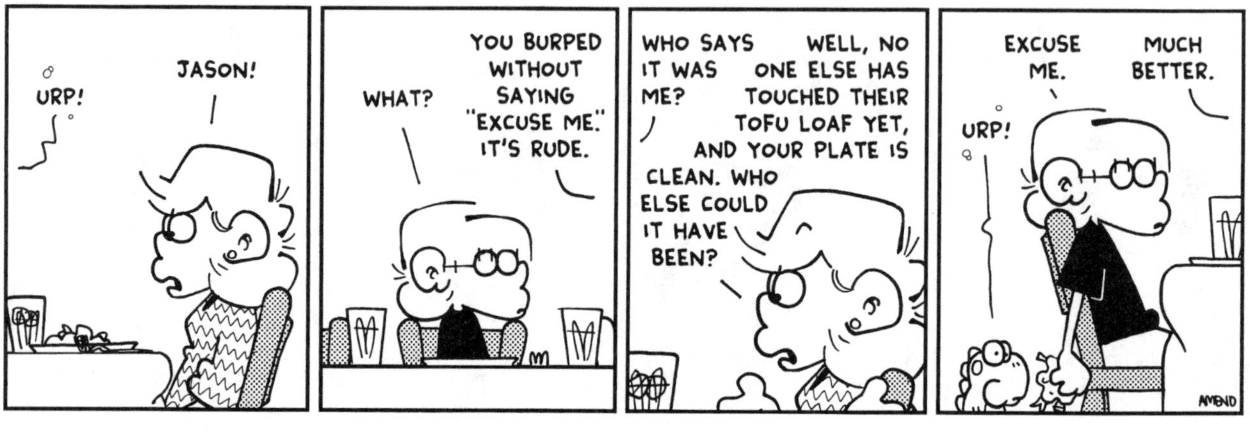
URP!
JASON!
WHAT?
YOU BURPED WITHOUT SAYING "EXCUSE ME." IT'S RUDE.
WHO SAYS IT WAS ME?
WELL, NO ONE ELSE HAS TOUCHED THEIR TOFU LOAF YET, AND YOUR PLATE IS CLEAN. WHO ELSE COULD IT HAVE BEEN?
URP!
EXCUSE ME.
MUCH BETTER.
AMEND

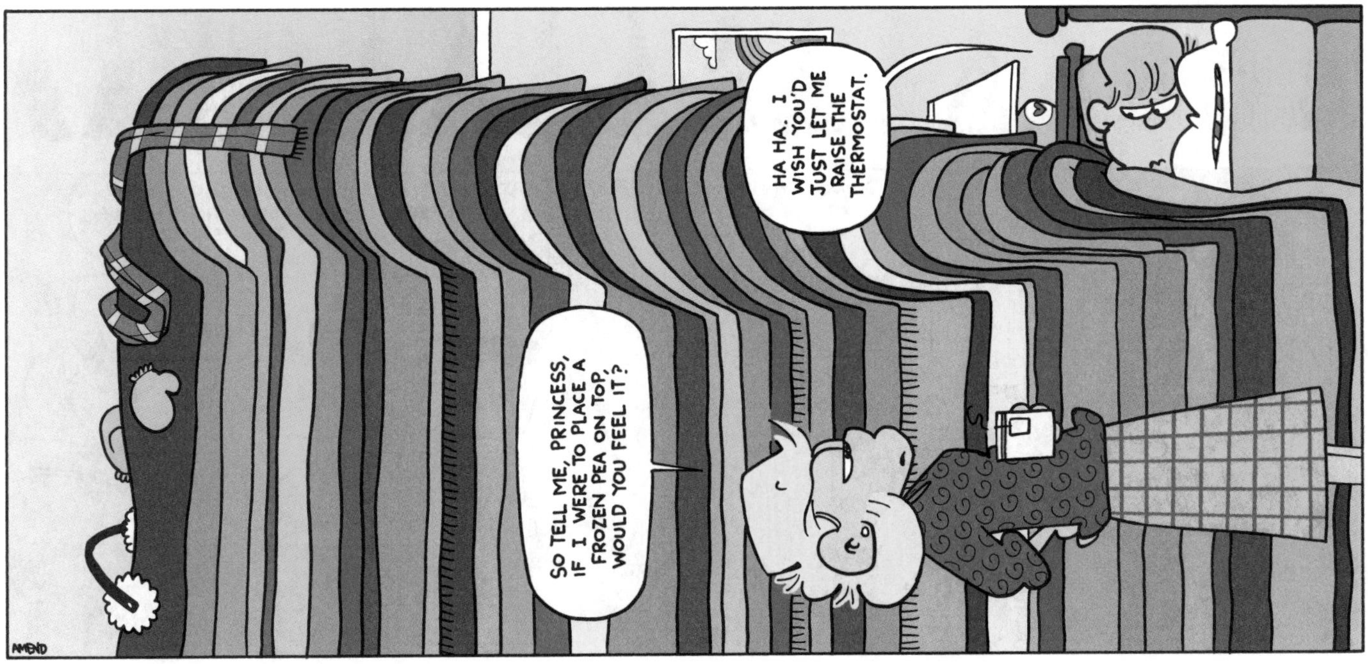
SO TELL ME, PRINCESS, IF I WERE TO PLACE A FROZEN PEA ON TOP, WOULD YOU FEEL IT?
HA HA. I WISH YOU'D JUST LET ME RAISE THE THERMOSTAT.
AMEND

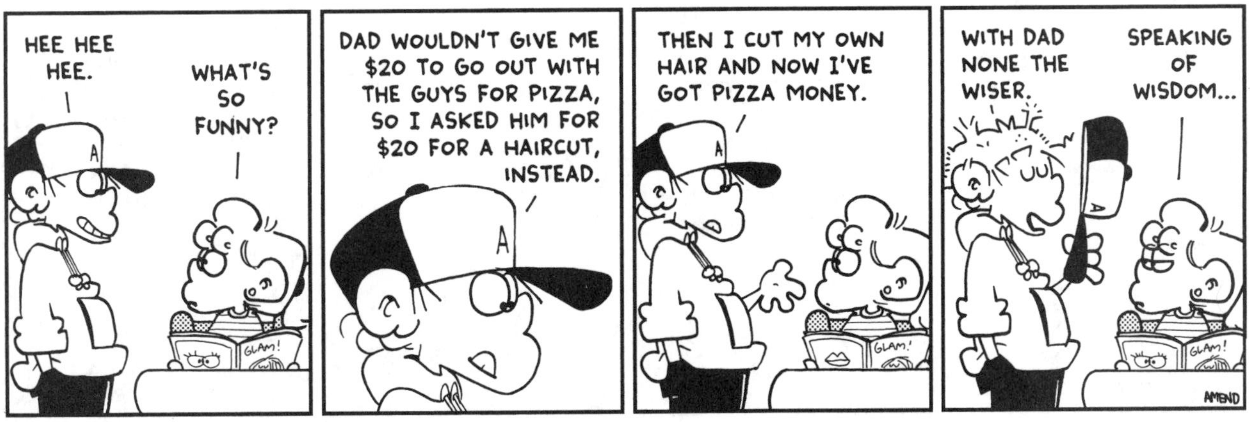
HEE HEE HEE.
WHAT'S SO FUNNY?
DAD WOULDN'T GIVE ME $20 TO GO OUT WITH THE GUYS FOR PIZZA, SO I ASKED HIM FOR $20 FOR A HAIRCUT, INSTEAD.
THEN I CUT MY OWN HAIR AND NOW I'VE GOT PIZZA MONEY.
WITH DAD NONE THE WISER.
SPEAKING OF WISDOM...
GLAM!
AMEND

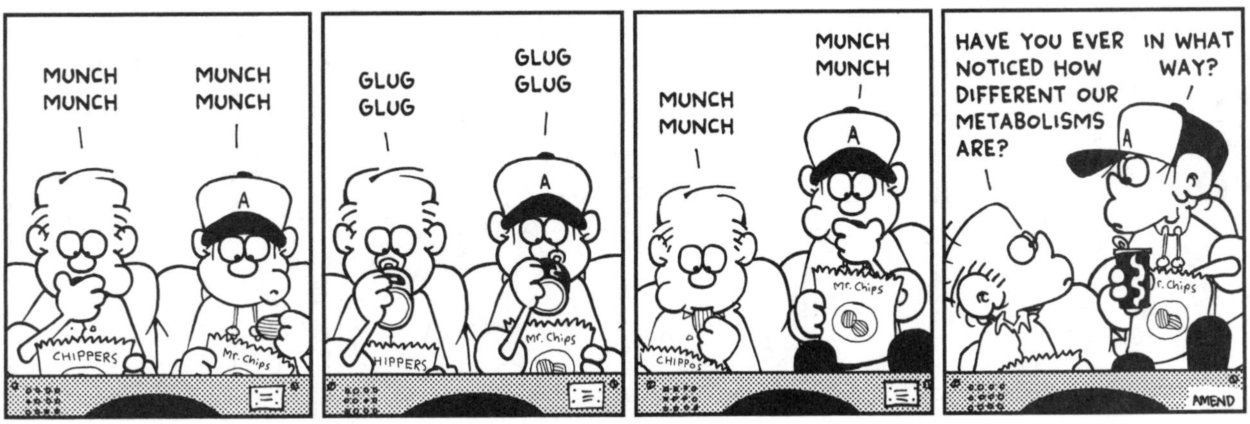
MUNCH MUNCH
MUNCH MUNCH
CHIPPERS
Mr. Chips
GLUG GLUG
GLUG GLUG
MUNCH MUNCH
MUNCH MUNCH
HAVE YOU EVER NOTICED HOW DIFFERENT OUR METABOLISMS ARE?
IN WHAT WAY?
AMEND

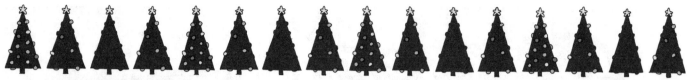

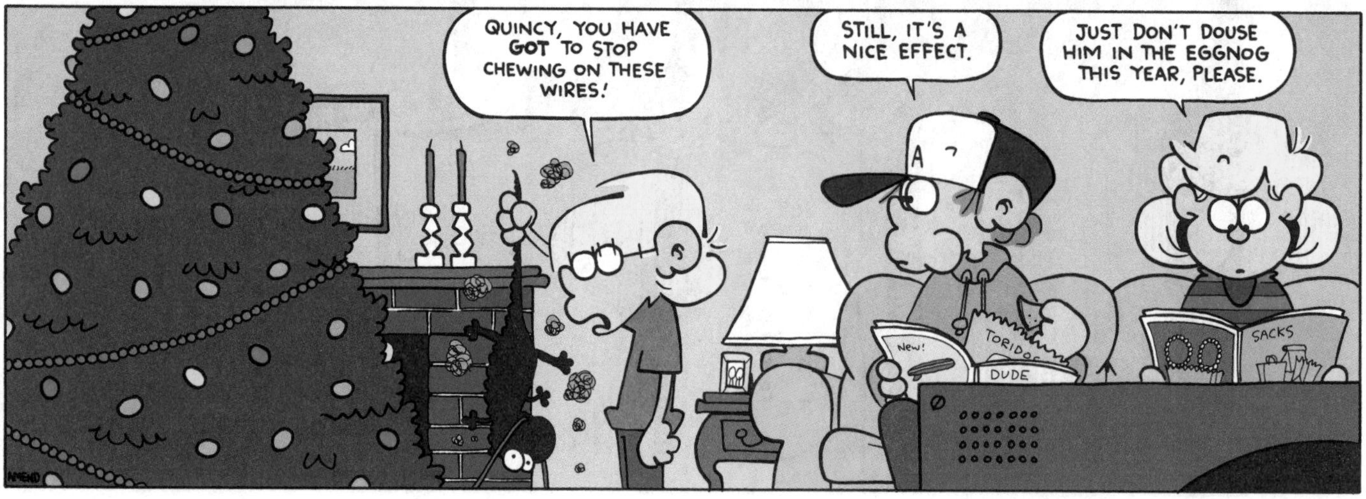
QUINCY, YOU HAVE **GOT** TO STOP CHEWING ON THESE WIRES!
STILL, IT'S A NICE EFFECT.
JUST DON'T DOUSE HIM IN THE EGGNOG THIS YEAR, PLEASE.
New!
DUDE
SACKS
AMEND

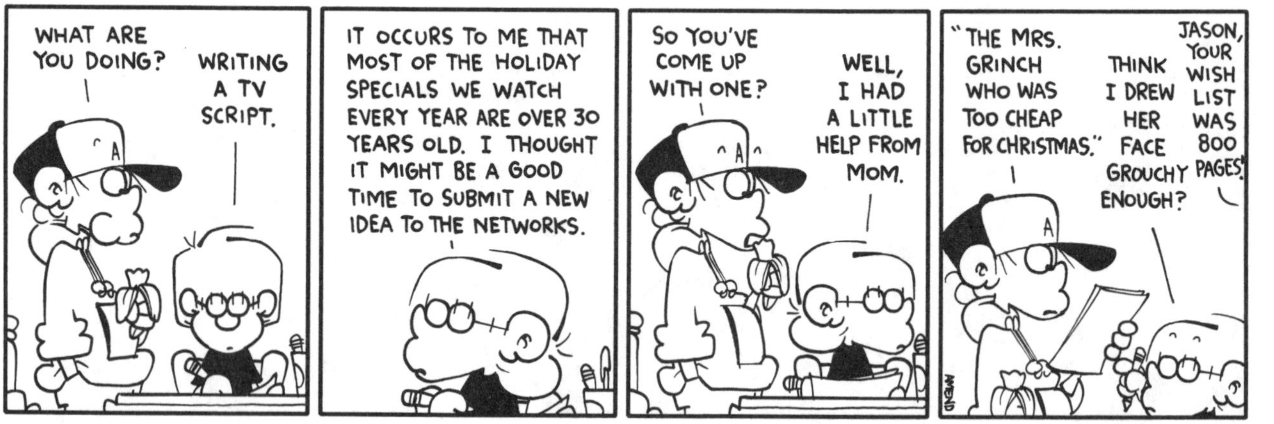
WHAT ARE YOU DOING?
WRITING A TV SCRIPT.
IT OCCURS TO ME THAT MOST OF THE HOLIDAY SPECIALS WE WATCH EVERY YEAR ARE OVER 30 YEARS OLD. I THOUGHT IT MIGHT BE A GOOD TIME TO SUBMIT A NEW IDEA TO THE NETWORKS.
SO YOU'VE COME UP WITH ONE?
WELL, I HAD A LITTLE HELP FROM MOM.
"THE MRS. GRINCH WHO WAS TOO CHEAP FOR CHRISTMAS."
THINK I DREW HER FACE GROUCHY ENOUGH?
JASON, YOUR WISH LIST WAS 800 PAGES!

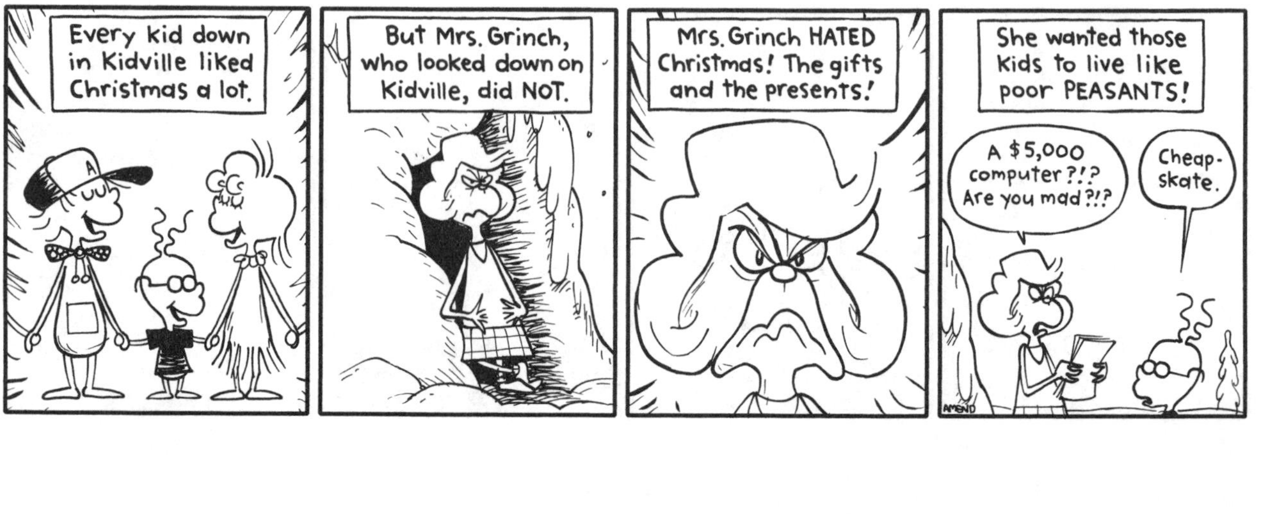
Every kid down in Kidville liked Christmas a lot.
But Mrs. Grinch, who looked down on Kidville, did NOT.
Mrs. Grinch HATED Christmas! The gifts and the presents!
She wanted those kids to live like poor PEASANTS!
A $5,000 computer?!? Are you mad?!?
Cheap-skate.
AMEND

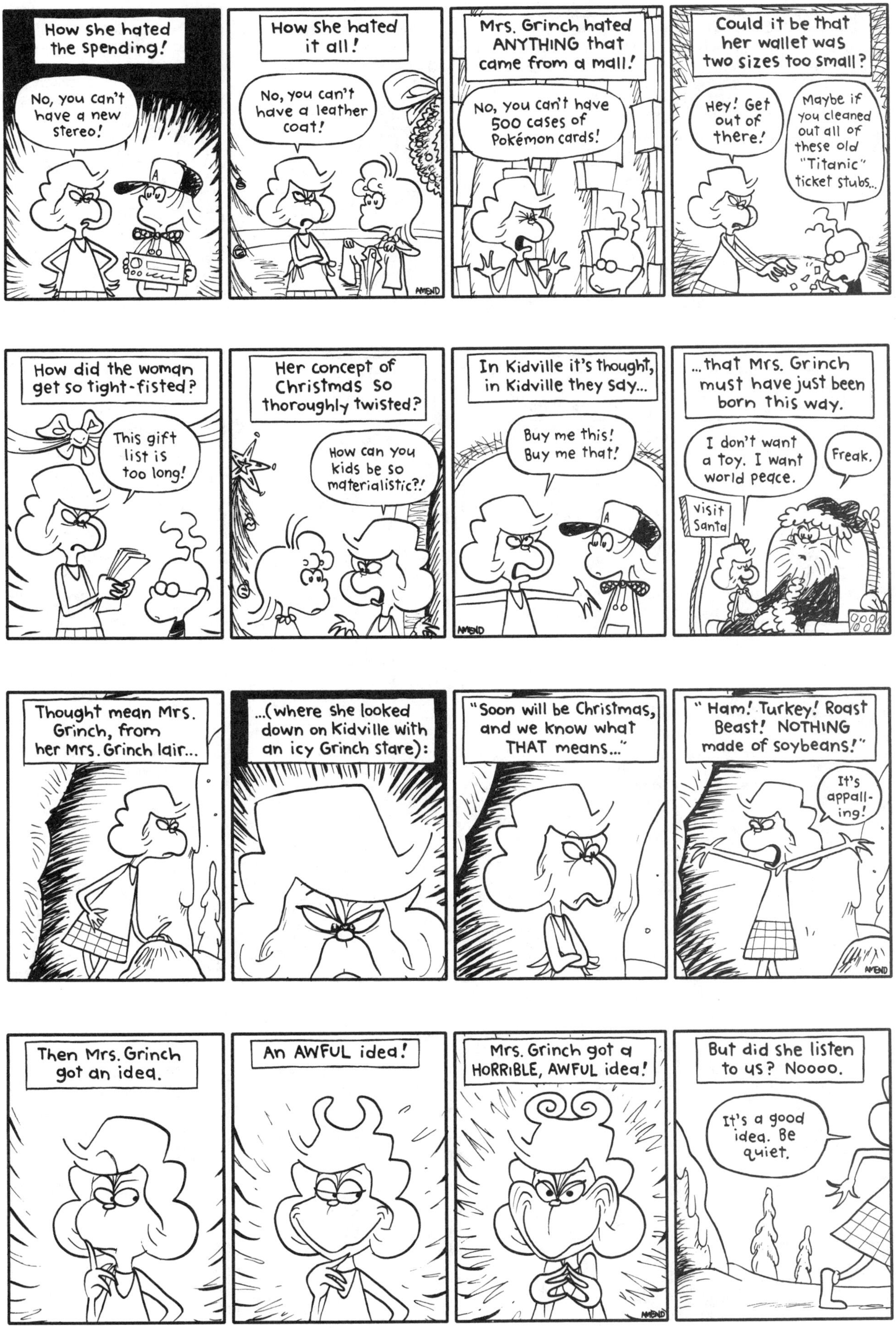
How she hated the spending!
No, you can't have a new stereo!
How she hated it all!
No, you can't have a leather coat!
Mrs. Grinch hated ANYTHING that came from a mall!
No, you can't have 500 cases of Pokémon cards!
Could it be that her wallet was two sizes too small?
Hey! Get out of there!
Maybe if you cleaned out all of these old "Titanic" ticket stubs...
How did the woman get so tight-fisted?
This gift list is too long!
Her concept of Christmas so thoroughly twisted?
How can you kids be so materialistic?!
In Kidville it's thought, in Kidville they say...
Buy me this! Buy me that!
...that Mrs. Grinch must have just been born this way.
I don't want a toy. I want world peace.
Freak.
Visit Santa
Thought mean Mrs. Grinch, from her Mrs. Grinch lair...
...(where she looked down on Kidville with an icy Grinch stare):
"Soon will be Christmas, and we know what THAT means..."
"Ham! Turkey! Roast Beast! NOTHING made of soybeans!"
It's appall-ing!
Then Mrs. Grinch got an idea.
An AWFUL idea!
Mrs. Grinch got a HORRIBLE, AWFUL idea!
But did she listen to us? Noooo.
It's a good idea. Be quiet.

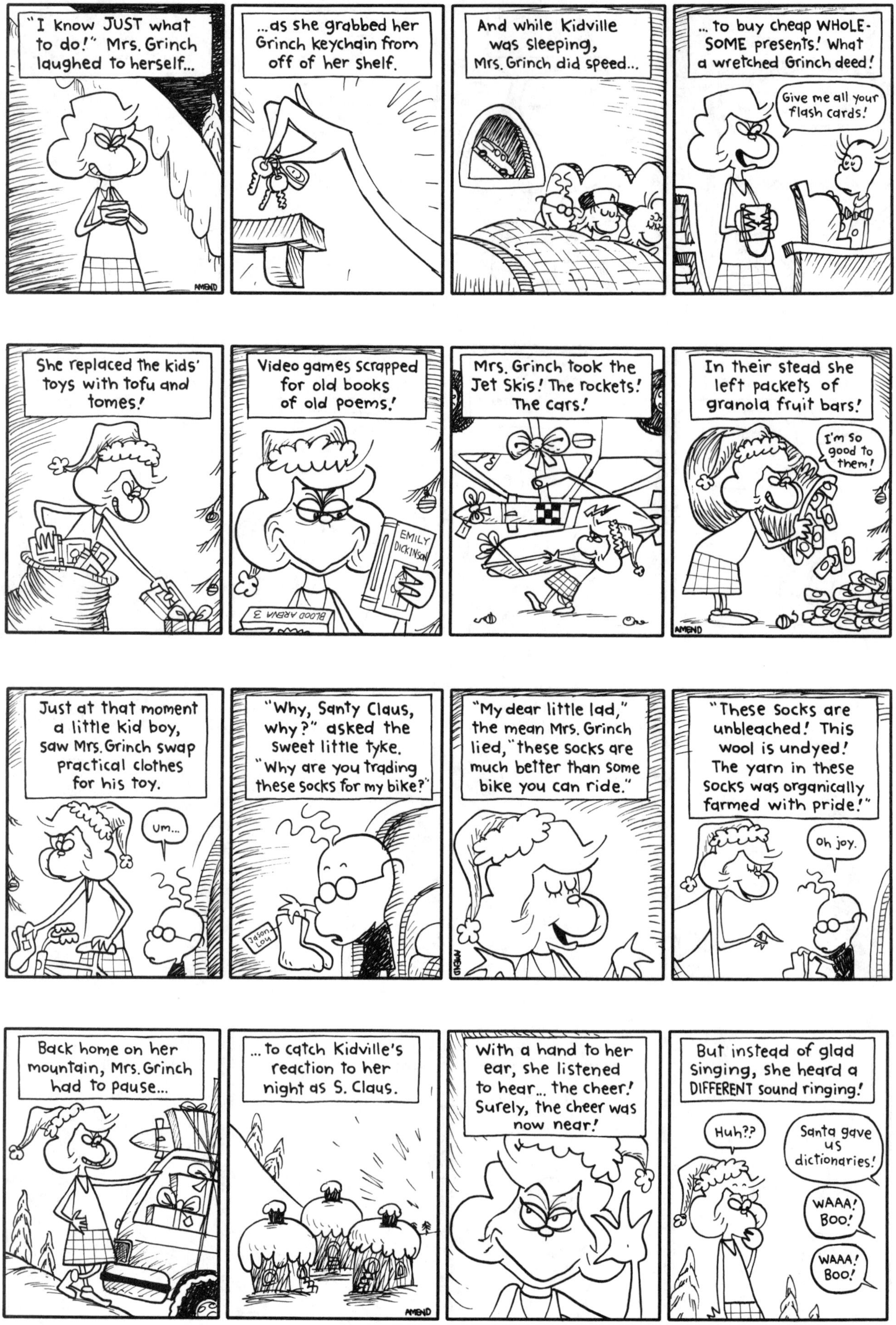
"I know JUST what to do!" Mrs. Grinch laughed to herself...
AMEND
...as she grabbed her Grinch keychain from off of her shelf.
And while Kidville was sleeping, Mrs. Grinch did speed...
... to buy cheap WHOLESOME presents! What a wretched Grinch deed!
Give me all your flash cards!
She replaced the kids' toys with tofu and tomes!
Video games scrapped for old books of old poems!
BLOOD ARENA 3
EMILY DICKINSON
Mrs. Grinch took the Jet Skis! The rockets! The cars!
In their stead she left packets of granola fruit bars!
I'm so good to them!
AMEND
Just at that moment a little kid boy, saw Mrs. Grinch swap practical clothes for his toy.
Um...
"Why, Santy Claus, why?" asked the sweet little tyke. "Why are you trading these socks for my bike?"
Jason Lou
"My dear little lad," the mean Mrs. Grinch lied, "these socks are much better than some bike you can ride."
AMEND
"These socks are unbleached! This wool is undyed! The yarn in these socks was organically farmed with pride!"
Oh joy.
Back home on her mountain, Mrs. Grinch had to pause...
... to catch Kidville's reaction to her night as S. Claus.
AMEND
With a hand to her ear, she listened to hear... the cheer! Surely, the cheer was now near!
But instead of glad singing, she heard a DIFFERENT sound ringing!
Huh??
Santa gave us dictionaries!
WAAA! BOO!
WAAA! BOO!

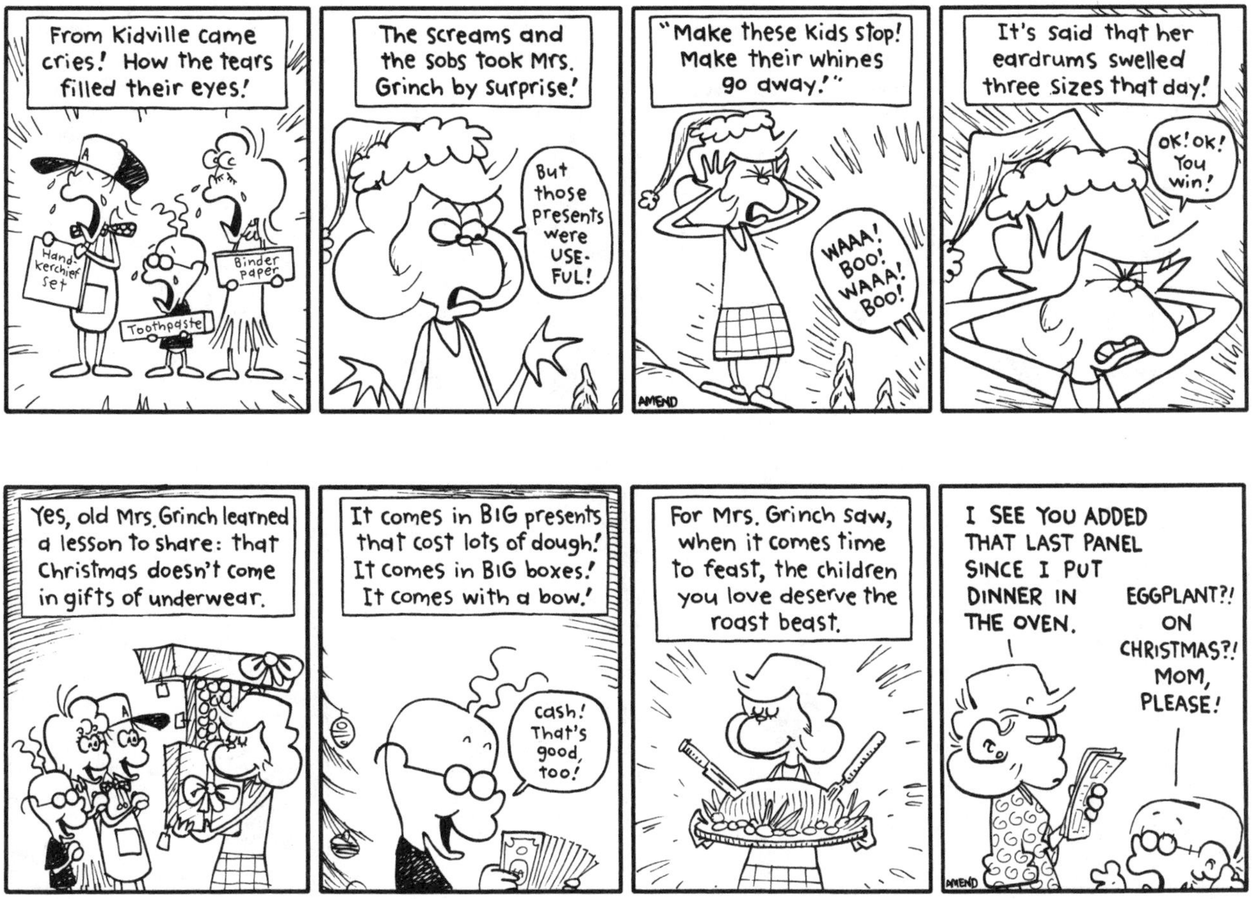
From Kidville came cries! How the tears filled their eyes!
Hand-kerchief set
Toothpaste
Binder paper
The screams and the sobs took Mrs. Grinch by surprise!
But those presents were USE-FUL!
"Make these kids stop! Make their whines go away!"
WAAA! BOO! WAAA! BOO!
It's said that her eardrums swelled three sizes that day!
OK! OK! You win!
Yes, old Mrs. Grinch learned a lesson to share: that Christmas doesn't come in gifts of underwear.
It comes in BIG presents that cost lots of dough! It comes in BIG boxes! It comes with a bow!
cash! That's good, too!
For Mrs. Grinch saw, when it comes time to feast, the children you love deserve the roast beast.
I SEE YOU ADDED THAT LAST PANEL SINCE I PUT DINNER IN THE OVEN.
EGGPLANT?! ON CHRISTMAS?! MOM, PLEASE!
AMEND

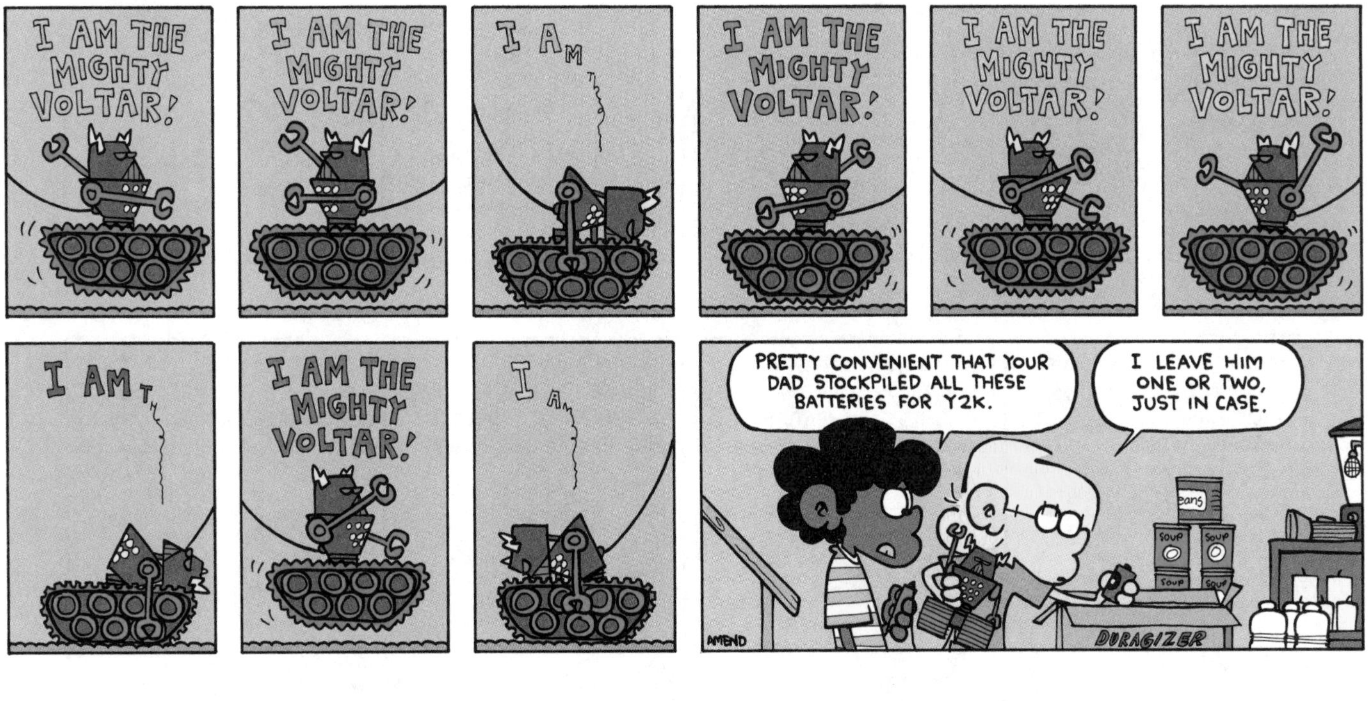
I AM THE MIGHTY VOLTAR!
I AM THE MIGHTY VOLTAR!
I AM
I AM THE MIGHTY VOLTAR!
I AM THE MIGHTY VOLTAR!
I AM THE MIGHTY VOLTAR!
I AM
I AM THE MIGHTY VOLTAR!
I A
PRETTY CONVENIENT THAT YOUR DAD STOCKPILED ALL THESE BATTERIES FOR Y2K.
I LEAVE HIM ONE OR TWO, JUST IN CASE.
Soup
Soup
DURAGIZER
AMEND

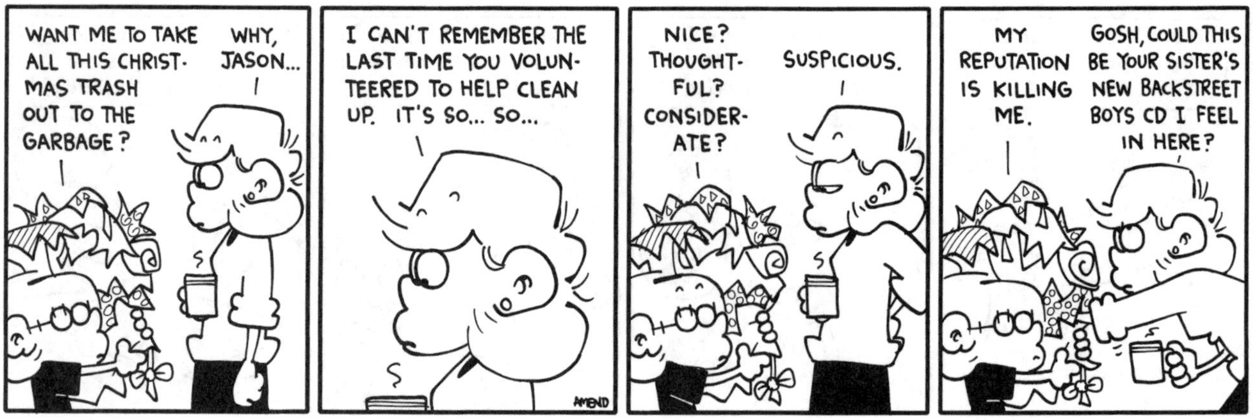
WANT ME TO TAKE ALL THIS CHRIST-MAS TRASH OUT TO THE GARBAGE?
WHY, JASON...
I CAN'T REMEMBER THE LAST TIME YOU VOLUN-TEERED TO HELP CLEAN UP. IT'S SO... SO...
NICE? THOUGHT-FUL? CONSIDER-ATE?
SUSPICIOUS.
MY REPUTATION IS KILLING ME.
GOSH, COULD THIS BE YOUR SISTER'S NEW BACKSTREET BOYS CD I FEEL IN HERE?
AMEND

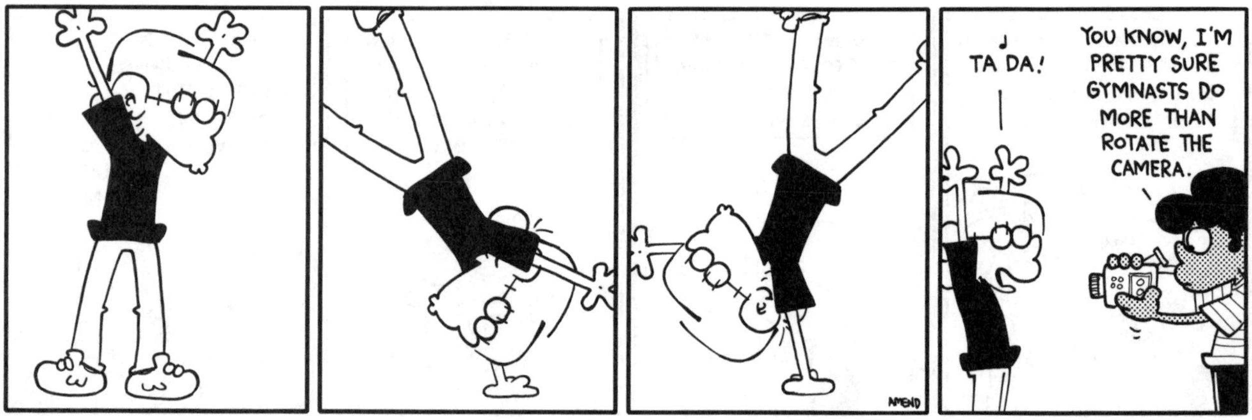
TA DA!
YOU KNOW, I'M PRETTY SURE GYMNASTS DO MORE THAN ROTATE THE CAMERA.
AMEND

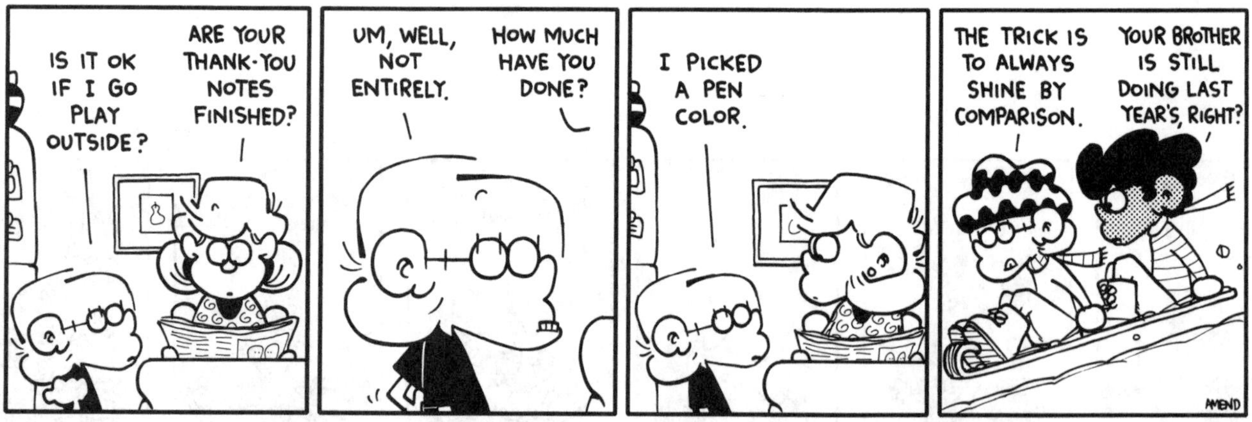
IS IT OK IF I GO PLAY OUTSIDE?
ARE YOUR THANK-YOU NOTES FINISHED?
UM, WELL, NOT ENTIRELY.
HOW MUCH HAVE YOU DONE?
I PICKED A PEN COLOR.
THE TRICK IS TO ALWAYS SHINE BY COMPARISON.
YOUR BROTHER IS STILL DOING LAST YEAR'S, RIGHT?
AMEND

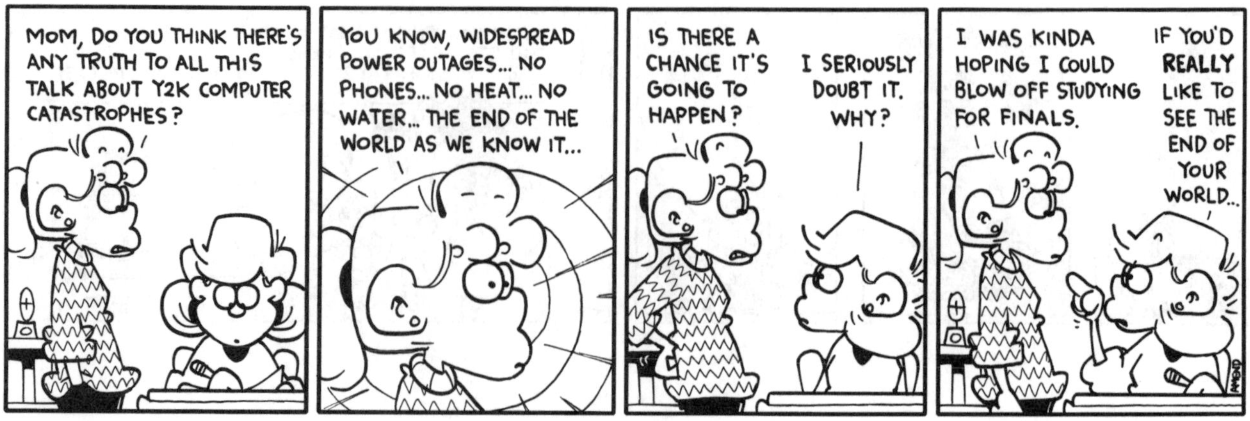
MOM, DO YOU THINK THERE'S ANY TRUTH TO ALL THIS TALK ABOUT Y2K COMPUTER CATASTROPHES?
YOU KNOW, WIDESPREAD POWER OUTAGES... NO PHONES... NO HEAT... NO WATER... THE END OF THE WORLD AS WE KNOW IT...
IS THERE A CHANCE IT'S GOING TO HAPPEN?
I SERIOUSLY DOUBT IT. WHY?
I WAS KINDA HOPING I COULD BLOW OFF STUDYING FOR FINALS.
IF YOU'D REALLY LIKE TO SEE THE END OF YOUR WORLD...
AMEND

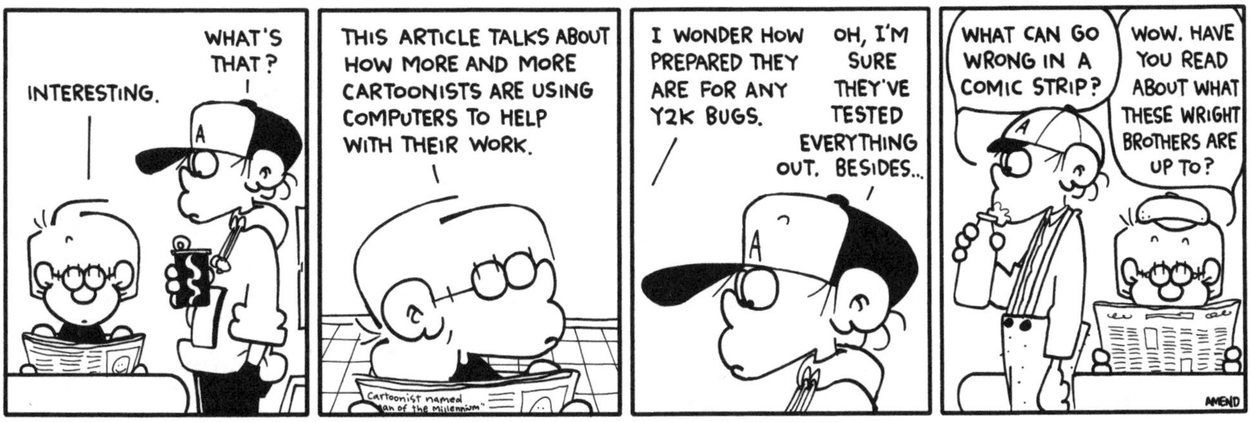
INTERESTING.
WHAT'S THAT?
THIS ARTICLE TALKS ABOUT HOW MORE AND MORE CARTOONISTS ARE USING COMPUTERS TO HELP WITH THEIR WORK.
Cartoonist named
I WONDER HOW PREPARED THEY ARE FOR ANY Y2K BUGS.
OH, I'M SURE THEY'VE TESTED EVERYTHING OUT. BESIDES...
WHAT CAN GO WRONG IN A COMIC STRIP?
WOW. HAVE YOU READ ABOUT WHAT THESE WRIGHT BROTHERS ARE UP TO?
AMEND

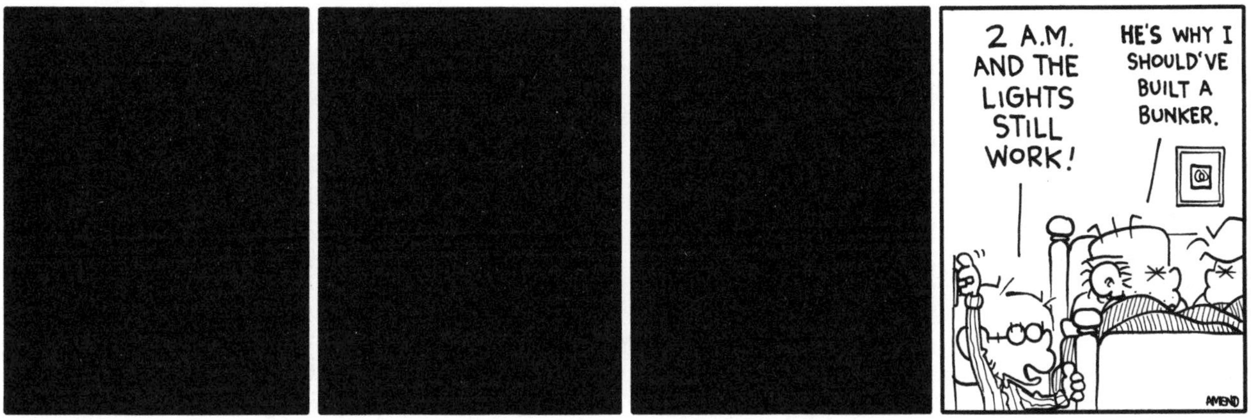
2 A.M. AND THE LIGHTS STILL WORK!
HE'S WHY I SHOULD'VE BUILT A BUNKER.
AMEND

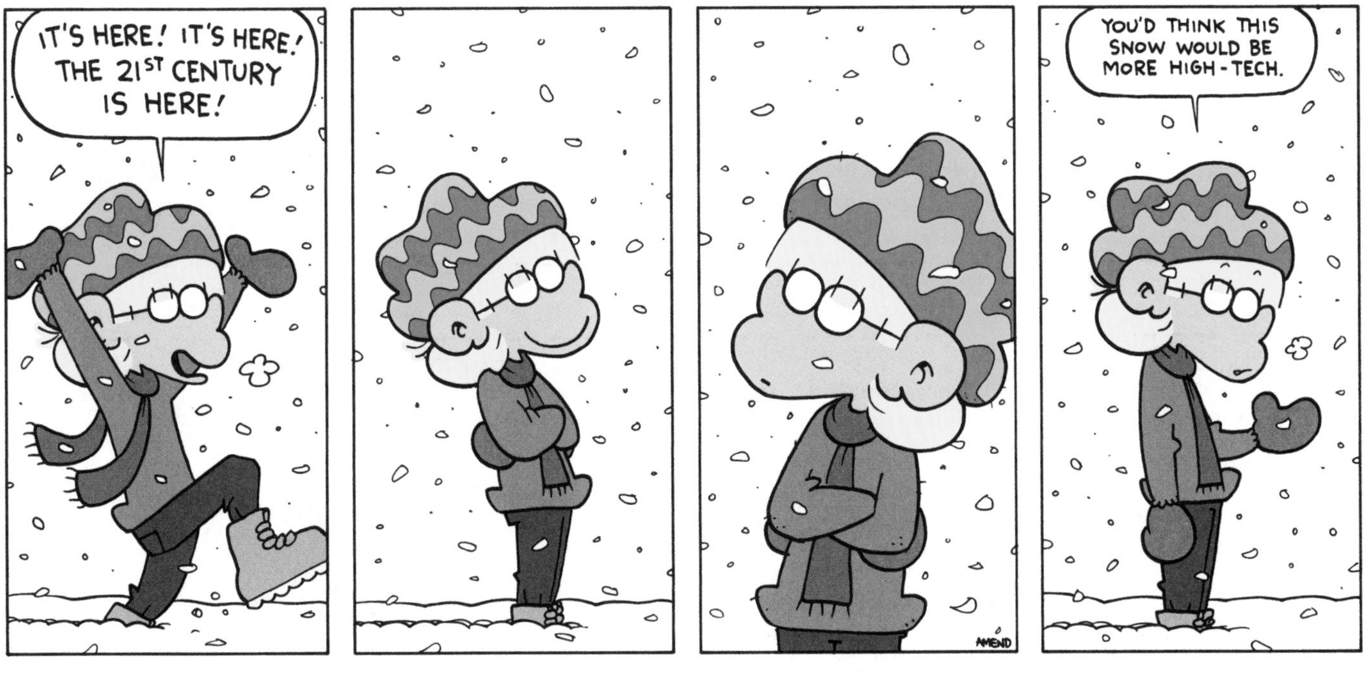
IT'S HERE! IT'S HERE! THE 21ST CENTURY IS HERE!
YOU'D THINK THIS SNOW WOULD BE MORE HIGH-TECH.
AMEND

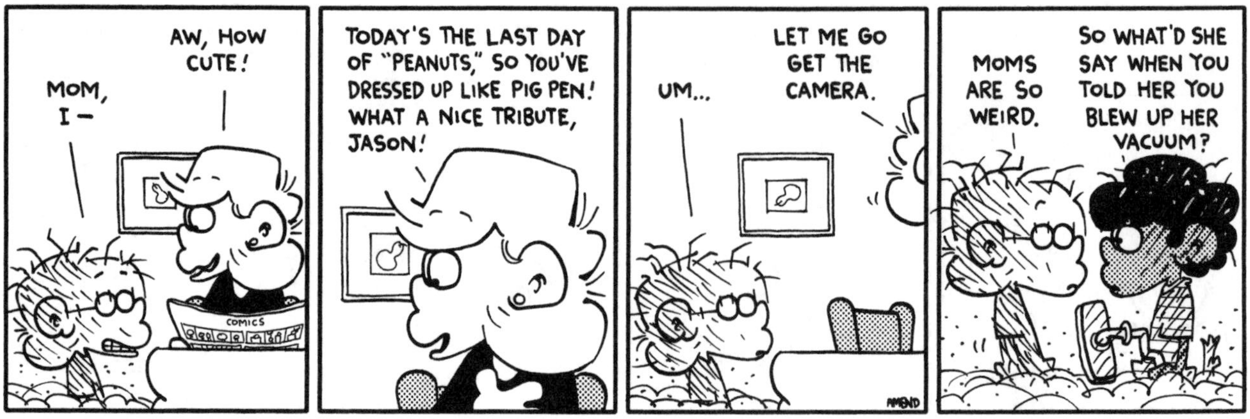
MOM, I—
AW, HOW CUTE!
TODAY'S THE LAST DAY OF "PEANUTS," SO YOU'VE DRESSED UP LIKE PIG PEN! WHAT A NICE TRIBUTE, JASON!
UM...
LET ME GO GET THE CAMERA.
MOMS ARE SO WEIRD.
SO WHAT'D SHE SAY WHEN YOU TOLD HER YOU BLEW UP HER VACUUM?

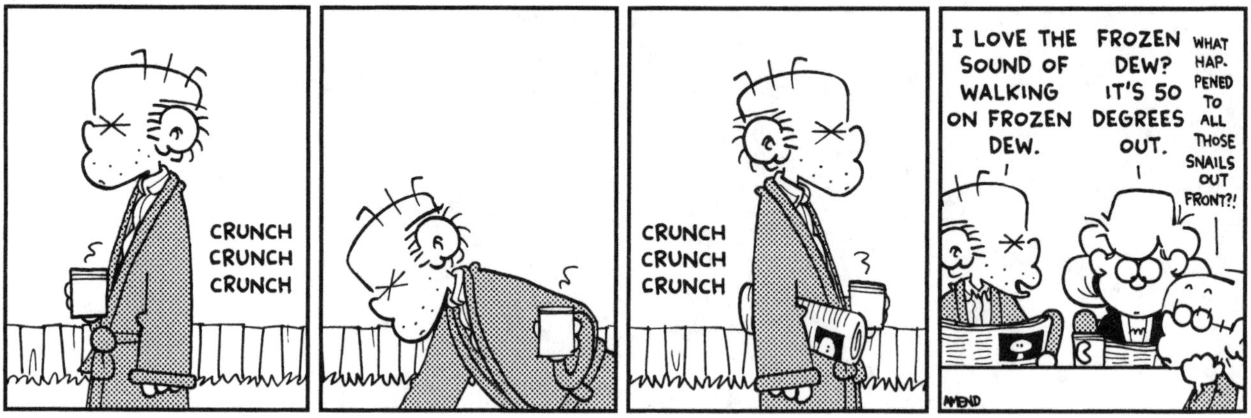
CRUNCH CRUNCH CRUNCH
CRUNCH CRUNCH CRUNCH
I LOVE THE SOUND OF WALKING ON FROZEN DEW.
FROZEN DEW? IT'S 50 DEGREES OUT.
WHAT HAP-PENED TO ALL THOSE SNAILS OUT FRONT?!

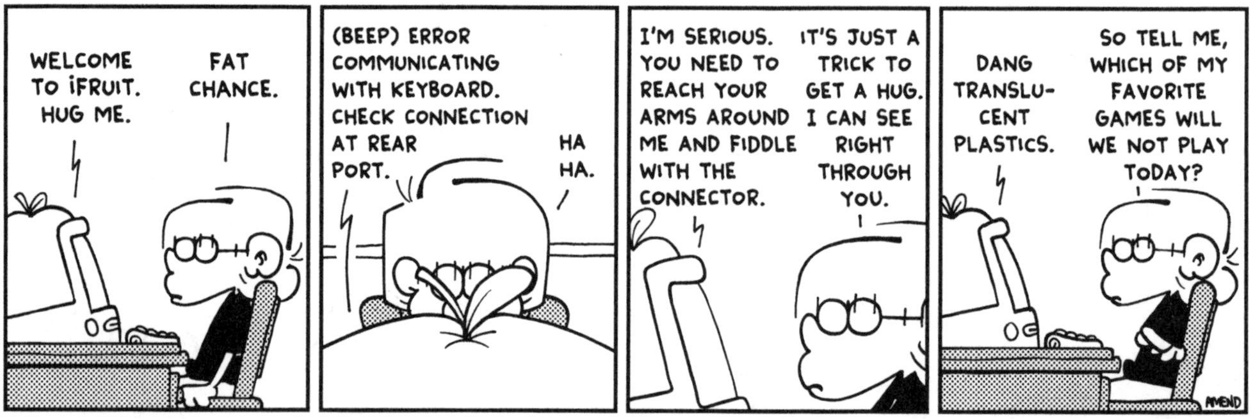
WELCOME TO iFRUIT. HUG ME.
FAT CHANCE.
(BEEP) ERROR COMMUNICATING WITH KEYBOARD. CHECK CONNECTION AT REAR PORT.
HA HA.
I'M SERIOUS. YOU NEED TO REACH YOUR ARMS AROUND ME AND FIDDLE WITH THE CONNECTOR.
IT'S JUST A TRICK TO GET A HUG. I CAN SEE RIGHT THROUGH YOU.
DANG TRANSLU-CENT PLASTICS.
SO TELL ME, WHICH OF MY FAVORITE GAMES WILL WE NOT PLAY TODAY?

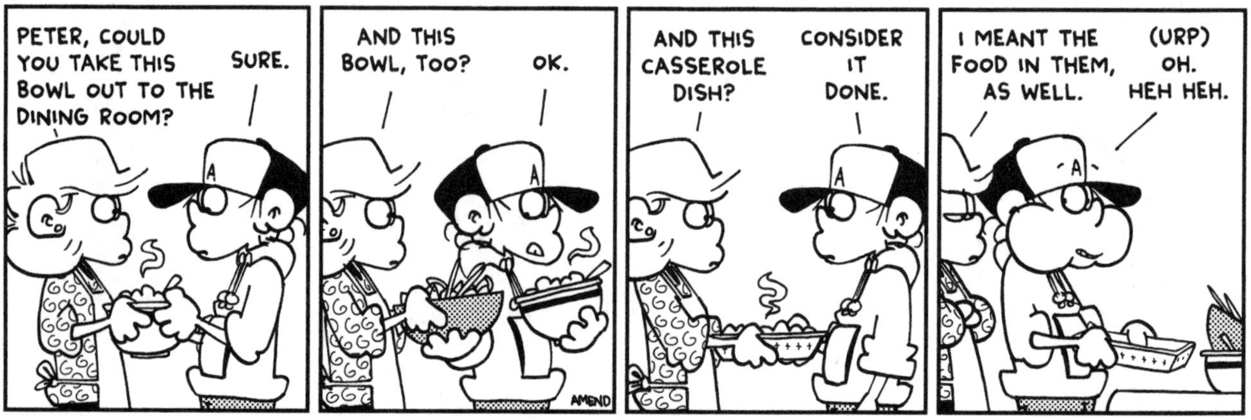
PETER, COULD YOU TAKE THIS BOWL OUT TO THE DINING ROOM?
SURE.
AND THIS BOWL, TOO?
OK.
AND THIS CASSEROLE DISH?
CONSIDER IT DONE.
I MEANT THE FOOD IN THEM, AS WELL.
(URP) OH. HEH HEH.

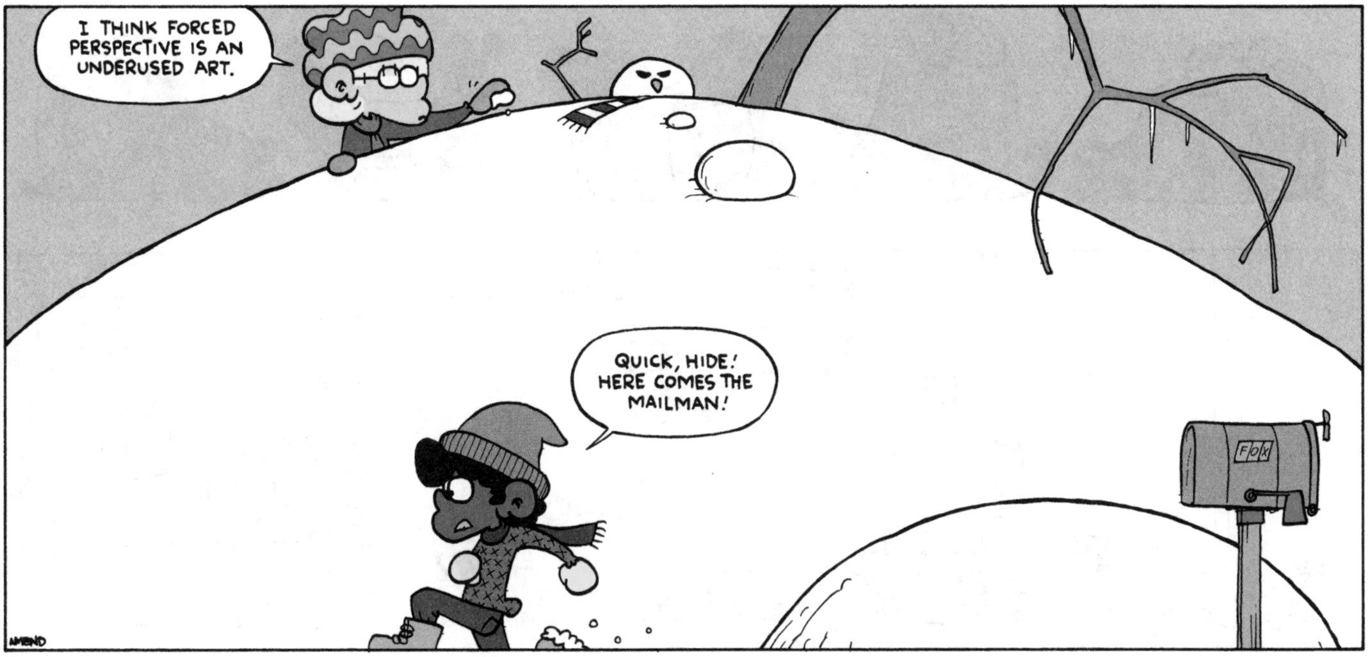
I THINK FORCED PERSPECTIVE IS AN UNDERUSED ART.
QUICK, HIDE! HERE COMES THE MAILMAN!

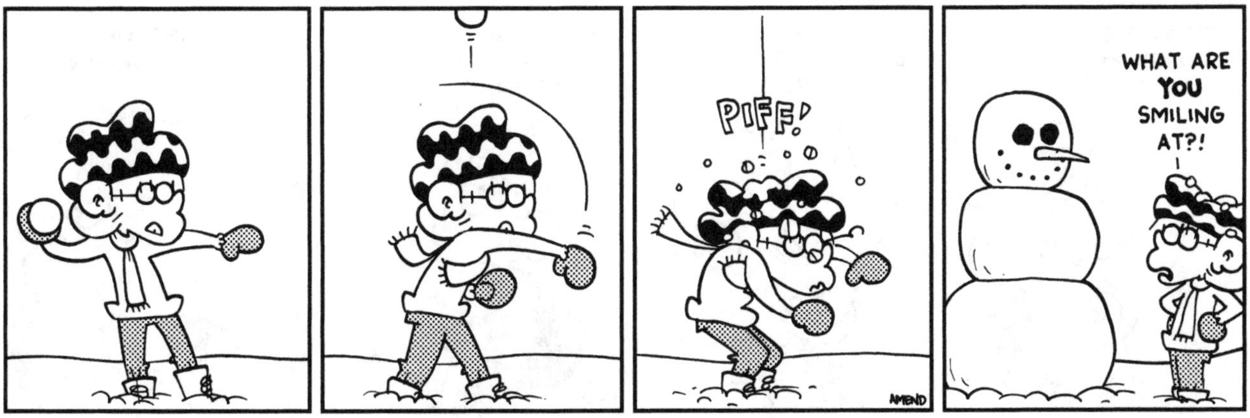
PIFF!
WHAT ARE **YOU** SMILING AT?!

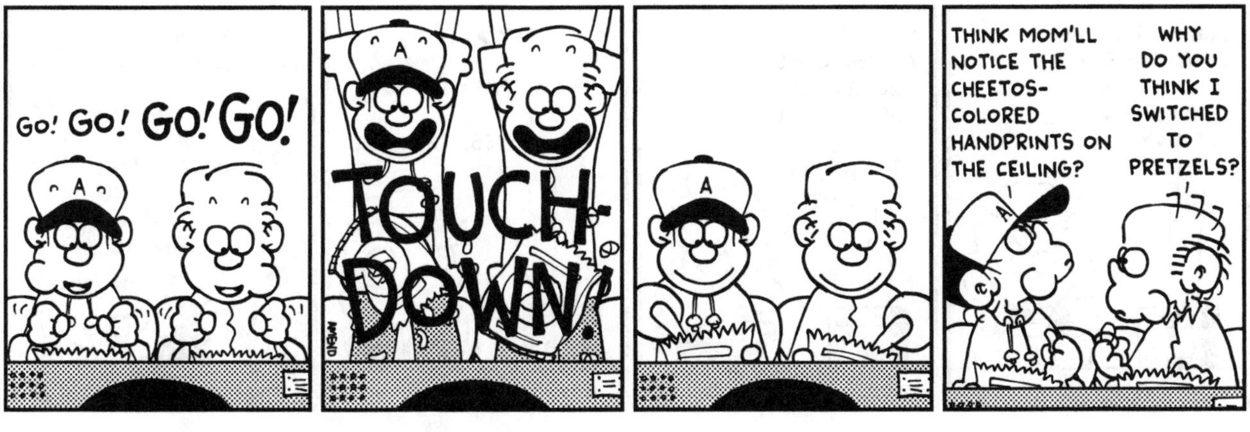
GO! GO! GO! GO!
TOUCH-DOWN!
THINK MOM'LL NOTICE THE CHEETOS-COLORED HANDPRINTS ON THE CEILING?
WHY DO YOU THINK I SWITCHED TO PRETZELS?

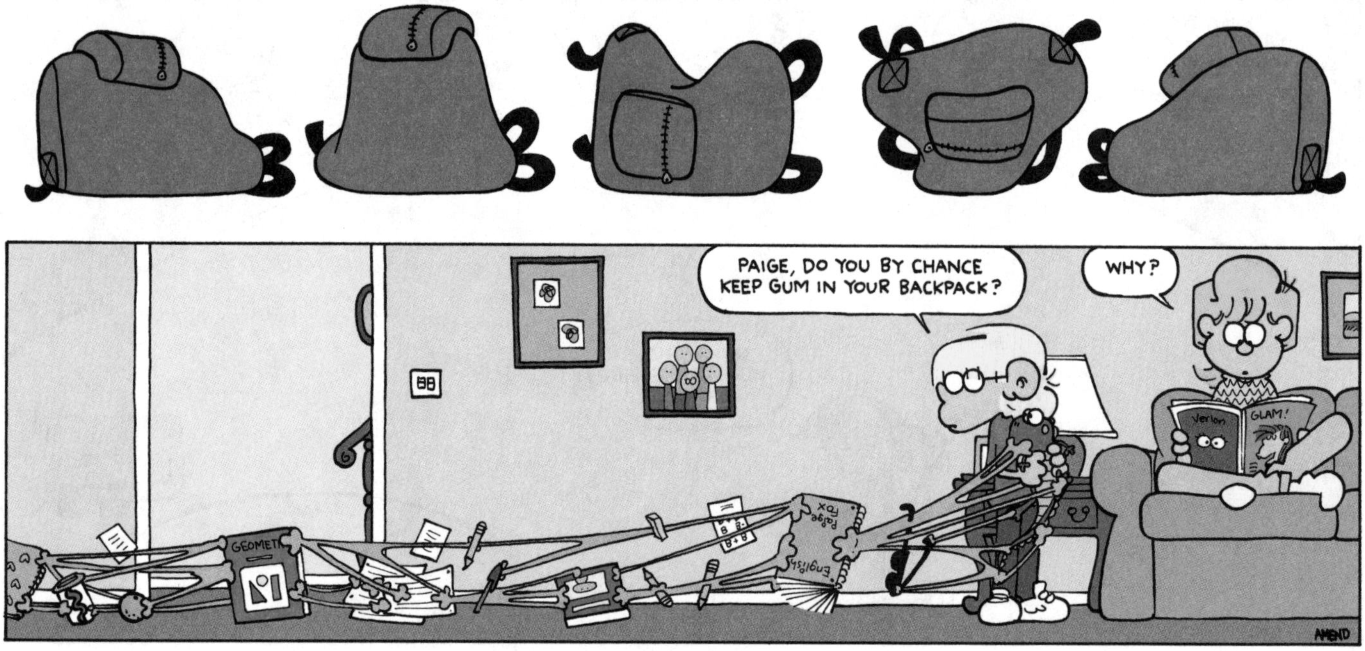
PAIGE, DO YOU BY CHANCE KEEP GUM IN YOUR BACKPACK?
WHY?
GLAM!
AMEND

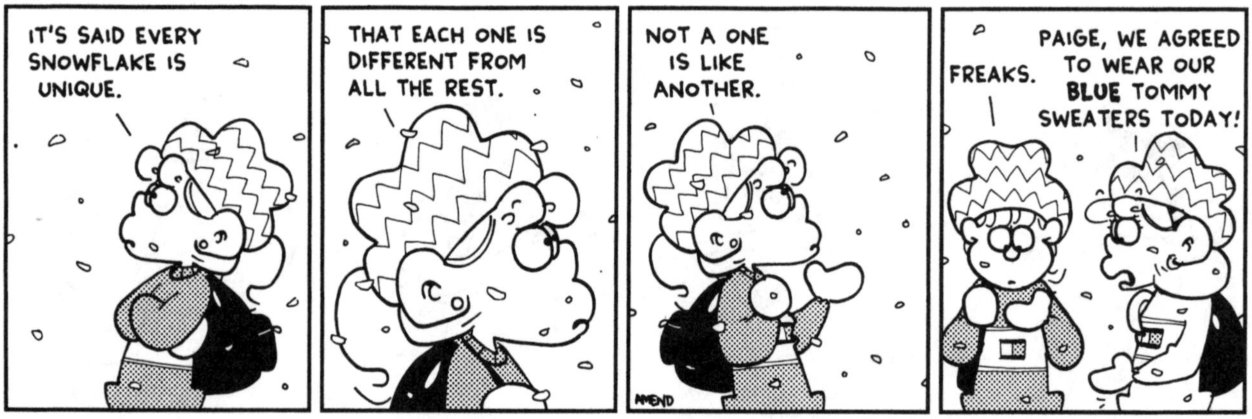
IT'S SAID EVERY SNOWFLAKE IS UNIQUE.
THAT EACH ONE IS DIFFERENT FROM ALL THE REST.
NOT A ONE IS LIKE ANOTHER.
AMEND
FREAKS.
PAIGE, WE AGREED TO WEAR OUR **BLUE** TOMMY SWEATERS TODAY!

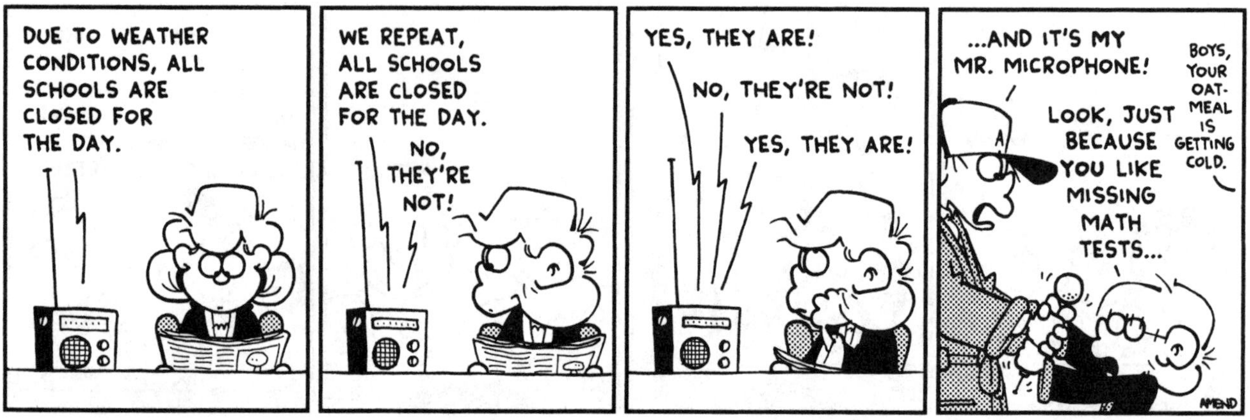
DUE TO WEATHER CONDITIONS, ALL SCHOOLS ARE CLOSED FOR THE DAY.
WE REPEAT, ALL SCHOOLS ARE CLOSED FOR THE DAY.
NO, THEY'RE NOT!
YES, THEY ARE!
NO, THEY'RE NOT!
YES, THEY ARE!
...AND IT'S MY MR. MICROPHONE!
BOYS, YOUR OAT-MEAL IS GETTING COLD.
LOOK, JUST BECAUSE YOU LIKE MISSING MATH TESTS...
AMEND

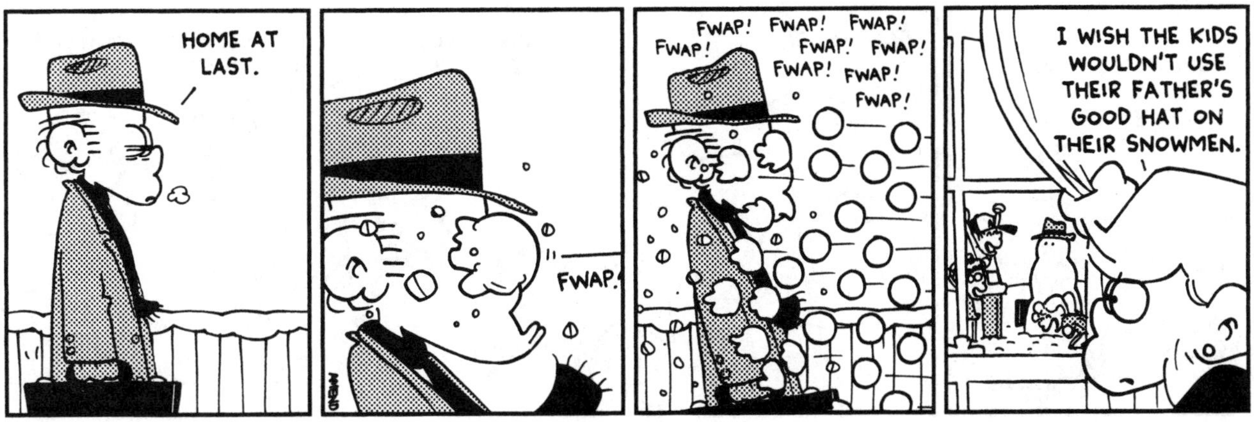
HOME AT LAST.
FWAP!
FWAP! FWAP! FWAP! FWAP! FWAP! FWAP! FWAP! FWAP!
I WISH THE KIDS WOULDN'T USE THEIR FATHER'S GOOD HAT ON THEIR SNOWMEN.

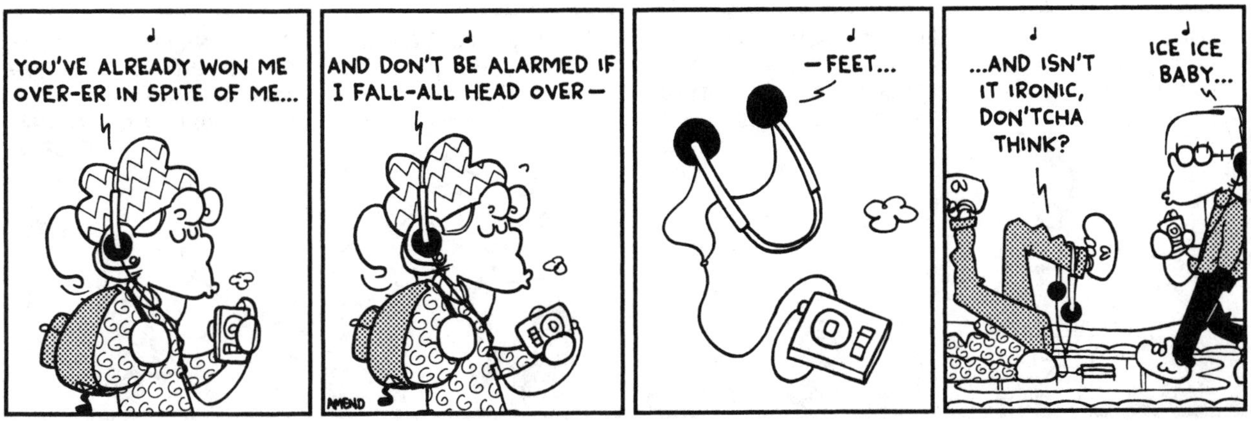
YOU'VE ALREADY WON ME OVER-ER IN SPITE OF ME...
AND DON'T BE ALARMED IF I FALL-ALL HEAD OVER—
—FEET...
...AND ISN'T IT IRONIC, DON'TCHA THINK?
ICE ICE BABY...

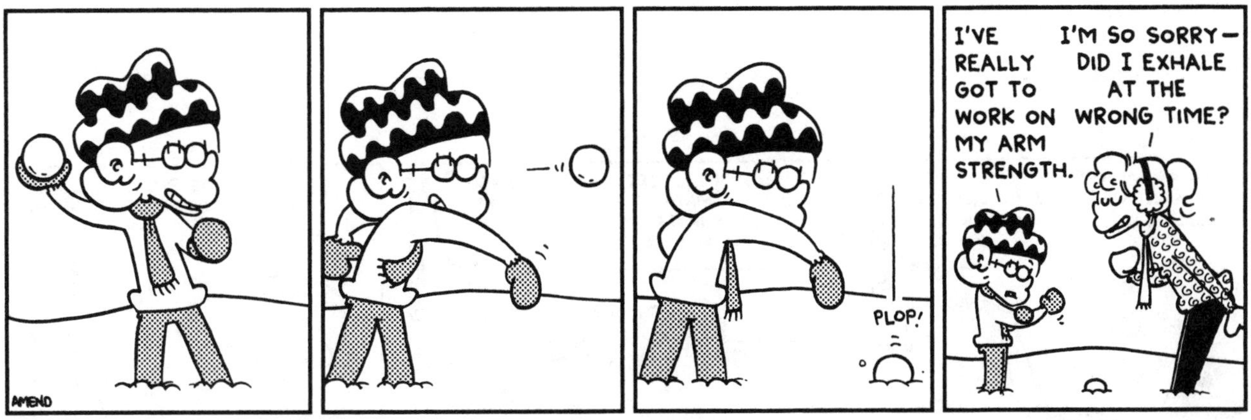
PLOP!
I'VE REALLY GOT TO WORK ON MY ARM STRENGTH.
I'M SO SORRY— DID I EXHALE AT THE WRONG TIME?

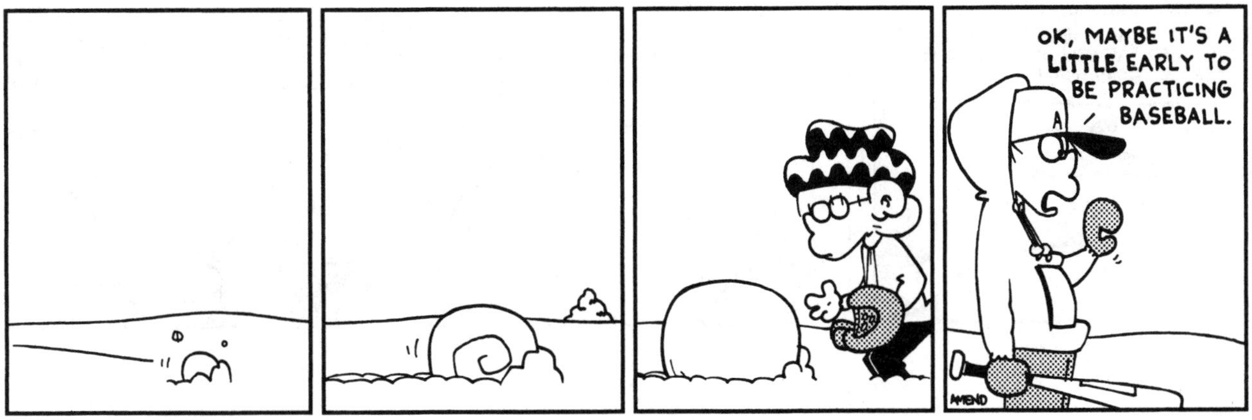
OK, MAYBE IT'S A LITTLE EARLY TO BE PRACTICING BASEBALL.

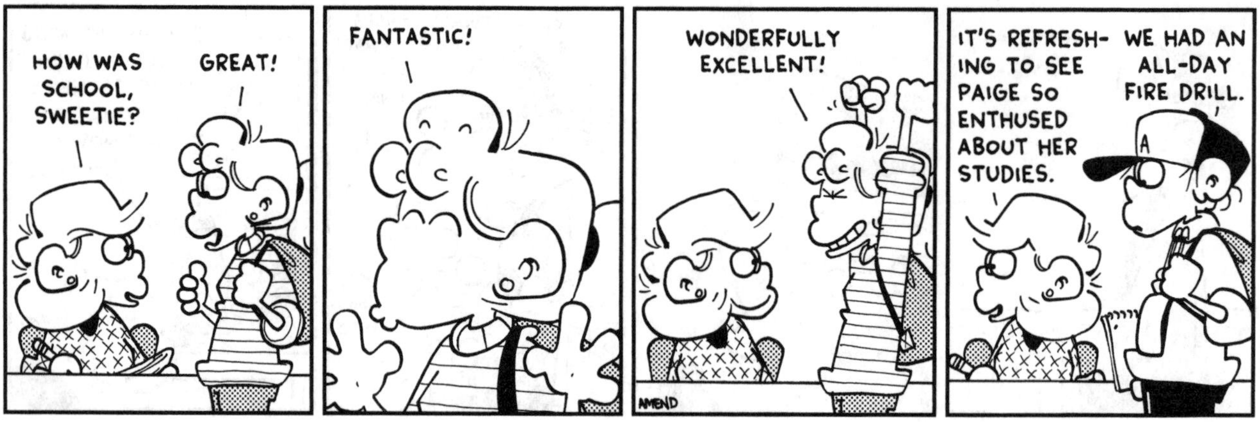
HOW WAS SCHOOL, SWEETIE?
GREAT!
FANTASTIC!
WONDERFULLY EXCELLENT!
IT'S REFRESH-ING TO SEE PAIGE SO ENTHUSED ABOUT HER STUDIES.
WE HAD AN ALL-DAY FIRE DRILL.
AMEND

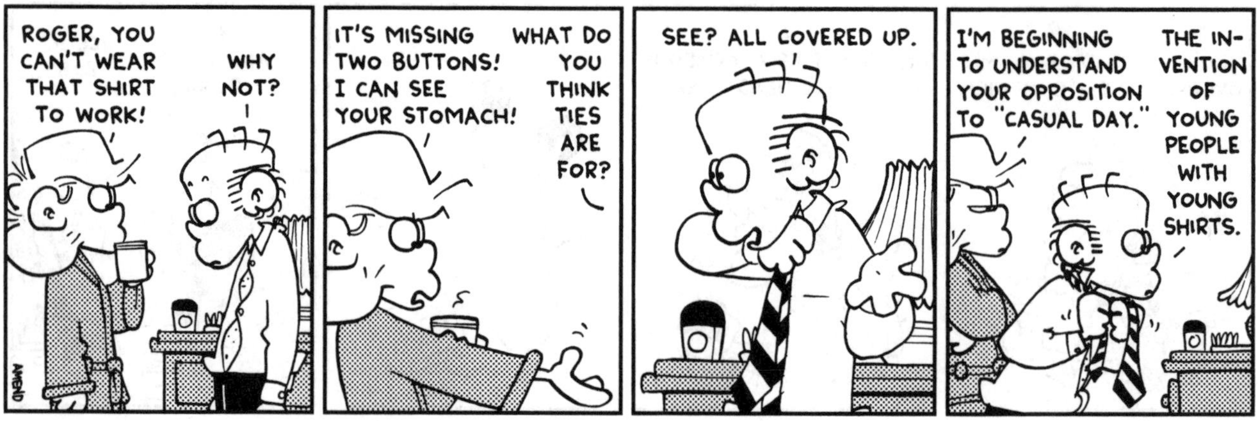
ROGER, YOU CAN'T WEAR THAT SHIRT TO WORK!
WHY NOT?
IT'S MISSING TWO BUTTONS! I CAN SEE YOUR STOMACH!
WHAT DO YOU THINK TIES ARE FOR?
SEE? ALL COVERED UP.
I'M BEGINNING TO UNDERSTAND YOUR OPPOSITION TO "CASUAL DAY."
THE IN-VENTION OF YOUNG PEOPLE WITH YOUNG SHIRTS.
AMEND

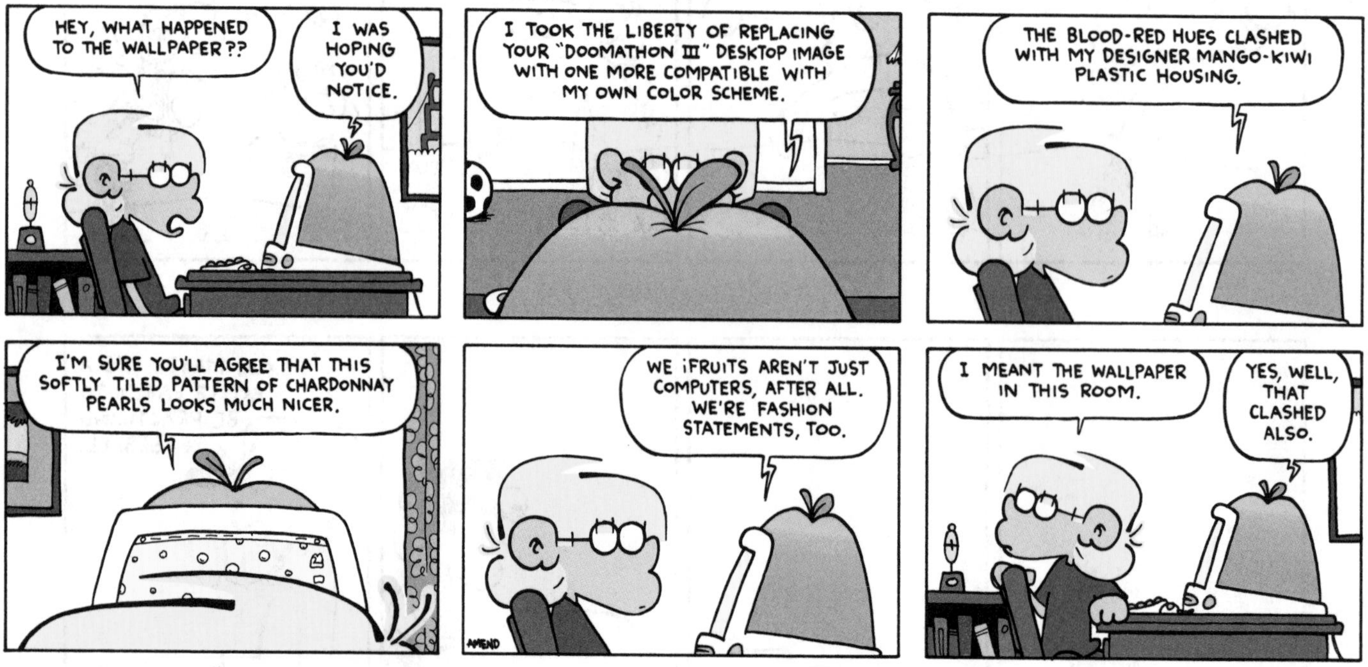
HEY, WHAT HAPPENED TO THE WALLPAPER??
I WAS HOPING YOU'D NOTICE.
I TOOK THE LIBERTY OF REPLACING YOUR "DOOMATHON III" DESKTOP IMAGE WITH ONE MORE COMPATIBLE WITH MY OWN COLOR SCHEME.
THE BLOOD-RED HUES CLASHED WITH MY DESIGNER MANGO-KIWI PLASTIC HOUSING.
I'M SURE YOU'LL AGREE THAT THIS SOFTLY TILED PATTERN OF CHARDONNAY PEARLS LOOKS MUCH NICER.
WE iFRUITS AREN'T JUST COMPUTERS, AFTER ALL. WE'RE FASHION STATEMENTS, TOO.
I MEANT THE WALLPAPER IN THIS ROOM.
YES, WELL, THAT CLASHED ALSO.
AMEND

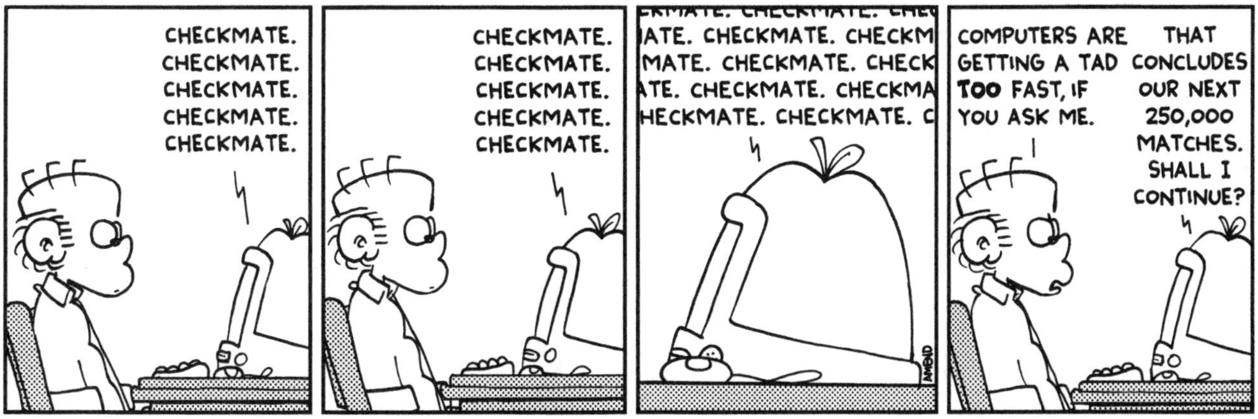
CHECKMATE. CHECKMATE. CHECKMATE. CHECKMATE. CHECKMATE.
CHECKMATE. CHECKMATE. CHECKMATE. CHECKMATE. CHECKMATE.
ATE. CHECKMATE. CHECKM MATE. CHECKMATE. CHECK TE. CHECKMATE. CHECKMA HECKMATE. CHECKMATE. C
COMPUTERS ARE GETTING A TAD **TOO** FAST, IF YOU ASK ME.
THAT CONCLUDES OUR NEXT 250,000 MATCHES. SHALL I CONTINUE?

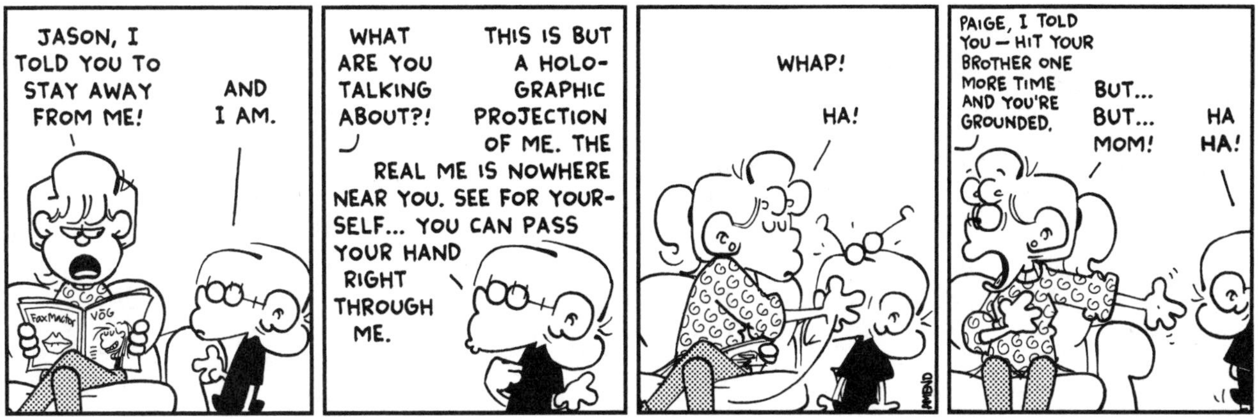
JASON, I TOLD YOU TO STAY AWAY FROM ME!
AND I AM.
WHAT ARE YOU TALKING ABOUT?!
THIS IS BUT A HOLOGRAPHIC PROJECTION OF ME. THE REAL ME IS NOWHERE NEAR YOU. SEE FOR YOURSELF... YOU CAN PASS YOUR HAND RIGHT THROUGH ME.
WHAP!
HA!
PAIGE, I TOLD YOU — HIT YOUR BROTHER ONE MORE TIME AND YOU'RE GROUNDED.
BUT... BUT... MOM!
HA HA!

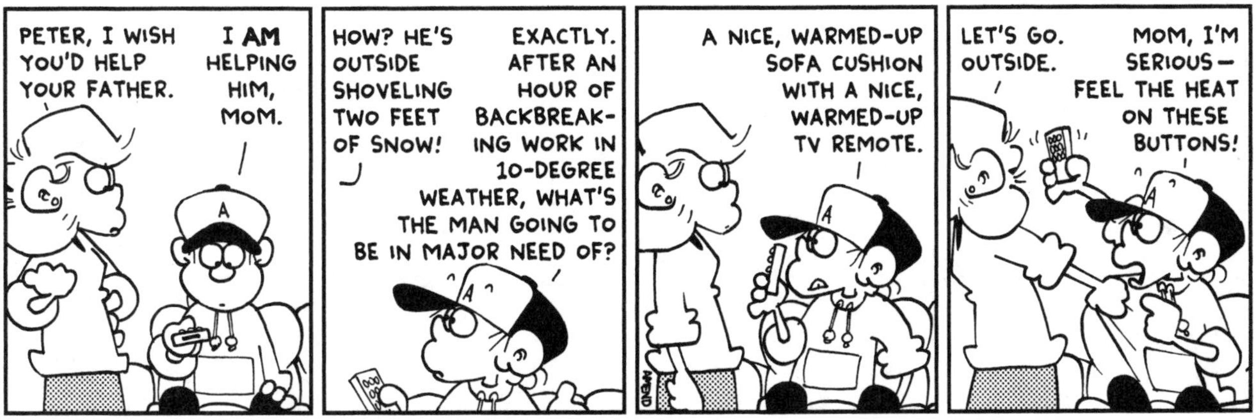
PETER, I WISH YOU'D HELP YOUR FATHER.
I **AM** HELPING HIM, MOM.
HOW? HE'S OUTSIDE SHOVELING TWO FEET OF SNOW!
EXACTLY. AFTER AN HOUR OF BACKBREAKING WORK IN 10-DEGREE WEATHER, WHAT'S THE MAN GOING TO BE IN MAJOR NEED OF?
A NICE, WARMED-UP SOFA CUSHION WITH A NICE, WARMED-UP TV REMOTE.
LET'S GO. OUTSIDE.
MOM, I'M SERIOUS — FEEL THE HEAT ON THESE BUTTONS!

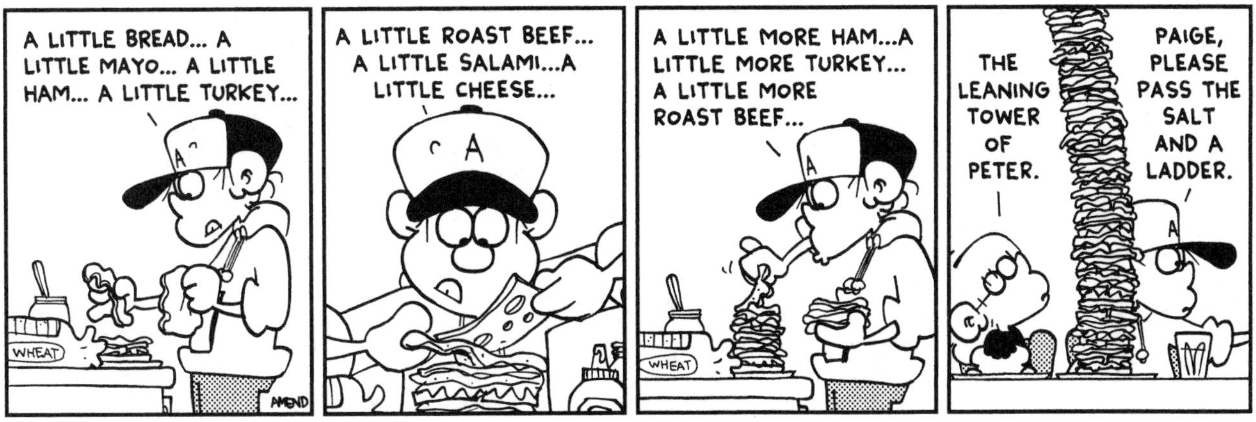
A LITTLE BREAD... A LITTLE MAYO... A LITTLE HAM... A LITTLE TURKEY...
WHEAT
A LITTLE ROAST BEEF... A LITTLE SALAMI...A LITTLE CHEESE...
A LITTLE MORE HAM...A LITTLE MORE TURKEY... A LITTLE MORE ROAST BEEF...
WHEAT
THE LEANING TOWER OF PETER.
PAIGE, PLEASE PASS THE SALT AND A LADDER.

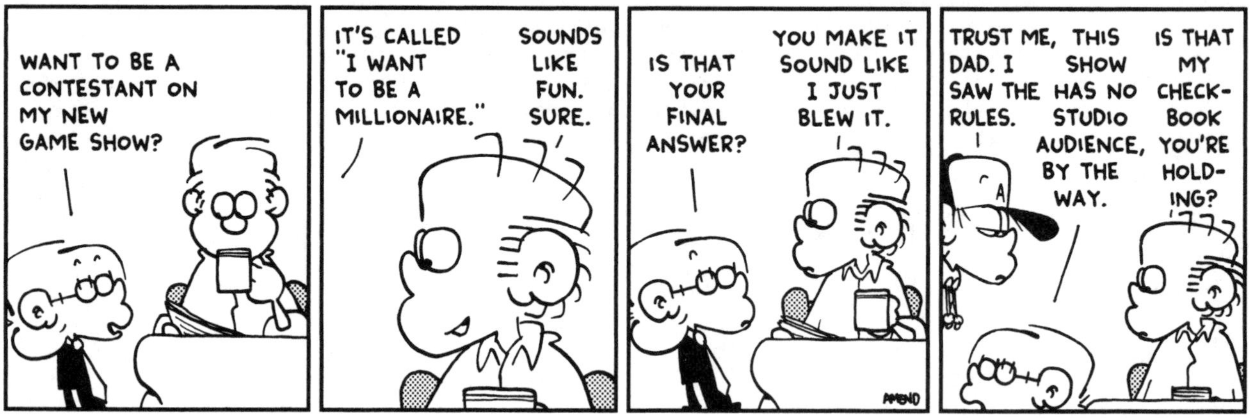
WANT TO BE A CONTESTANT ON MY NEW GAME SHOW?
IT'S CALLED "I WANT TO BE A MILLIONAIRE."
SOUNDS LIKE FUN. SURE.
IS THAT YOUR FINAL ANSWER?
YOU MAKE IT SOUND LIKE I JUST BLEW IT.
TRUST ME, DAD. I SAW THE RULES.
THIS SHOW HAS NO STUDIO AUDIENCE, BY THE WAY.
IS THAT MY CHECK-BOOK YOU'RE HOLD-ING?
AMEND

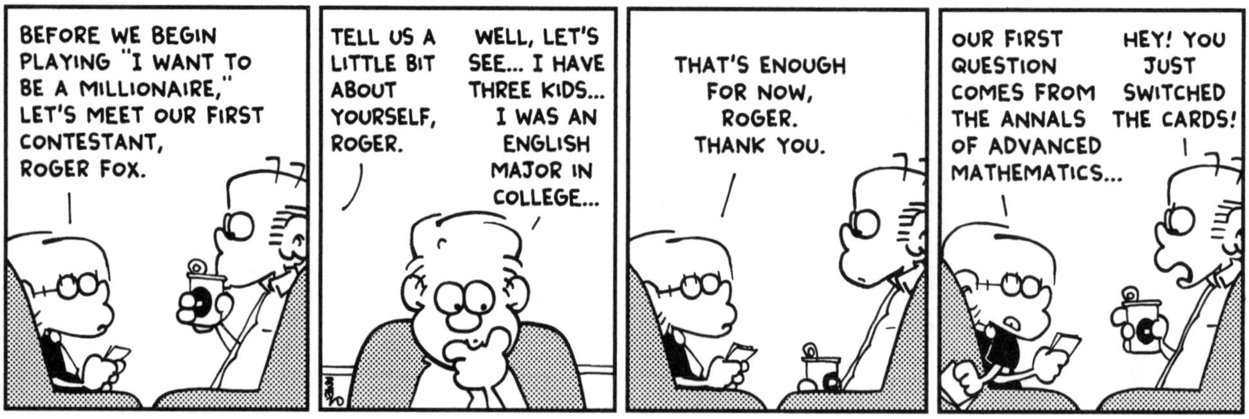
BEFORE WE BEGIN PLAYING "I WANT TO BE A MILLIONAIRE," LET'S MEET OUR FIRST CONTESTANT, ROGER FOX.
TELL US A LITTLE BIT ABOUT YOURSELF, ROGER.
WELL, LET'S SEE... I HAVE THREE KIDS... I WAS AN ENGLISH MAJOR IN COLLEGE...
AMEND
THAT'S ENOUGH FOR NOW, ROGER. THANK YOU.
OUR FIRST QUESTION COMES FROM THE ANNALS OF ADVANCED MATHEMATICS...
HEY! YOU JUST SWITCHED THE CARDS!

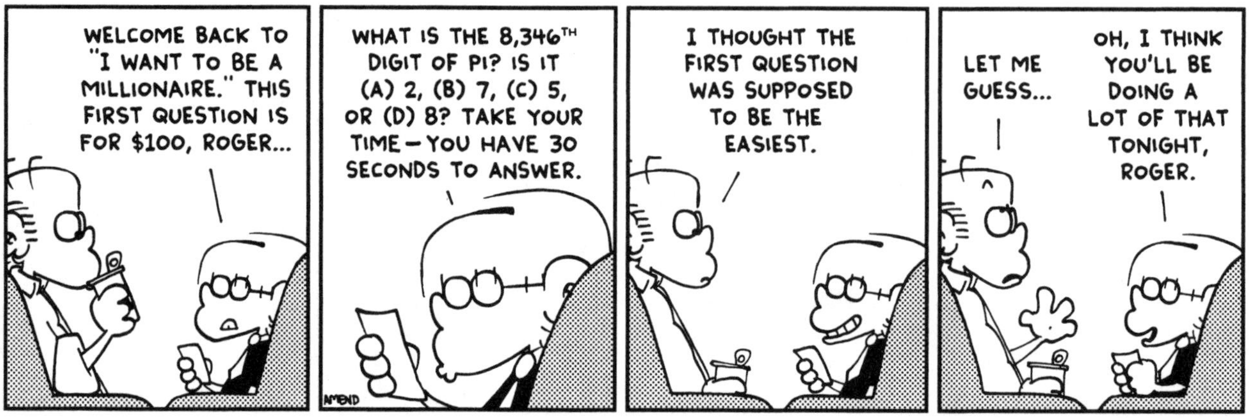
WELCOME BACK TO "I WANT TO BE A MILLIONAIRE." THIS FIRST QUESTION IS FOR $100, ROGER...
WHAT IS THE 8,346TH DIGIT OF PI? IS IT (A) 2, (B) 7, (C) 5, OR (D) 8? TAKE YOUR TIME—YOU HAVE 30 SECONDS TO ANSWER.
AMEND
I THOUGHT THE FIRST QUESTION WAS SUPPOSED TO BE THE EASIEST.
LET ME GUESS...
OH, I THINK YOU'LL BE DOING A LOT OF THAT TONIGHT, ROGER.

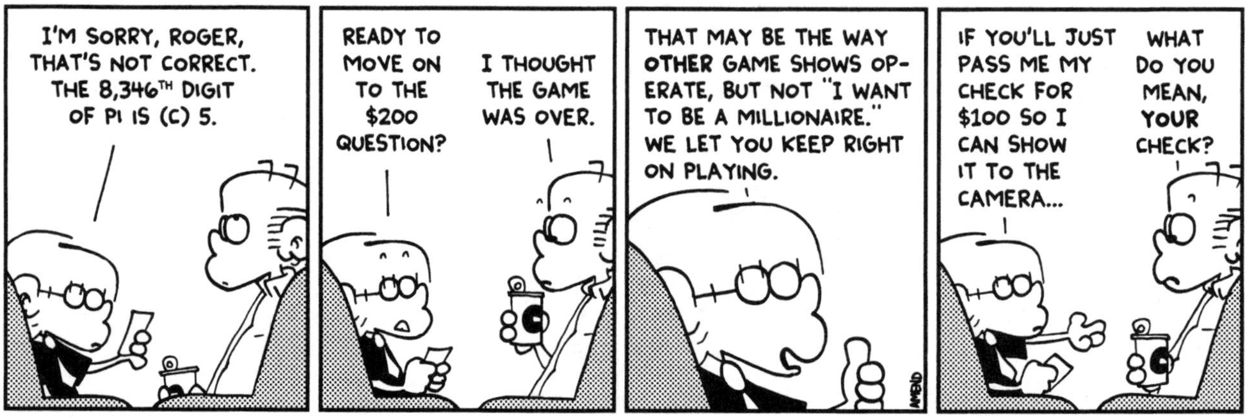
I'M SORRY, ROGER, THAT'S NOT CORRECT. THE 8,346TH DIGIT OF PI IS (C) 5.
READY TO MOVE ON TO THE $200 QUESTION?
I THOUGHT THE GAME WAS OVER.
THAT MAY BE THE WAY OTHER GAME SHOWS OP-ERATE, BUT NOT "I WANT TO BE A MILLIONAIRE." WE LET YOU KEEP RIGHT ON PLAYING.
AMEND
IF YOU'LL JUST PASS ME MY CHECK FOR $100 SO I CAN SHOW IT TO THE CAMERA...
WHAT DO YOU MEAN, YOUR CHECK?

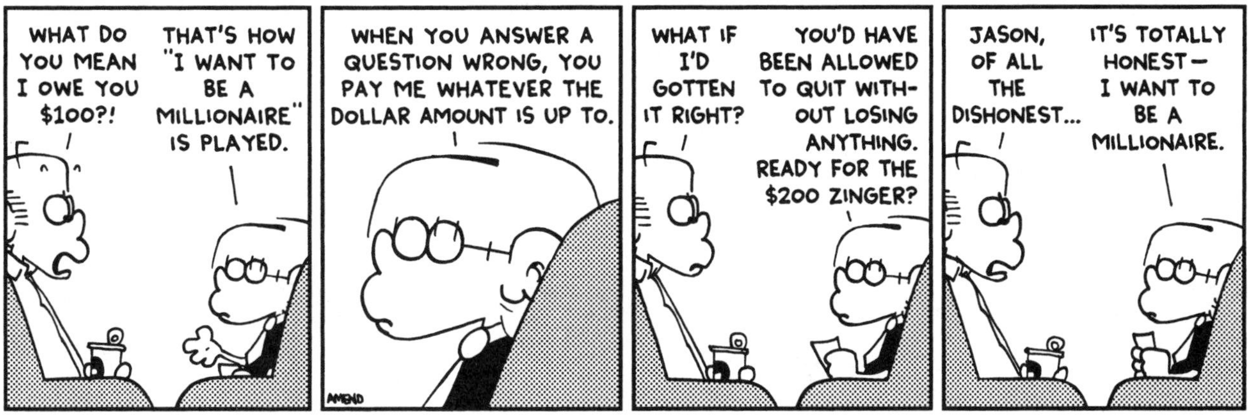
WHAT DO YOU MEAN I OWE YOU $100?!
THAT'S HOW "I WANT TO BE A MILLIONAIRE" IS PLAYED.
WHEN YOU ANSWER A QUESTION WRONG, YOU PAY ME WHATEVER THE DOLLAR AMOUNT IS UP TO.
WHAT IF I'D GOTTEN IT RIGHT?
YOU'D HAVE BEEN ALLOWED TO QUIT WITHOUT LOSING ANYTHING. READY FOR THE $200 ZINGER?
JASON, OF ALL THE DISHONEST...
IT'S TOTALLY HONEST— I WANT TO BE A MILLIONAIRE.
AMEND

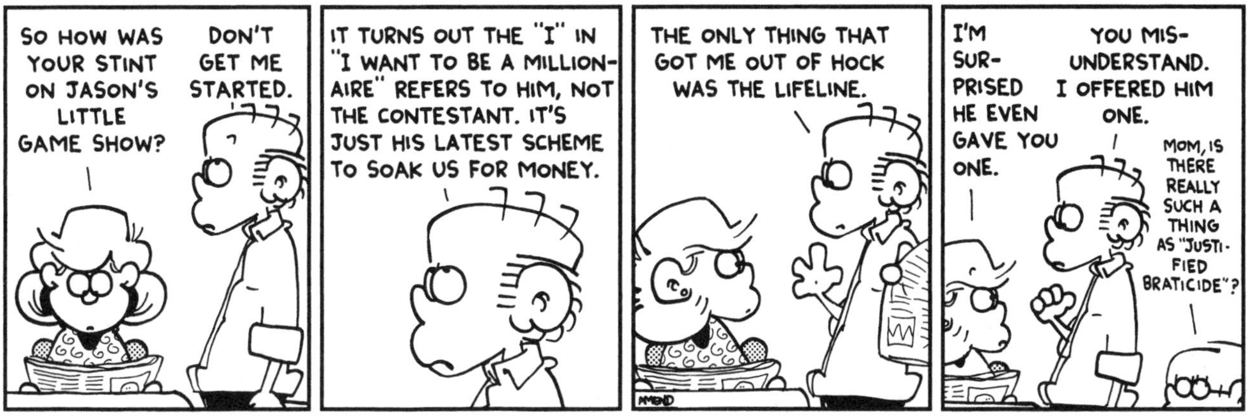
SO HOW WAS YOUR STINT ON JASON'S LITTLE GAME SHOW?
DON'T GET ME STARTED.
IT TURNS OUT THE "I" IN "I WANT TO BE A MILLIONAIRE" REFERS TO HIM, NOT THE CONTESTANT. IT'S JUST HIS LATEST SCHEME TO SOAK US FOR MONEY.
THE ONLY THING THAT GOT ME OUT OF HOCK WAS THE LIFELINE.
AMEND
I'M SURPRISED HE EVEN GAVE YOU ONE.
YOU MISUNDERSTAND. I OFFERED HIM ONE.
MOM, IS THERE REALLY SUCH A THING AS "JUSTIFIED BRATICIDE"?

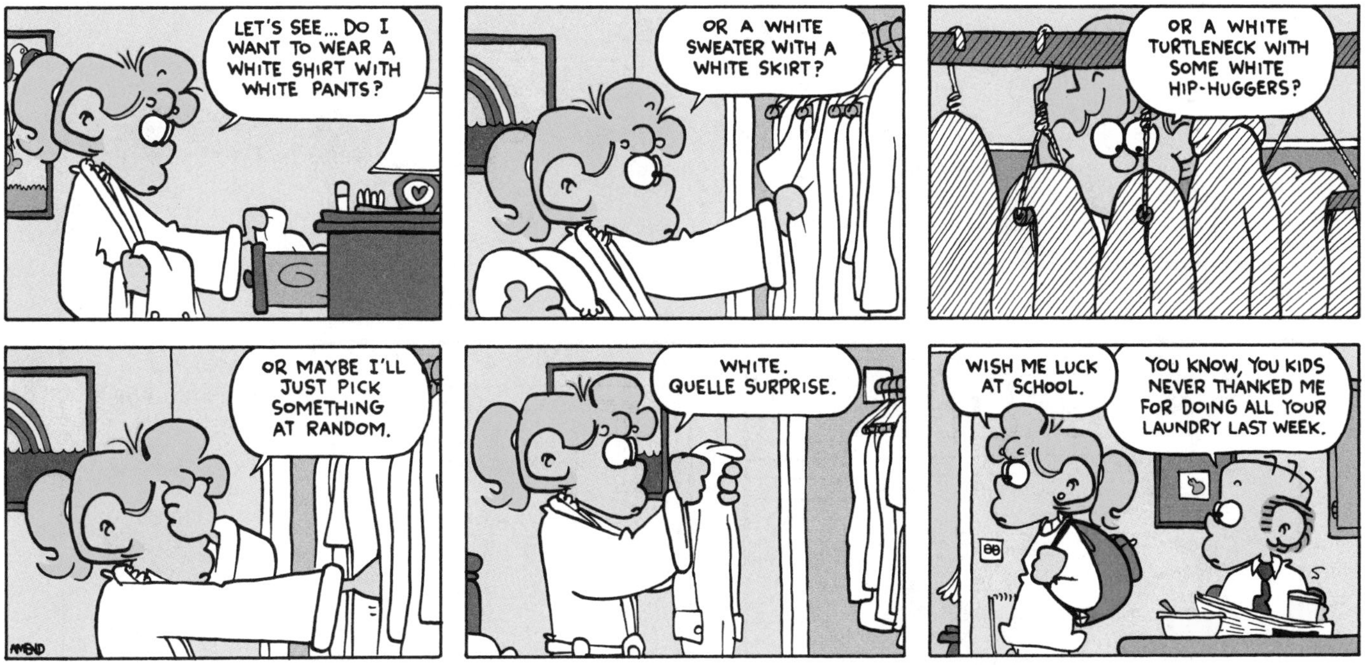
LET'S SEE... DO I WANT TO WEAR A WHITE SHIRT WITH WHITE PANTS?
OR A WHITE SWEATER WITH A WHITE SKIRT?
OR A WHITE TURTLENECK WITH SOME WHITE HIP-HUGGERS?
OR MAYBE I'LL JUST PICK SOMETHING AT RANDOM.
AMEND
WHITE. QUELLE SURPRISE.
WISH ME LUCK AT SCHOOL.
YOU KNOW, YOU KIDS NEVER THANKED ME FOR DOING ALL YOUR LAUNDRY LAST WEEK.

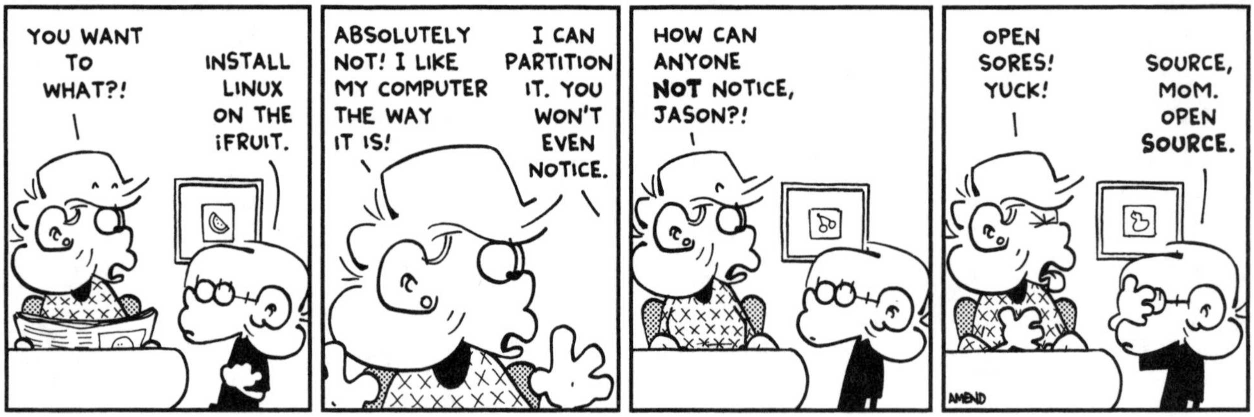
YOU WANT TO WHAT?!
INSTALL LINUX ON THE iFRUIT.
ABSOLUTELY NOT! I LIKE MY COMPUTER THE WAY IT IS!
I CAN PARTITION IT. YOU WON'T EVEN NOTICE.
HOW CAN ANYONE **NOT** NOTICE, JASON?!
OPEN SORES! YUCK!
SOURCE, MOM. OPEN **SOURCE.**
AMEND

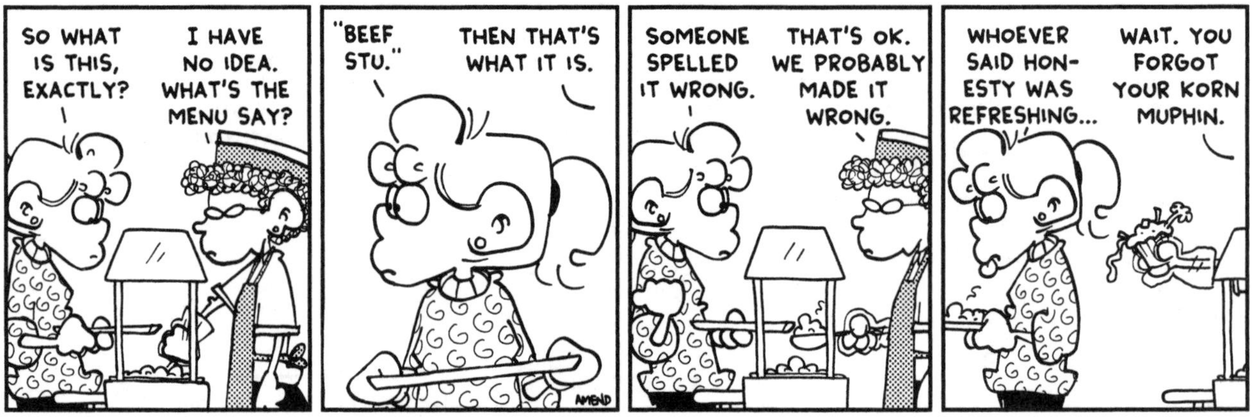
SO WHAT IS THIS, EXACTLY?
I HAVE NO IDEA. WHAT'S THE MENU SAY?
"BEEF STU."
THEN THAT'S WHAT IT IS.
SOMEONE SPELLED IT WRONG.
THAT'S OK. WE PROBABLY MADE IT WRONG.
WHOEVER SAID HON-ESTY WAS REFRESHING...
WAIT. YOU FORGOT YOUR KORN MUPHIN.
AMEND

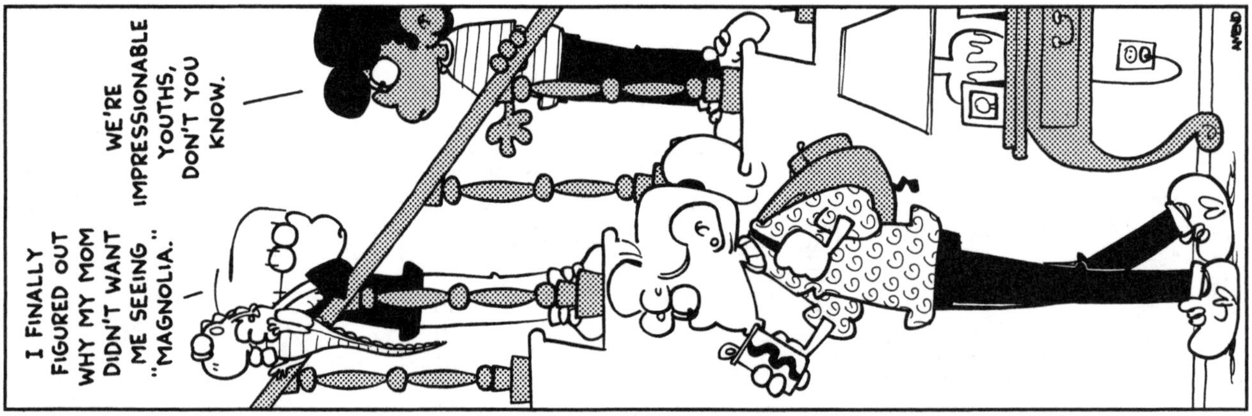
I FINALLY FIGURED OUT WHY MY MOM DIDN'T WANT ME SEEING "MAGNOLIA."
WE'RE IMPRESSIONABLE YOUTHS, DON'T YOU KNOW.
AMEND

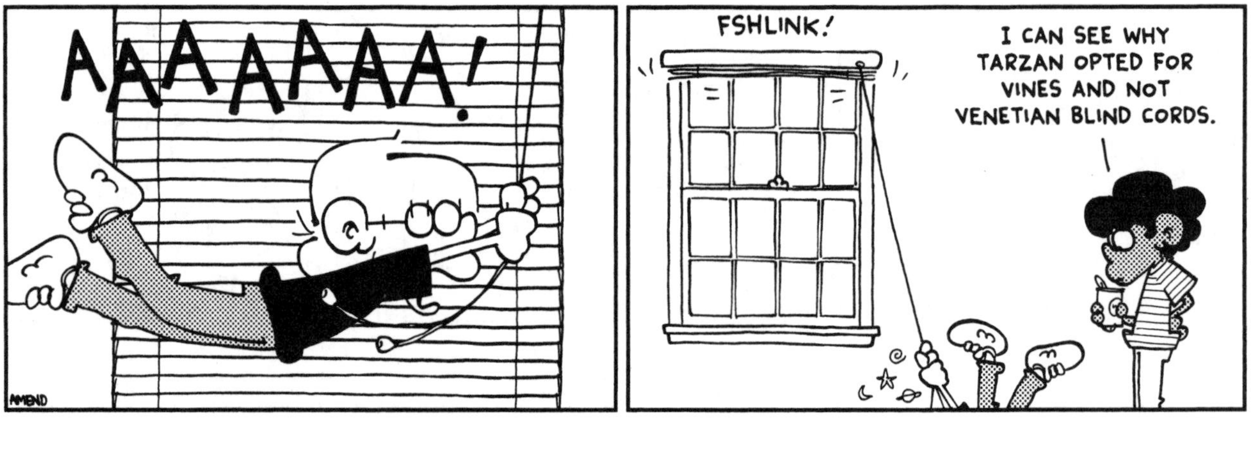
AAAAAAA!
FSHLINK!
I CAN SEE WHY TARZAN OPTED FOR VINES AND NOT VENETIAN BLIND CORDS.
AMEND

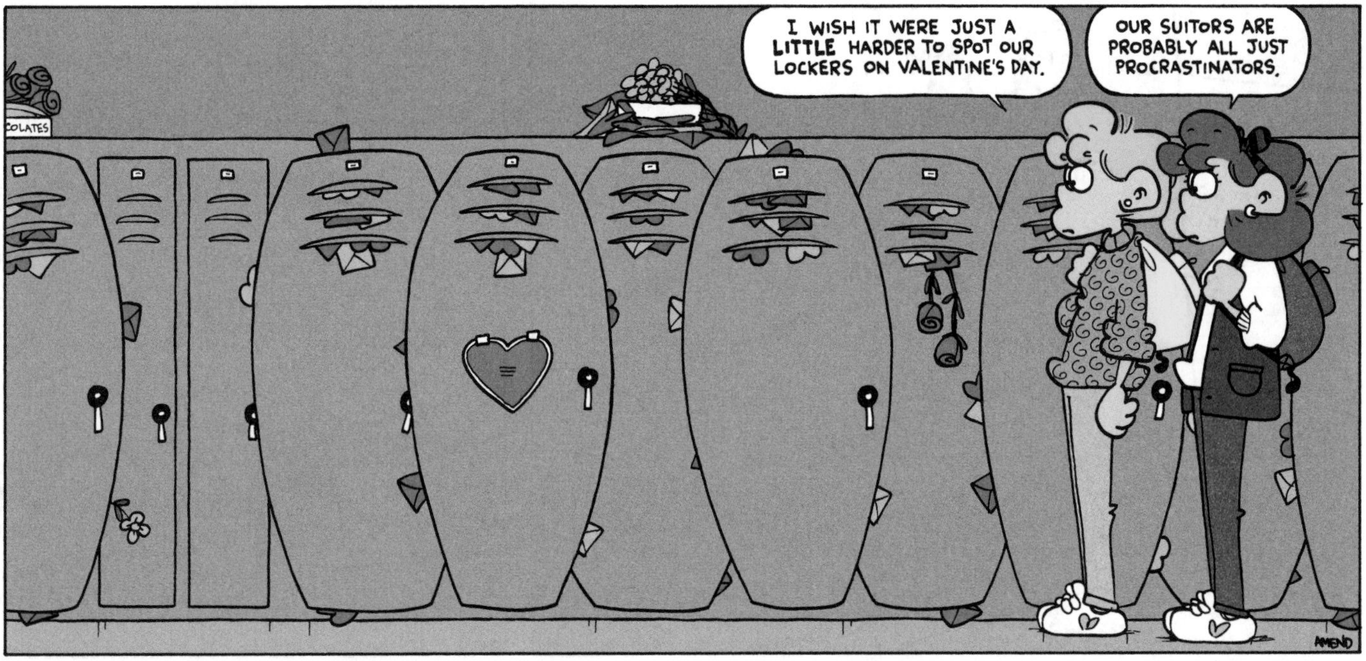
I WISH IT WERE JUST A LITTLE HARDER TO SPOT OUR LOCKERS ON VALENTINE'S DAY.
OUR SUITORS ARE PROBABLY ALL JUST PROCRASTINATORS.
AMEND

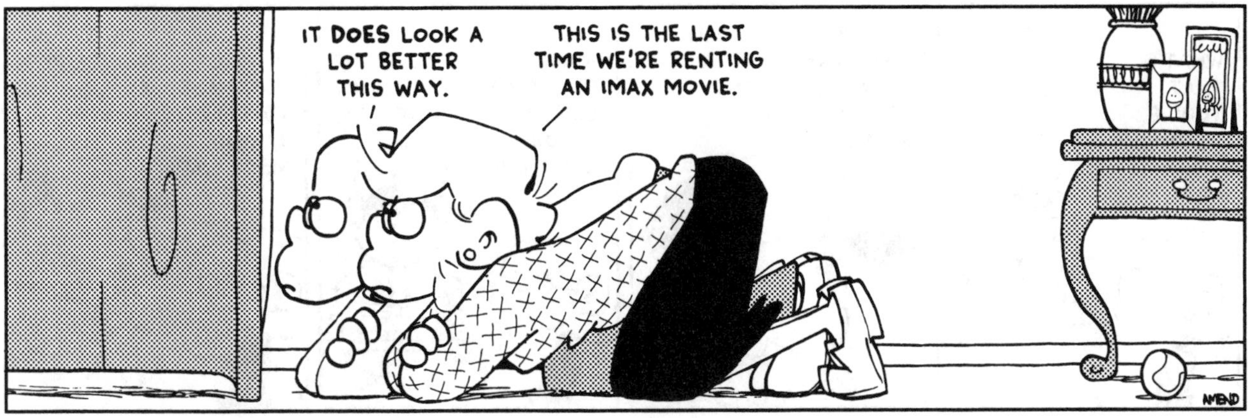
IT DOES LOOK A LOT BETTER THIS WAY.
THIS IS THE LAST TIME WE'RE RENTING AN IMAX MOVIE.
AMEND

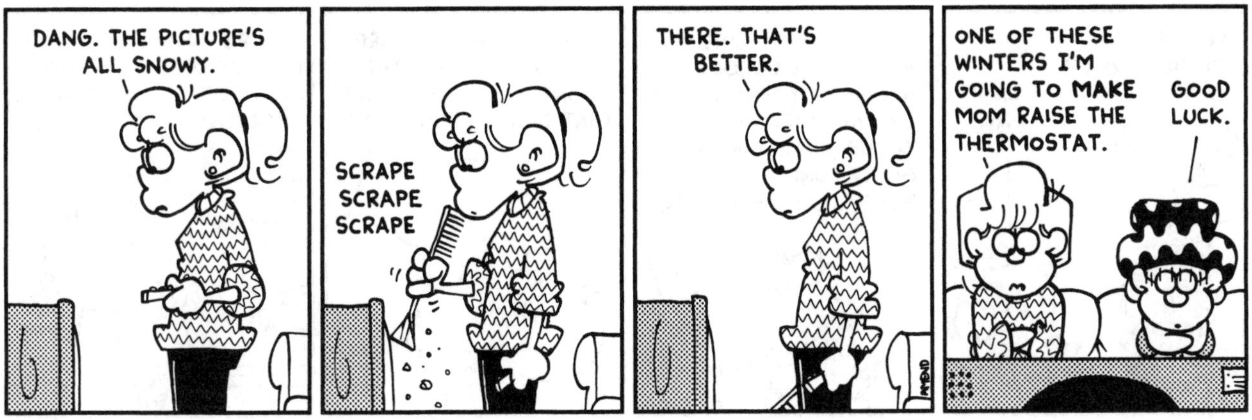
DANG. THE PICTURE'S ALL SNOWY.
SCRAPE SCRAPE SCRAPE
THERE. THAT'S BETTER.
ONE OF THESE WINTERS I'M GOING TO MAKE MOM RAISE THE THERMOSTAT.
GOOD LUCK.

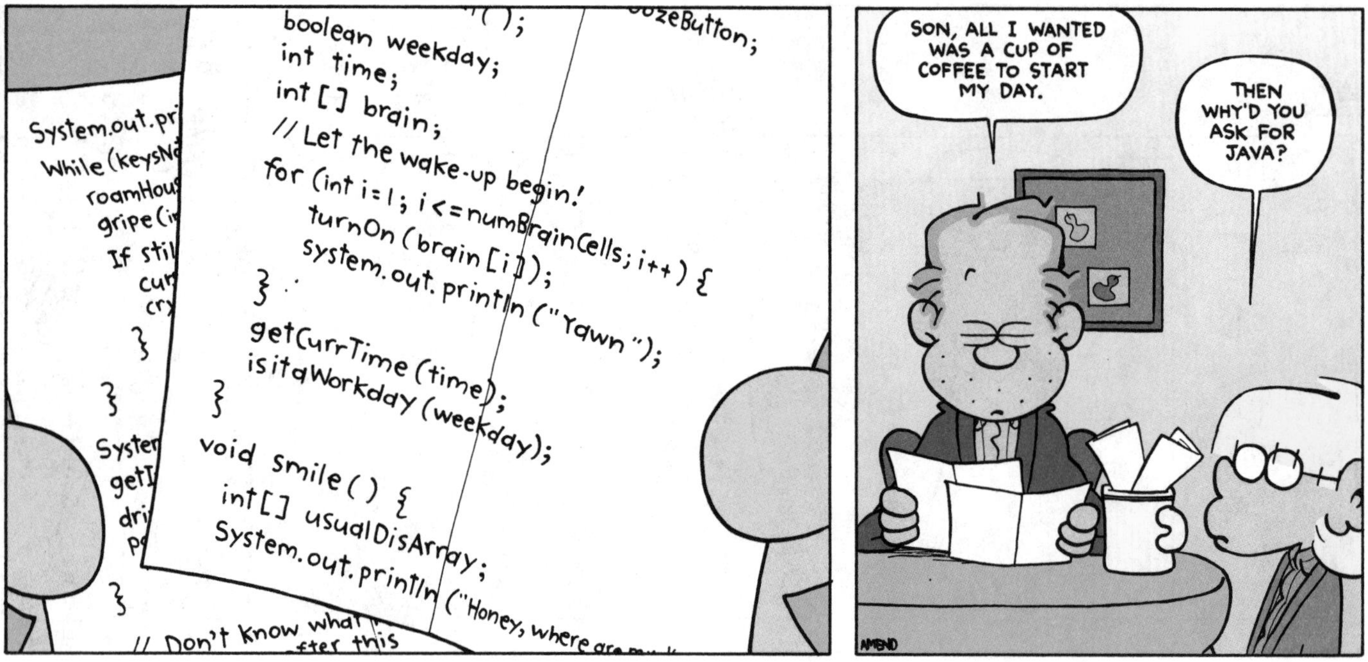
boolean weekday;
int time;
int [] brain;
// Let the wake-up begin!
for (int i=1; i<=numBrainCells; i++) {
turnOn (brain[i]);
system.out.println ("Yawn");
}
getCurrTime (time);
isitaWorkday (weekday);
}
void smile() {
int[] usualDisArray;
SON, ALL I WANTED WAS A CUP OF COFFEE TO START MY DAY.
THEN WHY'D YOU ASK FOR JAVA?
AMEND

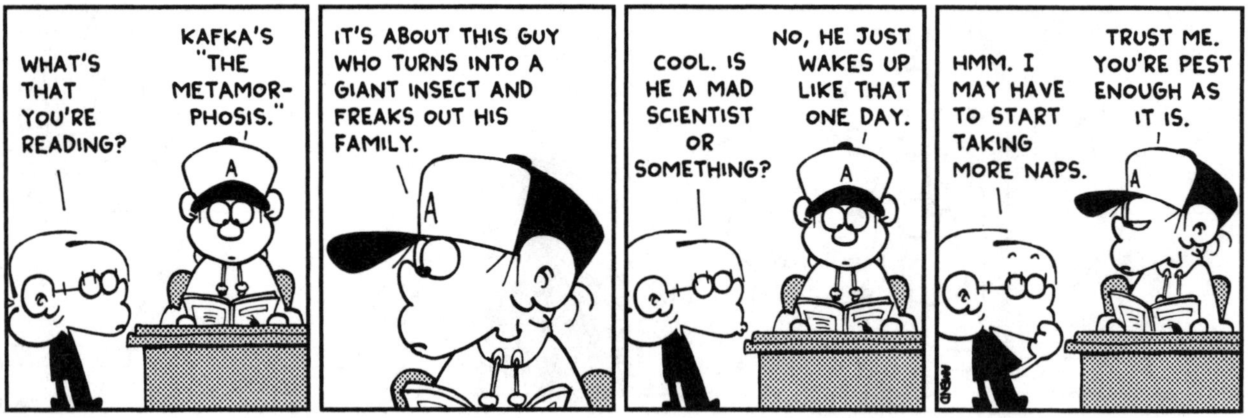
WHAT'S THAT YOU'RE READING?
KAFKA'S "THE METAMORPHOSIS."
IT'S ABOUT THIS GUY WHO TURNS INTO A GIANT INSECT AND FREAKS OUT HIS FAMILY.
COOL. IS HE A MAD SCIENTIST OR SOMETHING?
NO, HE JUST WAKES UP LIKE THAT ONE DAY.
HMM. I MAY HAVE TO START TAKING MORE NAPS.
TRUST ME. YOU'RE PEST ENOUGH AS IT IS.
AMEND

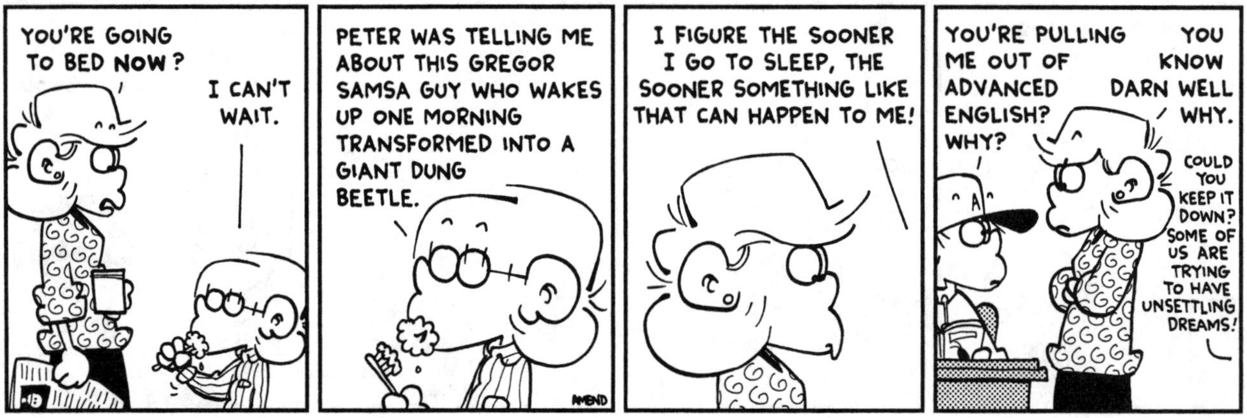
YOU'RE GOING TO BED NOW?
I CAN'T WAIT.
PETER WAS TELLING ME ABOUT THIS GREGOR SAMSA GUY WHO WAKES UP ONE MORNING TRANSFORMED INTO A GIANT DUNG BEETLE.
I FIGURE THE SOONER I GO TO SLEEP, THE SOONER SOMETHING LIKE THAT CAN HAPPEN TO ME!
YOU'RE PULLING ME OUT OF ADVANCED ENGLISH? WHY?
YOU KNOW DARN WELL WHY.
COULD YOU KEEP IT DOWN? SOME OF US ARE TRYING TO HAVE UNSETTLING DREAMS!
AMEND

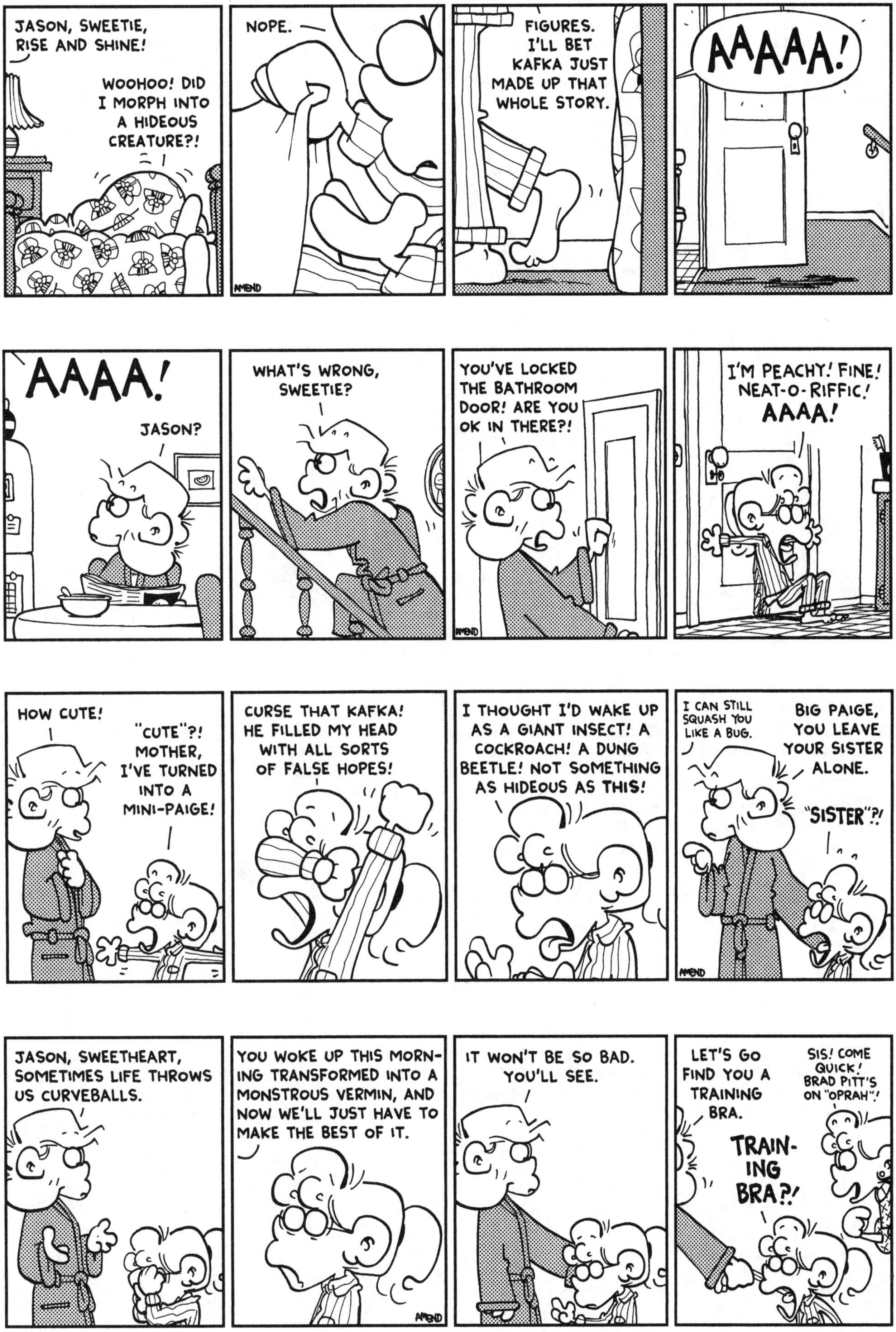
JASON, SWEETIE, RISE AND SHINE!
WOOHOO! DID I MORPH INTO A HIDEOUS CREATURE?!
NOPE.
FIGURES. I'LL BET KAFKA JUST MADE UP THAT WHOLE STORY.
AAAAA!
AMEND
AAAA!
JASON?
WHAT'S WRONG, SWEETIE?
YOU'VE LOCKED THE BATHROOM DOOR! ARE YOU OK IN THERE?!
I'M PEACHY! FINE! NEAT-O-RIFFIC! AAAA!
AMEND
HOW CUTE!
"CUTE"?! MOTHER, I'VE TURNED INTO A MINI-PAIGE!
CURSE THAT KAFKA! HE FILLED MY HEAD WITH ALL SORTS OF FALSE HOPES!
I THOUGHT I'D WAKE UP AS A GIANT INSECT! A COCKROACH! A DUNG BEETLE! NOT SOMETHING AS HIDEOUS AS THIS!
I CAN STILL SQUASH YOU LIKE A BUG.
BIG PAIGE, YOU LEAVE YOUR SISTER ALONE.
"SISTER"?!
AMEND
JASON, SWEETHEART, SOMETIMES LIFE THROWS US CURVEBALLS.
YOU WOKE UP THIS MORNING TRANSFORMED INTO A MONSTROUS VERMIN, AND NOW WE'LL JUST HAVE TO MAKE THE BEST OF IT.
AMEND
IT WON'T BE SO BAD. YOU'LL SEE.
LET'S GO FIND YOU A TRAINING BRA.
SIS! COME QUICK! BRAD PITT'S ON "OPRAH"!
TRAINING BRA?!

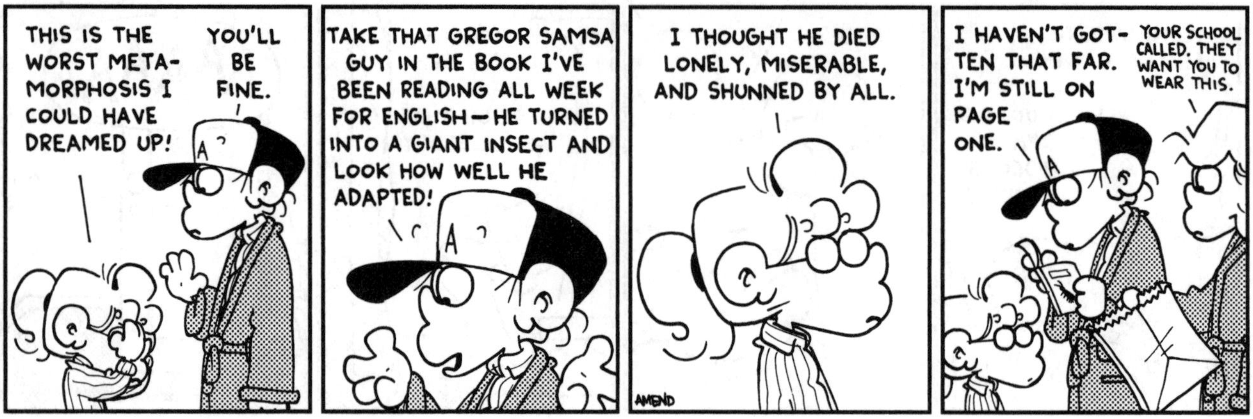
THIS IS THE WORST META-MORPHOSIS I COULD HAVE DREAMED UP!
YOU'LL BE FINE.
TAKE THAT GREGOR SAMSA GUY IN THE BOOK I'VE BEEN READING ALL WEEK FOR ENGLISH—HE TURNED INTO A GIANT INSECT AND LOOK HOW WELL HE ADAPTED!
I THOUGHT HE DIED LONELY, MISERABLE, AND SHUNNED BY ALL.
I HAVEN'T GOT-TEN THAT FAR. I'M STILL ON PAGE ONE.
YOUR SCHOOL CALLED. THEY WANT YOU TO WEAR THIS.
AMEND

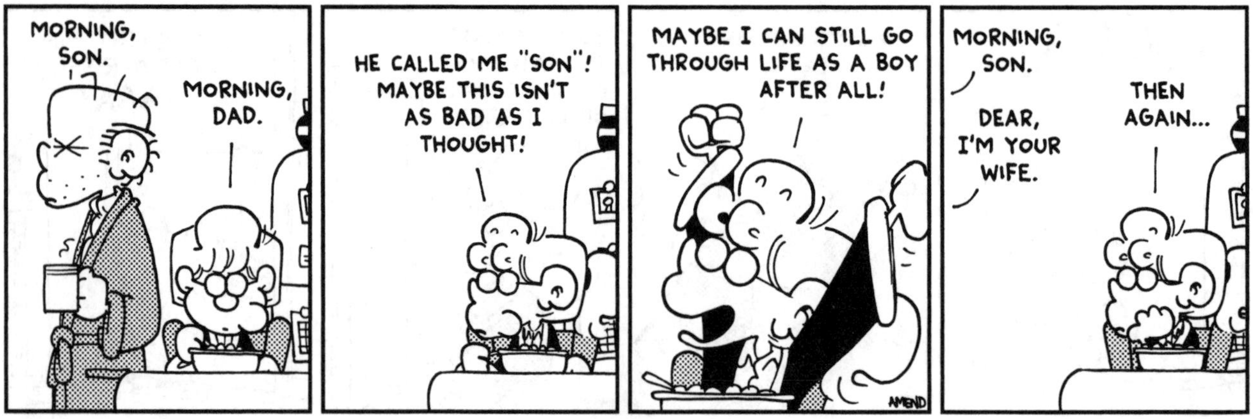
MORNING, SON.
MORNING, DAD.
HE CALLED ME "SON"! MAYBE THIS ISN'T AS BAD AS I THOUGHT!
MAYBE I CAN STILL GO THROUGH LIFE AS A BOY AFTER ALL!
MORNING, SON.
DEAR, I'M YOUR WIFE.
THEN AGAIN...
AMEND

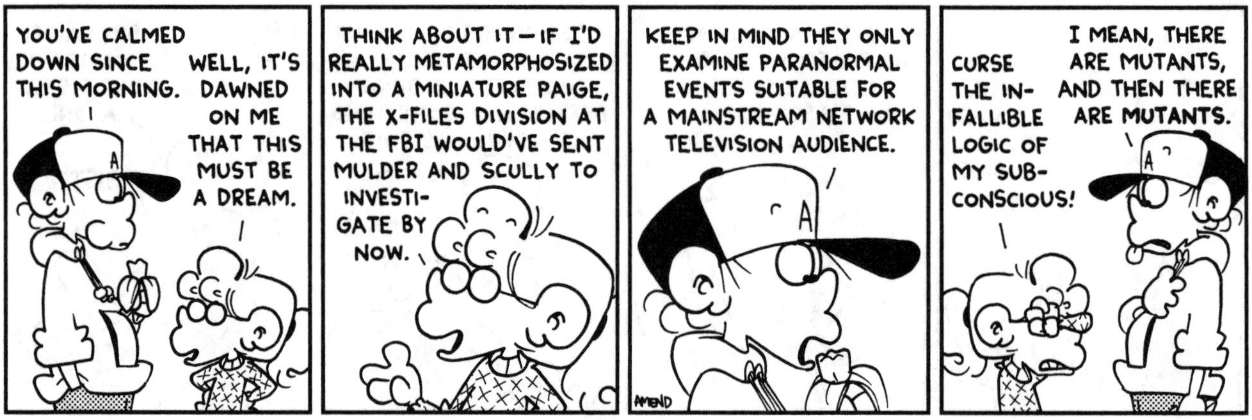
YOU'VE CALMED DOWN SINCE THIS MORNING.
WELL, IT'S DAWNED ON ME THAT THIS MUST BE A DREAM.
THINK ABOUT IT—IF I'D REALLY METAMORPHOSIZED INTO A MINIATURE PAIGE, THE X-FILES DIVISION AT THE FBI WOULD'VE SENT MULDER AND SCULLY TO INVESTI-GATE BY NOW.
KEEP IN MIND THEY ONLY EXAMINE PARANORMAL EVENTS SUITABLE FOR A MAINSTREAM NETWORK TELEVISION AUDIENCE.
CURSE THE IN-FALLIBLE LOGIC OF MY SUB-CONSCIOUS!
I MEAN, THERE ARE MUTANTS, AND THEN THERE ARE MUTANTS.
AMEND

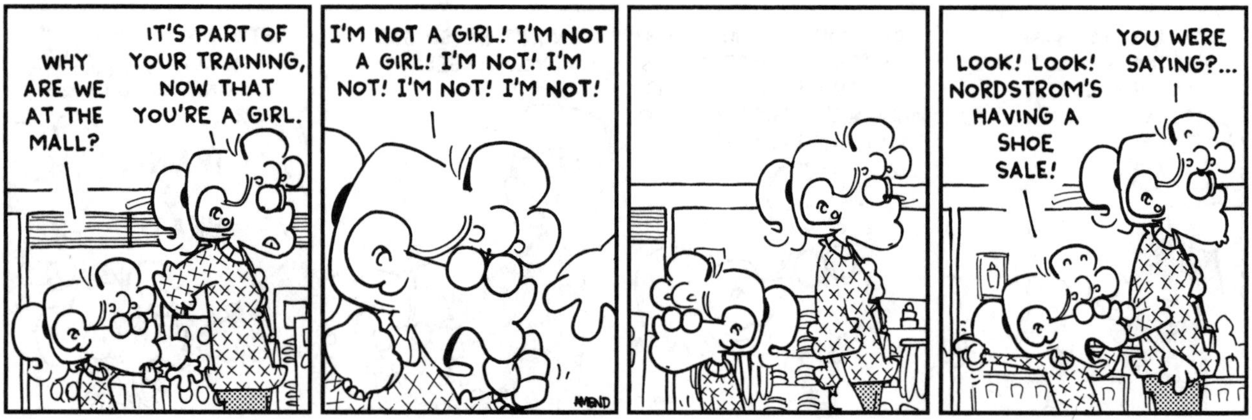
WHY ARE WE AT THE MALL?
IT'S PART OF YOUR TRAINING, NOW THAT YOU'RE A GIRL.
I'M NOT A GIRL! I'M NOT A GIRL! I'M NOT! I'M NOT! I'M NOT! I'M NOT!
LOOK! LOOK! NORDSTROM'S HAVING A SHOE SALE!
YOU WERE SAYING?...
AMEND

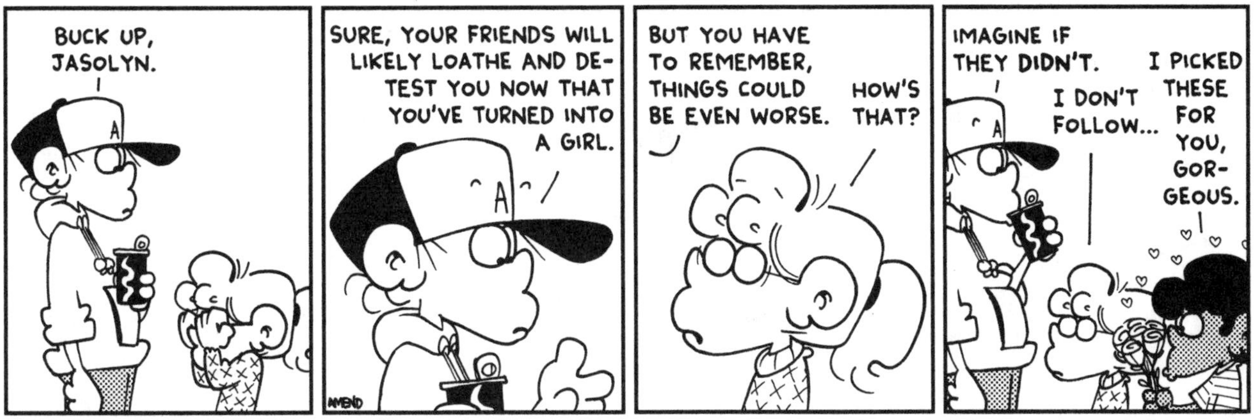
BUCK UP, JASOLYN.
SURE, YOUR FRIENDS WILL LIKELY LOATHE AND DETEST YOU NOW THAT YOU'VE TURNED INTO A GIRL.
BUT YOU HAVE TO REMEMBER, THINGS COULD BE EVEN WORSE.
HOW'S THAT?
IMAGINE IF THEY DIDN'T.
I DON'T FOLLOW...
I PICKED THESE FOR YOU, GORGEOUS.
AMEND

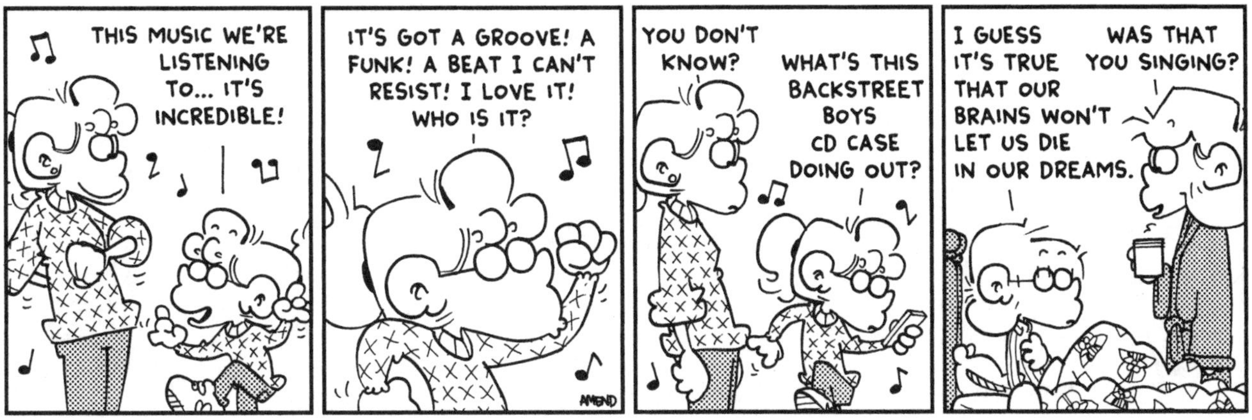
THIS MUSIC WE'RE LISTENING TO... IT'S INCREDIBLE!
IT'S GOT A GROOVE! A FUNK! A BEAT I CAN'T RESIST! I LOVE IT! WHO IS IT?
YOU DON'T KNOW?
WHAT'S THIS BACKSTREET BOYS CD CASE DOING OUT?
I GUESS IT'S TRUE THAT OUR BRAINS WON'T LET US DIE IN OUR DREAMS.
WAS THAT YOU SINGING?
AMEND

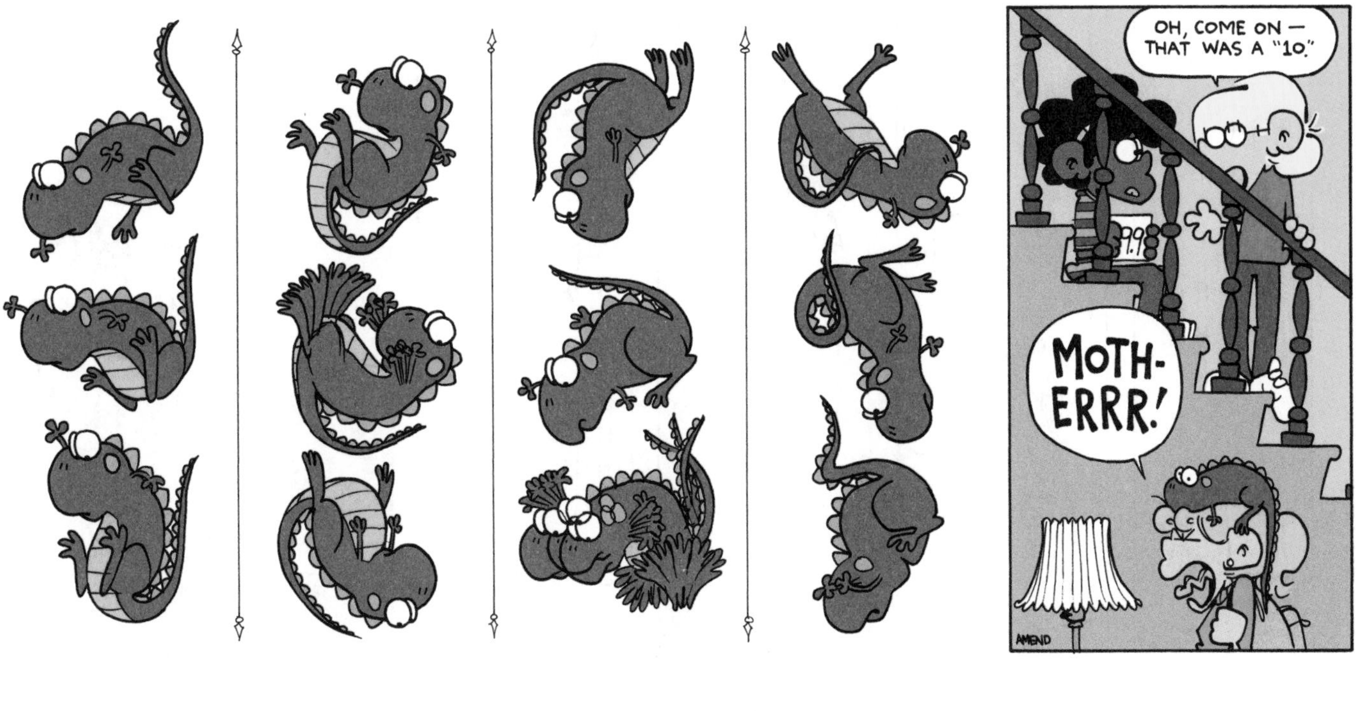
OH, COME ON — THAT WAS A "10."
MOTH-ERRR!
AMEND

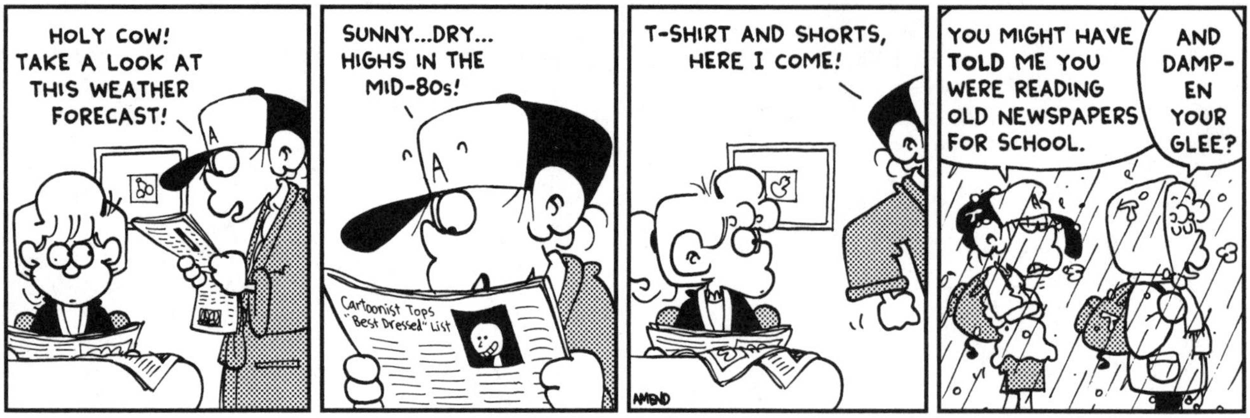
HOLY COW! TAKE A LOOK AT THIS WEATHER FORECAST!
SUNNY...DRY... HIGHS IN THE MID-80s!
Cartoonist Tops "Best Dressed" List
T-SHIRT AND SHORTS, HERE I COME!
YOU MIGHT HAVE TOLD ME YOU WERE READING OLD NEWSPAPERS FOR SCHOOL.
AND DAMPEN YOUR GLEE?

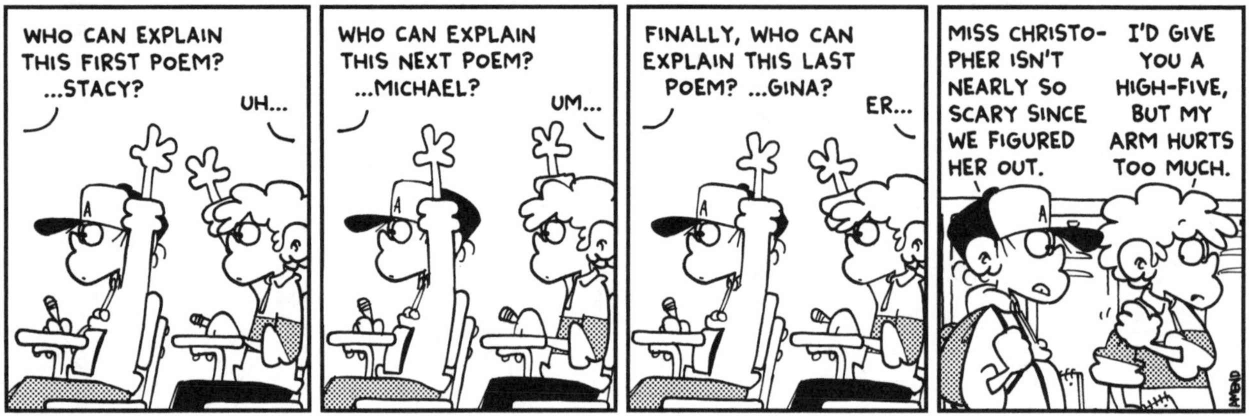
WHO CAN EXPLAIN THIS FIRST POEM? ...STACY?
UH...
WHO CAN EXPLAIN THIS NEXT POEM? ...MICHAEL?
UM...
FINALLY, WHO CAN EXPLAIN THIS LAST POEM? ...GINA?
ER...
MISS CHRISTOPHER ISN'T NEARLY SO SCARY SINCE WE FIGURED HER OUT.
I'D GIVE YOU A HIGH-FIVE, BUT MY ARM HURTS TOO MUCH.

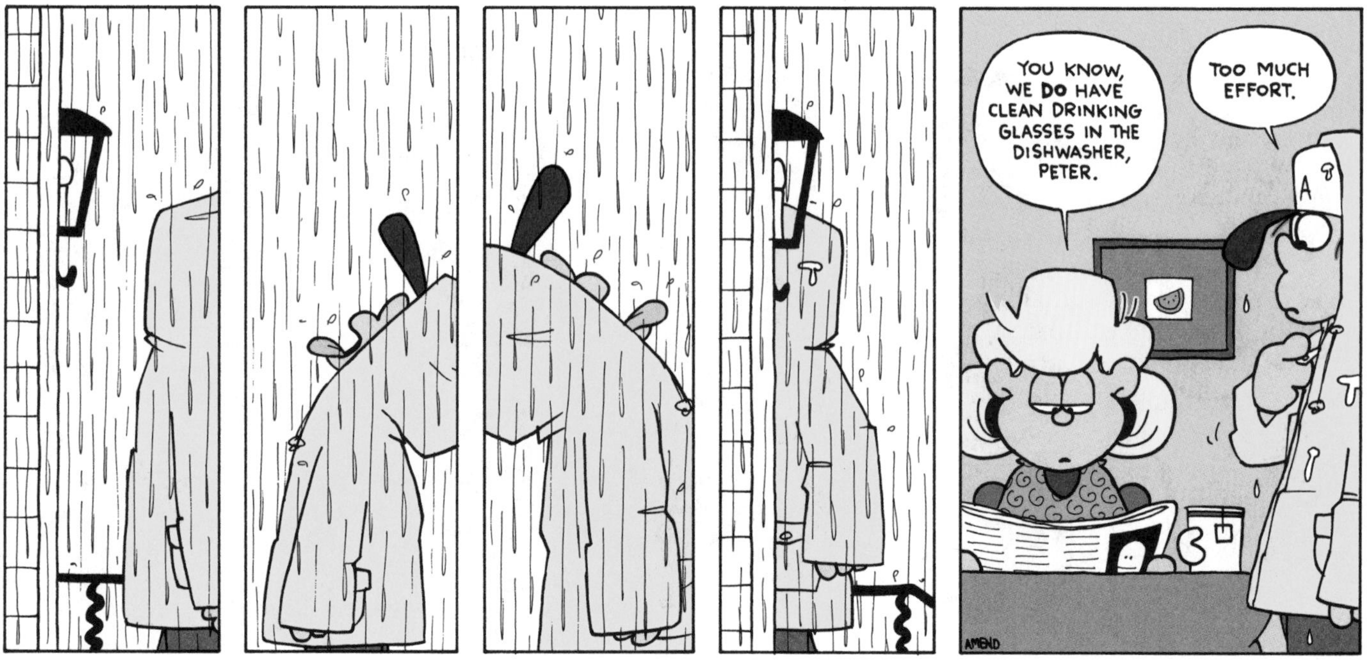
YOU KNOW, WE DO HAVE CLEAN DRINKING GLASSES IN THE DISHWASHER, PETER.
TOO MUCH EFFORT.

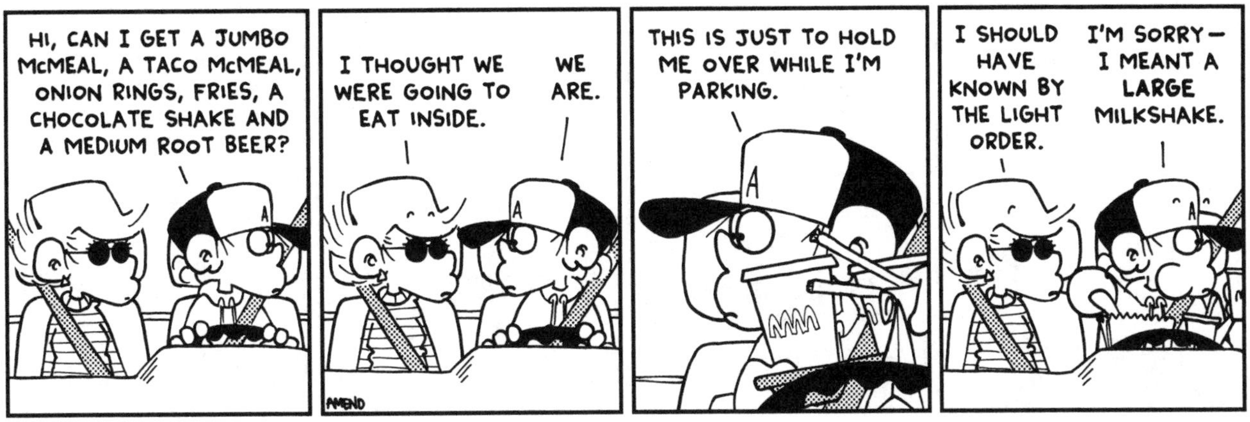
HI, CAN I GET A JUMBO McMEAL, A TACO McMEAL, ONION RINGS, FRIES, A CHOCOLATE SHAKE AND A MEDIUM ROOT BEER?
I THOUGHT WE WERE GOING TO EAT INSIDE.
WE ARE.
AMEND
THIS IS JUST TO HOLD ME OVER WHILE I'M PARKING.
I SHOULD HAVE KNOWN BY THE LIGHT ORDER.
I'M SORRY— I MEANT A **LARGE** MILKSHAKE.

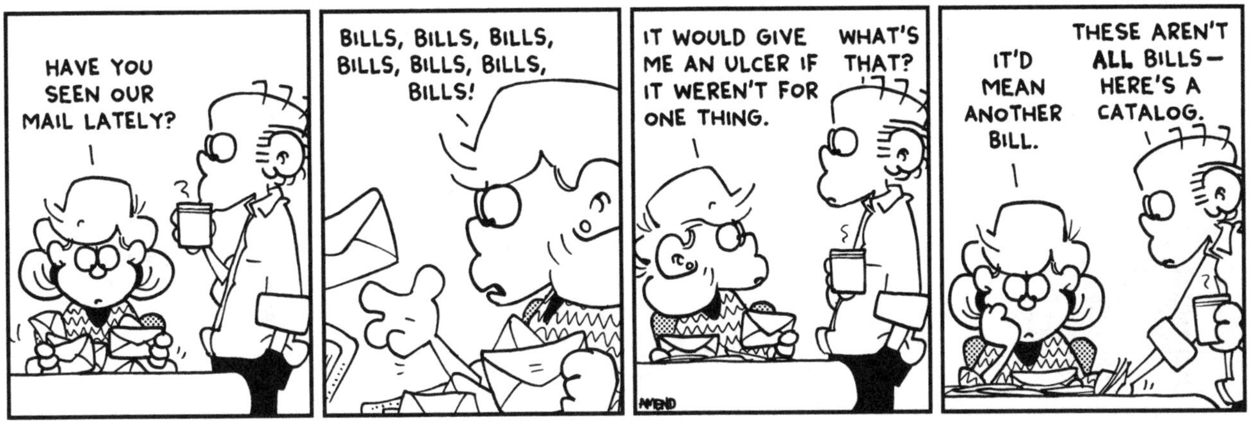
HAVE YOU SEEN OUR MAIL LATELY?
BILLS, BILLS, BILLS, BILLS, BILLS, BILLS, BILLS!
IT WOULD GIVE ME AN ULCER IF IT WEREN'T FOR ONE THING.
WHAT'S THAT?
AMEND
IT'D MEAN ANOTHER BILL.
THESE AREN'T **ALL** BILLS— HERE'S A CATALOG.

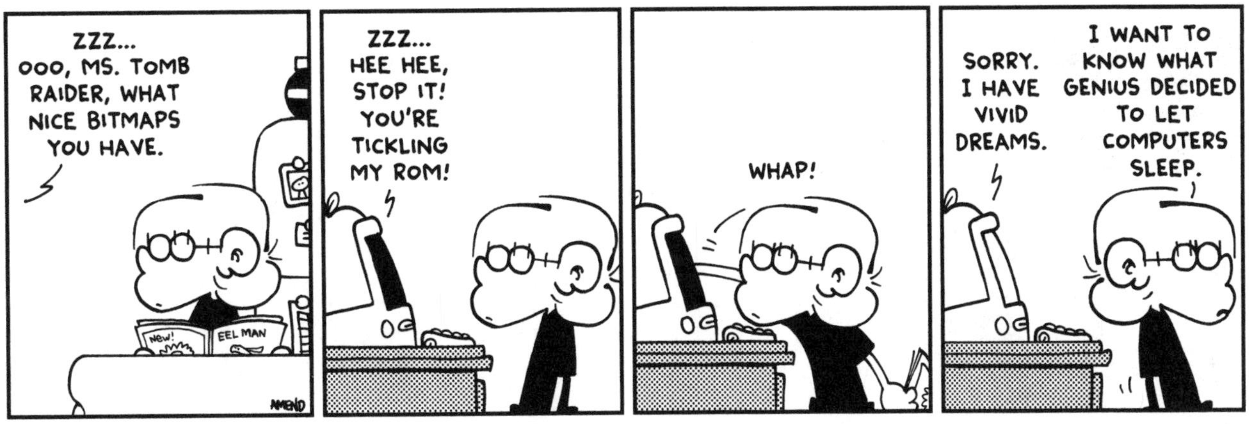
ZZZ... OOO, MS. TOMB RAIDER, WHAT NICE BITMAPS YOU HAVE.
NEW!
EEL MAN
AMEND
ZZZ... HEE HEE, STOP IT! YOU'RE TICKLING MY ROM!
WHAP!
SORRY. I HAVE VIVID DREAMS.
I WANT TO KNOW WHAT GENIUS DECIDED TO LET COMPUTERS SLEEP.

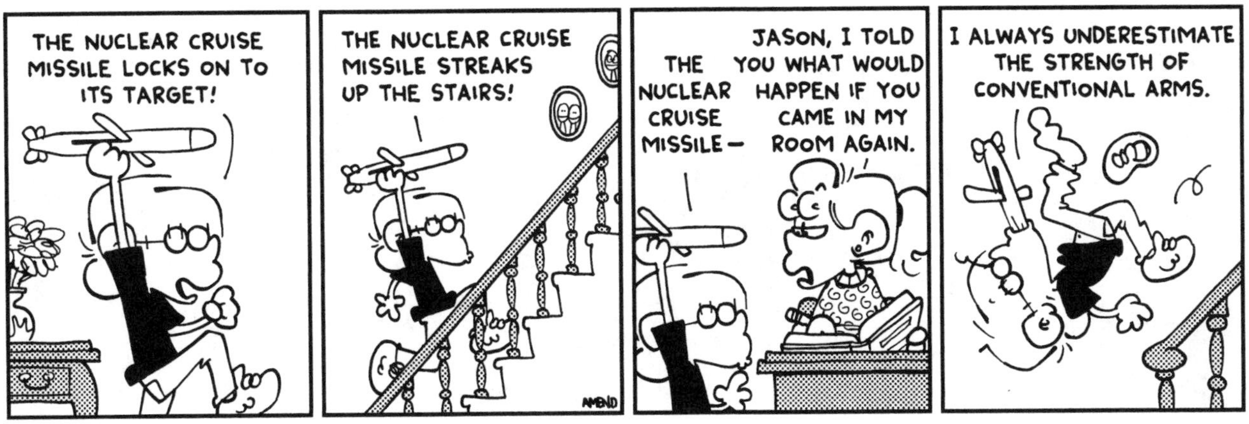
THE NUCLEAR CRUISE MISSILE LOCKS ON TO ITS TARGET!
THE NUCLEAR CRUISE MISSILE STREAKS UP THE STAIRS!
AMEND
THE NUCLEAR CRUISE MISSILE—
JASON, I TOLD YOU WHAT WOULD HAPPEN IF YOU CAME IN MY ROOM AGAIN.
I ALWAYS UNDERESTIMATE THE STRENGTH OF CONVENTIONAL ARMS.

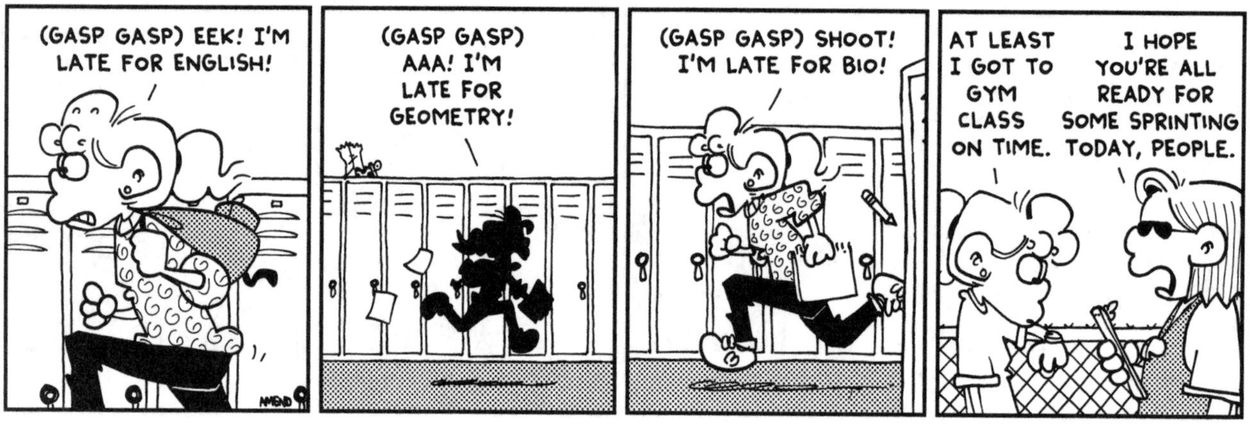
(GASP GASP) EEK! I'M LATE FOR ENGLISH!
(GASP GASP) AAA! I'M LATE FOR GEOMETRY!
(GASP GASP) SHOOT! I'M LATE FOR BIO!
AT LEAST I GOT TO GYM CLASS ON TIME.
I HOPE YOU'RE ALL READY FOR SOME SPRINTING TODAY, PEOPLE.

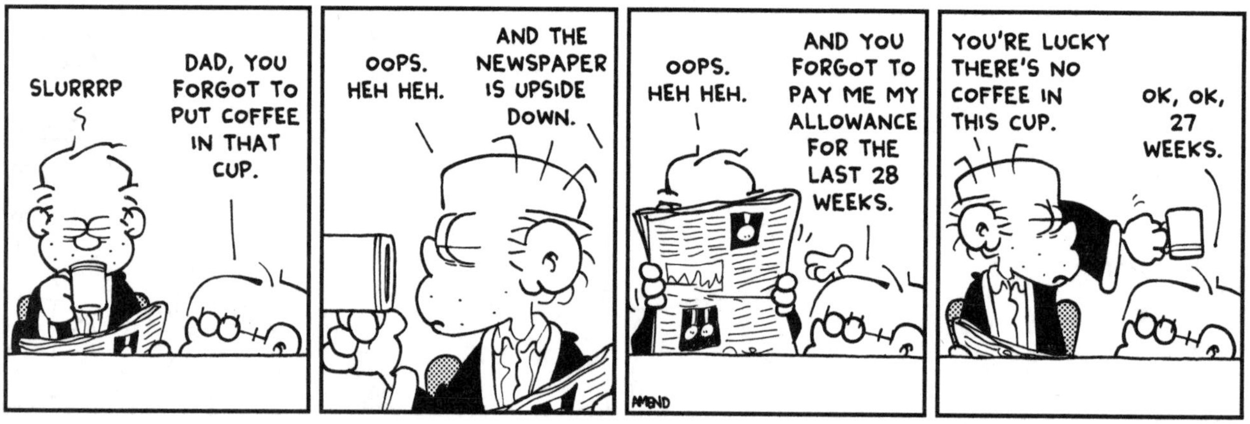
SLURRRP
DAD, YOU FORGOT TO PUT COFFEE IN THAT CUP.
OOPS. HEH HEH.
AND THE NEWSPAPER IS UPSIDE DOWN.
OOPS. HEH HEH.
AND YOU FORGOT TO PAY ME MY ALLOWANCE FOR THE LAST 28 WEEKS.
YOU'RE LUCKY THERE'S NO COFFEE IN THIS CUP.
OK, OK, 27 WEEKS.

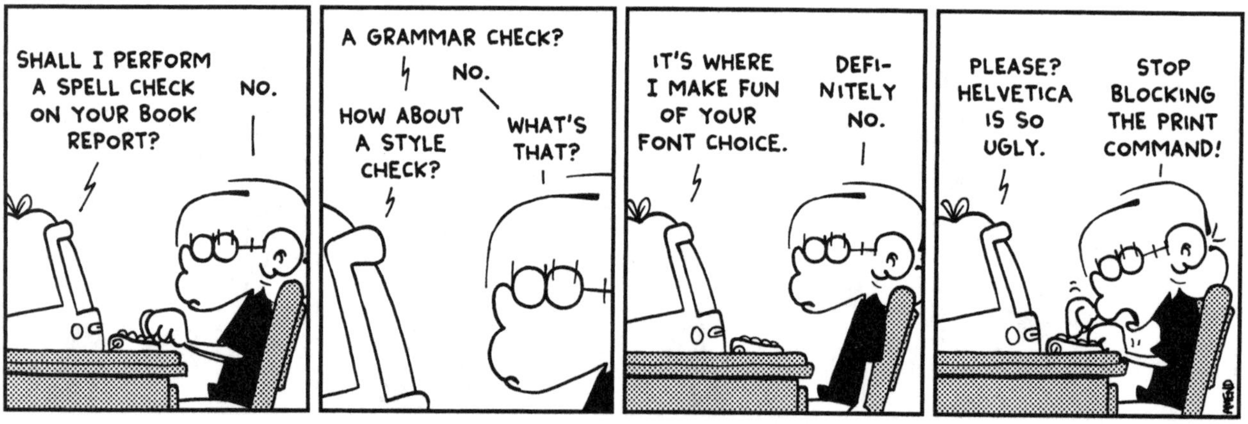
SHALL I PERFORM A SPELL CHECK ON YOUR BOOK REPORT?
NO.
A GRAMMAR CHECK?
NO.
HOW ABOUT A STYLE CHECK?
WHAT'S THAT?
IT'S WHERE I MAKE FUN OF YOUR FONT CHOICE.
DEFI-NITELY NO.
PLEASE? HELVETICA IS SO UGLY.
STOP BLOCKING THE PRINT COMMAND!

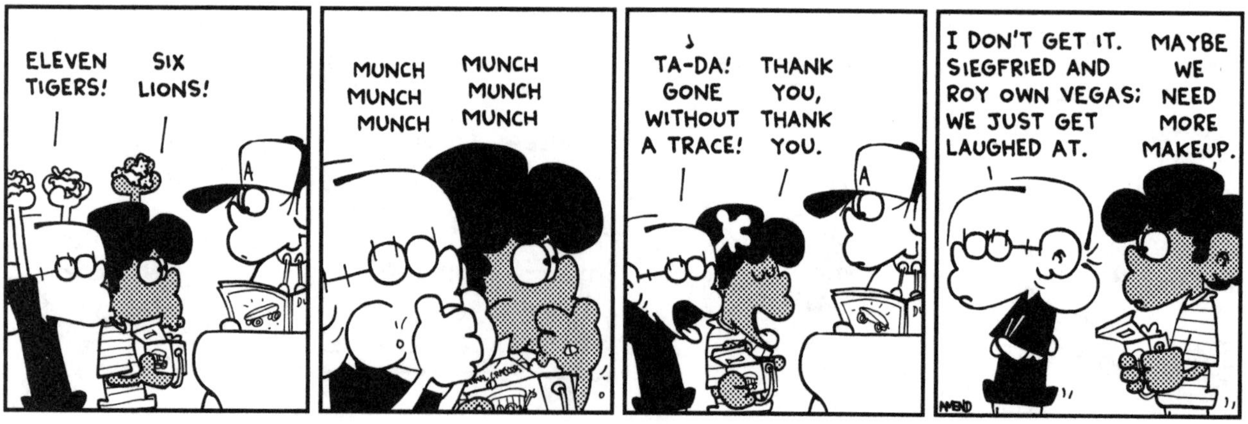
ELEVEN TIGERS!
SIX LIONS!
MUNCH MUNCH MUNCH
MUNCH MUNCH MUNCH
TA-DA! GONE WITHOUT A TRACE!
THANK YOU, THANK YOU.
I DON'T GET IT. SIEGFRIED AND ROY OWN VEGAS; WE JUST GET LAUGHED AT.
MAYBE WE NEED MORE MAKEUP.

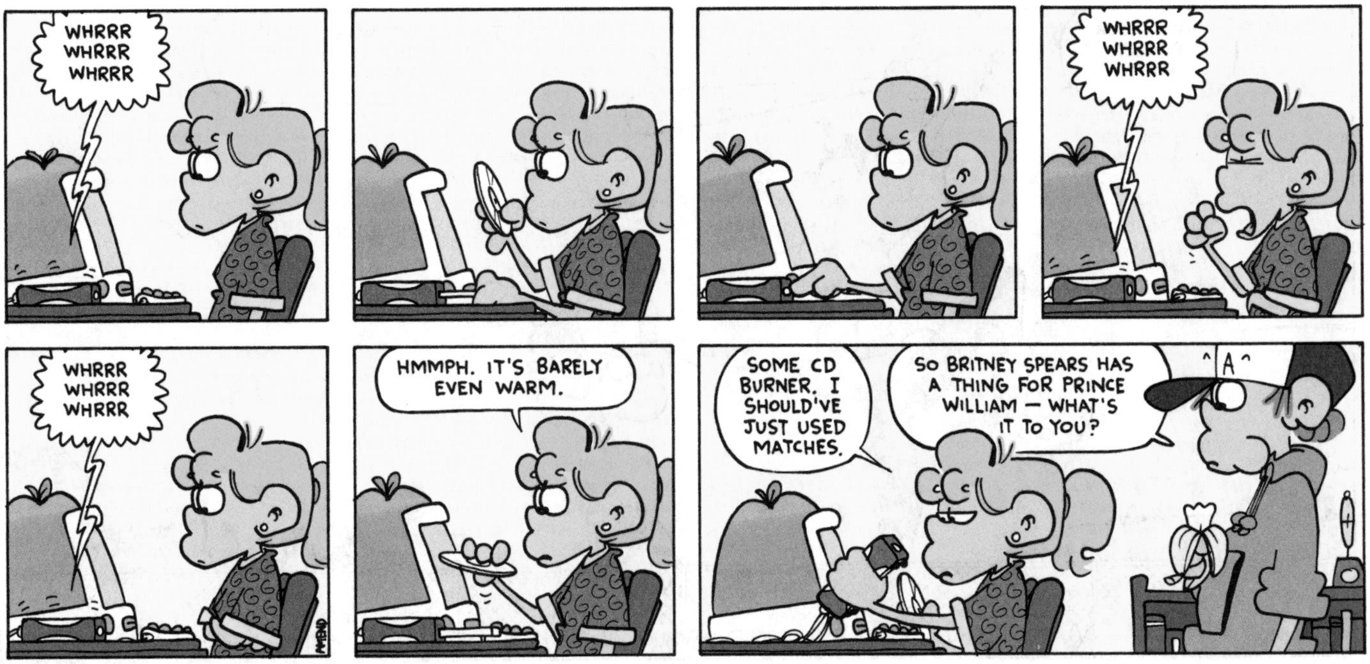
WHRRR
WHRRR
WHRRR
WHRRR
WHRRR
WHRRR
WHRRR
WHRRR
WHRRR
HMMPH. IT'S BARELY EVEN WARM.
SOME CD BURNER. I SHOULD'VE JUST USED MATCHES.
SO BRITNEY SPEARS HAS A THING FOR PRINCE WILLIAM — WHAT'S IT TO YOU?

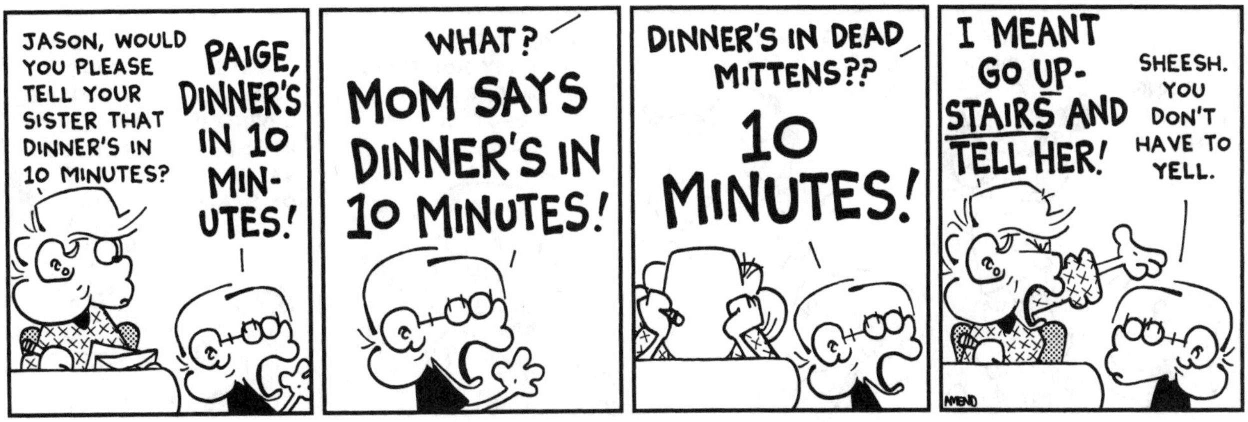
JASON, WOULD YOU PLEASE TELL YOUR SISTER THAT DINNER'S IN 10 MINUTES?
PAIGE, DINNER'S IN 10 MIN-UTES!
WHAT?
MOM SAYS DINNER'S IN 10 MINUTES!
DINNER'S IN DEAD MITTENS??
10 MINUTES!
I MEANT GO UP-STAIRS AND TELL HER!
SHEESH. YOU DON'T HAVE TO YELL.

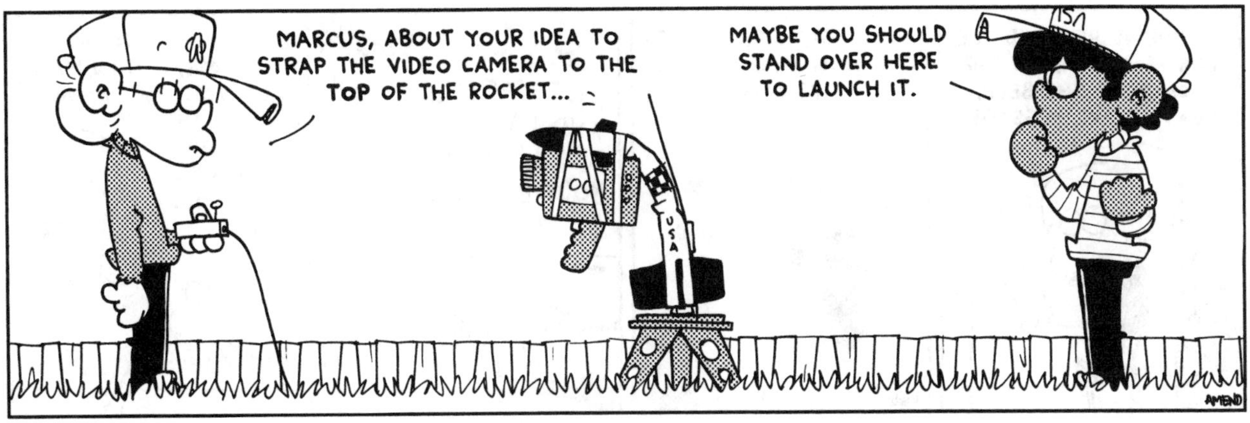
MARCUS, ABOUT YOUR IDEA TO STRAP THE VIDEO CAMERA TO THE TOP OF THE ROCKET...
MAYBE YOU SHOULD STAND OVER HERE TO LAUNCH IT.

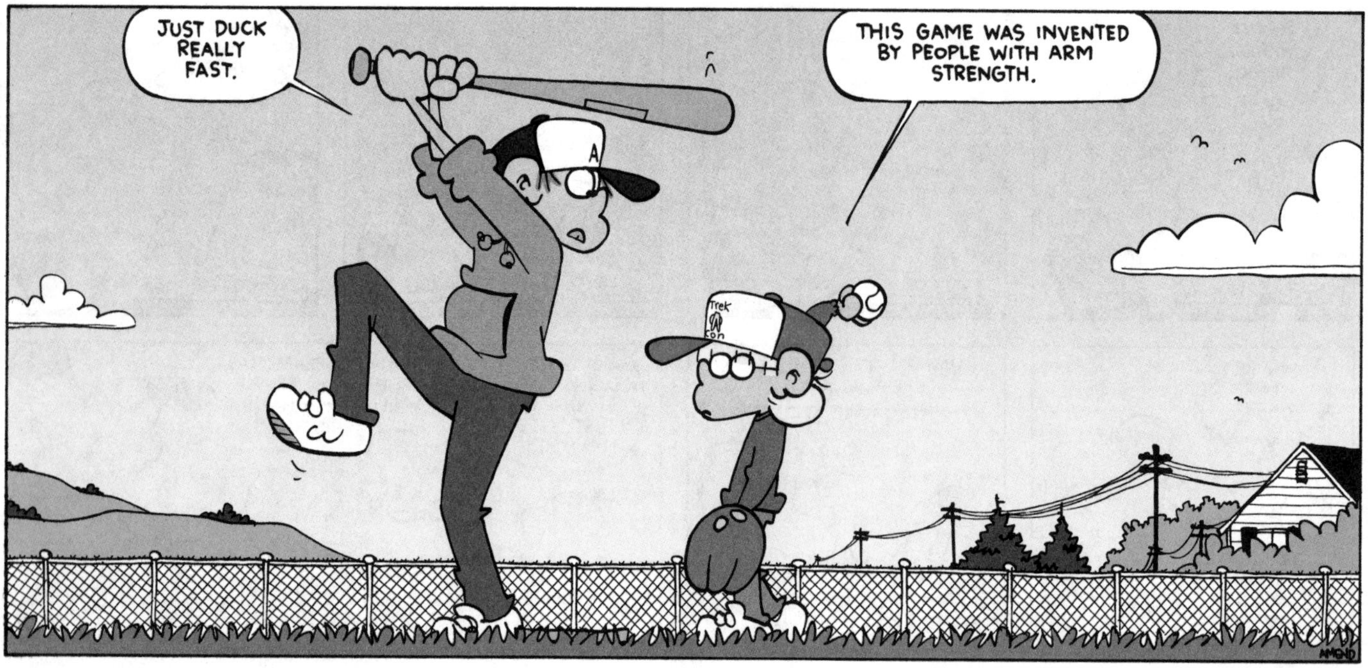
JUST DUCK REALLY FAST.
THIS GAME WAS INVENTED BY PEOPLE WITH ARM STRENGTH.
AMEND

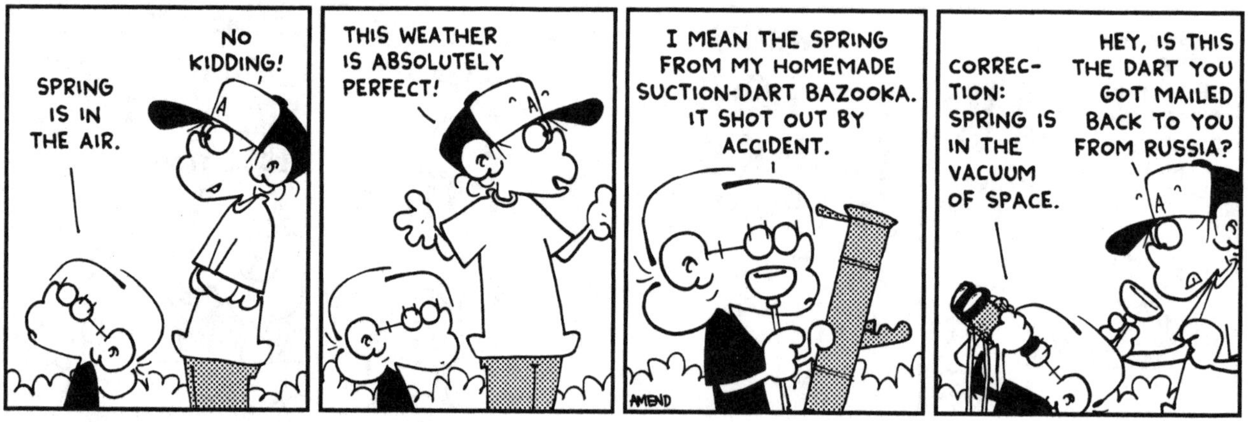
SPRING IS IN THE AIR.
NO KIDDING!
THIS WEATHER IS ABSOLUTELY PERFECT!
I MEAN THE SPRING FROM MY HOMEMADE SUCTION-DART BAZOOKA. IT SHOT OUT BY ACCIDENT.
AMEND
CORREC-TION: SPRING IS IN THE VACUUM OF SPACE.
HEY, IS THIS THE DART YOU GOT MAILED BACK TO YOU FROM RUSSIA?

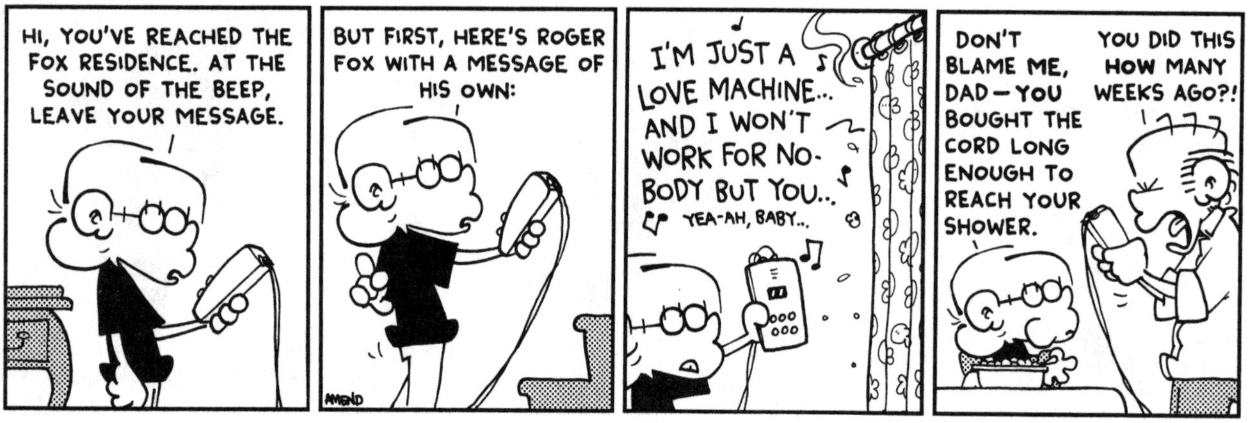
HI, YOU'VE REACHED THE FOX RESIDENCE. AT THE SOUND OF THE BEEP, LEAVE YOUR MESSAGE.
BUT FIRST, HERE'S ROGER FOX WITH A MESSAGE OF HIS OWN:
AMEND
I'M JUST A LOVE MACHINE... AND I WON'T WORK FOR NO-BODY BUT YOU...
YEA-AH, BABY...
DON'T BLAME ME, DAD—YOU BOUGHT THE CORD LONG ENOUGH TO REACH YOUR SHOWER.
YOU DID THIS HOW MANY WEEKS AGO?!

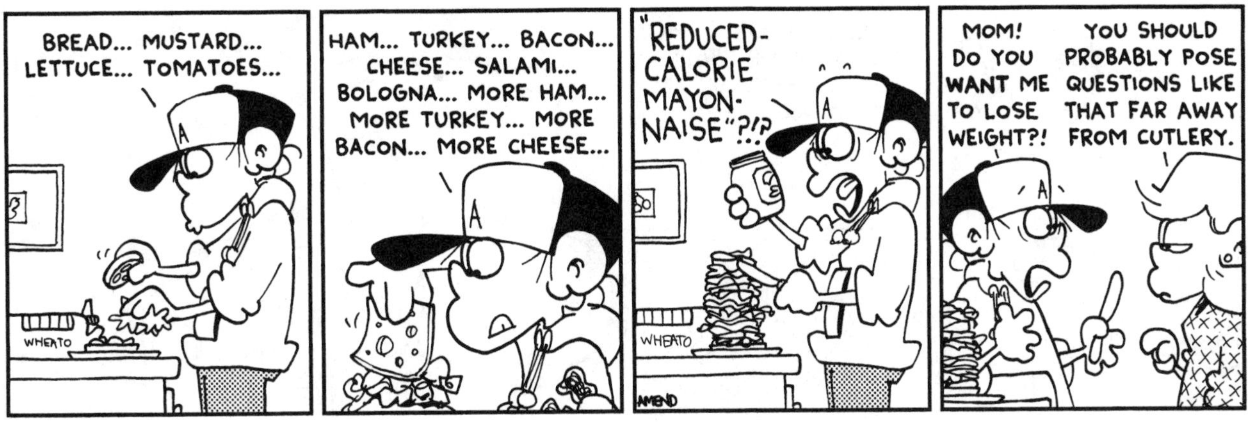
BREAD... MUSTARD... LETTUCE... TOMATOES...
HAM... TURKEY... BACON... CHEESE... SALAMI... BOLOGNA... MORE HAM... MORE TURKEY... MORE BACON... MORE CHEESE...
"REDUCED-CALORIE MAYONNAISE"?!?
MOM! DO YOU WANT ME TO LOSE WEIGHT?!
YOU SHOULD PROBABLY POSE QUESTIONS LIKE THAT FAR AWAY FROM CUTLERY.

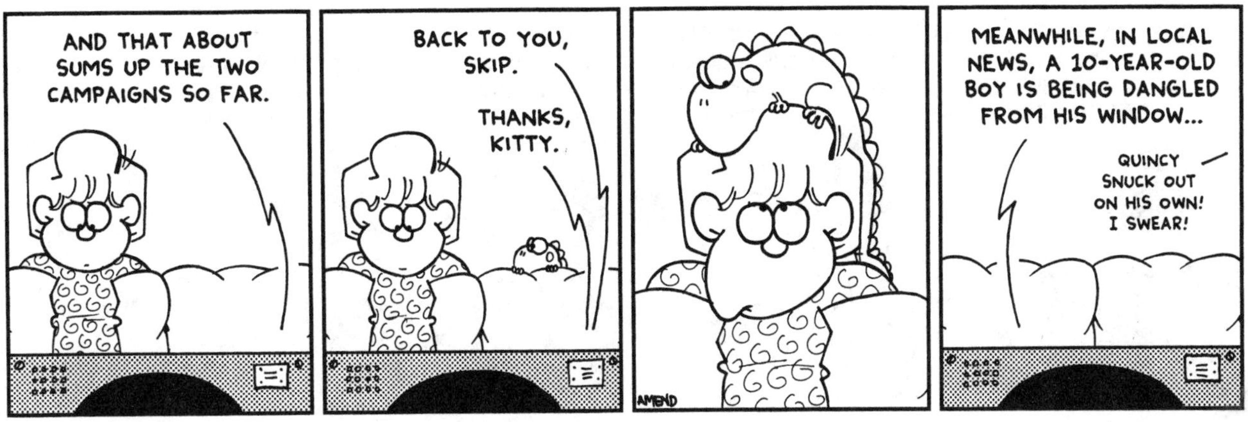
AND THAT ABOUT SUMS UP THE TWO CAMPAIGNS SO FAR.
BACK TO YOU, SKIP.
THANKS, KITTY.
MEANWHILE, IN LOCAL NEWS, A 10-YEAR-OLD BOY IS BEING DANGLED FROM HIS WINDOW...
QUINCY SNUCK OUT ON HIS OWN! I SWEAR!

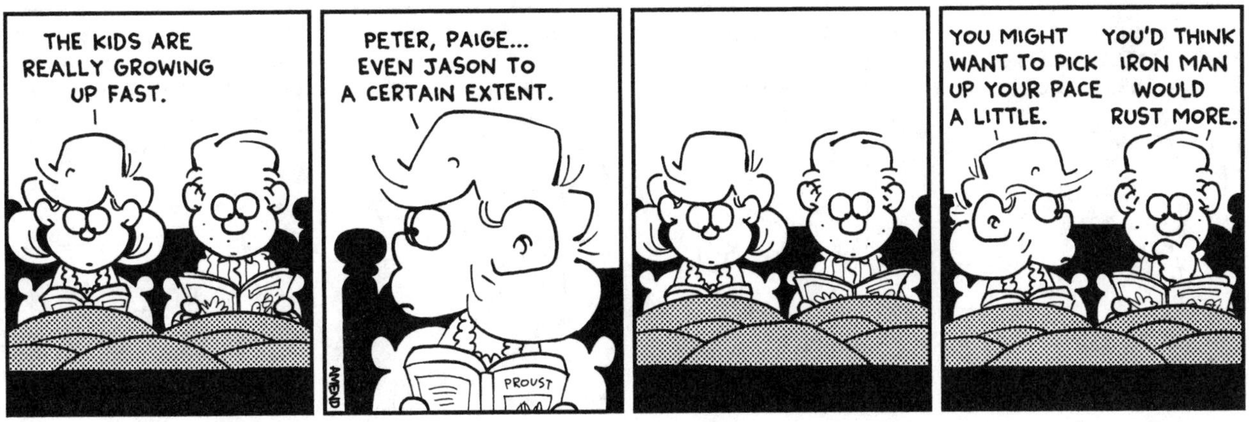
THE KIDS ARE REALLY GROWING UP FAST.
PETER, PAIGE... EVEN JASON TO A CERTAIN EXTENT.
PROUST
YOU MIGHT WANT TO PICK UP YOUR PACE A LITTLE.
YOU'D THINK IRON MAN WOULD RUST MORE.

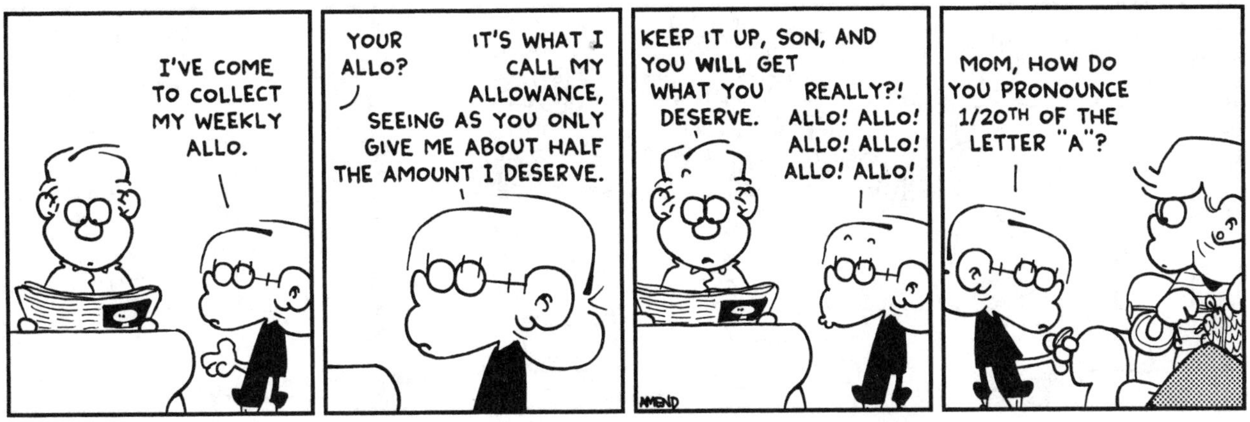
I'VE COME TO COLLECT MY WEEKLY ALLO.
YOUR ALLO?
IT'S WHAT I CALL MY ALLOWANCE, SEEING AS YOU ONLY GIVE ME ABOUT HALF THE AMOUNT I DESERVE.
KEEP IT UP, SON, AND YOU WILL GET WHAT YOU DESERVE.
REALLY?! ALLO! ALLO! ALLO! ALLO! ALLO! ALLO!
MOM, HOW DO YOU PRONOUNCE 1/20TH OF THE LETTER "A"?

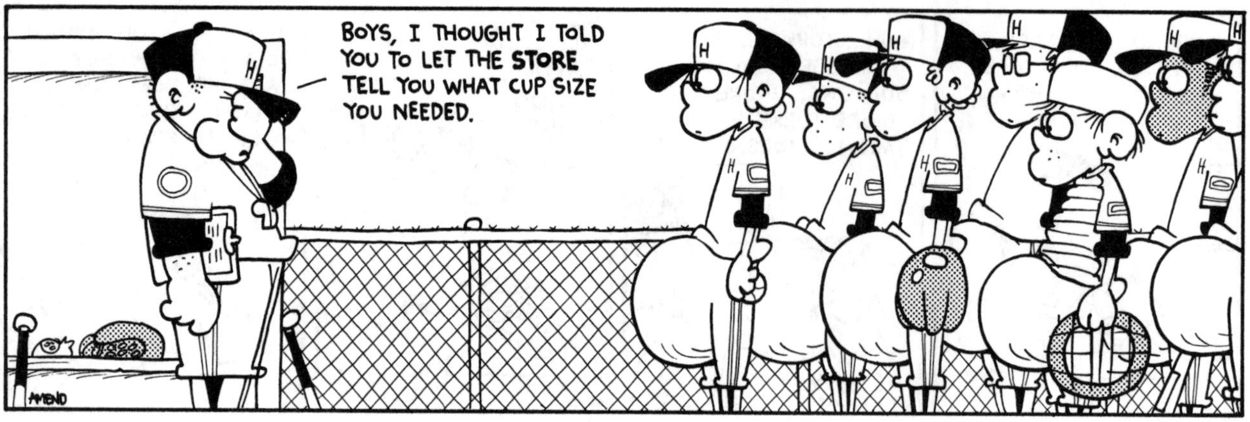
BOYS, I THOUGHT I TOLD YOU TO LET THE STORE TELL YOU WHAT CUP SIZE YOU NEEDED.

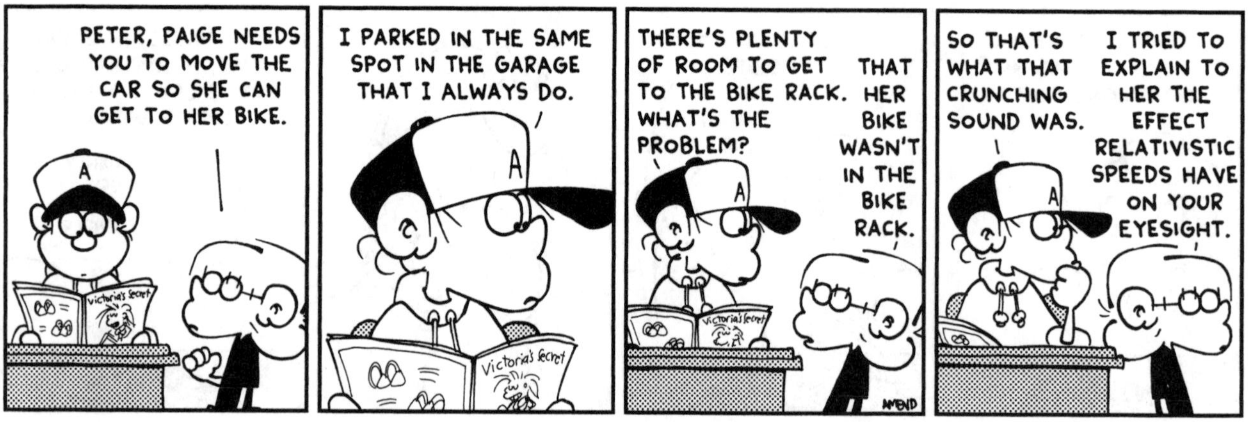
PETER, PAIGE NEEDS YOU TO MOVE THE CAR SO SHE CAN GET TO HER BIKE.
I PARKED IN THE SAME SPOT IN THE GARAGE THAT I ALWAYS DO.
THERE'S PLENTY OF ROOM TO GET TO THE BIKE RACK. WHAT'S THE PROBLEM?
THAT HER BIKE WASN'T IN THE BIKE RACK.
SO THAT'S WHAT THAT CRUNCHING SOUND WAS.
I TRIED TO EXPLAIN TO HER THE EFFECT RELATIVISTIC SPEEDS HAVE ON YOUR EYESIGHT.

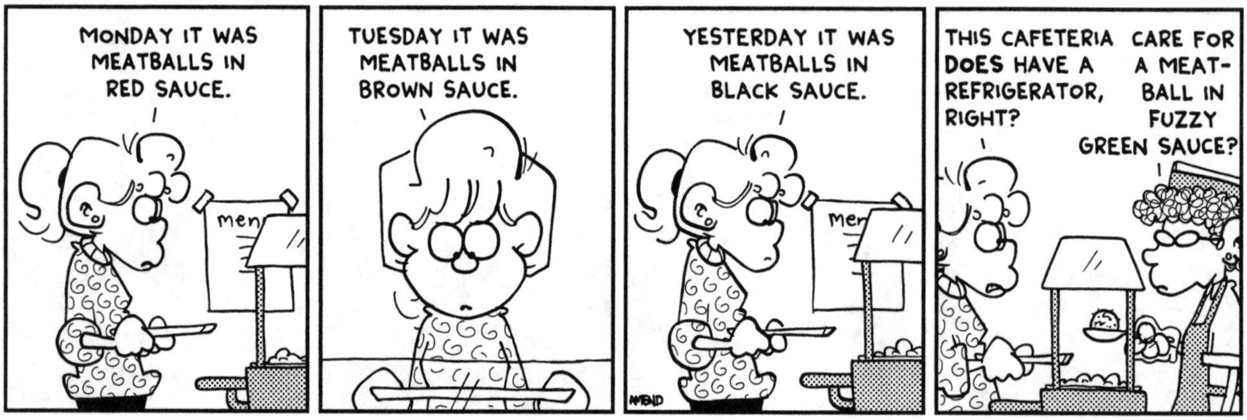
MONDAY IT WAS MEATBALLS IN RED SAUCE.
TUESDAY IT WAS MEATBALLS IN BROWN SAUCE.
YESTERDAY IT WAS MEATBALLS IN BLACK SAUCE.
THIS CAFETERIA DOES HAVE A REFRIGERATOR, RIGHT?
CARE FOR A MEAT-BALL IN FUZZY GREEN SAUCE?

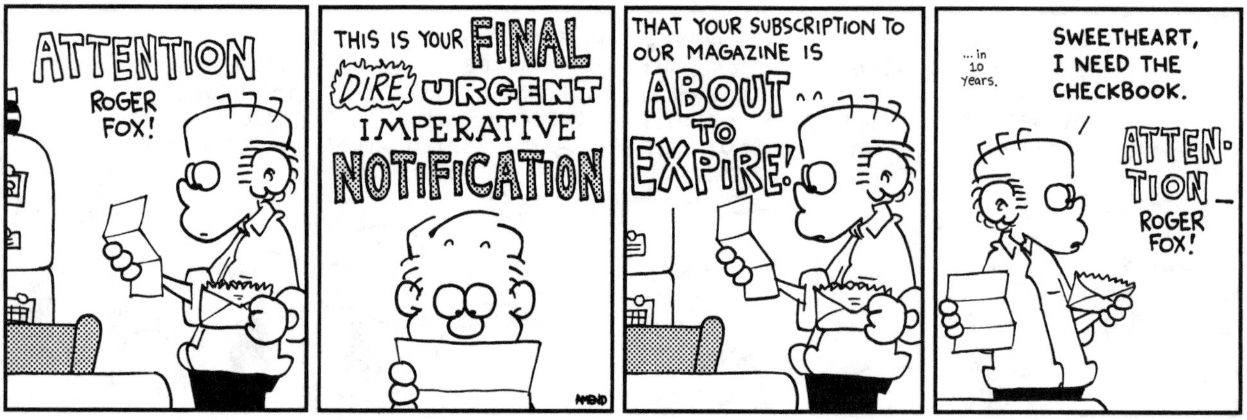
ATTENTION ROGER FOX!
THIS IS YOUR FINAL DIRE URGENT IMPERATIVE NOTIFICATION
THAT YOUR SUBSCRIPTION TO OUR MAGAZINE IS ABOUT TO EXPIRE!
...in 10 years.
SWEETHEART, I NEED THE CHECKBOOK.
ATTEN-TION ROGER FOX!

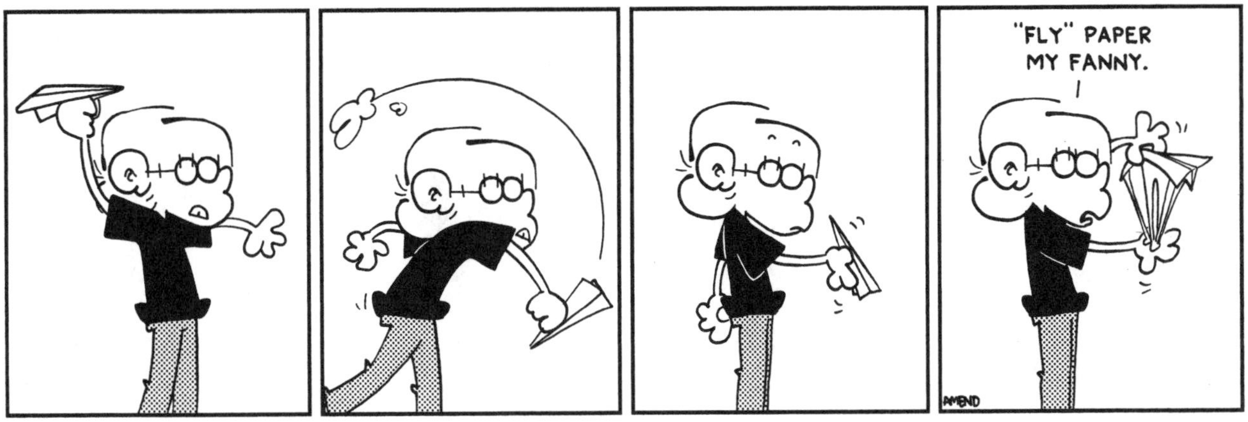
"FLY" PAPER MY FANNY.
AMEND

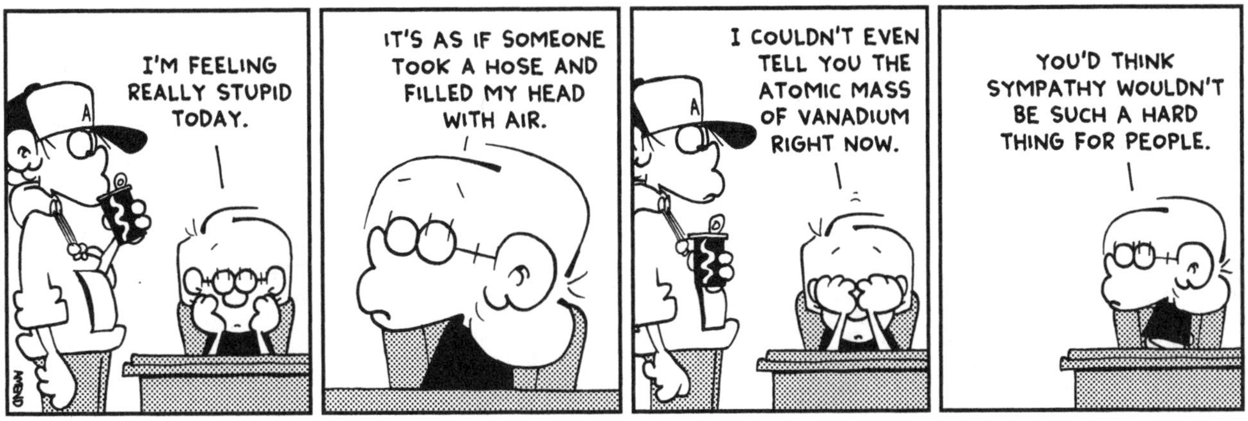
I'M FEELING REALLY STUPID TODAY.
IT'S AS IF SOMEONE TOOK A HOSE AND FILLED MY HEAD WITH AIR.
I COULDN'T EVEN TELL YOU THE ATOMIC MASS OF VANADIUM RIGHT NOW.
YOU'D THINK SYMPATHY WOULDN'T BE SUCH A HARD THING FOR PEOPLE.

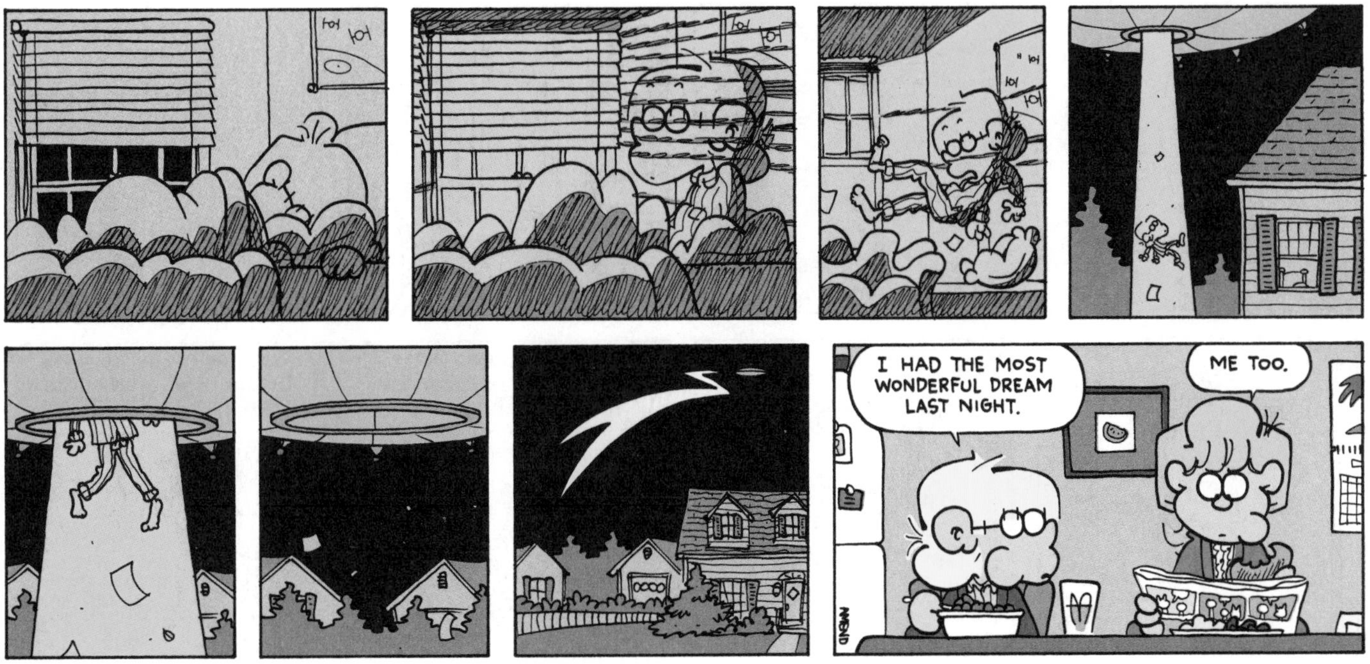
I HAD THE MOST WONDERFUL DREAM LAST NIGHT.
ME TOO.

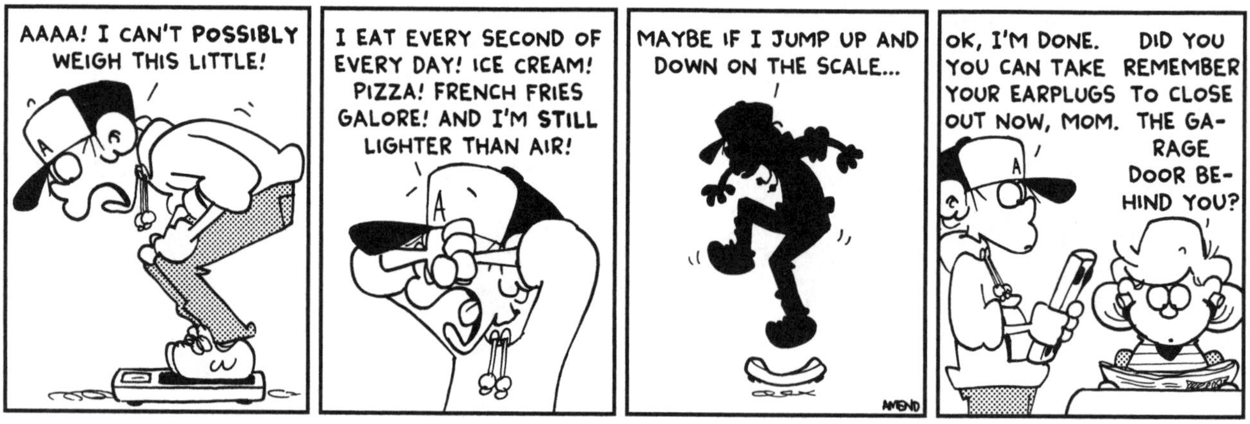
AAAA! I CAN'T POSSIBLY WEIGH THIS LITTLE!
I EAT EVERY SECOND OF EVERY DAY! ICE CREAM! PIZZA! FRENCH FRIES GALORE! AND I'M STILL LIGHTER THAN AIR!
MAYBE IF I JUMP UP AND DOWN ON THE SCALE...
OK, I'M DONE. YOU CAN TAKE YOUR EARPLUGS OUT NOW, MOM.
DID YOU REMEMBER TO CLOSE THE GA-RAGE DOOR BE-HIND YOU?
AMEND

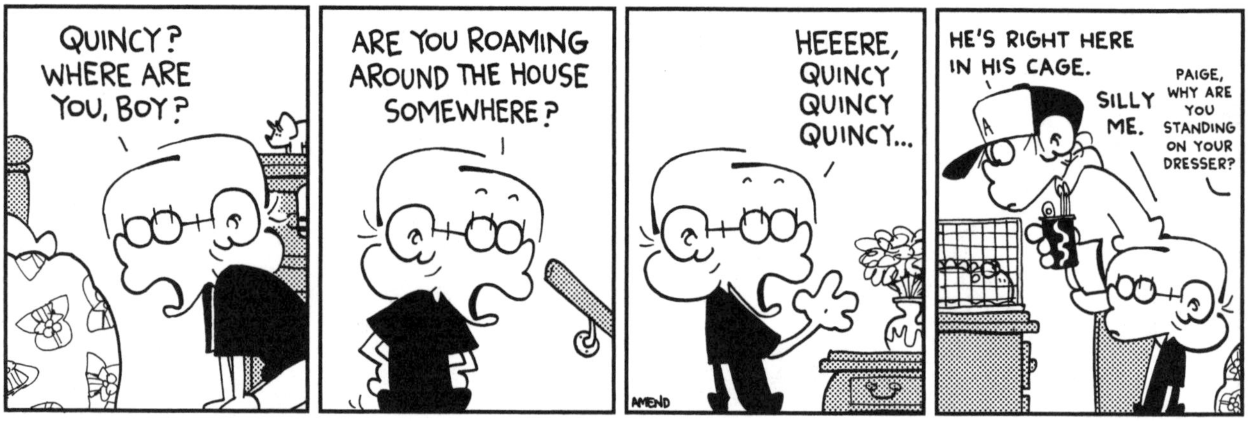
QUINCY? WHERE ARE YOU, BOY?
ARE YOU ROAMING AROUND THE HOUSE SOMEWHERE?
HEEERE, QUINCY QUINCY QUINCY...
AMEND
HE'S RIGHT HERE IN HIS CAGE.
SILLY ME.
PAIGE, WHY ARE YOU STANDING ON YOUR DRESSER?

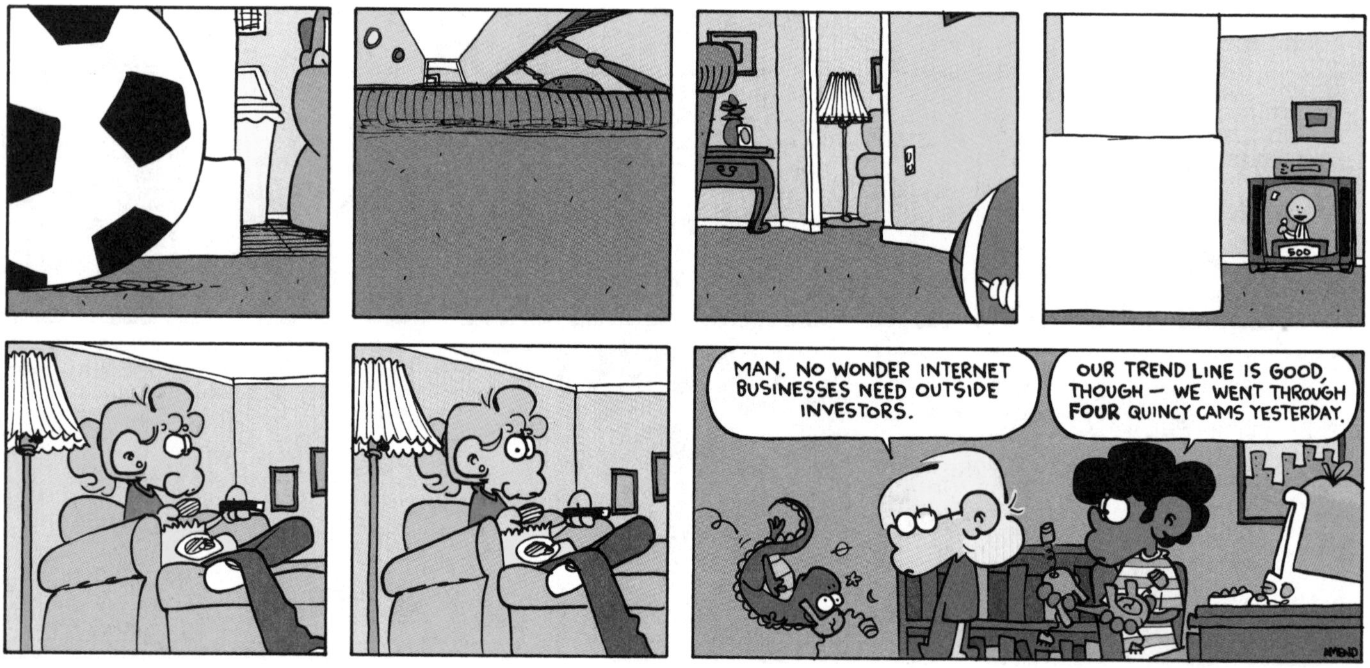
500
MAN. NO WONDER INTERNET BUSINESSES NEED OUTSIDE INVESTORS.
OUR TREND LINE IS GOOD, THOUGH — WE WENT THROUGH FOUR QUINCY CAMS YESTERDAY.
AMEND

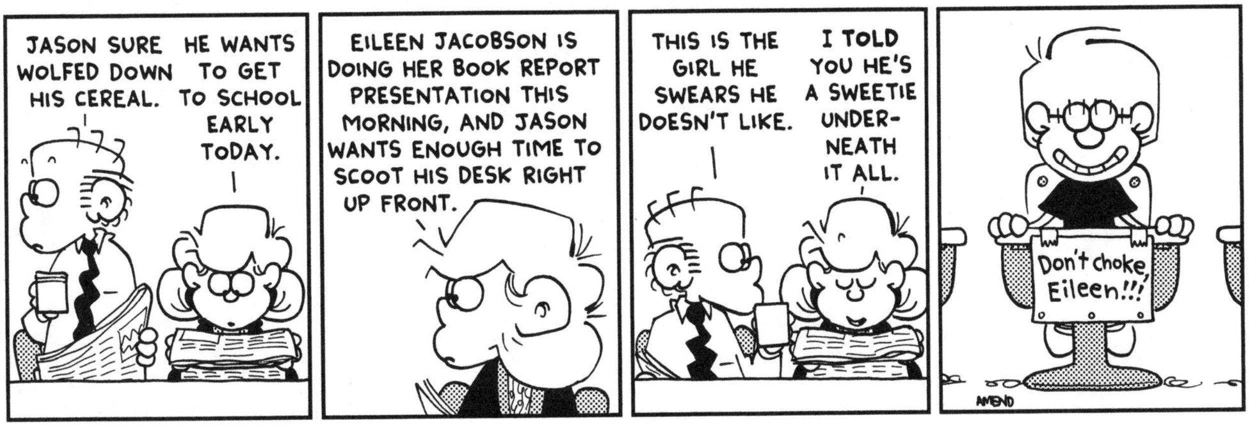
JASON SURE WOLFED DOWN HIS CEREAL.
HE WANTS TO GET TO SCHOOL EARLY TODAY.
EILEEN JACOBSON IS DOING HER BOOK REPORT PRESENTATION THIS MORNING, AND JASON WANTS ENOUGH TIME TO SCOOT HIS DESK RIGHT UP FRONT.
THIS IS THE GIRL HE SWEARS HE DOESN'T LIKE.
I TOLD YOU HE'S A SWEETIE UNDER-NEATH IT ALL.
Don't choke, Eileen!!!
AMEND

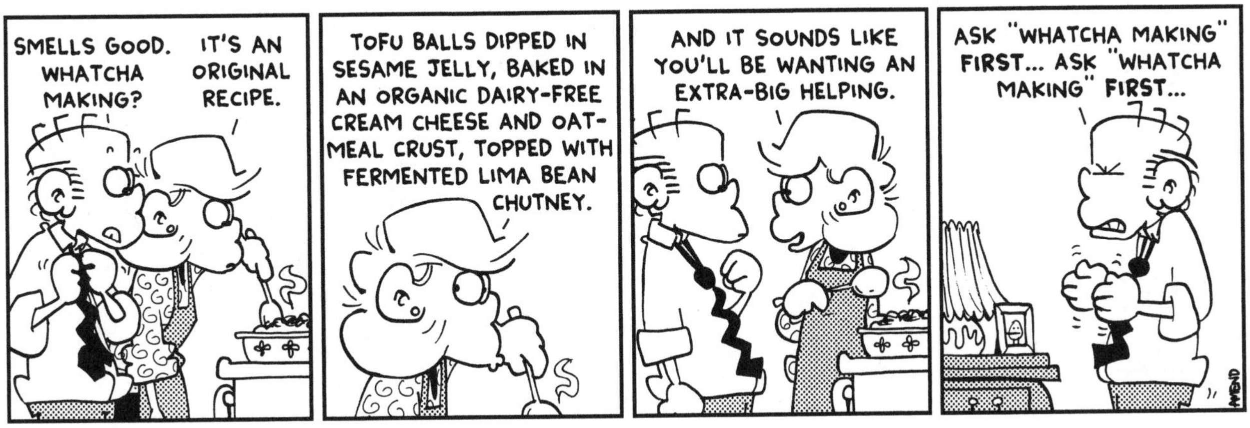
SMELLS GOOD. WHATCHA MAKING?
IT'S AN ORIGINAL RECIPE.
TOFU BALLS DIPPED IN SESAME JELLY, BAKED IN AN ORGANIC DAIRY-FREE CREAM CHEESE AND OAT-MEAL CRUST, TOPPED WITH FERMENTED LIMA BEAN CHUTNEY.
AND IT SOUNDS LIKE YOU'LL BE WANTING AN EXTRA-BIG HELPING.
ASK "WHATCHA MAKING" FIRST... ASK "WHATCHA MAKING" FIRST...
AMEND

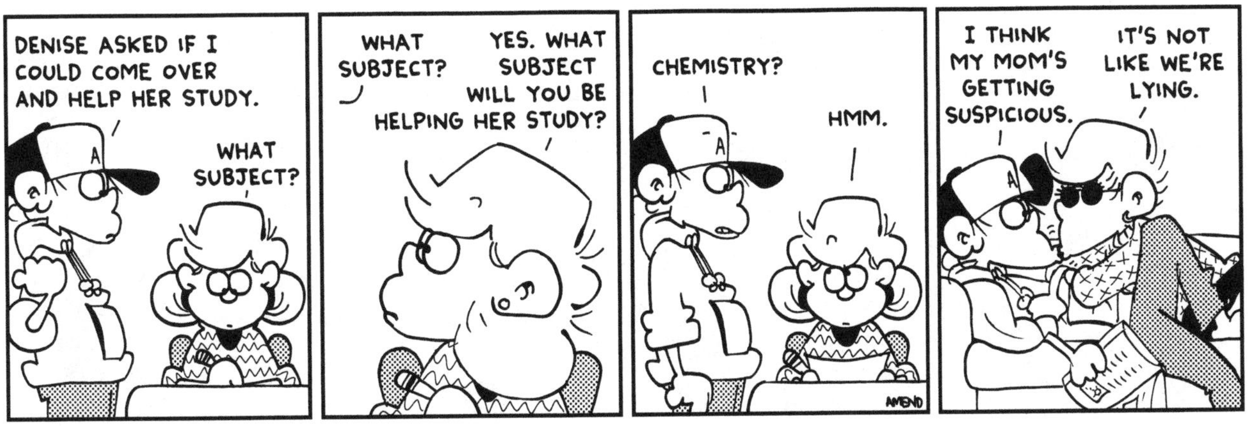
DENISE ASKED IF I COULD COME OVER AND HELP HER STUDY.
WHAT SUBJECT?
WHAT SUBJECT?
YES. WHAT SUBJECT WILL YOU BE HELPING HER STUDY?
CHEMISTRY?
HMM.
AMEND
I THINK MY MOM'S GETTING SUSPICIOUS.
IT'S NOT LIKE WE'RE LYING.

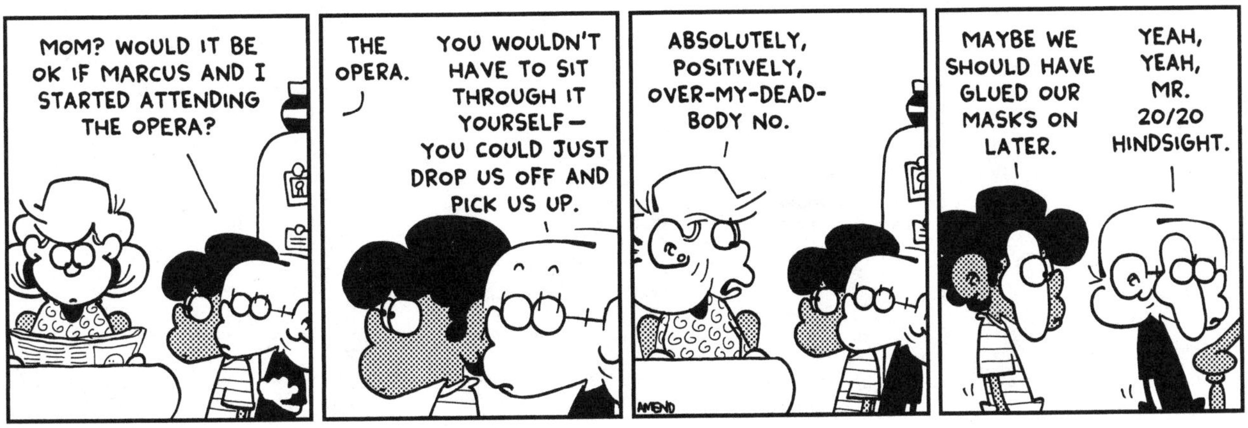
MOM? WOULD IT BE OK IF MARCUS AND I STARTED ATTENDING THE OPERA?
THE OPERA.
YOU WOULDN'T HAVE TO SIT THROUGH IT YOURSELF— YOU COULD JUST DROP US OFF AND PICK US UP.
ABSOLUTELY, POSITIVELY, OVER-MY-DEAD-BODY NO.
AMEND
MAYBE WE SHOULD HAVE GLUED OUR MASKS ON LATER.
YEAH, YEAH, MR. 20/20 HINDSIGHT.

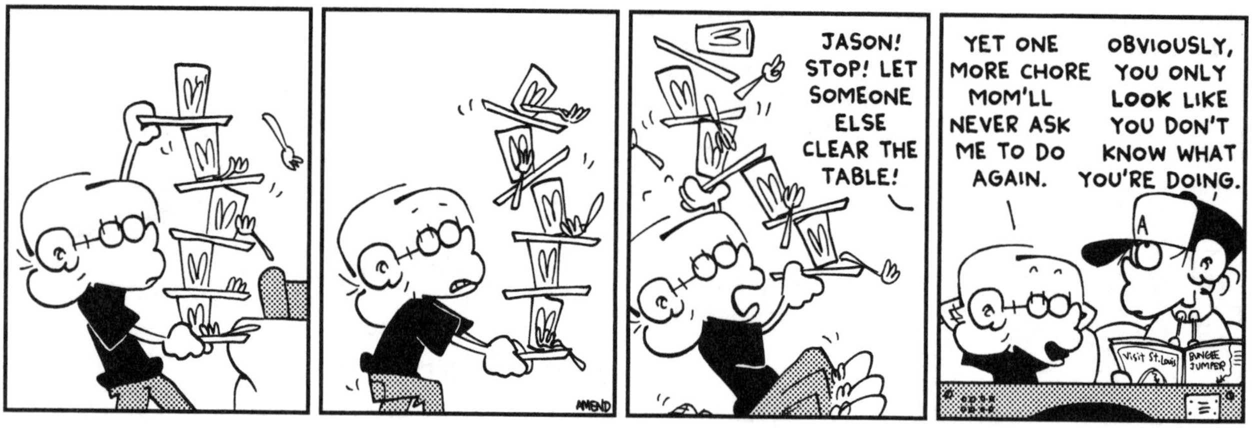
JASON! STOP! LET SOMEONE ELSE CLEAR THE TABLE!
YET ONE MORE CHORE MOM'LL NEVER ASK ME TO DO AGAIN.
OBVIOUSLY, YOU ONLY **LOOK** LIKE YOU DON'T KNOW WHAT YOU'RE DOING.
Visit St. Louis
BUNGEE JUMPER
AMEND

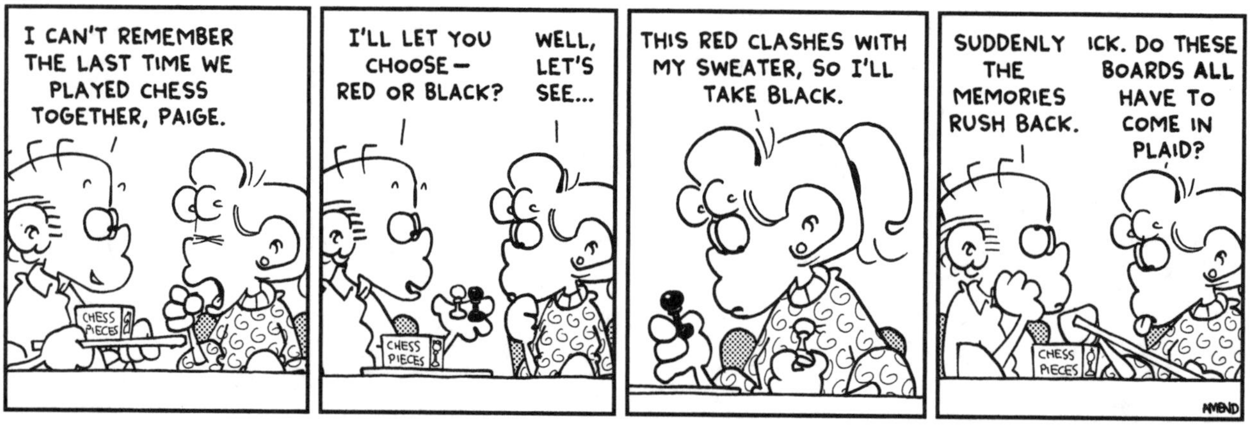
I CAN'T REMEMBER THE LAST TIME WE PLAYED CHESS TOGETHER, PAIGE.
CHESS PIECES
I'LL LET YOU CHOOSE— RED OR BLACK?
WELL, LET'S SEE...
THIS RED CLASHES WITH MY SWEATER, SO I'LL TAKE BLACK.
SUDDENLY THE MEMORIES RUSH BACK.
ICK. DO THESE BOARDS **ALL** HAVE TO COME IN PLAID?
AMEND

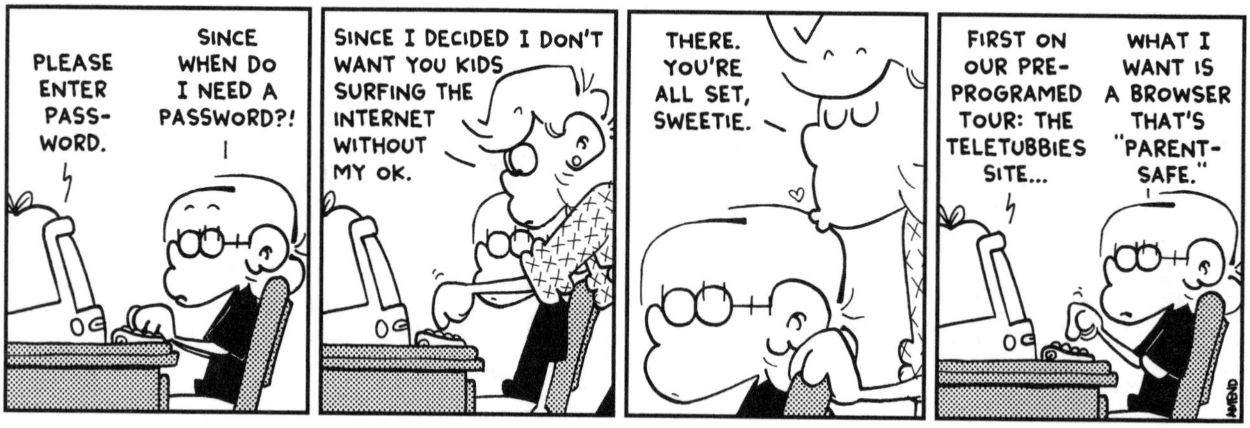
PLEASE ENTER PASS-WORD.
SINCE WHEN DO I NEED A PASSWORD?!
SINCE I DECIDED I DON'T WANT YOU KIDS SURFING THE INTERNET WITHOUT MY OK.
THERE. YOU'RE ALL SET, SWEETIE.
FIRST ON OUR PRE-PROGRAMED TOUR: THE TELETUBBIES SITE...
WHAT I WANT IS A BROWSER THAT'S "PARENT-SAFE."
AMEND

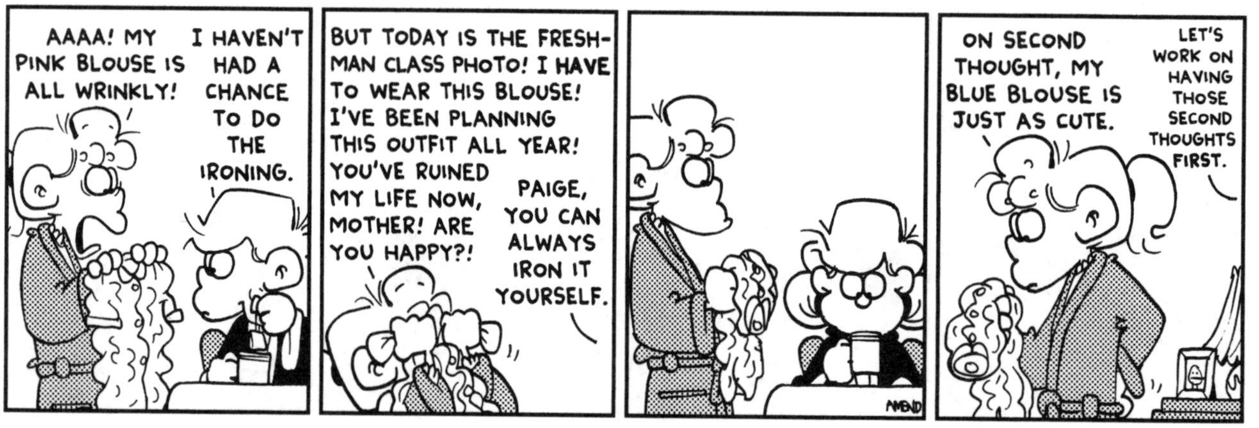
AAAA! MY PINK BLOUSE IS ALL WRINKLY!
I HAVEN'T HAD A CHANCE TO DO THE IRONING.
BUT TODAY IS THE FRESH-MAN CLASS PHOTO! I HAVE TO WEAR THIS BLOUSE! I'VE BEEN PLANNING THIS OUTFIT ALL YEAR! YOU'VE RUINED MY LIFE NOW, MOTHER! ARE YOU HAPPY?!
PAIGE, YOU CAN ALWAYS IRON IT YOURSELF.
AMEND
ON SECOND THOUGHT, MY BLUE BLOUSE IS JUST AS CUTE.
LET'S WORK ON HAVING THOSE SECOND THOUGHTS FIRST.

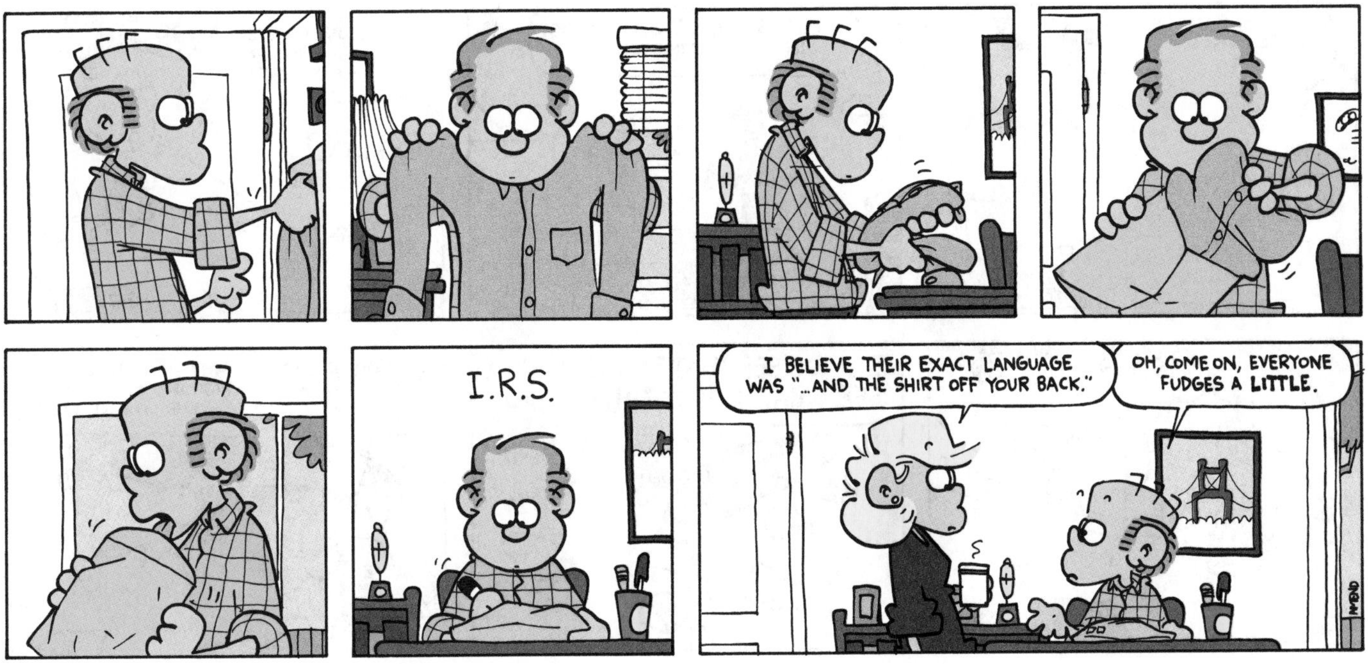
I.R.S.
I BELIEVE THEIR EXACT LANGUAGE WAS "...AND THE SHIRT OFF YOUR BACK."
OH, COME ON, EVERYONE FUDGES A LITTLE.
AMEND

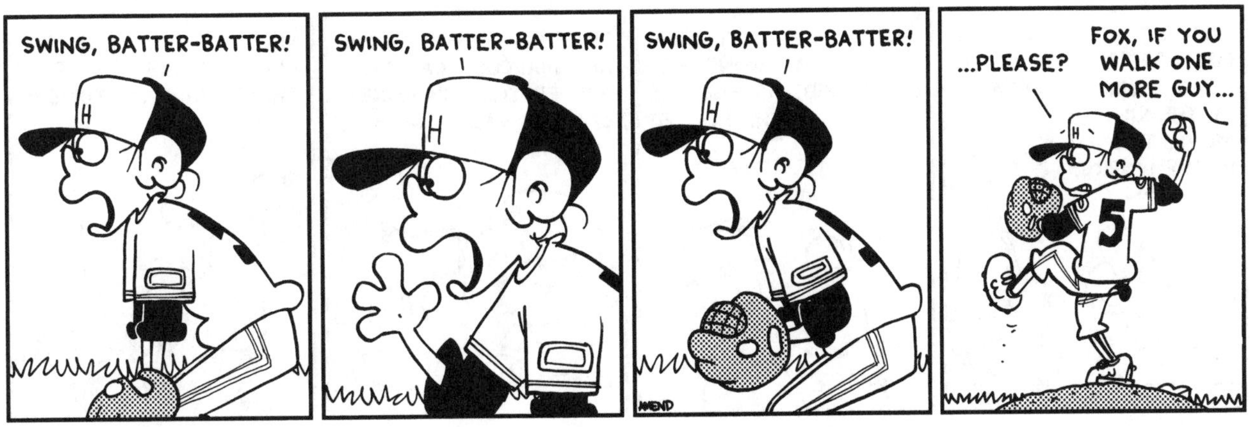
SWING, BATTER-BATTER!
SWING, BATTER-BATTER!
SWING, BATTER-BATTER!
AMEND
...PLEASE?
FOX, IF YOU WALK ONE MORE GUY...

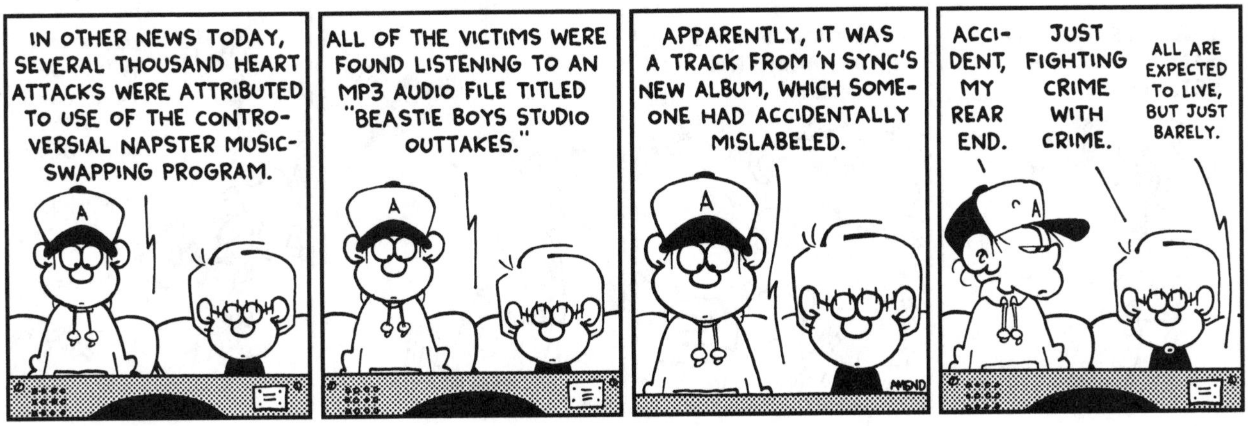
IN OTHER NEWS TODAY, SEVERAL THOUSAND HEART ATTACKS WERE ATTRIBUTED TO USE OF THE CONTROVERSIAL NAPSTER MUSIC-SWAPPING PROGRAM.
ALL OF THE VICTIMS WERE FOUND LISTENING TO AN MP3 AUDIO FILE TITLED "BEASTIE BOYS STUDIO OUTTAKES."
APPARENTLY, IT WAS A TRACK FROM 'N SYNC'S NEW ALBUM, WHICH SOMEONE HAD ACCIDENTALLY MISLABELED.
AMEND
ACCIDENT, MY REAR END.
JUST FIGHTING CRIME WITH CRIME.
ALL ARE EXPECTED TO LIVE, BUT JUST BARELY.

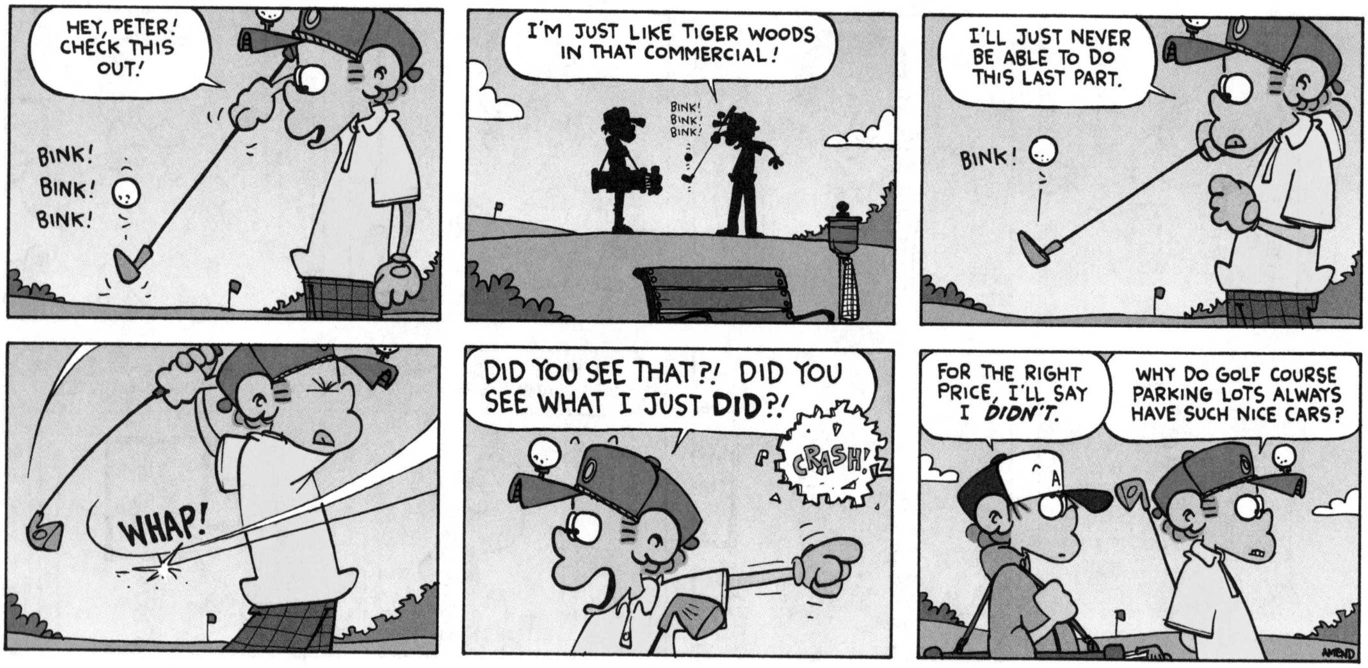
HEY, PETER! CHECK THIS OUT!
BINK! BINK! BINK!
I'M JUST LIKE TIGER WOODS IN THAT COMMERCIAL!
BINK! BINK! BINK!
I'LL JUST NEVER BE ABLE TO DO THIS LAST PART.
BINK!
WHAP!
DID YOU SEE THAT?! DID YOU SEE WHAT I JUST DID?!
CRASH!
FOR THE RIGHT PRICE, I'LL SAY I DIDN'T.
WHY DO GOLF COURSE PARKING LOTS ALWAYS HAVE SUCH NICE CARS?
AMEND

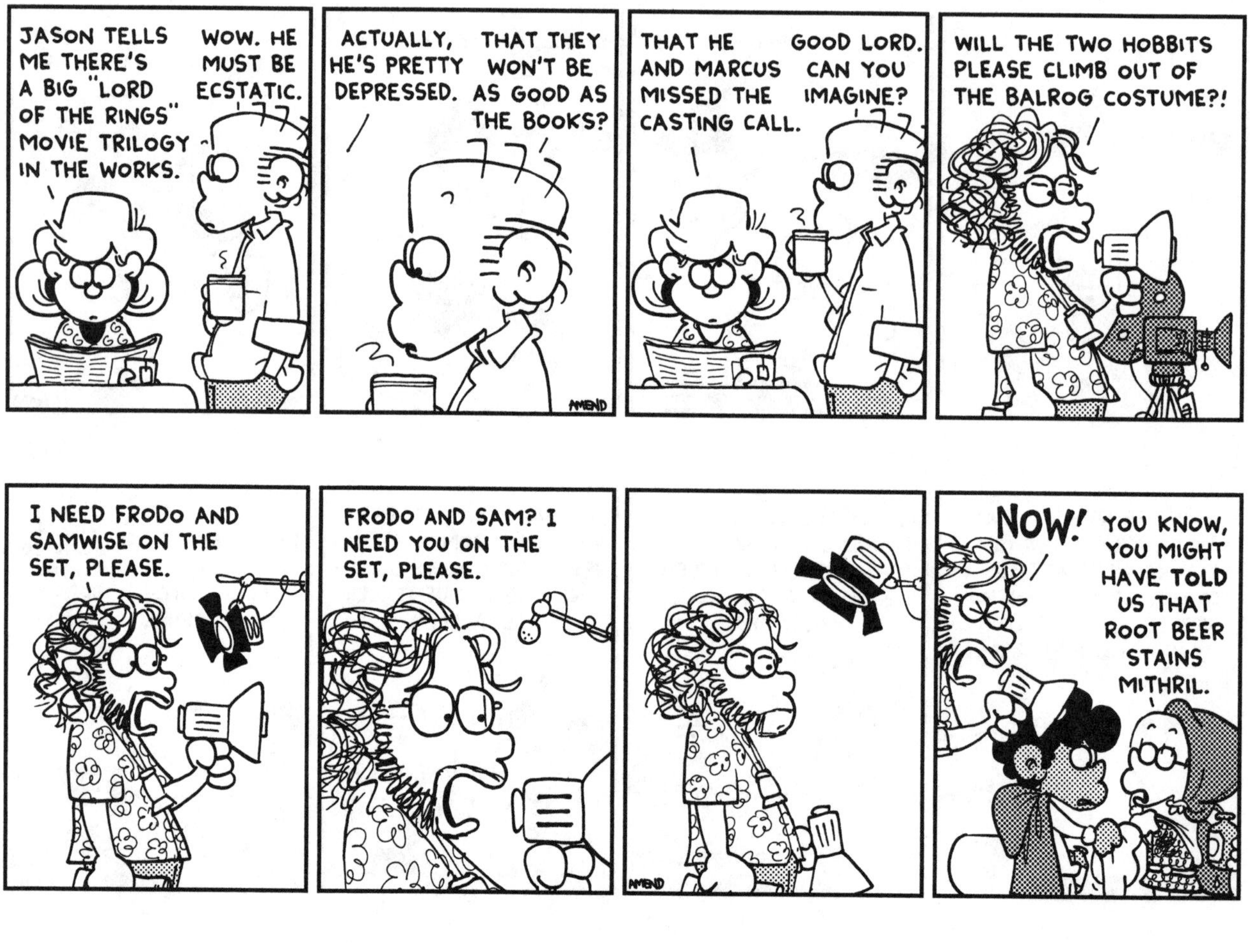
JASON TELLS ME THERE'S A BIG "LORD OF THE RINGS" MOVIE TRILOGY IN THE WORKS.
WOW. HE MUST BE ECSTATIC.
ACTUALLY, HE'S PRETTY DEPRESSED.
THAT THEY WON'T BE AS GOOD AS THE BOOKS?
AMEND
THAT HE AND MARCUS MISSED THE CASTING CALL.
GOOD LORD. CAN YOU IMAGINE?
WILL THE TWO HOBBITS PLEASE CLIMB OUT OF THE BALROG COSTUME?!
I NEED FRODO AND SAMWISE ON THE SET, PLEASE.
FRODO AND SAM? I NEED YOU ON THE SET, PLEASE.
AMEND
NOW!
YOU KNOW, YOU MIGHT HAVE TOLD US THAT ROOT BEER STAINS MITHRIL.

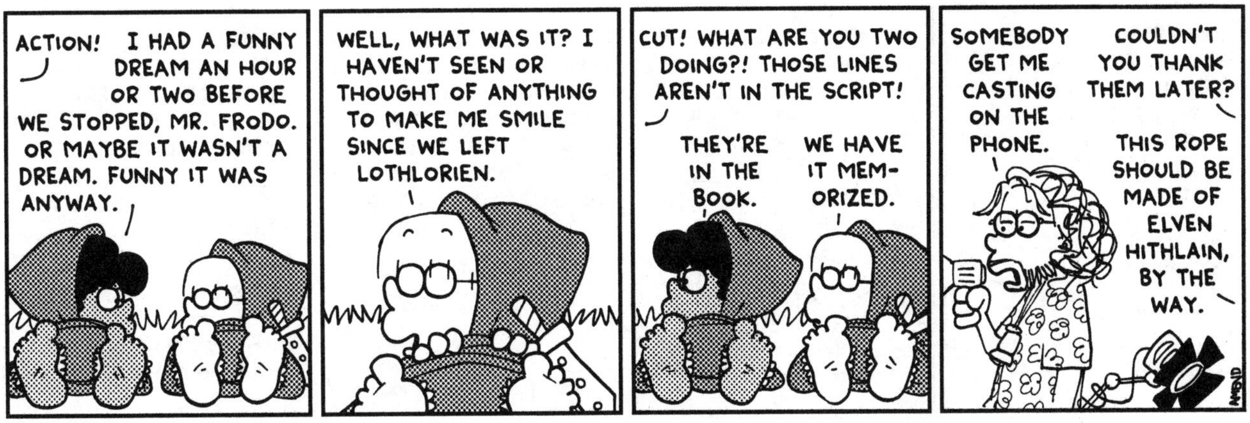
ACTION!
I HAD A FUNNY DREAM AN HOUR OR TWO BEFORE WE STOPPED, MR. FRODO. OR MAYBE IT WASN'T A DREAM. FUNNY IT WAS ANYWAY.
WELL, WHAT WAS IT? I HAVEN'T SEEN OR THOUGHT OF ANYTHING TO MAKE ME SMILE SINCE WE LEFT LOTHLORIEN.
CUT! WHAT ARE YOU TWO DOING?! THOSE LINES AREN'T IN THE SCRIPT!
THEY'RE IN THE BOOK.
WE HAVE IT MEMORIZED.
SOMEBODY GET ME CASTING ON THE PHONE.
COULDN'T YOU THANK THEM LATER?
THIS ROPE SHOULD BE MADE OF ELVEN HITHLAIN, BY THE WAY.
AMEND

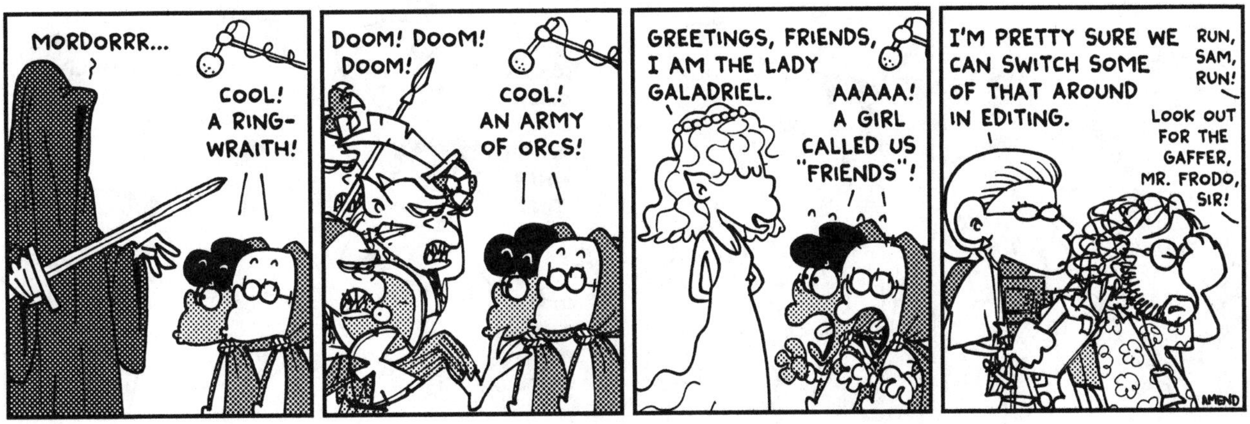
MORDORRR...
COOL! A RING-WRAITH!
DOOM! DOOM! DOOM!
COOL! AN ARMY OF ORCS!
GREETINGS, FRIENDS, I AM THE LADY GALADRIEL.
AAAAA! A GIRL CALLED US "FRIENDS"!
I'M PRETTY SURE WE CAN SWITCH SOME OF THAT AROUND IN EDITING.
RUN, SAM, RUN!
LOOK OUT FOR THE GAFFER, MR. FRODO, SIR!
AMEND

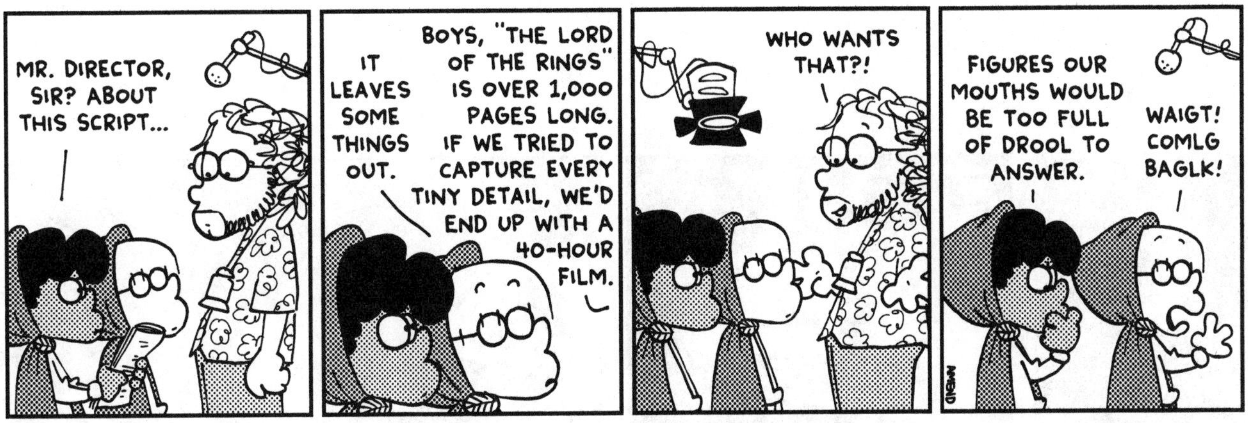
MR. DIRECTOR, SIR? ABOUT THIS SCRIPT...
IT LEAVES SOME THINGS OUT.
BOYS, "THE LORD OF THE RINGS" IS OVER 1,000 PAGES LONG. IF WE TRIED TO CAPTURE EVERY TINY DETAIL, WE'D END UP WITH A 40-HOUR FILM.
WHO WANTS THAT?!
AMEND
FIGURES OUR MOUTHS WOULD BE TOO FULL OF DROOL TO ANSWER.
WAIGT! COMLG BAGLK!

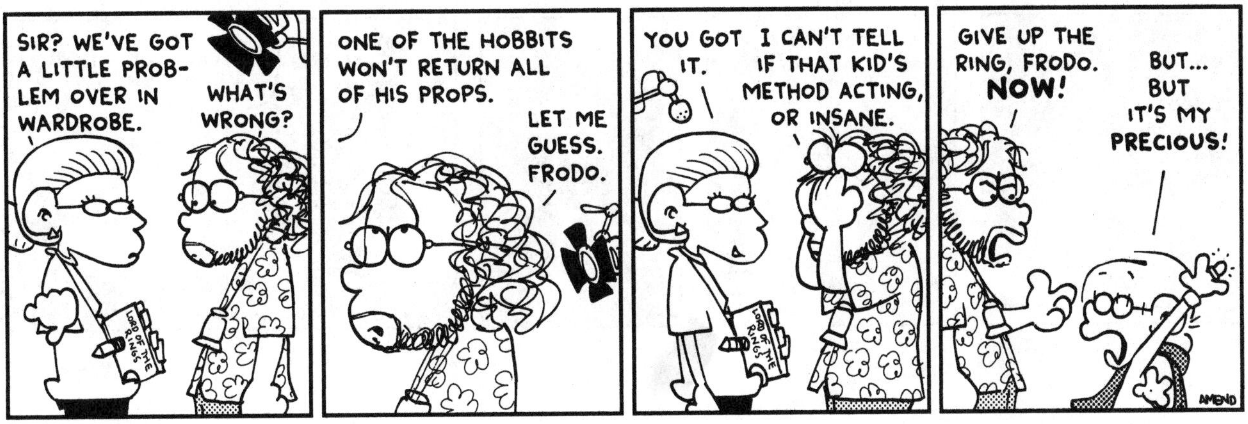
SIR? WE'VE GOT A LITTLE PROBLEM OVER IN WARDROBE.
WHAT'S WRONG?
LORD OF THE RINGS
ONE OF THE HOBBITS WON'T RETURN ALL OF HIS PROPS.
LET ME GUESS. FRODO.
YOU GOT IT.
I CAN'T TELL IF THAT KID'S METHOD ACTING, OR INSANE.
LORD OF THE RINGS
GIVE UP THE RING, FRODO. NOW!
BUT... BUT IT'S MY PRECIOUS!
AMEND

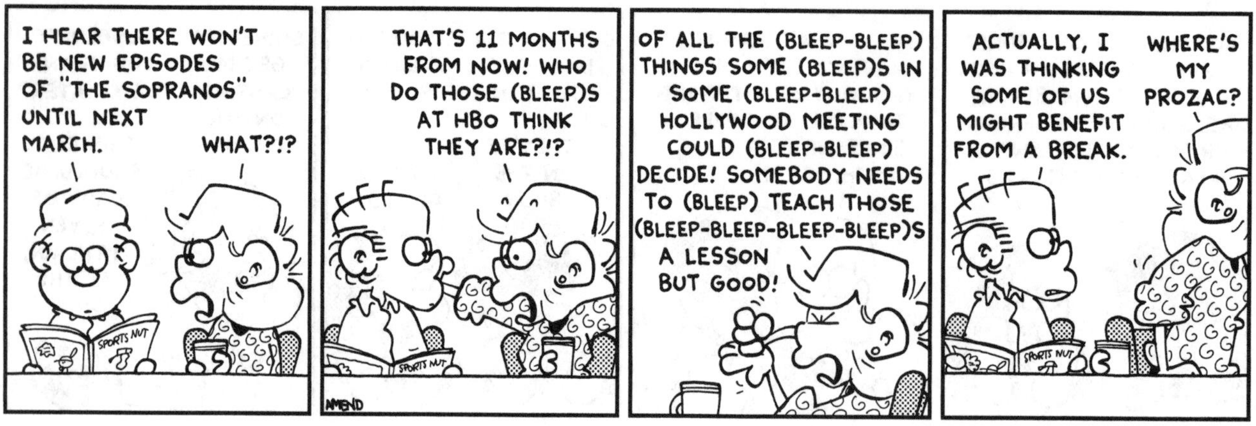
I HEAR THERE WON'T BE NEW EPISODES OF "THE SOPRANOS" UNTIL NEXT MARCH.
WHAT?!?
SPORTS NUT
THAT'S 11 MONTHS FROM NOW! WHO DO THOSE (BLEEP)S AT HBO THINK THEY ARE?!?
SPORTS NUT
AMEND
OF ALL THE (BLEEP-BLEEP) THINGS SOME (BLEEP)S IN SOME (BLEEP-BLEEP) HOLLYWOOD MEETING COULD (BLEEP-BLEEP) DECIDE! SOMEBODY NEEDS TO (BLEEP) TEACH THOSE (BLEEP-BLEEP-BLEEP-BLEEP)S A LESSON BUT GOOD!
ACTUALLY, I WAS THINKING SOME OF US MIGHT BENEFIT FROM A BREAK.
WHERE'S MY PROZAC?
SPORTS NUT

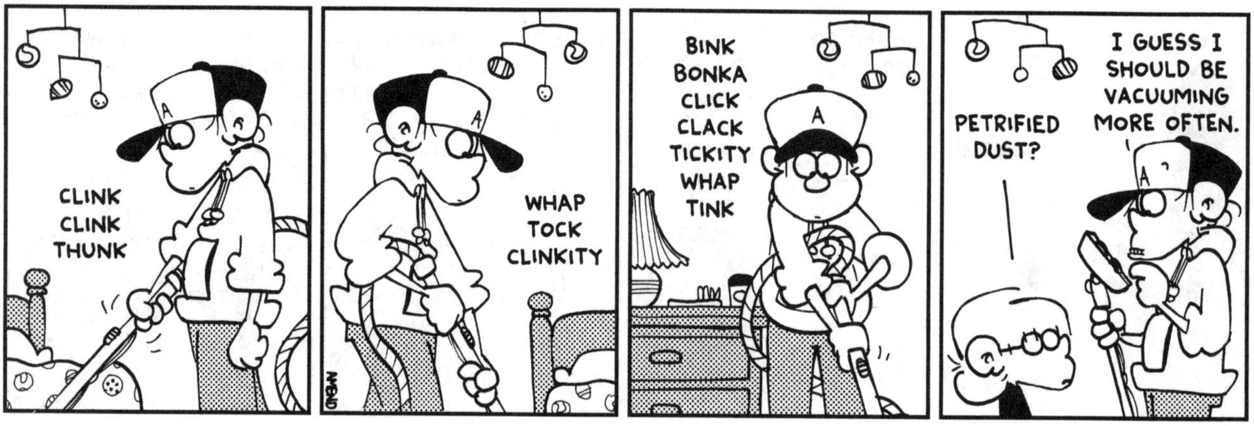
CLINK CLINK THUNK
WHAP TOCK CLINKITY
AMEND
BINK BONKA CLICK CLACK TICKITY WHAP TINK
PETRIFIED DUST?
I GUESS I SHOULD BE VACUUMING MORE OFTEN.

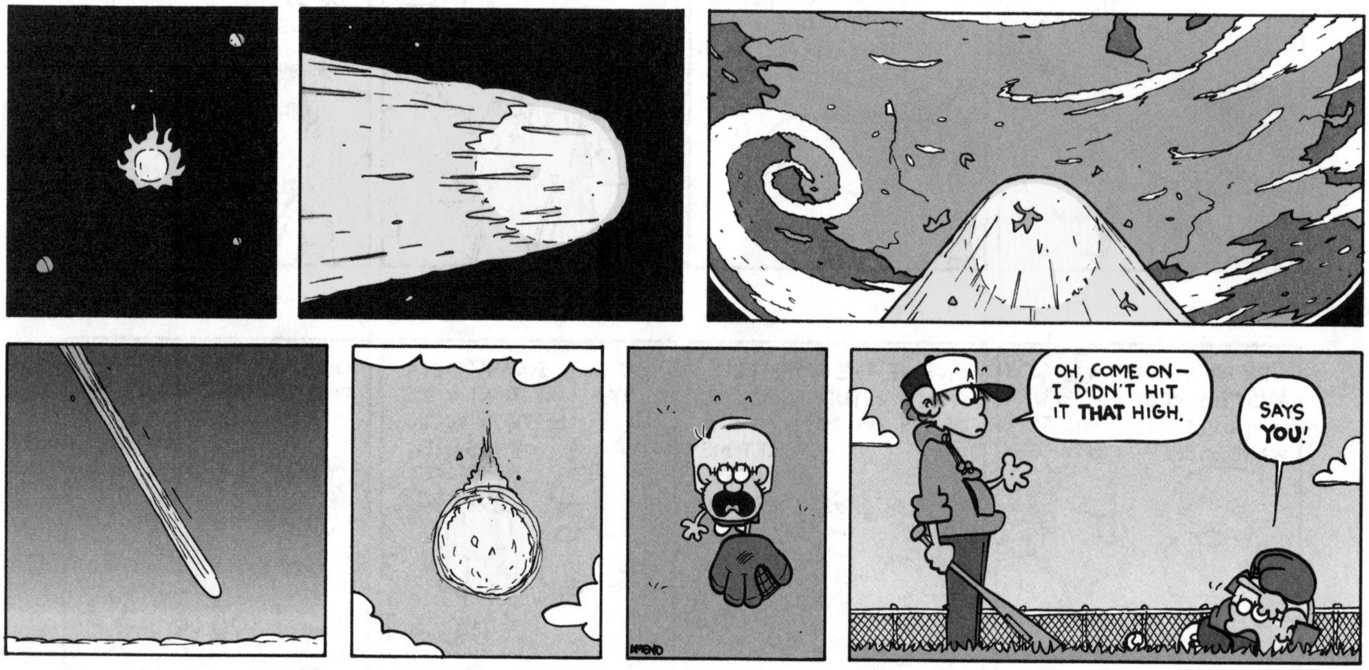
AMEND
OH, COME ON— I DIDN'T HIT IT THAT HIGH.
SAYS YOU!

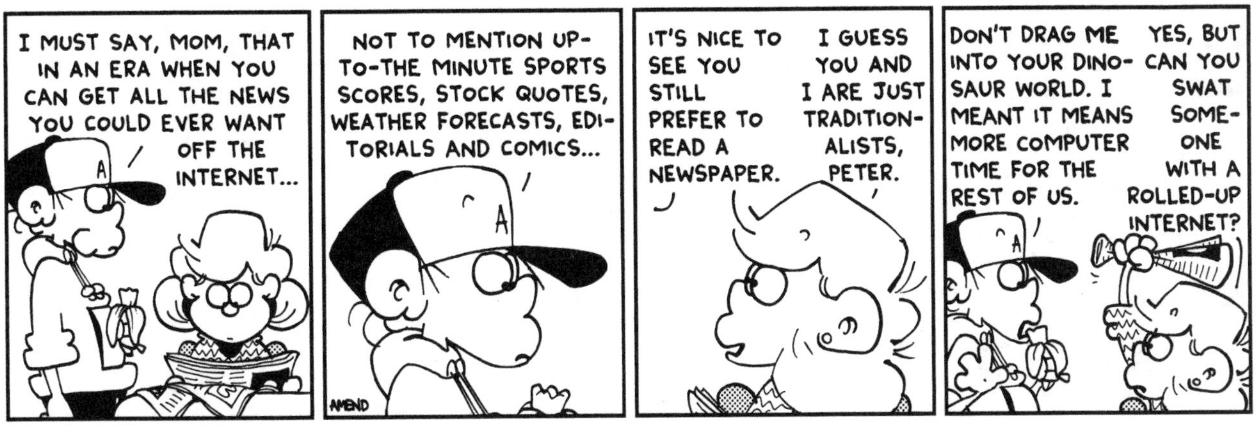
I MUST SAY, MOM, THAT IN AN ERA WHEN YOU CAN GET ALL THE NEWS YOU COULD EVER WANT OFF THE INTERNET...
NOT TO MENTION UP-TO-THE MINUTE SPORTS SCORES, STOCK QUOTES, WEATHER FORECASTS, EDITORIALS AND COMICS...
IT'S NICE TO SEE YOU STILL PREFER TO READ A NEWSPAPER.
I GUESS YOU AND I ARE JUST TRADITIONALISTS, PETER.
DON'T DRAG ME INTO YOUR DINOSAUR WORLD. I MEANT IT MEANS MORE COMPUTER TIME FOR THE REST OF US.
YES, BUT CAN YOU SWAT SOMEONE WITH A ROLLED-UP INTERNET?
AMEND

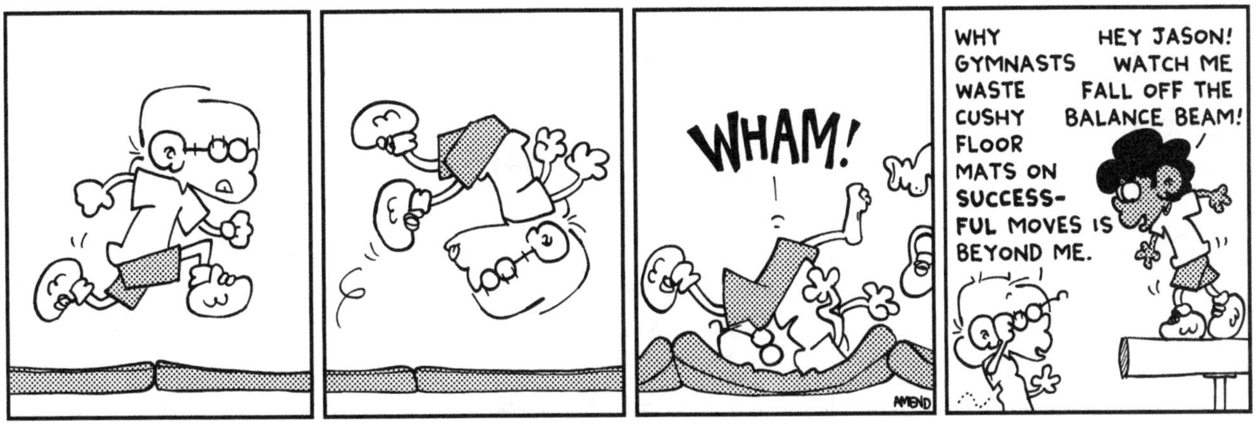
WHAM!
WHY GYMNASTS WASTE CUSHY FLOOR MATS ON SUCCESSFUL MOVES IS BEYOND ME.
HEY JASON! WATCH ME FALL OFF THE BALANCE BEAM!
AMEND

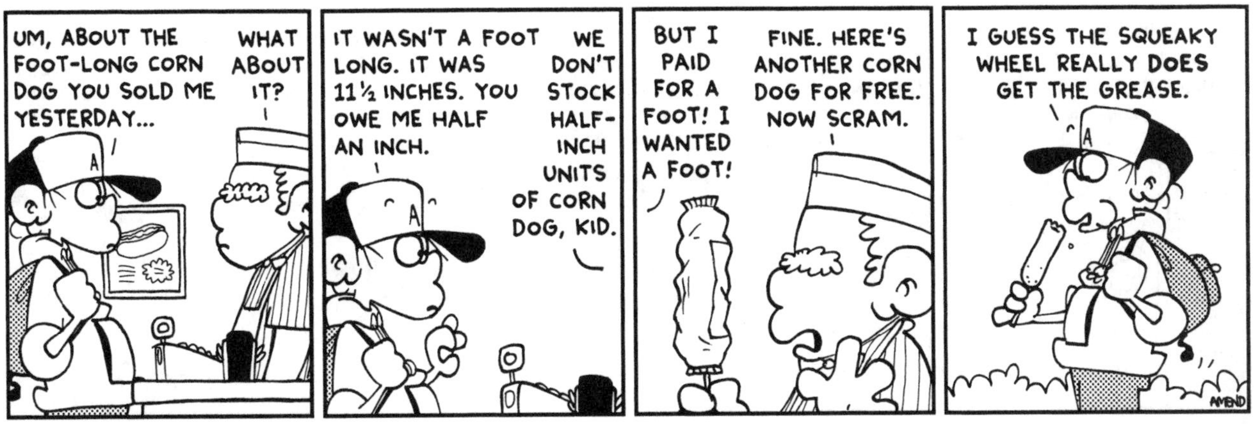
UM, ABOUT THE FOOT-LONG CORN DOG YOU SOLD ME YESTERDAY...
WHAT ABOUT IT?
IT WASN'T A FOOT LONG. IT WAS 11½ INCHES. YOU OWE ME HALF AN INCH.
WE DON'T STOCK HALF-INCH UNITS OF CORN DOG, KID.
BUT I PAID FOR A FOOT! I WANTED A FOOT!
FINE. HERE'S ANOTHER CORN DOG FOR FREE. NOW SCRAM.
I GUESS THE SQUEAKY WHEEL REALLY DOES GET THE GREASE.
AMEND

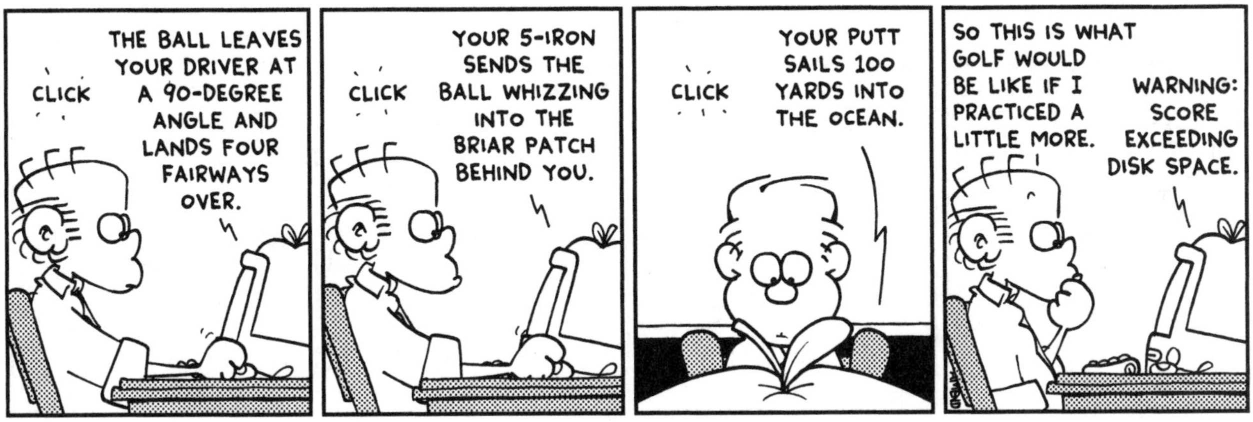
CLICK
THE BALL LEAVES YOUR DRIVER AT A 90-DEGREE ANGLE AND LANDS FOUR FAIRWAYS OVER.
CLICK
YOUR 5-IRON SENDS THE BALL WHIZZING INTO THE BRIAR PATCH BEHIND YOU.
CLICK
YOUR PUTT SAILS 100 YARDS INTO THE OCEAN.
SO THIS IS WHAT GOLF WOULD BE LIKE IF I PRACTICED A LITTLE MORE.
WARNING: SCORE EXCEEDING DISK SPACE.

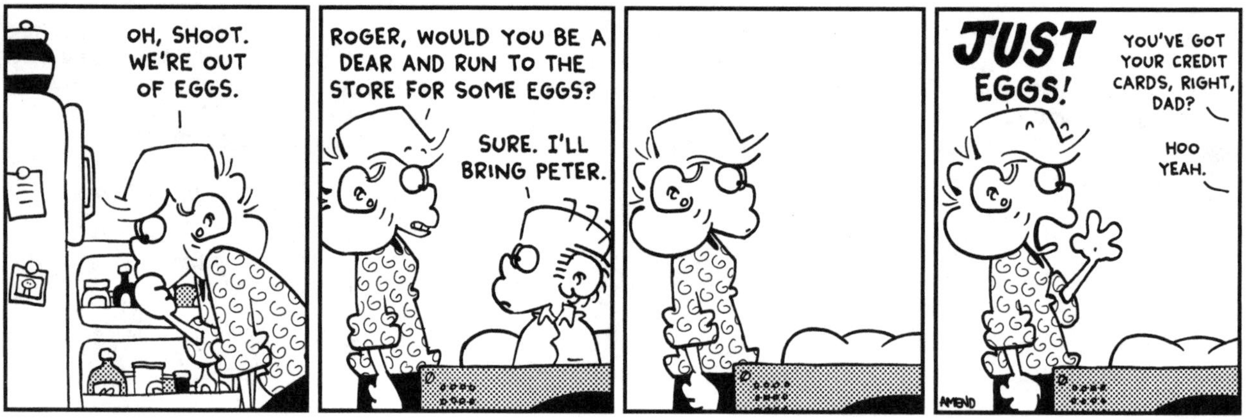
OH, SHOOT. WE'RE OUT OF EGGS.
ROGER, WOULD YOU BE A DEAR AND RUN TO THE STORE FOR SOME EGGS?
SURE. I'LL BRING PETER.
JUST EGGS!
YOU'VE GOT YOUR CREDIT CARDS, RIGHT, DAD?
HOO YEAH.

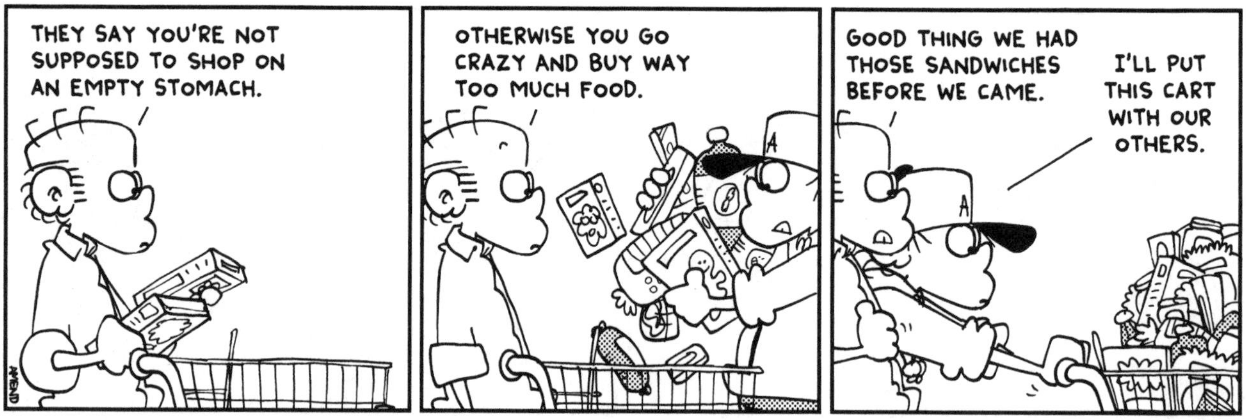
THEY SAY YOU'RE NOT SUPPOSED TO SHOP ON AN EMPTY STOMACH.
OTHERWISE YOU GO CRAZY AND BUY WAY TOO MUCH FOOD.
GOOD THING WE HAD THOSE SANDWICHES BEFORE WE CAME.
I'LL PUT THIS CART WITH OUR OTHERS.

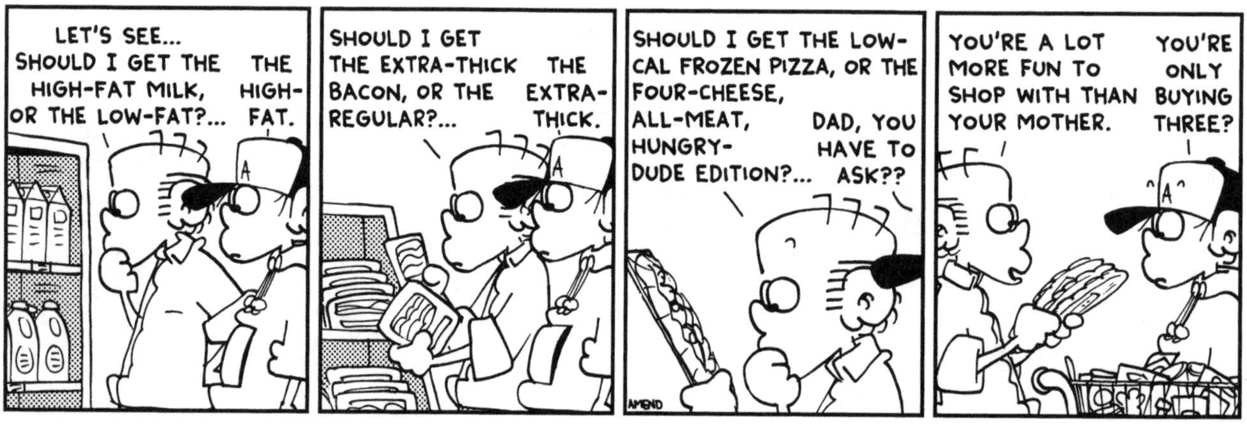
LET'S SEE... SHOULD I GET THE HIGH-FAT MILK, OR THE LOW-FAT?...
THE HIGH-FAT.
SHOULD I GET THE EXTRA-THICK BACON, OR THE REGULAR?...
THE EXTRA-THICK.
SHOULD I GET THE LOW-CAL FROZEN PIZZA, OR THE FOUR-CHEESE, ALL-MEAT, HUNGRY-DUDE EDITION?...
DAD, YOU HAVE TO ASK??
YOU'RE A LOT MORE FUN TO SHOP WITH THAN YOUR MOTHER.
YOU'RE ONLY BUYING THREE?

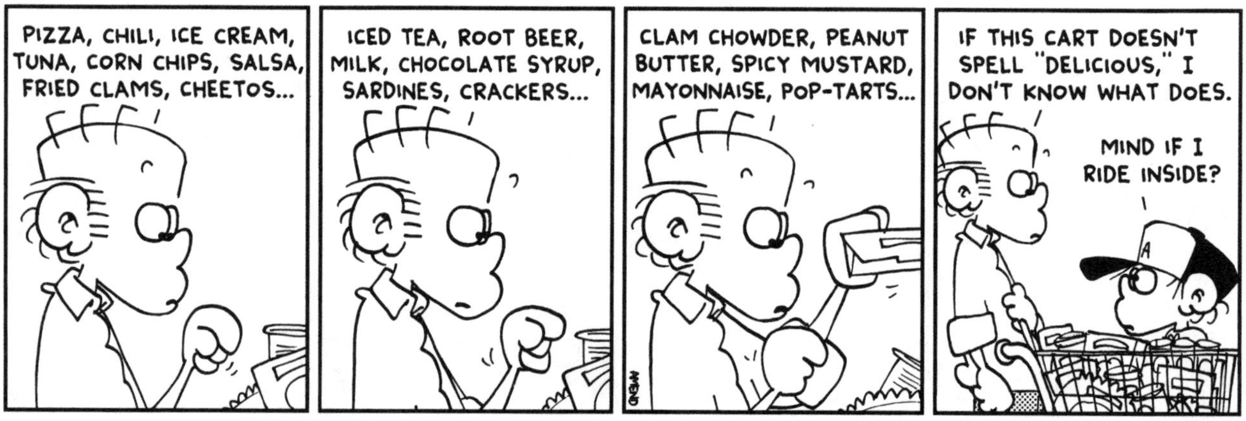
PIZZA, CHILI, ICE CREAM, TUNA, CORN CHIPS, SALSA, FRIED CLAMS, CHEETOS...
ICED TEA, ROOT BEER, MILK, CHOCOLATE SYRUP, SARDINES, CRACKERS...
CLAM CHOWDER, PEANUT BUTTER, SPICY MUSTARD, MAYONNAISE, POP-TARTS...
IF THIS CART DOESN'T SPELL "DELICIOUS," I DON'T KNOW WHAT DOES.
MIND IF I RIDE INSIDE?

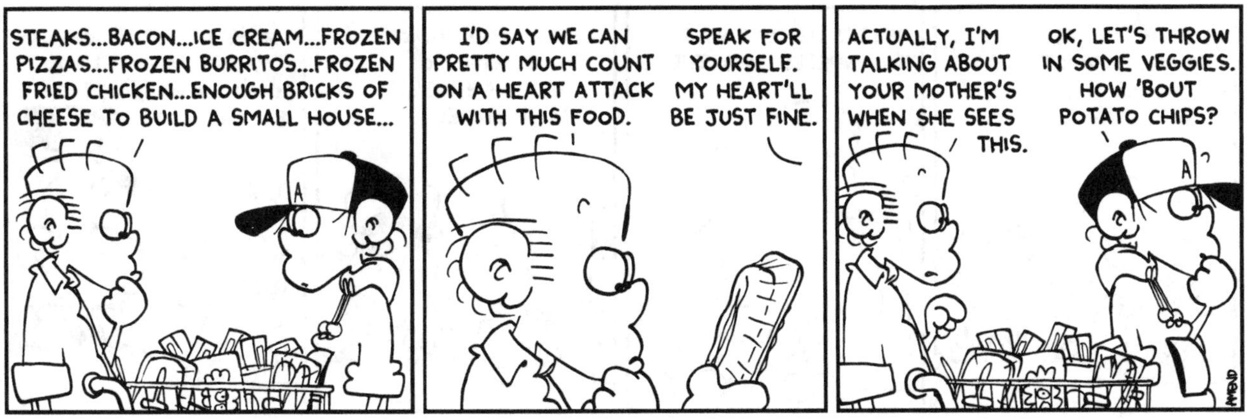
STEAKS...BACON...ICE CREAM...FROZEN PIZZAS...FROZEN BURRITOS...FROZEN FRIED CHICKEN...ENOUGH BRICKS OF CHEESE TO BUILD A SMALL HOUSE...
I'D SAY WE CAN PRETTY MUCH COUNT ON A HEART ATTACK WITH THIS FOOD.
SPEAK FOR YOURSELF. MY HEART'LL BE JUST FINE.
ACTUALLY, I'M TALKING ABOUT YOUR MOTHER'S WHEN SHE SEES THIS.
OK, LET'S THROW IN SOME VEGGIES. HOW 'BOUT POTATO CHIPS?
AMEND

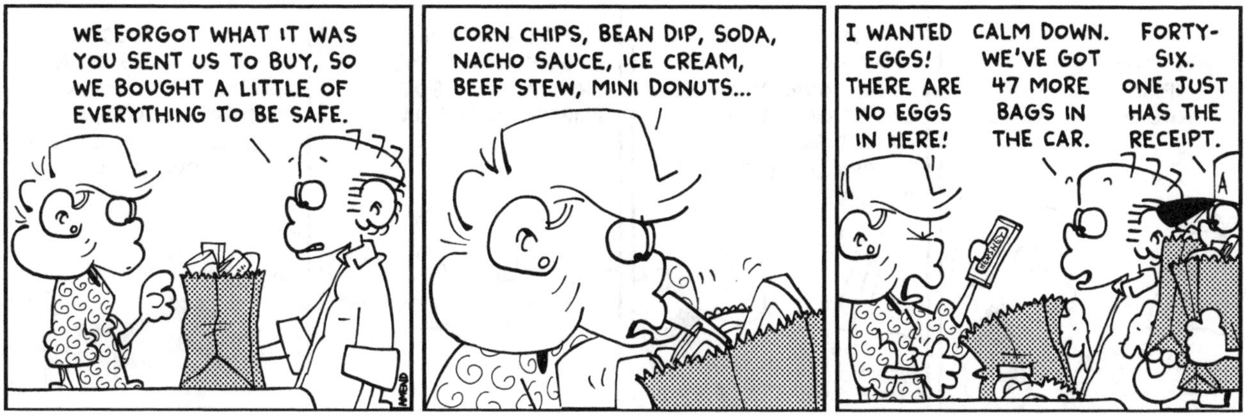
WE FORGOT WHAT IT WAS YOU SENT US TO BUY, SO WE BOUGHT A LITTLE OF EVERYTHING TO BE SAFE.
AMEND
CORN CHIPS, BEAN DIP, SODA, NACHO SAUCE, ICE CREAM, BEEF STEW, MINI DONUTS...
I WANTED EGGS! THERE ARE NO EGGS IN HERE!
CALM DOWN. WE'VE GOT 47 MORE BAGS IN THE CAR.
FORTY-SIX. ONE JUST HAS THE RECEIPT.

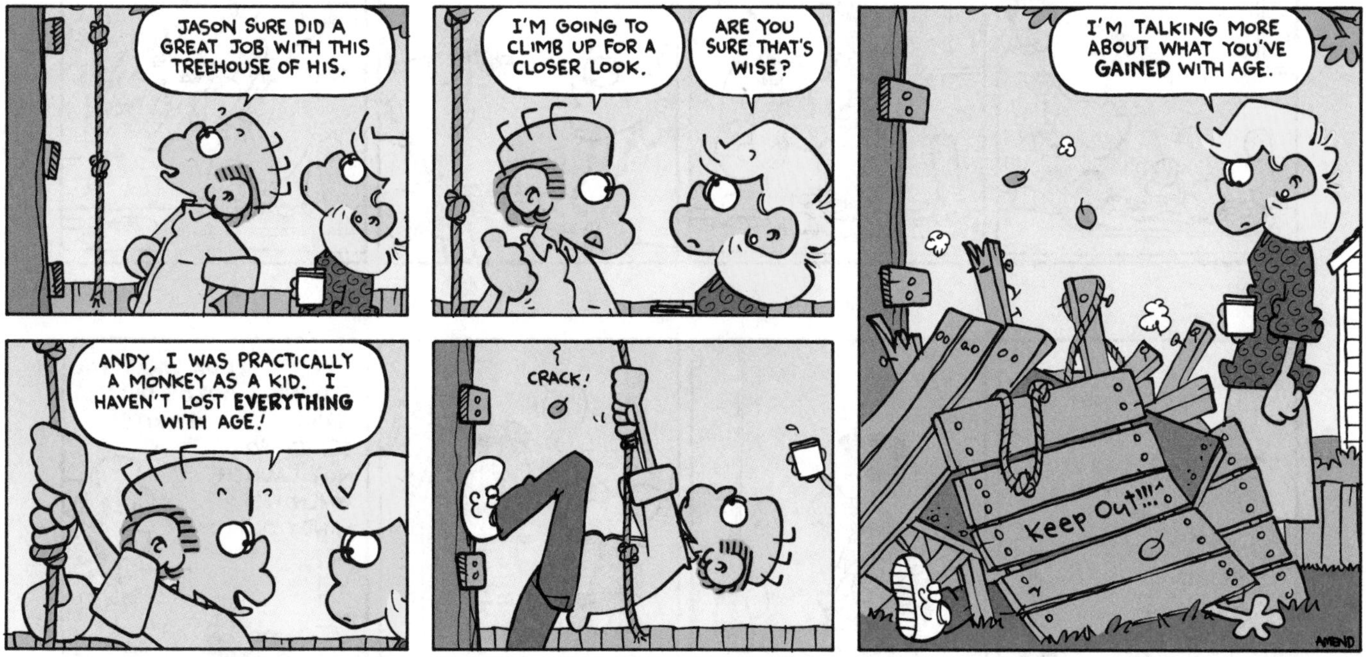
JASON SURE DID A GREAT JOB WITH THIS TREEHOUSE OF HIS.
I'M GOING TO CLIMB UP FOR A CLOSER LOOK.
ARE YOU SURE THAT'S WISE?
ANDY, I WAS PRACTICALLY A MONKEY AS A KID. I HAVEN'T LOST **EVERYTHING** WITH AGE!
CRACK!
I'M TALKING MORE ABOUT WHAT YOU'VE **GAINED** WITH AGE.
Keep Out!!!
AMEND

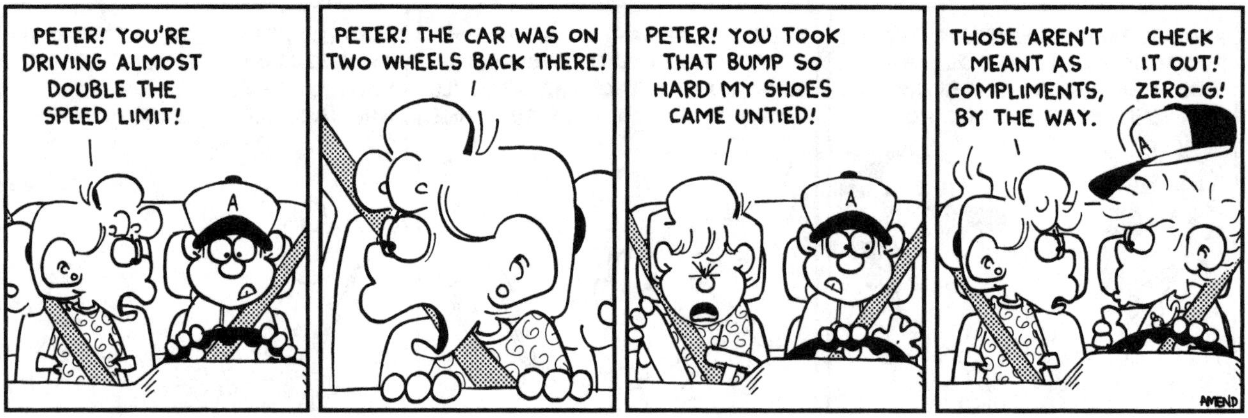
PETER! YOU'RE DRIVING ALMOST DOUBLE THE SPEED LIMIT!
PETER! THE CAR WAS ON TWO WHEELS BACK THERE!
PETER! YOU TOOK THAT BUMP SO HARD MY SHOES CAME UNTIED!
THOSE AREN'T MEANT AS COMPLIMENTS, BY THE WAY.
CHECK IT OUT! ZERO-G!
AMEND

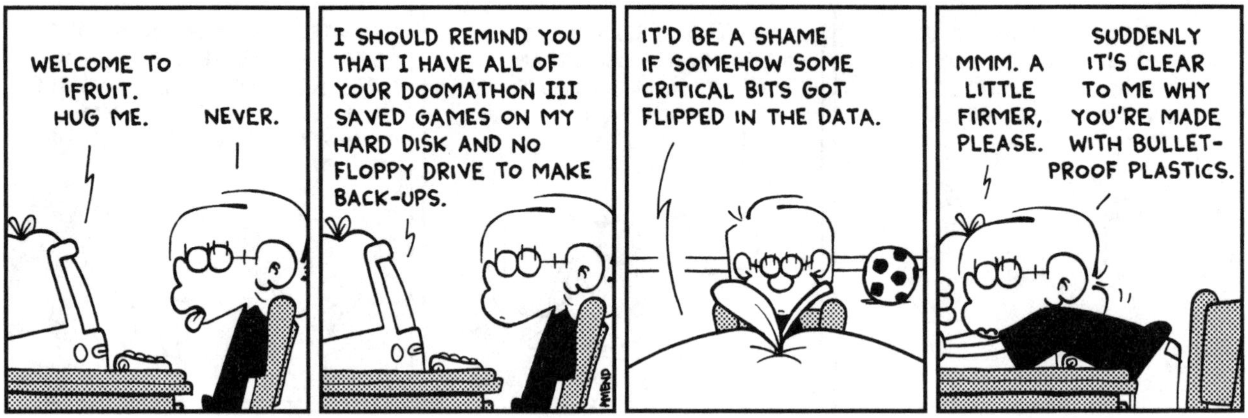
WELCOME TO iFRUIT. HUG ME.
NEVER.
I SHOULD REMIND YOU THAT I HAVE ALL OF YOUR DOOMATHON III SAVED GAMES ON MY HARD DISK AND NO FLOPPY DRIVE TO MAKE BACK-UPS.
AMEND
IT'D BE A SHAME IF SOMEHOW SOME CRITICAL BITS GOT FLIPPED IN THE DATA.
MMM. A LITTLE FIRMER, PLEASE.
SUDDENLY IT'S CLEAR TO ME WHY YOU'RE MADE WITH BULLET-PROOF PLASTICS.

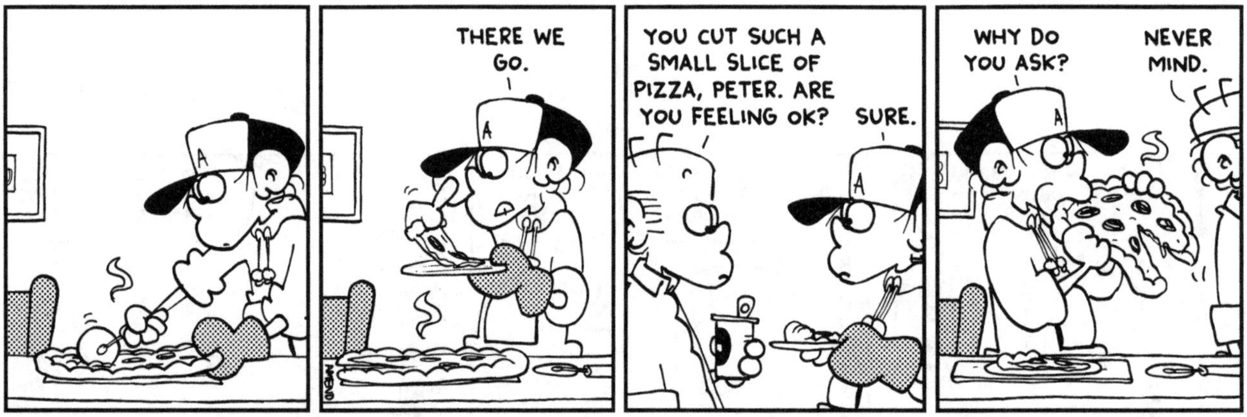
THERE WE GO.
AMEND
YOU CUT SUCH A SMALL SLICE OF PIZZA, PETER. ARE YOU FEELING OK?
SURE.
WHY DO YOU ASK?
NEVER MIND.

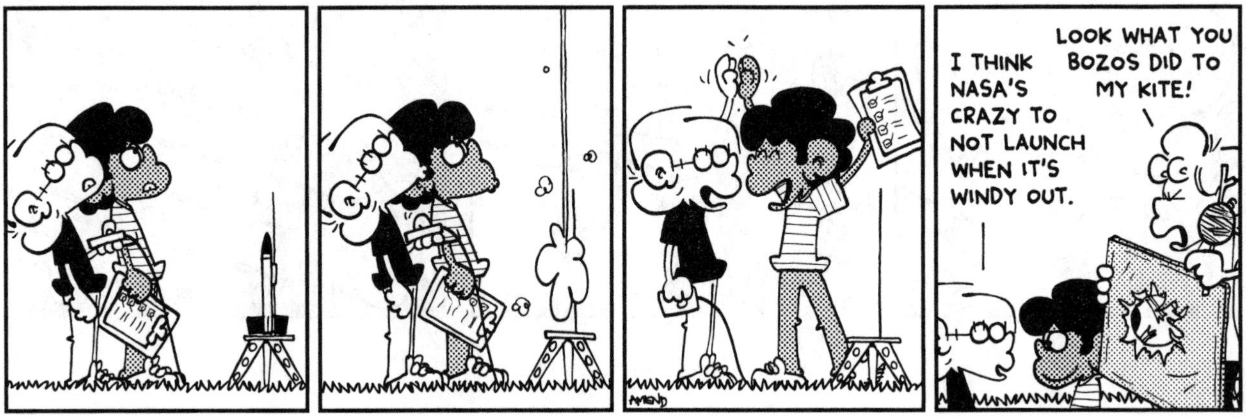
AMEND
I THINK NASA'S CRAZY TO NOT LAUNCH WHEN IT'S WINDY OUT.
LOOK WHAT YOU BOZOS DID TO MY KITE!

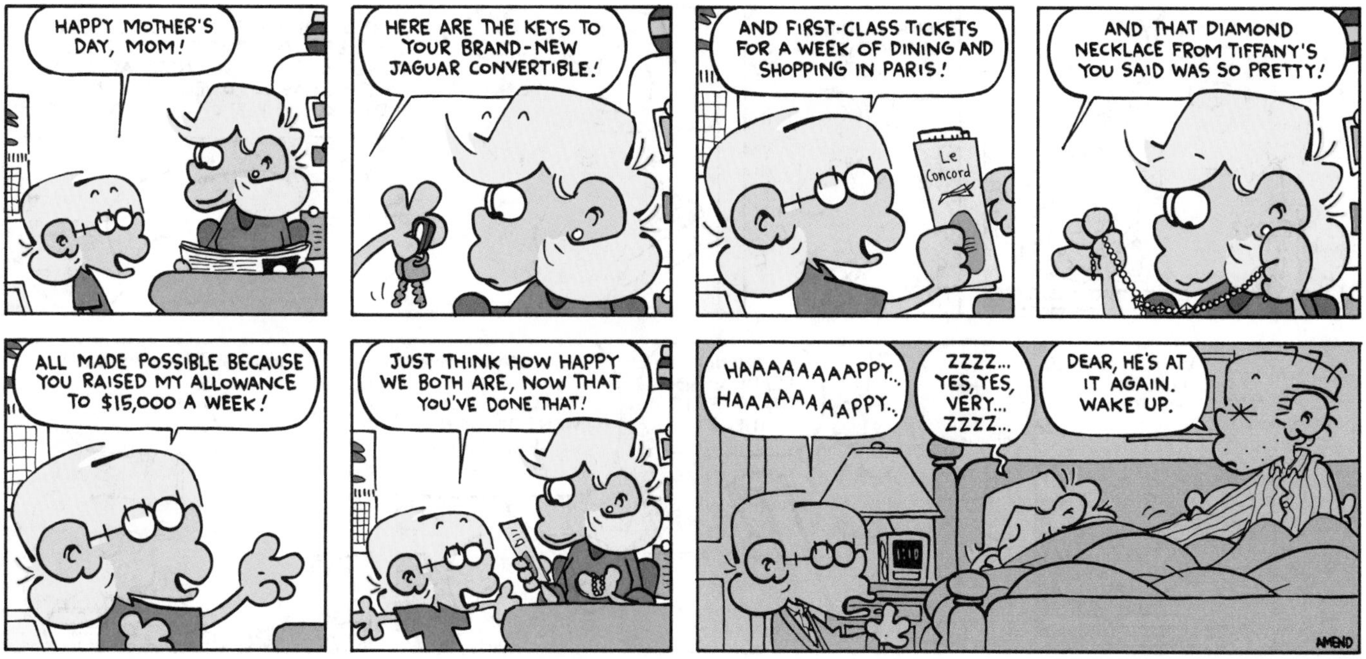
HAPPY MOTHER'S DAY, MOM!
HERE ARE THE KEYS TO YOUR BRAND-NEW JAGUAR CONVERTIBLE!
AND FIRST-CLASS TICKETS FOR A WEEK OF DINING AND SHOPPING IN PARIS!
Le Concord
AND THAT DIAMOND NECKLACE FROM TIFFANY'S YOU SAID WAS SO PRETTY!
ALL MADE POSSIBLE BECAUSE YOU RAISED MY ALLOWANCE TO $15,000 A WEEK!
JUST THINK HOW HAPPY WE BOTH ARE, NOW THAT YOU'VE DONE THAT!
HAAAAAAAAPPY... HAAAAAAAAPPY...
ZZZZ... YES, YES, VERY... ZZZZ...
DEAR, HE'S AT IT AGAIN. WAKE UP.
AMEND

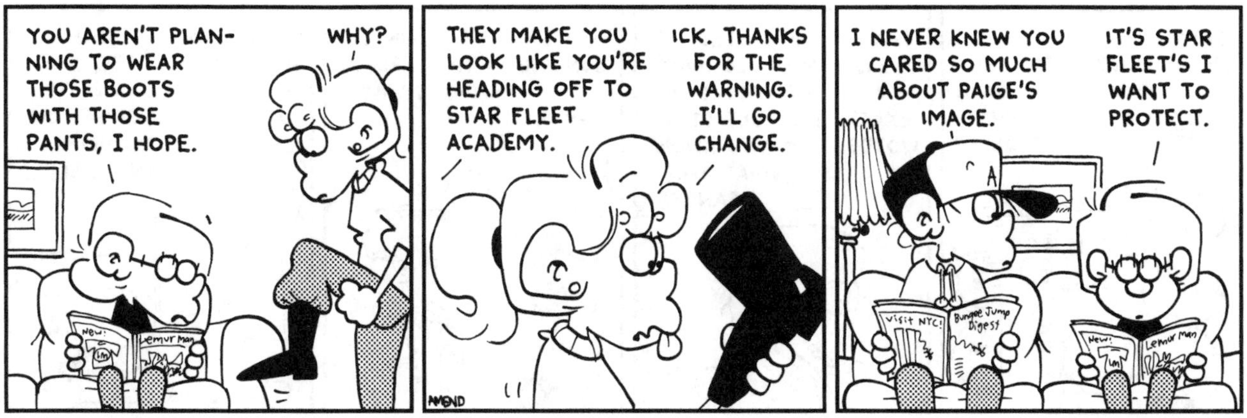
YOU AREN'T PLANNING TO WEAR THOSE BOOTS WITH THOSE PANTS, I HOPE.
WHY?
THEY MAKE YOU LOOK LIKE YOU'RE HEADING OFF TO STAR FLEET ACADEMY.
ICK. THANKS FOR THE WARNING. I'LL GO CHANGE.
AMEND
I NEVER KNEW YOU CARED SO MUCH ABOUT PAIGE'S IMAGE.
IT'S STAR FLEET'S I WANT TO PROTECT.

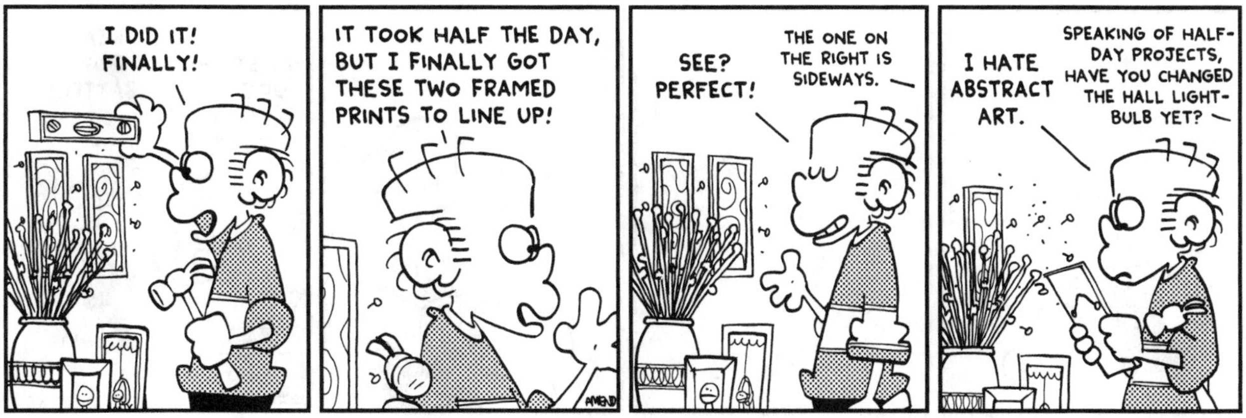
I DID IT! FINALLY!
IT TOOK HALF THE DAY, BUT I FINALLY GOT THESE TWO FRAMED PRINTS TO LINE UP!
AMEND
SEE? PERFECT!
THE ONE ON THE RIGHT IS SIDEWAYS.
I HATE ABSTRACT ART.
SPEAKING OF HALF-DAY PROJECTS, HAVE YOU CHANGED THE HALL LIGHT-BULB YET?

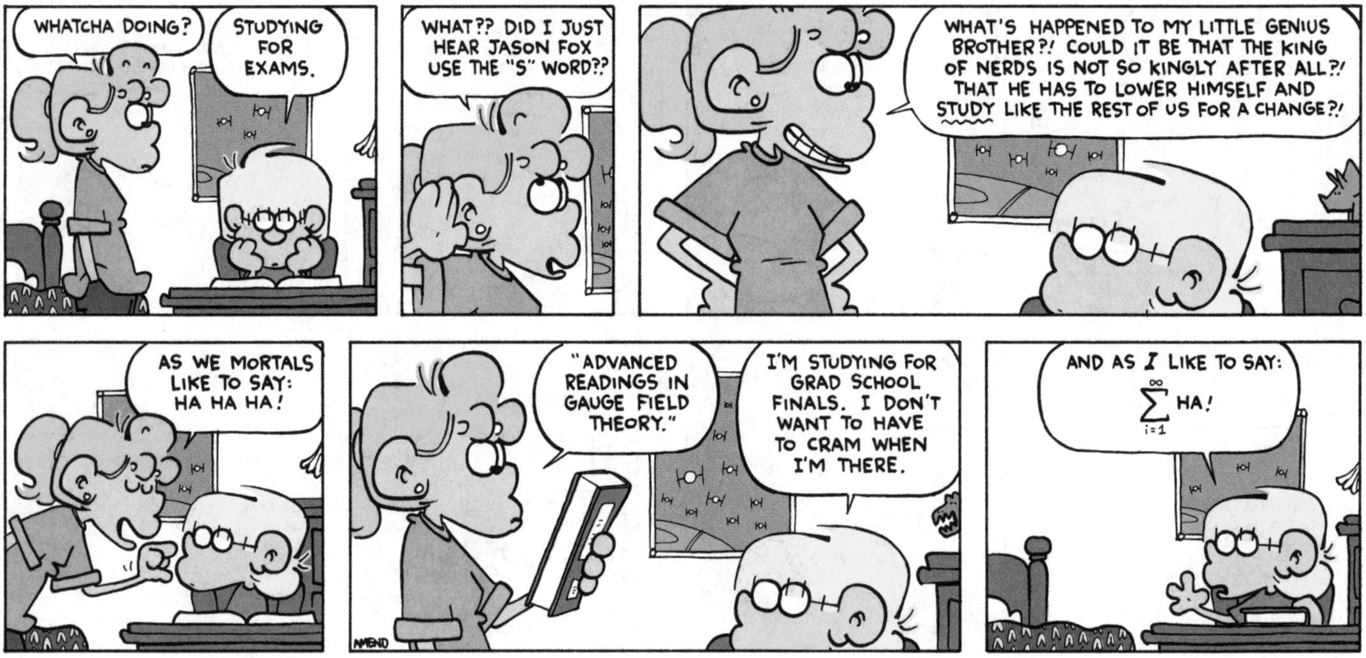
WHATCHA DOING?
STUDYING FOR EXAMS.
WHAT?? DID I JUST HEAR JASON FOX USE THE "S" WORD??
WHAT'S HAPPENED TO MY LITTLE GENIUS BROTHER?! COULD IT BE THAT THE KING OF NERDS IS NOT SO KINGLY AFTER ALL?! THAT HE HAS TO LOWER HIMSELF AND STUDY LIKE THE REST OF US FOR A CHANGE?!
AS WE MORTALS LIKE TO SAY: HA HA HA!
"ADVANCED READINGS IN GAUGE FIELD THEORY."
I'M STUDYING FOR GRAD SCHOOL FINALS. I DON'T WANT TO HAVE TO CRAM WHEN I'M THERE.
AND AS *I* LIKE TO SAY: $\sum_{i=1}^{\infty}$ HA!

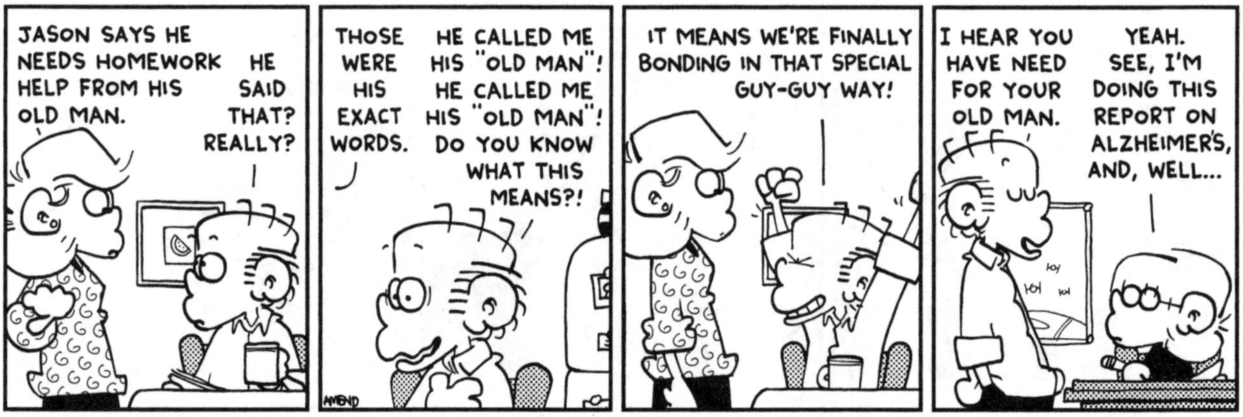
JASON SAYS HE NEEDS HOMEWORK HELP FROM HIS OLD MAN.
HE SAID THAT? REALLY?
THOSE WERE HIS EXACT WORDS.
HE CALLED ME HIS "OLD MAN"! HE CALLED ME HIS "OLD MAN"! DO YOU KNOW WHAT THIS MEANS?!
IT MEANS WE'RE FINALLY BONDING IN THAT SPECIAL GUY-GUY WAY!
I HEAR YOU HAVE NEED FOR YOUR OLD MAN.
YEAH. SEE, I'M DOING THIS REPORT ON ALZHEIMER'S, AND, WELL...

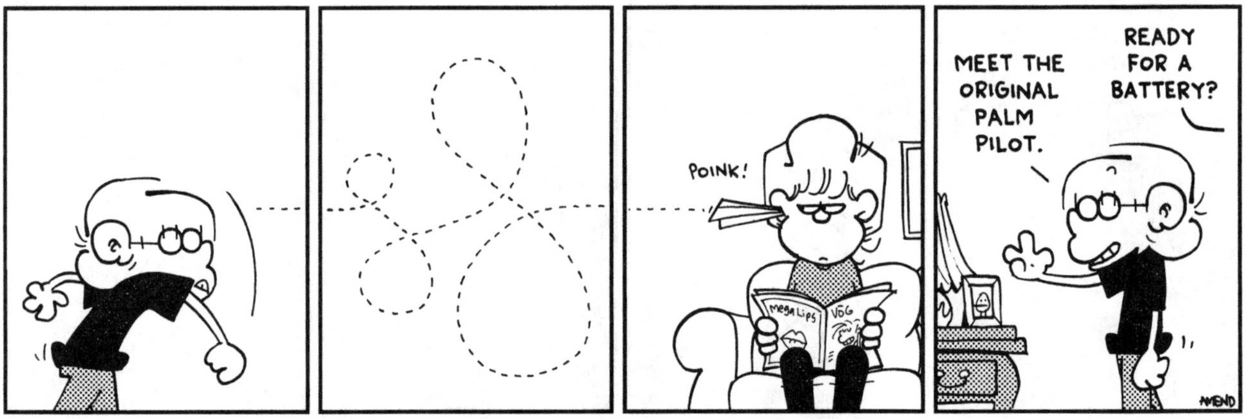
POINK!
MEET THE ORIGINAL PALM PILOT.
READY FOR A BATTERY?

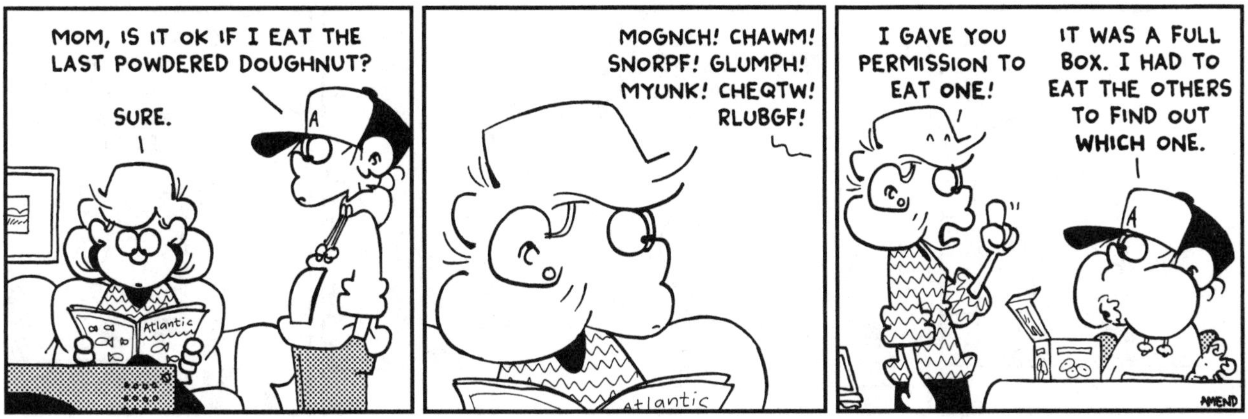
MOM, IS IT OK IF I EAT THE LAST POWDERED DOUGHNUT?
SURE.
Atlantic
MOGNCH! CHAWM! SNORPF! GLUMPH! MYUNK! CHEQTW! RLUBGF!
Atlantic
I GAVE YOU PERMISSION TO EAT ONE!
IT WAS A FULL BOX. I HAD TO EAT THE OTHERS TO FIND OUT WHICH ONE.
AMEND

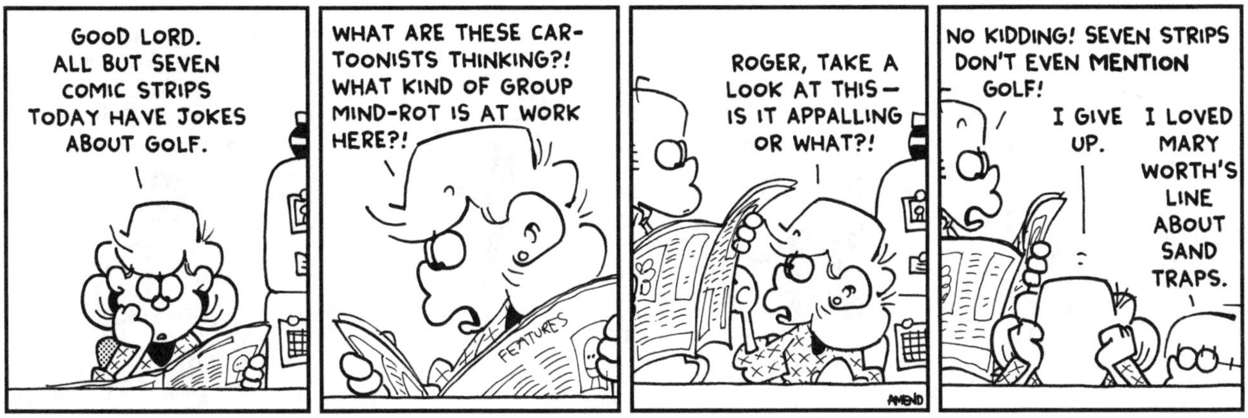
GOOD LORD. ALL BUT SEVEN COMIC STRIPS TODAY HAVE JOKES ABOUT GOLF.
WHAT ARE THESE CARTOONISTS THINKING?! WHAT KIND OF GROUP MIND-ROT IS AT WORK HERE?!
FEATURES
ROGER, TAKE A LOOK AT THIS— IS IT APPALLING OR WHAT?!
AMEND
NO KIDDING! SEVEN STRIPS DON'T EVEN MENTION GOLF!
I GIVE UP.
I LOVED MARY WORTH'S LINE ABOUT SAND TRAPS.

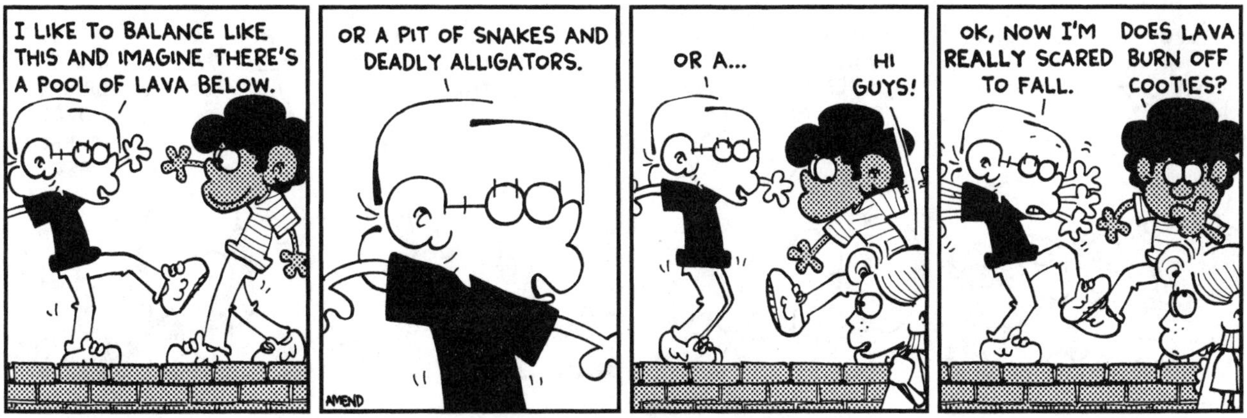
I LIKE TO BALANCE LIKE THIS AND IMAGINE THERE'S A POOL OF LAVA BELOW.
OR A PIT OF SNAKES AND DEADLY ALLIGATORS.
AMEND
OR A...
HI GUYS!
OK, NOW I'M REALLY SCARED TO FALL.
DOES LAVA BURN OFF COOTIES?

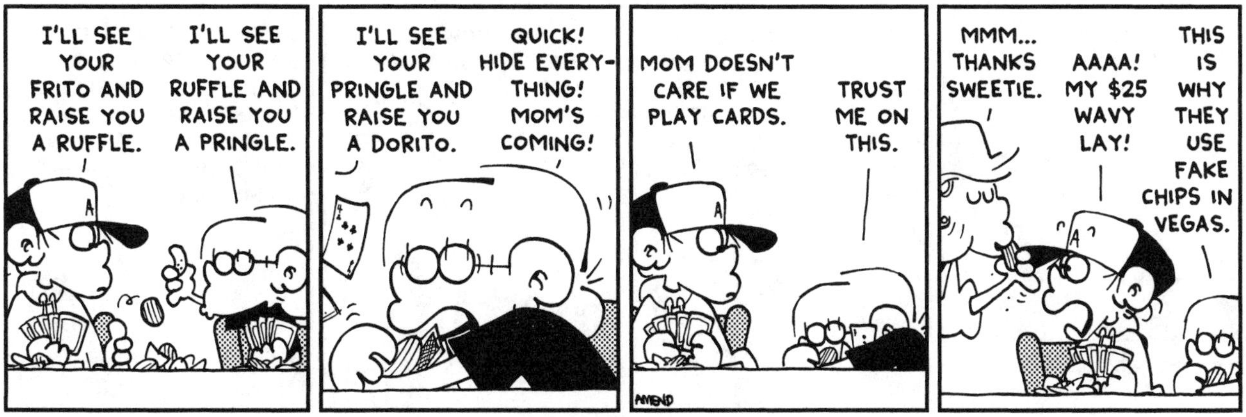
I'LL SEE YOUR FRITO AND RAISE YOU A RUFFLE.
I'LL SEE YOUR RUFFLE AND RAISE YOU A PRINGLE.
I'LL SEE YOUR PRINGLE AND RAISE YOU A DORITO.
QUICK! HIDE EVERYTHING! MOM'S COMING!
MOM DOESN'T CARE IF WE PLAY CARDS.
TRUST ME ON THIS.
AMEND
MMM... THANKS SWEETIE.
AAAA! MY $25 WAVY LAY!
THIS IS WHY THEY USE FAKE CHIPS IN VEGAS.

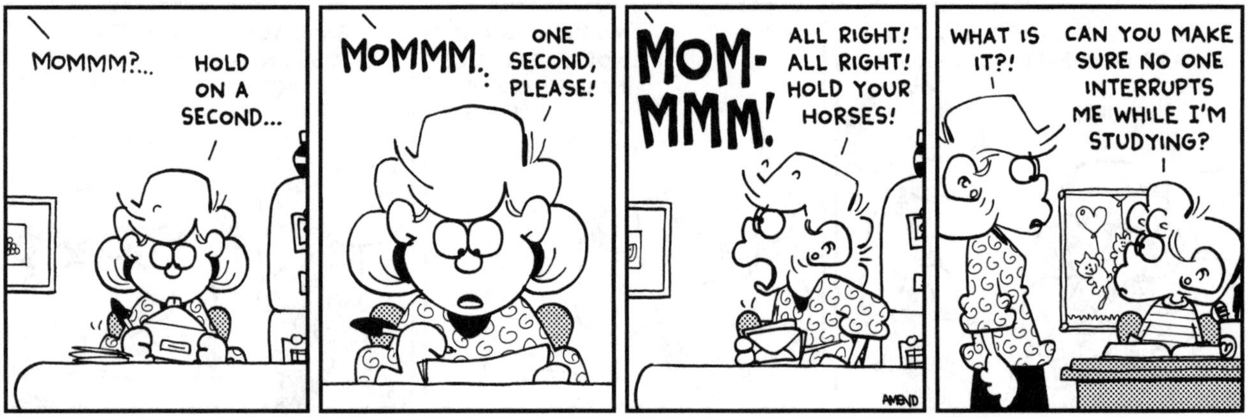
MOMMM?...
HOLD ON A SECOND...
MOMMM.
ONE SECOND, PLEASE!
MOM-MMM!
ALL RIGHT! ALL RIGHT! HOLD YOUR HORSES!
AMEND
WHAT IS IT?!
CAN YOU MAKE SURE NO ONE INTERRUPTS ME WHILE I'M STUDYING?

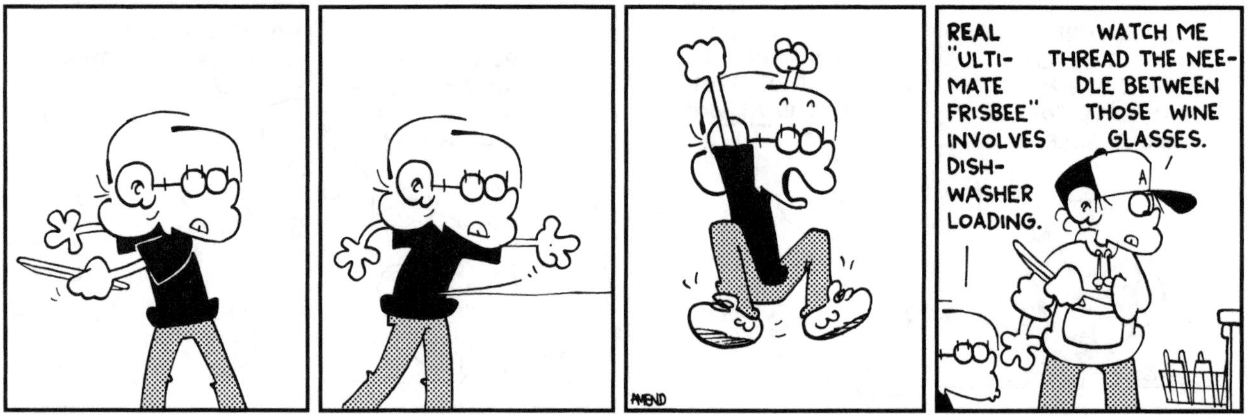
AMEND
REAL "ULTIMATE FRISBEE" INVOLVES DISH-WASHER LOADING.
WATCH ME THREAD THE NEE-DLE BETWEEN THOSE WINE GLASSES.

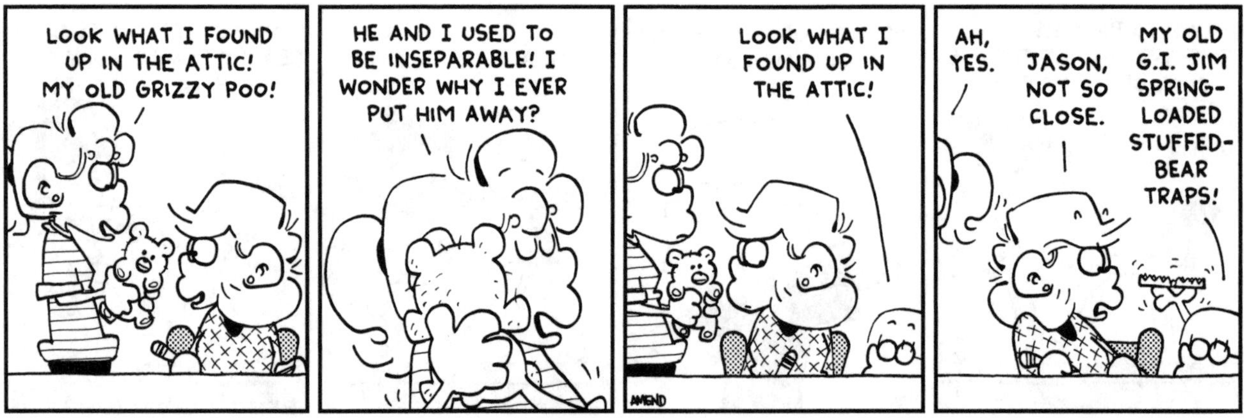
LOOK WHAT I FOUND UP IN THE ATTIC! MY OLD GRIZZY POO!
HE AND I USED TO BE INSEPARABLE! I WONDER WHY I EVER PUT HIM AWAY?
LOOK WHAT I FOUND UP IN THE ATTIC!
AMEND
AH, YES.
JASON, NOT SO CLOSE.
MY OLD G.I. JIM SPRING-LOADED STUFFED-BEAR TRAPS!

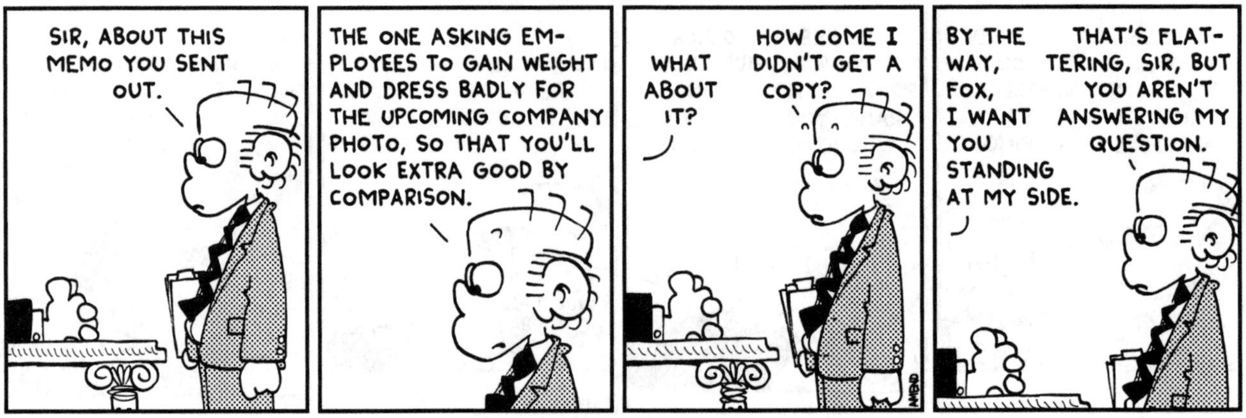
SIR, ABOUT THIS MEMO YOU SENT OUT.
THE ONE ASKING EM-PLOYEES TO GAIN WEIGHT AND DRESS BADLY FOR THE UPCOMING COMPANY PHOTO, SO THAT YOU'LL LOOK EXTRA GOOD BY COMPARISON.
WHAT ABOUT IT?
HOW COME I DIDN'T GET A COPY?
AMEND
BY THE WAY, FOX, I WANT YOU STANDING AT MY SIDE.
THAT'S FLAT-TERING, SIR, BUT YOU AREN'T ANSWERING MY QUESTION.

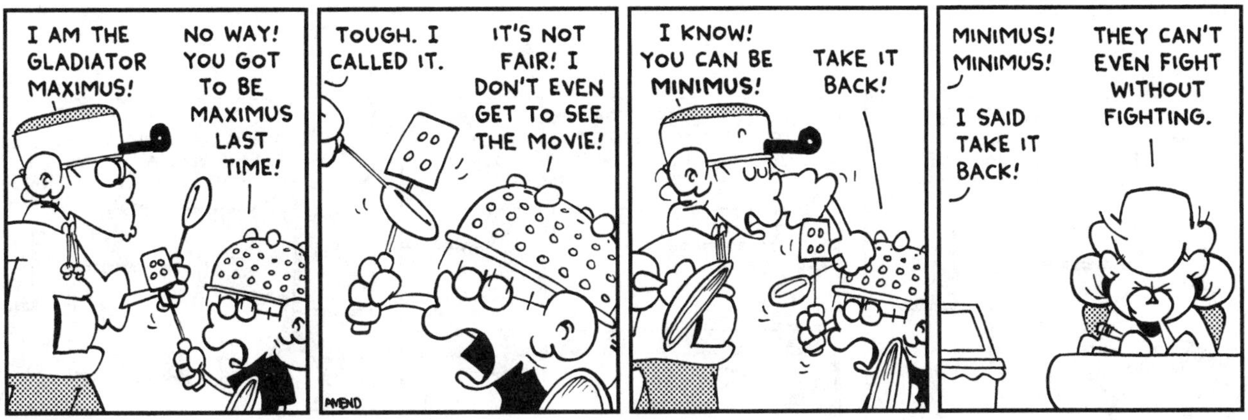
I AM THE GLADIATOR MAXIMUS!
NO WAY! YOU GOT TO BE MAXIMUS LAST TIME!
TOUGH. I CALLED IT.
IT'S NOT FAIR! I DON'T EVEN GET TO SEE THE MOVIE!
I KNOW! YOU CAN BE MINIMUS!
TAKE IT BACK!
MINIMUS! MINIMUS!
I SAID TAKE IT BACK!
THEY CAN'T EVEN FIGHT WITHOUT FIGHTING.
AMEND

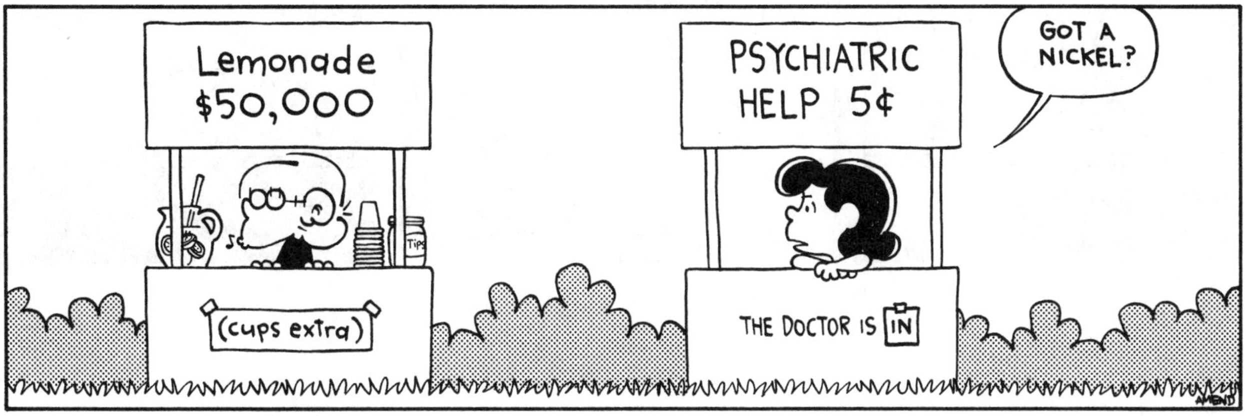
Lemonade $50,000
Tips
(cups extra)
PSYCHIATRIC HELP 5¢
GOT A NICKEL?
THE DOCTOR IS IN
AMEND

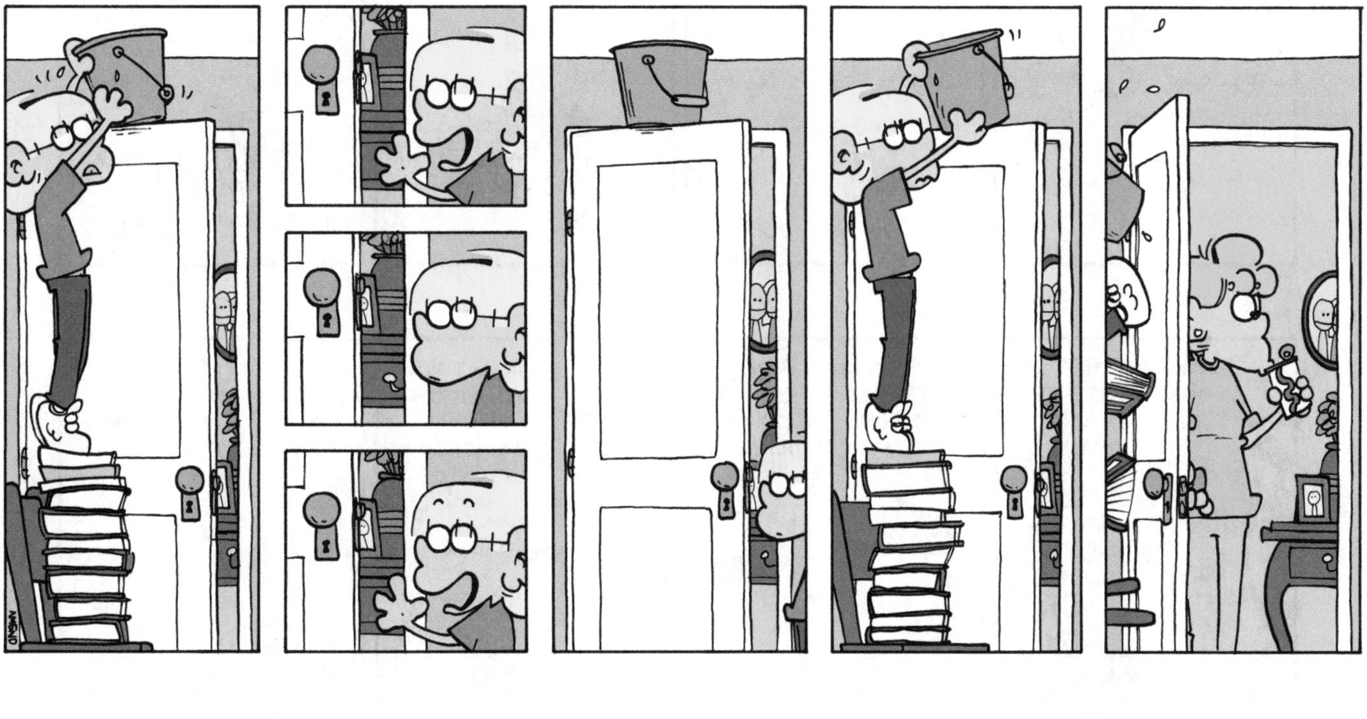

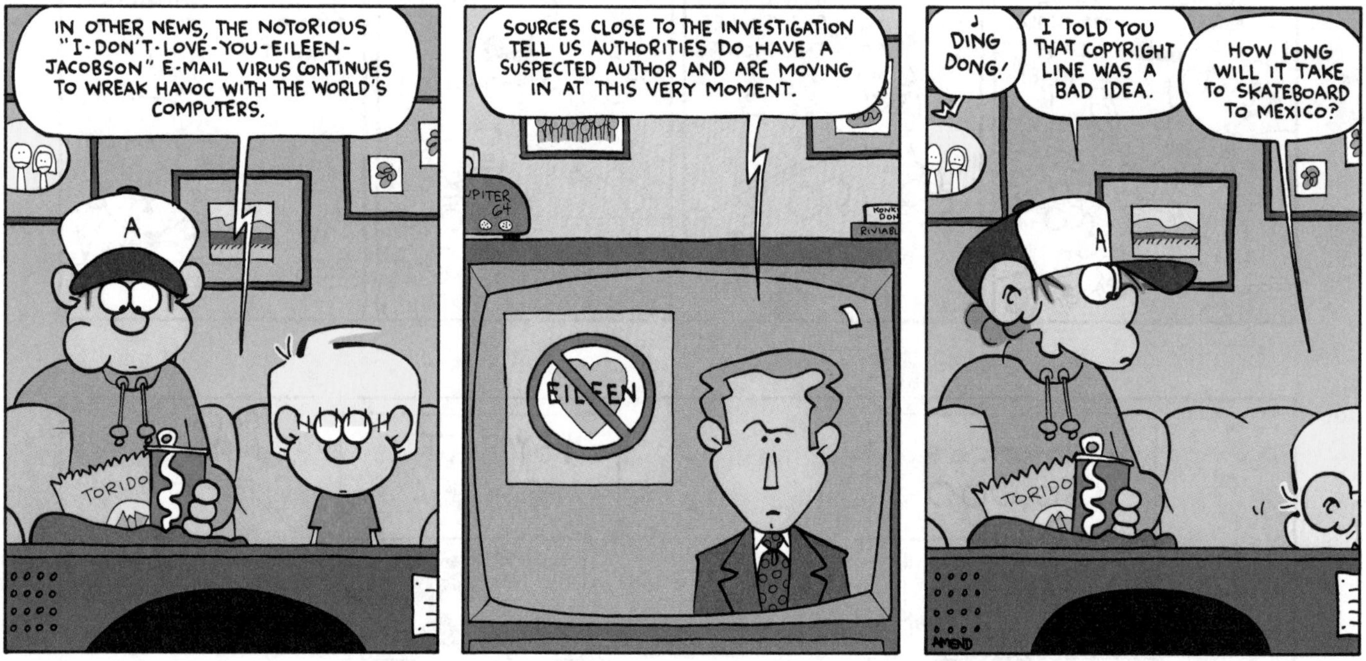
IN OTHER NEWS, THE NOTORIOUS "I-DON'T-LOVE-YOU-EILEEN-JACOBSON" E-MAIL VIRUS CONTINUES TO WREAK HAVOC WITH THE WORLD'S COMPUTERS.
TORIDO
SOURCES CLOSE TO THE INVESTIGATION TELL US AUTHORITIES DO HAVE A SUSPECTED AUTHOR AND ARE MOVING IN AT THIS VERY MOMENT.
EILEEN
DING DONG!
I TOLD YOU THAT COPYRIGHT LINE WAS A BAD IDEA.
HOW LONG WILL IT TAKE TO SKATEBOARD TO MEXICO?
AMEND

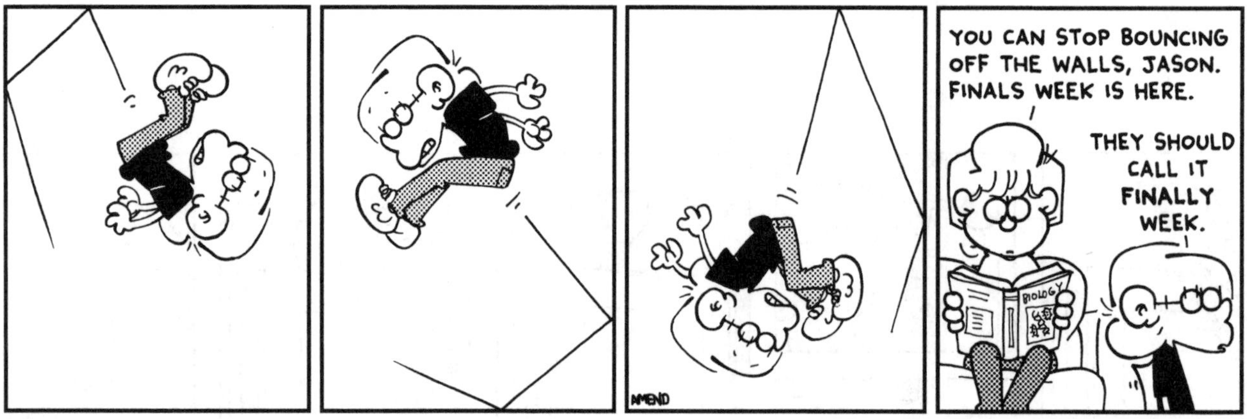
AMEND
YOU CAN STOP BOUNCING OFF THE WALLS, JASON. FINALS WEEK IS HERE.
THEY SHOULD CALL IT FINALLY WEEK.
BIOLOGY

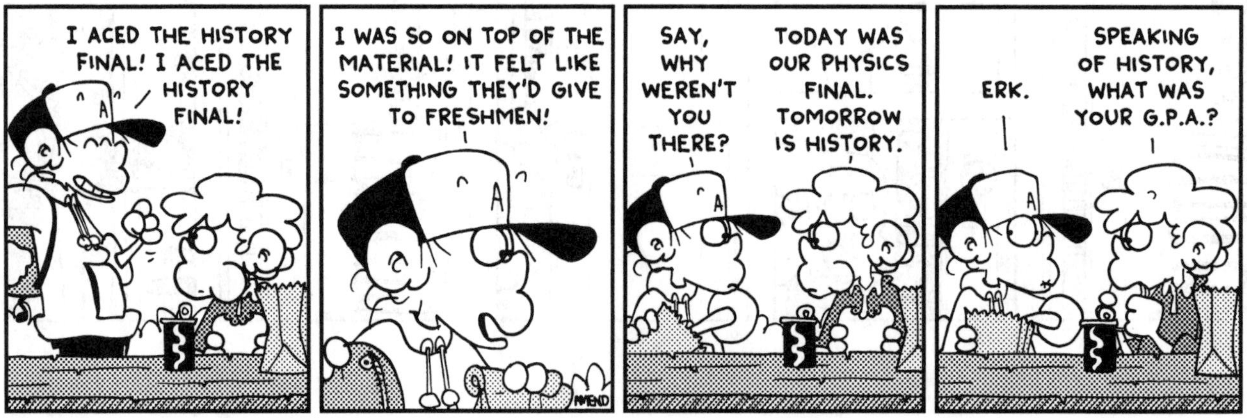
I ACED THE HISTORY FINAL! I ACED THE HISTORY FINAL!
I WAS SO ON TOP OF THE MATERIAL! IT FELT LIKE SOMETHING THEY'D GIVE TO FRESHMEN!
AMEND
SAY, WHY WEREN'T YOU THERE?
TODAY WAS OUR PHYSICS FINAL. TOMORROW IS HISTORY.
ERK.
SPEAKING OF HISTORY, WHAT WAS YOUR G.P.A.?

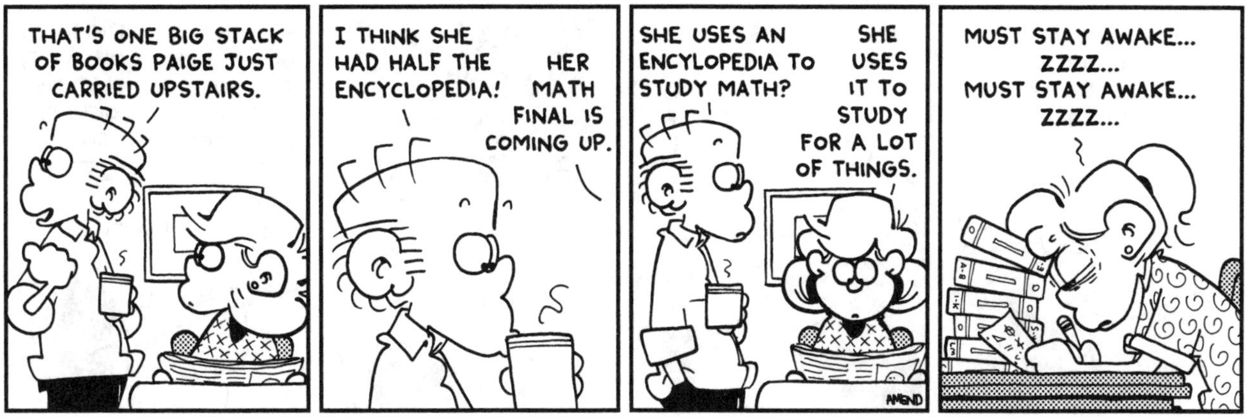
THAT'S ONE BIG STACK OF BOOKS PAIGE JUST CARRIED UPSTAIRS.
I THINK SHE HAD HALF THE ENCYCLOPEDIA!
HER MATH FINAL IS COMING UP.
SHE USES AN ENCYCLOPEDIA TO STUDY MATH?
SHE USES IT TO STUDY FOR A LOT OF THINGS.
MUST STAY AWAKE... ZZZZ... MUST STAY AWAKE... ZZZZ...

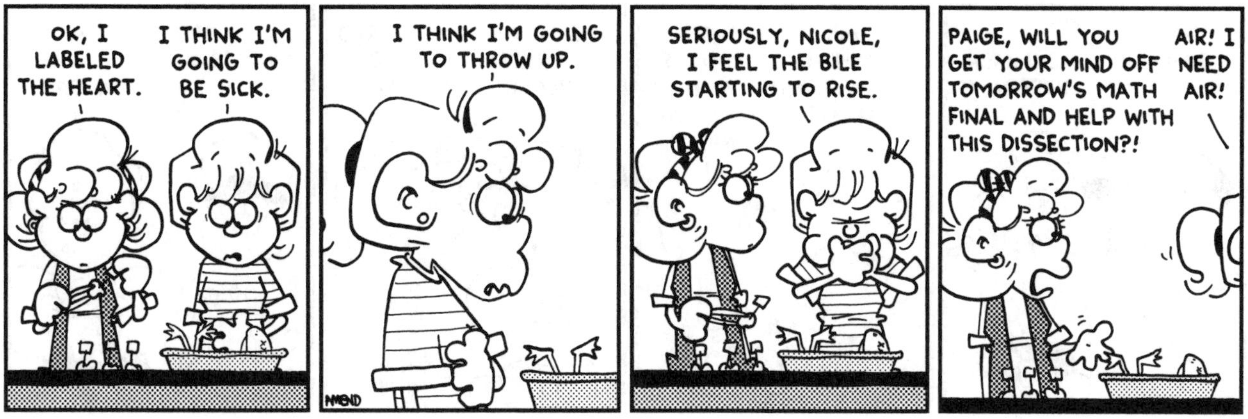
OK, I LABELED THE HEART.
I THINK I'M GOING TO BE SICK.
I THINK I'M GOING TO THROW UP.
SERIOUSLY, NICOLE, I FEEL THE BILE STARTING TO RISE.
PAIGE, WILL YOU GET YOUR MIND OFF TOMORROW'S MATH FINAL AND HELP WITH THIS DISSECTION?!
AIR! I NEED AIR!

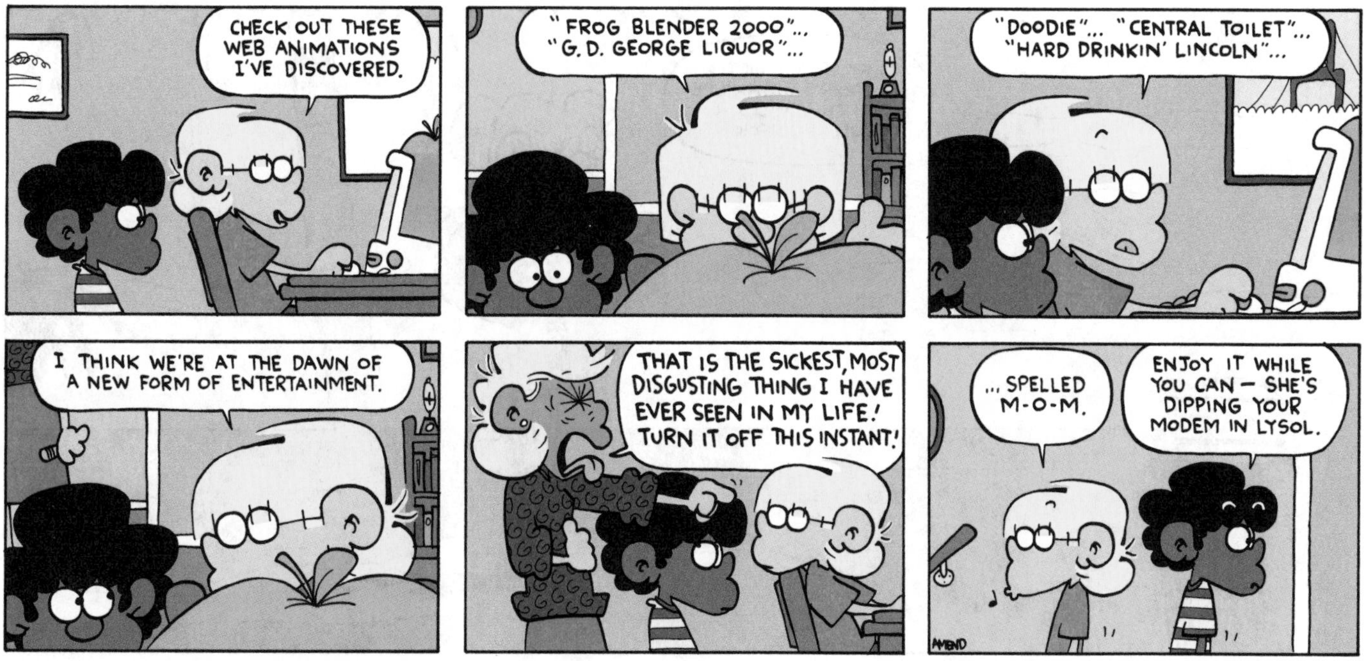
CHECK OUT THESE WEB ANIMATIONS I'VE DISCOVERED.
"FROG BLENDER 2000"... "G. D. GEORGE LIQUOR"...
"DOODIE"... "CENTRAL TOILET"... "HARD DRINKIN' LINCOLN"...
I THINK WE'RE AT THE DAWN OF A NEW FORM OF ENTERTAINMENT.
THAT IS THE SICKEST, MOST DISGUSTING THING I HAVE EVER SEEN IN MY LIFE! TURN IT OFF THIS INSTANT!
... SPELLED M-O-M.
ENJOY IT WHILE YOU CAN – SHE'S DIPPING YOUR MODEM IN LYSOL.

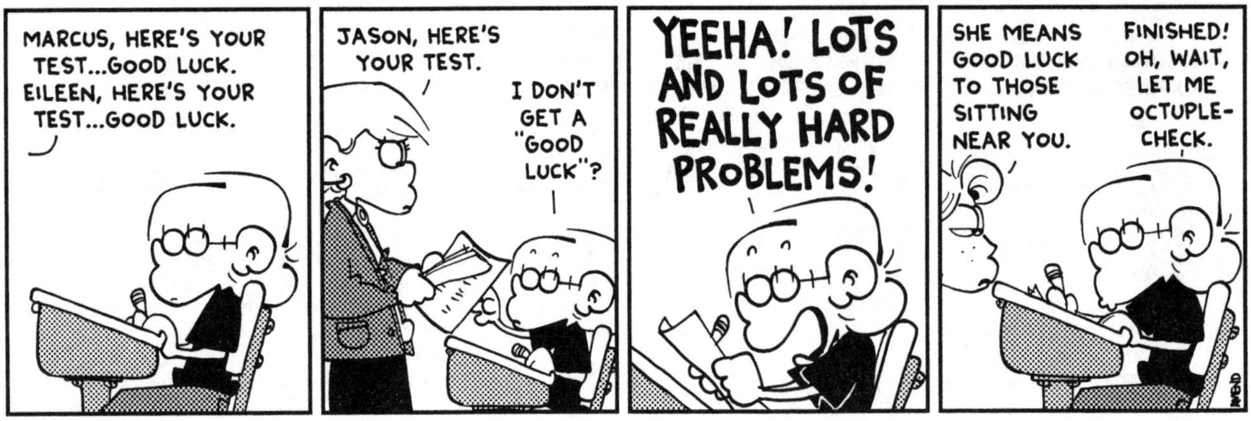
MARCUS, HERE'S YOUR TEST...GOOD LUCK. EILEEN, HERE'S YOUR TEST...GOOD LUCK.
JASON, HERE'S YOUR TEST.
I DON'T GET A "GOOD LUCK"?
YEEHA! LOTS AND LOTS OF REALLY HARD PROBLEMS!
SHE MEANS GOOD LUCK TO THOSE SITTING NEAR YOU.
FINISHED! OH, WAIT, LET ME OCTUPLE-CHECK.
AMEND

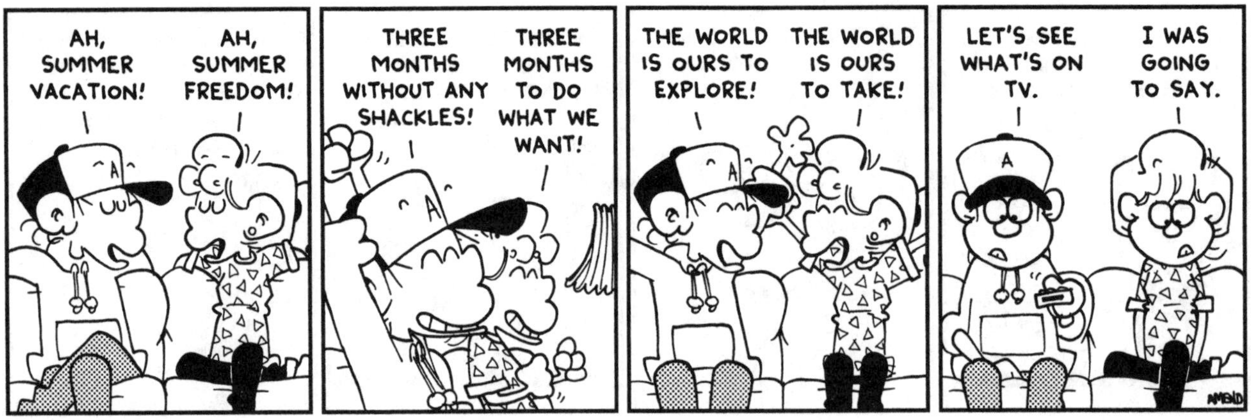
AH, SUMMER VACATION!
AH, SUMMER FREEDOM!
THREE MONTHS WITHOUT ANY SHACKLES!
THREE MONTHS TO DO WHAT WE WANT!
THE WORLD IS OURS TO EXPLORE!
THE WORLD IS OURS TO TAKE!
LET'S SEE WHAT'S ON TV.
I WAS GOING TO SAY.
AMEND

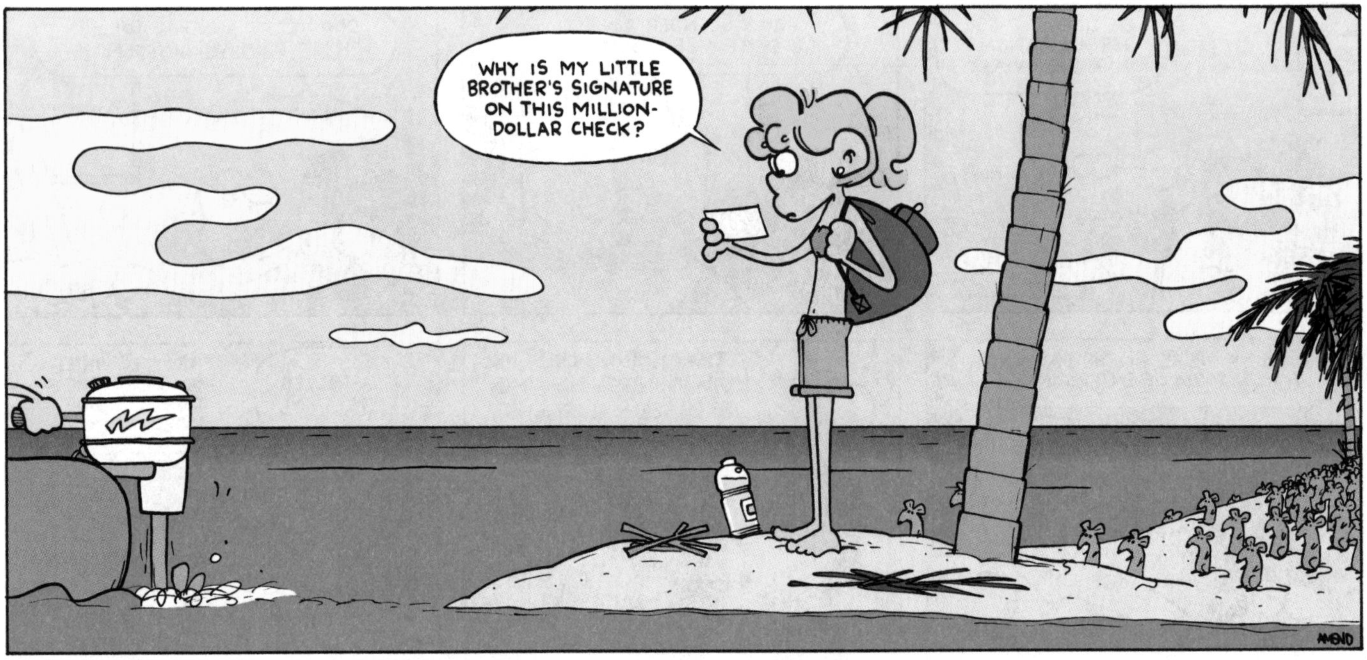
WHY IS MY LITTLE BROTHER'S SIGNATURE ON THIS MILLION-DOLLAR CHECK?
AMEND

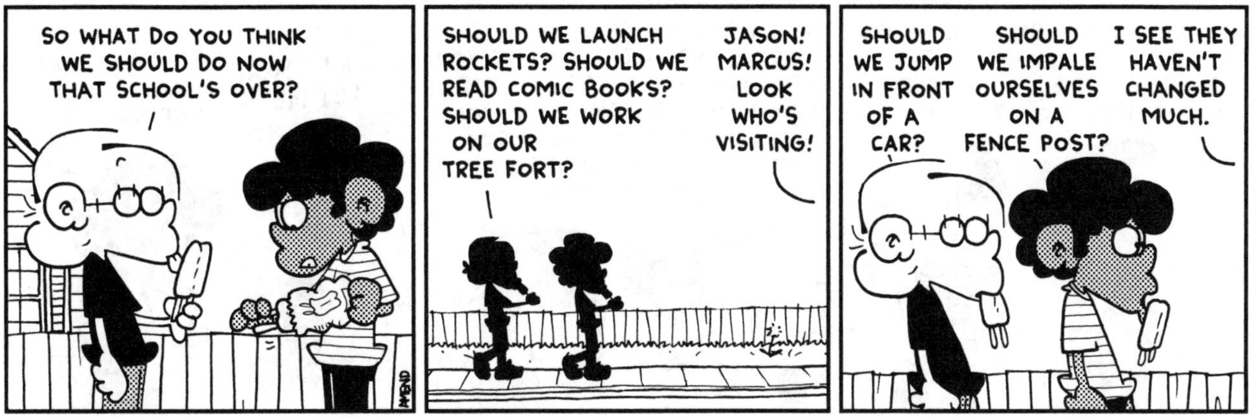
SO WHAT DO YOU THINK WE SHOULD DO NOW THAT SCHOOL'S OVER?
SHOULD WE LAUNCH ROCKETS? SHOULD WE READ COMIC BOOKS? SHOULD WE WORK ON OUR TREE FORT?
JASON! MARCUS! LOOK WHO'S VISITING!
AMEND
SHOULD WE JUMP IN FRONT OF A CAR?
SHOULD WE IMPALE OURSELVES ON A FENCE POST?
I SEE THEY HAVEN'T CHANGED MUCH.

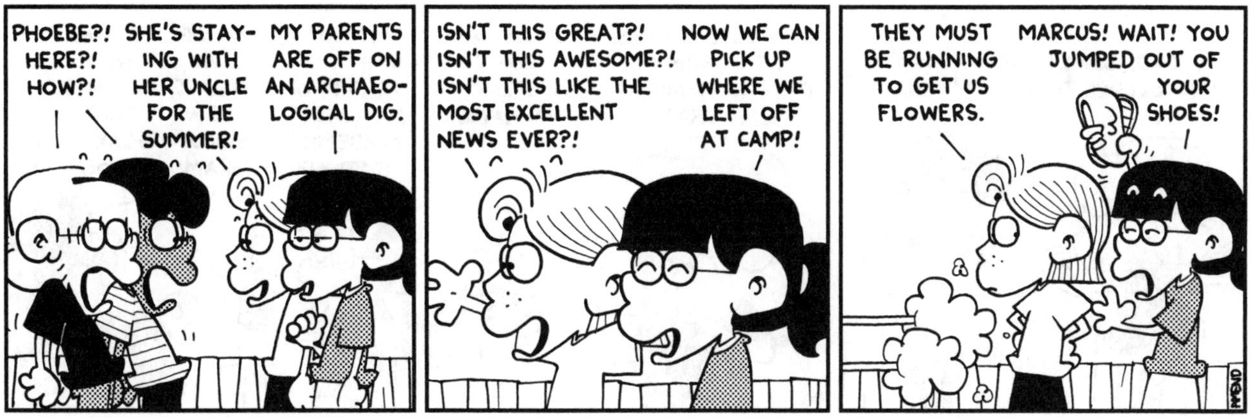
PHOEBE?! HERE?! HOW?!
SHE'S STAY-ING WITH HER UNCLE FOR THE SUMMER!
MY PARENTS ARE OFF ON AN ARCHAEO-LOGICAL DIG.
ISN'T THIS GREAT?! ISN'T THIS AWESOME?! ISN'T THIS LIKE THE MOST EXCELLENT NEWS EVER?!
NOW WE CAN PICK UP WHERE WE LEFT OFF AT CAMP!
THEY MUST BE RUNNING TO GET US FLOWERS.
MARCUS! WAIT! YOU JUMPED OUT OF YOUR SHOES!
AMEND

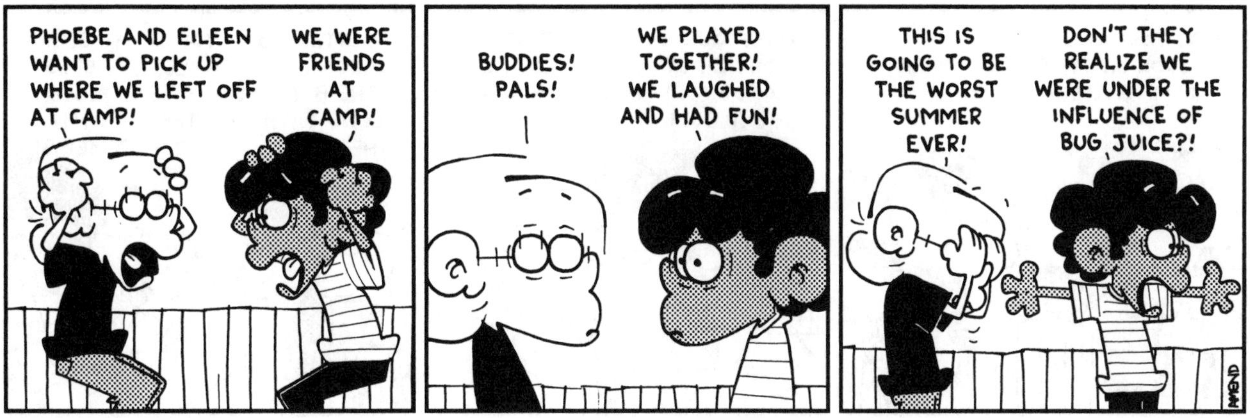
PHOEBE AND EILEEN WANT TO PICK UP WHERE WE LEFT OFF AT CAMP!
WE WERE FRIENDS AT CAMP!
BUDDIES! PALS!
WE PLAYED TOGETHER! WE LAUGHED AND HAD FUN!
THIS IS GOING TO BE THE WORST SUMMER EVER!
DON'T THEY REALIZE WE WERE UNDER THE INFLUENCE OF BUG JUICE?!
AMEND

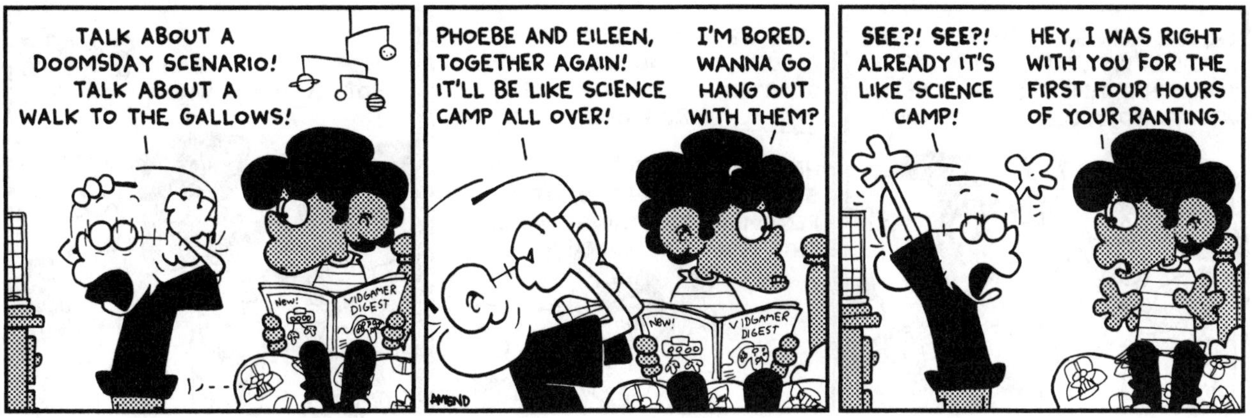
TALK ABOUT A DOOMSDAY SCENARIO! TALK ABOUT A WALK TO THE GALLOWS!
NEW!
VIDGAMER DIGEST
PHOEBE AND EILEEN, TOGETHER AGAIN! IT'LL BE LIKE SCIENCE CAMP ALL OVER!
I'M BORED. WANNA GO HANG OUT WITH THEM?
AMEND
SEE?! SEE?! ALREADY IT'S LIKE SCIENCE CAMP!
HEY, I WAS RIGHT WITH YOU FOR THE FIRST FOUR HOURS OF YOUR RANTING.

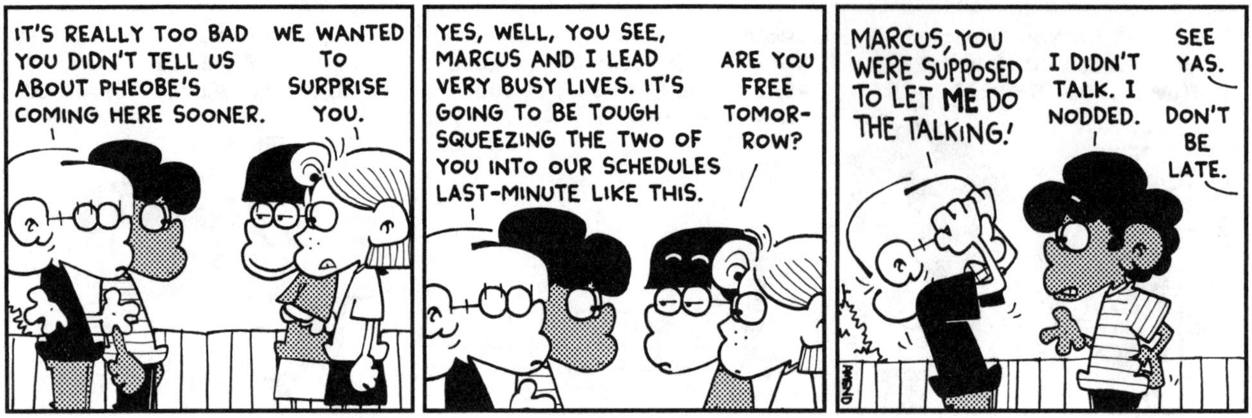
IT'S REALLY TOO BAD YOU DIDN'T TELL US ABOUT PHEOBE'S COMING HERE SOONER.
WE WANTED TO SURPRISE YOU.
YES, WELL, YOU SEE, MARCUS AND I LEAD VERY BUSY LIVES. IT'S GOING TO BE TOUGH SQUEEZING THE TWO OF YOU INTO OUR SCHEDULES LAST-MINUTE LIKE THIS.
ARE YOU FREE TOMORROW?
MARCUS, YOU WERE SUPPOSED TO LET ME DO THE TALKING!
I DIDN'T TALK. I NODDED.
SEE YAS.
DON'T BE LATE.

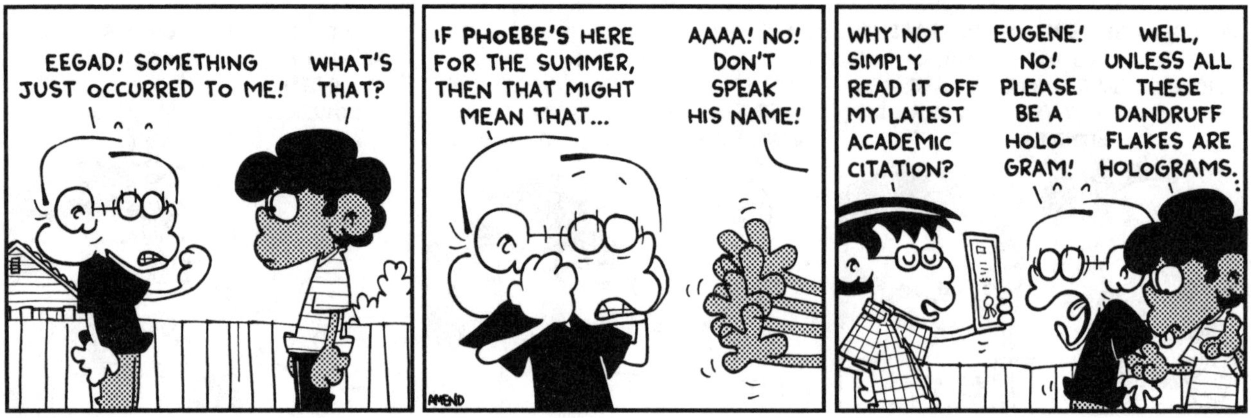
EEGAD! SOMETHING JUST OCCURRED TO ME!
WHAT'S THAT?
IF PHOEBE'S HERE FOR THE SUMMER, THEN THAT MIGHT MEAN THAT...
AAAA! NO! DON'T SPEAK HIS NAME!
WHY NOT SIMPLY READ IT OFF MY LATEST ACADEMIC CITATION?
EUGENE! NO! PLEASE BE A HOLOGRAM!
WELL, UNLESS ALL THESE DANDRUFF FLAKES ARE HOLOGRAMS.

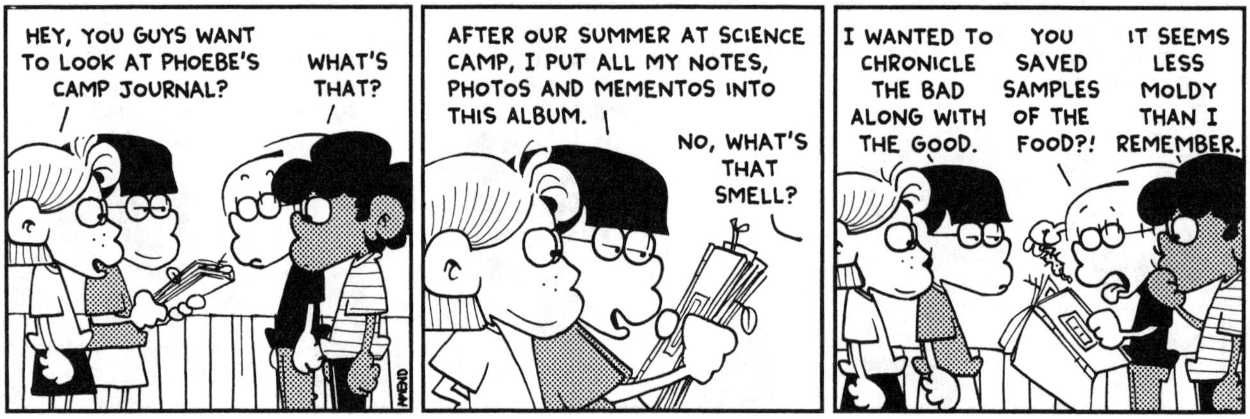
HEY, YOU GUYS WANT TO LOOK AT PHOEBE'S CAMP JOURNAL?
WHAT'S THAT?
AFTER OUR SUMMER AT SCIENCE CAMP, I PUT ALL MY NOTES, PHOTOS AND MEMENTOS INTO THIS ALBUM.
NO, WHAT'S THAT SMELL?
I WANTED TO CHRONICLE THE BAD ALONG WITH THE GOOD.
YOU SAVED SAMPLES OF THE FOOD?!
IT SEEMS LESS MOLDY THAN I REMEMBER.

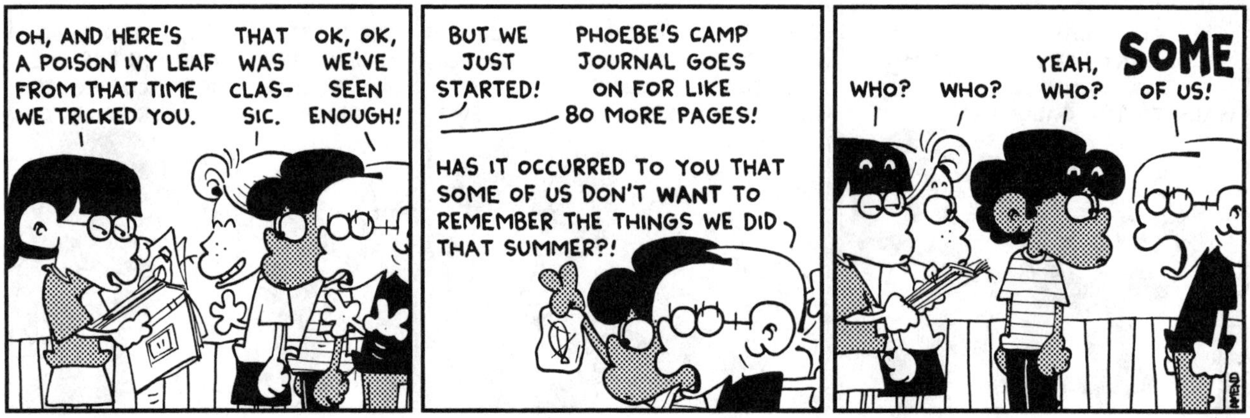
OH, AND HERE'S A POISON IVY LEAF FROM THAT TIME WE TRICKED YOU.
THAT WAS CLASSIC.
OK, OK, WE'VE SEEN ENOUGH!
BUT WE JUST STARTED!
PHOEBE'S CAMP JOURNAL GOES ON FOR LIKE 80 MORE PAGES!
HAS IT OCCURRED TO YOU THAT SOME OF US DON'T WANT TO REMEMBER THE THINGS WE DID THAT SUMMER?!
WHO?
WHO?
YEAH, WHO?
SOME OF US!

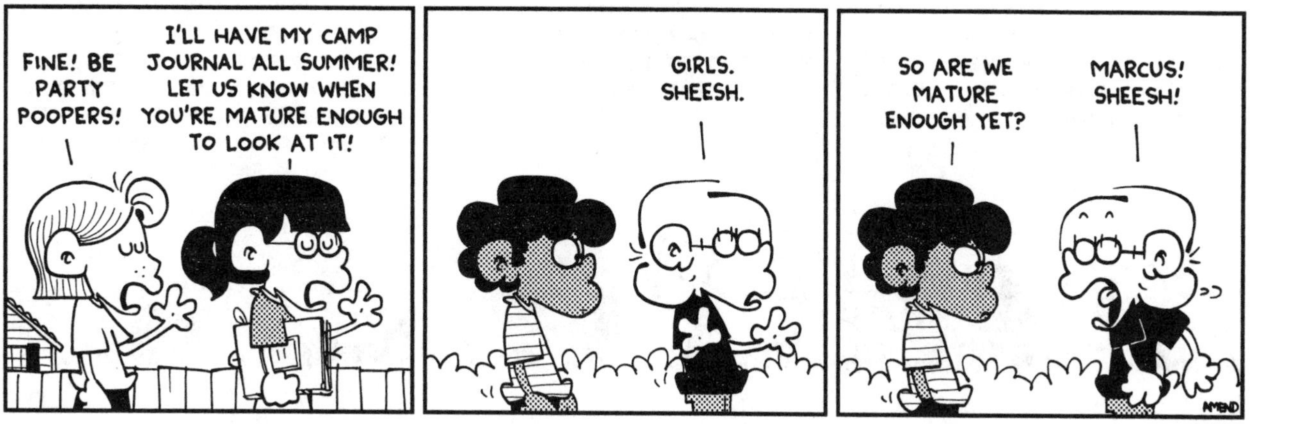
FINE! BE PARTY POOPERS!
I'LL HAVE MY CAMP JOURNAL ALL SUMMER! LET US KNOW WHEN YOU'RE MATURE ENOUGH TO LOOK AT IT!
GIRLS. SHEESH.
SO ARE WE MATURE ENOUGH YET?
MARCUS! SHEESH!
AMEND

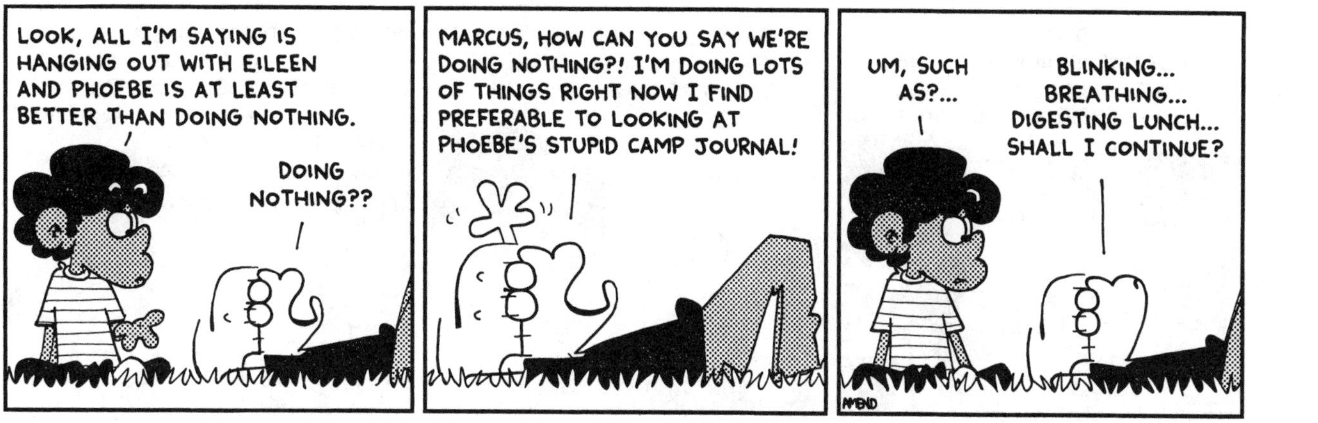
LOOK, ALL I'M SAYING IS HANGING OUT WITH EILEEN AND PHOEBE IS AT LEAST BETTER THAN DOING NOTHING.
DOING NOTHING??
MARCUS, HOW CAN YOU SAY WE'RE DOING NOTHING?! I'M DOING LOTS OF THINGS RIGHT NOW I FIND PREFERABLE TO LOOKING AT PHOEBE'S STUPID CAMP JOURNAL!
UM, SUCH AS?...
BLINKING... BREATHING... DIGESTING LUNCH... SHALL I CONTINUE?
AMEND

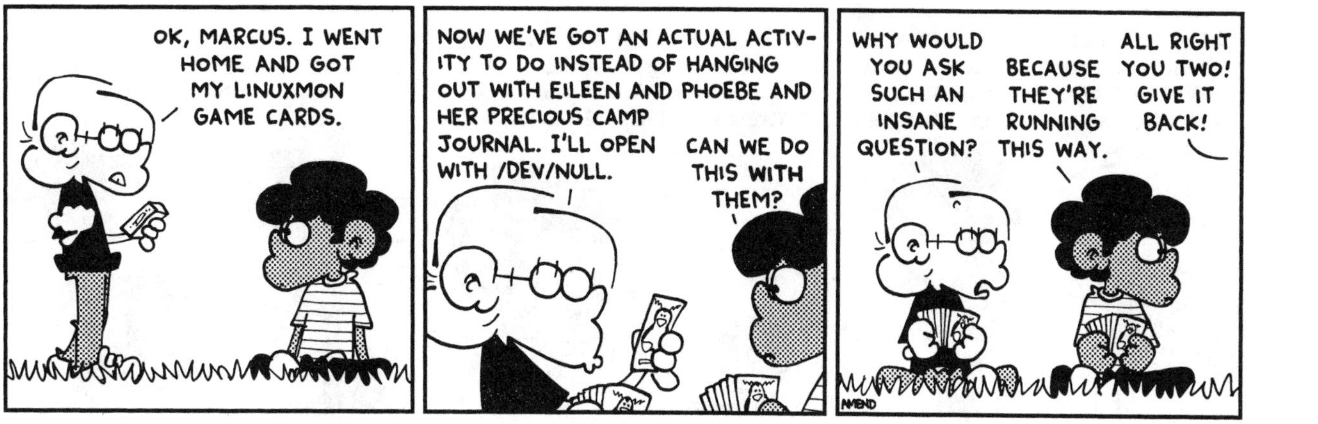
OK, MARCUS. I WENT HOME AND GOT MY LINUXMON GAME CARDS.
NOW WE'VE GOT AN ACTUAL ACTIVITY TO DO INSTEAD OF HANGING OUT WITH EILEEN AND PHOEBE AND HER PRECIOUS CAMP JOURNAL. I'LL OPEN WITH /DEV/NULL.
CAN WE DO THIS WITH THEM?
WHY WOULD YOU ASK SUCH AN INSANE QUESTION?
BECAUSE THEY'RE RUNNING THIS WAY.
ALL RIGHT YOU TWO! GIVE IT BACK!
AMEND

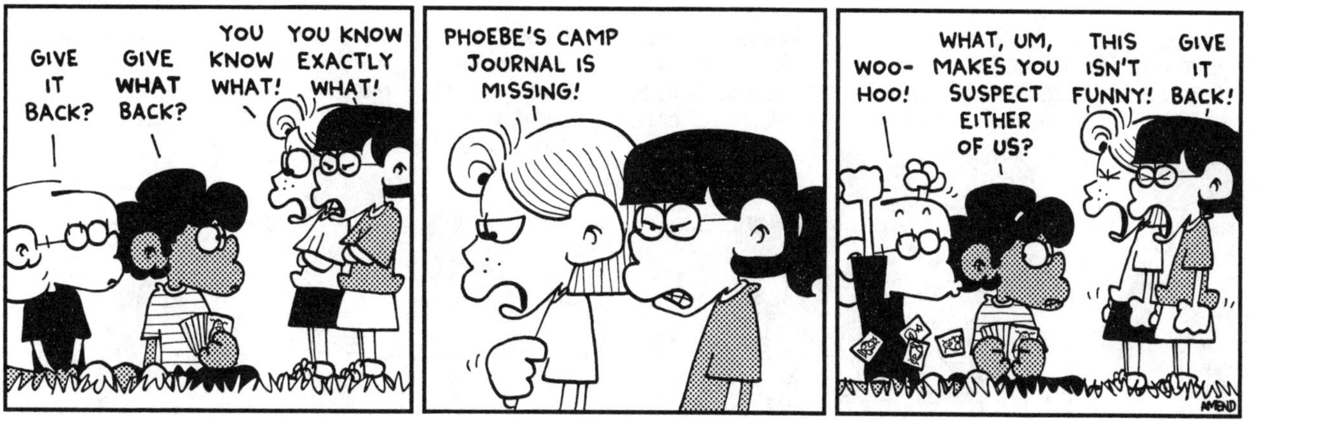
GIVE IT BACK?
GIVE WHAT BACK?
YOU KNOW WHAT!
YOU KNOW EXACTLY WHAT!
PHOEBE'S CAMP JOURNAL IS MISSING!
WOO-HOO!
WHAT, UM, MAKES YOU SUSPECT EITHER OF US?
THIS ISN'T FUNNY!
GIVE IT BACK!
AMEND

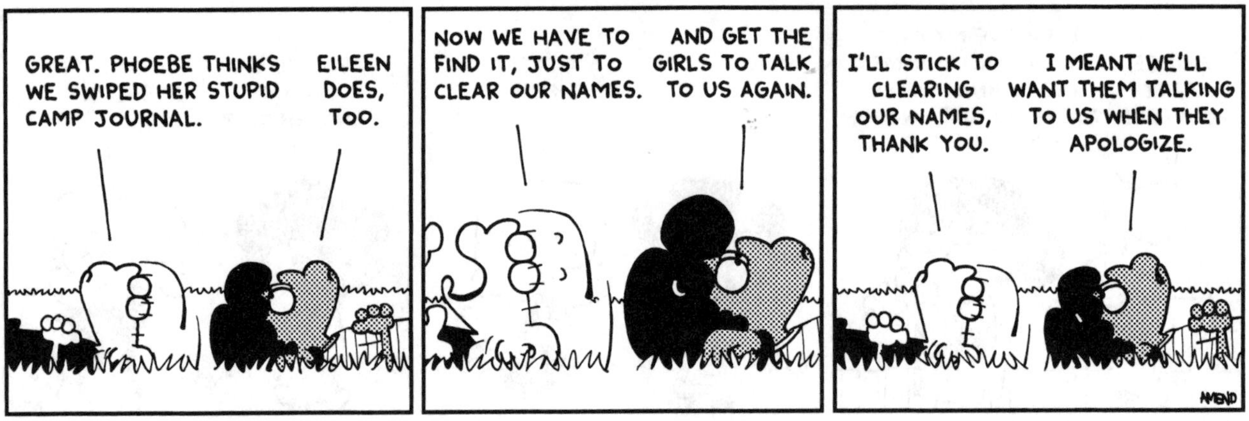
GREAT. PHOEBE THINKS WE SWIPED HER STUPID CAMP JOURNAL.
EILEEN DOES, TOO.
NOW WE HAVE TO FIND IT, JUST TO CLEAR OUR NAMES.
AND GET THE GIRLS TO TALK TO US AGAIN.
I'LL STICK TO CLEARING OUR NAMES, THANK YOU.
I MEANT WE'LL WANT THEM TALKING TO US WHEN THEY APOLOGIZE.

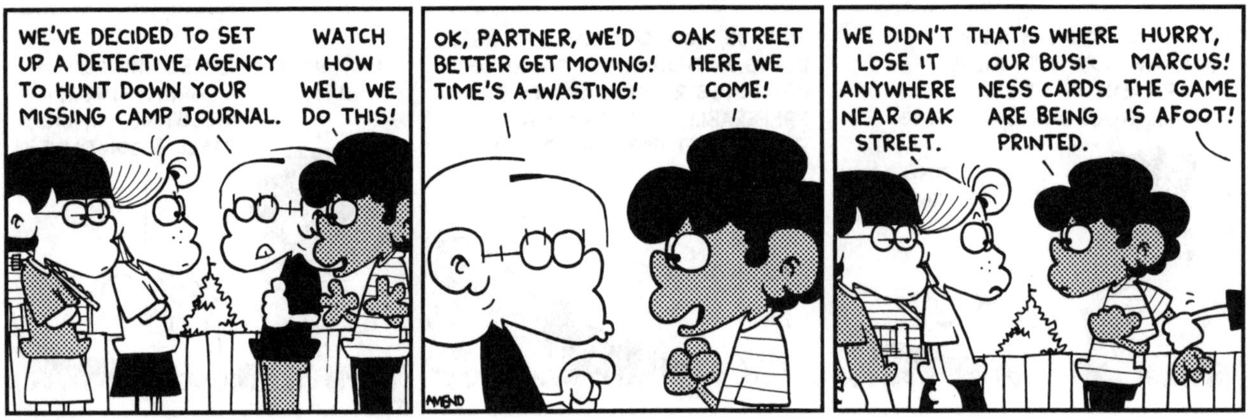
WE'VE DECIDED TO SET UP A DETECTIVE AGENCY TO HUNT DOWN YOUR MISSING CAMP JOURNAL.
WATCH HOW WELL WE DO THIS!
OK, PARTNER, WE'D BETTER GET MOVING! TIME'S A-WASTING!
OAK STREET HERE WE COME!
WE DIDN'T LOSE IT ANYWHERE NEAR OAK STREET.
THAT'S WHERE OUR BUSINESS CARDS ARE BEING PRINTED.
HURRY, MARCUS! THE GAME IS AFOOT!

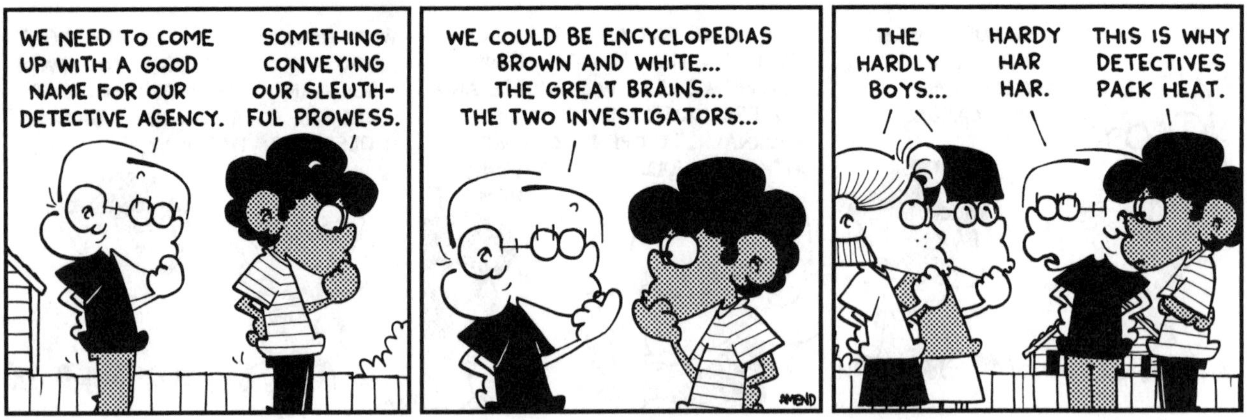
WE NEED TO COME UP WITH A GOOD NAME FOR OUR DETECTIVE AGENCY.
SOMETHING CONVEYING OUR SLEUTHFUL PROWESS.
WE COULD BE ENCYCLOPEDIAS BROWN AND WHITE... THE GREAT BRAINS... THE TWO INVESTIGATORS...
THE HARDLY BOYS...
HARDY HAR HAR.
THIS IS WHY DETECTIVES PACK HEAT.

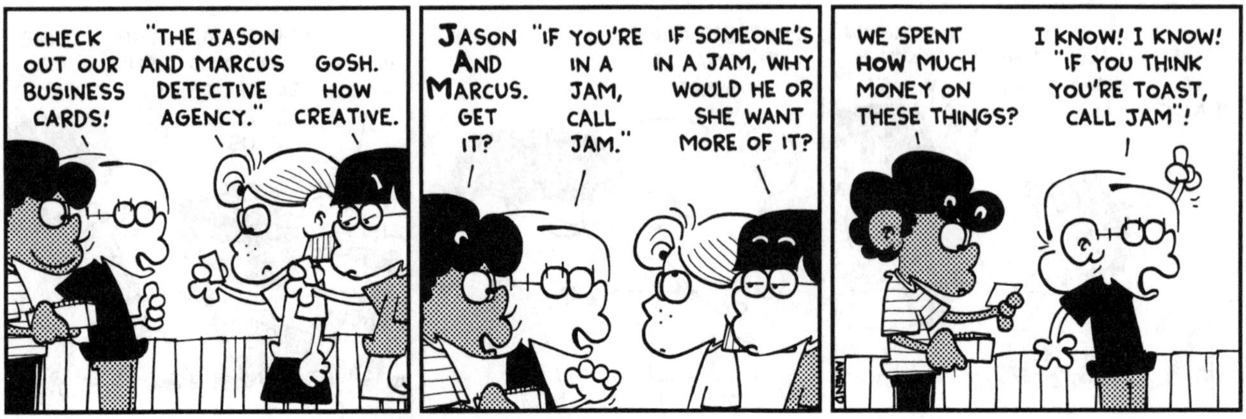
CHECK OUT OUR BUSINESS CARDS!
"THE JASON AND MARCUS DETECTIVE AGENCY."
GOSH. HOW CREATIVE.
JASON AND MARCUS. GET IT?
"IF YOU'RE IN A JAM, CALL JAM."
IF SOMEONE'S IN A JAM, WHY WOULD HE OR SHE WANT MORE OF IT?
WE SPENT HOW MUCH MONEY ON THESE THINGS?
I KNOW! I KNOW! "IF YOU THINK YOU'RE TOAST, CALL JAM"!

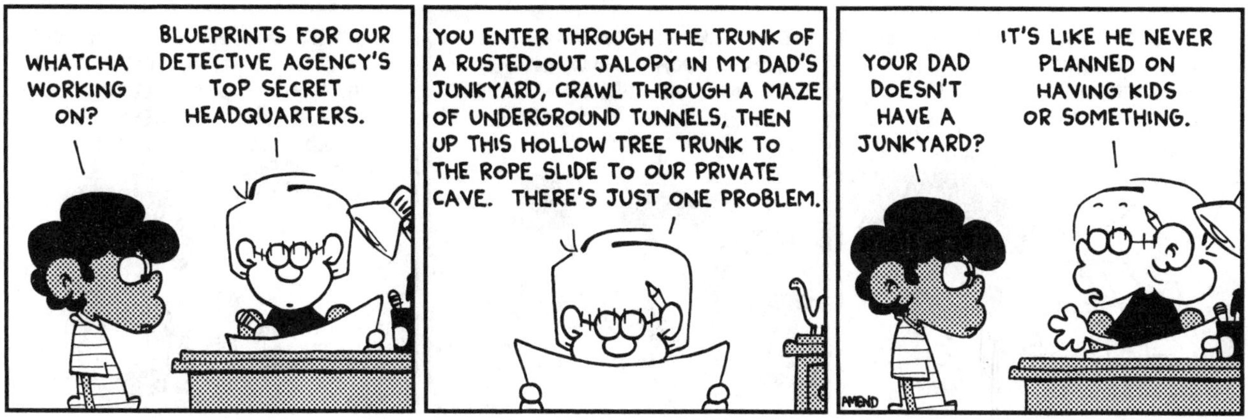
WHATCHA WORKING ON?
BLUEPRINTS FOR OUR DETECTIVE AGENCY'S TOP SECRET HEADQUARTERS.
YOU ENTER THROUGH THE TRUNK OF A RUSTED-OUT JALOPY IN MY DAD'S JUNKYARD, CRAWL THROUGH A MAZE OF UNDERGROUND TUNNELS, THEN UP THIS HOLLOW TREE TRUNK TO THE ROPE SLIDE TO OUR PRIVATE CAVE. THERE'S JUST ONE PROBLEM.
YOUR DAD DOESN'T HAVE A JUNKYARD?
IT'S LIKE HE NEVER PLANNED ON HAVING KIDS OR SOMETHING.
AMEND

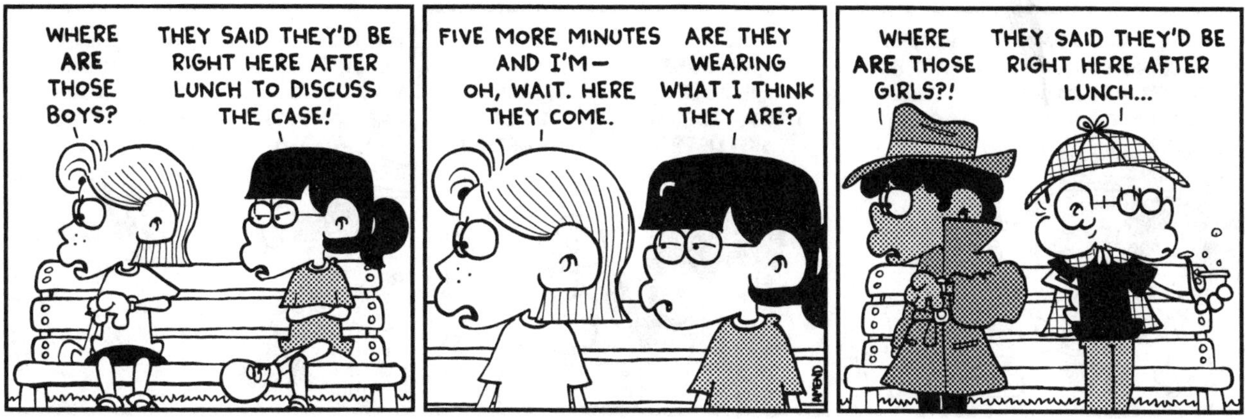
WHERE ARE THOSE BOYS?
THEY SAID THEY'D BE RIGHT HERE AFTER LUNCH TO DISCUSS THE CASE!
FIVE MORE MINUTES AND I'M— OH, WAIT. HERE THEY COME.
ARE THEY WEARING WHAT I THINK THEY ARE?
AMEND
WHERE ARE THOSE GIRLS?!
THEY SAID THEY'D BE RIGHT HERE AFTER LUNCH...

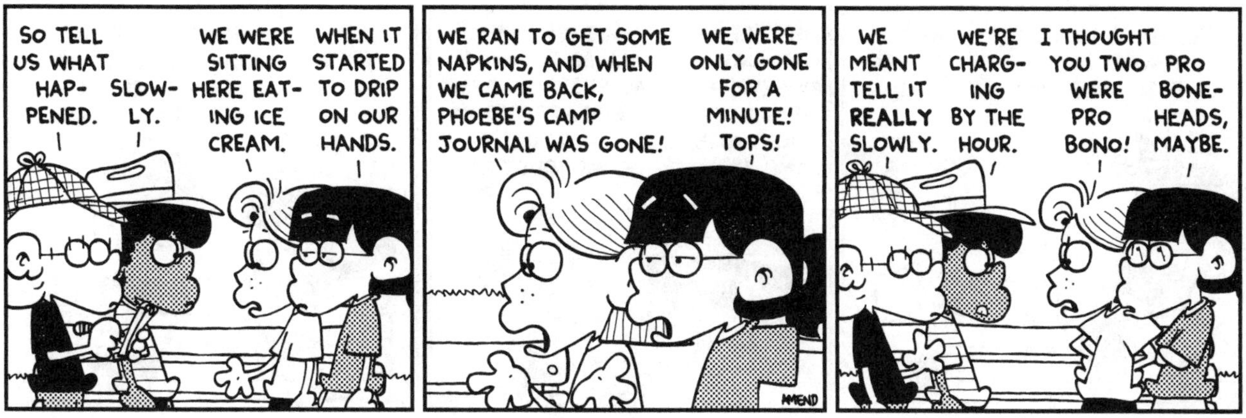
SO TELL US WHAT HAP-PENED.
SLOW-LY.
WE WERE SITTING HERE EAT-ING ICE CREAM.
WHEN IT STARTED TO DRIP ON OUR HANDS.
WE RAN TO GET SOME NAPKINS, AND WHEN WE CAME BACK, PHOEBE'S CAMP JOURNAL WAS GONE!
WE WERE ONLY GONE FOR A MINUTE! TOPS!
AMEND
WE MEANT TELL IT REALLY SLOWLY.
WE'RE CHARG-ING BY THE HOUR.
I THOUGHT YOU TWO WERE PRO BONO!
PRO BONE-HEADS, MAYBE.

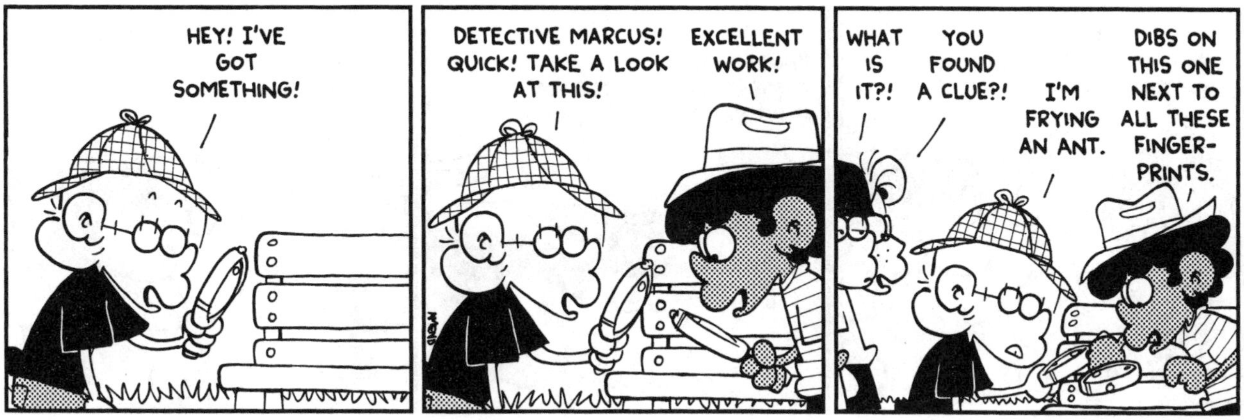
HEY! I'VE GOT SOMETHING!
DETECTIVE MARCUS! QUICK! TAKE A LOOK AT THIS!
EXCELLENT WORK!
AMEND
WHAT IS IT?!
YOU FOUND A CLUE?!
I'M FRYING AN ANT.
DIBS ON THIS ONE NEXT TO ALL THESE FINGER-PRINTS.

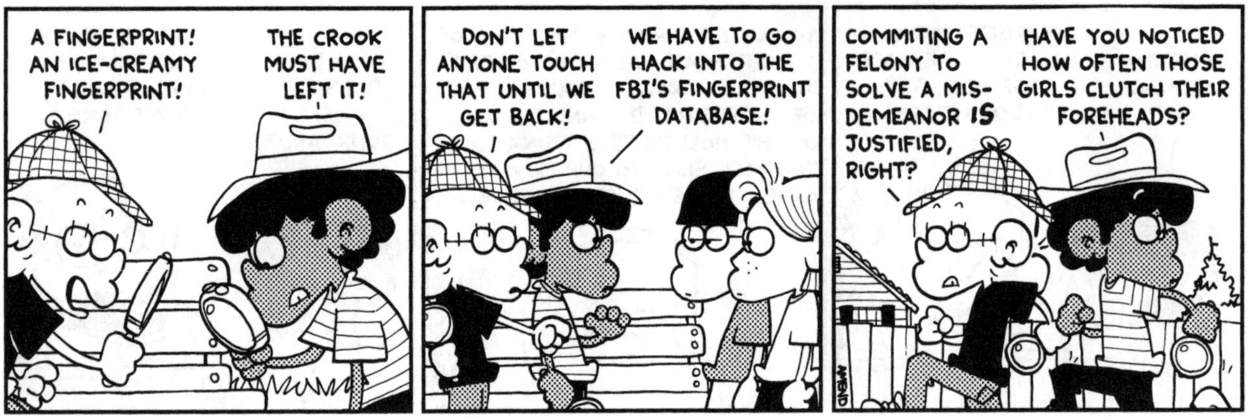
A FINGERPRINT! AN ICE-CREAMY FINGERPRINT!
THE CROOK MUST HAVE LEFT IT!
DON'T LET ANYONE TOUCH THAT UNTIL WE GET BACK!
WE HAVE TO GO HACK INTO THE FBI'S FINGERPRINT DATABASE!
COMMITING A FELONY TO SOLVE A MIS-DEMEANOR **IS** JUSTIFIED, RIGHT?
HAVE YOU NOTICED HOW OFTEN THOSE GIRLS CLUTCH THEIR FOREHEADS?
AMEND

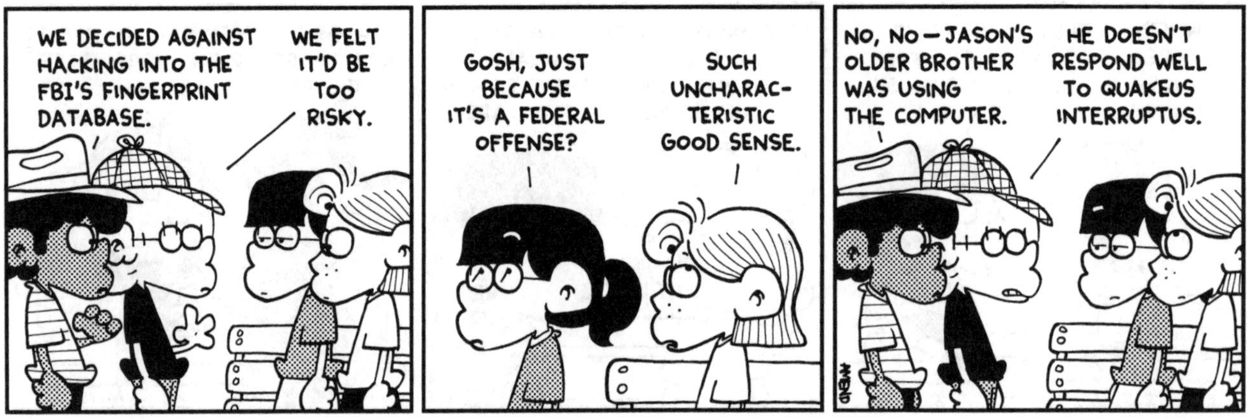
WE DECIDED AGAINST HACKING INTO THE FBI'S FINGERPRINT DATABASE.
WE FELT IT'D BE TOO RISKY.
GOSH, JUST BECAUSE IT'S A FEDERAL OFFENSE?
SUCH UNCHARAC-TERISTIC GOOD SENSE.
NO, NO — JASON'S OLDER BROTHER WAS USING THE COMPUTER.
HE DOESN'T RESPOND WELL TO QUAKEUS INTERRUPTUS.
AMEND

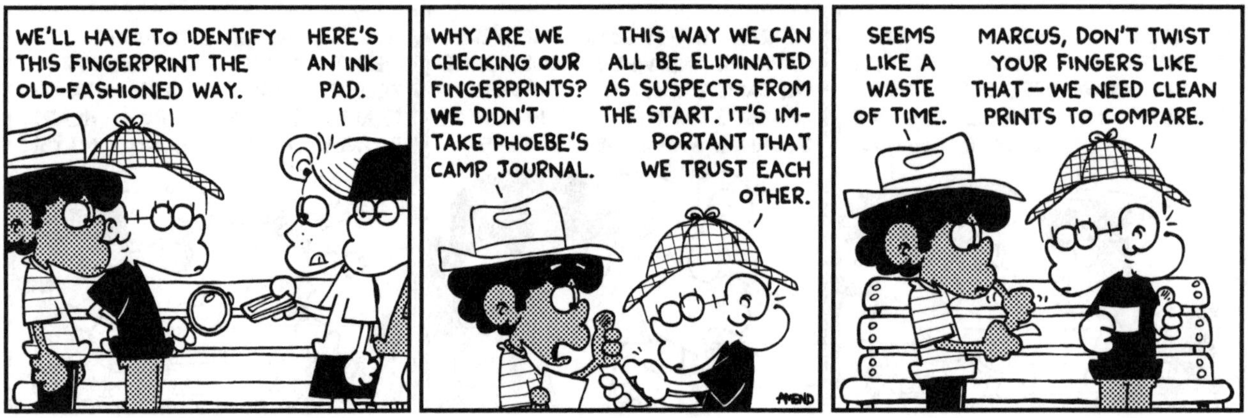
WE'LL HAVE TO IDENTIFY THIS FINGERPRINT THE OLD-FASHIONED WAY.
HERE'S AN INK PAD.
WHY ARE WE CHECKING OUR FINGERPRINTS? WE DIDN'T TAKE PHOEBE'S CAMP JOURNAL.
THIS WAY WE CAN ALL BE ELIMINATED AS SUSPECTS FROM THE START. IT'S IM-PORTANT THAT WE TRUST EACH OTHER.
AMEND
SEEMS LIKE A WASTE OF TIME.
MARCUS, DON'T TWIST YOUR FINGERS LIKE THAT — WE NEED CLEAN PRINTS TO COMPARE.

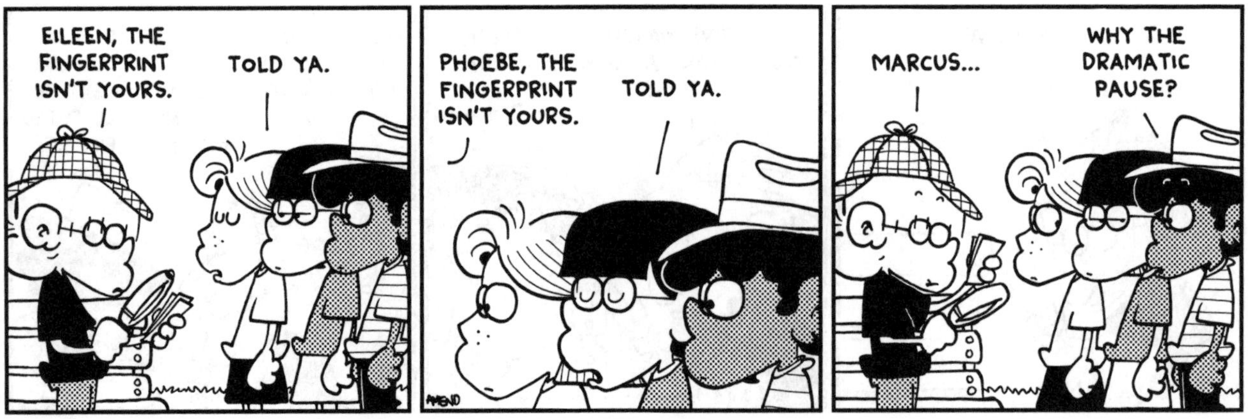
EILEEN, THE FINGERPRINT ISN'T YOURS.
TOLD YA.
PHOEBE, THE FINGERPRINT ISN'T YOURS.
TOLD YA.
AMEND
MARCUS...
WHY THE DRAMATIC PAUSE?

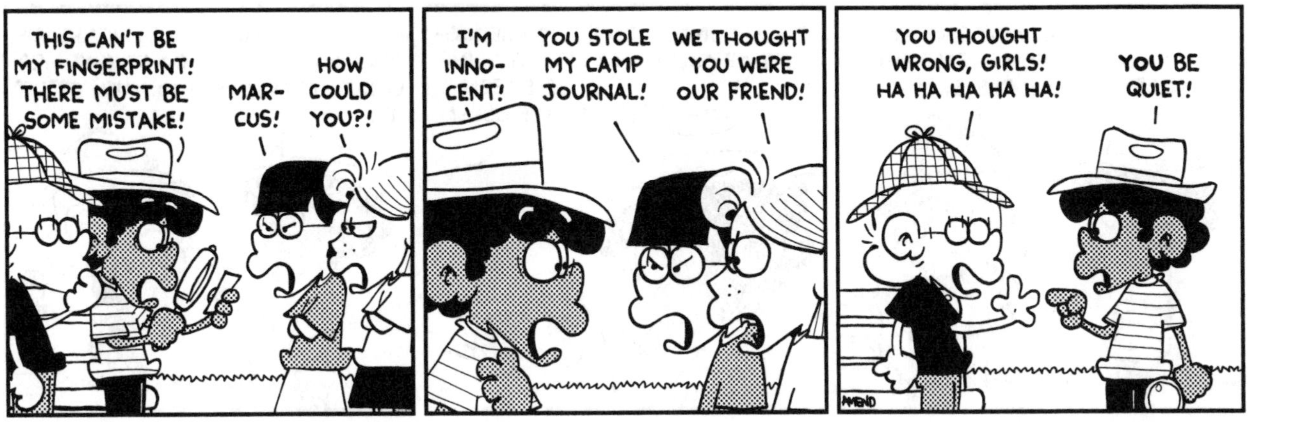
THIS CAN'T BE MY FINGERPRINT! THERE MUST BE SOME MISTAKE!
MAR-CUS!
HOW COULD YOU?!
I'M INNO-CENT!
YOU STOLE MY CAMP JOURNAL!
WE THOUGHT YOU WERE OUR FRIEND!
YOU THOUGHT WRONG, GIRLS! HA HA HA HA HA!
YOU BE QUIET!
AMEND

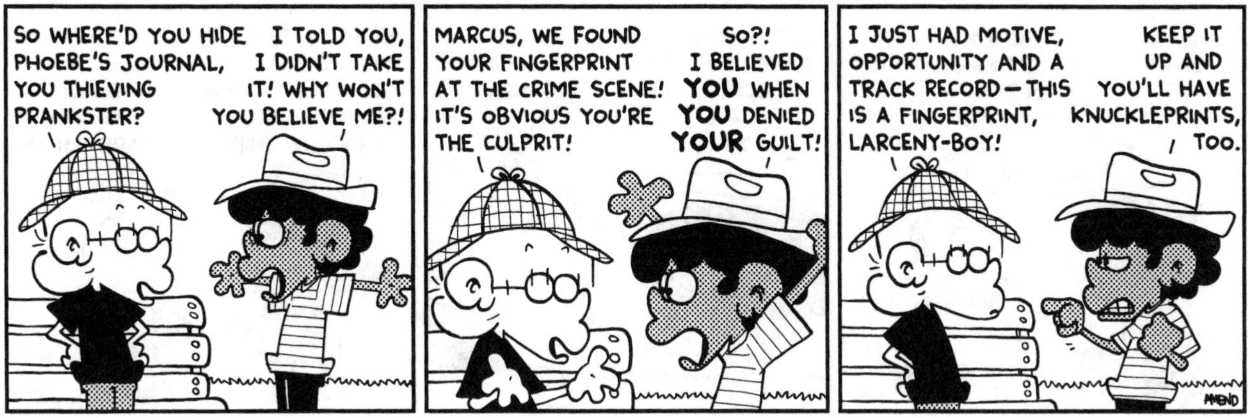
SO WHERE'D YOU HIDE PHOEBE'S JOURNAL, YOU THIEVING PRANKSTER?
I TOLD YOU, I DIDN'T TAKE IT! WHY WON'T YOU BELIEVE ME?!
MARCUS, WE FOUND YOUR FINGERPRINT AT THE CRIME SCENE! IT'S OBVIOUS YOU'RE THE CULPRIT!
SO?! I BELIEVED YOU WHEN YOU DENIED YOUR GUILT!
I JUST HAD MOTIVE, OPPORTUNITY AND A TRACK RECORD—THIS IS A FINGERPRINT, LARCENY-BOY!
KEEP IT UP AND YOU'LL HAVE KNUCKLEPRINTS, TOO.
AMEND

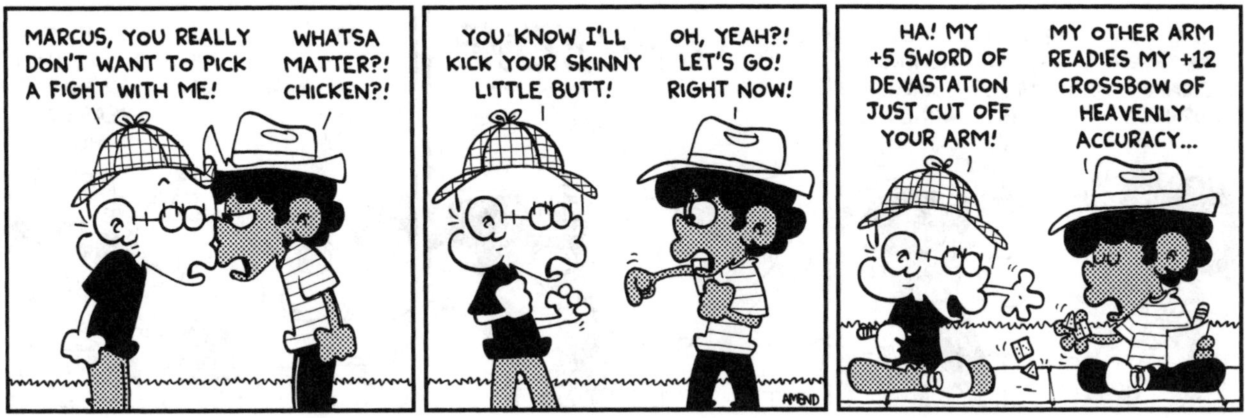
MARCUS, YOU REALLY DON'T WANT TO PICK A FIGHT WITH ME!
WHATSA MATTER?! CHICKEN?!
YOU KNOW I'LL KICK YOUR SKINNY LITTLE BUTT!
OH, YEAH?! LET'S GO! RIGHT NOW!
HA! MY +5 SWORD OF DEVASTATION JUST CUT OFF YOUR ARM!
MY OTHER ARM READIES MY +12 CROSSBOW OF HEAVENLY ACCURACY...
AMEND

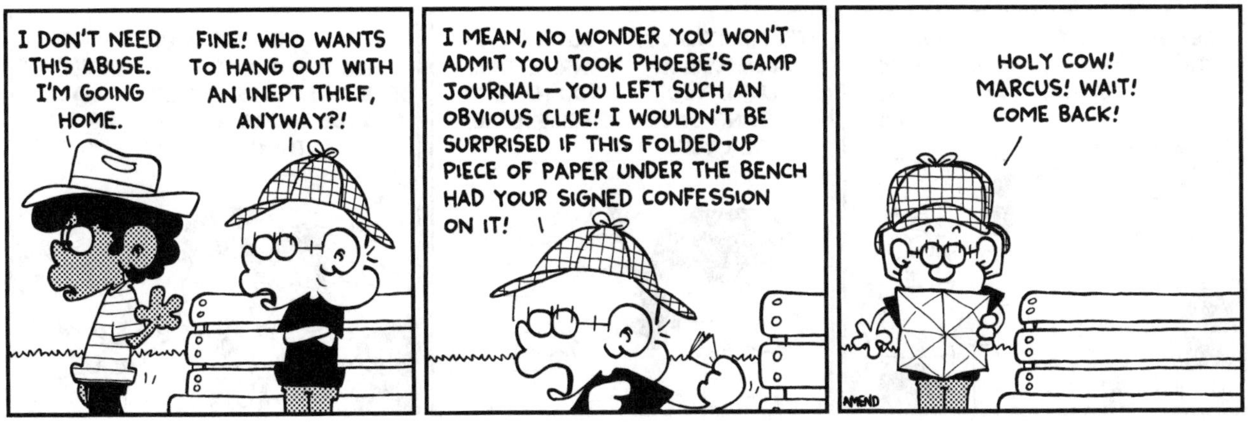
I DON'T NEED THIS ABUSE. I'M GOING HOME.
FINE! WHO WANTS TO HANG OUT WITH AN INEPT THIEF, ANYWAY?!
I MEAN, NO WONDER YOU WON'T ADMIT YOU TOOK PHOEBE'S CAMP JOURNAL—YOU LEFT SUCH AN OBVIOUS CLUE! I WOULDN'T BE SURPRISED IF THIS FOLDED-UP PIECE OF PAPER UNDER THE BENCH HAD YOUR SIGNED CONFESSION ON IT!
HOLY COW! MARCUS! WAIT! COME BACK!
AMEND

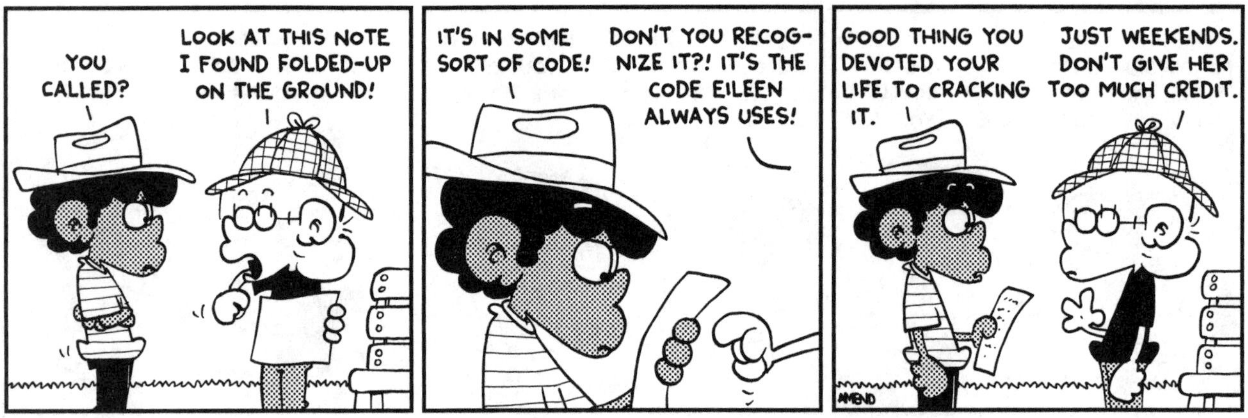
YOU CALLED?
LOOK AT THIS NOTE I FOUND FOLDED-UP ON THE GROUND!
IT'S IN SOME SORT OF CODE!
DON'T YOU RECOGNIZE IT?! IT'S THE CODE EILEEN ALWAYS USES!
GOOD THING YOU DEVOTED YOUR LIFE TO CRACKING IT.
JUST WEEKENDS. DON'T GIVE HER TOO MUCH CREDIT.
AMEND

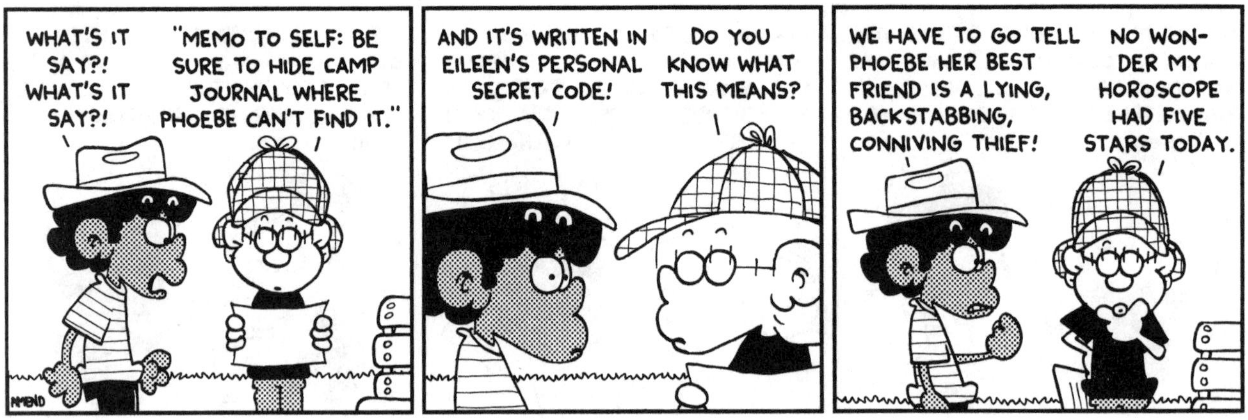
WHAT'S IT SAY?! WHAT'S IT SAY?!
"MEMO TO SELF: BE SURE TO HIDE CAMP JOURNAL WHERE PHOEBE CAN'T FIND IT."
AND IT'S WRITTEN IN EILEEN'S PERSONAL SECRET CODE!
DO YOU KNOW WHAT THIS MEANS?
WE HAVE TO GO TELL PHOEBE HER BEST FRIEND IS A LYING, BACKSTABBING, CONNIVING THIEF!
NO WONDER MY HOROSCOPE HAD FIVE STARS TODAY.
AMEND

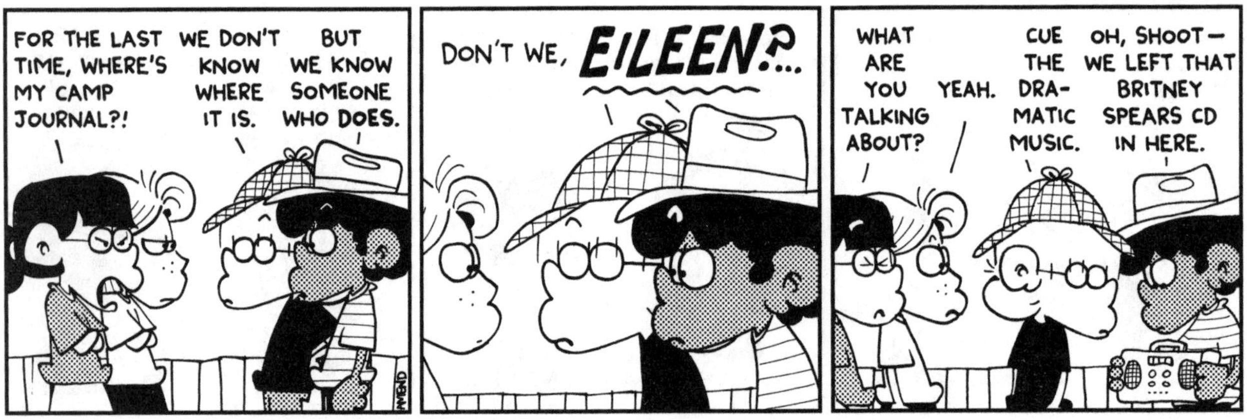
FOR THE LAST TIME, WHERE'S MY CAMP JOURNAL?!
WE DON'T KNOW WHERE IT IS.
BUT WE KNOW SOMEONE WHO DOES.
DON'T WE, EILEEN?...
WHAT ARE YOU TALKING ABOUT?
YEAH.
CUE THE DRAMATIC MUSIC.
OH, SHOOT— WE LEFT THAT BRITNEY SPEARS CD IN HERE.
AMEND

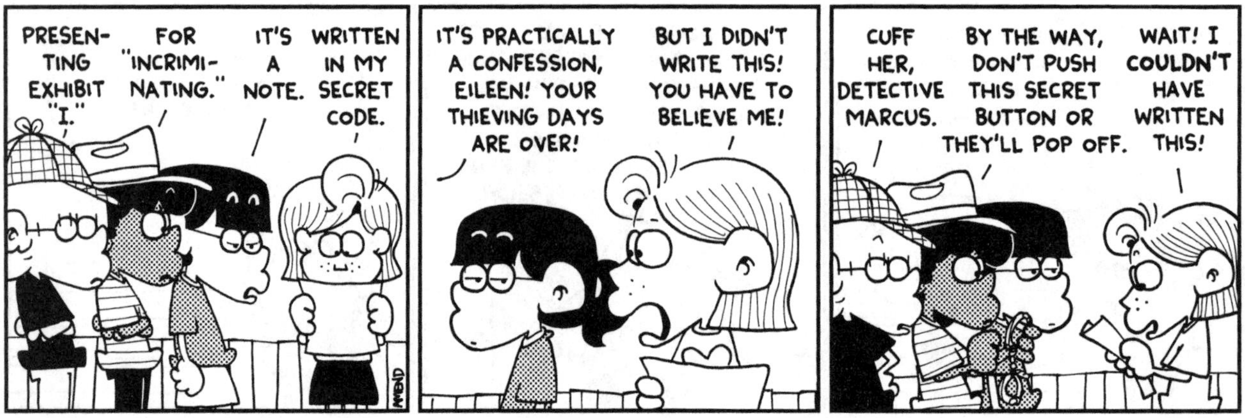
PRESENTING EXHIBIT "I."
FOR "INCRIMINATING."
IT'S A NOTE.
WRITTEN IN MY SECRET CODE.
IT'S PRACTICALLY A CONFESSION, EILEEN! YOUR THIEVING DAYS ARE OVER!
BUT I DIDN'T WRITE THIS! YOU HAVE TO BELIEVE ME!
CUFF HER, DETECTIVE MARCUS.
BY THE WAY, DON'T PUSH THIS SECRET BUTTON OR THEY'LL POP OFF.
WAIT! I COULDN'T HAVE WRITTEN THIS!
AMEND

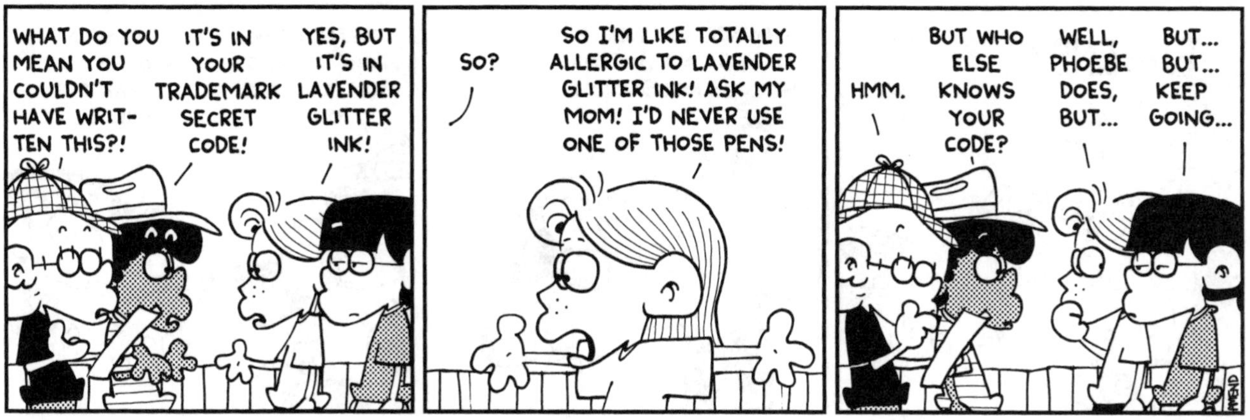
WHAT DO YOU MEAN YOU COULDN'T HAVE WRITTEN THIS?!
IT'S IN YOUR TRADEMARK SECRET CODE!
YES, BUT IT'S IN LAVENDER GLITTER INK!
SO?
SO I'M LIKE TOTALLY ALLERGIC TO LAVENDER GLITTER INK! ASK MY MOM! I'D NEVER USE ONE OF THOSE PENS!
HMM.
BUT WHO ELSE KNOWS YOUR CODE?
WELL, PHOEBE DOES, BUT...
BUT... BUT... KEEP GOING...
AMEND

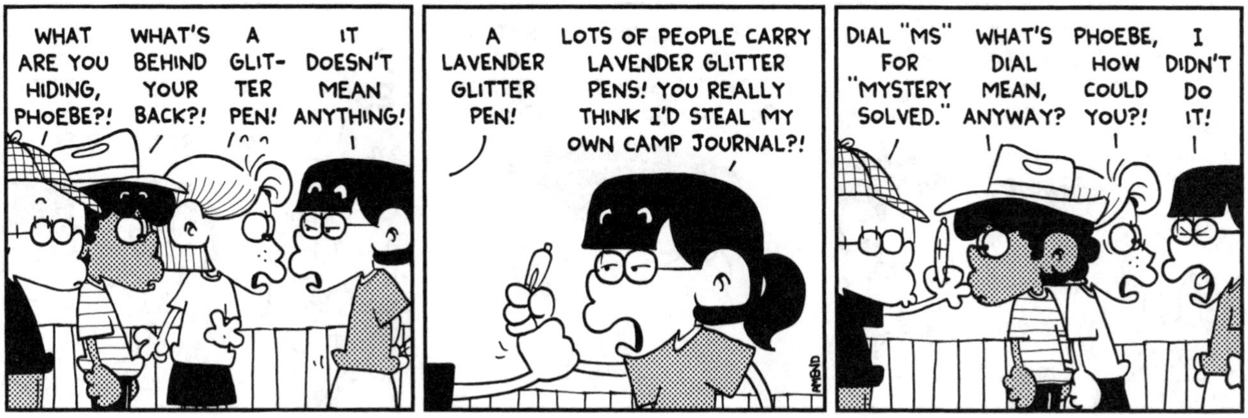
WHAT ARE YOU HIDING, PHOEBE?!
WHAT'S BEHIND YOUR BACK?!
A GLITTER PEN!
IT DOESN'T MEAN ANYTHING!
A LAVENDER GLITTER PEN!
LOTS OF PEOPLE CARRY LAVENDER GLITTER PENS! YOU REALLY THINK I'D STEAL MY OWN CAMP JOURNAL?!
AMEND
DIAL "MS" FOR "MYSTERY SOLVED."
WHAT'S DIAL MEAN, ANYWAY?
PHOEBE, HOW COULD YOU?!
I DIDN'T DO IT!

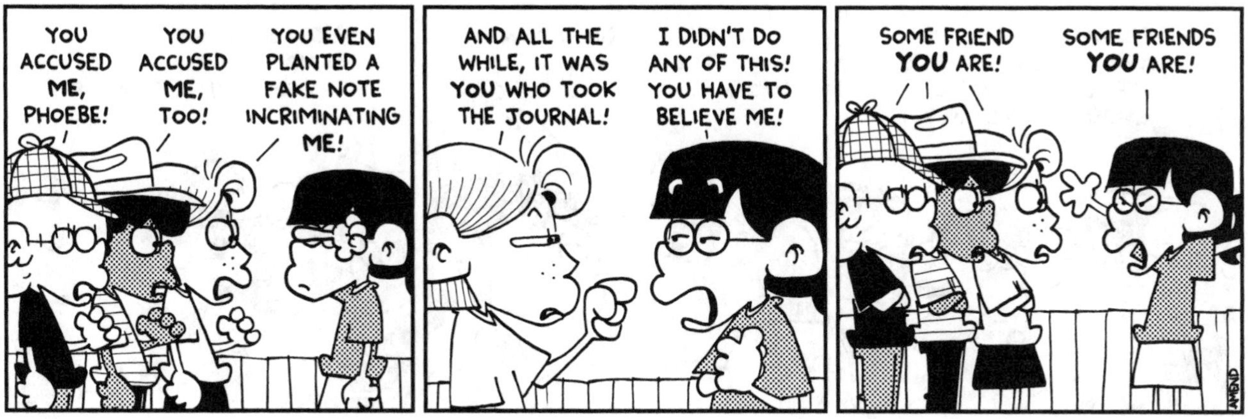
YOU ACCUSED ME, PHOEBE!
YOU ACCUSED ME, TOO!
YOU EVEN PLANTED A FAKE NOTE INCRIMINATING ME!
AND ALL THE WHILE, IT WAS YOU WHO TOOK THE JOURNAL!
I DIDN'T DO ANY OF THIS! YOU HAVE TO BELIEVE ME!
SOME FRIEND YOU ARE!
SOME FRIENDS YOU ARE!
AMEND

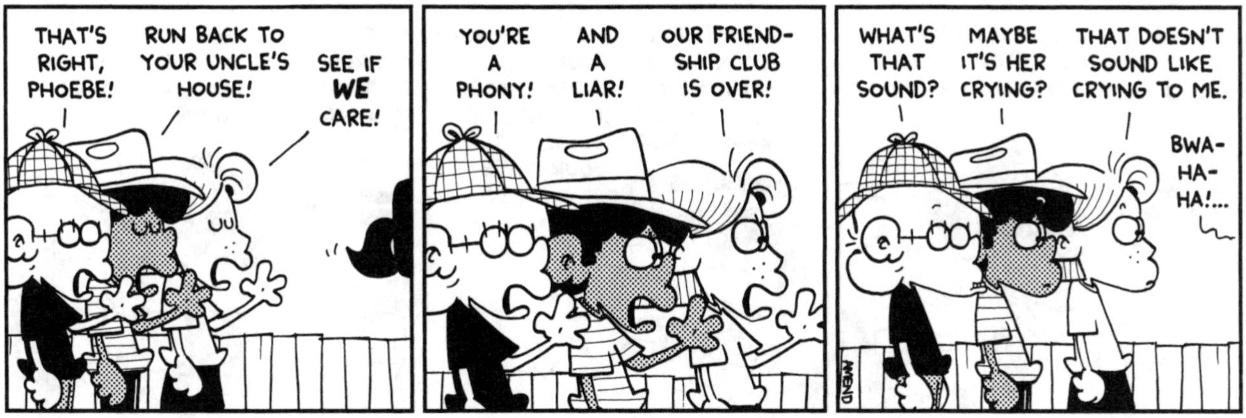
THAT'S RIGHT, PHOEBE!
RUN BACK TO YOUR UNCLE'S HOUSE!
SEE IF WE CARE!
YOU'RE A PHONY!
AND A LIAR!
OUR FRIENDSHIP CLUB IS OVER!
AMEND
WHAT'S THAT SOUND?
MAYBE IT'S HER CRYING?
THAT DOESN'T SOUND LIKE CRYING TO ME.
BWA-HA-HA!...

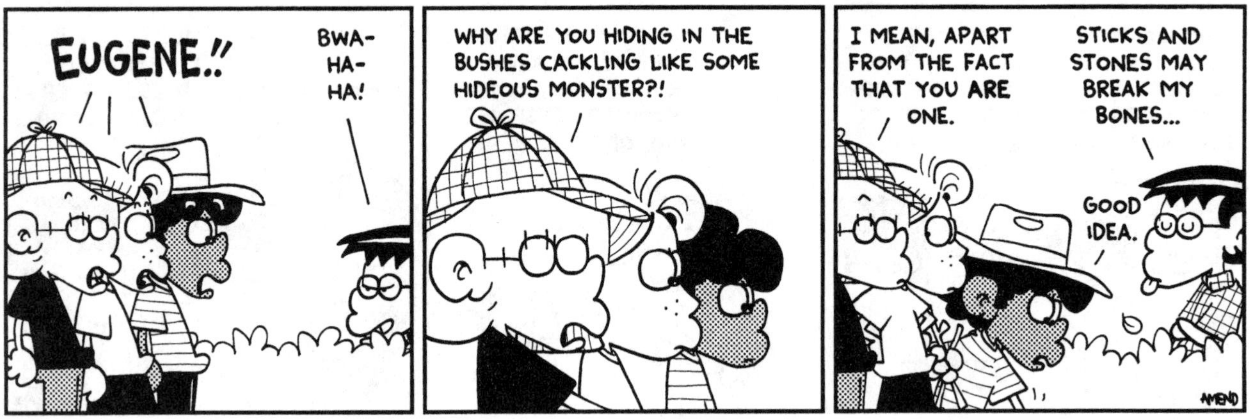
EUGENE.!!
BWA-HA-HA!
WHY ARE YOU HIDING IN THE BUSHES CACKLING LIKE SOME HIDEOUS MONSTER?!
I MEAN, APART FROM THE FACT THAT YOU ARE ONE.
STICKS AND STONES MAY BREAK MY BONES...
GOOD IDEA.
AMEND

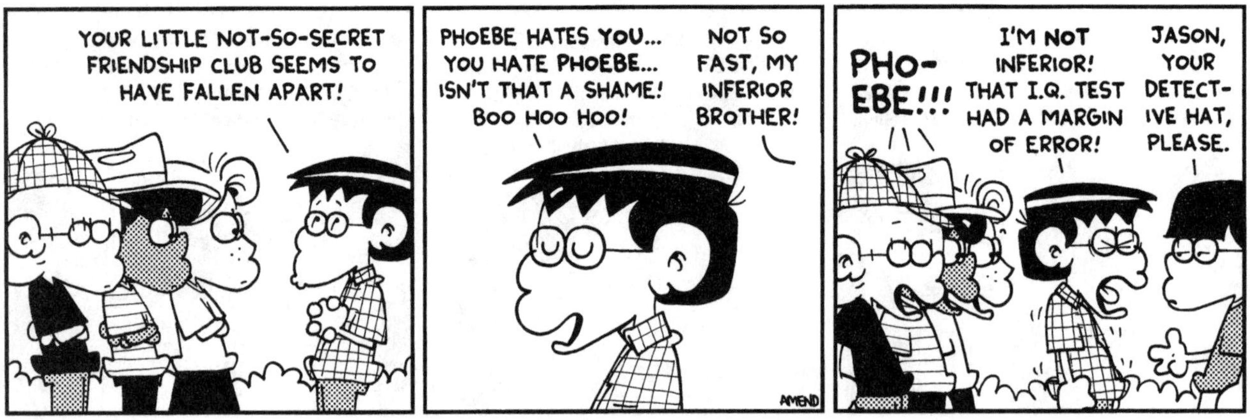
YOUR LITTLE NOT-SO-SECRET FRIENDSHIP CLUB SEEMS TO HAVE FALLEN APART!
PHOEBE HATES YOU... YOU HATE PHOEBE... ISN'T THAT A SHAME! BOO HOO HOO!
NOT SO FAST, MY INFERIOR BROTHER!
PHO-EBE!!!
I'M NOT INFERIOR! THAT I.Q. TEST HAD A MARGIN OF ERROR!
JASON, YOUR DETECT-IVE HAT, PLEASE.
AMEND

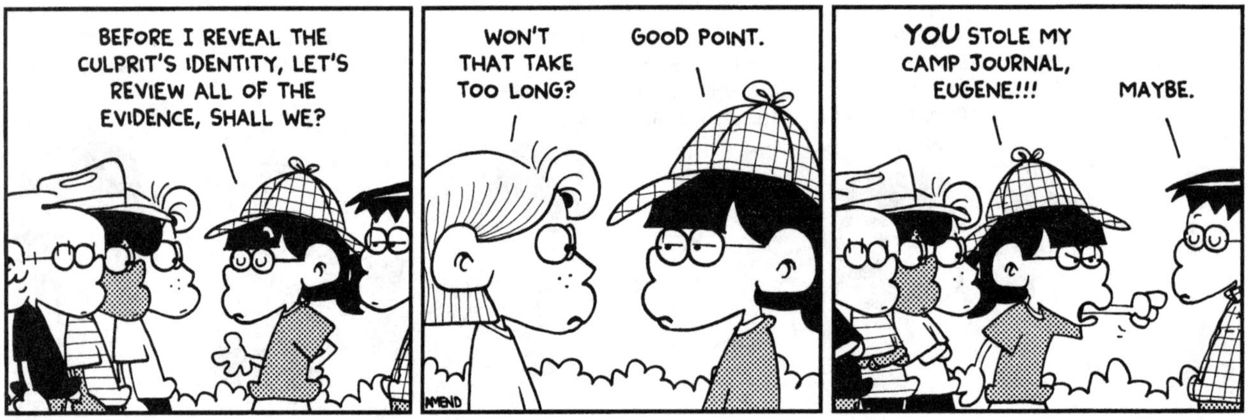
BEFORE I REVEAL THE CULPRIT'S IDENTITY, LET'S REVIEW ALL OF THE EVIDENCE, SHALL WE?
WON'T THAT TAKE TOO LONG?
GOOD POINT.
YOU STOLE MY CAMP JOURNAL, EUGENE!!!
MAYBE.
AMEND

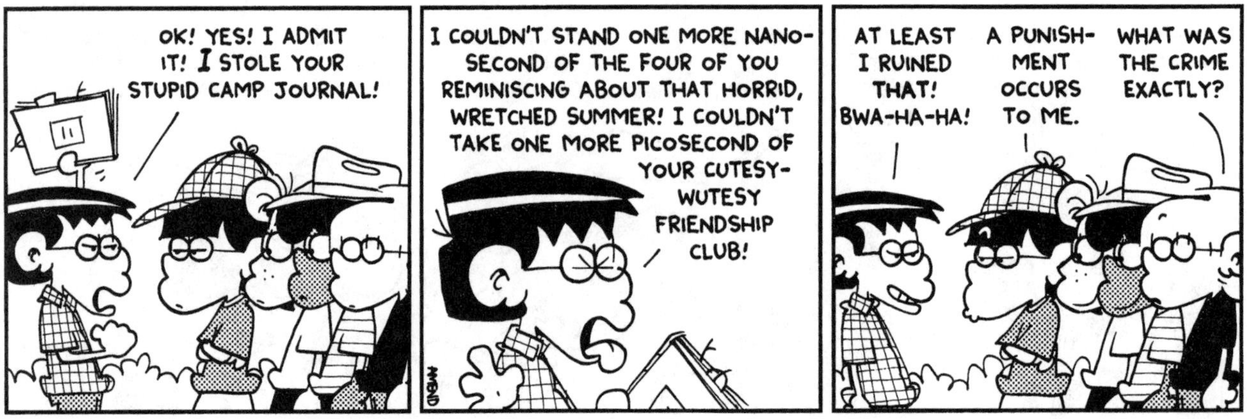
OK! YES! I ADMIT IT! I STOLE YOUR STUPID CAMP JOURNAL!
I COULDN'T STAND ONE MORE NANO-SECOND OF THE FOUR OF YOU REMINISCING ABOUT THAT HORRID, WRETCHED SUMMER! I COULDN'T TAKE ONE MORE PICOSECOND OF YOUR CUTESY-WUTESY FRIENDSHIP CLUB!
AT LEAST I RUINED THAT! BWA-HA-HA!
A PUNISH-MENT OCCURS TO ME.
WHAT WAS THE CRIME EXACTLY?
AMEND

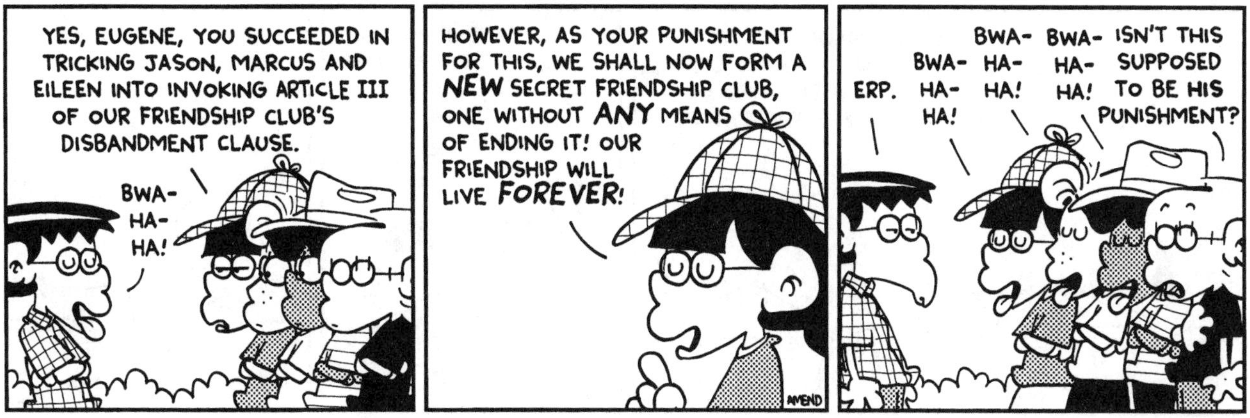
YES, EUGENE, YOU SUCCEEDED IN TRICKING JASON, MARCUS AND EILEEN INTO INVOKING ARTICLE III OF OUR FRIENDSHIP CLUB'S DISBANDMENT CLAUSE.
BWA-HA-HA!
HOWEVER, AS YOUR PUNISHMENT FOR THIS, WE SHALL NOW FORM A NEW SECRET FRIENDSHIP CLUB, ONE WITHOUT ANY MEANS OF ENDING IT! OUR FRIENDSHIP WILL LIVE FOREVER!
AMEND
ERP.
BWA-HA-HA!
BWA-HA-HA!
BWA-HA-HA!
ISN'T THIS SUPPOSED TO BE HIS PUNISHMENT?

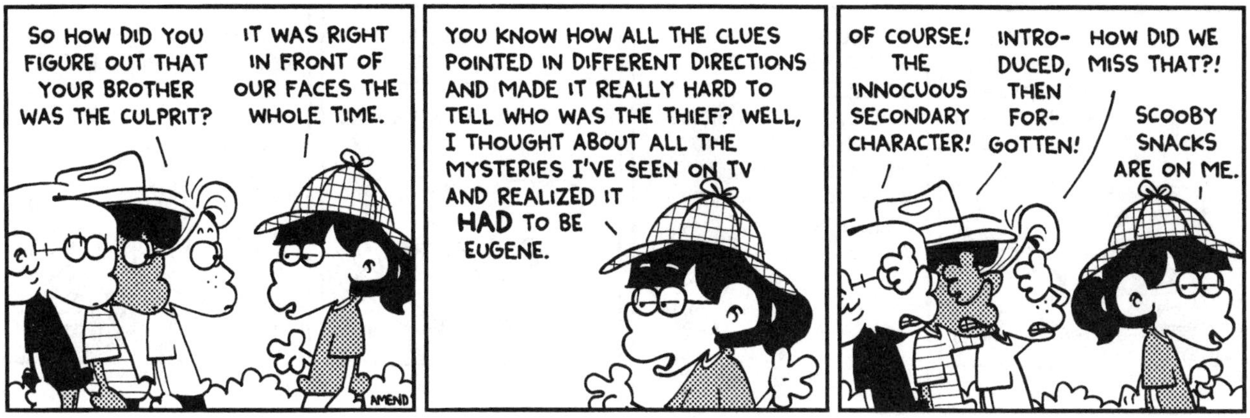
SO HOW DID YOU FIGURE OUT THAT YOUR BROTHER WAS THE CULPRIT?
IT WAS RIGHT IN FRONT OF OUR FACES THE WHOLE TIME.
AMEND
YOU KNOW HOW ALL THE CLUES POINTED IN DIFFERENT DIRECTIONS AND MADE IT REALLY HARD TO TELL WHO WAS THE THIEF? WELL, I THOUGHT ABOUT ALL THE MYSTERIES I'VE SEEN ON TV AND REALIZED IT HAD TO BE EUGENE.
OF COURSE! THE INNOCUOUS SECONDARY CHARACTER!
INTRO-DUCED, THEN FOR-GOTTEN!
HOW DID WE MISS THAT?!
SCOOBY SNACKS ARE ON ME.

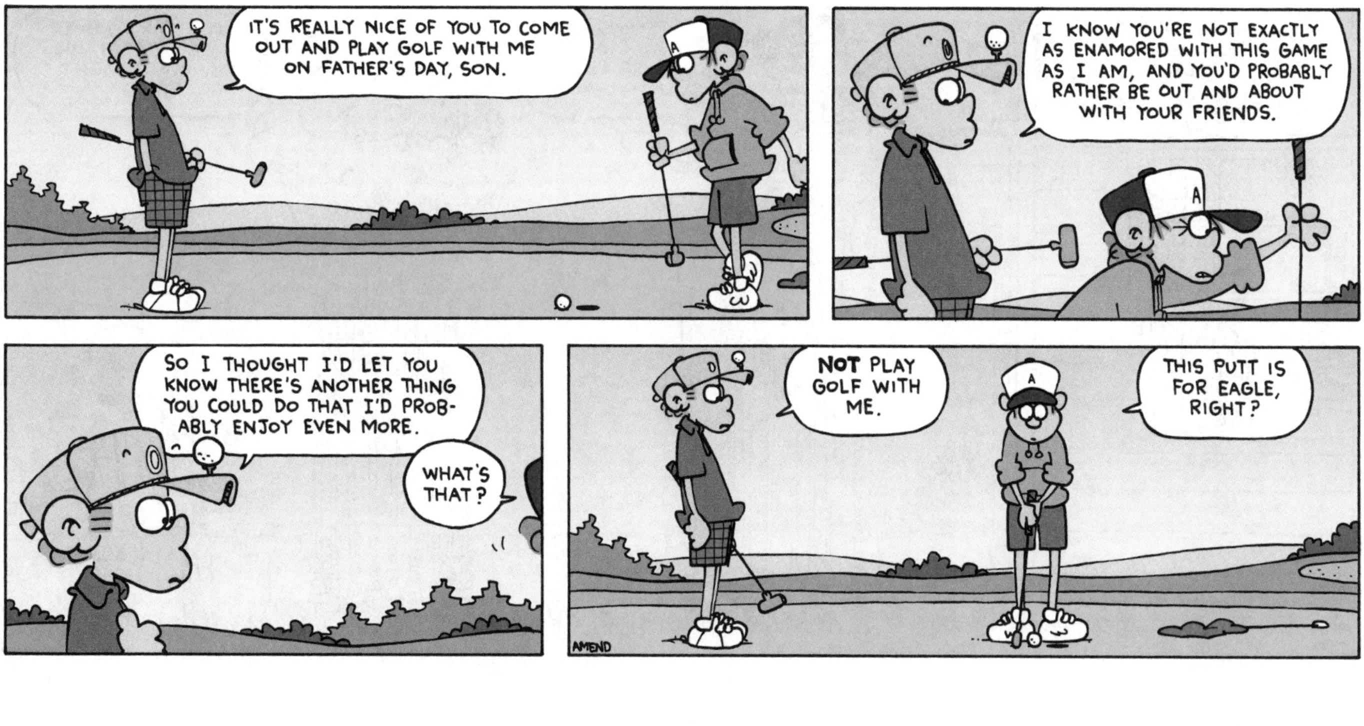
IT'S REALLY NICE OF YOU TO COME OUT AND PLAY GOLF WITH ME ON FATHER'S DAY, SON.
I KNOW YOU'RE NOT EXACTLY AS ENAMORED WITH THIS GAME AS I AM, AND YOU'D PROBABLY RATHER BE OUT AND ABOUT WITH YOUR FRIENDS.
SO I THOUGHT I'D LET YOU KNOW THERE'S ANOTHER THING YOU COULD DO THAT I'D PROBABLY ENJOY EVEN MORE.
WHAT'S THAT?
NOT PLAY GOLF WITH ME.
THIS PUTT IS FOR EAGLE, RIGHT?
AMEND

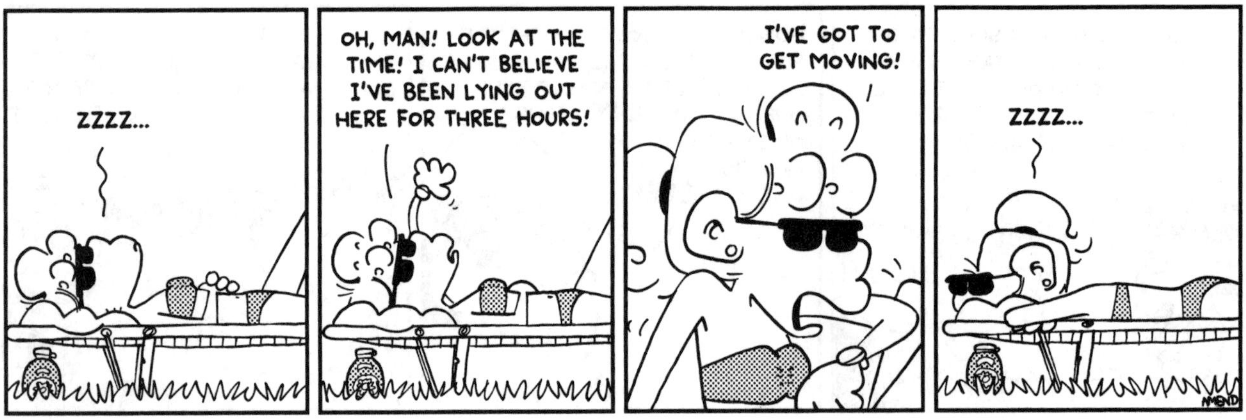
ZZZZ...
OH, MAN! LOOK AT THE TIME! I CAN'T BELIEVE I'VE BEEN LYING OUT HERE FOR THREE HOURS!
I'VE GOT TO GET MOVING!
ZZZZ...

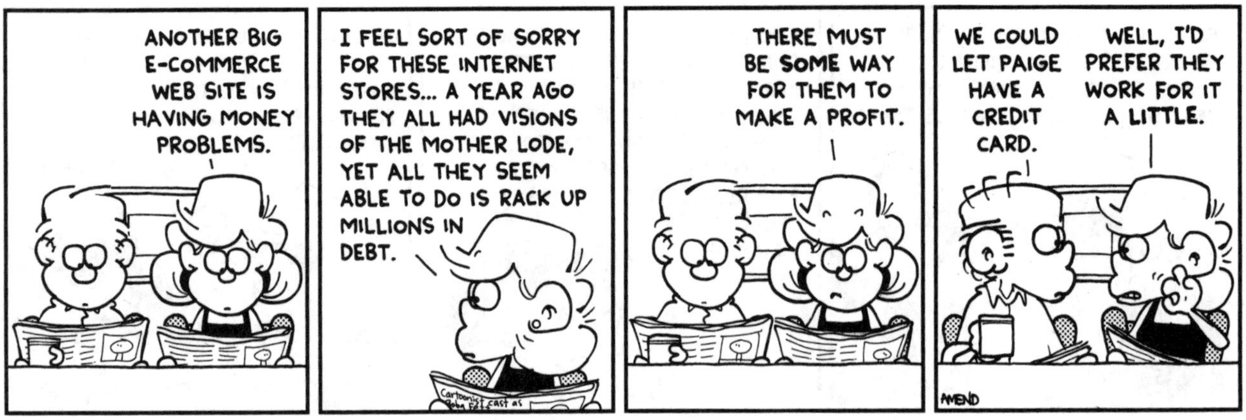
ANOTHER BIG E-COMMERCE WEB SITE IS HAVING MONEY PROBLEMS.
I FEEL SORT OF SORRY FOR THESE INTERNET STORES... A YEAR AGO THEY ALL HAD VISIONS OF THE MOTHER LODE, YET ALL THEY SEEM ABLE TO DO IS RACK UP MILLIONS IN DEBT.
THERE MUST BE SOME WAY FOR THEM TO MAKE A PROFIT.
WE COULD LET PAIGE HAVE A CREDIT CARD.
WELL, I'D PREFER THEY WORK FOR IT A LITTLE.

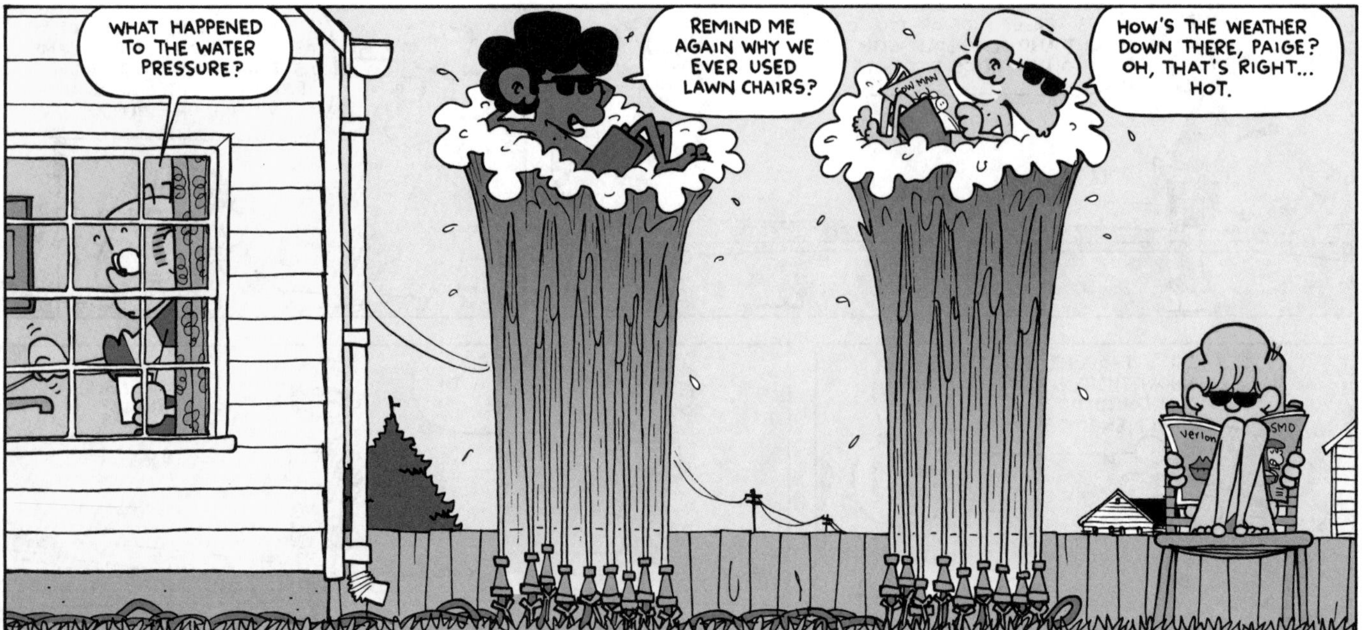
WHAT HAPPENED TO THE WATER PRESSURE?
REMIND ME AGAIN WHY WE EVER USED LAWN CHAIRS?
HOW'S THE WEATHER DOWN THERE, PAIGE? OH, THAT'S RIGHT... HOT.

OOOOOOOOO!
AHHHHHHHHH!
OHHHHHHHHH!
CLAP! CLAP! CLAP! CLAP! CLAP! CLAP! CLAP!
SERIOUSLY, WHO NEEDS FIREWORKS WHEN YOU'VE GOT DAD'S HOLIDAY BARBECUE?
CAN YOU KIDS GO SEE IF WE'VE GOT ANY MORE LIGHTER FLUID?
AMEND

Tofu Casserole
Tofu Casserole
TOFU CASSEROLE
I'M SORRY, MOM, BUT TONIGHT'S DINNER HAS BEEN VOTED OFF THE TABLE.
HA HA. NOW IF YOU COMEDIANS HAVE ANY HOPES OF SURVIVING UNTIL DESSERT...
AMEND

HAVE I EVER TOLD YOU, SIR, HOW MUCH THIS JOB MEANS TO ME?
HOW GRATEFUL I AM FOR THE OPPORTUNITY TO BE HERE?
HOW THANKFUL I AM TO BE A PART OF THE PAVILIONPLEX-22 TEAM?
PRETTY MUCH EVERY DAY OF THIS HEAT WAVE, YES.
COULD YOU DUCK JUST A LITTLE? YOU'RE BLOCKING THE AC VENT.
AMEND

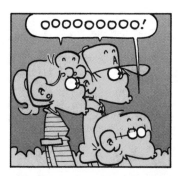

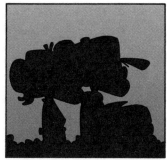

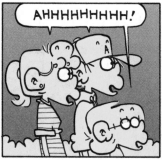

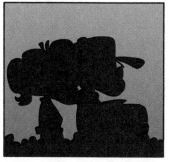

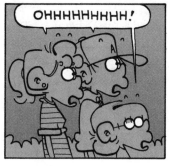

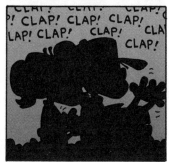

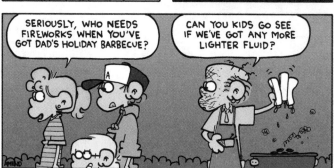

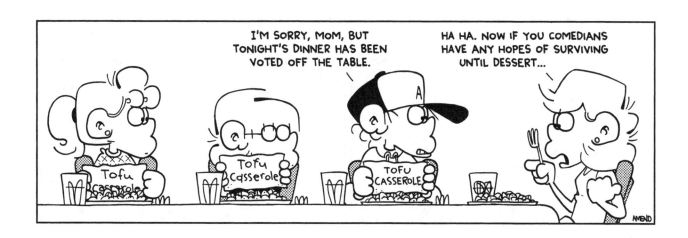

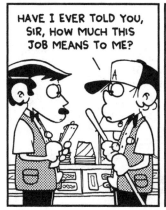

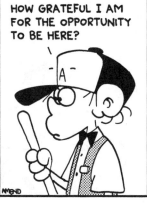

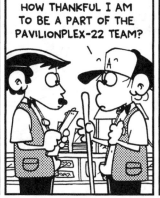

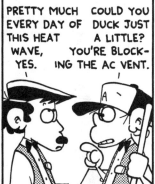

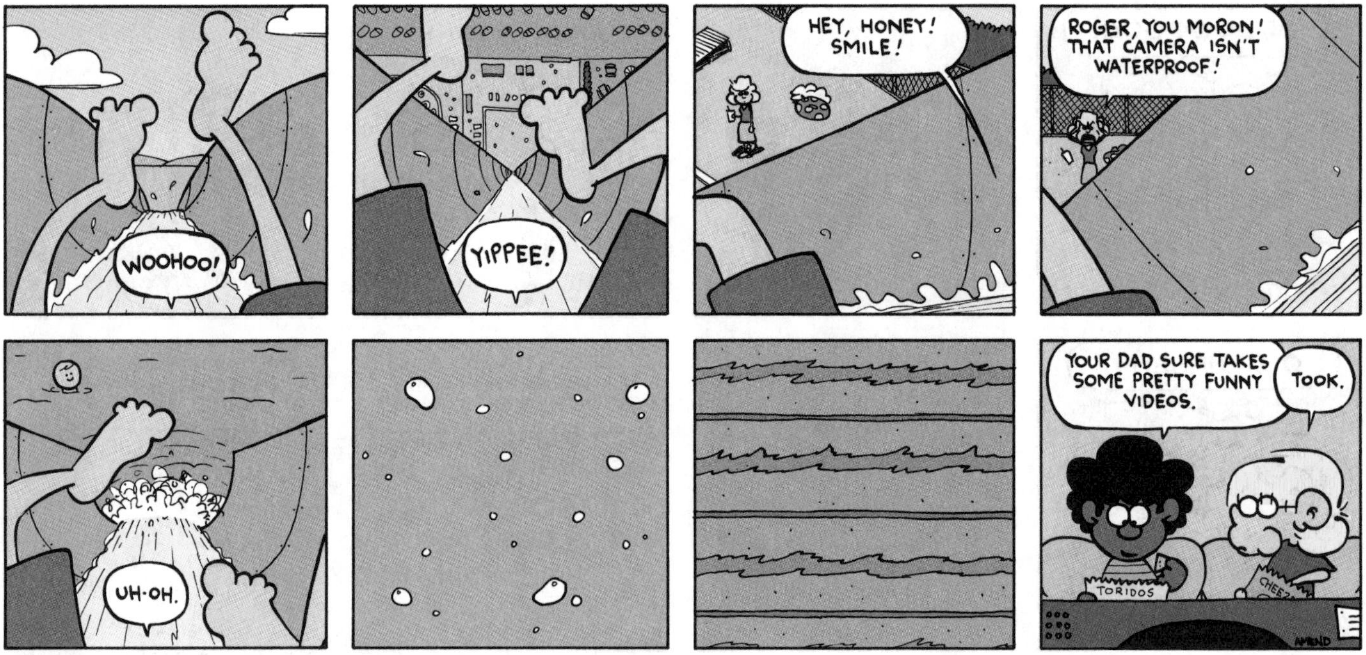
WOOHOO!
YIPPEE!
HEY, HONEY! SMILE!
ROGER, YOU MORON! THAT CAMERA ISN'T WATERPROOF!
UH-OH.
YOUR DAD SURE TAKES SOME PRETTY FUNNY VIDEOS.
TOOK.
TORIDOS

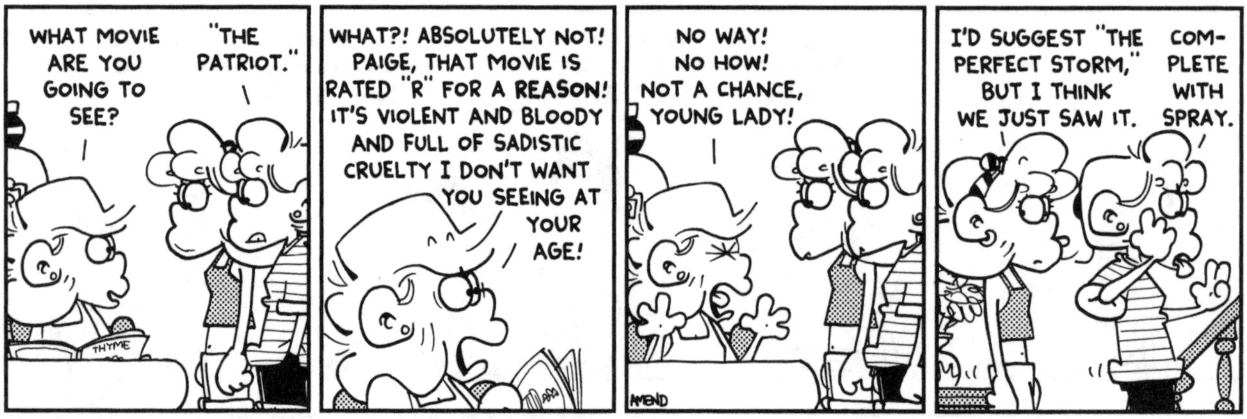
WHAT MOVIE ARE YOU GOING TO SEE?
"THE PATRIOT."
THYME
WHAT?! ABSOLUTELY NOT! PAIGE, THAT MOVIE IS RATED "R" FOR A **REASON**! IT'S VIOLENT AND BLOODY AND FULL OF SADISTIC CRUELTY I DON'T WANT YOU SEEING AT YOUR AGE!
NO WAY! NO HOW! NOT A CHANCE, YOUNG LADY!
I'D SUGGEST "THE PERFECT STORM," BUT I THINK WE JUST SAW IT.
COMPLETE WITH SPRAY.

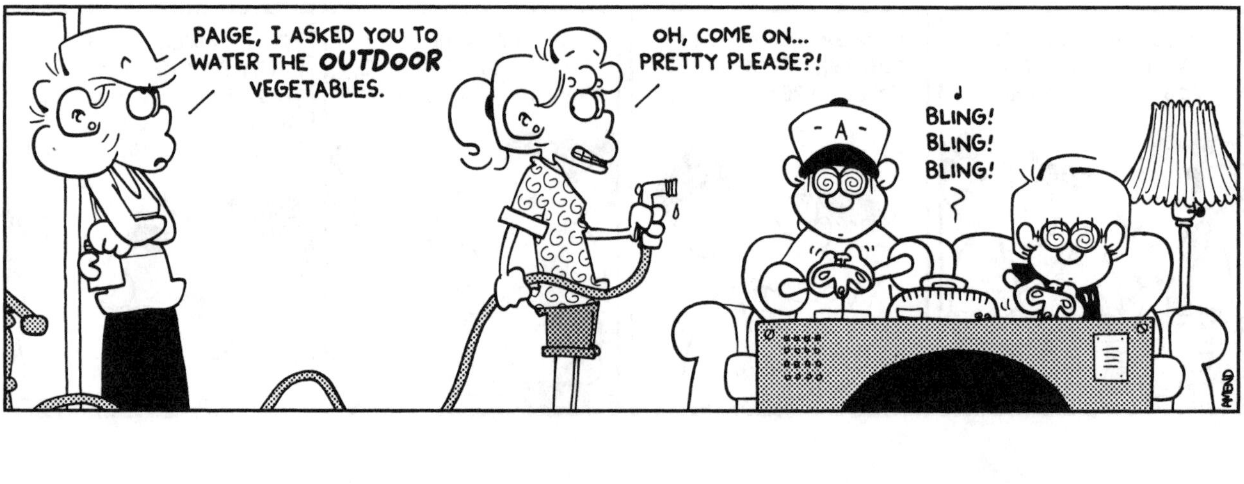
PAIGE, I ASKED YOU TO WATER THE ***OUTDOOR*** VEGETABLES.
OH, COME ON... PRETTY PLEASE?!
BLING! BLING! BLING!

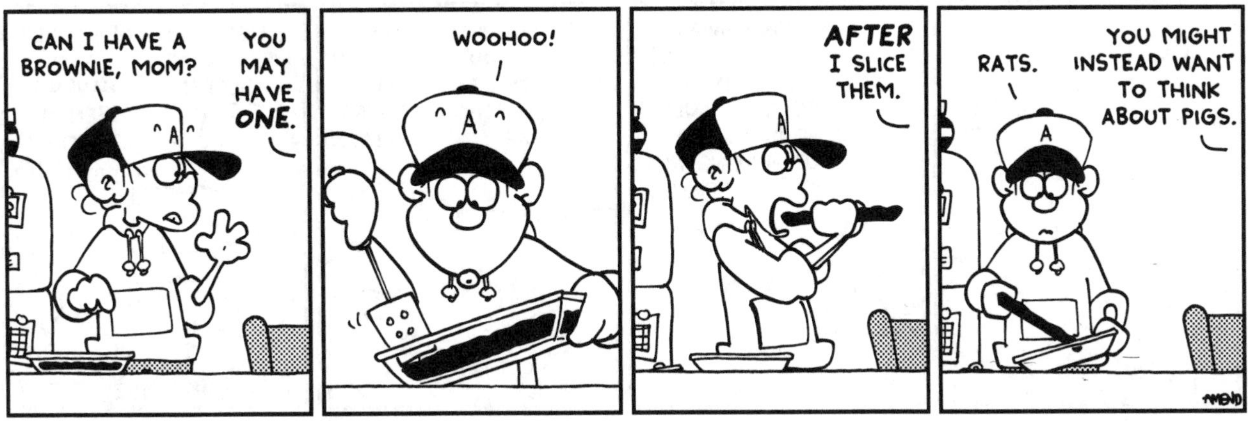
CAN I HAVE A BROWNIE, MOM?
YOU MAY HAVE **ONE**.
WOOHOO!
**AFTER** I SLICE THEM.
RATS.
YOU MIGHT INSTEAD WANT TO THINK ABOUT PIGS.
AMEND

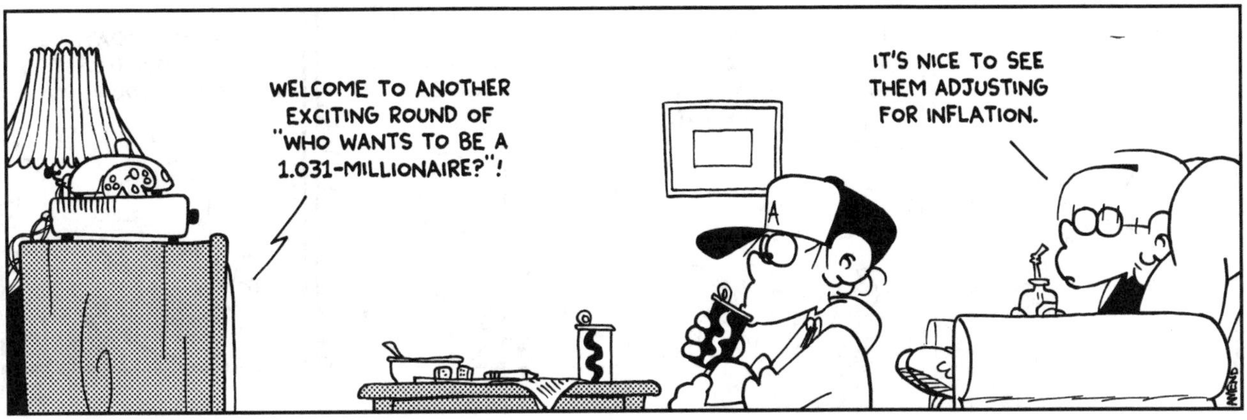
WELCOME TO ANOTHER EXCITING ROUND OF "WHO WANTS TO BE A 1.031-MILLIONAIRE?"!
IT'S NICE TO SEE THEM ADJUSTING FOR INFLATION.
AMEND

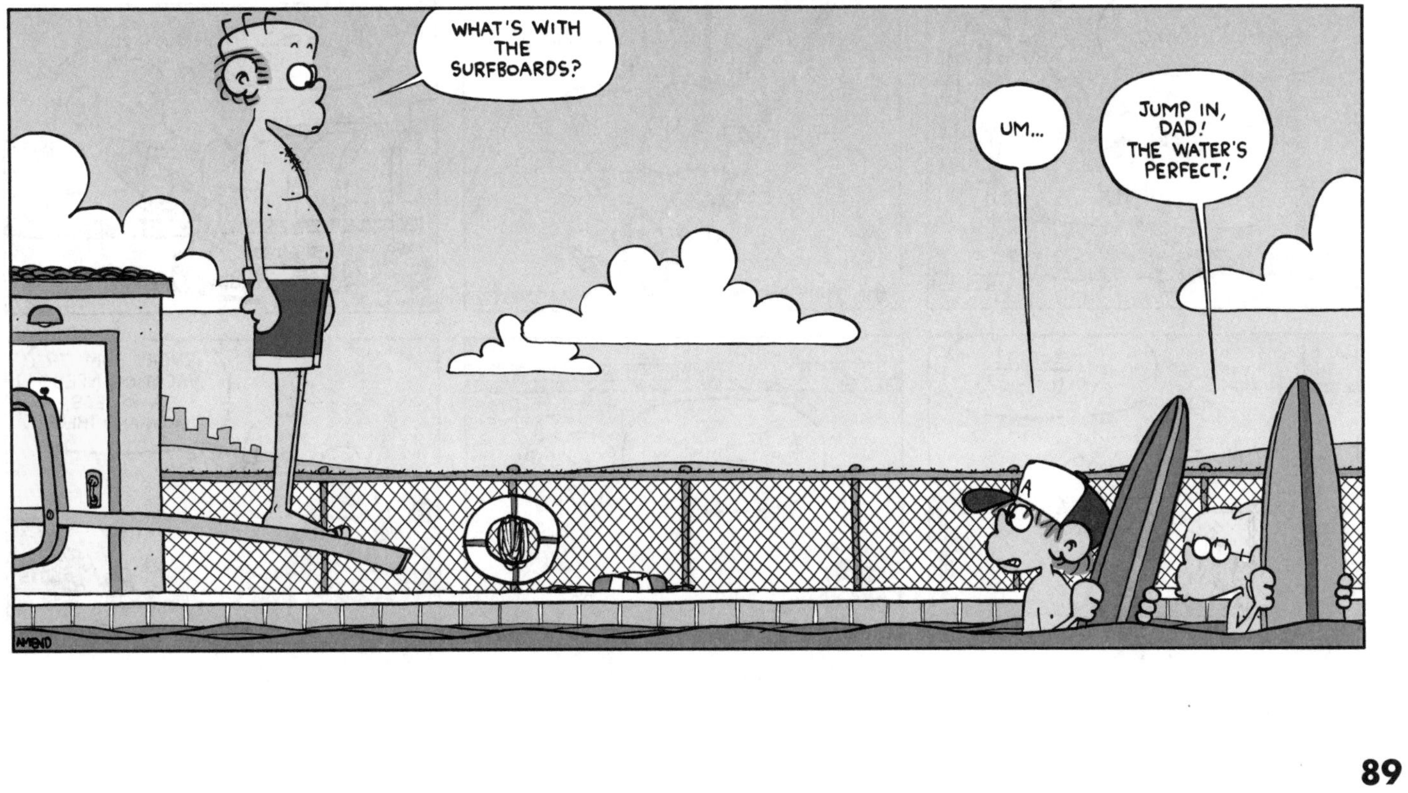
WHAT'S WITH THE SURFBOARDS?
UM...
JUMP IN, DAD! THE WATER'S PERFECT!
AMEND

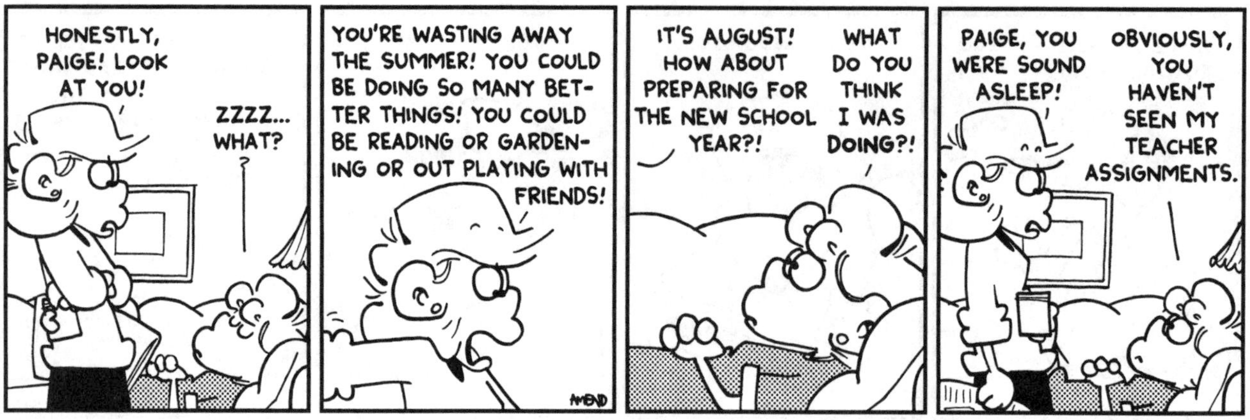
HONESTLY, PAIGE! LOOK AT YOU!
ZZZZ... WHAT?
YOU'RE WASTING AWAY THE SUMMER! YOU COULD BE DOING SO MANY BETTER THINGS! YOU COULD BE READING OR GARDENING OR OUT PLAYING WITH FRIENDS!
IT'S AUGUST! HOW ABOUT PREPARING FOR THE NEW SCHOOL YEAR?!
WHAT DO YOU THINK I WAS DOING?!
PAIGE, YOU WERE SOUND ASLEEP!
OBVIOUSLY, YOU HAVEN'T SEEN MY TEACHER ASSIGNMENTS.
AMEND

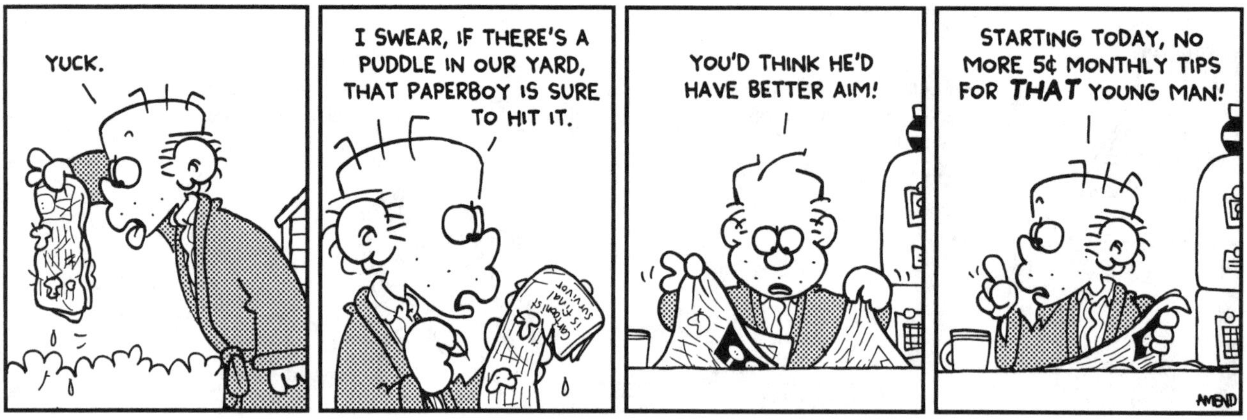
YUCK.
I SWEAR, IF THERE'S A PUDDLE IN OUR YARD, THAT PAPERBOY IS SURE TO HIT IT.
YOU'D THINK HE'D HAVE BETTER AIM!
STARTING TODAY, NO MORE 5¢ MONTHLY TIPS FOR **THAT** YOUNG MAN!
AMEND

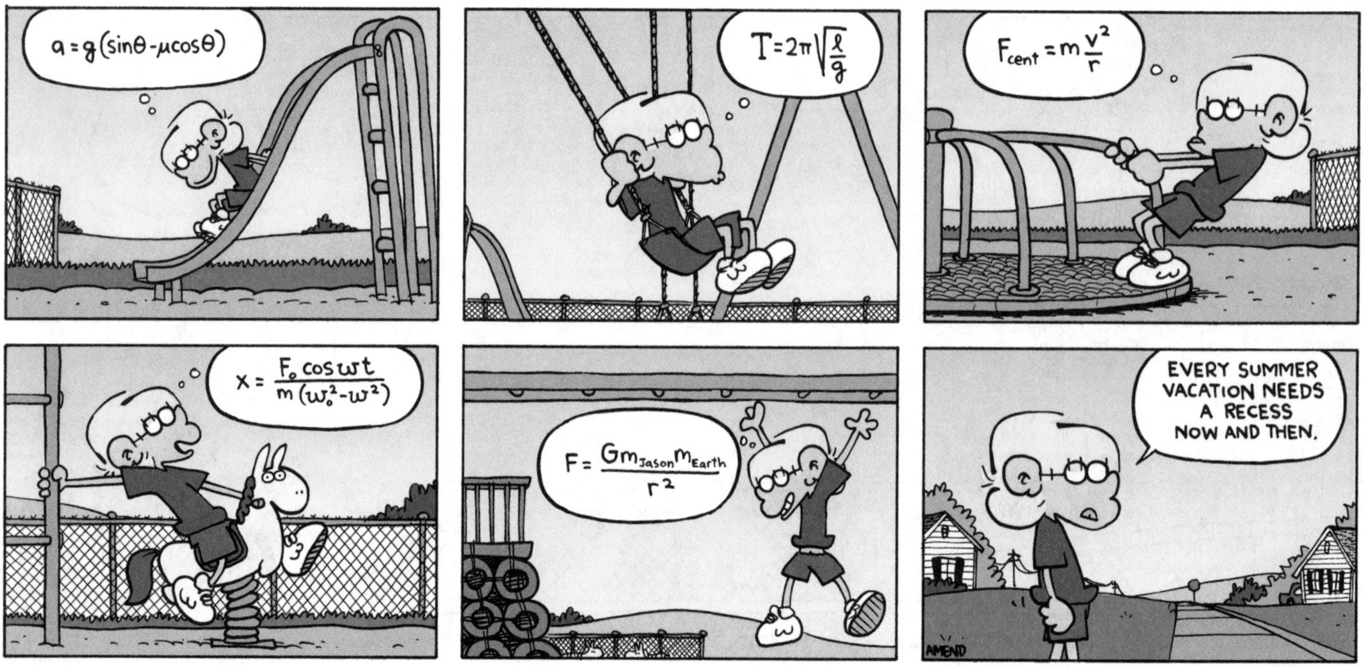
$a = g(\sin\theta - \mu\cos\theta)$
$T = 2\pi\sqrt{\frac{l}{g}}$
$F_{cent} = m\frac{v^2}{r}$
$x = \frac{F_0 \cos\omega t}{m(\omega_0^2 - \omega^2)}$
$F = \frac{G m_{Jason} m_{Earth}}{r^2}$
EVERY SUMMER VACATION NEEDS A RECESS NOW AND THEN.
AMEND

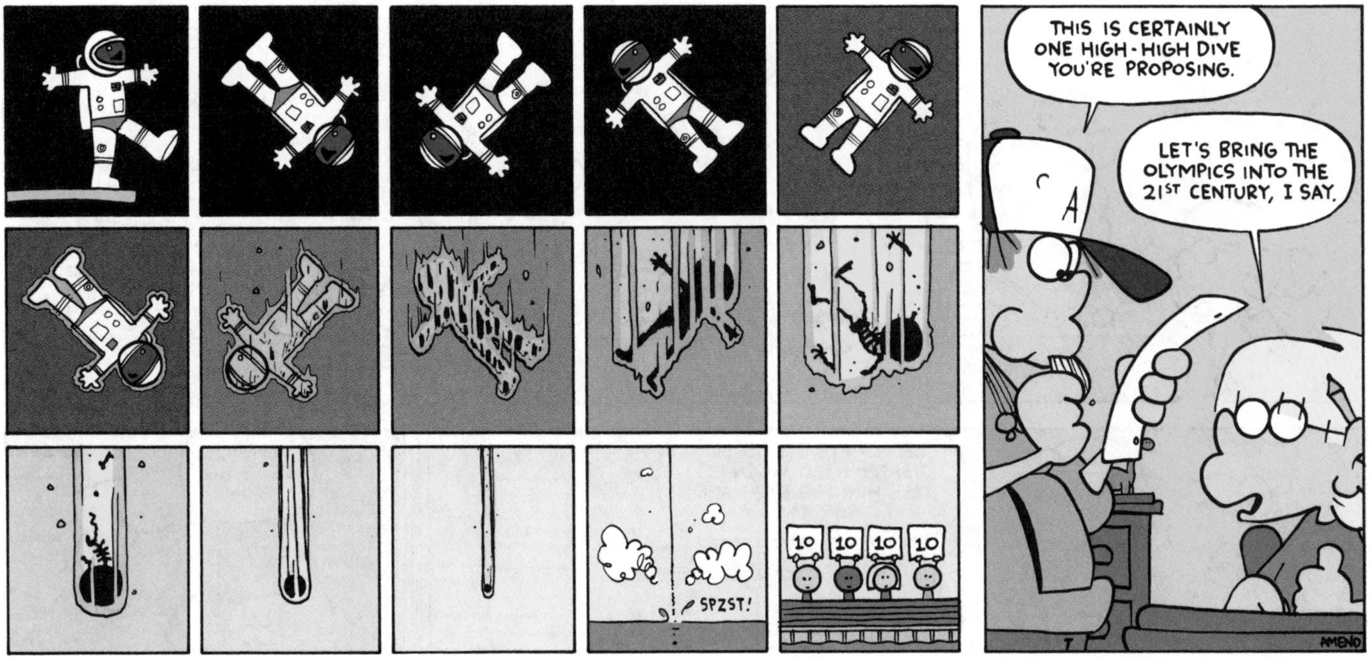
SPZST!
10 10 10 10
THIS IS CERTAINLY ONE HIGH-HIGH DIVE YOU'RE PROPOSING.
LET'S BRING THE OLYMPICS INTO THE 21ST CENTURY, I SAY.
AMEND

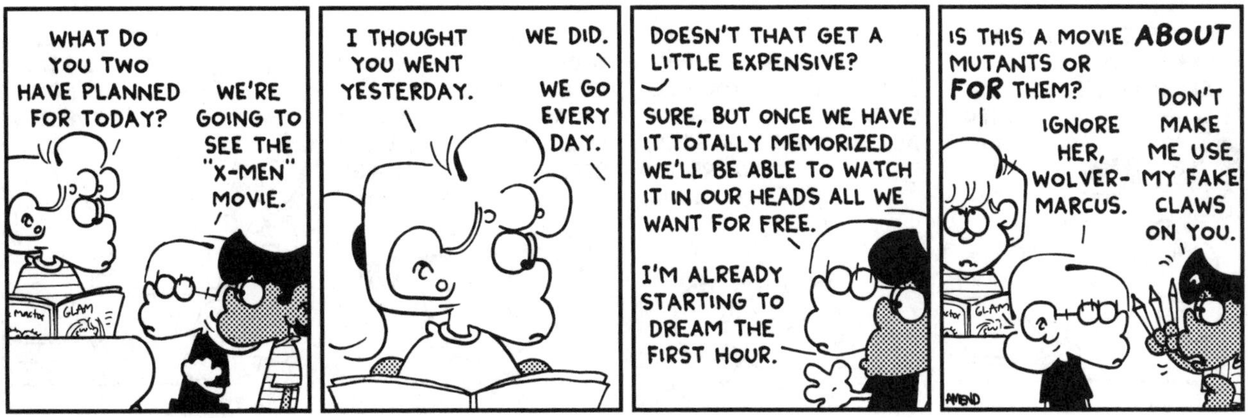
WHAT DO YOU TWO HAVE PLANNED FOR TODAY?
WE'RE GOING TO SEE THE "X-MEN" MOVIE.
I THOUGHT YOU WENT YESTERDAY.
WE DID.
WE GO EVERY DAY.
DOESN'T THAT GET A LITTLE EXPENSIVE?
SURE, BUT ONCE WE HAVE IT TOTALLY MEMORIZED WE'LL BE ABLE TO WATCH IT IN OUR HEADS ALL WE WANT FOR FREE.
I'M ALREADY STARTING TO DREAM THE FIRST HOUR.
IS THIS A MOVIE ABOUT MUTANTS OR FOR THEM?
IGNORE HER, WOLVER-MARCUS.
DON'T MAKE ME USE MY FAKE CLAWS ON YOU.
AMEND

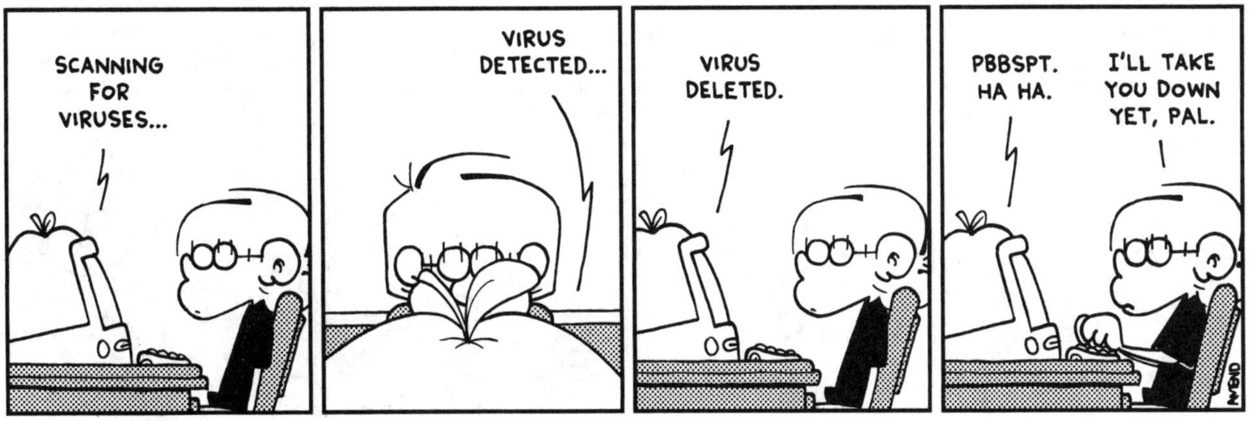
SCANNING FOR VIRUSES...
VIRUS DETECTED...
VIRUS DELETED.
PBBSPT. HA HA.
I'LL TAKE YOU DOWN YET, PAL.
AMEND

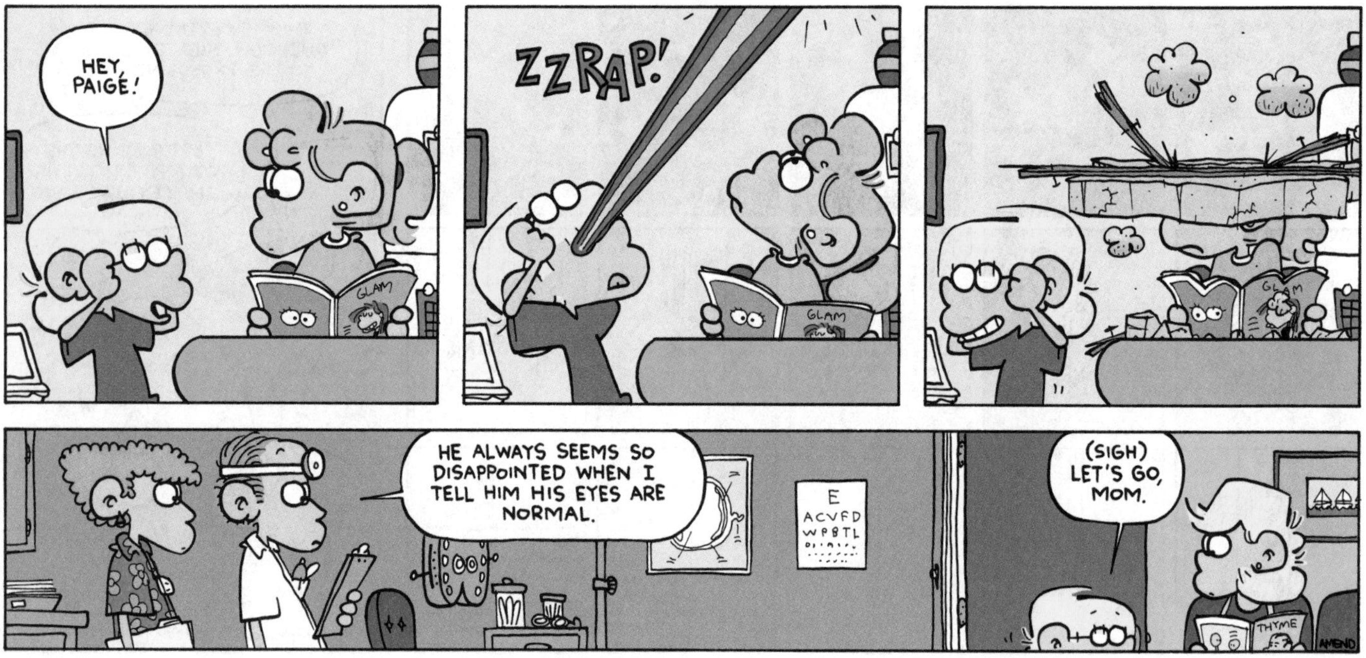

HEY, PAIGE!
ZZRAP!
HE ALWAYS SEEMS SO DISAPPOINTED WHEN I TELL HIM HIS EYES ARE NORMAL.
(SIGH) LET'S GO, MOM.


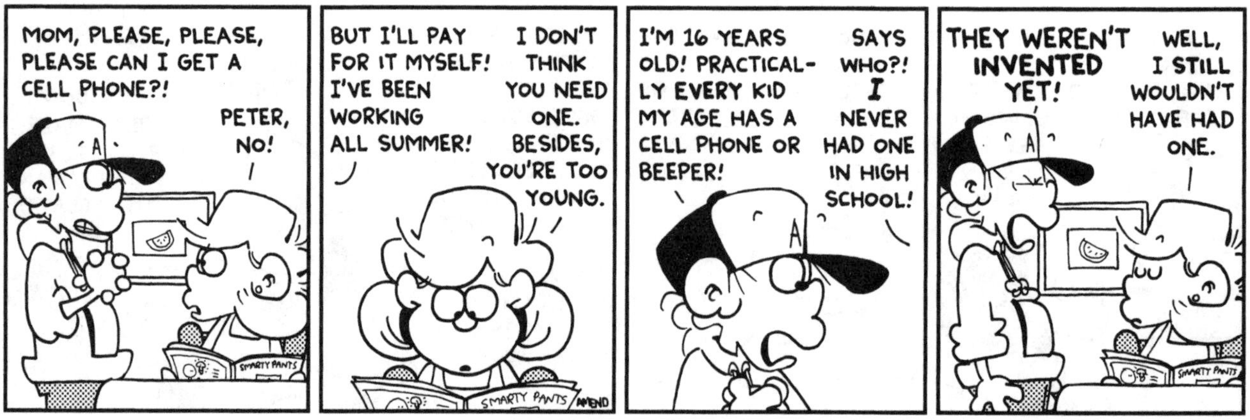

MOM, PLEASE, PLEASE, PLEASE CAN I GET A CELL PHONE?!
PETER, NO!
BUT I'LL PAY FOR IT MYSELF! I'VE BEEN WORKING ALL SUMMER!
I DON'T THINK YOU NEED ONE. BESIDES, YOU'RE TOO YOUNG.
I'M 16 YEARS OLD! PRACTICAL-LY EVERY KID MY AGE HAS A CELL PHONE OR BEEPER!
SAYS WHO?! I NEVER HAD ONE IN HIGH SCHOOL!
THEY WEREN'T INVENTED YET!
WELL, I STILL WOULDN'T HAVE HAD ONE.


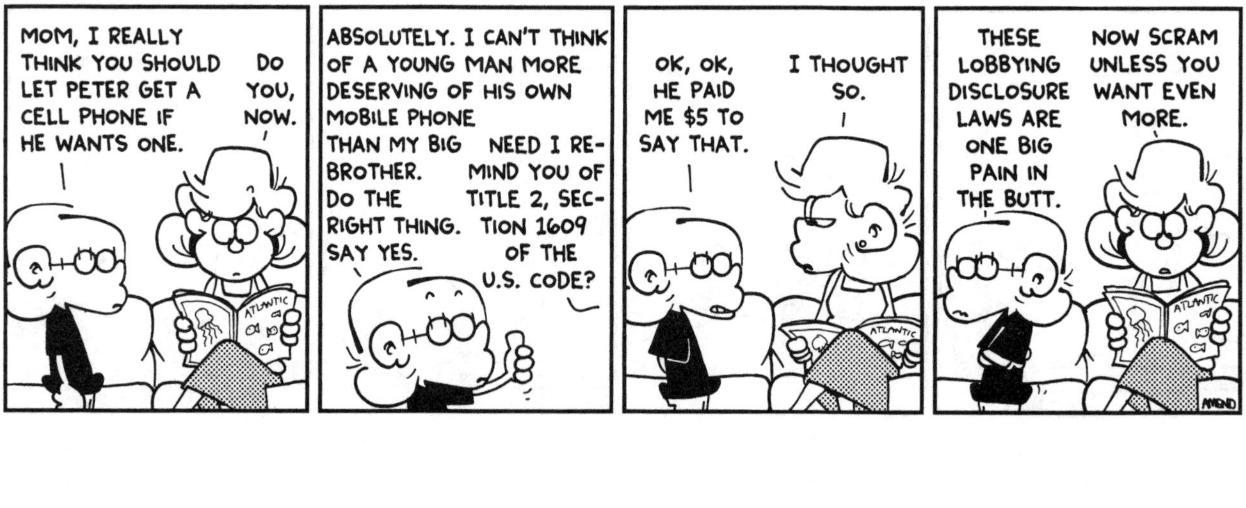

MOM, I REALLY THINK YOU SHOULD LET PETER GET A CELL PHONE IF HE WANTS ONE.
DO YOU, NOW.
ABSOLUTELY. I CAN'T THINK OF A YOUNG MAN MORE DESERVING OF HIS OWN MOBILE PHONE THAN MY BIG BROTHER. DO THE RIGHT THING. SAY YES.
NEED I RE-MIND YOU OF TITLE 2, SEC-TION 1609 OF THE U.S. CODE?
OK, OK, HE PAID ME $5 TO SAY THAT.
I THOUGHT SO.
THESE LOBBYING DISCLOSURE LAWS ARE ONE BIG PAIN IN THE BUTT.
NOW SCRAM UNLESS YOU WANT EVEN MORE.

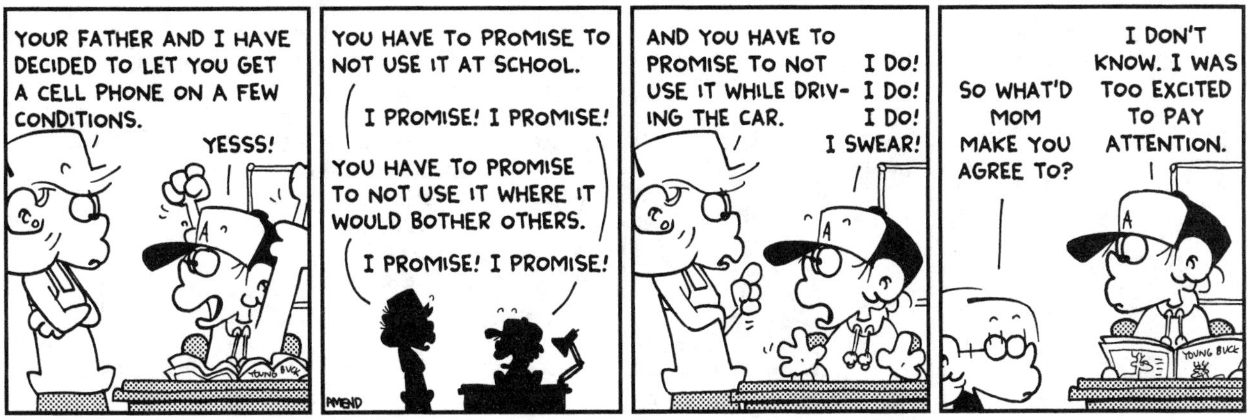
YOUR FATHER AND I HAVE DECIDED TO LET YOU GET A CELL PHONE ON A FEW CONDITIONS.
YESSS!
YOU HAVE TO PROMISE TO NOT USE IT AT SCHOOL.
I PROMISE! I PROMISE!
YOU HAVE TO PROMISE TO NOT USE IT WHERE IT WOULD BOTHER OTHERS.
I PROMISE! I PROMISE!
AND YOU HAVE TO PROMISE TO NOT USE IT WHILE DRIVING THE CAR.
I DO! I DO! I DO! I SWEAR!
SO WHAT'D MOM MAKE YOU AGREE TO?
I DON'T KNOW. I WAS TOO EXCITED TO PAY ATTENTION.

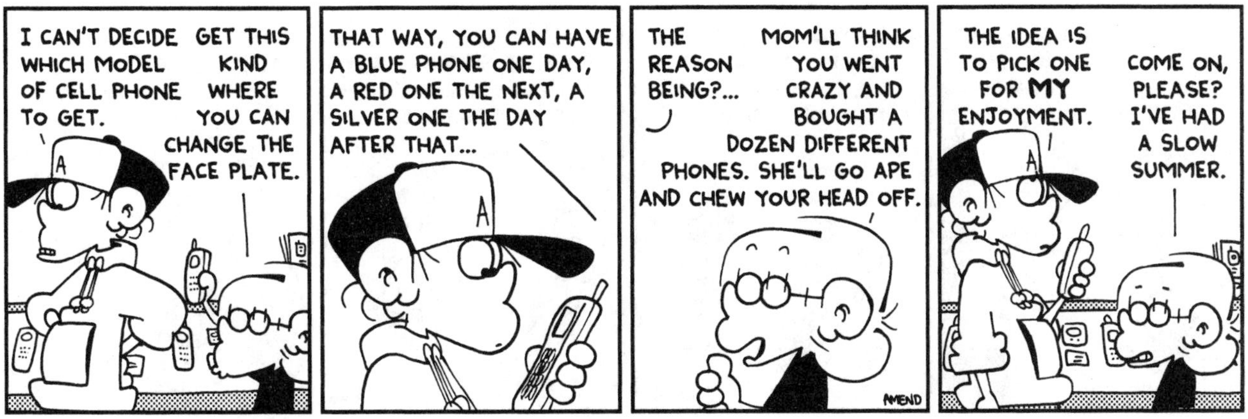
I CAN'T DECIDE WHICH MODEL OF CELL PHONE TO GET.
GET THIS KIND WHERE YOU CAN CHANGE THE FACE PLATE.
THAT WAY, YOU CAN HAVE A BLUE PHONE ONE DAY, A RED ONE THE NEXT, A SILVER ONE THE DAY AFTER THAT...
THE REASON BEING?...
MOM'LL THINK YOU WENT CRAZY AND BOUGHT A DOZEN DIFFERENT PHONES. SHE'LL GO APE AND CHEW YOUR HEAD OFF.
THE IDEA IS TO PICK ONE FOR **MY** ENJOYMENT.
COME ON, PLEASE? I'VE HAD A SLOW SUMMER.

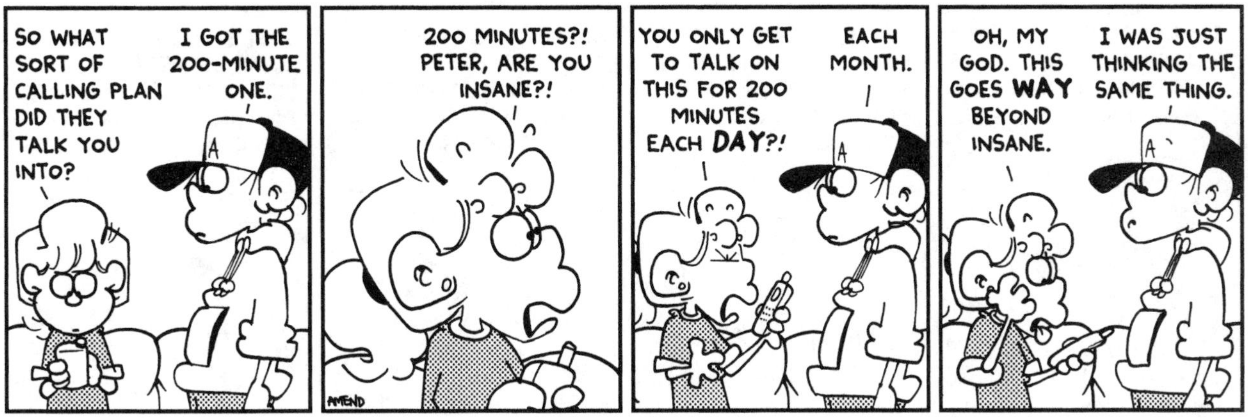
SO WHAT SORT OF CALLING PLAN DID THEY TALK YOU INTO?
I GOT THE 200-MINUTE ONE.
200 MINUTES?! PETER, ARE YOU INSANE?!
YOU ONLY GET TO TALK ON THIS FOR 200 MINUTES EACH **DAY**?!
EACH MONTH.
OH, MY GOD. THIS GOES **WAY** BEYOND INSANE.
I WAS JUST THINKING THE SAME THING.

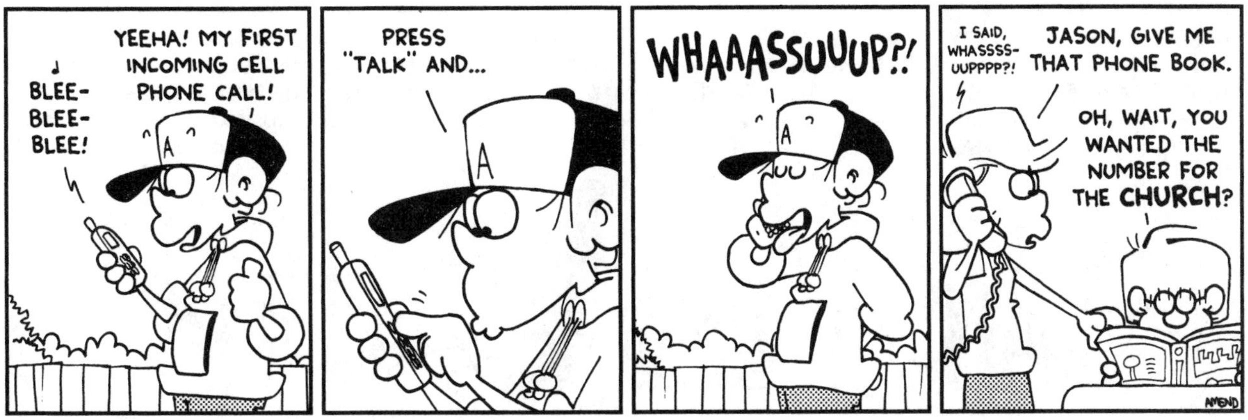
BLEE-BLEE-BLEE!
YEEHA! MY FIRST INCOMING CELL PHONE CALL!
PRESS "TALK" AND...
WHAAASSUUUP?!
I SAID, WHASSSS-UUPPPP?!
JASON, GIVE ME THAT PHONE BOOK.
OH, WAIT, YOU WANTED THE NUMBER FOR THE **CHURCH**?

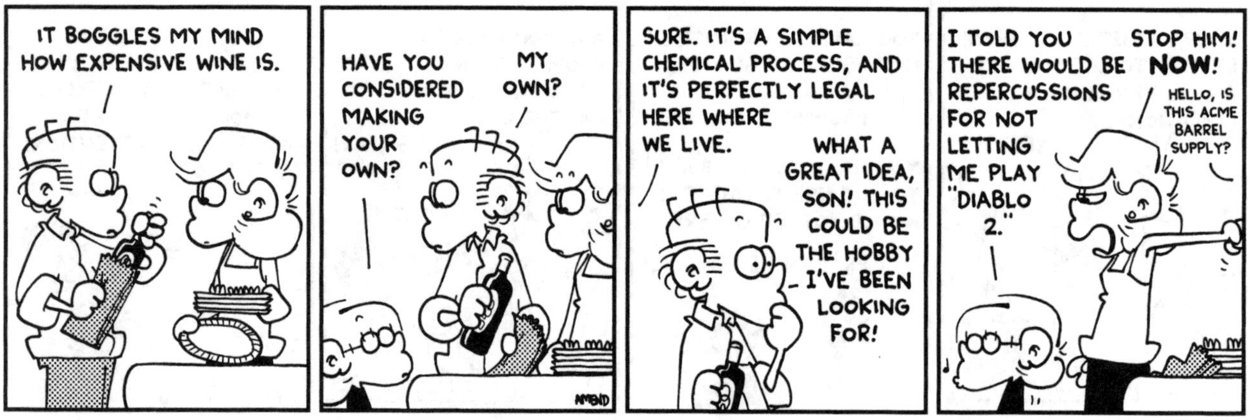
IT BOGGLES MY MIND HOW EXPENSIVE WINE IS.
HAVE YOU CONSIDERED MAKING YOUR OWN?
MY OWN?
SURE. IT'S A SIMPLE CHEMICAL PROCESS, AND IT'S PERFECTLY LEGAL HERE WHERE WE LIVE.
WHAT A GREAT IDEA, SON! THIS COULD BE THE HOBBY I'VE BEEN LOOKING FOR!
I TOLD YOU THERE WOULD BE REPERCUSSIONS FOR NOT LETTING ME PLAY "DIABLO 2."
STOP HIM! NOW!
HELLO, IS THIS ACME BARREL SUPPLY?
AMEND

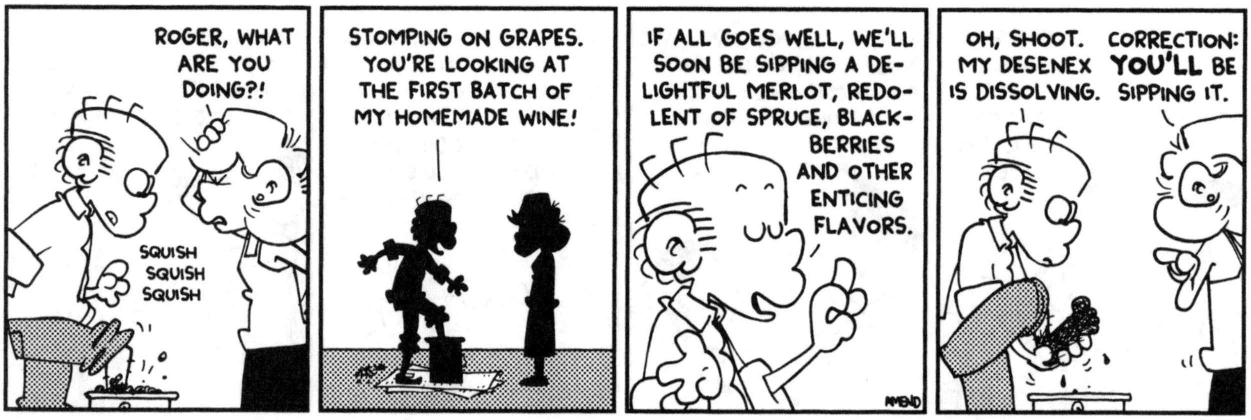
ROGER, WHAT ARE YOU DOING?!
SQUISH SQUISH SQUISH
STOMPING ON GRAPES. YOU'RE LOOKING AT THE FIRST BATCH OF MY HOMEMADE WINE!
IF ALL GOES WELL, WE'LL SOON BE SIPPING A DELIGHTFUL MERLOT, REDOLENT OF SPRUCE, BLACKBERRIES AND OTHER ENTICING FLAVORS.
OH, SHOOT. MY DESENEX IS DISSOLVING.
CORRECTION: YOU'LL BE SIPPING IT.
AMEND

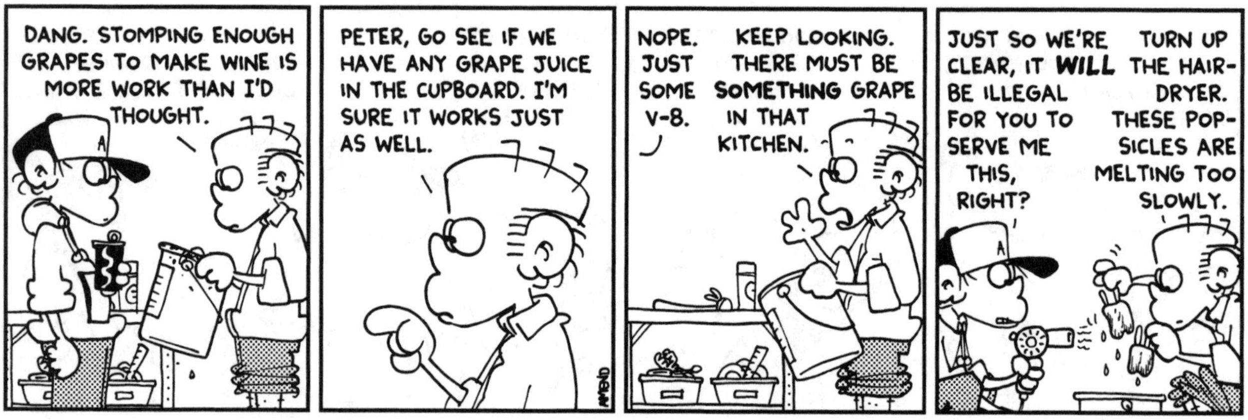
DANG. STOMPING ENOUGH GRAPES TO MAKE WINE IS MORE WORK THAN I'D THOUGHT.
PETER, GO SEE IF WE HAVE ANY GRAPE JUICE IN THE CUPBOARD. I'M SURE IT WORKS JUST AS WELL.
NOPE. JUST SOME V-8.
KEEP LOOKING. THERE MUST BE SOMETHING GRAPE IN THAT KITCHEN.
JUST SO WE'RE CLEAR, IT WILL BE ILLEGAL FOR YOU TO SERVE ME THIS, RIGHT?
TURN UP THE HAIR-DRYER. THESE POPSICLES ARE MELTING TOO SLOWLY.
AMEND

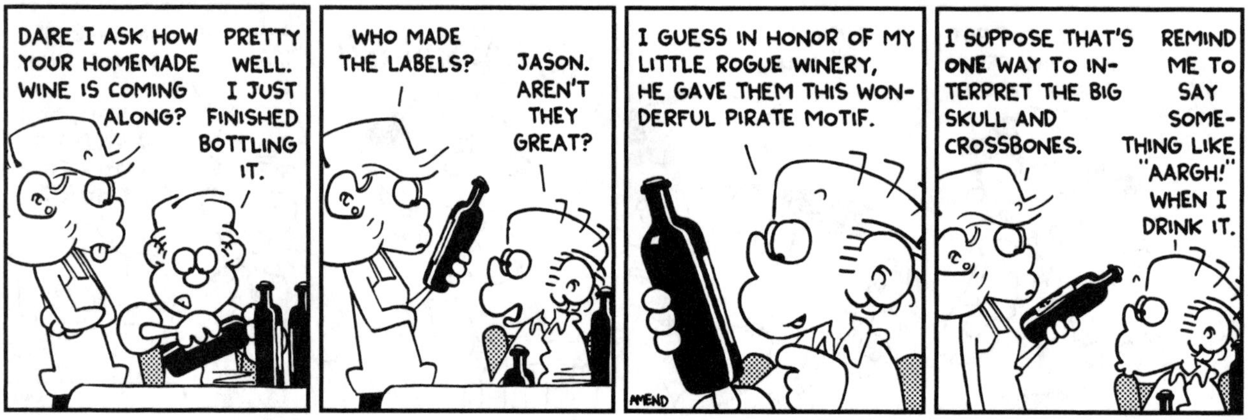
DARE I ASK HOW YOUR HOMEMADE WINE IS COMING ALONG?
PRETTY WELL. I JUST FINISHED BOTTLING IT.
WHO MADE THE LABELS?
JASON. AREN'T THEY GREAT?
I GUESS IN HONOR OF MY LITTLE ROGUE WINERY, HE GAVE THEM THIS WONDERFUL PIRATE MOTIF.
I SUPPOSE THAT'S ONE WAY TO INTERPRET THE BIG SKULL AND CROSSBONES.
REMIND ME TO SAY SOMETHING LIKE "AARGH!" WHEN I DRINK IT.
AMEND

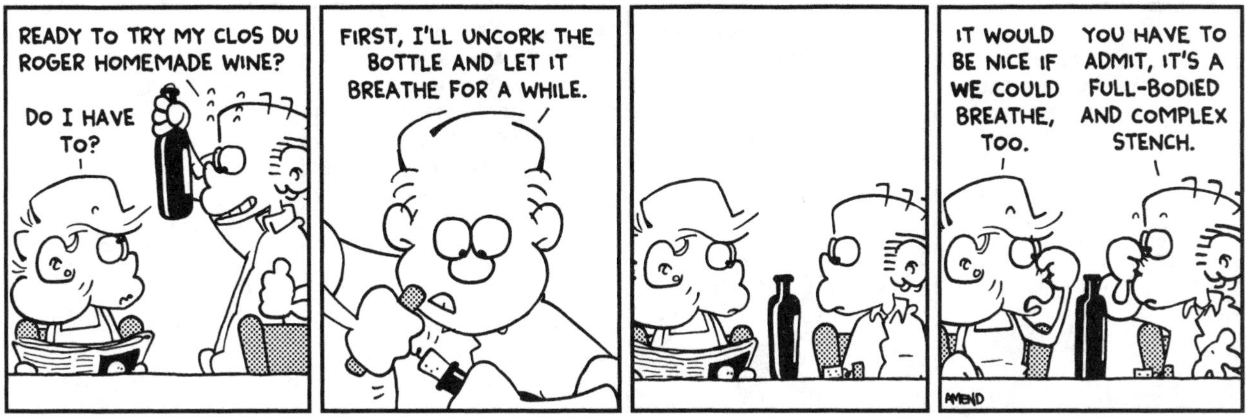
READY TO TRY MY CLOS DU ROGER HOMEMADE WINE?
DO I HAVE TO?
FIRST, I'LL UNCORK THE BOTTLE AND LET IT BREATHE FOR A WHILE.
IT WOULD BE NICE IF WE COULD BREATHE, TOO.
YOU HAVE TO ADMIT, IT'S A FULL-BODIED AND COMPLEX STENCH.
AMEND

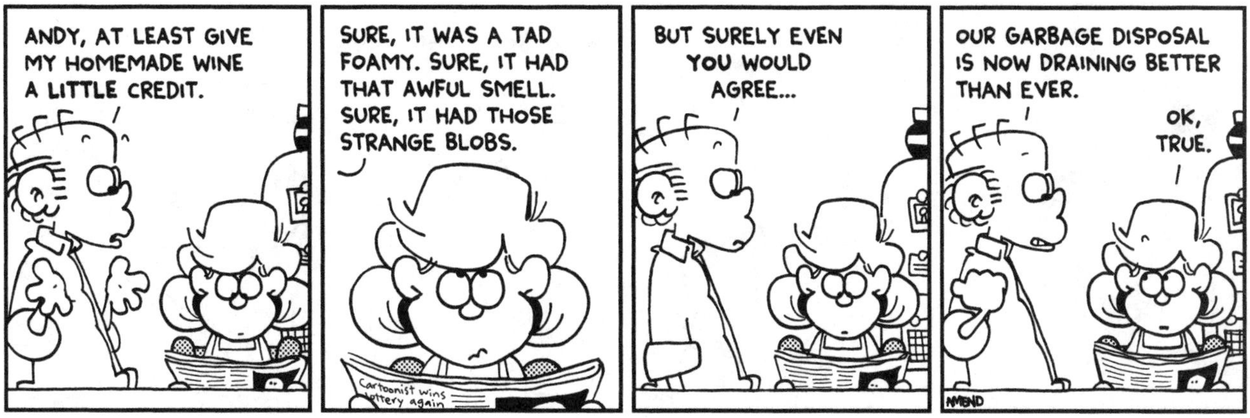
ANDY, AT LEAST GIVE MY HOMEMADE WINE A LITTLE CREDIT.
SURE, IT WAS A TAD FOAMY. SURE, IT HAD THAT AWFUL SMELL. SURE, IT HAD THOSE STRANGE BLOBS.
Cartoonist wins lottery again
BUT SURELY EVEN YOU WOULD AGREE...
OUR GARBAGE DISPOSAL IS NOW DRAINING BETTER THAN EVER.
OK, TRUE.
AMEND

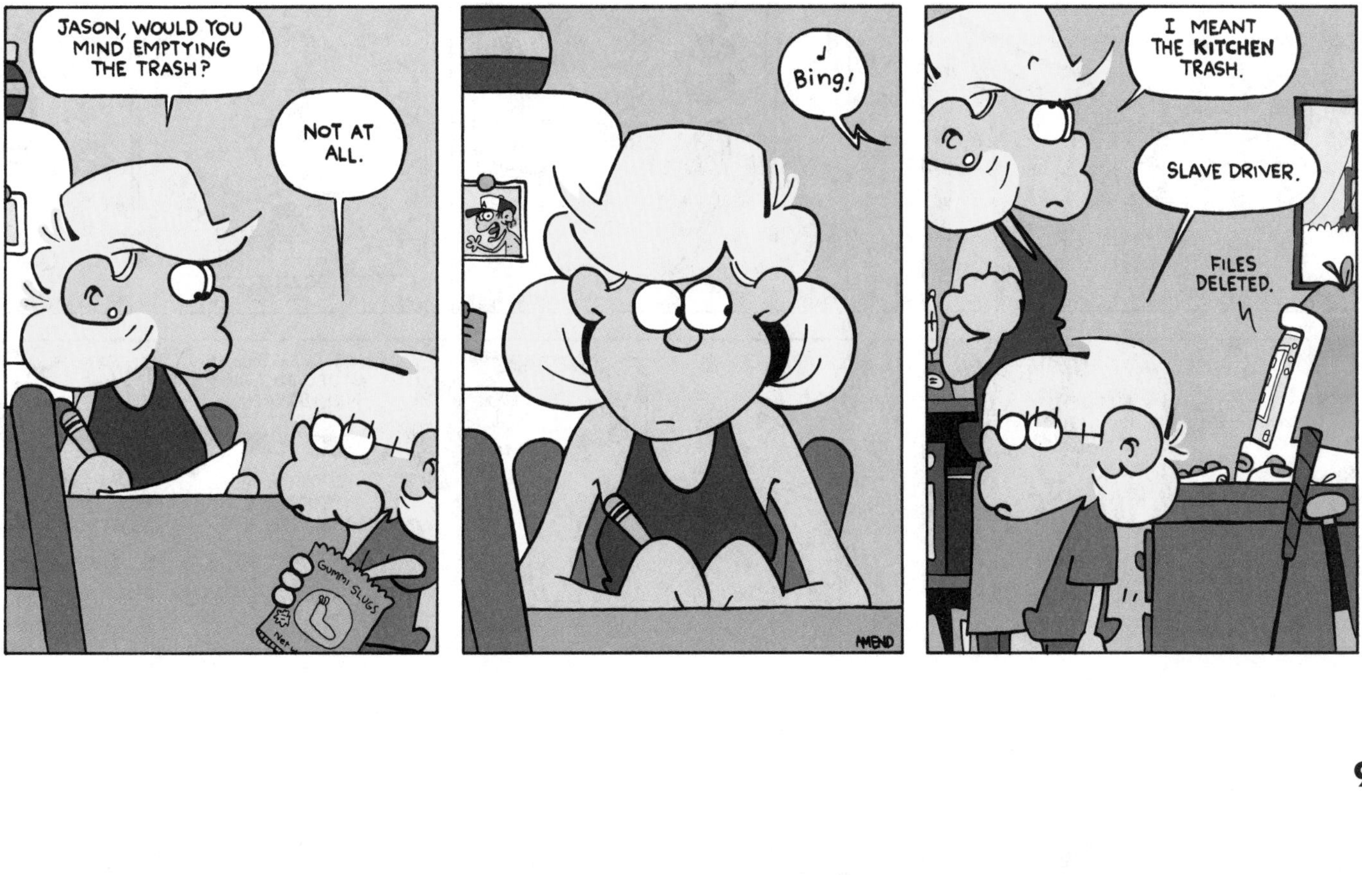
JASON, WOULD YOU MIND EMPTYING THE TRASH?
NOT AT ALL.
GUMMI SLUGS
Bing!
AMEND
I MEANT THE KITCHEN TRASH.
SLAVE DRIVER.
FILES DELETED.

 MOM! YOU PUT MY CLEAN SHIRTS AWAY WRONG!

 YOU **KNOW** I LIKE THEM PILED IN ORDER! YOU PUT MY "DEEP SPACE NINE" SHIRT AFTER MY "VOYAGER" SHIRT, WHEN ANY FOOL COULD TELL YOU "DS9" COMES FIRST!

 AND WHAT'S THIS "PHANTOM MENACE" SHIRT DOING IN HERE?! IT SHOULD BE IN MY LUCASFILM DRAWER! NEXT TIME YOU DO THE LAUNDRY, PUT MY CLOTHES WHERE THEY BELONG!

I SORTA SHOULDA SEEN THAT COMING.

 Bee Bee Boop Beep Bee Bee Boop

 Beep Bee Bee Boop Beep Bee Bee Boop Beep Bee Bee Boop Beep Bee Bee Boop Beep

 Beee Beee Beeeeeee

 CHECK IT OUT— I'M PLAYING LED ZEPPELIN!

THIS WOULD EXPLAIN OUR LAST PHONE BILL.

 PAIGE SURE SEEMS GLUED TO THAT FIRE BREATHER.

I THINK HER BODY HAS CARAMELIZED.

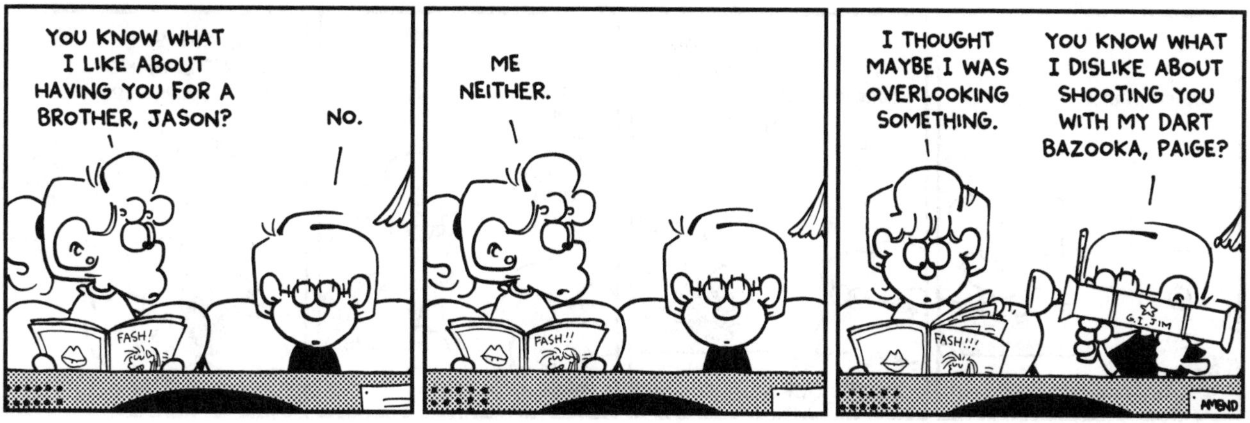
YOU KNOW WHAT I LIKE ABOUT HAVING YOU FOR A BROTHER, JASON?
NO.
ME NEITHER.
I THOUGHT MAYBE I WAS OVERLOOKING SOMETHING.
YOU KNOW WHAT I DISLIKE ABOUT SHOOTING YOU WITH MY DART BAZOOKA, PAIGE?
AMEND

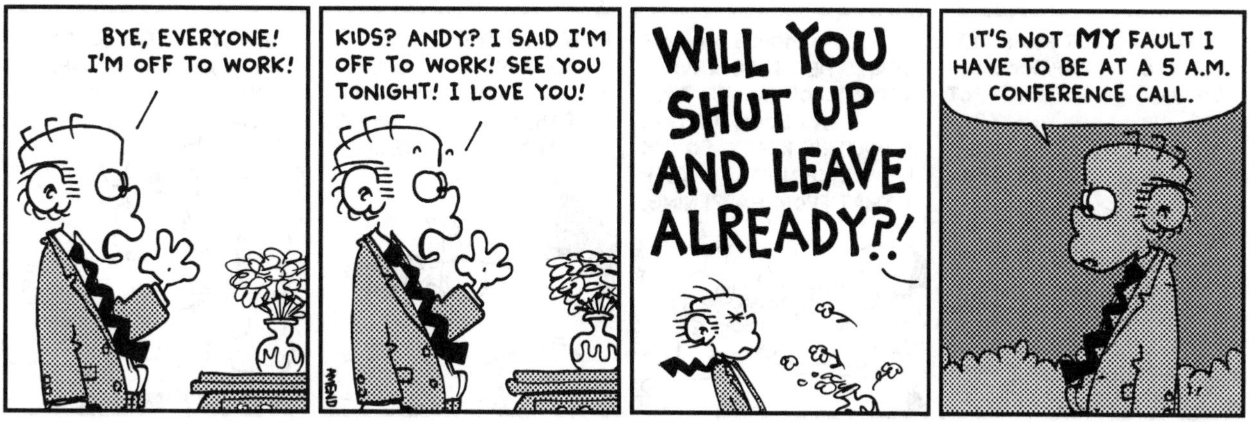
BYE, EVERYONE! I'M OFF TO WORK!
KIDS? ANDY? I SAID I'M OFF TO WORK! SEE YOU TONIGHT! I LOVE YOU!
AMEND
WILL YOU SHUT UP AND LEAVE ALREADY?!
IT'S NOT **MY** FAULT I HAVE TO BE AT A 5 A.M. CONFERENCE CALL.

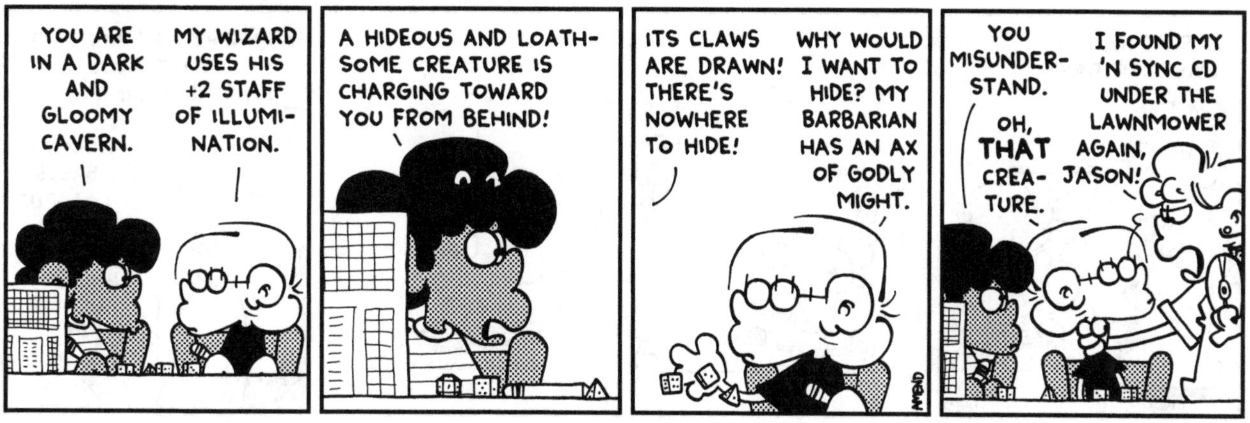
YOU ARE IN A DARK AND GLOOMY CAVERN.
MY WIZARD USES HIS +2 STAFF OF ILLUMINATION.
A HIDEOUS AND LOATHSOME CREATURE IS CHARGING TOWARD YOU FROM BEHIND!
ITS CLAWS ARE DRAWN! THERE'S NOWHERE TO HIDE!
WHY WOULD I WANT TO HIDE? MY BARBARIAN HAS AN AX OF GODLY MIGHT.
AMEND
YOU MISUNDERSTAND.
I FOUND MY 'N SYNC CD UNDER THE LAWNMOWER AGAIN, JASON!
OH, **THAT** CREATURE.

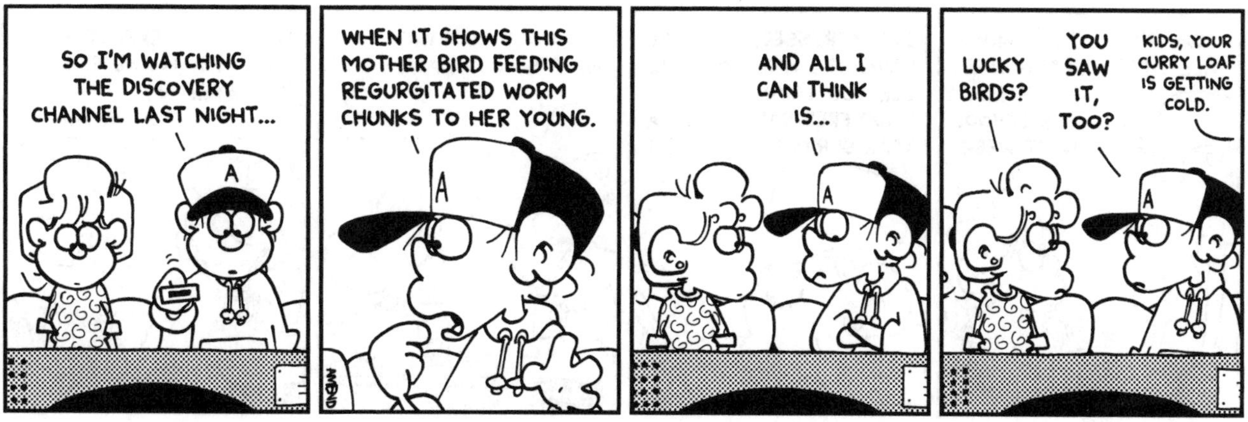
SO I'M WATCHING THE DISCOVERY CHANNEL LAST NIGHT...
WHEN IT SHOWS THIS MOTHER BIRD FEEDING REGURGITATED WORM CHUNKS TO HER YOUNG.
AMEND
AND ALL I CAN THINK IS...
LUCKY BIRDS?
YOU SAW IT, TOO?
KIDS, YOUR CURRY LOAF IS GETTING COLD.

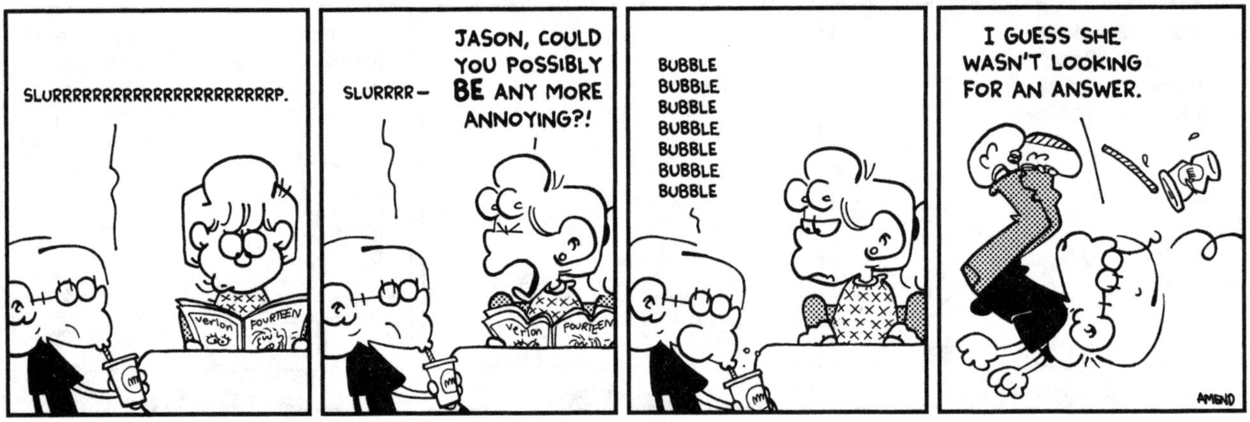
SLURRRRRRRRRRRRRRRRRRRRRP.
SLURRRR–
JASON, COULD YOU POSSIBLY BE ANY MORE ANNOYING?!
BUBBLE BUBBLE BUBBLE BUBBLE BUBBLE BUBBLE BUBBLE
I GUESS SHE WASN'T LOOKING FOR AN ANSWER.
AMEND

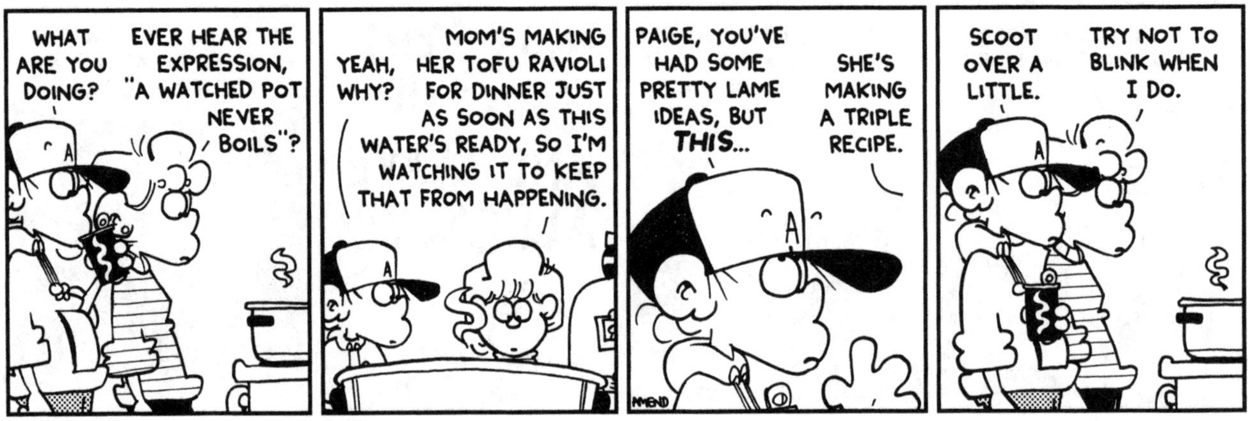
WHAT ARE YOU DOING?
EVER HEAR THE EXPRESSION, "A WATCHED POT NEVER BOILS"?
YEAH, WHY?
MOM'S MAKING HER TOFU RAVIOLI FOR DINNER JUST AS SOON AS THIS WATER'S READY, SO I'M WATCHING IT TO KEEP THAT FROM HAPPENING.
PAIGE, YOU'VE HAD SOME PRETTY LAME IDEAS, BUT THIS...
SHE'S MAKING A TRIPLE RECIPE.
AMEND
SCOOT OVER A LITTLE.
TRY NOT TO BLINK WHEN I DO.

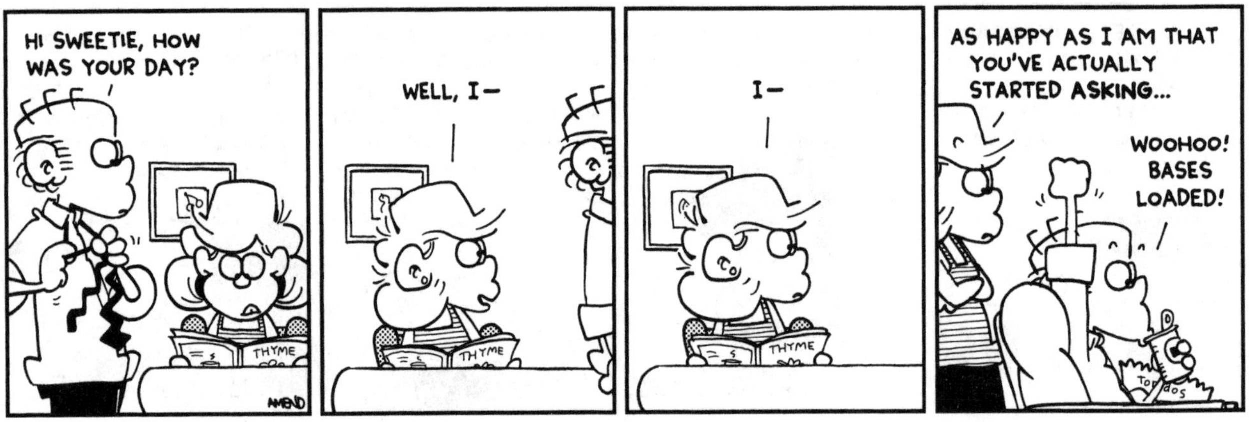
HI SWEETIE, HOW WAS YOUR DAY?
THYME
AMEND
WELL, I–
I–
AS HAPPY AS I AM THAT YOU'VE ACTUALLY STARTED ASKING...
WOOHOO! BASES LOADED!

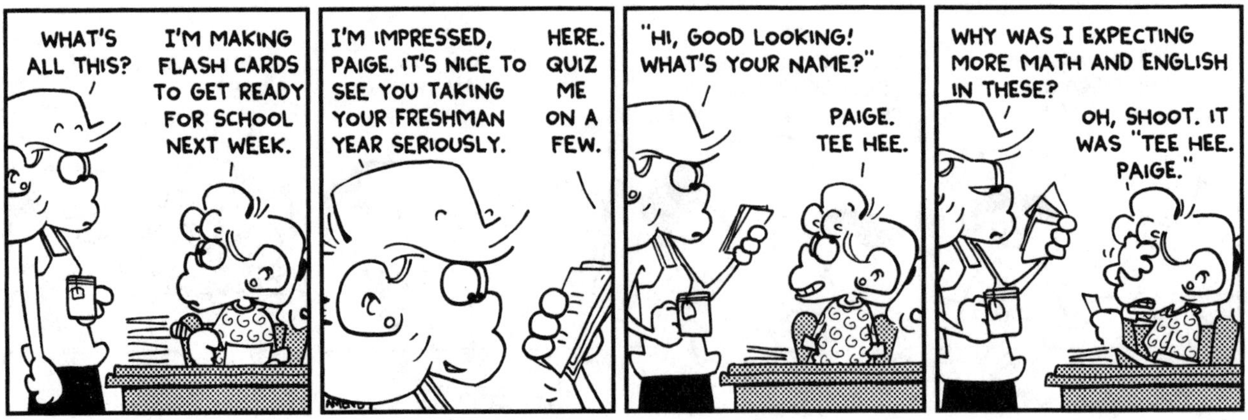
WHAT'S ALL THIS?
I'M MAKING FLASH CARDS TO GET READY FOR SCHOOL NEXT WEEK.
I'M IMPRESSED, PAIGE. IT'S NICE TO SEE YOU TAKING YOUR FRESHMAN YEAR SERIOUSLY.
HERE. QUIZ ME ON A FEW.
"HI, GOOD LOOKING! WHAT'S YOUR NAME?"
PAIGE. TEE HEE.
WHY WAS I EXPECTING MORE MATH AND ENGLISH IN THESE?
OH, SHOOT. IT WAS "TEE HEE. PAIGE."

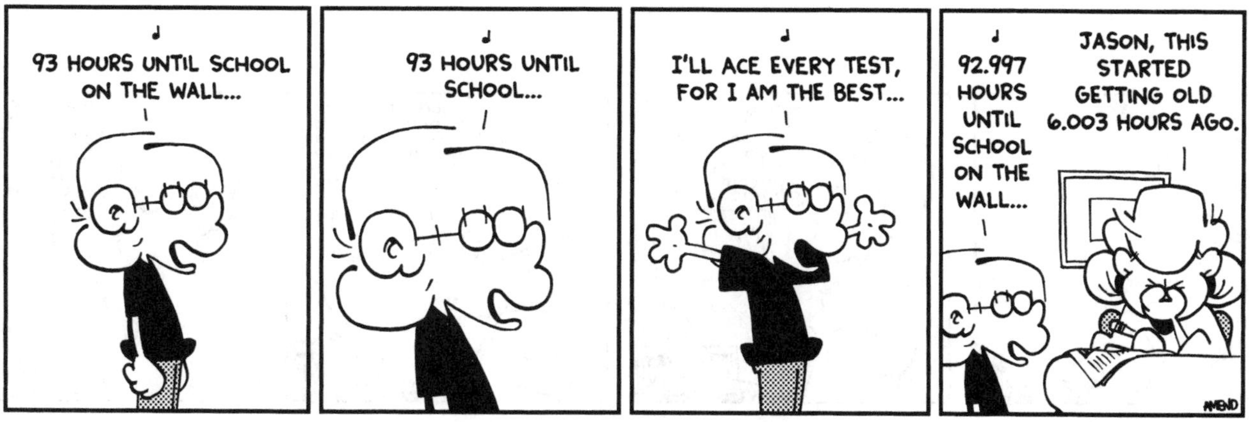
93 HOURS UNTIL SCHOOL ON THE WALL...
93 HOURS UNTIL SCHOOL...
I'LL ACE EVERY TEST, FOR I AM THE BEST...
92.997 HOURS UNTIL SCHOOL ON THE WALL...
JASON, THIS STARTED GETTING OLD 6.003 HOURS AGO.
AMEND

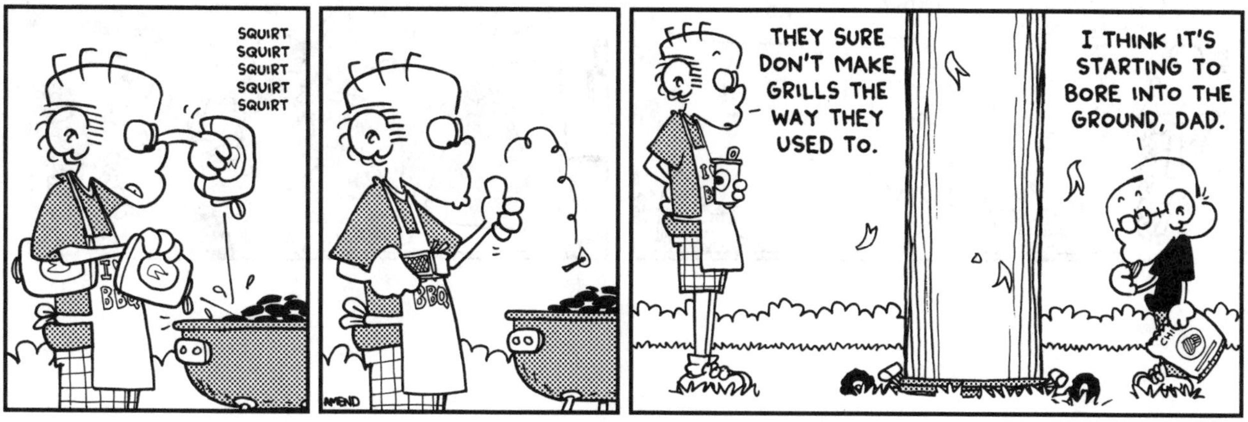
SQUIRT SQUIRT SQUIRT SQUIRT SQUIRT
I BBQ
AMEND
THEY SURE DON'T MAKE GRILLS THE WAY THEY USED TO.
I THINK IT'S STARTING TO BORE INTO THE GROUND, DAD.

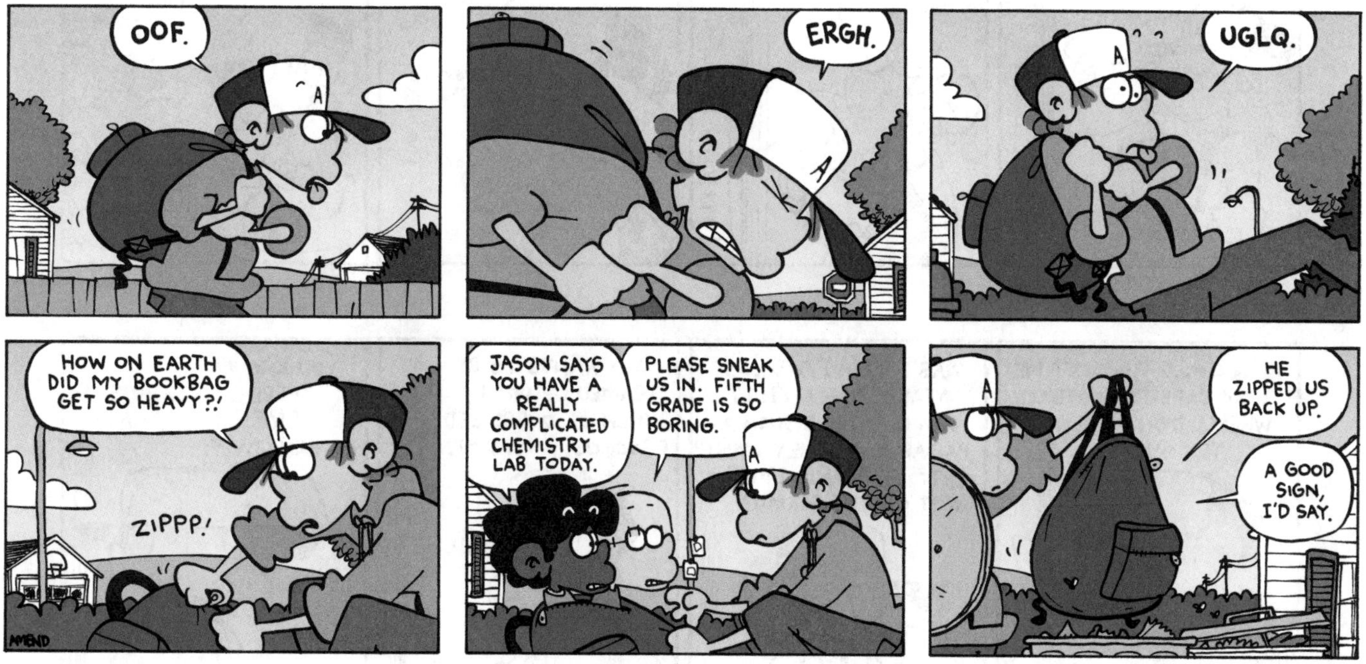
OOF.
ERGH.
UGLQ.
HOW ON EARTH DID MY BOOKBAG GET SO HEAVY?!
ZIPPP!
AMEND
JASON SAYS YOU HAVE A REALLY COMPLICATED CHEMISTRY LAB TODAY.
PLEASE SNEAK US IN. FIFTH GRADE IS SO BORING.
HE ZIPPED US BACK UP.
A GOOD SIGN, I'D SAY.

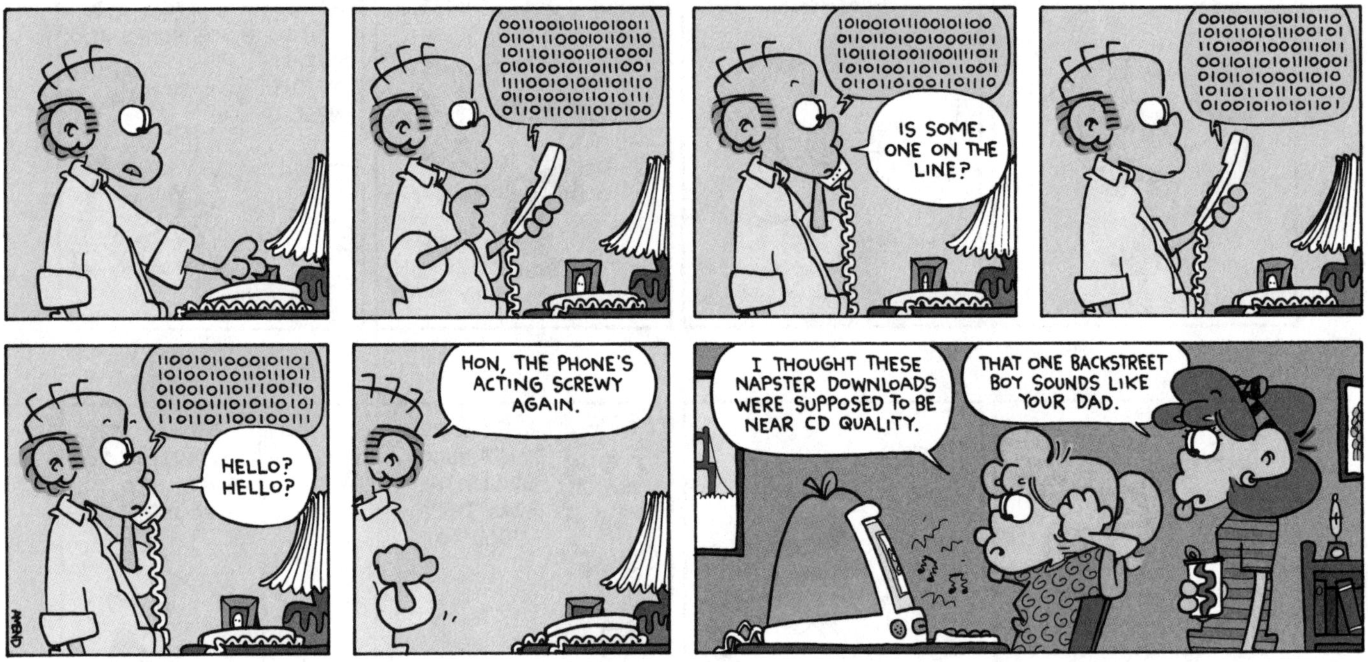
IS SOME-
ONE ON THE
LINE?
HELLO?
HELLO?
HON, THE PHONE'S
ACTING SCREWY
AGAIN.
I THOUGHT THESE
NAPSTER DOWNLOADS
WERE SUPPOSED TO BE
NEAR CD QUALITY.
THAT ONE BACKSTREET
BOY SOUNDS LIKE
YOUR DAD.
AMEND

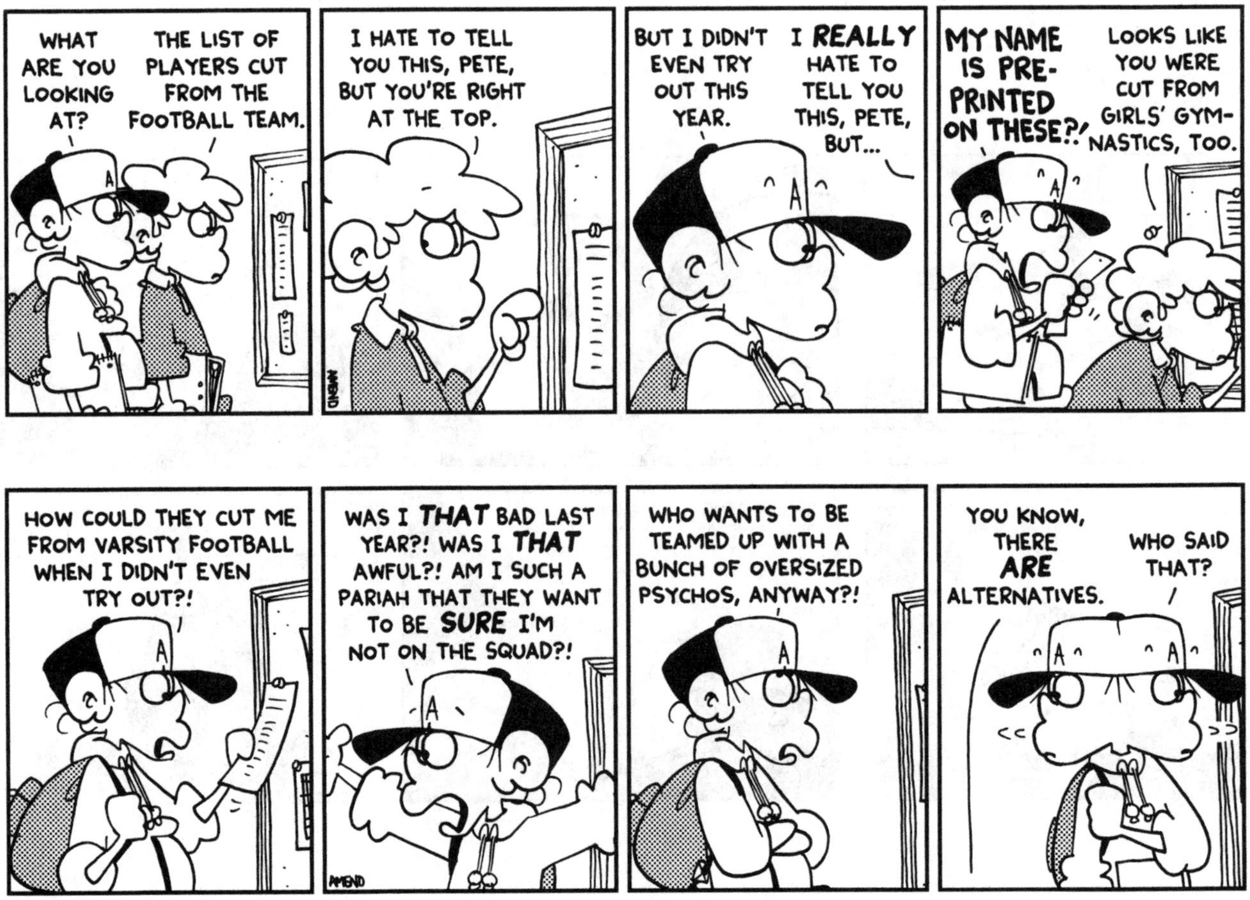
WHAT ARE YOU LOOKING AT?
THE LIST OF PLAYERS CUT FROM THE FOOTBALL TEAM.
I HATE TO TELL YOU THIS, PETE, BUT YOU'RE RIGHT AT THE TOP.
AMEND
BUT I DIDN'T EVEN TRY OUT THIS YEAR.
I REALLY HATE TO TELL YOU THIS, PETE, BUT...
MY NAME IS PRE-PRINTED ON THESE?!
LOOKS LIKE YOU WERE CUT FROM GIRLS' GYM-NASTICS, TOO.
HOW COULD THEY CUT ME FROM VARSITY FOOTBALL WHEN I DIDN'T EVEN TRY OUT?!
WAS I THAT BAD LAST YEAR?! WAS I THAT AWFUL?! AM I SUCH A PARIAH THAT THEY WANT TO BE SURE I'M NOT ON THE SQUAD?!
AMEND
WHO WANTS TO BE TEAMED UP WITH A BUNCH OF OVERSIZED PSYCHOS, ANYWAY?!
YOU KNOW, THERE ARE ALTERNATIVES.
WHO SAID THAT?

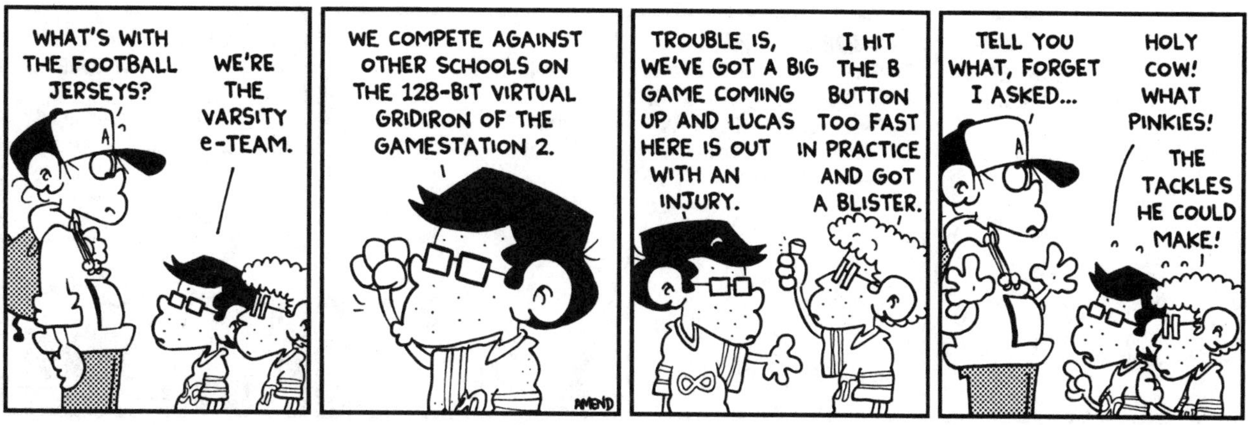
WHAT'S WITH THE FOOTBALL JERSEYS?
WE'RE THE VARSITY e-TEAM.
WE COMPETE AGAINST OTHER SCHOOLS ON THE 128-BIT VIRTUAL GRIDIRON OF THE GAMESTATION 2.
AMEND
TROUBLE IS, WE'VE GOT A BIG GAME COMING UP AND LUCAS HERE IS OUT WITH AN INJURY.
I HIT THE B BUTTON TOO FAST IN PRACTICE AND GOT A BLISTER.
TELL YOU WHAT, FORGET I ASKED...
HOLY COW! WHAT PINKIES!
THE TACKLES HE COULD MAKE!

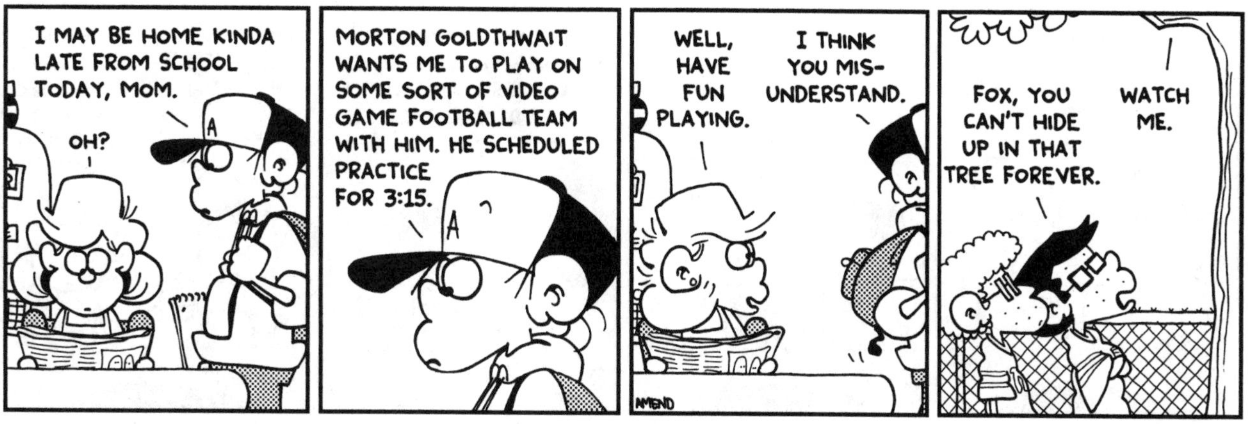
I MAY BE HOME KINDA LATE FROM SCHOOL TODAY, MOM.
OH?
MORTON GOLDTHWAIT WANTS ME TO PLAY ON SOME SORT OF VIDEO GAME FOOTBALL TEAM WITH HIM. HE SCHEDULED PRACTICE FOR 3:15.
WELL, HAVE FUN PLAYING.
I THINK YOU MIS-UNDERSTAND.
AMEND
FOX, YOU CAN'T HIDE UP IN THAT TREE FOREVER.
WATCH ME.

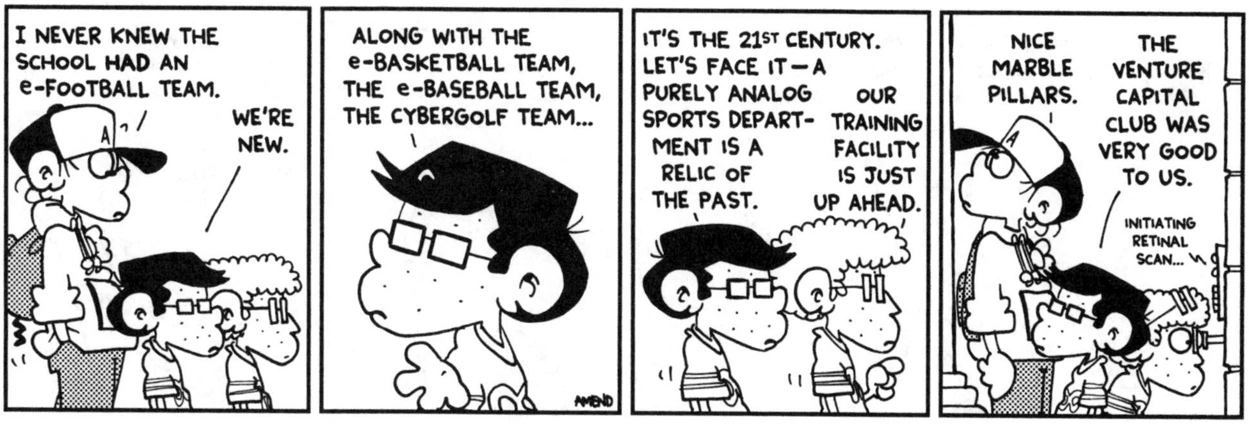
I NEVER KNEW THE SCHOOL HAD AN e-FOOTBALL TEAM.
WE'RE NEW.
ALONG WITH THE e-BASKETBALL TEAM, THE e-BASEBALL TEAM, THE CYBERGOLF TEAM...
AMEND
IT'S THE 21ST CENTURY. LET'S FACE IT—A PURELY ANALOG SPORTS DEPARTMENT IS A RELIC OF THE PAST.
OUR TRAINING FACILITY IS JUST UP AHEAD.
NICE MARBLE PILLARS.
THE VENTURE CAPITAL CLUB WAS VERY GOOD TO US.
INITIATING RETINAL SCAN...

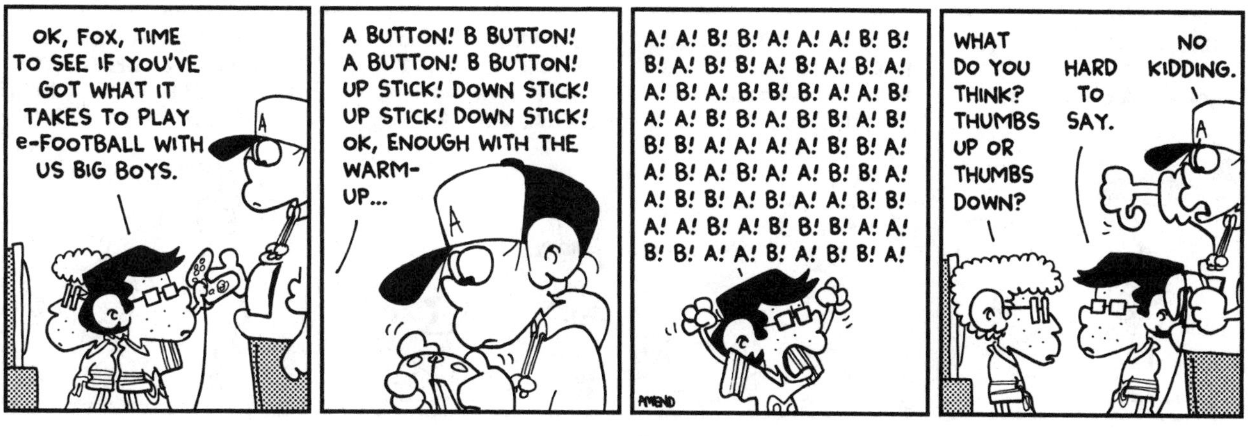
OK, FOX, TIME TO SEE IF YOU'VE GOT WHAT IT TAKES TO PLAY e-FOOTBALL WITH US BIG BOYS.
A BUTTON! B BUTTON! A BUTTON! B BUTTON! UP STICK! DOWN STICK! UP STICK! DOWN STICK! OK, ENOUGH WITH THE WARM-UP...
A! A! B! B! A! A! A! B! B! B! A! B! B! A! B! A! B! A! A! B! A! B! B! B! A! A! B! A! A! B! A! B! A! B! A! B! B! A! B! A! A! A! B! B! A! A! B! A! B! A! A! B! B! A! A! B! B! A! B! A! A! B! B! A! A! B! A! B! B! B! A! A! B! B! A! A! B! A! B! B! A!
AMEND
WHAT DO YOU THINK? THUMBS UP OR THUMBS DOWN?
HARD TO SAY.
NO KIDDING.

I GOT AN A+++ ON MY MATH QUIZ.

THAT'S WONDERFUL, JASON!

WONDERFUL?! MOM, THIS IS THE WORST SCORE I'VE RECEIVED ON A QUIZ IN TWO YEARS! I'LL NEVER BREAK MY RECORD A+++++ AVERAGE AT THIS RATE!

I THINK I NEED A PRIVATE TUTOR.

LESSON ONE: "HOW NOT TO BE SUCH A WEENIE"...

THIS ISN'T WHAT I MEANT, MOM!

CLICK
CLICK
CLICK
CLICK
CLICK

CLICK
CLICK
CLICK
CLICK
CLICK

PAIGE, WILL YOU STOP SURFING THROUGH THE CHANNELS LIKE THAT?! YOU'RE DRIVING ME NUTS!

CLICK
CLICK
CLICK
CLICK
CLICK
CLICK

THIS IS HOW TO DO IT.

PETER, SLOW DOWN FOR A SEC. I NEED TO BLINK.

WELCOME, PAIGE.

CHECK YOUR E-MAIL! CHECK YOUR E-MAIL!

YOU HAVE 23,291 NEW MESSAGES FROM JASON.

HEE HEE.

DELETING ALL.

WHAT?! YOU AREN'T GOING TO READ ANY OF THEM?!

HAND-CRAFTED SPAM JUST ISN'T WORTH THE TROUBLE.

WAS THAT YOU I HEARD TYPING ALL NIGHT?

TELL ME IF IT'S NOT OK FOR ME TO BLOW OFF HOMEWORK TONIGHT.

TELL ME IF IT'S NOT OK FOR ME TO ORDER THIS SWEATER ON YOUR CREDIT CARD.

TELL ME IF IT'S NOT OK FOR ME TO EAT THIS BOX OF HO-HOS BEFORE DINNER.

TELL ME YOU HAVEN'T BEEN WEARING HEAD-PHONES ALL AFTERNOON.

THE KIDS BOUGHT ME A WALKMAN. ISN'T THAT SWEET?

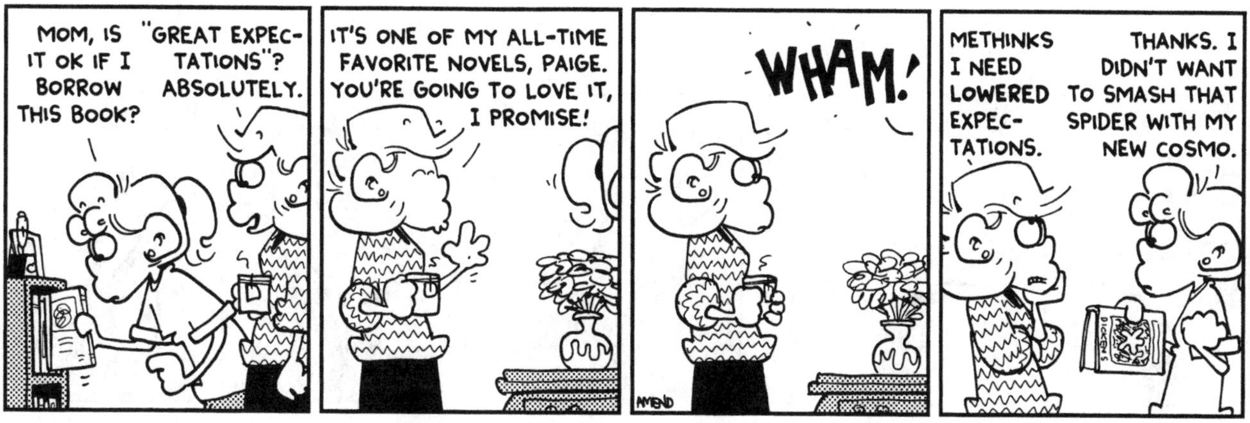
MOM, IS IT OK IF I BORROW THIS BOOK?
"GREAT EXPECTATIONS"? ABSOLUTELY.
IT'S ONE OF MY ALL-TIME FAVORITE NOVELS, PAIGE. YOU'RE GOING TO LOVE IT, I PROMISE!
WHAM!
METHINKS I NEED LOWERED EXPECTATIONS.
THANKS. I DIDN'T WANT TO SMASH THAT SPIDER WITH MY NEW COSMO.
AMEND

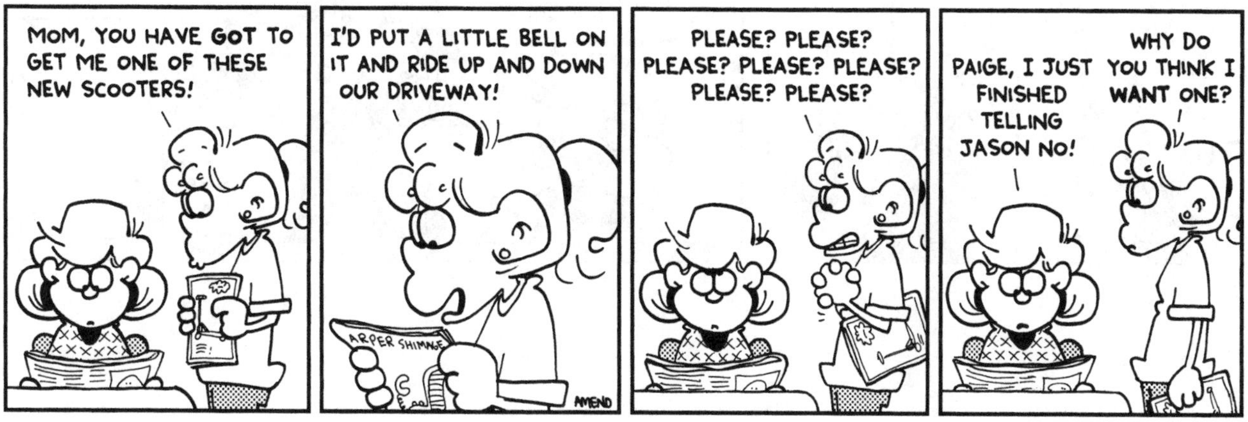
MOM, YOU HAVE GOT TO GET ME ONE OF THESE NEW SCOOTERS!
I'D PUT A LITTLE BELL ON IT AND RIDE UP AND DOWN OUR DRIVEWAY!
PLEASE? PLEASE? PLEASE? PLEASE? PLEASE? PLEASE? PLEASE?
PAIGE, I JUST FINISHED TELLING JASON NO!
WHY DO YOU THINK I WANT ONE?
AMEND

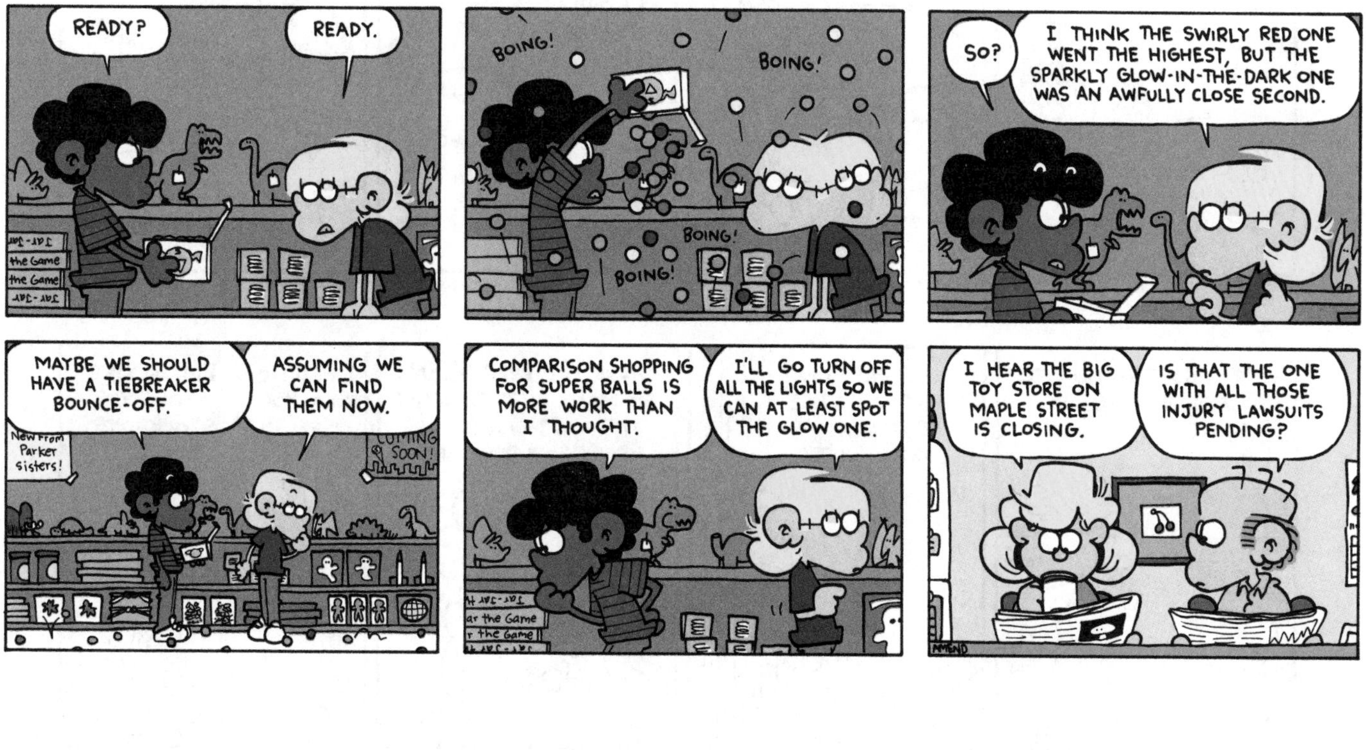
READY?
READY.
BOING!
BOING!
BOING!
BOING!
SO?
I THINK THE SWIRLY RED ONE WENT THE HIGHEST, BUT THE SPARKLY GLOW-IN-THE-DARK ONE WAS AN AWFULLY CLOSE SECOND.
MAYBE WE SHOULD HAVE A TIEBREAKER BOUNCE-OFF.
ASSUMING WE CAN FIND THEM NOW.
New from Parker sisters!
COMING SOON!
COMPARISON SHOPPING FOR SUPER BALLS IS MORE WORK THAN I THOUGHT.
I'LL GO TURN OFF ALL THE LIGHTS SO WE CAN AT LEAST SPOT THE GLOW ONE.
I HEAR THE BIG TOY STORE ON MAPLE STREET IS CLOSING.
IS THAT THE ONE WITH ALL THOSE INJURY LAWSUITS PENDING?
AMEND

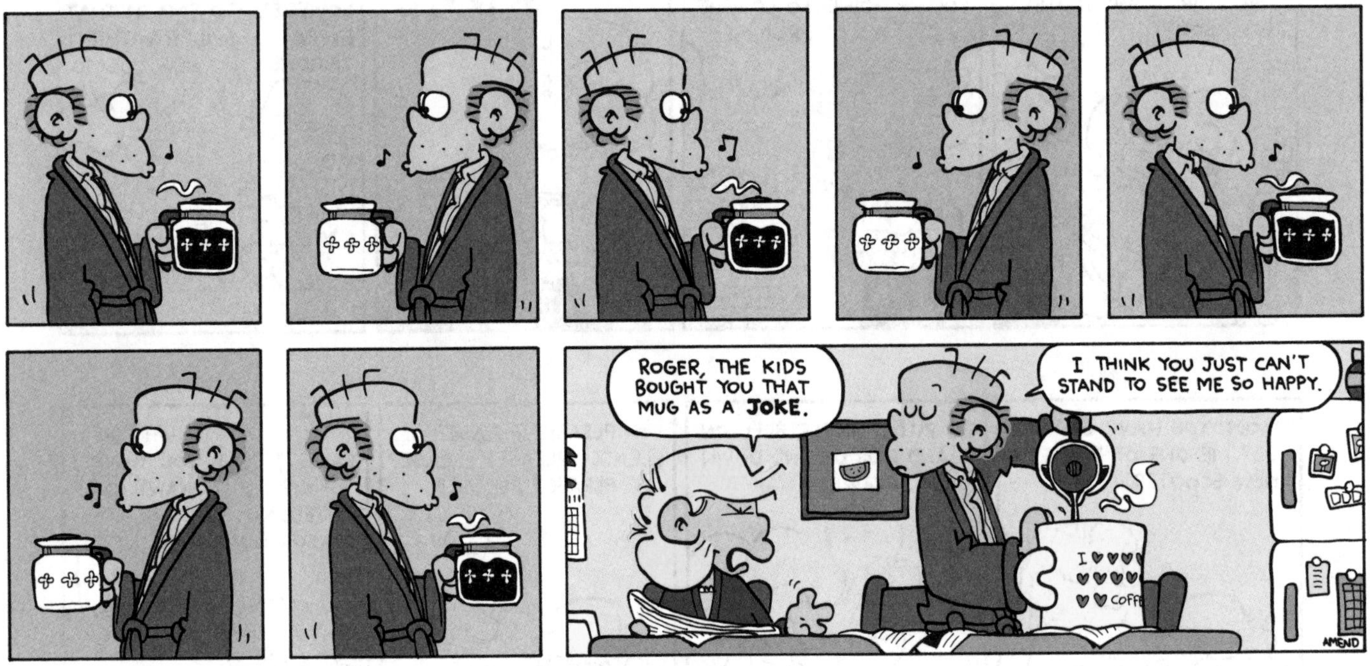
ROGER, THE KIDS BOUGHT YOU THAT MUG AS A **JOKE.**
I THINK YOU JUST CAN'T STAND TO SEE ME SO HAPPY.
AMEND

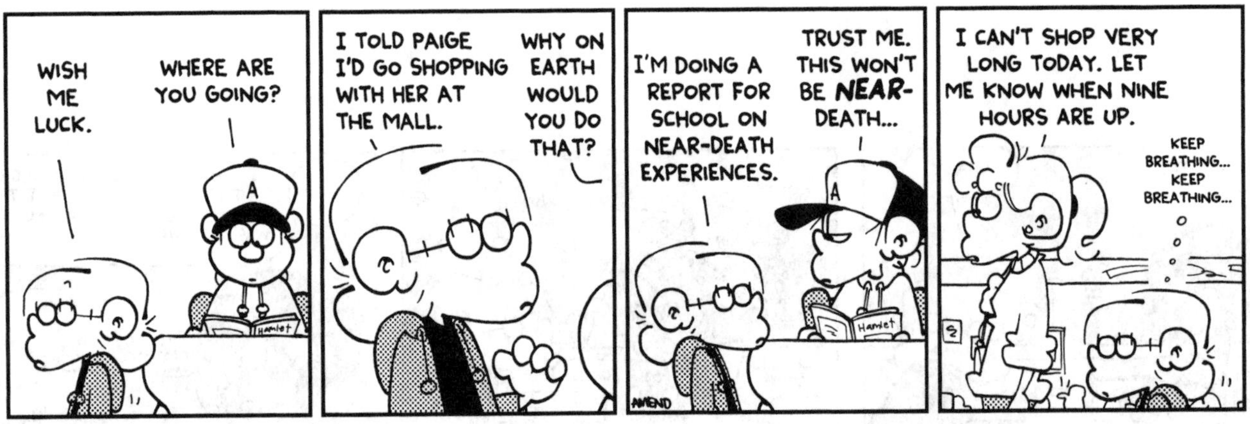
WISH ME LUCK.
WHERE ARE YOU GOING?
Hamlet
I TOLD PAIGE I'D GO SHOPPING WITH HER AT THE MALL.
WHY ON EARTH WOULD YOU DO THAT?
I'M DOING A REPORT FOR SCHOOL ON NEAR-DEATH EXPERIENCES.
TRUST ME. THIS WON'T BE **NEAR**-DEATH...
Hamlet
AMEND
I CAN'T SHOP VERY LONG TODAY. LET ME KNOW WHEN NINE HOURS ARE UP.
KEEP BREATHING... KEEP BREATHING...

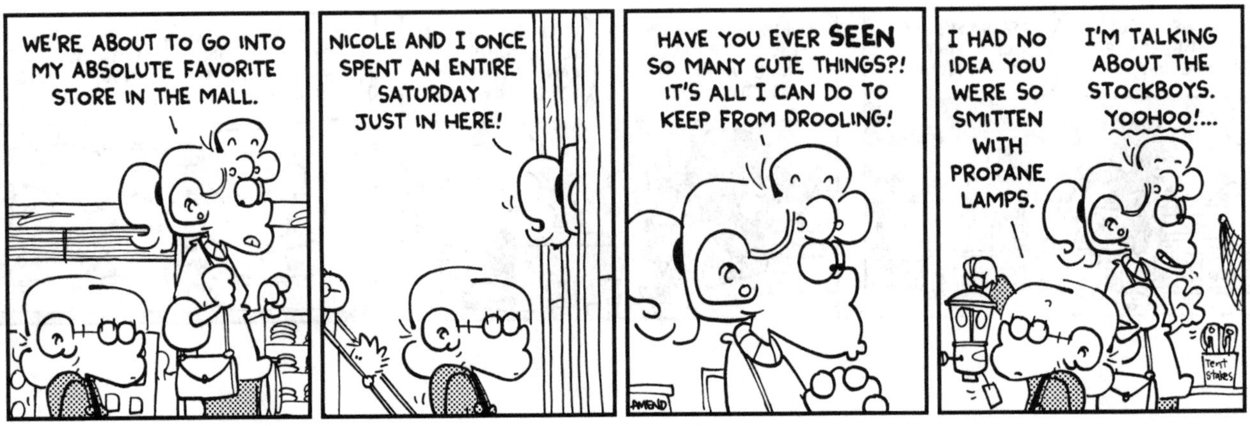
WE'RE ABOUT TO GO INTO MY ABSOLUTE FAVORITE STORE IN THE MALL.
NICOLE AND I ONCE SPENT AN ENTIRE SATURDAY JUST IN HERE!
HAVE YOU EVER **SEEN** SO MANY CUTE THINGS?! IT'S ALL I CAN DO TO KEEP FROM DROOLING!
AMEND
I HAD NO IDEA YOU WERE SO SMITTEN WITH PROPANE LAMPS.
I'M TALKING ABOUT THE STOCKBOYS. YOOHOO!...
Tent Stakes

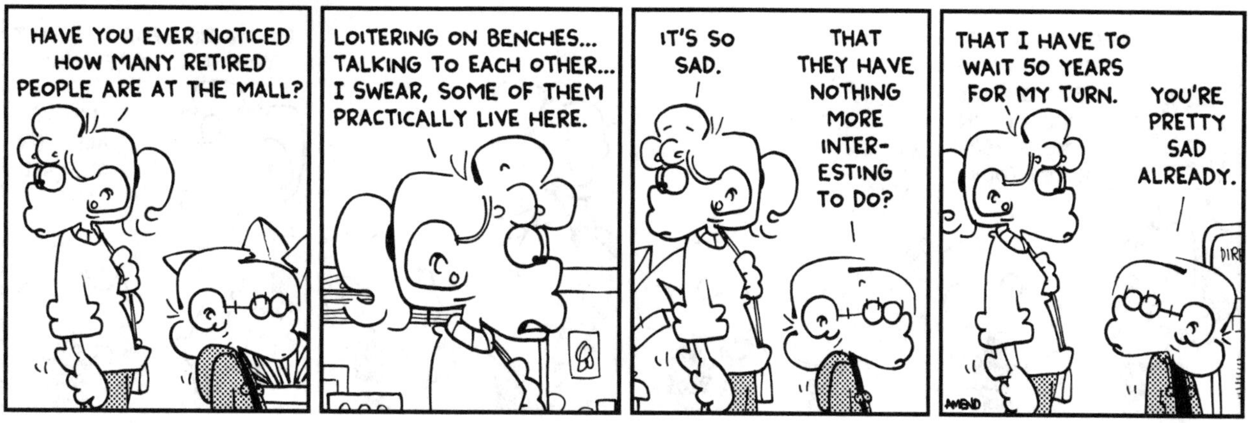
HAVE YOU EVER NOTICED HOW MANY RETIRED PEOPLE ARE AT THE MALL?
LOITERING ON BENCHES... TALKING TO EACH OTHER... I SWEAR, SOME OF THEM PRACTICALLY LIVE HERE.
IT'S SO SAD.
THAT THEY HAVE NOTHING MORE INTERESTING TO DO?
THAT I HAVE TO WAIT 50 YEARS FOR MY TURN.
YOU'RE PRETTY SAD ALREADY.

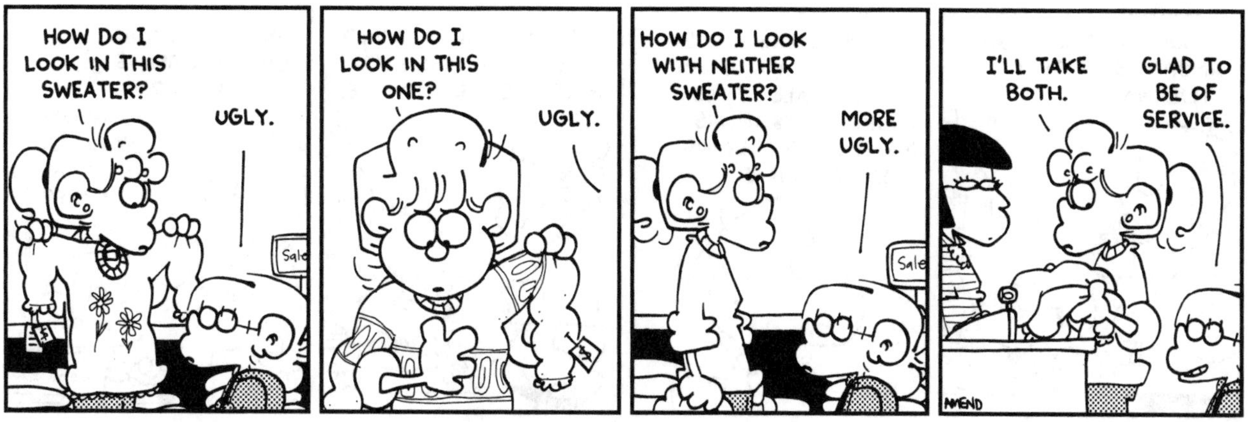
HOW DO I LOOK IN THIS SWEATER?
UGLY.
HOW DO I LOOK IN THIS ONE?
UGLY.
HOW DO I LOOK WITH NEITHER SWEATER?
MORE UGLY.
I'LL TAKE BOTH.
GLAD TO BE OF SERVICE.

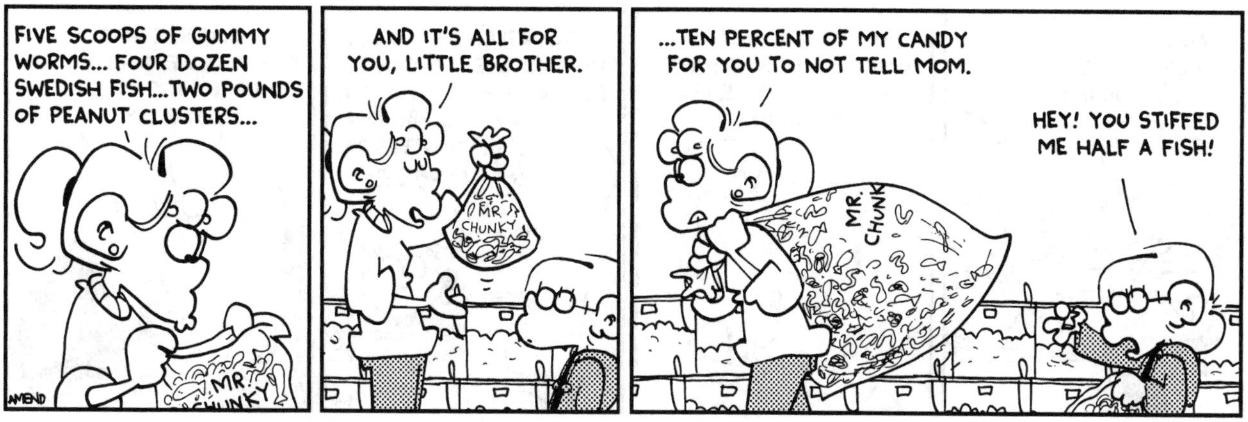
FIVE SCOOPS OF GUMMY WORMS... FOUR DOZEN SWEDISH FISH...TWO POUNDS OF PEANUT CLUSTERS...
AND IT'S ALL FOR YOU, LITTLE BROTHER.
...TEN PERCENT OF MY CANDY FOR YOU TO NOT TELL MOM.
HEY! YOU STIFFED ME HALF A FISH!

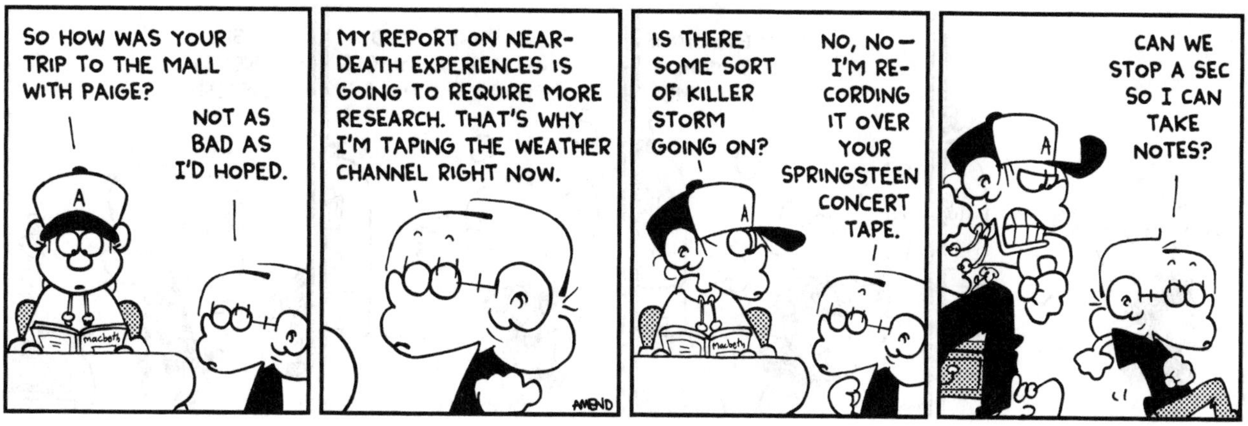
SO HOW WAS YOUR TRIP TO THE MALL WITH PAIGE?
NOT AS BAD AS I'D HOPED.
MY REPORT ON NEAR-DEATH EXPERIENCES IS GOING TO REQUIRE MORE RESEARCH. THAT'S WHY I'M TAPING THE WEATHER CHANNEL RIGHT NOW.
IS THERE SOME SORT OF KILLER STORM GOING ON?
NO, NO— I'M RECORDING IT OVER YOUR SPRINGSTEEN CONCERT TAPE.
CAN WE STOP A SEC SO I CAN TAKE NOTES?

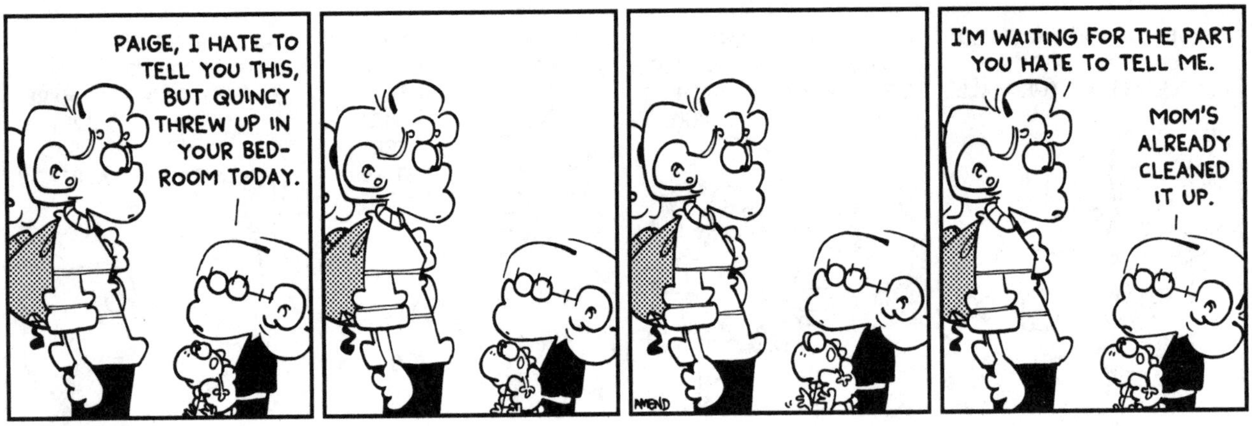
PAIGE, I HATE TO TELL YOU THIS, BUT QUINCY THREW UP IN YOUR BEDROOM TODAY.
I'M WAITING FOR THE PART YOU HATE TO TELL ME.
MOM'S ALREADY CLEANED IT UP.

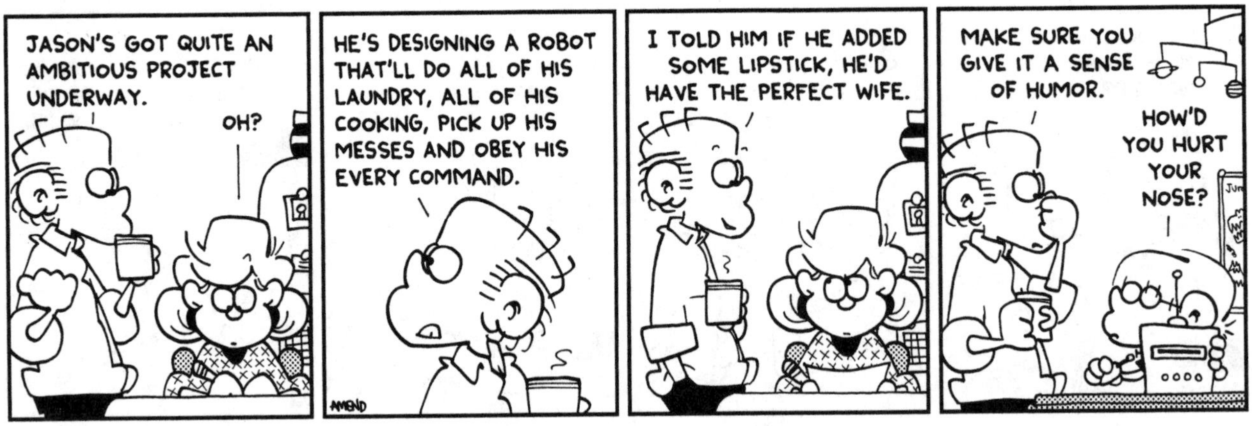
JASON'S GOT QUITE AN AMBITIOUS PROJECT UNDERWAY.
OH?
HE'S DESIGNING A ROBOT THAT'LL DO ALL OF HIS LAUNDRY, ALL OF HIS COOKING, PICK UP HIS MESSES AND OBEY HIS EVERY COMMAND.
I TOLD HIM IF HE ADDED SOME LIPSTICK, HE'D HAVE THE PERFECT WIFE.
MAKE SURE YOU GIVE IT A SENSE OF HUMOR.
HOW'D YOU HURT YOUR NOSE?

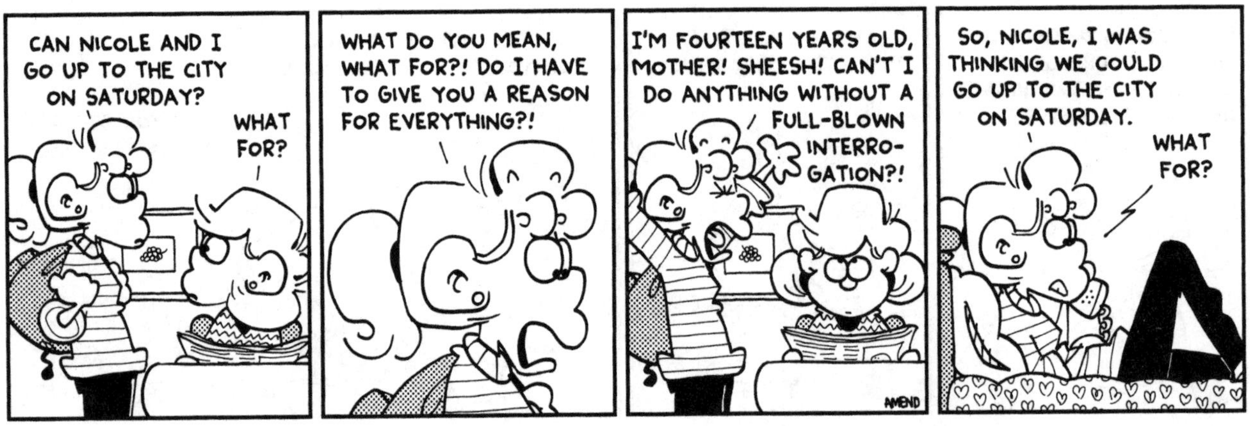
CAN NICOLE AND I GO UP TO THE CITY ON SATURDAY?
WHAT FOR?
WHAT DO YOU MEAN, WHAT FOR?! DO I HAVE TO GIVE YOU A REASON FOR EVERYTHING?!
I'M FOURTEEN YEARS OLD, MOTHER! SHEESH! CAN'T I DO ANYTHING WITHOUT A FULL-BLOWN INTERROGATION?!
SO, NICOLE, I WAS THINKING WE COULD GO UP TO THE CITY ON SATURDAY.
WHAT FOR?

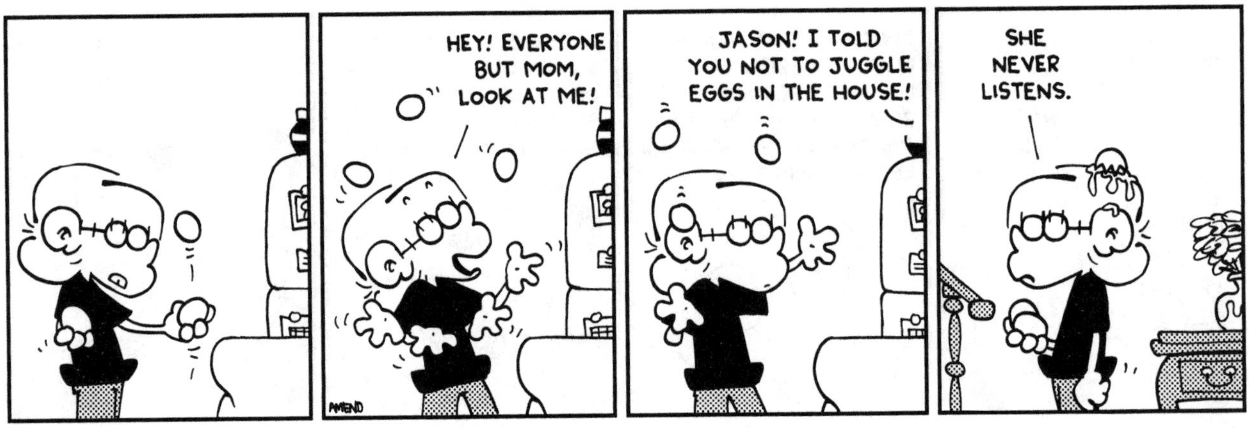
HEY! EVERYONE BUT MOM, LOOK AT ME!
JASON! I TOLD YOU NOT TO JUGGLE EGGS IN THE HOUSE!
SHE NEVER LISTENS.

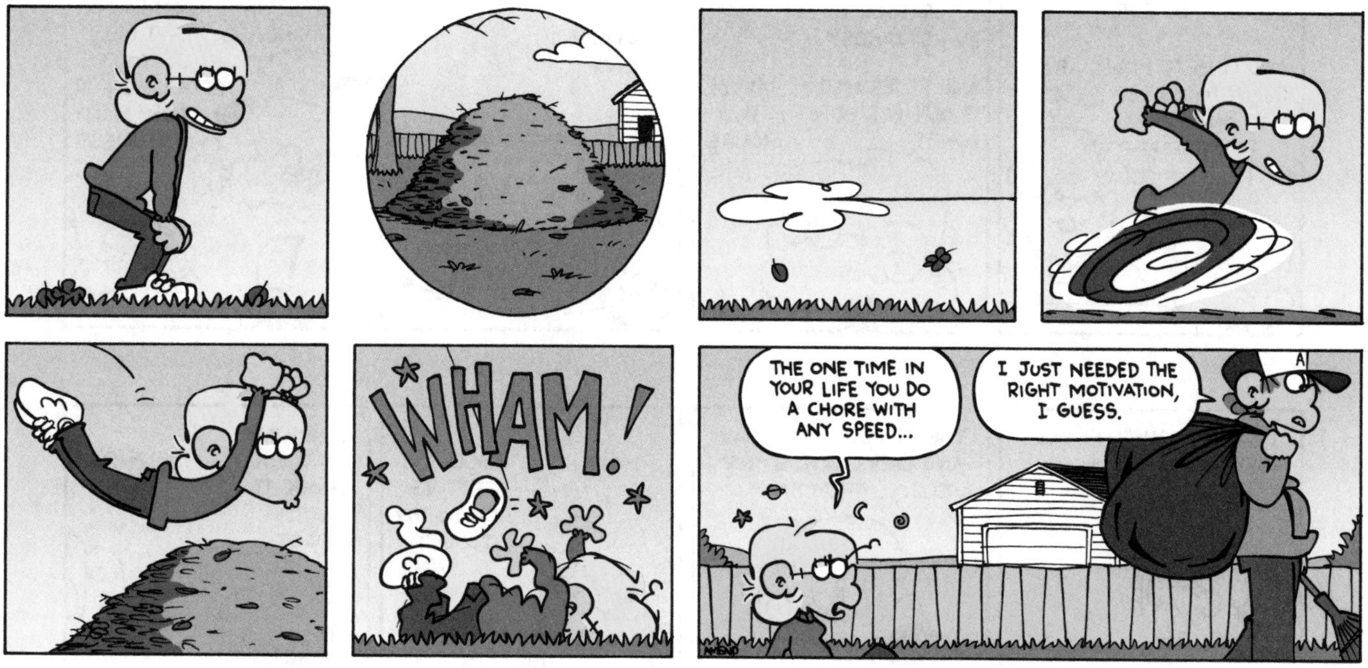
WHAM!
THE ONE TIME IN YOUR LIFE YOU DO A CHORE WITH ANY SPEED...
I JUST NEEDED THE RIGHT MOTIVATION, I GUESS.

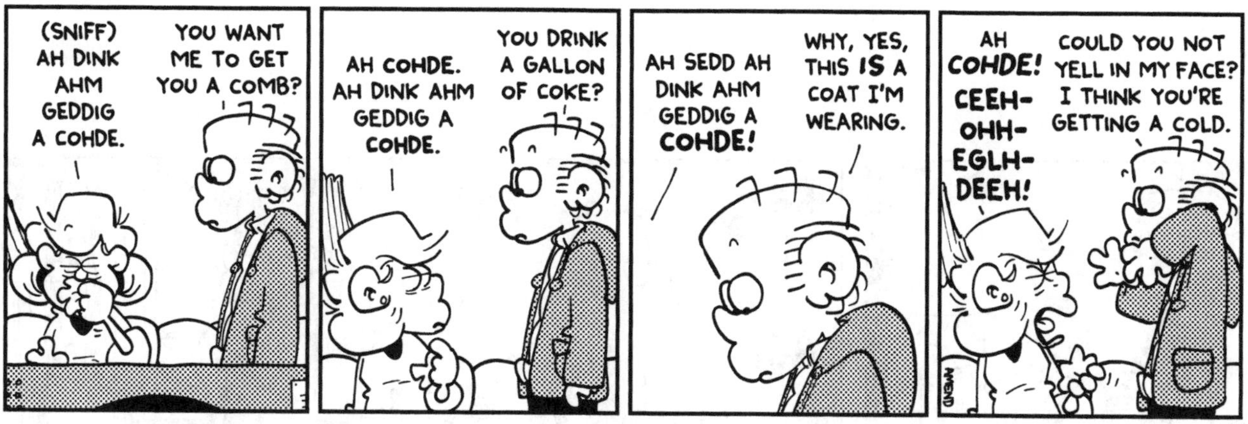
(SNIFF) AH DINK AHM GEDDIG A COHDE.
YOU WANT ME TO GET YOU A COMB?
AH COHDE. AH DINK AHM GEDDIG A COHDE.
YOU DRINK A GALLON OF COKE?
AH SEDD AH DINK AHM GEDDIG A COHDE!
WHY, YES, THIS IS A COAT I'M WEARING.
AH COHDE! CEEH-OHH-EGLH-DEEH!
COULD YOU NOT YELL IN MY FACE? I THINK YOU'RE GETTING A COLD.

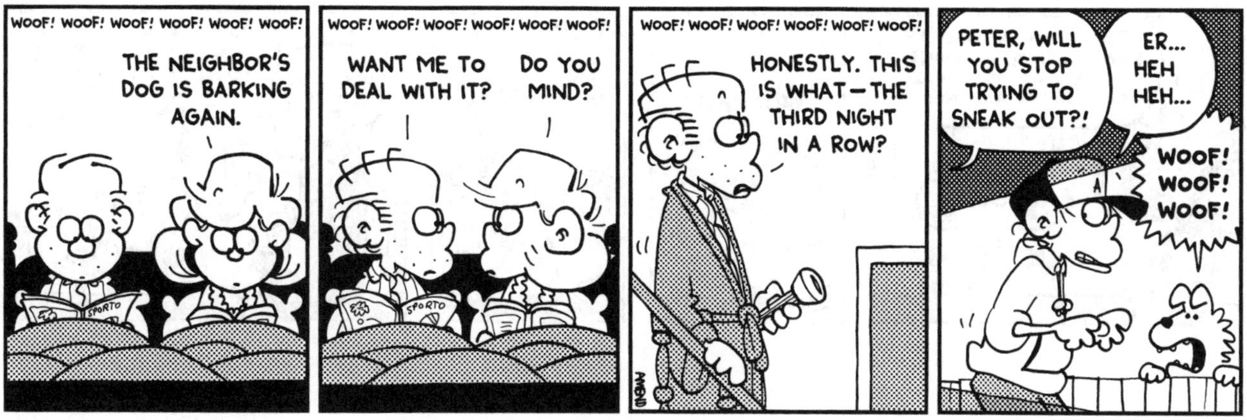
WOOF! WOOF! WOOF! WOOF! WOOF! WOOF!
THE NEIGHBOR'S DOG IS BARKING AGAIN.
WOOF! WOOF! WOOF! WOOF! WOOF! WOOF!
WANT ME TO DEAL WITH IT?
DO YOU MIND?
WOOF! WOOF! WOOF! WOOF! WOOF! WOOF!
HONESTLY. THIS IS WHAT—THE THIRD NIGHT IN A ROW?
PETER, WILL YOU STOP TRYING TO SNEAK OUT?!
ER... HEH HEH...
WOOF! WOOF! WOOF!

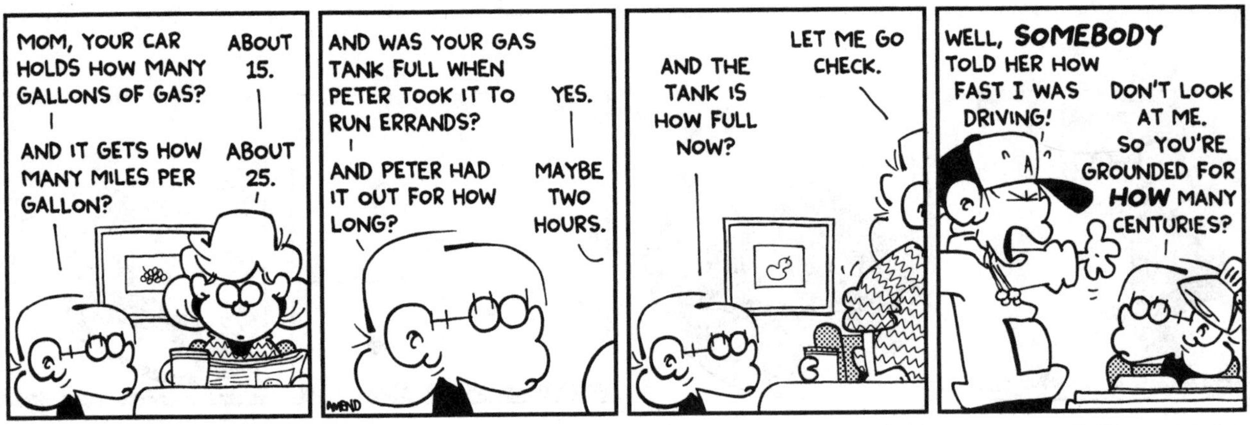
MOM, YOUR CAR HOLDS HOW MANY GALLONS OF GAS?
ABOUT 15.
AND IT GETS HOW MANY MILES PER GALLON?
ABOUT 25.
AND WAS YOUR GAS TANK FULL WHEN PETER TOOK IT TO RUN ERRANDS?
YES.
AND PETER HAD IT OUT FOR HOW LONG?
MAYBE TWO HOURS.
AND THE TANK IS HOW FULL NOW?
LET ME GO CHECK.
WELL, SOMEBODY TOLD HER HOW FAST I WAS DRIVING!
DON'T LOOK AT ME. SO YOU'RE GROUNDED FOR HOW MANY CENTURIES?
AMEND

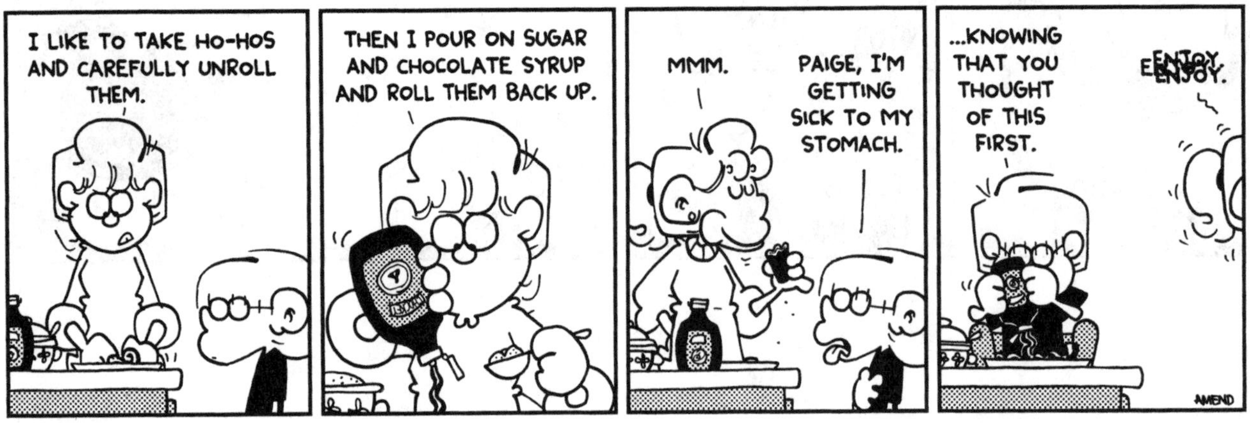
I LIKE TO TAKE HO-HOS AND CAREFULLY UNROLL THEM.
THEN I POUR ON SUGAR AND CHOCOLATE SYRUP AND ROLL THEM BACK UP.
MMM.
PAIGE, I'M GETTING SICK TO MY STOMACH.
...KNOWING THAT YOU THOUGHT OF THIS FIRST.
ENJOY. ENJOY.
AMEND

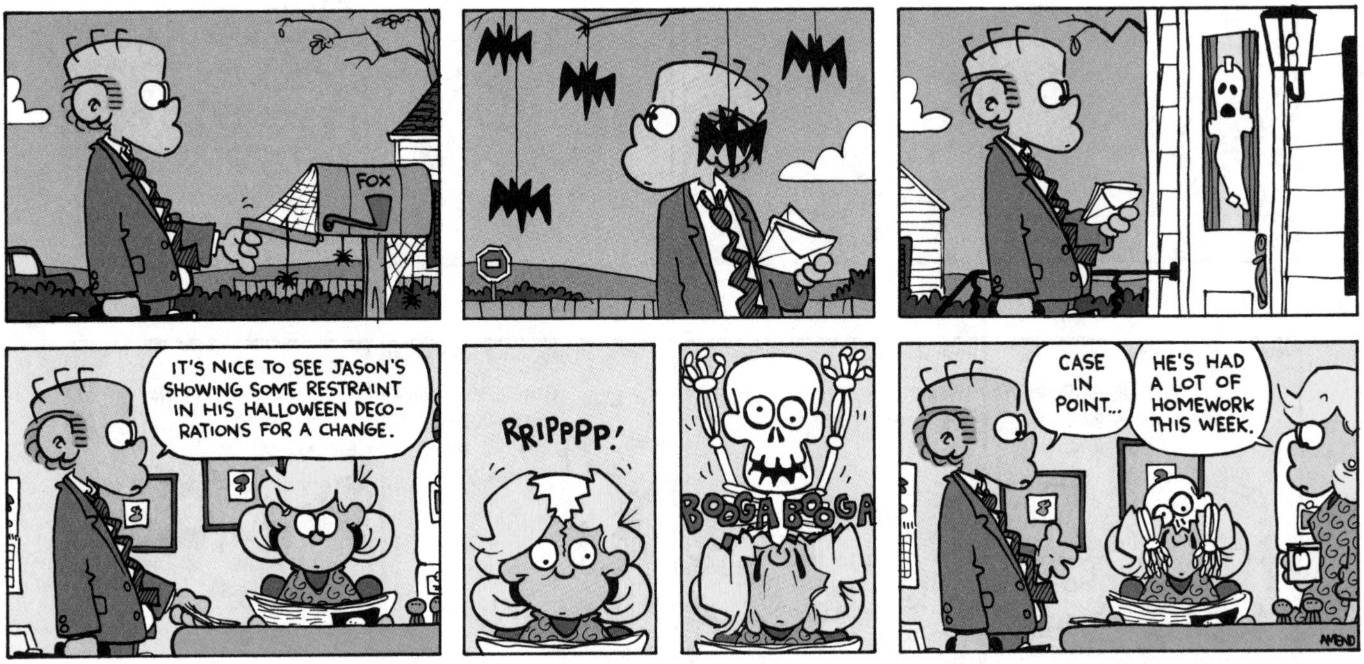
FOX
IT'S NICE TO SEE JASON'S SHOWING SOME RESTRAINT IN HIS HALLOWEEN DECORATIONS FOR A CHANGE.
RRIPPPP!
BOOGA BOOGA
CASE IN POINT...
HE'S HAD A LOT OF HOMEWORK THIS WEEK.
AMEND

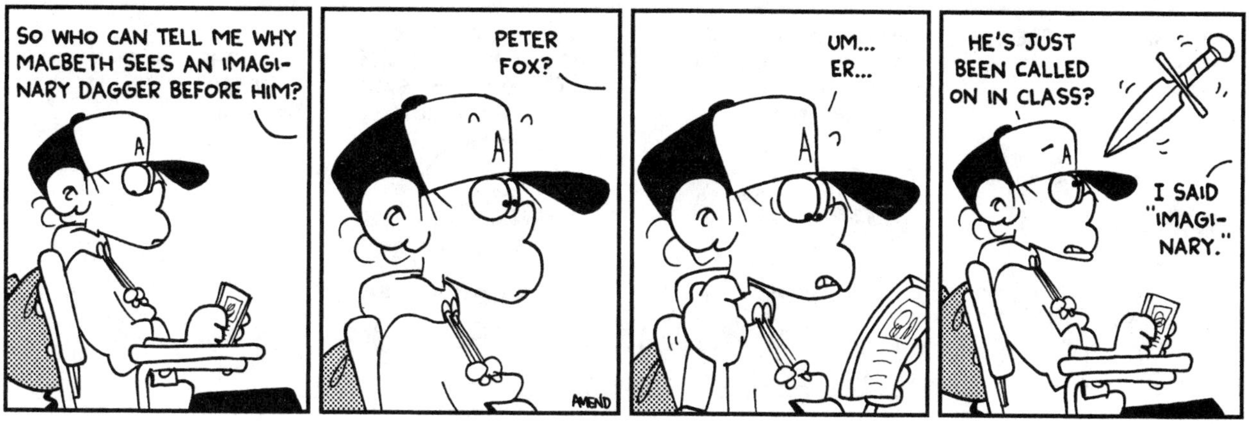
SO WHO CAN TELL ME WHY MACBETH SEES AN IMAGINARY DAGGER BEFORE HIM?
PETER FOX?
UM... ER...
HE'S JUST BEEN CALLED ON IN CLASS?
I SAID "IMAGINARY."
AMEND

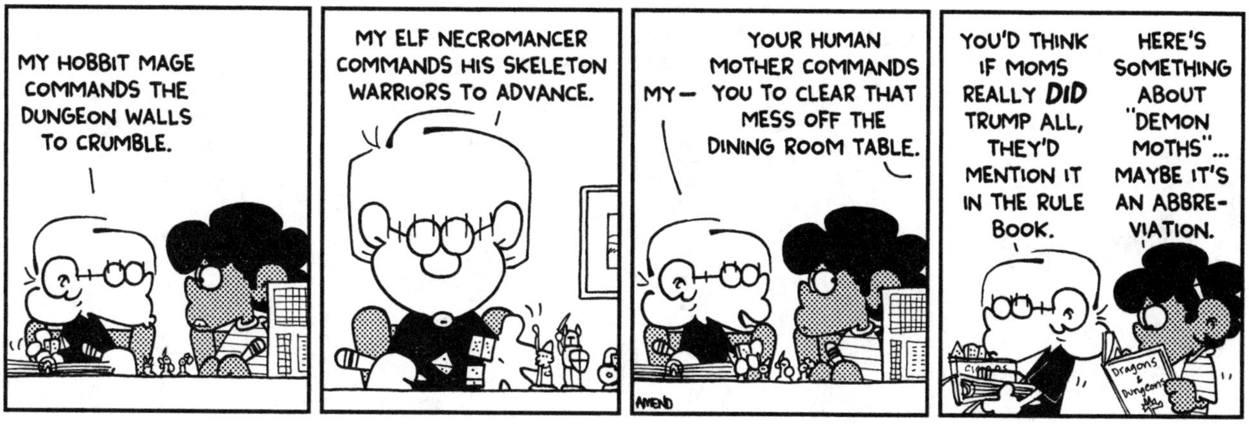
MY HOBBIT MAGE COMMANDS THE DUNGEON WALLS TO CRUMBLE.
MY ELF NECROMANCER COMMANDS HIS SKELETON WARRIORS TO ADVANCE.
MY—
YOUR HUMAN MOTHER COMMANDS YOU TO CLEAR THAT MESS OFF THE DINING ROOM TABLE.
YOU'D THINK IF MOMS REALLY DID TRUMP ALL, THEY'D MENTION IT IN THE RULE BOOK.
HERE'S SOMETHING ABOUT "DEMON MOTHS"... MAYBE IT'S AN ABBREVIATION.
Dragons & Dungeons
AMEND

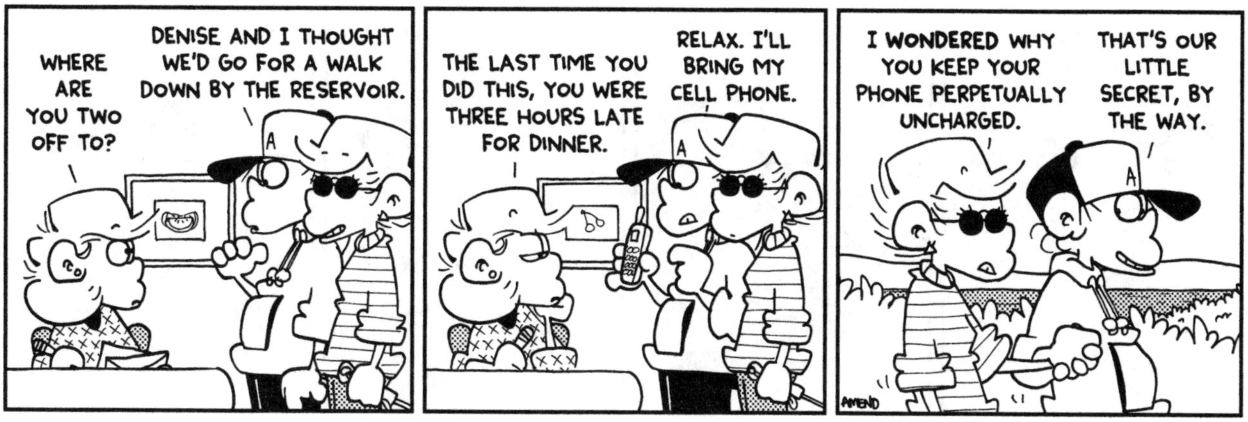
WHERE ARE YOU TWO OFF TO?
DENISE AND I THOUGHT WE'D GO FOR A WALK DOWN BY THE RESERVOIR.
THE LAST TIME YOU DID THIS, YOU WERE THREE HOURS LATE FOR DINNER.
RELAX. I'LL BRING MY CELL PHONE.
I WONDERED WHY YOU KEEP YOUR PHONE PERPETUALLY UNCHARGED.
THAT'S OUR LITTLE SECRET, BY THE WAY.
AMEND

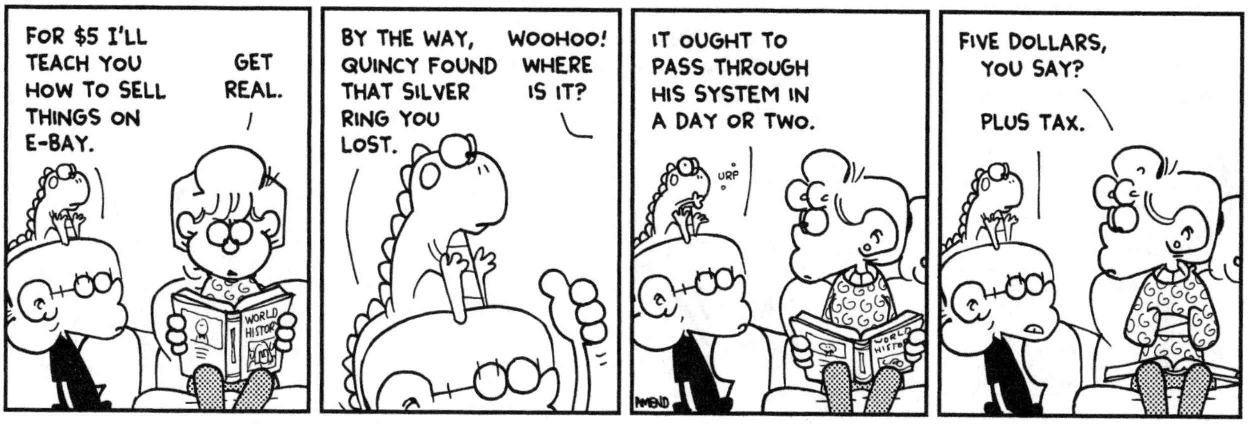
FOR $5 I'LL TEACH YOU HOW TO SELL THINGS ON E-BAY.
GET REAL.
BY THE WAY, QUINCY FOUND THAT SILVER RING YOU LOST.
WOOHOO! WHERE IS IT?
IT OUGHT TO PASS THROUGH HIS SYSTEM IN A DAY OR TWO.
URP
FIVE DOLLARS, YOU SAY?
PLUS TAX.
AMEND

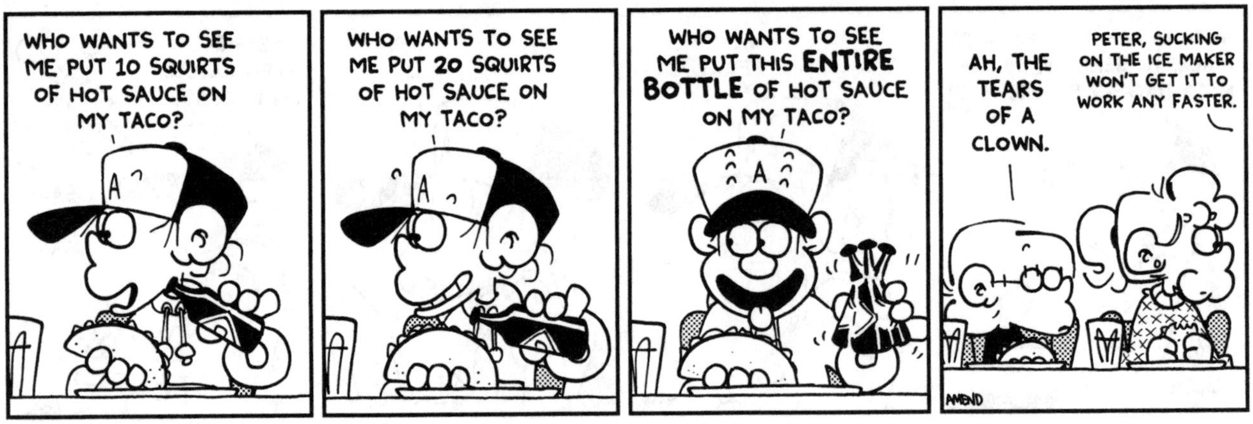
WHO WANTS TO SEE ME PUT 10 SQUIRTS OF HOT SAUCE ON MY TACO?
WHO WANTS TO SEE ME PUT 20 SQUIRTS OF HOT SAUCE ON MY TACO?
WHO WANTS TO SEE ME PUT THIS **ENTIRE BOTTLE** OF HOT SAUCE ON MY TACO?
AH, THE TEARS OF A CLOWN.
PETER, SUCKING ON THE ICE MAKER WON'T GET IT TO WORK ANY FASTER.
AMEND

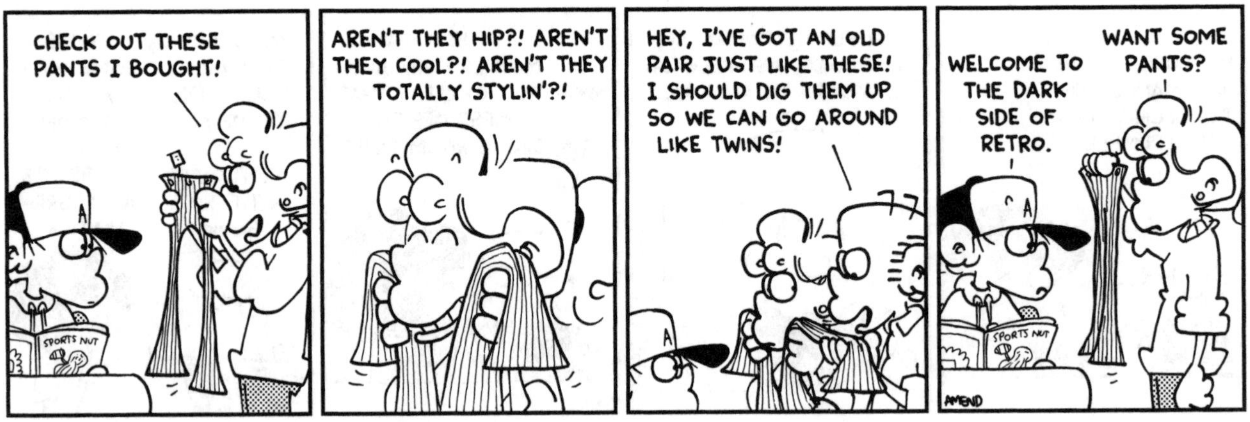
CHECK OUT THESE PANTS I BOUGHT!
SPORTS NUT
AREN'T THEY HIP?! AREN'T THEY COOL?! AREN'T THEY TOTALLY STYLIN'?!
HEY, I'VE GOT AN OLD PAIR JUST LIKE THESE! I SHOULD DIG THEM UP SO WE CAN GO AROUND LIKE TWINS!
WELCOME TO THE DARK SIDE OF RETRO.
WANT SOME PANTS?
SPORTS NUT
AMEND

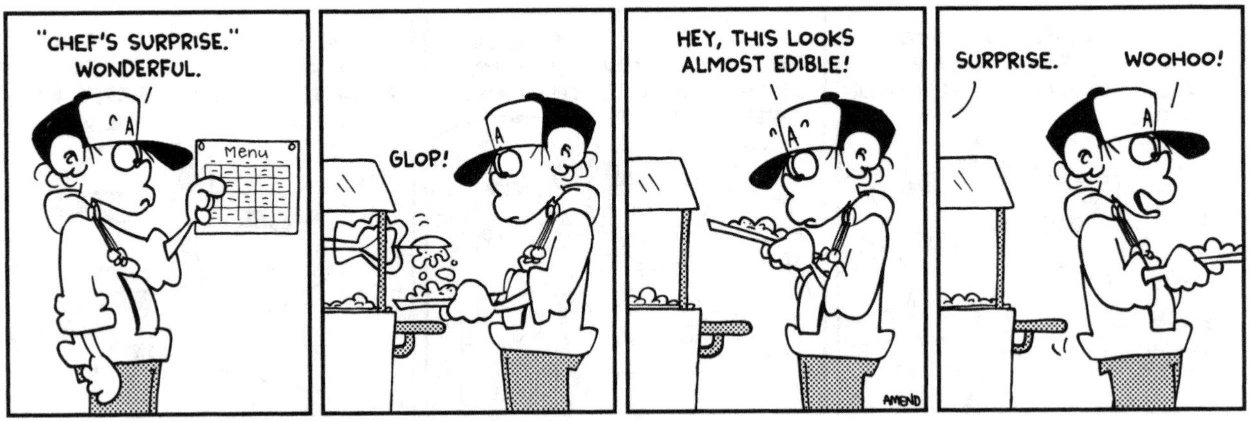
"CHEF'S SURPRISE." WONDERFUL.
Menu
GLOP!
HEY, THIS LOOKS ALMOST EDIBLE!
AMEND
SURPRISE.
WOOHOO!

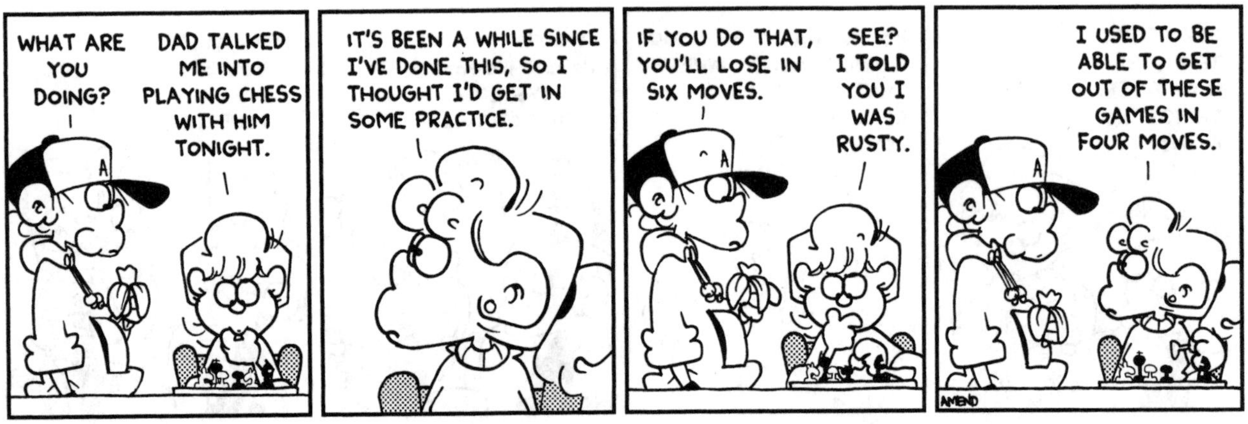
WHAT ARE YOU DOING?
DAD TALKED ME INTO PLAYING CHESS WITH HIM TONIGHT.
IT'S BEEN A WHILE SINCE I'VE DONE THIS, SO I THOUGHT I'D GET IN SOME PRACTICE.
IF YOU DO THAT, YOU'LL LOSE IN SIX MOVES.
SEE? I TOLD YOU I WAS RUSTY.
I USED TO BE ABLE TO GET OUT OF THESE GAMES IN FOUR MOVES.
AMEND

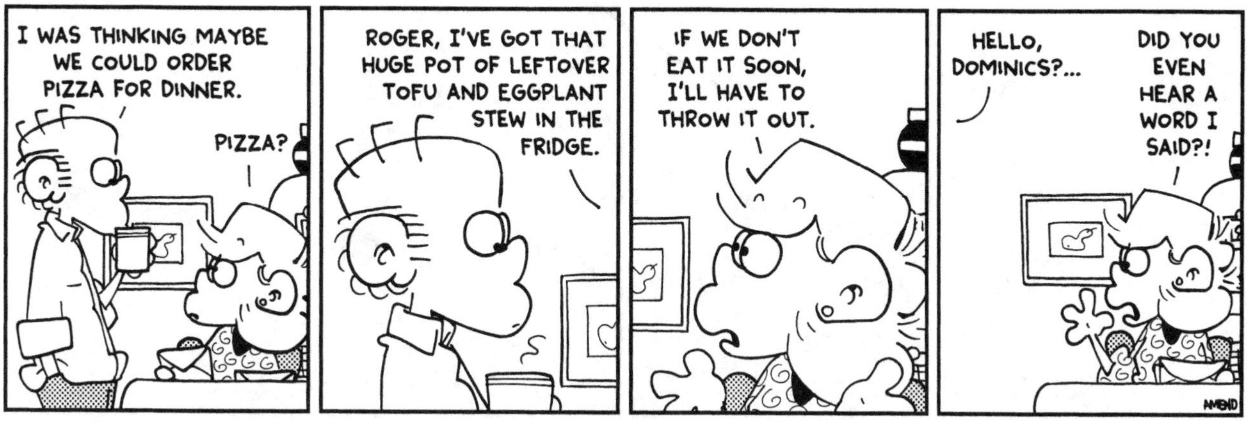
I WAS THINKING MAYBE WE COULD ORDER PIZZA FOR DINNER.
PIZZA?
ROGER, I'VE GOT THAT HUGE POT OF LEFTOVER TOFU AND EGGPLANT STEW IN THE FRIDGE.
IF WE DON'T EAT IT SOON, I'LL HAVE TO THROW IT OUT.
HELLO, DOMINICS?...
DID YOU EVEN HEAR A WORD I SAID?!
AMEND

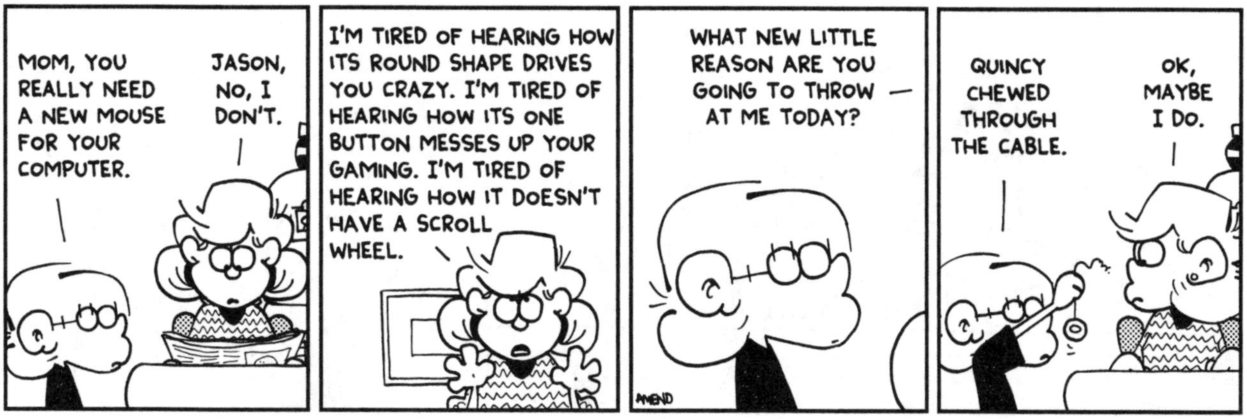
MOM, YOU REALLY NEED A NEW MOUSE FOR YOUR COMPUTER.
JASON, NO, I DON'T.
I'M TIRED OF HEARING HOW ITS ROUND SHAPE DRIVES YOU CRAZY. I'M TIRED OF HEARING HOW ITS ONE BUTTON MESSES UP YOUR GAMING. I'M TIRED OF HEARING HOW IT DOESN'T HAVE A SCROLL WHEEL.
AMEND
WHAT NEW LITTLE REASON ARE YOU GOING TO THROW AT ME TODAY?
QUINCY CHEWED THROUGH THE CABLE.
OK, MAYBE I DO.

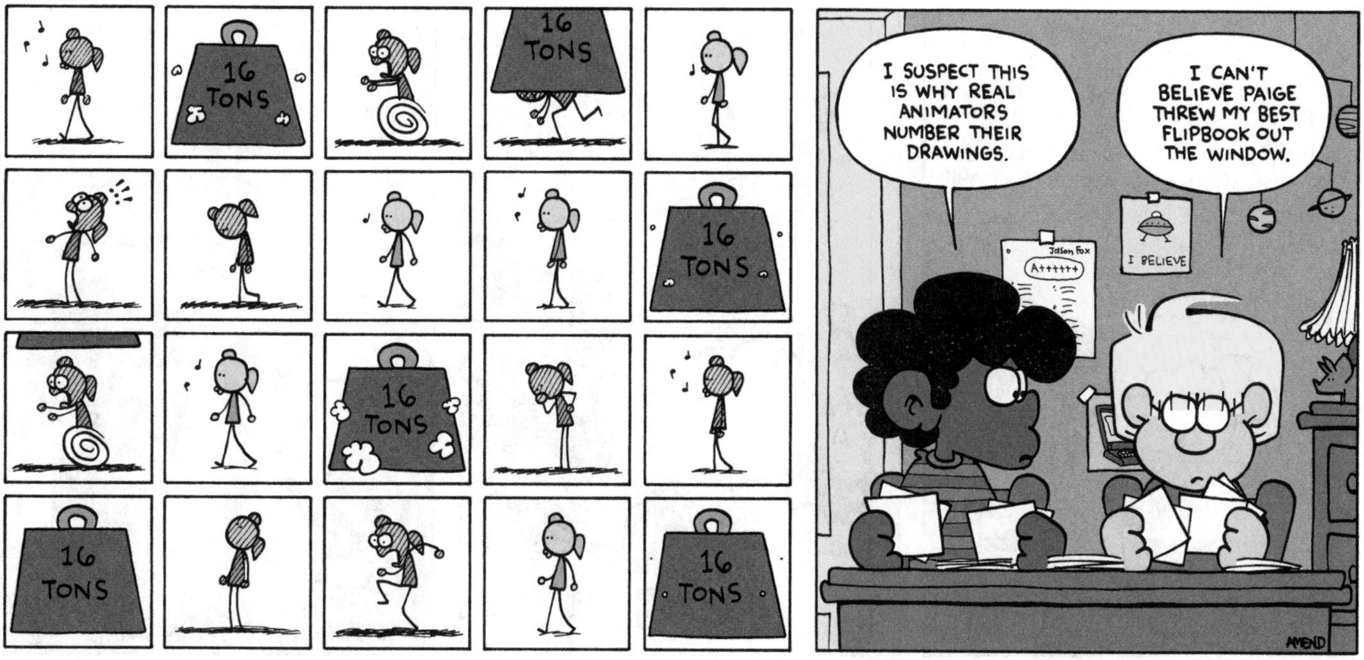
16 TONS
16 TONS
16 TONS
16 TONS
16 TONS
16 TONS
16 TONS
I SUSPECT THIS IS WHY REAL ANIMATORS NUMBER THEIR DRAWINGS.
I CAN'T BELIEVE PAIGE THREW MY BEST FLIPBOOK OUT THE WINDOW.
Jason Fox
A++++++
I BELIEVE
AMEND

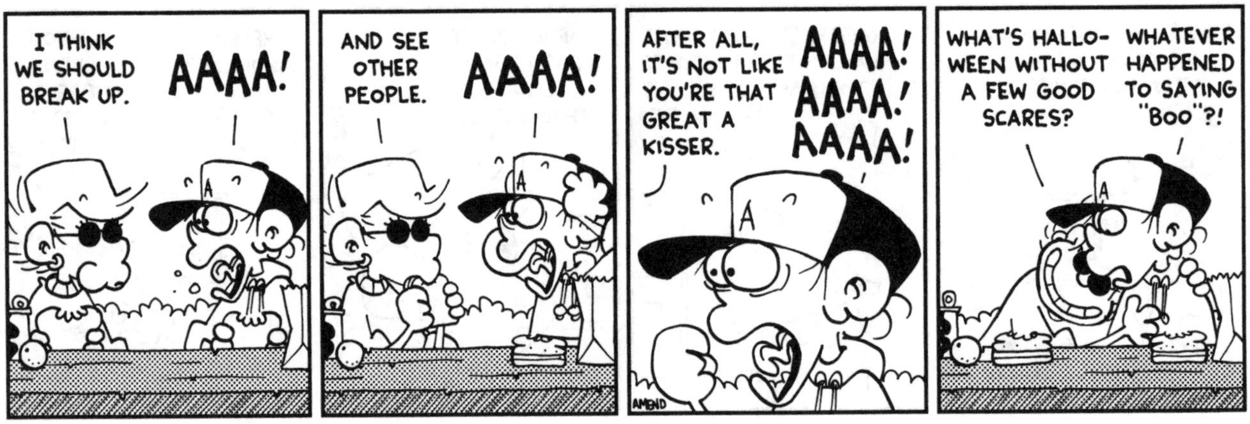
I THINK WE SHOULD BREAK UP.
AAAA!
AND SEE OTHER PEOPLE.
AAAA!
AFTER ALL, IT'S NOT LIKE YOU'RE THAT GREAT A KISSER.
AAAA! AAAA! AAAA!
WHAT'S HALLOWEEN WITHOUT A FEW GOOD SCARES?
WHATEVER HAPPENED TO SAYING "BOO"?!
AMEND

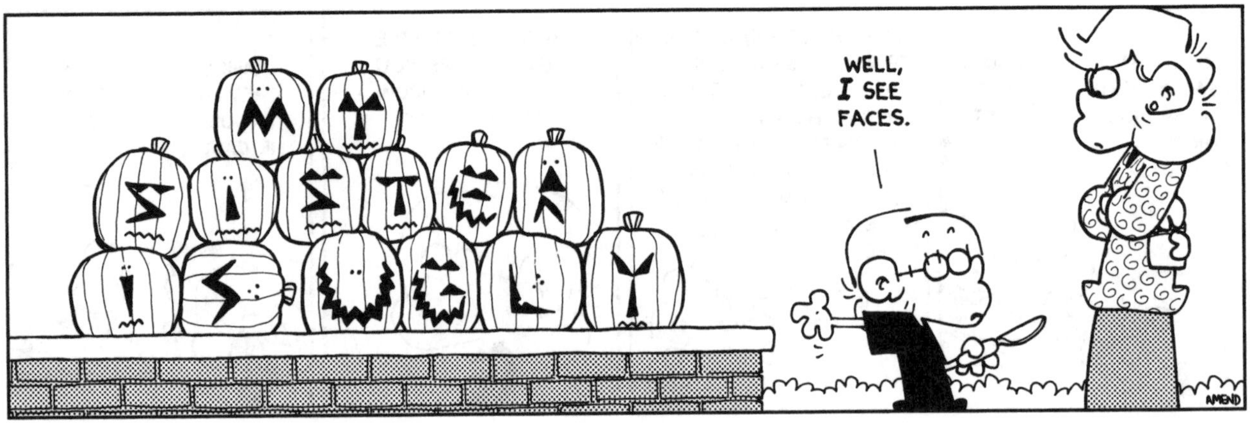
MY SISTER IS UGLY
WELL, I SEE FACES.
AMEND

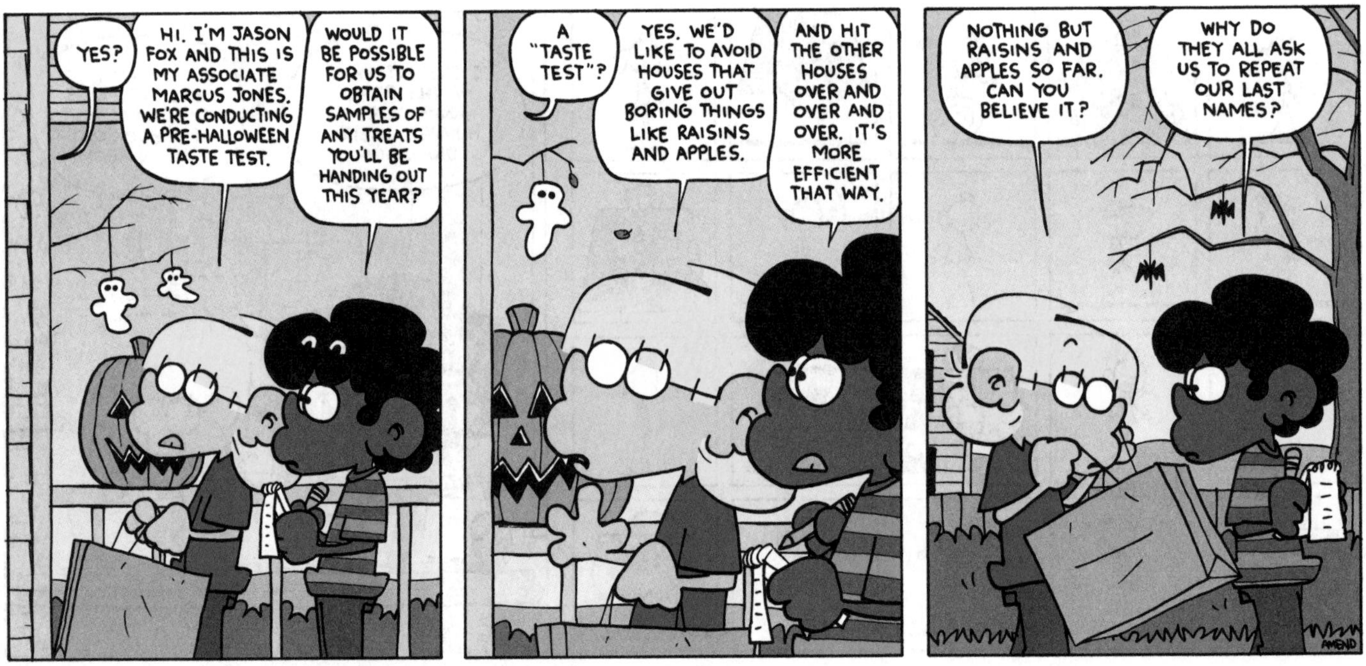
YES?
HI. I'M JASON FOX AND THIS IS MY ASSOCIATE MARCUS JONES. WE'RE CONDUCTING A PRE-HALLOWEEN TASTE TEST.
WOULD IT BE POSSIBLE FOR US TO OBTAIN SAMPLES OF ANY TREATS YOU'LL BE HANDING OUT THIS YEAR?
A "TASTE TEST"?
YES. WE'D LIKE TO AVOID HOUSES THAT GIVE OUT BORING THINGS LIKE RAISINS AND APPLES.
AND HIT THE OTHER HOUSES OVER AND OVER AND OVER. IT'S MORE EFFICIENT THAT WAY.
NOTHING BUT RAISINS AND APPLES SO FAR. CAN YOU BELIEVE IT?
WHY DO THEY ALL ASK US TO REPEAT OUR LAST NAMES?
AMEND

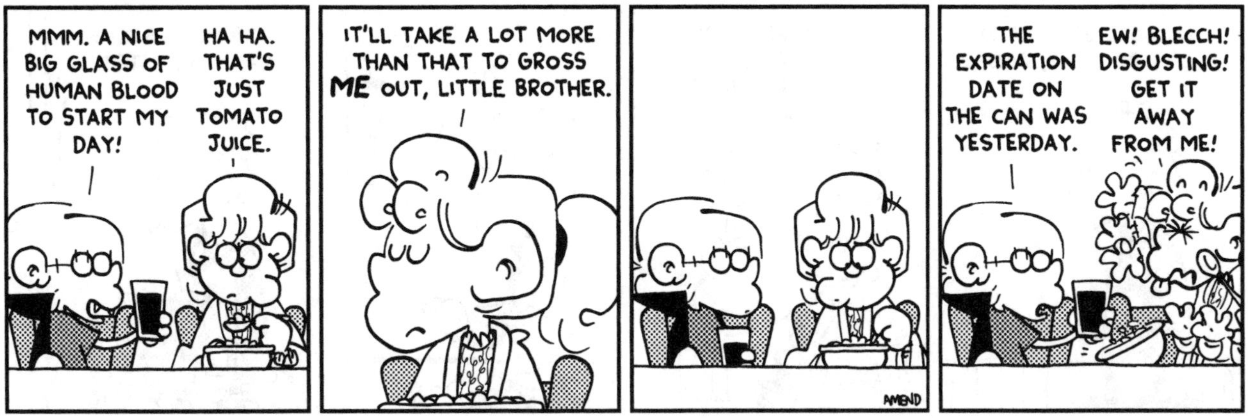
MMM. A NICE BIG GLASS OF HUMAN BLOOD TO START MY DAY!
HA HA. THAT'S JUST TOMATO JUICE.
IT'LL TAKE A LOT MORE THAN THAT TO GROSS **ME** OUT, LITTLE BROTHER.
THE EXPIRATION DATE ON THE CAN WAS YESTERDAY.
EW! BLECCH! DISGUSTING! GET IT AWAY FROM ME!
AMEND

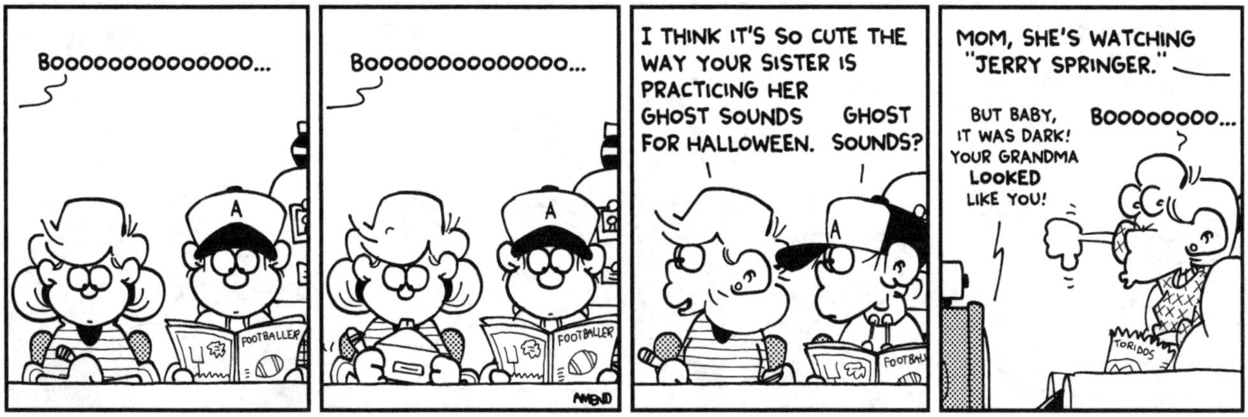
BOOOOOOOOOOOOOO...
FOOTBALLER
BOOOOOOOOOOOOOO...
FOOTBALLER
AMEND
I THINK IT'S SO CUTE THE WAY YOUR SISTER IS PRACTICING HER GHOST SOUNDS FOR HALLOWEEN.
GHOST SOUNDS?
MOM, SHE'S WATCHING "JERRY SPRINGER."
BUT BABY, IT WAS DARK! YOUR GRANDMA **LOOKED** LIKE YOU!
BOOOOOOOO...
TORIDOS

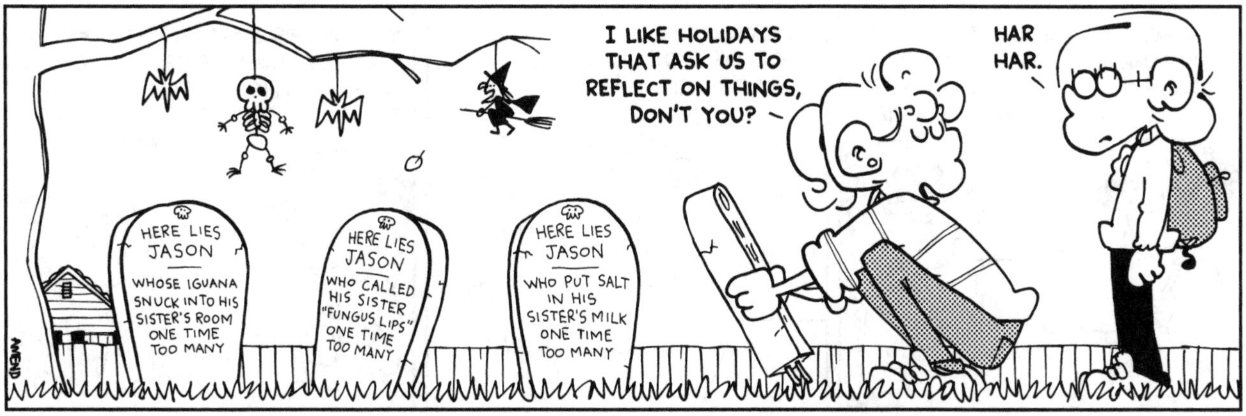
HERE LIES JASON
WHOSE IGUANA SNUCK INTO HIS SISTER'S ROOM ONE TIME TOO MANY
HERE LIES JASON
WHO CALLED HIS SISTER "FUNGUS LIPS" ONE TIME TOO MANY
HERE LIES JASON
WHO PUT SALT IN HIS SISTER'S MILK ONE TIME TOO MANY
I LIKE HOLIDAYS THAT ASK US TO REFLECT ON THINGS, DON'T YOU?
HAR HAR.
AMEND

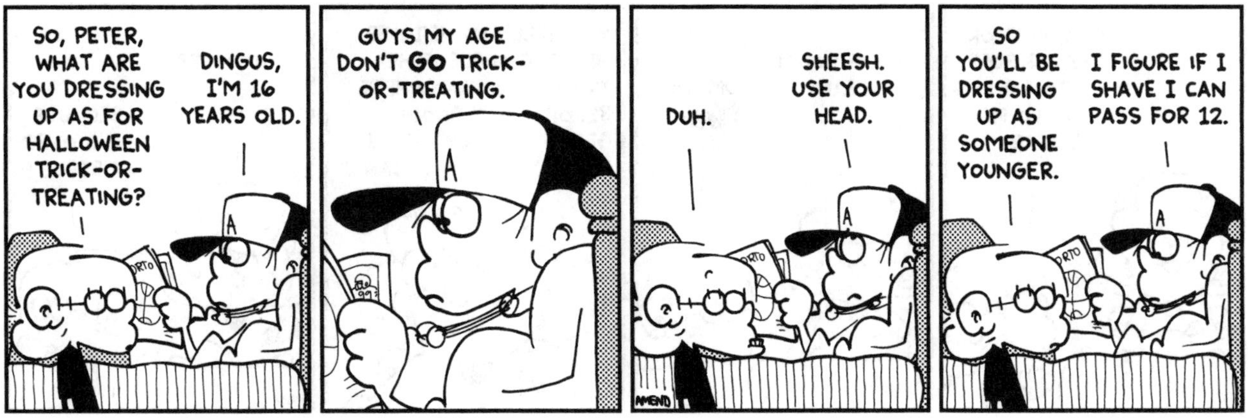
SO, PETER, WHAT ARE YOU DRESSING UP AS FOR HALLOWEEN TRICK-OR-TREATING?
DINGUS, I'M 16 YEARS OLD.
GUYS MY AGE DON'T **GO** TRICK-OR-TREATING.
DUH.
SHEESH. USE YOUR HEAD.
SO YOU'LL BE DRESSING UP AS SOMEONE YOUNGER.
I FIGURE IF I SHAVE I CAN PASS FOR 12.
AMEND

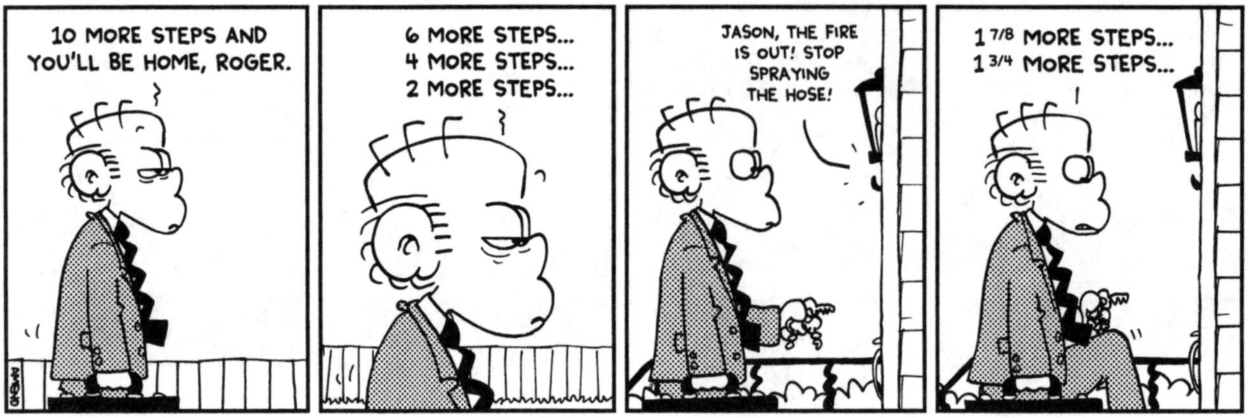
10 MORE STEPS AND YOU'LL BE HOME, ROGER.
6 MORE STEPS... 4 MORE STEPS... 2 MORE STEPS...
JASON, THE FIRE IS OUT! STOP SPRAYING THE HOSE!
1 7/8 MORE STEPS... 1 3/4 MORE STEPS...

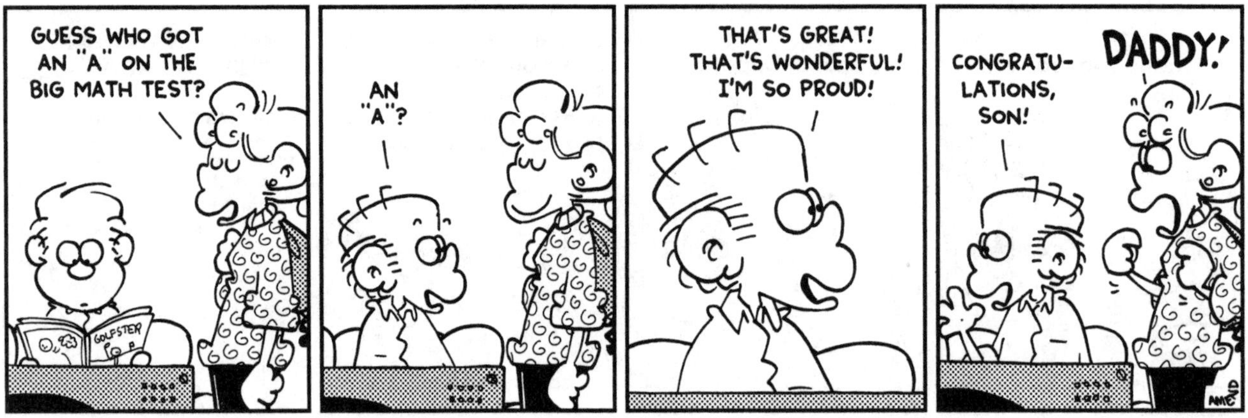
GUESS WHO GOT AN "A" ON THE BIG MATH TEST?
GOLFSTER
AN "A"?
THAT'S GREAT! THAT'S WONDERFUL! I'M SO PROUD!
CONGRATU-LATIONS, SON!
DADDY!

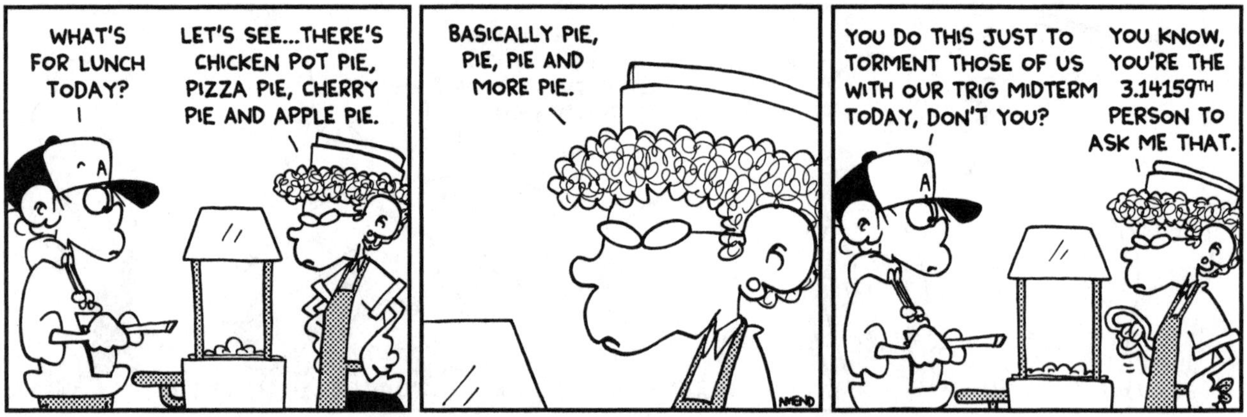
WHAT'S FOR LUNCH TODAY?
LET'S SEE...THERE'S CHICKEN POT PIE, PIZZA PIE, CHERRY PIE AND APPLE PIE.
BASICALLY PIE, PIE, PIE AND MORE PIE.
YOU DO THIS JUST TO TORMENT THOSE OF US WITH OUR TRIG MIDTERM TODAY, DON'T YOU?
YOU KNOW, YOU'RE THE 3.14159TH PERSON TO ASK ME THAT.

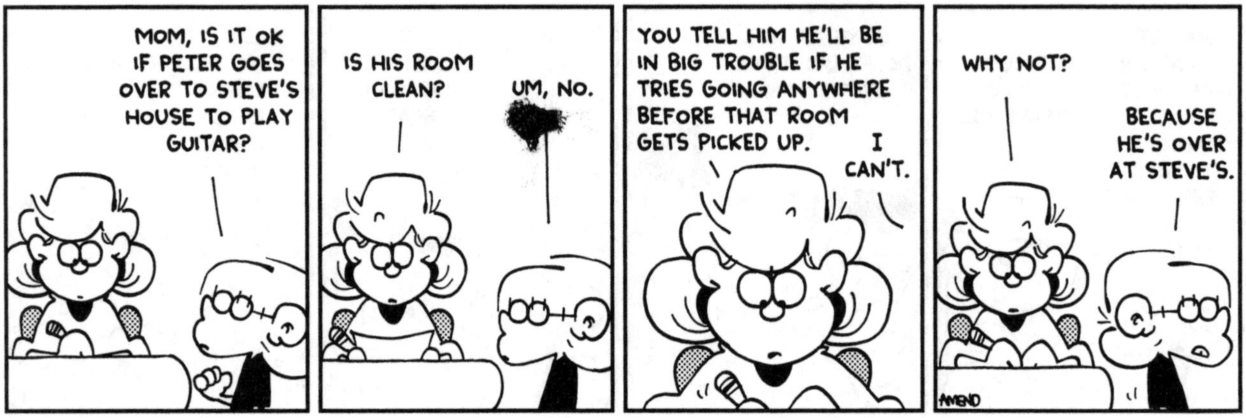
MOM, IS IT OK IF PETER GOES OVER TO STEVE'S HOUSE TO PLAY GUITAR?
IS HIS ROOM CLEAN?
UM, NO.
YOU TELL HIM HE'LL BE IN BIG TROUBLE IF HE TRIES GOING ANYWHERE BEFORE THAT ROOM GETS PICKED UP.
I CAN'T.
WHY NOT?
BECAUSE HE'S OVER AT STEVE'S.

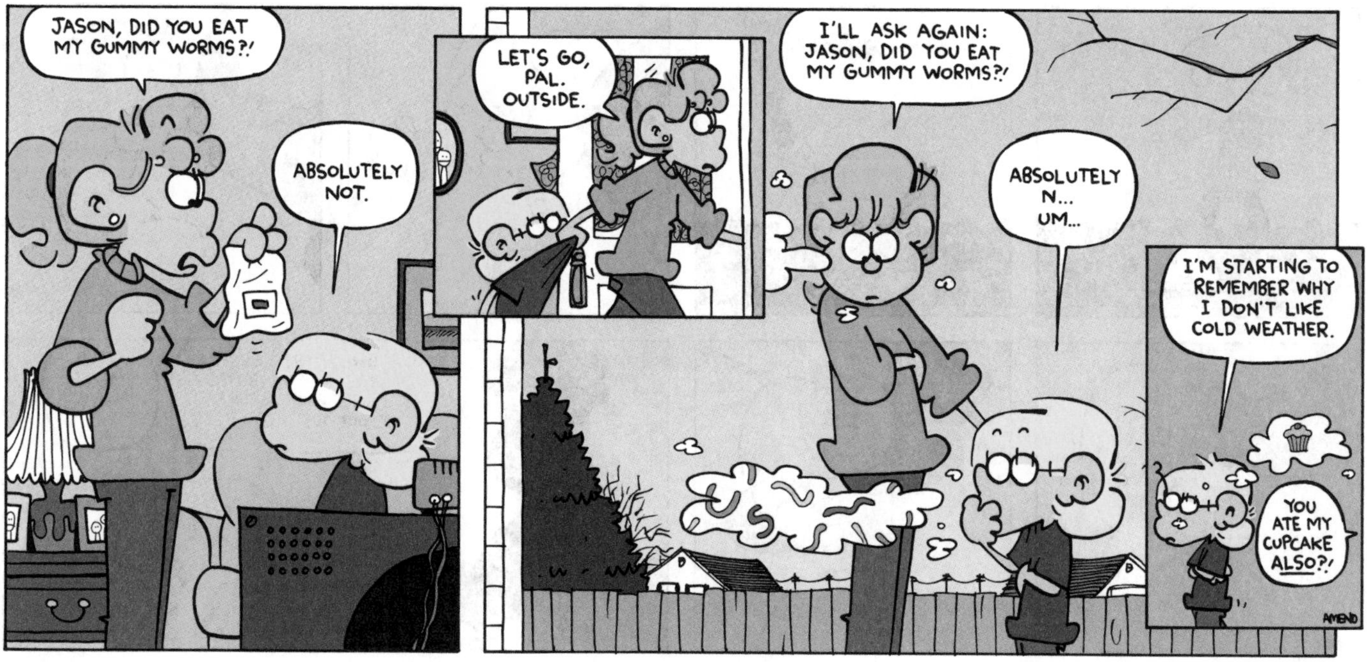
JASON, DID YOU EAT MY GUMMY WORMS?!
ABSOLUTELY NOT.
LET'S GO, PAL. OUTSIDE.
I'LL ASK AGAIN: JASON, DID YOU EAT MY GUMMY WORMS?!
ABSOLUTELY N... UM...
I'M STARTING TO REMEMBER WHY I DON'T LIKE COLD WEATHER.
YOU ATE MY CUPCAKE ALSO?!
AMEND

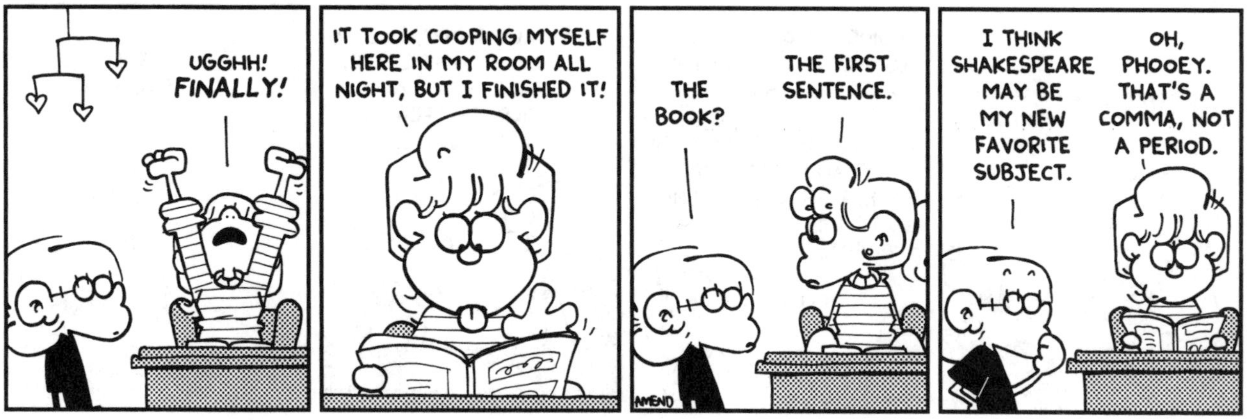
UGGHH! FINALLY!
IT TOOK COOPING MYSELF HERE IN MY ROOM ALL NIGHT, BUT I FINISHED IT!
THE BOOK?
THE FIRST SENTENCE.
I THINK SHAKESPEARE MAY BE MY NEW FAVORITE SUBJECT.
OH, PHOOEY. THAT'S A COMMA, NOT A PERIOD.
AMEND

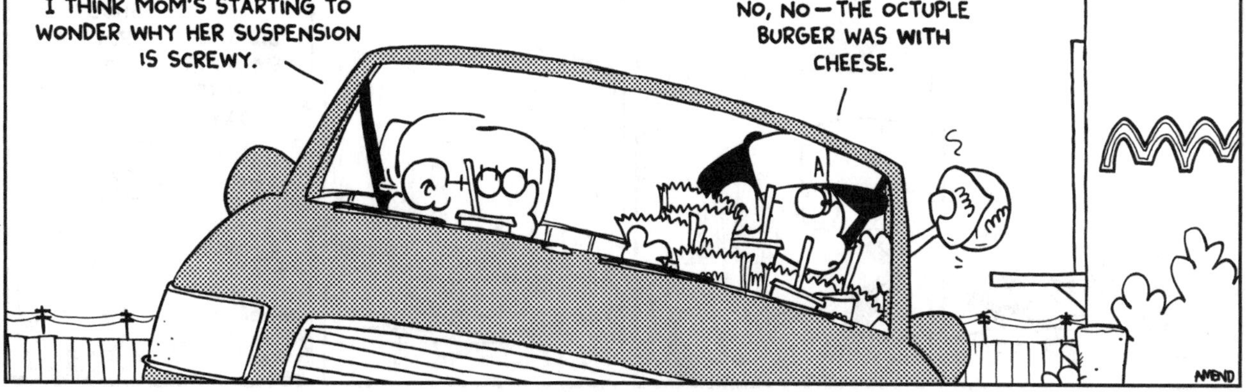
I THINK MOM'S STARTING TO WONDER WHY HER SUSPENSION IS SCREWY.
NO, NO—THE OCTUPLE BURGER WAS WITH CHEESE.
AMEND

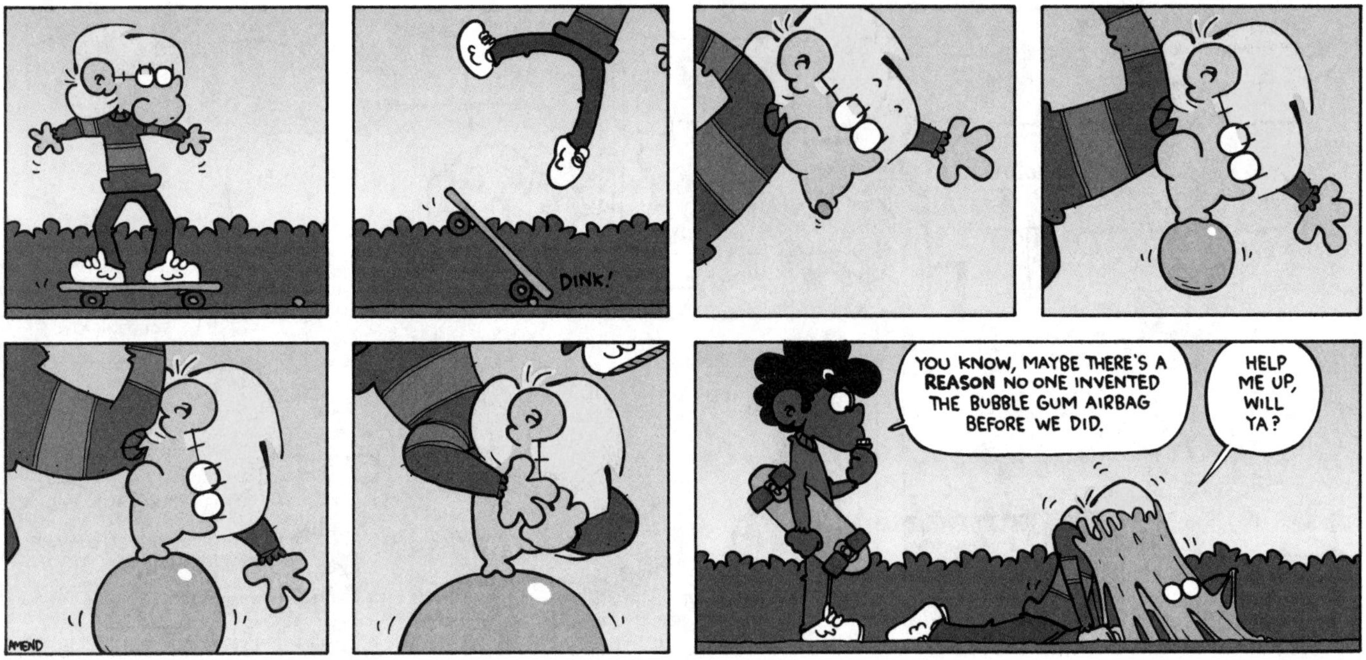
DINK!
AMEND
YOU KNOW, MAYBE THERE'S A REASON NO ONE INVENTED THE BUBBLE GUM AIRBAG BEFORE WE DID.
HELP ME UP, WILL YA?

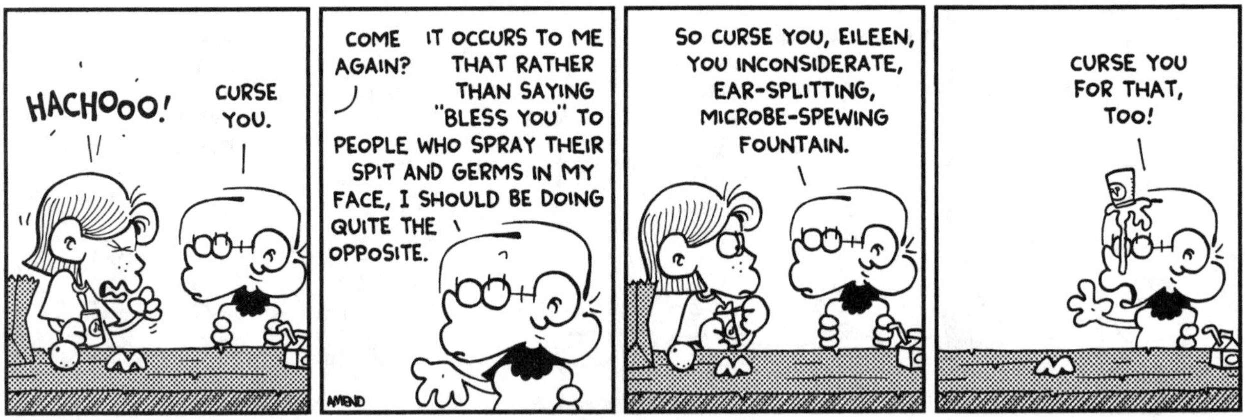
HACHOOO!
CURSE YOU.
COME AGAIN?
IT OCCURS TO ME THAT RATHER THAN SAYING "BLESS YOU" TO PEOPLE WHO SPRAY THEIR SPIT AND GERMS IN MY FACE, I SHOULD BE DOING QUITE THE OPPOSITE.
AMEND
SO CURSE YOU, EILEEN, YOU INCONSIDERATE, EAR-SPLITTING, MICROBE-SPEWING FOUNTAIN.
CURSE YOU FOR THAT, TOO!

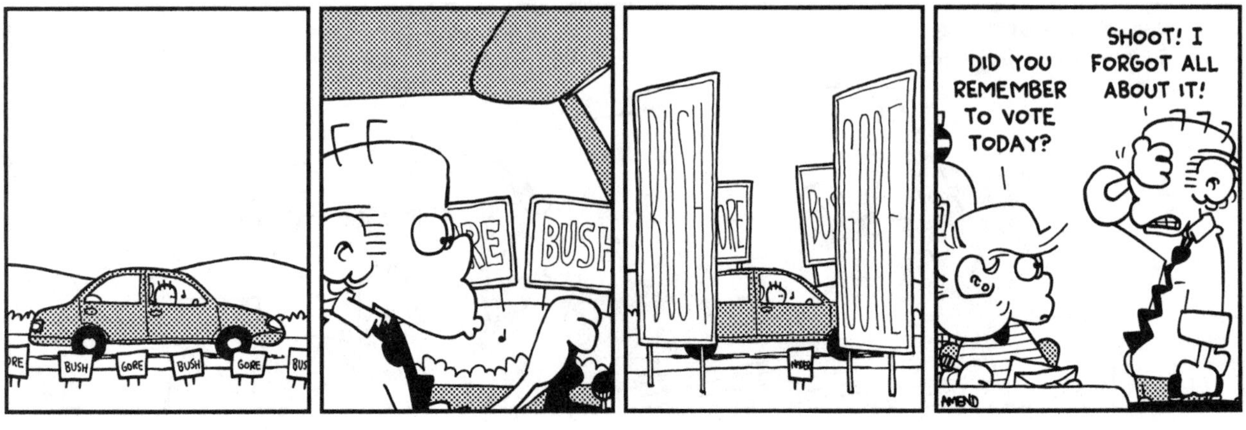
BUSH
GORE
BUSH
GORE
BUSH
BUSH
GORE
DID YOU REMEMBER TO VOTE TODAY?
SHOOT! I FORGOT ALL ABOUT IT!
AMEND

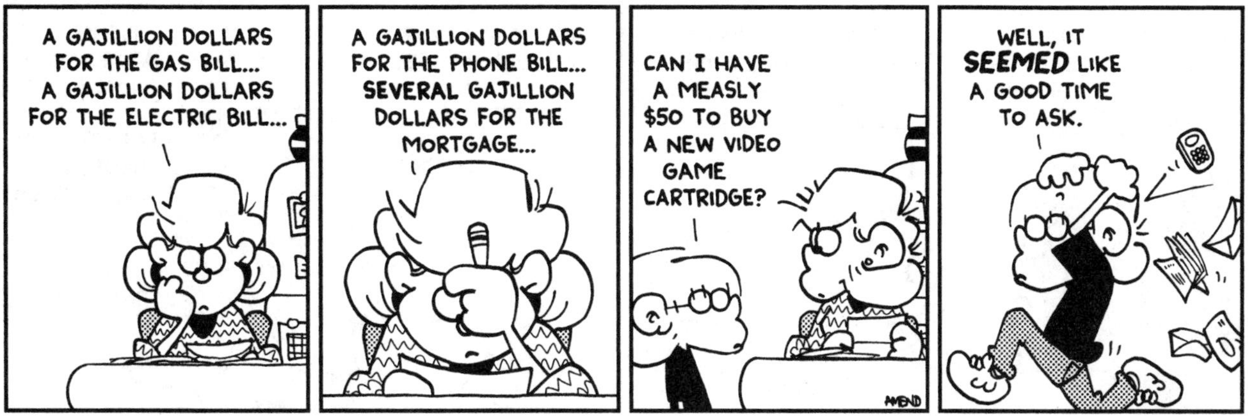
A GAJILLION DOLLARS FOR THE GAS BILL... A GAJILLION DOLLARS FOR THE ELECTRIC BILL...
A GAJILLION DOLLARS FOR THE PHONE BILL... **SEVERAL** GAJILLION DOLLARS FOR THE MORTGAGE...
CAN I HAVE A MEASLY $50 TO BUY A NEW VIDEO GAME CARTRIDGE?
WELL, IT **SEEMED** LIKE A GOOD TIME TO ASK.

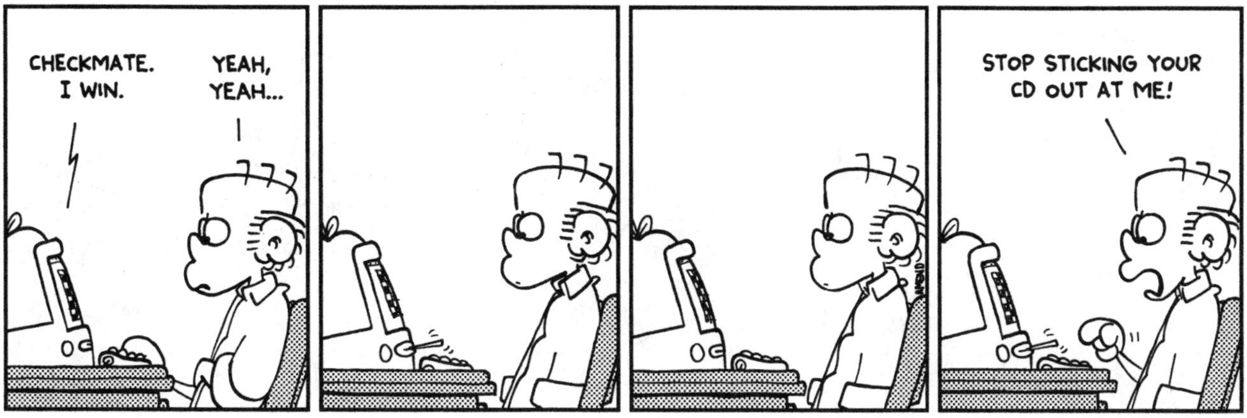
CHECKMATE. I WIN.
YEAH, YEAH...
STOP STICKING YOUR CD OUT AT ME!

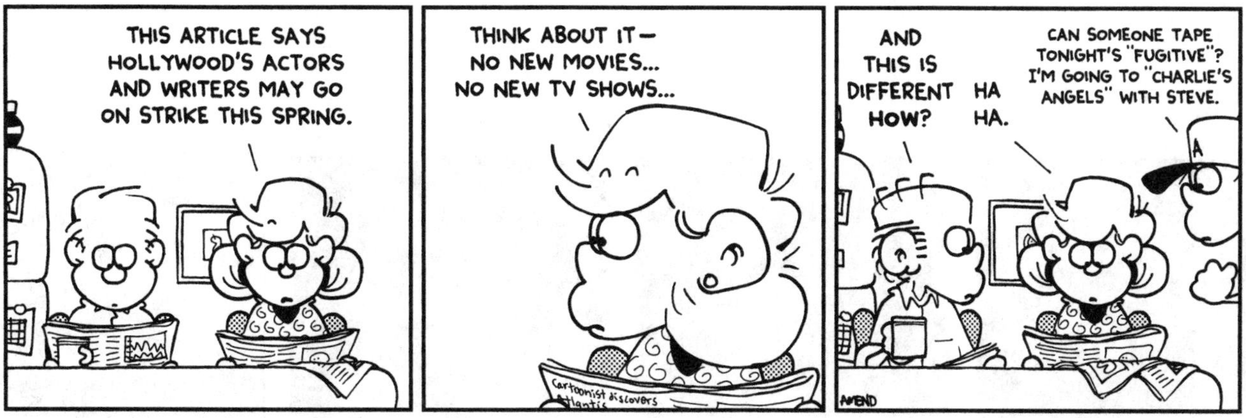
THIS ARTICLE SAYS HOLLYWOOD'S ACTORS AND WRITERS MAY GO ON STRIKE THIS SPRING.
THINK ABOUT IT— NO NEW MOVIES... NO NEW TV SHOWS...
Cartoonist discovers
AND THIS IS DIFFERENT **HOW**?
HA HA.
CAN SOMEONE TAPE TONIGHT'S "FUGITIVE"? I'M GOING TO "CHARLIE'S ANGELS" WITH STEVE.

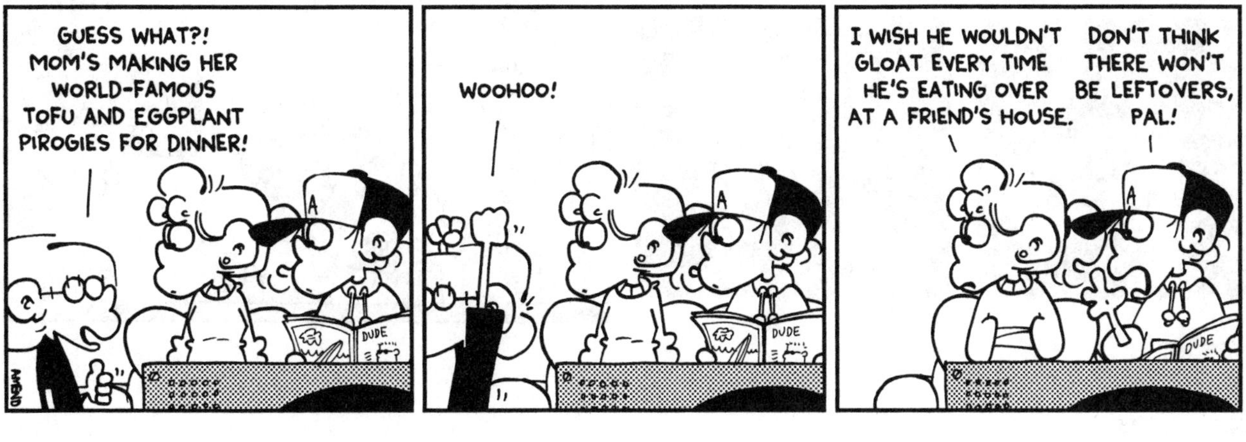
GUESS WHAT?! MOM'S MAKING HER WORLD-FAMOUS TOFU AND EGGPLANT PIROGIES FOR DINNER!
WOOHOO!
I WISH HE WOULDN'T GLOAT EVERY TIME HE'S EATING OVER AT A FRIEND'S HOUSE.
DON'T THINK THERE WON'T BE LEFTOVERS, PAL!

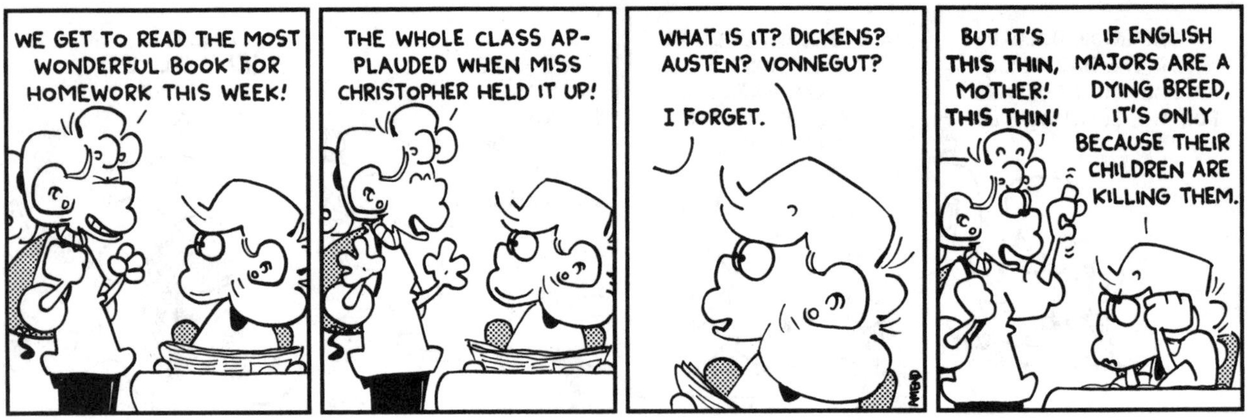
WE GET TO READ THE MOST WONDERFUL BOOK FOR HOMEWORK THIS WEEK!
THE WHOLE CLASS APPLAUDED WHEN MISS CHRISTOPHER HELD IT UP!
WHAT IS IT? DICKENS? AUSTEN? VONNEGUT?
I FORGET.
BUT IT'S THIS THIN, MOTHER! THIS THIN!
IF ENGLISH MAJORS ARE A DYING BREED, IT'S ONLY BECAUSE THEIR CHILDREN ARE KILLING THEM.
AMEND

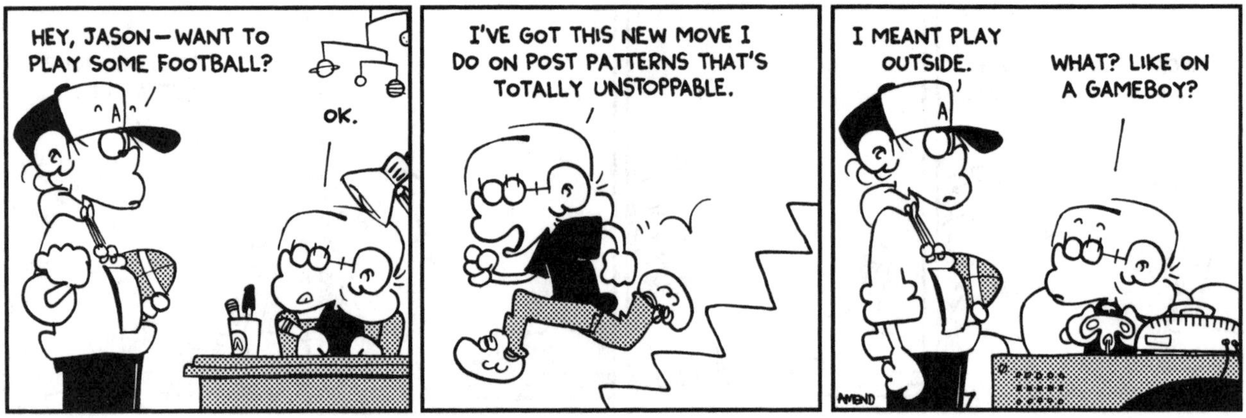
HEY, JASON—WANT TO PLAY SOME FOOTBALL?
OK.
I'VE GOT THIS NEW MOVE I DO ON POST PATTERNS THAT'S TOTALLY UNSTOPPABLE.
I MEANT PLAY OUTSIDE.
WHAT? LIKE ON A GAMEBOY?
AMEND

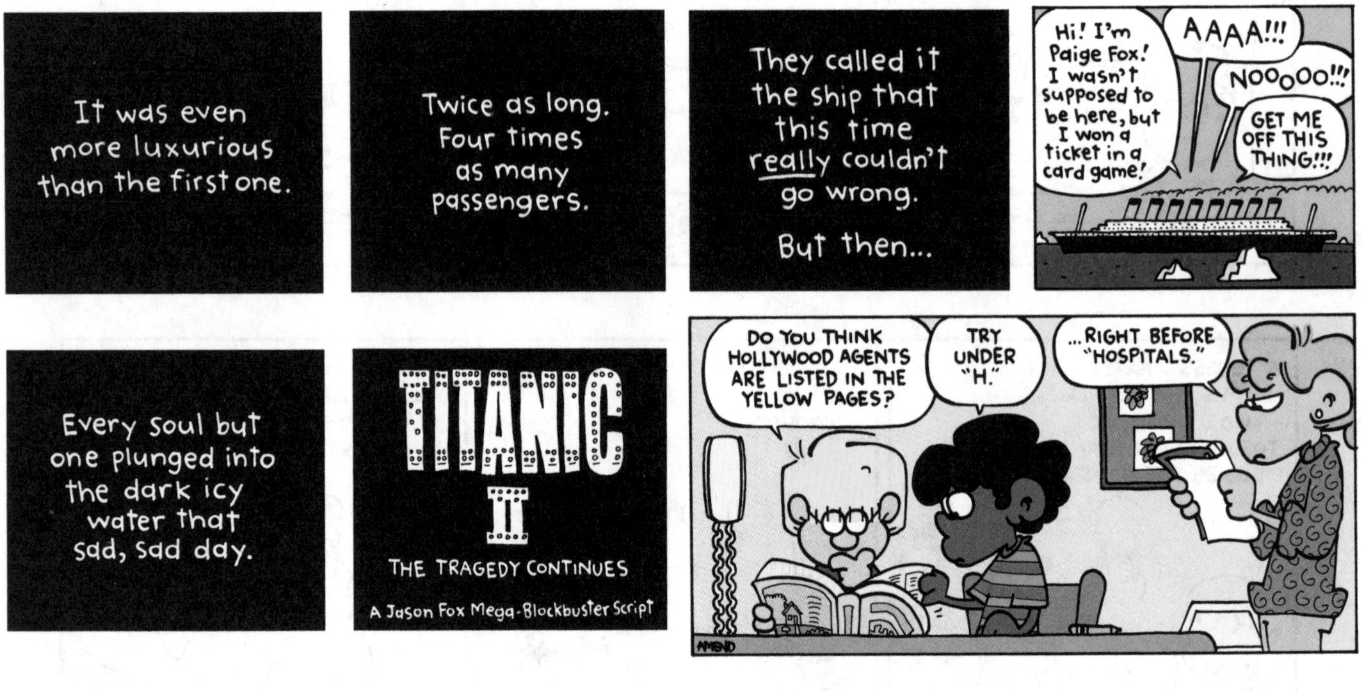
It was even more luxurious than the first one.
Twice as long. Four times as many passengers.
They called it the ship that this time really couldn't go wrong.
But then...
Hi! I'm Paige Fox! I wasn't supposed to be here, but I won a ticket in a card game!
AAAA!!!
NOOOOO!!!
GET ME OFF THIS THING!!!
Every soul but one plunged into the dark icy water that sad, sad day.
TITANIC II
THE TRAGEDY CONTINUES
A Jason Fox Mega-Blockbuster Script
DO YOU THINK HOLLYWOOD AGENTS ARE LISTED IN THE YELLOW PAGES?
TRY UNDER "H."
...RIGHT BEFORE "HOSPITALS."
AMEND

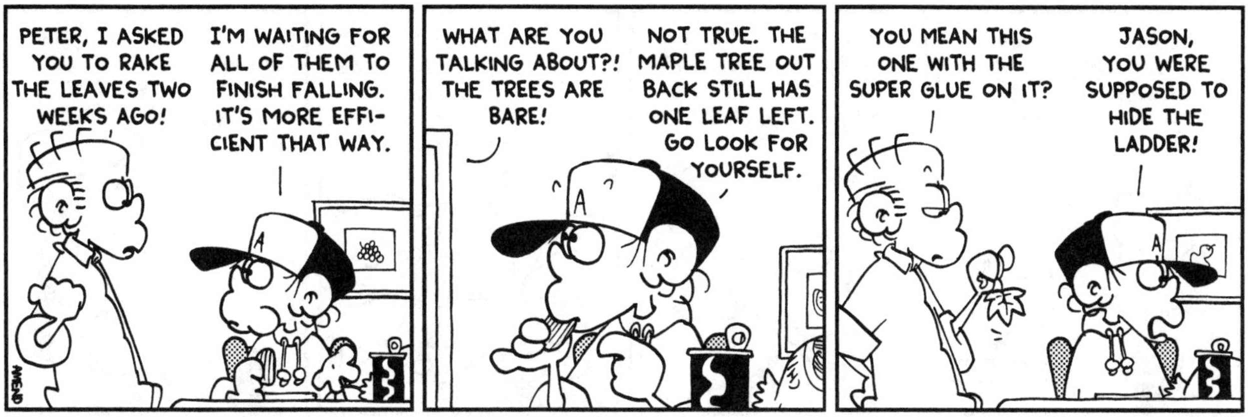
PETER, I ASKED YOU TO RAKE THE LEAVES TWO WEEKS AGO!
I'M WAITING FOR ALL OF THEM TO FINISH FALLING. IT'S MORE EFFICIENT THAT WAY.
WHAT ARE YOU TALKING ABOUT?! THE TREES ARE BARE!
NOT TRUE. THE MAPLE TREE OUT BACK STILL HAS ONE LEAF LEFT. GO LOOK FOR YOURSELF.
YOU MEAN THIS ONE WITH THE SUPER GLUE ON IT?
JASON, YOU WERE SUPPOSED TO HIDE THE LADDER!

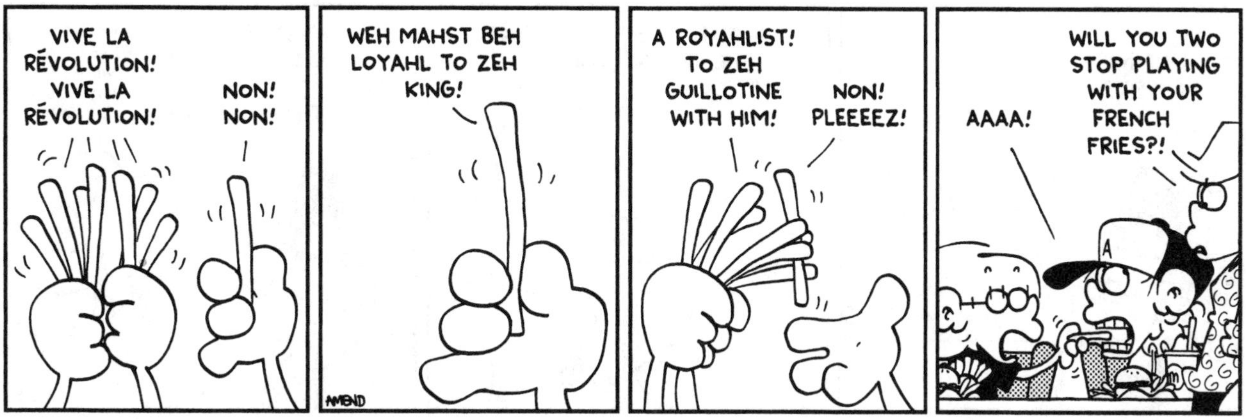
VIVE LA RÉVOLUTION! VIVE LA RÉVOLUTION!
NON! NON!
WEH MAHST BEH LOYAHL TO ZEH KING!
A ROYAHLIST! TO ZEH GUILLOTINE WITH HIM!
NON! PLEEEEZ!
AAAA!
WILL YOU TWO STOP PLAYING WITH YOUR FRENCH FRIES?!

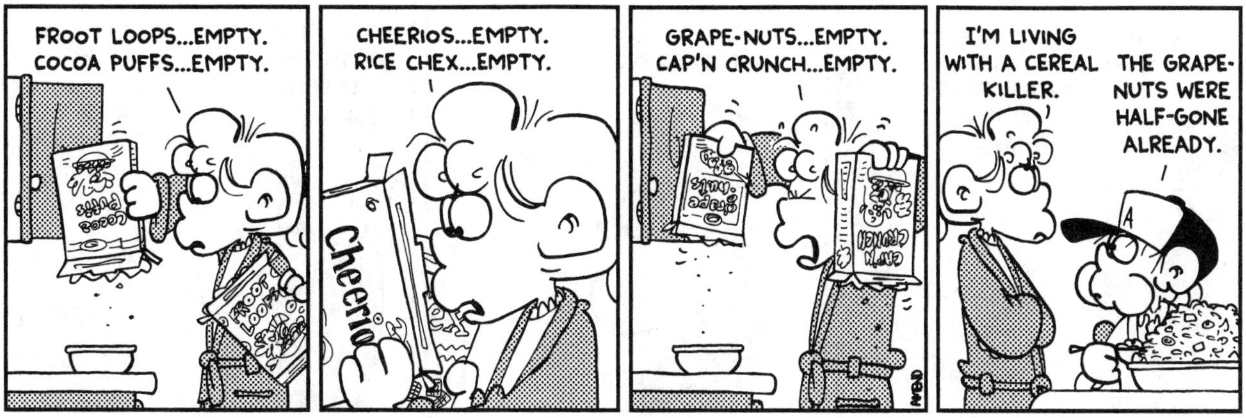
FROOT LOOPS...EMPTY. COCOA PUFFS...EMPTY.
CHEERIOS...EMPTY. RICE CHEX...EMPTY.
GRAPE-NUTS...EMPTY. CAP'N CRUNCH...EMPTY.
I'M LIVING WITH A CEREAL KILLER.
THE GRAPE-NUTS WERE HALF-GONE ALREADY.

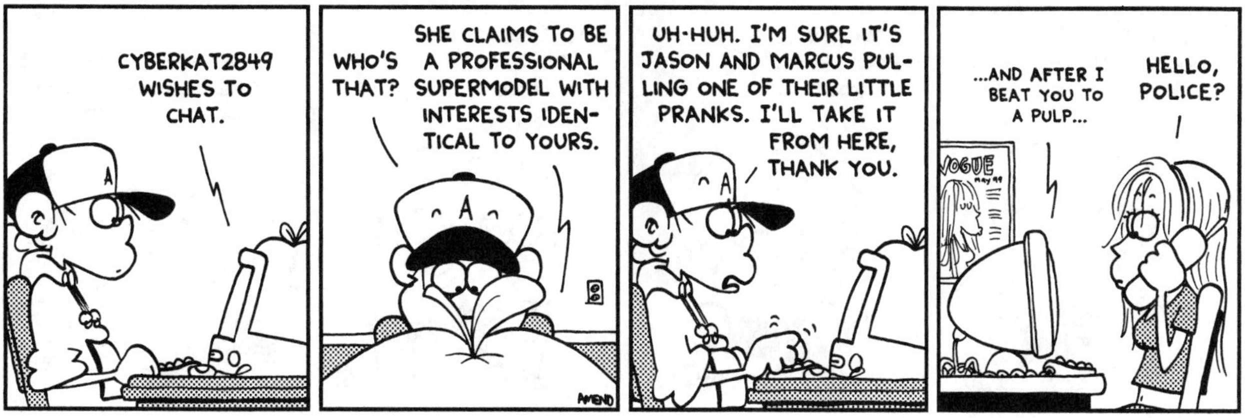
CYBERKAT2849 WISHES TO CHAT.
WHO'S THAT?
SHE CLAIMS TO BE A PROFESSIONAL SUPERMODEL WITH INTERESTS IDENTICAL TO YOURS.
UH-HUH. I'M SURE IT'S JASON AND MARCUS PULLING ONE OF THEIR LITTLE PRANKS. I'LL TAKE IT FROM HERE, THANK YOU.
...AND AFTER I BEAT YOU TO A PULP...
HELLO, POLICE?

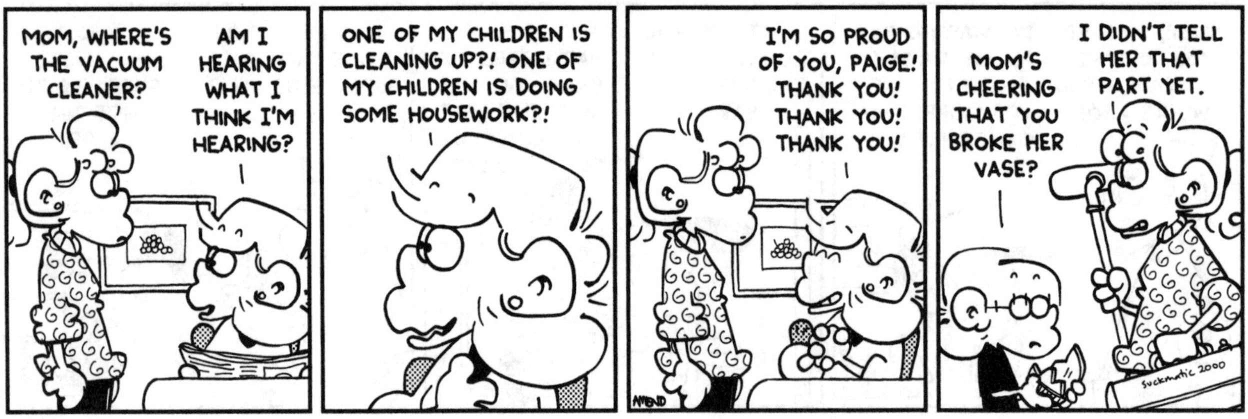
MOM, WHERE'S THE VACUUM CLEANER?
AM I HEARING WHAT I THINK I'M HEARING?
ONE OF MY CHILDREN IS CLEANING UP?! ONE OF MY CHILDREN IS DOING SOME HOUSEWORK?!
I'M SO PROUD OF YOU, PAIGE! THANK YOU! THANK YOU! THANK YOU!
AMEND
MOM'S CHEERING THAT YOU BROKE HER VASE?
I DIDN'T TELL HER THAT PART YET.
Suckmatic 2000

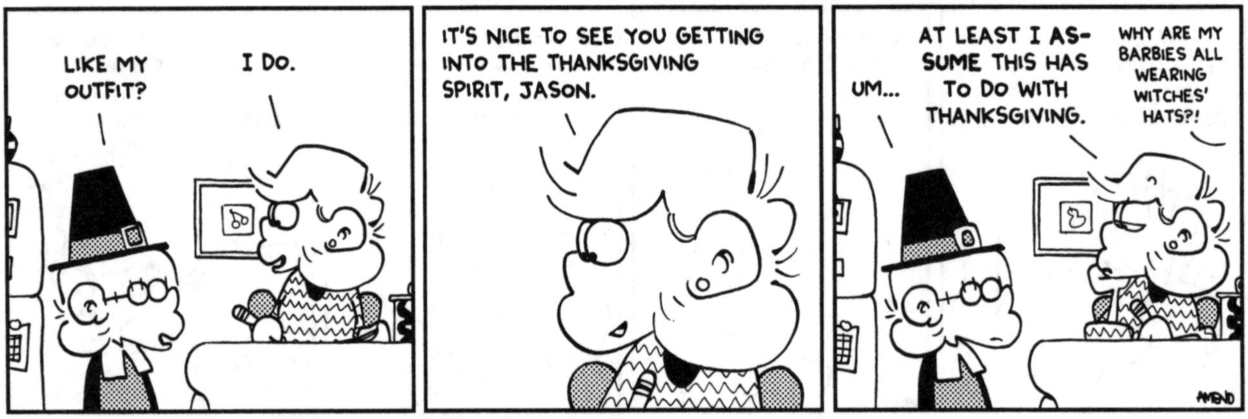
LIKE MY OUTFIT?
I DO.
IT'S NICE TO SEE YOU GETTING INTO THE THANKSGIVING SPIRIT, JASON.
UM...
AT LEAST I ASSUME THIS HAS TO DO WITH THANKSGIVING.
WHY ARE MY BARBIES ALL WEARING WITCHES' HATS?!
AMEND

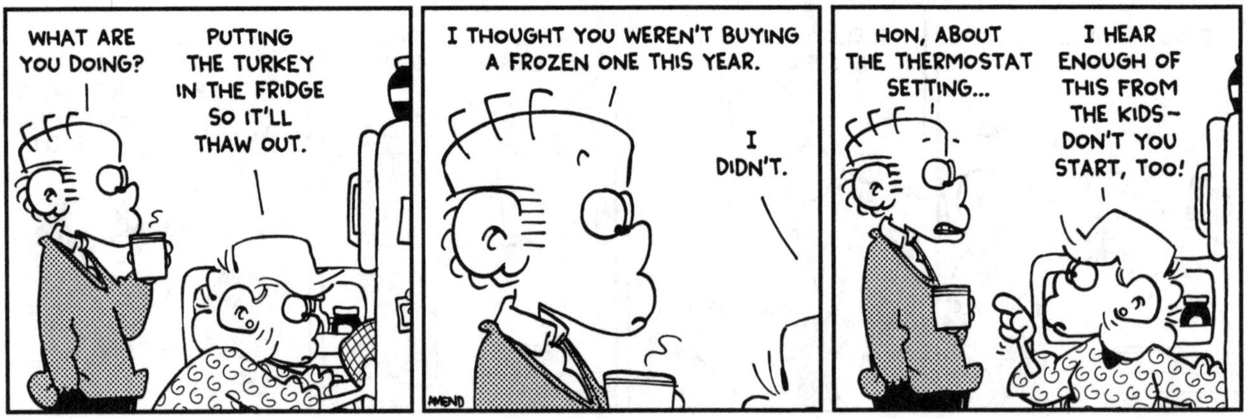
WHAT ARE YOU DOING?
PUTTING THE TURKEY IN THE FRIDGE SO IT'LL THAW OUT.
I THOUGHT YOU WEREN'T BUYING A FROZEN ONE THIS YEAR.
I DIDN'T.
AMEND
HON, ABOUT THE THERMOSTAT SETTING...
I HEAR ENOUGH OF THIS FROM THE KIDS— DON'T YOU START, TOO!

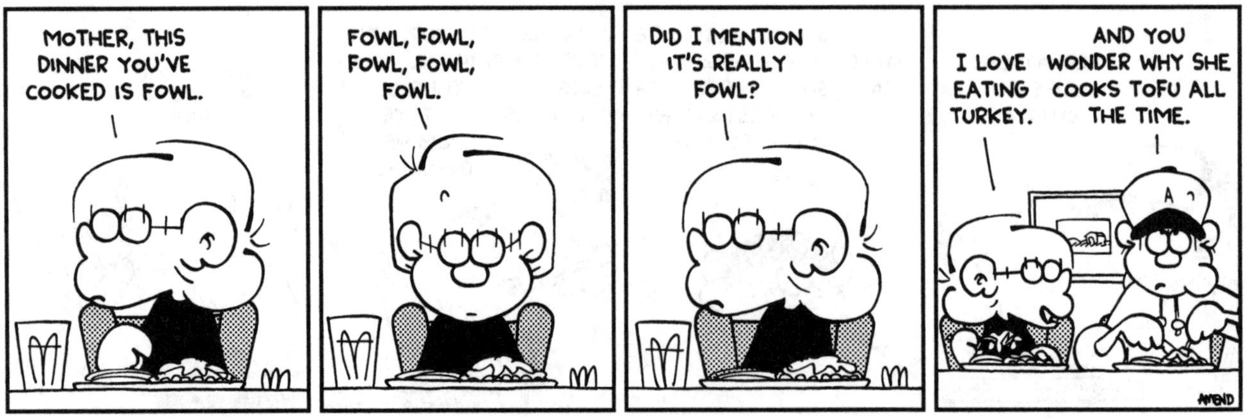
MOTHER, THIS DINNER YOU'VE COOKED IS FOWL.
FOWL, FOWL, FOWL, FOWL, FOWL.
DID I MENTION IT'S REALLY FOWL?
I LOVE EATING TURKEY.
AND YOU WONDER WHY SHE COOKS TOFU ALL THE TIME.
AMEND

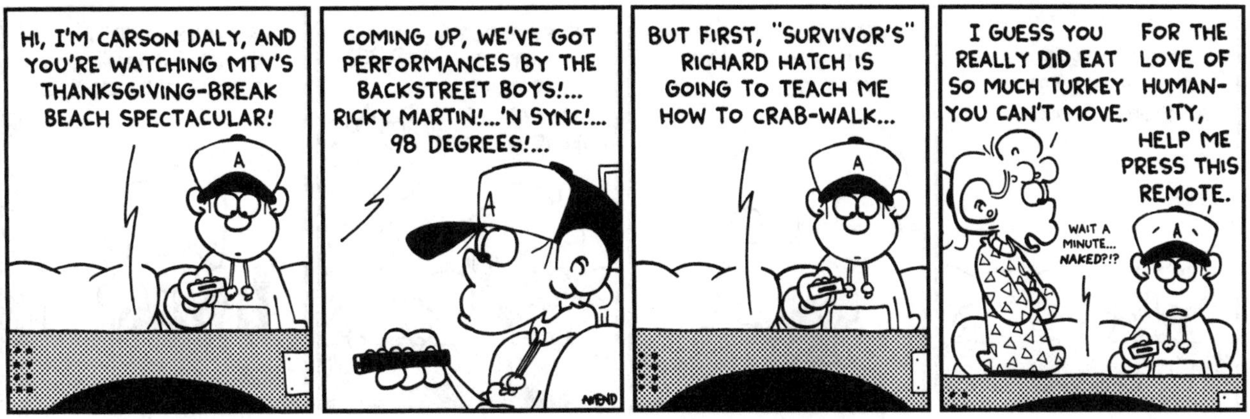
HI, I'M CARSON DALY, AND YOU'RE WATCHING MTV'S THANKSGIVING-BREAK BEACH SPECTACULAR!
COMING UP, WE'VE GOT PERFORMANCES BY THE BACKSTREET BOYS!... RICKY MARTIN!...'N SYNC!... 98 DEGREES!...
BUT FIRST, "SURVIVOR'S" RICHARD HATCH IS GOING TO TEACH ME HOW TO CRAB-WALK...
I GUESS YOU REALLY DID EAT SO MUCH TURKEY YOU CAN'T MOVE.
FOR THE LOVE OF HUMAN-ITY, HELP ME PRESS THIS REMOTE.
WAIT A MINUTE... NAKED?!?
AMEND

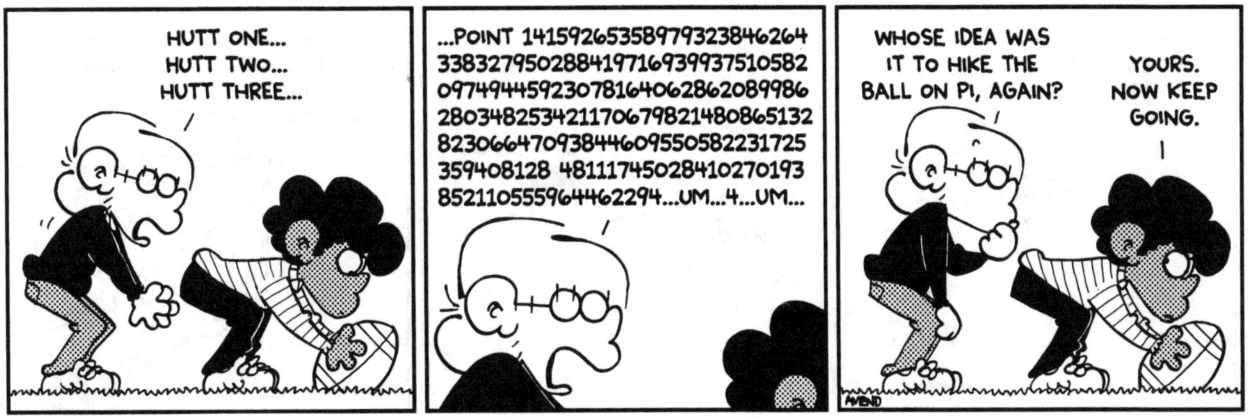
HUTT ONE... HUTT TWO... HUTT THREE...
...POINT 14159265358979323846264 33832795028841971693993751058 2097494459230781640628620899862 8034825342117067982148086513282 306647093844609550582231725 359408128 48111745028410270193 852110555964462294...UM...4...UM...
WHOSE IDEA WAS IT TO HIKE THE BALL ON PI, AGAIN?
YOURS. NOW KEEP GOING.
AMEND

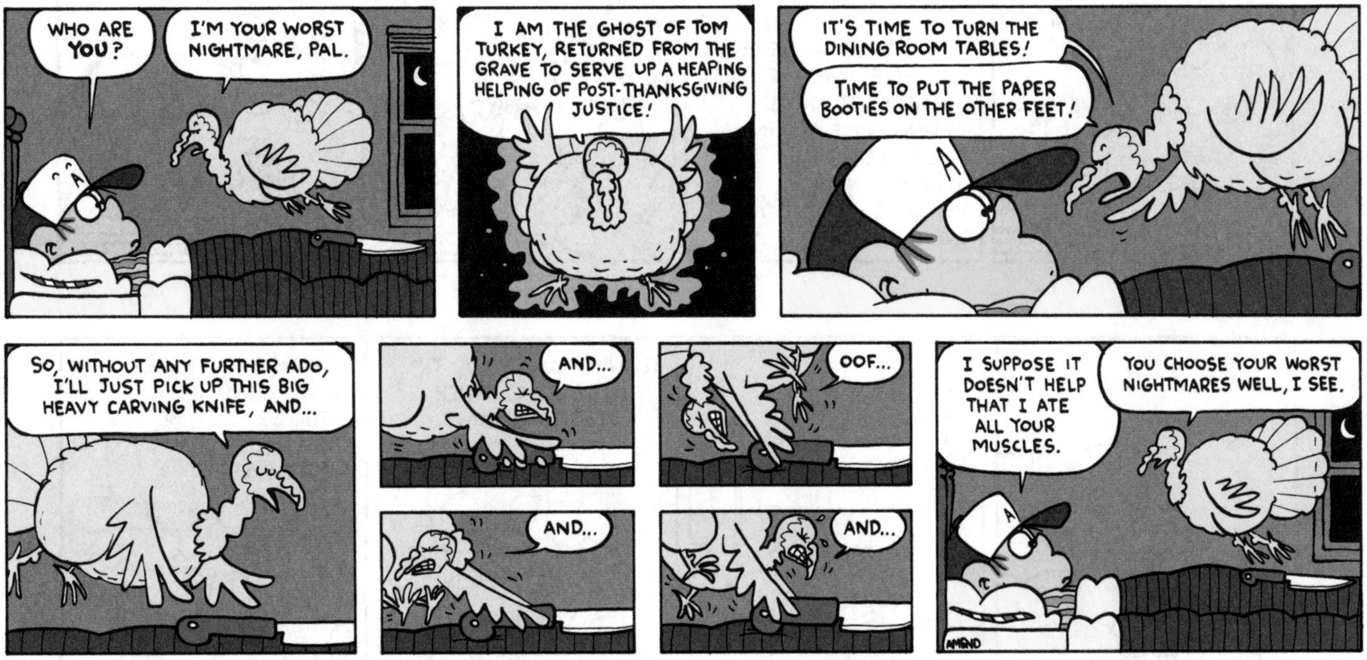
WHO ARE YOU?
I'M YOUR WORST NIGHTMARE, PAL.
I AM THE GHOST OF TOM TURKEY, RETURNED FROM THE GRAVE TO SERVE UP A HEAPING HELPING OF POST-THANKSGIVING JUSTICE!
IT'S TIME TO TURN THE DINING ROOM TABLES!
TIME TO PUT THE PAPER BOOTIES ON THE OTHER FEET!
SO, WITHOUT ANY FURTHER ADO, I'LL JUST PICK UP THIS BIG HEAVY CARVING KNIFE, AND...
AND...
OOF...
AND...
AND...
I SUPPOSE IT DOESN'T HELP THAT I ATE ALL YOUR MUSCLES.
YOU CHOOSE YOUR WORST NIGHTMARES WELL, I SEE.
AMEND

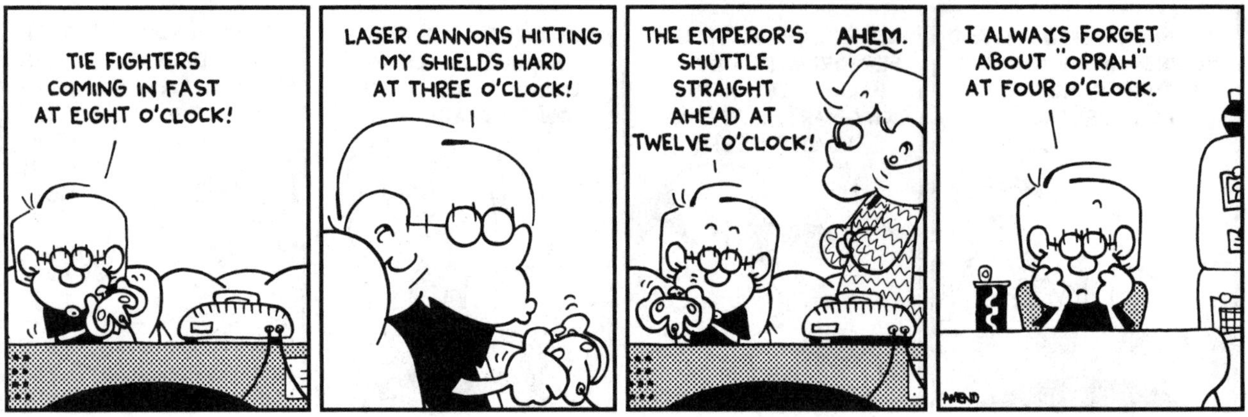
TIE FIGHTERS COMING IN FAST AT EIGHT O'CLOCK!
LASER CANNONS HITTING MY SHIELDS HARD AT THREE O'CLOCK!
THE EMPEROR'S SHUTTLE STRAIGHT AHEAD AT TWELVE O'CLOCK!
AHEM.
I ALWAYS FORGET ABOUT "OPRAH" AT FOUR O'CLOCK.
AMEND

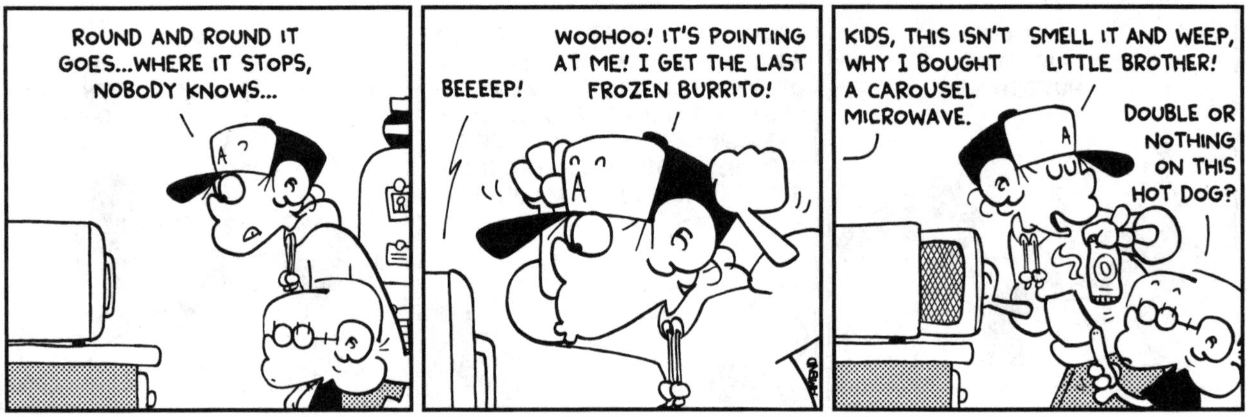
ROUND AND ROUND IT GOES...WHERE IT STOPS, NOBODY KNOWS...
BEEEEP!
WOOHOO! IT'S POINTING AT ME! I GET THE LAST FROZEN BURRITO!
AMEND
KIDS, THIS ISN'T WHY I BOUGHT A CAROUSEL MICROWAVE.
SMELL IT AND WEEP, LITTLE BROTHER!
DOUBLE OR NOTHING ON THIS HOT DOG?

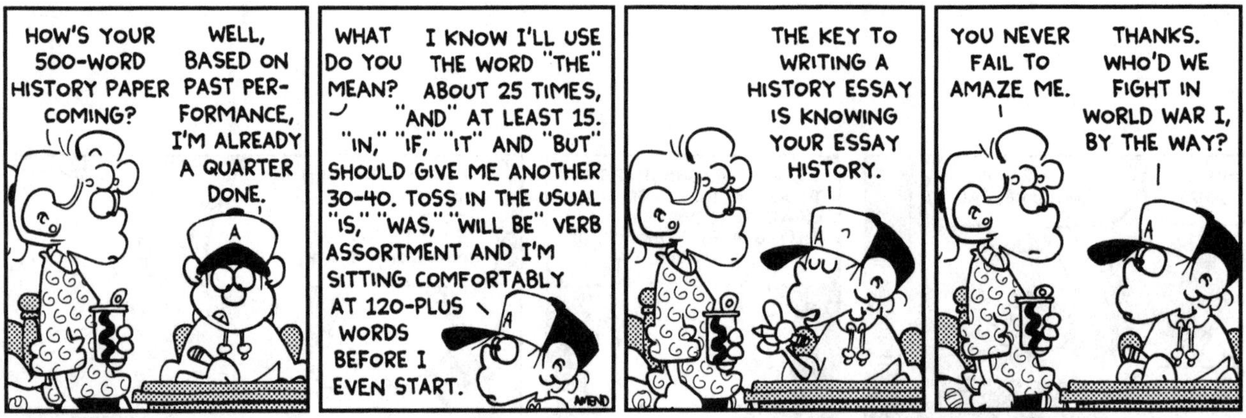
HOW'S YOUR 500-WORD HISTORY PAPER COMING?
WELL, BASED ON PAST PERFORMANCE, I'M ALREADY A QUARTER DONE.
WHAT DO YOU MEAN?
I KNOW I'LL USE THE WORD "THE" ABOUT 25 TIMES, "AND" AT LEAST 15. "IN," "IF," "IT" AND "BUT" SHOULD GIVE ME ANOTHER 30-40. TOSS IN THE USUAL "IS," "WAS," "WILL BE" VERB ASSORTMENT AND I'M SITTING COMFORTABLY AT 120-PLUS WORDS BEFORE I EVEN START.
AMEND
THE KEY TO WRITING A HISTORY ESSAY IS KNOWING YOUR ESSAY HISTORY.
YOU NEVER FAIL TO AMAZE ME.
THANKS. WHO'D WE FIGHT IN WORLD WAR I, BY THE WAY?

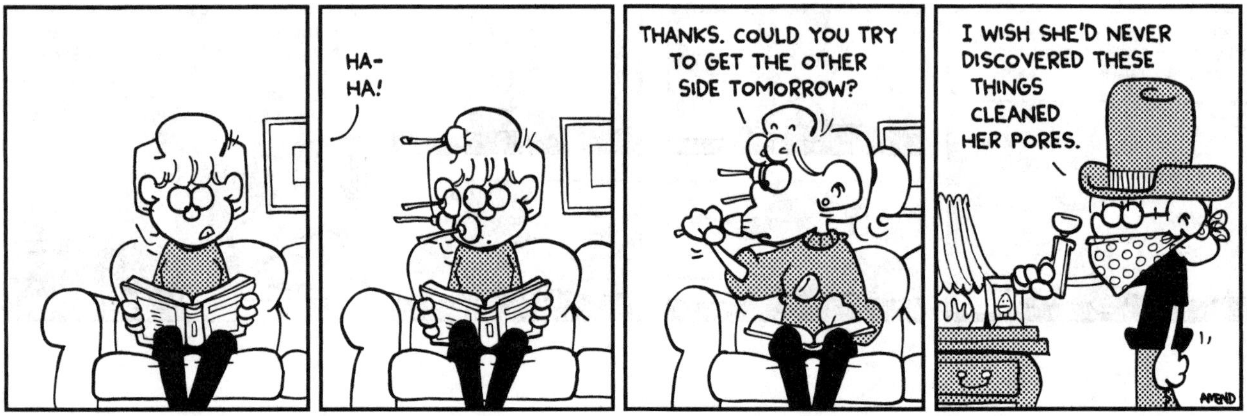
HA-HA!
THANKS. COULD YOU TRY TO GET THE OTHER SIDE TOMORROW?
I WISH SHE'D NEVER DISCOVERED THESE THINGS CLEANED HER PORES.
AMEND

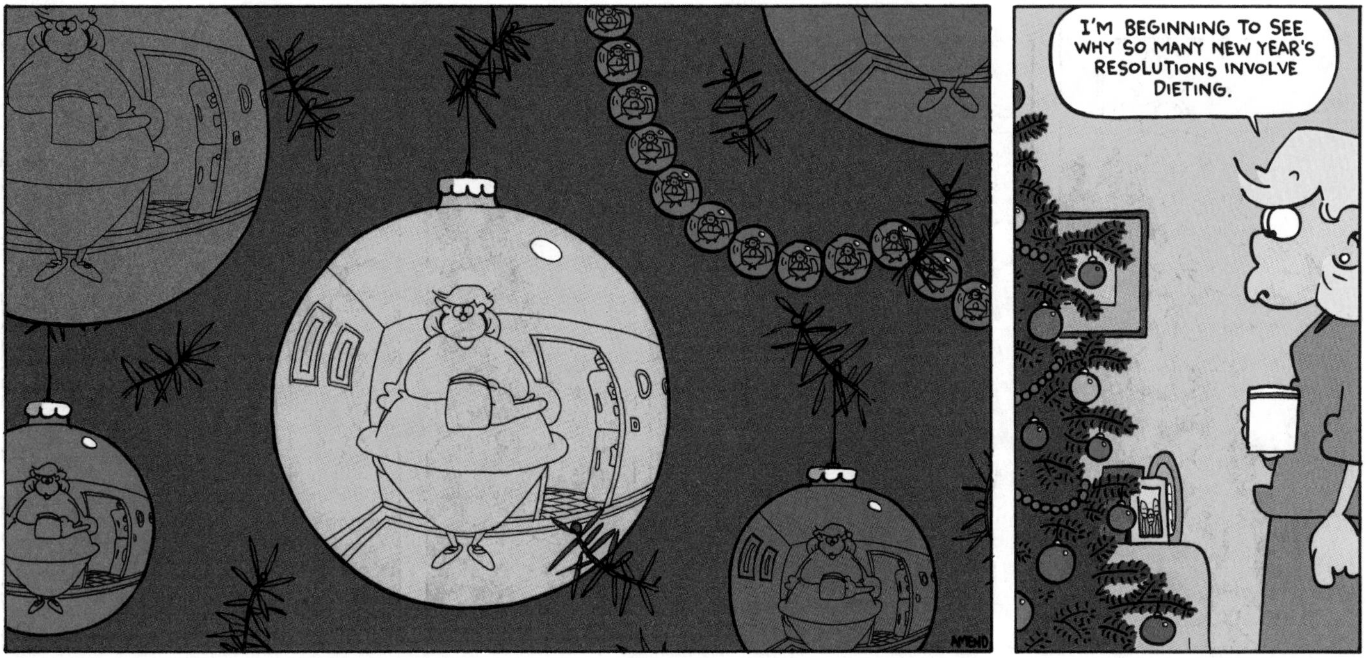
I'M BEGINNING TO SEE WHY SO MANY NEW YEAR'S RESOLUTIONS INVOLVE DIETING.
AMEND

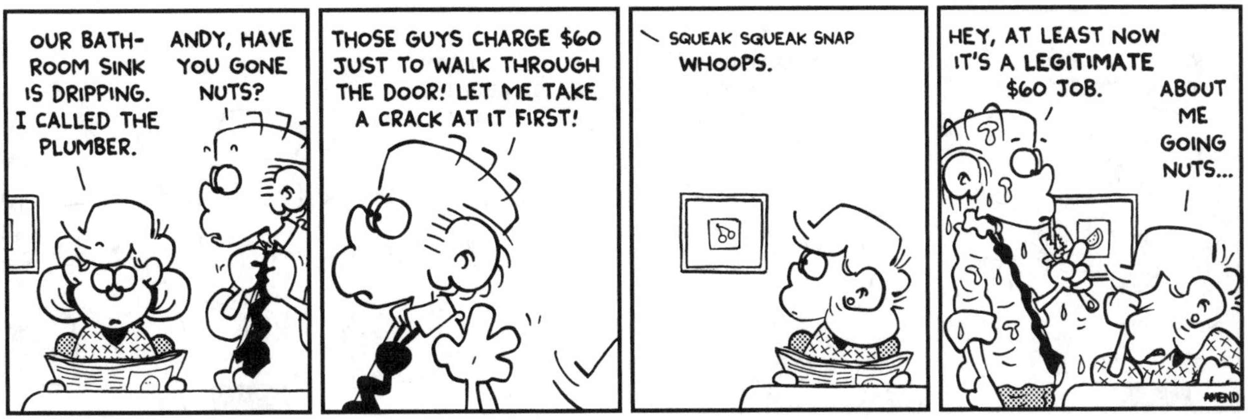
OUR BATH-ROOM SINK IS DRIPPING. I CALLED THE PLUMBER.
ANDY, HAVE YOU GONE NUTS?
THOSE GUYS CHARGE $60 JUST TO WALK THROUGH THE DOOR! LET ME TAKE A CRACK AT IT FIRST!
SQUEAK SQUEAK SNAP
WHOOPS.
HEY, AT LEAST NOW IT'S A LEGITIMATE $60 JOB.
ABOUT ME GOING NUTS...
AMEND

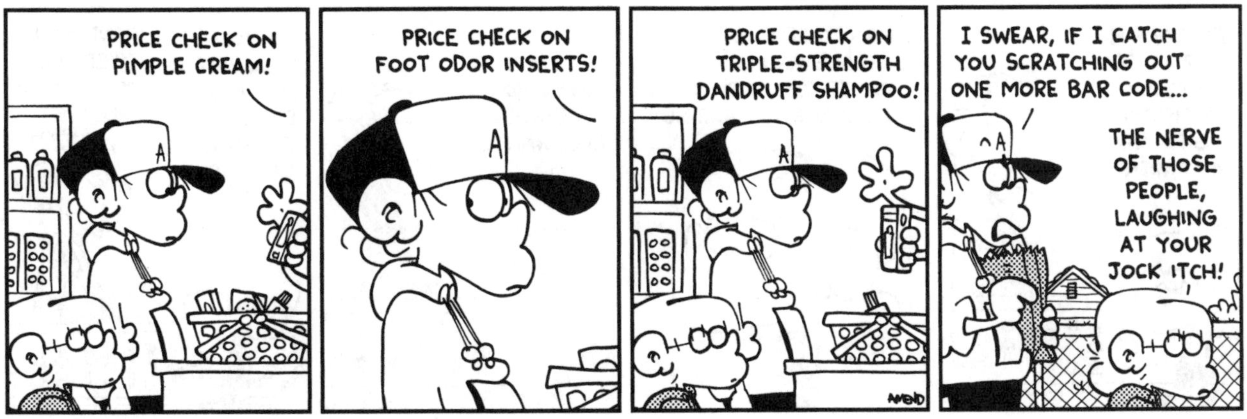
PRICE CHECK ON PIMPLE CREAM!
PRICE CHECK ON FOOT ODOR INSERTS!
PRICE CHECK ON TRIPLE-STRENGTH DANDRUFF SHAMPOO!
I SWEAR, IF I CATCH YOU SCRATCHING OUT ONE MORE BAR CODE...
THE NERVE OF THOSE PEOPLE, LAUGHING AT YOUR JOCK ITCH!
AMEND

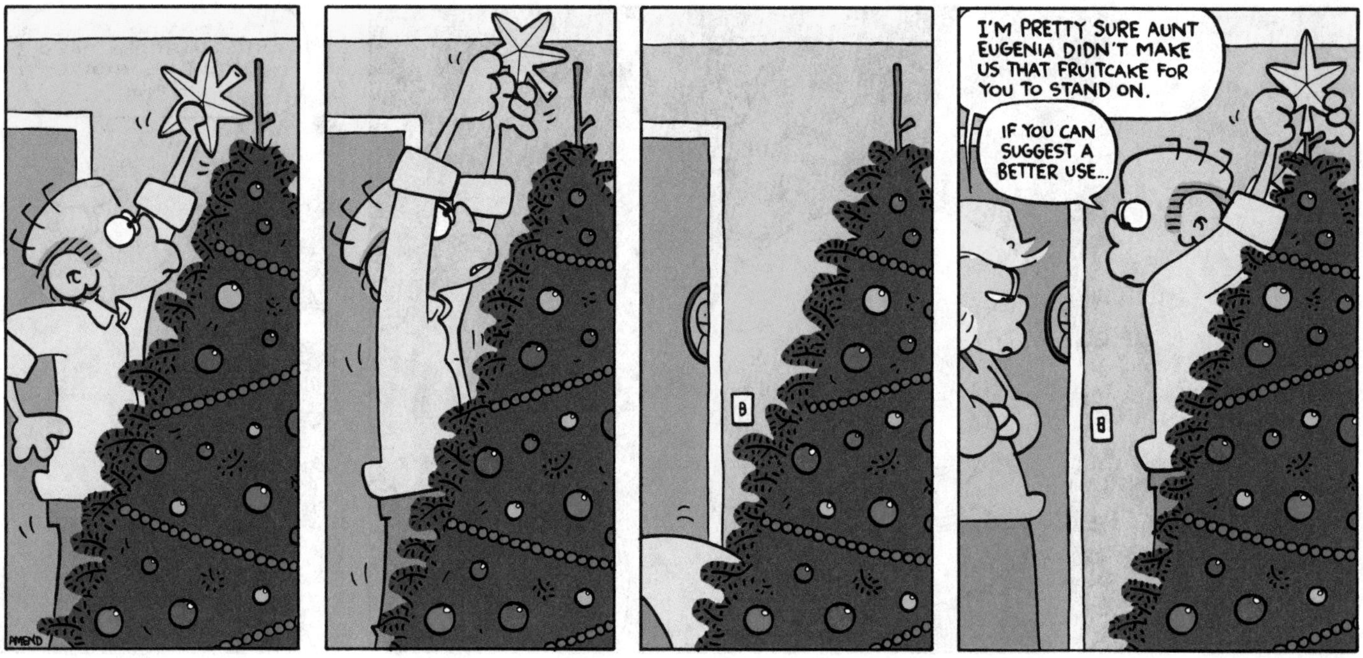
I'M PRETTY SURE AUNT EUGENIA DIDN'T MAKE US THAT FRUITCAKE FOR YOU TO STAND ON.
IF YOU CAN SUGGEST A BETTER USE...

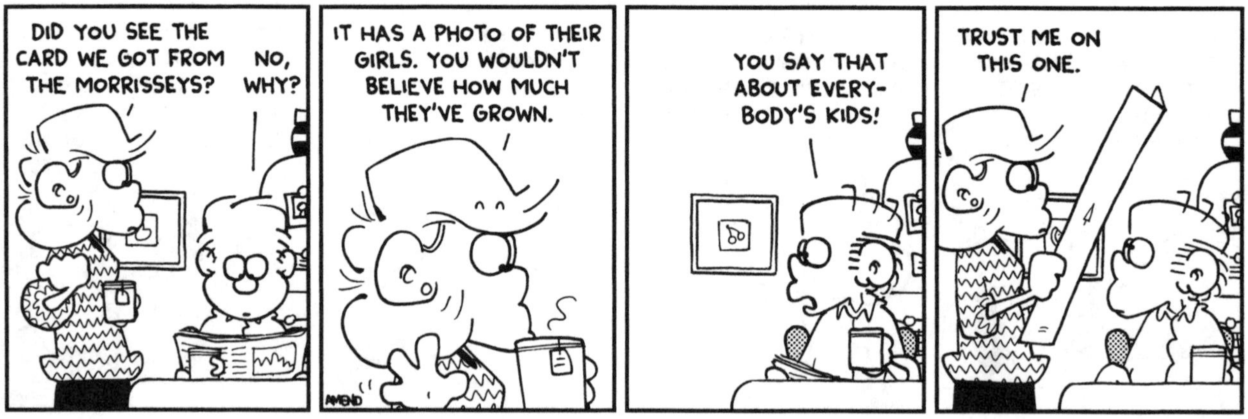
DID YOU SEE THE CARD WE GOT FROM THE MORRISSEYS?
NO, WHY?
IT HAS A PHOTO OF THEIR GIRLS. YOU WOULDN'T BELIEVE HOW MUCH THEY'VE GROWN.
YOU SAY THAT ABOUT EVERY-BODY'S KIDS!
TRUST ME ON THIS ONE.

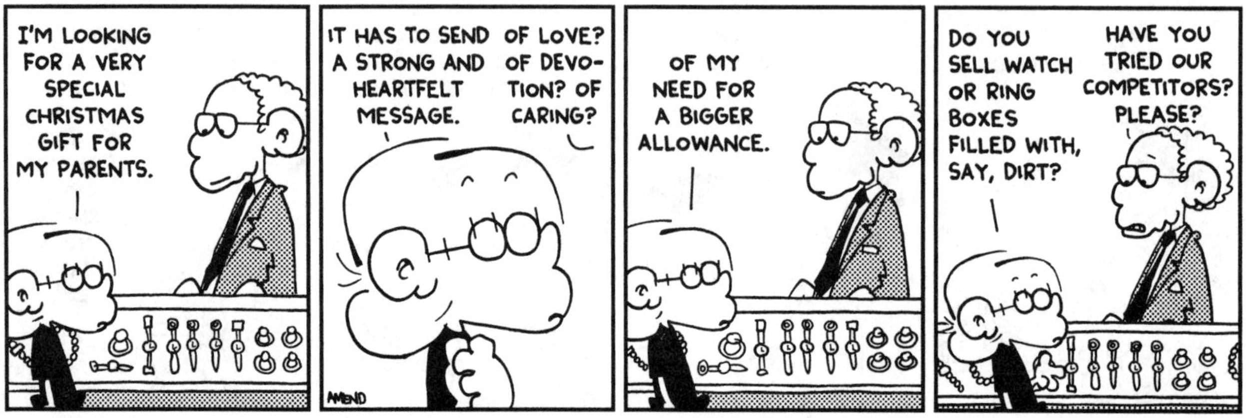
I'M LOOKING FOR A VERY SPECIAL CHRISTMAS GIFT FOR MY PARENTS.
IT HAS TO SEND A STRONG AND HEARTFELT MESSAGE.
OF LOVE? OF DEVO-TION? OF CARING?
OF MY NEED FOR A BIGGER ALLOWANCE.
DO YOU SELL WATCH OR RING BOXES FILLED WITH, SAY, DIRT?
HAVE YOU TRIED OUR COMPETITORS? PLEASE?

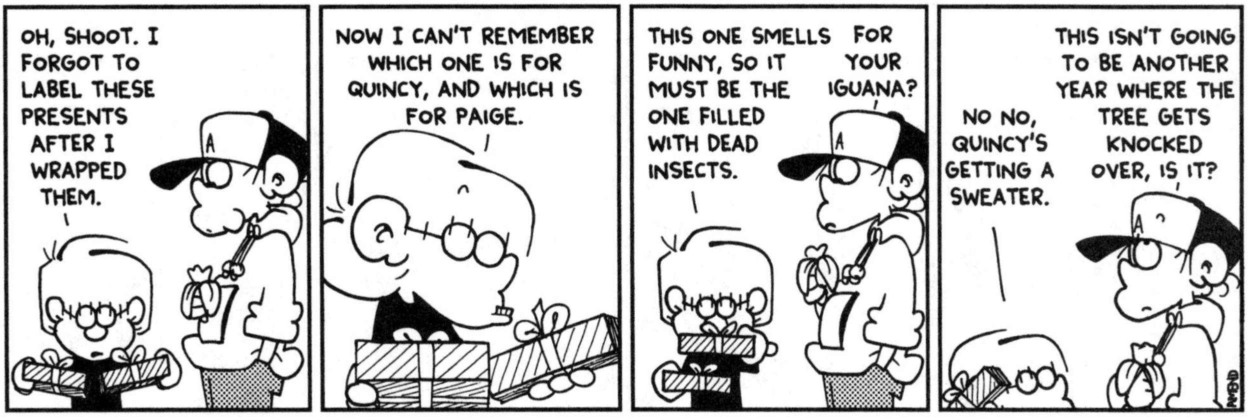
OH, SHOOT. I FORGOT TO LABEL THESE PRESENTS AFTER I WRAPPED THEM.
NOW I CAN'T REMEMBER WHICH ONE IS FOR QUINCY, AND WHICH IS FOR PAIGE.
THIS ONE SMELLS FUNNY, SO IT MUST BE THE ONE FILLED WITH DEAD INSECTS.
FOR YOUR IGUANA?
NO NO, QUINCY'S GETTING A SWEATER.
THIS ISN'T GOING TO BE ANOTHER YEAR WHERE THE TREE GETS KNOCKED OVER, IS IT?

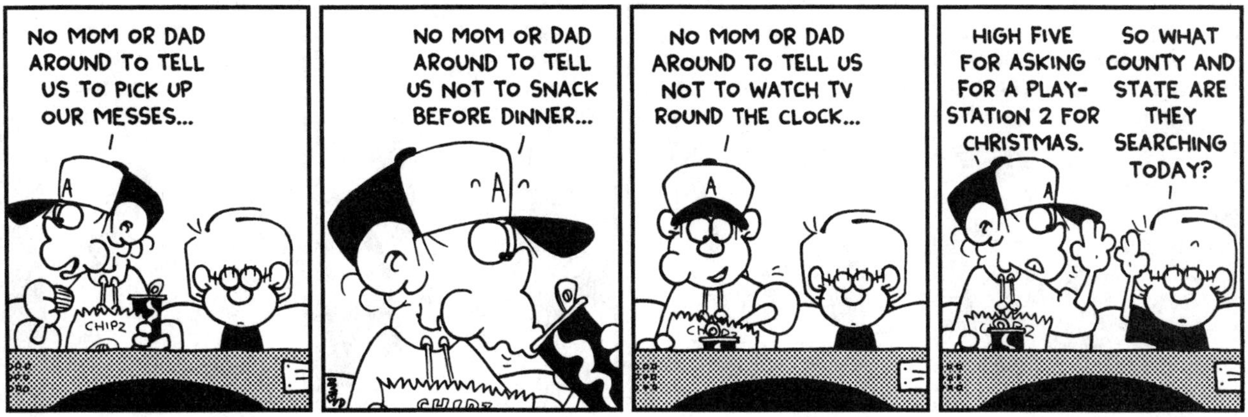
NO MOM OR DAD AROUND TO TELL US TO PICK UP OUR MESSES...
CHIPZ
NO MOM OR DAD AROUND TO TELL US NOT TO SNACK BEFORE DINNER...
NO MOM OR DAD AROUND TO TELL US NOT TO WATCH TV ROUND THE CLOCK...
HIGH FIVE FOR ASKING FOR A PLAY-STATION 2 FOR CHRISTMAS.
SO WHAT COUNTY AND STATE ARE THEY SEARCHING TODAY?

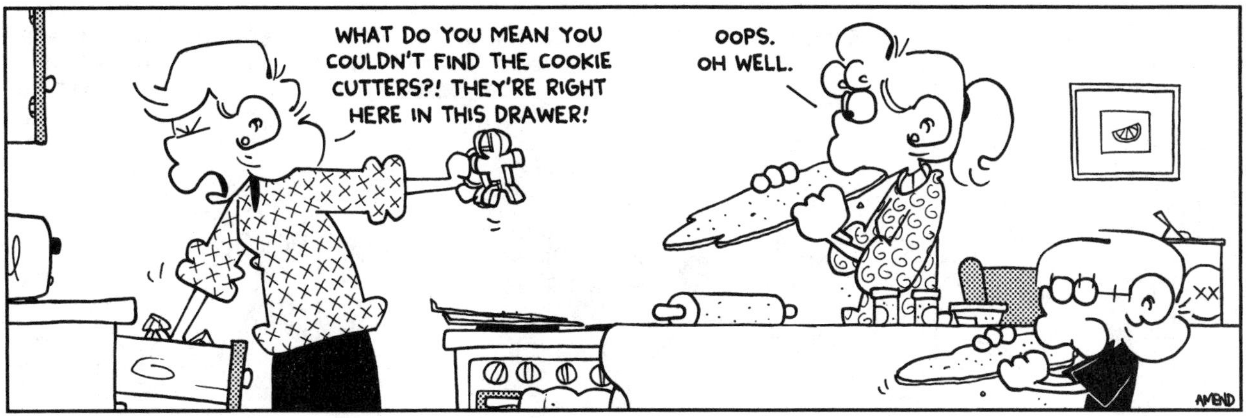
WHAT DO YOU MEAN YOU COULDN'T FIND THE COOKIE CUTTERS?! THEY'RE RIGHT HERE IN THIS DRAWER!
OOPS. OH WELL.
AMEND

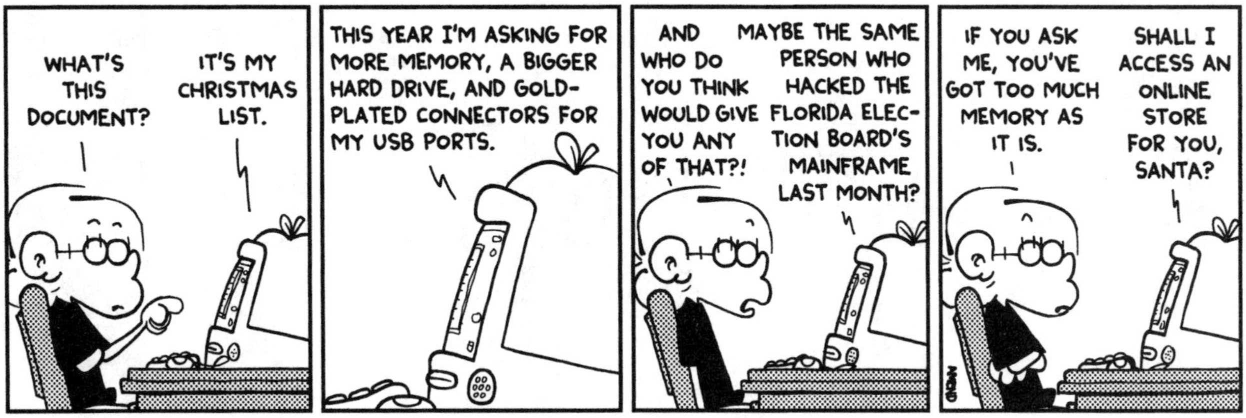
WHAT'S THIS DOCUMENT?
IT'S MY CHRISTMAS LIST.
THIS YEAR I'M ASKING FOR MORE MEMORY, A BIGGER HARD DRIVE, AND GOLD-PLATED CONNECTORS FOR MY USB PORTS.
AND WHO DO YOU THINK WOULD GIVE YOU ANY OF THAT?!
MAYBE THE SAME PERSON WHO HACKED THE FLORIDA ELECTION BOARD'S MAINFRAME LAST MONTH?
IF YOU ASK ME, YOU'VE GOT TOO MUCH MEMORY AS IT IS.
SHALL I ACCESS AN ONLINE STORE FOR YOU, SANTA?

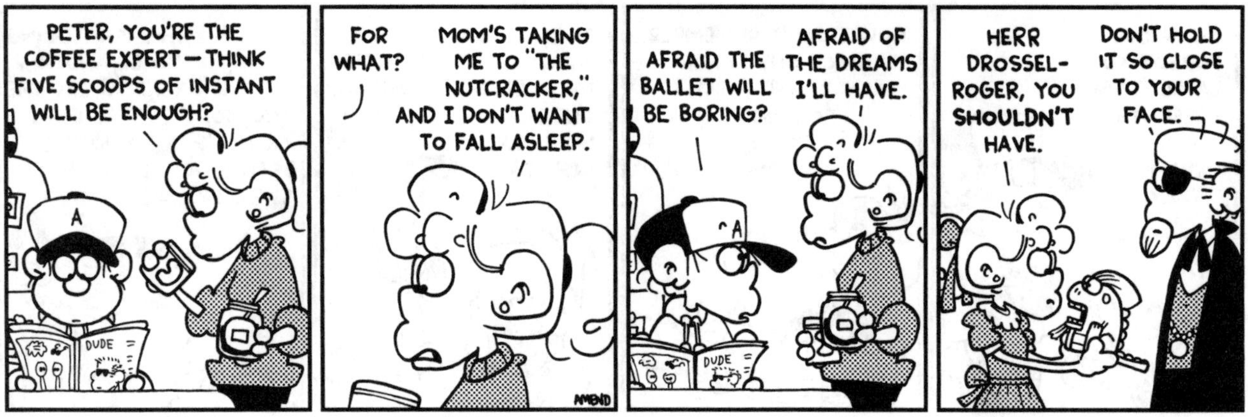
PETER, YOU'RE THE COFFEE EXPERT—THINK FIVE SCOOPS OF INSTANT WILL BE ENOUGH?
FOR WHAT?
MOM'S TAKING ME TO "THE NUTCRACKER," AND I DON'T WANT TO FALL ASLEEP.
AFRAID THE BALLET WILL BE BORING?
AFRAID OF THE DREAMS I'LL HAVE.
DUDE
HERR DROSSEL-ROGER, YOU SHOULDN'T HAVE.
DON'T HOLD IT SO CLOSE TO YOUR FACE.
AMEND

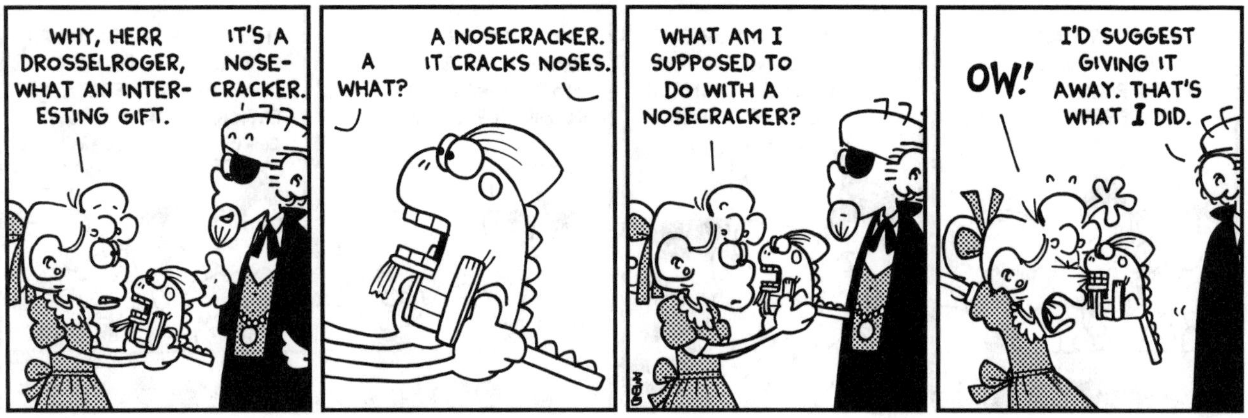
WHY, HERR DROSSELROGER, WHAT AN INTER-ESTING GIFT.
IT'S A NOSE-CRACKER.
A WHAT?
A NOSECRACKER. IT CRACKS NOSES.
WHAT AM I SUPPOSED TO DO WITH A NOSECRACKER?
OW!
I'D SUGGEST GIVING IT AWAY. THAT'S WHAT I DID.
AMEND

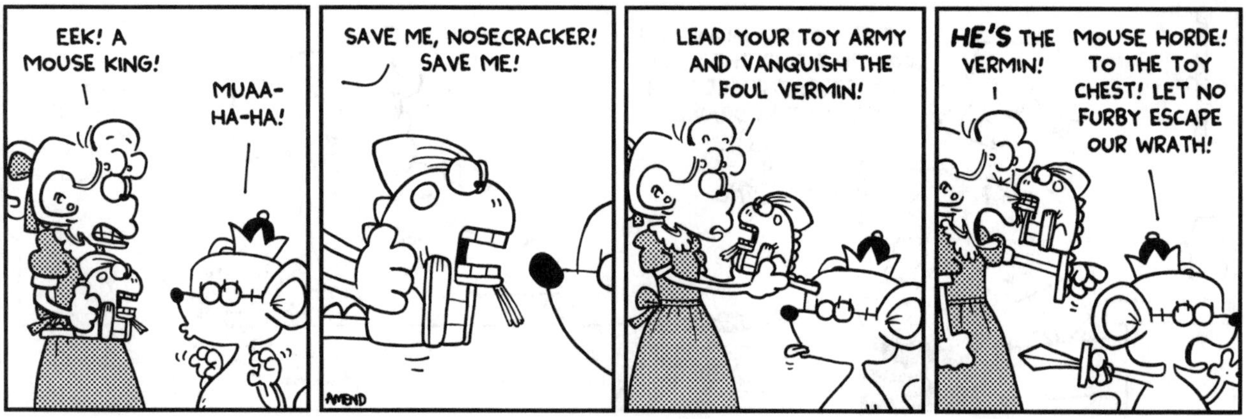
EEK! A MOUSE KING!
MUAA-HA-HA!
SAVE ME, NOSECRACKER! SAVE ME!
LEAD YOUR TOY ARMY AND VANQUISH THE FOUL VERMIN!
HE'S THE VERMIN!
MOUSE HORDE! TO THE TOY CHEST! LET NO FURBY ESCAPE OUR WRATH!
AMEND

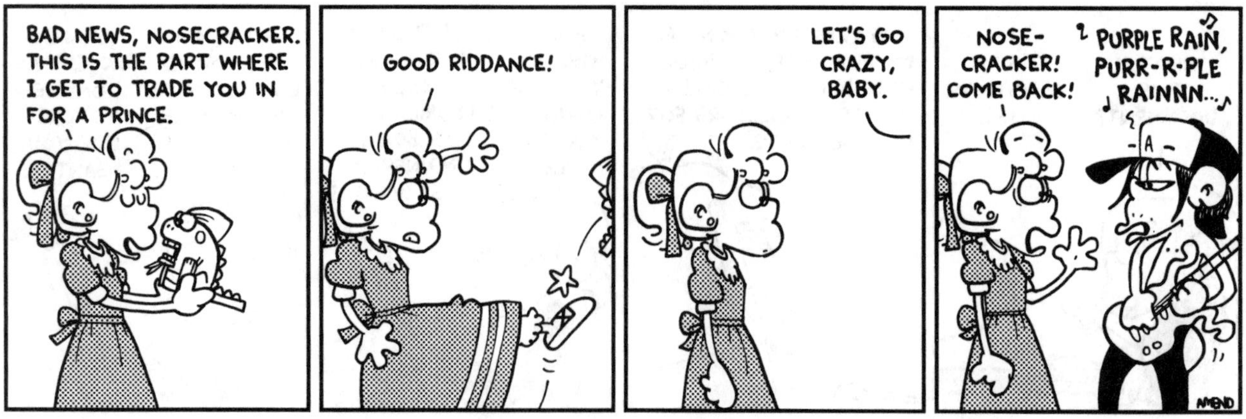
BAD NEWS, NOSECRACKER. THIS IS THE PART WHERE I GET TO TRADE YOU IN FOR A PRINCE.
GOOD RIDDANCE!
LET'S GO CRAZY, BABY.
NOSE-CRACKER! COME BACK!
PURPLE RAIN, PURR-R-PLE RAINNN...
AMEND

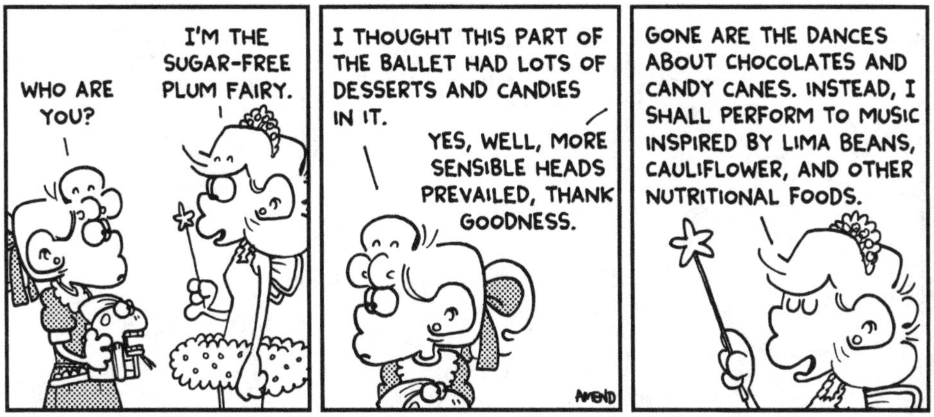
WHO ARE YOU?
I'M THE SUGAR-FREE PLUM FAIRY.
I THOUGHT THIS PART OF THE BALLET HAD LOTS OF DESSERTS AND CANDIES IN IT.
YES, WELL, MORE SENSIBLE HEADS PREVAILED, THANK GOODNESS.
GONE ARE THE DANCES ABOUT CHOCOLATES AND CANDY CANES. INSTEAD, I SHALL PERFORM TO MUSIC INSPIRED BY LIMA BEANS, CAULIFLOWER, AND OTHER NUTRITIONAL FOODS.
ALL I HEAR ARE CRICKETS CHIRPING.
THOSE ARE PICCOLOS, I'M SURE.
AMEND

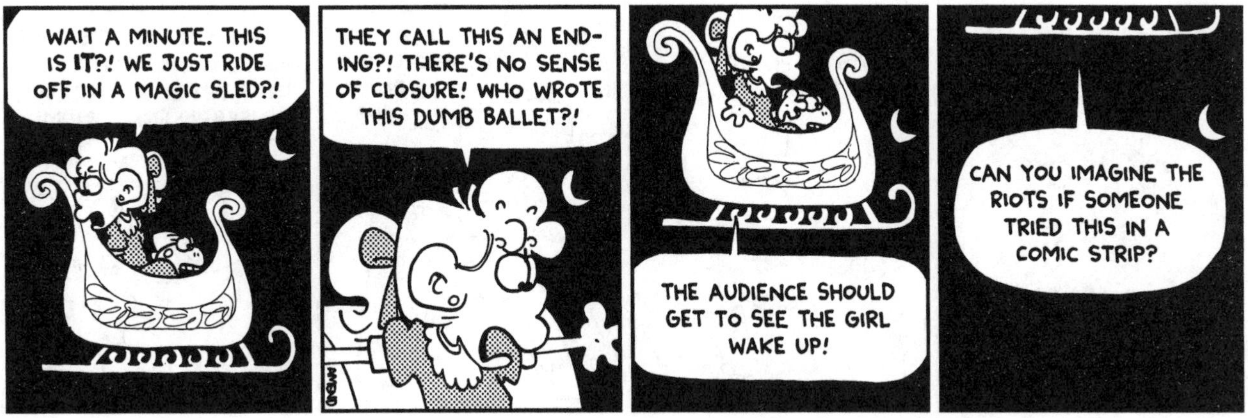
WAIT A MINUTE. THIS IS IT?! WE JUST RIDE OFF IN A MAGIC SLED?!
THEY CALL THIS AN ENDING?! THERE'S NO SENSE OF CLOSURE! WHO WROTE THIS DUMB BALLET?!
AMEND
THE AUDIENCE SHOULD GET TO SEE THE GIRL WAKE UP!
CAN YOU IMAGINE THE RIOTS IF SOMEONE TRIED THIS IN A COMIC STRIP?

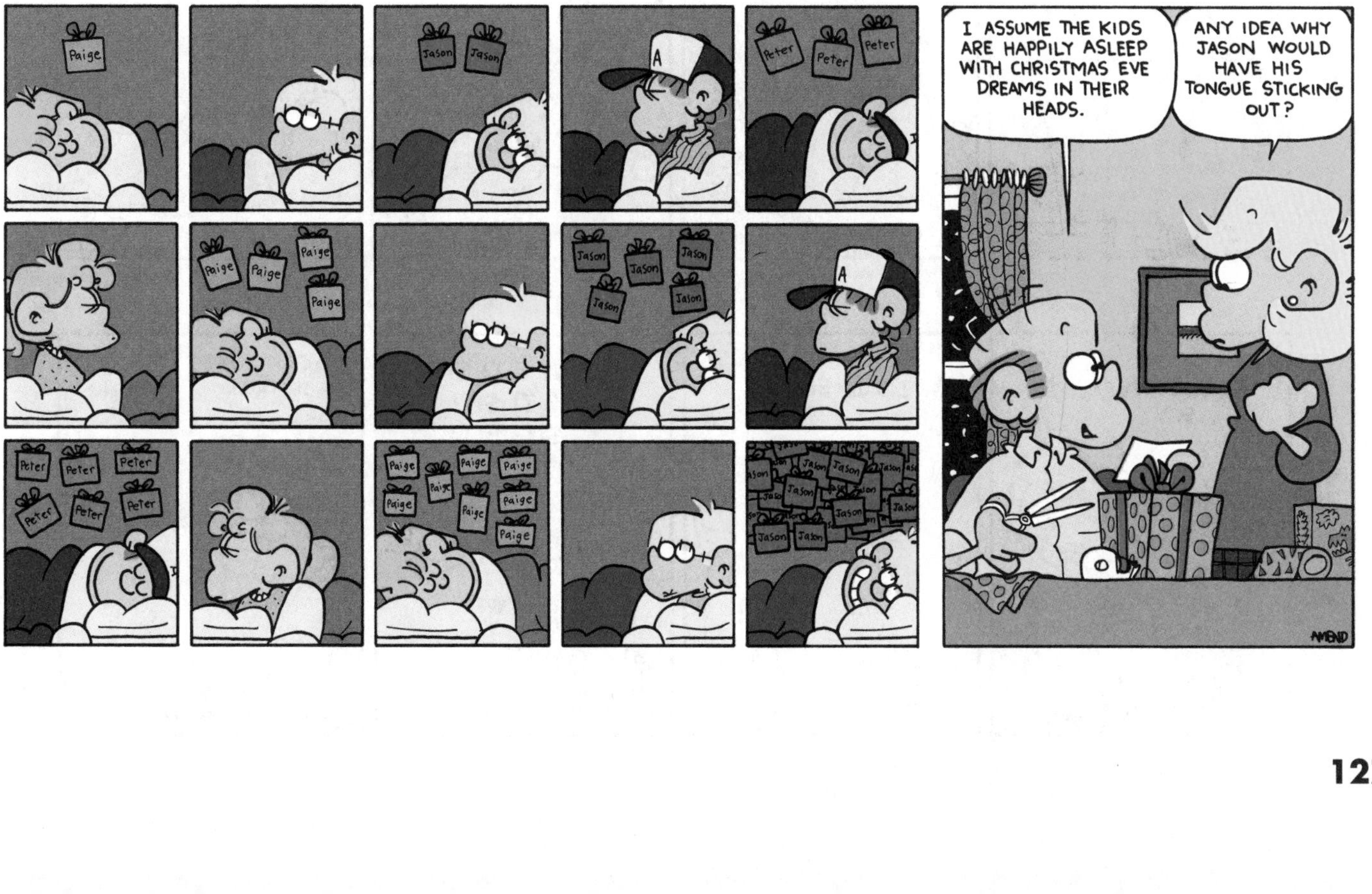
I ASSUME THE KIDS ARE HAPPILY ASLEEP WITH CHRISTMAS EVE DREAMS IN THEIR HEADS.
ANY IDEA WHY JASON WOULD HAVE HIS TONGUE STICKING OUT?
AMEND

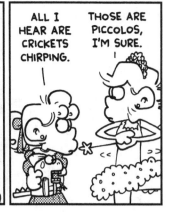

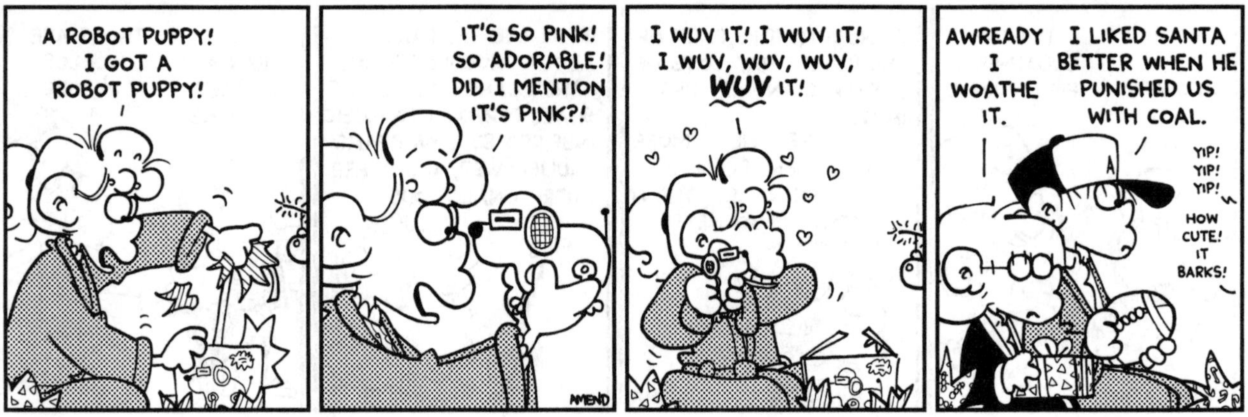
A ROBOT PUPPY! I GOT A ROBOT PUPPY!
IT'S SO PINK! SO ADORABLE! DID I MENTION IT'S PINK?!
I WUV IT! I WUV IT! I WUV, WUV, WUV, WUV IT!
AWREADY I WOATHE IT.
I LIKED SANTA BETTER WHEN HE PUNISHED US WITH COAL.
YIP! YIP! YIP!
HOW CUTE! IT BARKS!
AMEND

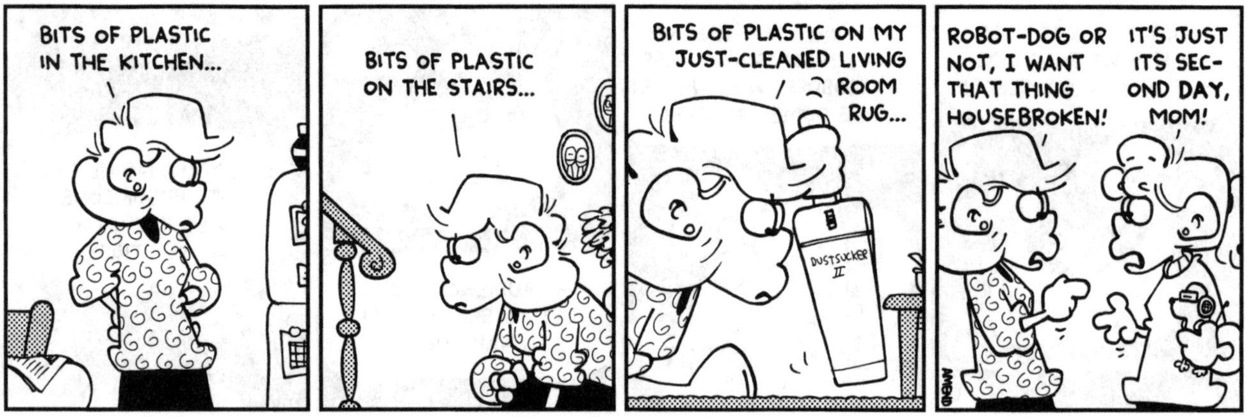
BITS OF PLASTIC IN THE KITCHEN...
BITS OF PLASTIC ON THE STAIRS...
BITS OF PLASTIC ON MY JUST-CLEANED LIVING ROOM RUG...
DUSTSUCKER II
ROBOT-DOG OR NOT, I WANT THAT THING HOUSEBROKEN!
IT'S JUST ITS SECOND DAY, MOM!
AMEND

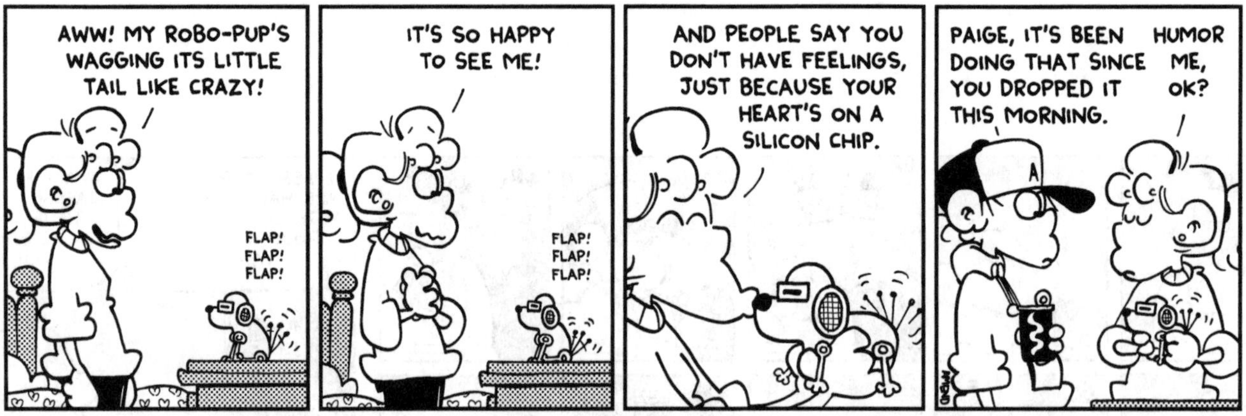
AWW! MY ROBO-PUP'S WAGGING ITS LITTLE TAIL LIKE CRAZY!
FLAP! FLAP! FLAP!
IT'S SO HAPPY TO SEE ME!
FLAP! FLAP! FLAP!
AND PEOPLE SAY YOU DON'T HAVE FEELINGS, JUST BECAUSE YOUR HEART'S ON A SILICON CHIP.
PAIGE, IT'S BEEN DOING THAT SINCE YOU DROPPED IT THIS MORNING.
HUMOR ME, OK?
AMEND

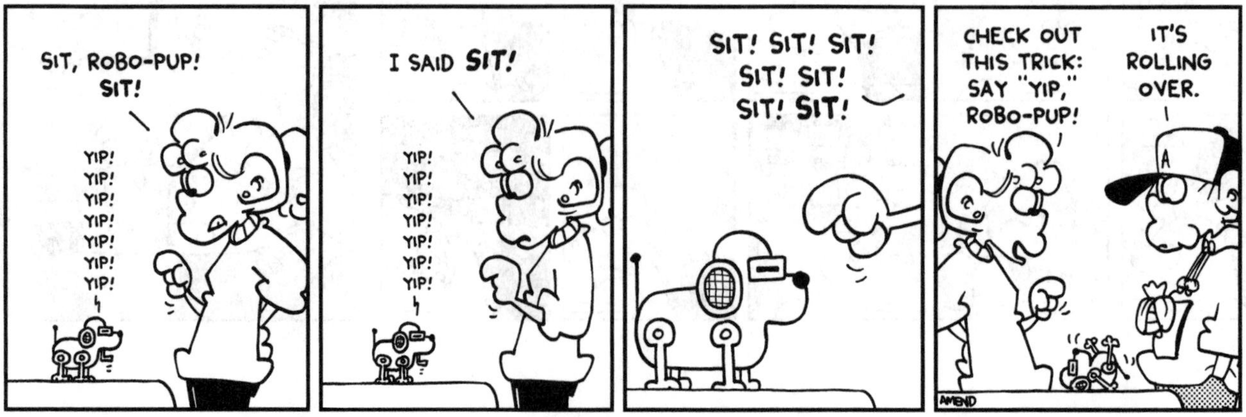
SIT, ROBO-PUP! SIT!
YIP! YIP! YIP! YIP! YIP! YIP! YIP!
I SAID SIT!
YIP! YIP! YIP! YIP! YIP! YIP! YIP!
SIT! SIT! SIT! SIT! SIT! SIT! SIT!
CHECK OUT THIS TRICK: SAY "YIP," ROBO-PUP!
IT'S ROLLING OVER.
AMEND

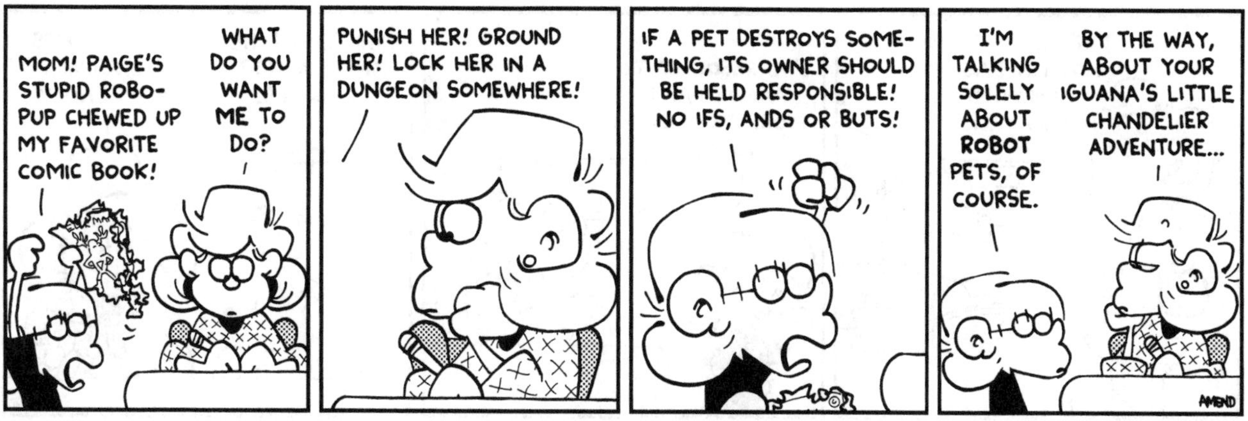
MOM! PAIGE'S STUPID ROBO-PUP CHEWED UP MY FAVORITE COMIC BOOK!
WHAT DO YOU WANT ME TO DO?
PUNISH HER! GROUND HER! LOCK HER IN A DUNGEON SOMEWHERE!
IF A PET DESTROYS SOMETHING, ITS OWNER SHOULD BE HELD RESPONSIBLE! NO IFS, ANDS OR BUTS!
I'M TALKING SOLELY ABOUT **ROBOT** PETS, OF COURSE.
BY THE WAY, ABOUT YOUR IGUANA'S LITTLE CHANDELIER ADVENTURE...
AMEND

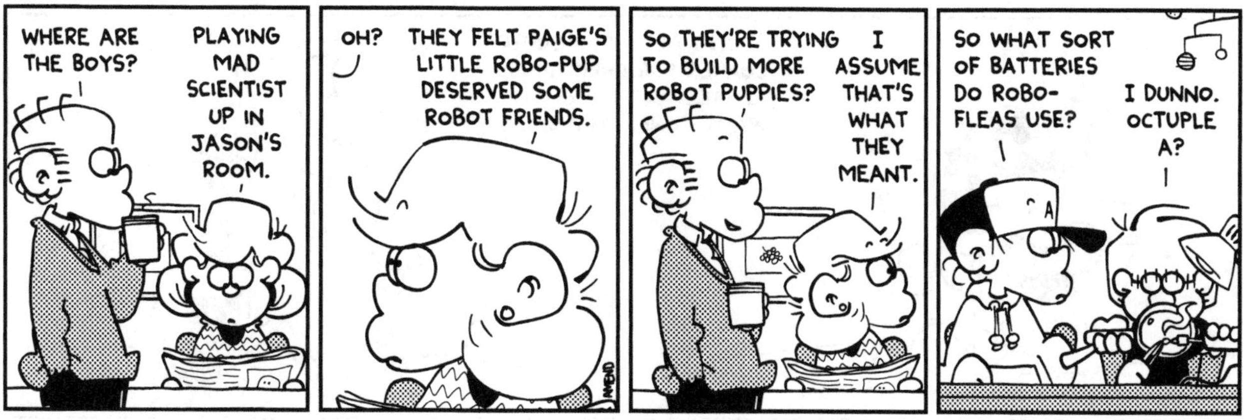
WHERE ARE THE BOYS?
PLAYING MAD SCIENTIST UP IN JASON'S ROOM.
OH?
THEY FELT PAIGE'S LITTLE ROBO-PUP DESERVED SOME ROBOT FRIENDS.
AMEND
SO THEY'RE TRYING TO BUILD MORE ROBOT PUPPIES?
I ASSUME THAT'S WHAT THEY MEANT.
SO WHAT SORT OF BATTERIES DO ROBO-FLEAS USE?
I DUNNO. OCTUPLE A?

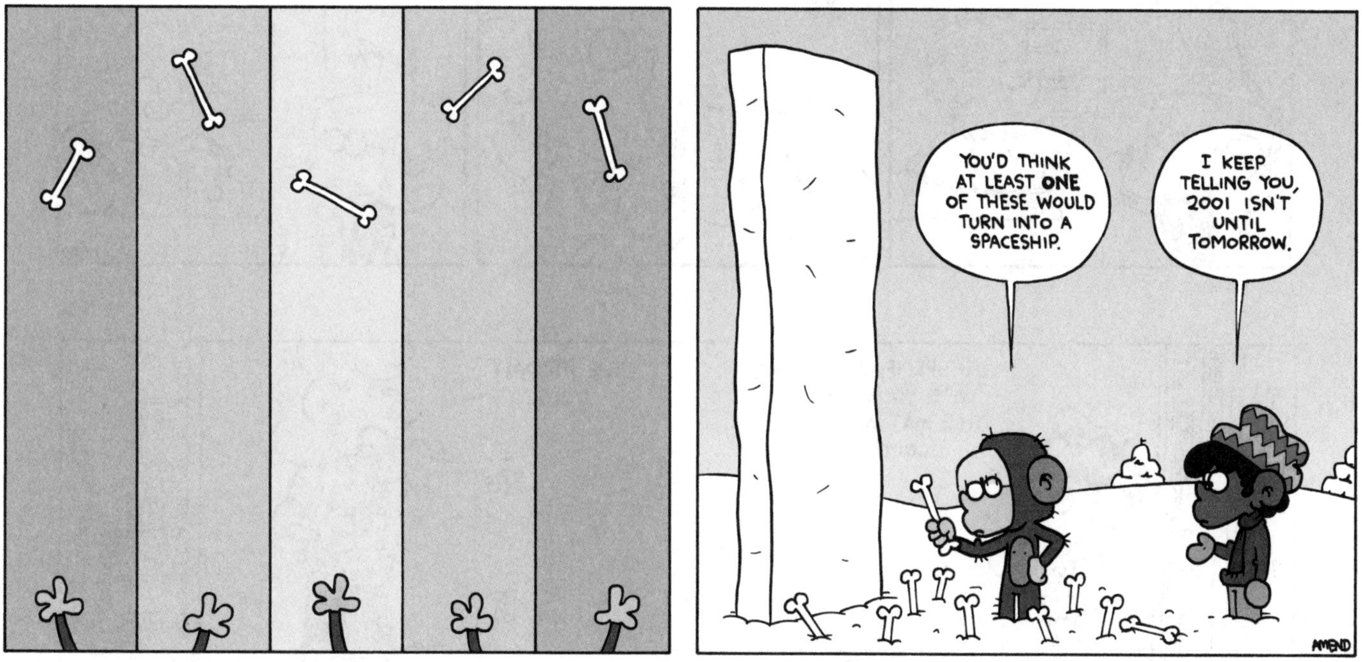
YOU'D THINK AT LEAST **ONE** OF THESE WOULD TURN INTO A SPACESHIP.
I KEEP TELLING YOU, 2001 ISN'T UNTIL TOMORROW.
AMEND

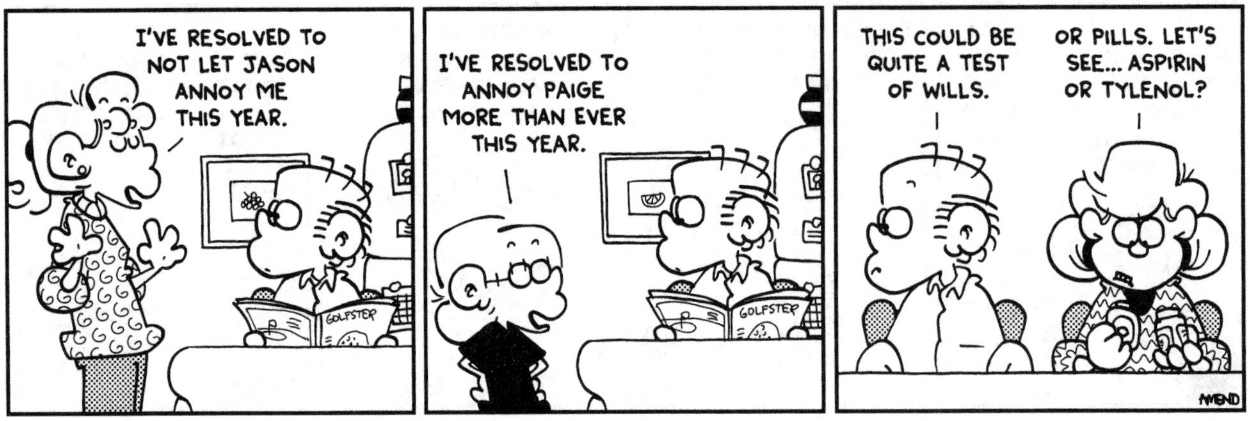
I'VE RESOLVED TO NOT LET JASON ANNOY ME THIS YEAR.
GOLFSTER
I'VE RESOLVED TO ANNOY PAIGE MORE THAN EVER THIS YEAR.
GOLFSTER
THIS COULD BE QUITE A TEST OF WILLS.
OR PILLS. LET'S SEE... ASPIRIN OR TYLENOL?
AMEND

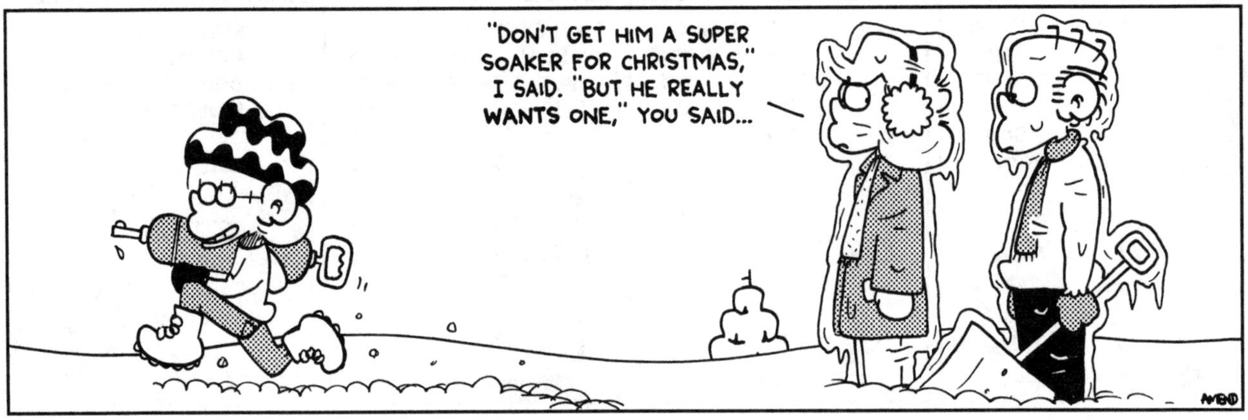
"DON'T GET HIM A SUPER SOAKER FOR CHRISTMAS," I SAID. "BUT HE REALLY **WANTS** ONE," YOU SAID...
AMEND

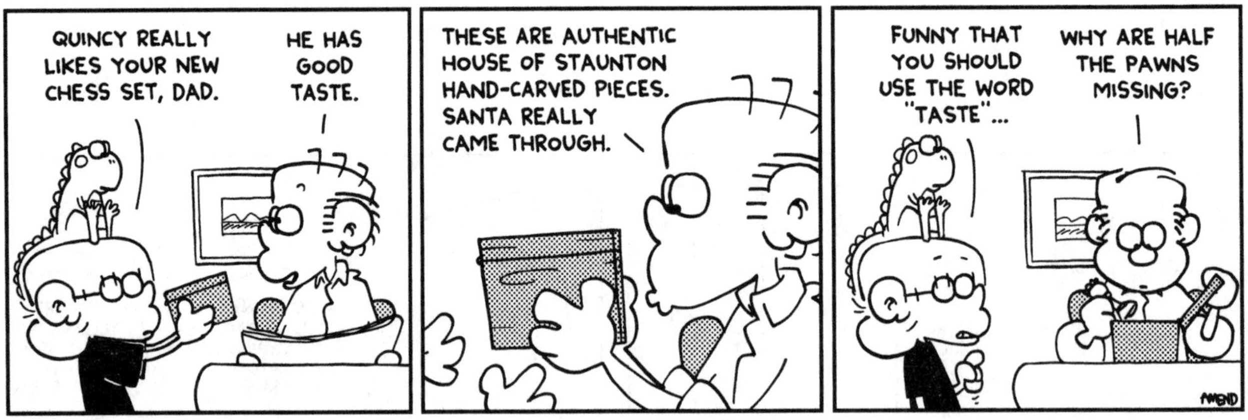
QUINCY REALLY LIKES YOUR NEW CHESS SET, DAD.
HE HAS GOOD TASTE.
THESE ARE AUTHENTIC HOUSE OF STAUNTON HAND-CARVED PIECES. SANTA REALLY CAME THROUGH.
FUNNY THAT YOU SHOULD USE THE WORD "TASTE"...
WHY ARE HALF THE PAWNS MISSING?
AMEND

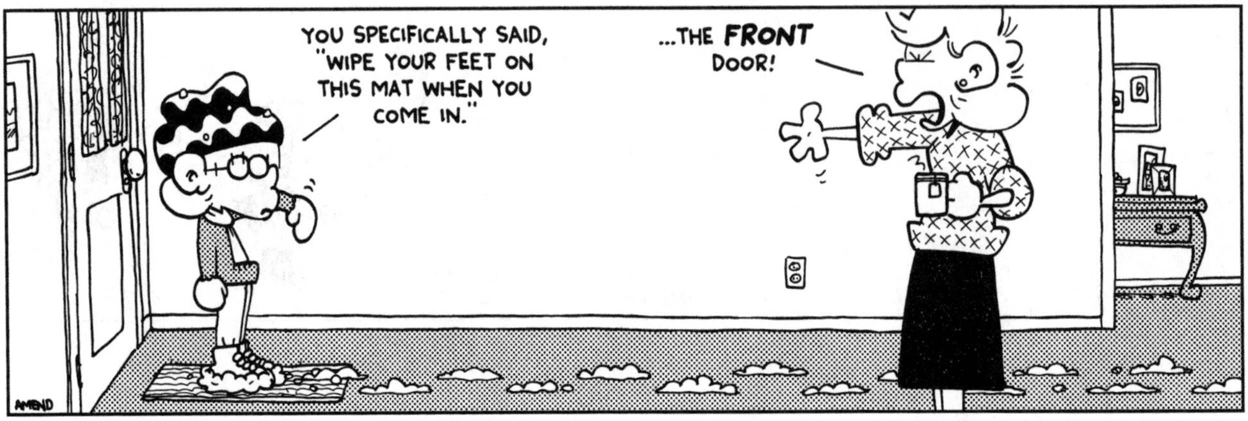
YOU SPECIFICALLY SAID, "WIPE YOUR FEET ON THIS MAT WHEN YOU COME IN."
...THE **FRONT** DOOR!
AMEND

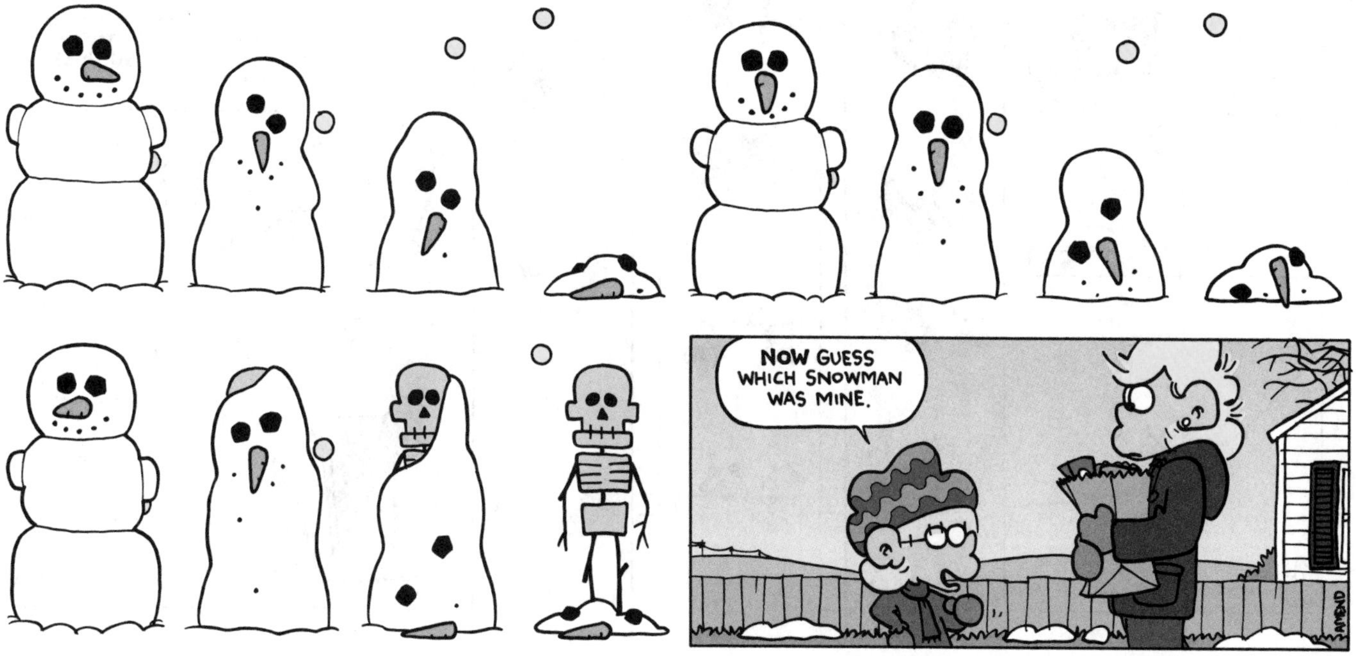
NOW GUESS WHICH SNOWMAN WAS MINE.
AMEND

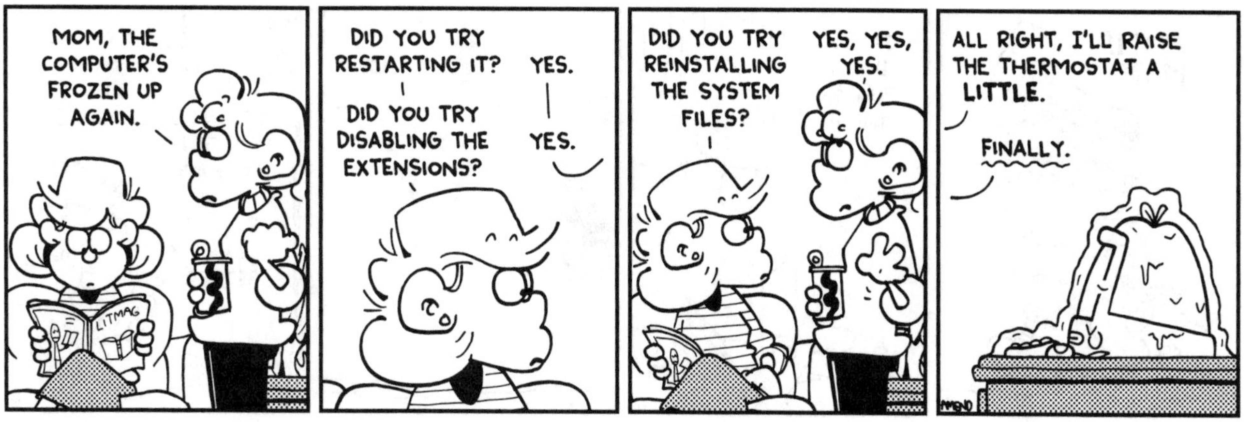
MOM, THE COMPUTER'S FROZEN UP AGAIN.
LITMAG
DID YOU TRY RESTARTING IT?
YES.
DID YOU TRY DISABLING THE EXTENSIONS?
YES.
DID YOU TRY REINSTALLING THE SYSTEM FILES?
YES, YES, YES.
ALL RIGHT, I'LL RAISE THE THERMOSTAT A LITTLE.
FINALLY.
AMEND

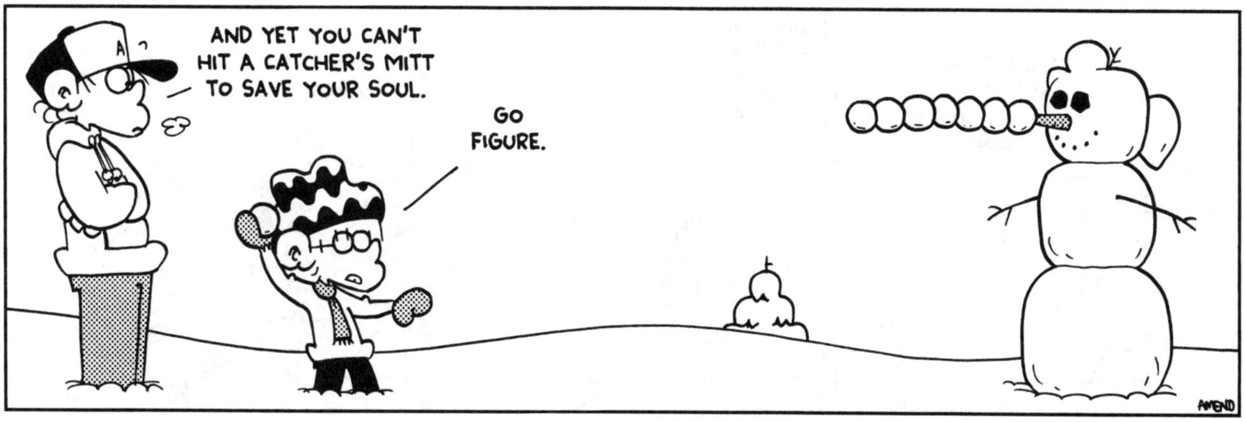
A
AND YET YOU CAN'T HIT A CATCHER'S MITT TO SAVE YOUR SOUL.
GO FIGURE.
AMEND

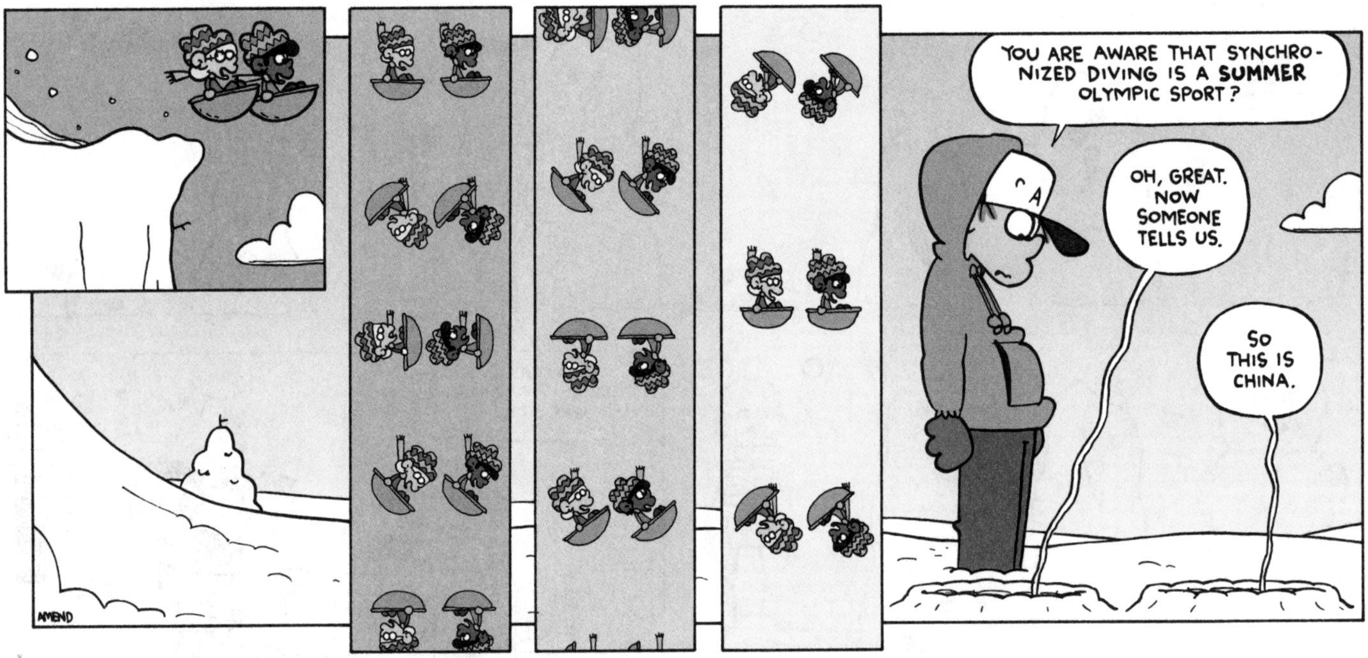
AMEND
YOU ARE AWARE THAT SYNCHRONIZED DIVING IS A SUMMER OLYMPIC SPORT?
OH, GREAT. NOW SOMEONE TELLS US.
SO THIS IS CHINA.

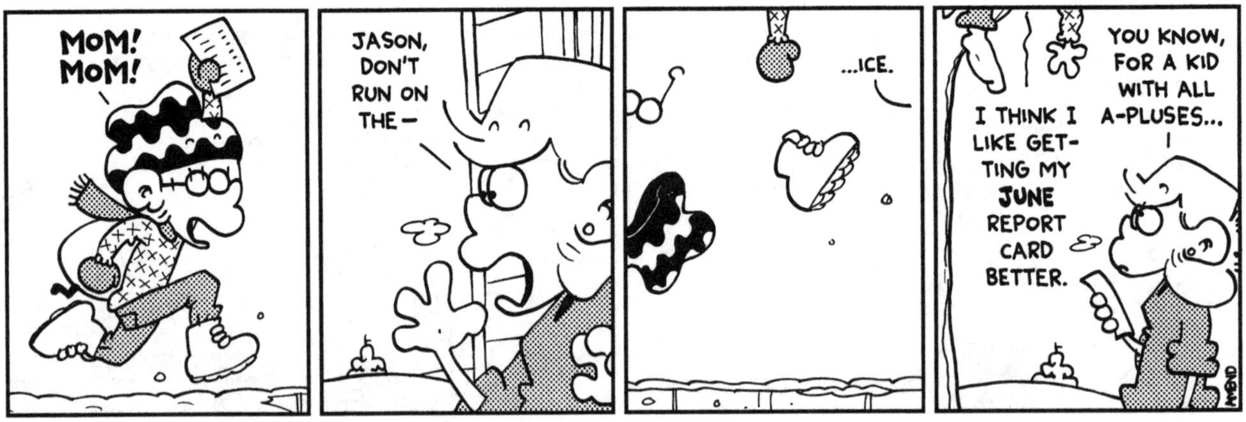
MOM! MOM!
JASON, DON'T RUN ON THE—
...ICE.
I THINK I LIKE GETTING MY JUNE REPORT CARD BETTER.
YOU KNOW, FOR A KID WITH ALL A-PLUSES...
AMEND

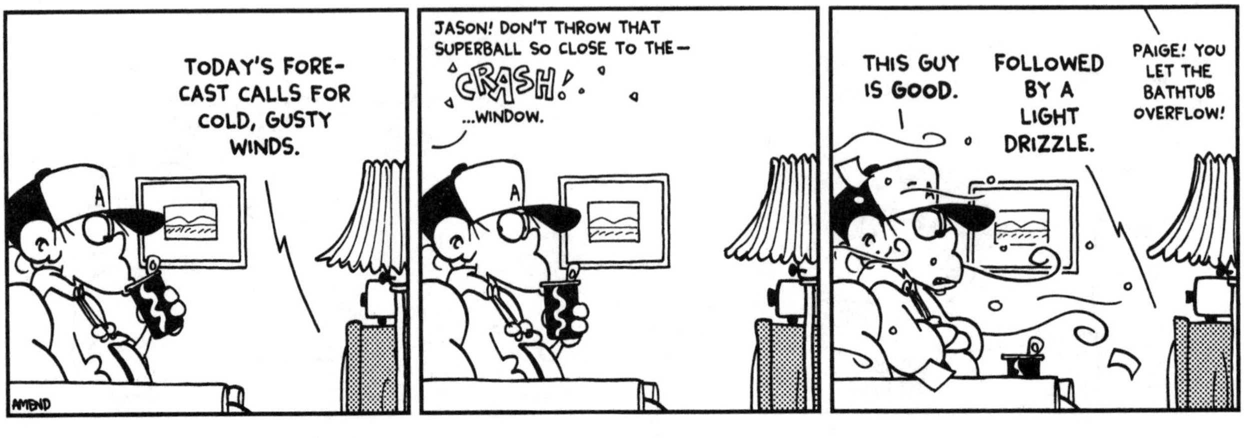
TODAY'S FORECAST CALLS FOR COLD, GUSTY WINDS.
AMEND
JASON! DON'T THROW THAT SUPERBALL SO CLOSE TO THE—
CRASH!
...WINDOW.
THIS GUY IS GOOD.
FOLLOWED BY A LIGHT DRIZZLE.
PAIGE! YOU LET THE BATHTUB OVERFLOW!

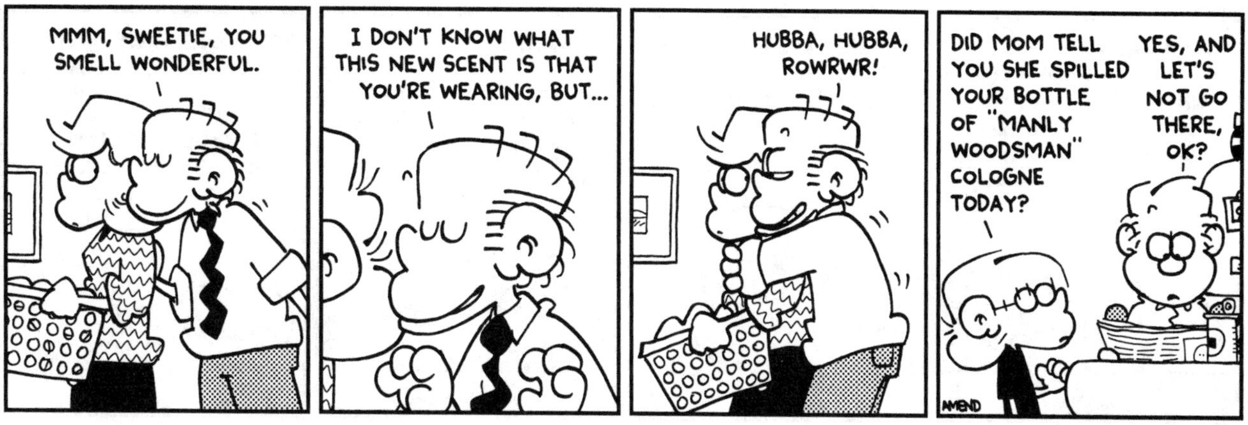
MMM, SWEETIE, YOU SMELL WONDERFUL.
I DON'T KNOW WHAT THIS NEW SCENT IS THAT YOU'RE WEARING, BUT...
HUBBA, HUBBA, ROWRWR!
DID MOM TELL YOU SHE SPILLED YOUR BOTTLE OF "MANLY WOODSMAN" COLOGNE TODAY?
YES, AND LET'S NOT GO THERE, OK?

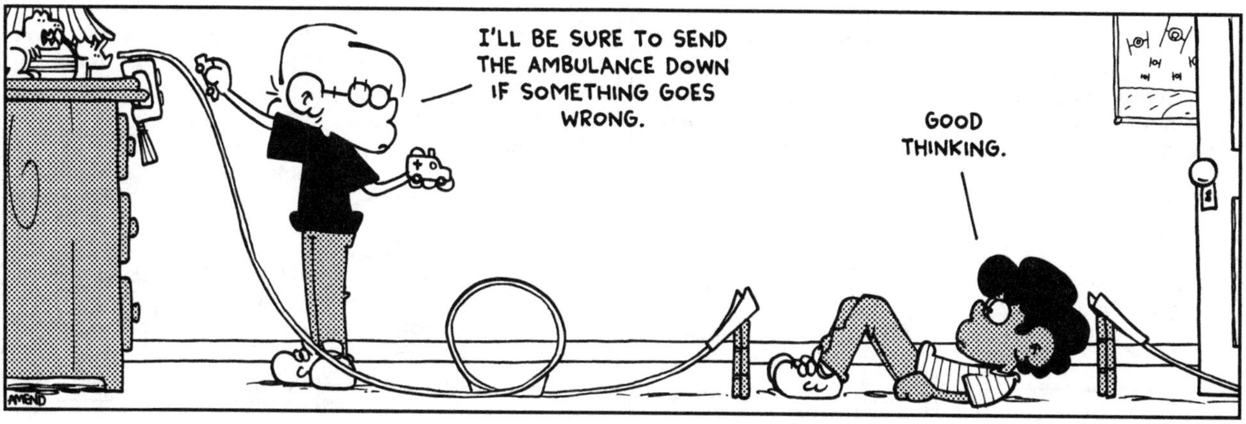
I'LL BE SURE TO SEND THE AMBULANCE DOWN IF SOMETHING GOES WRONG.
GOOD THINKING.

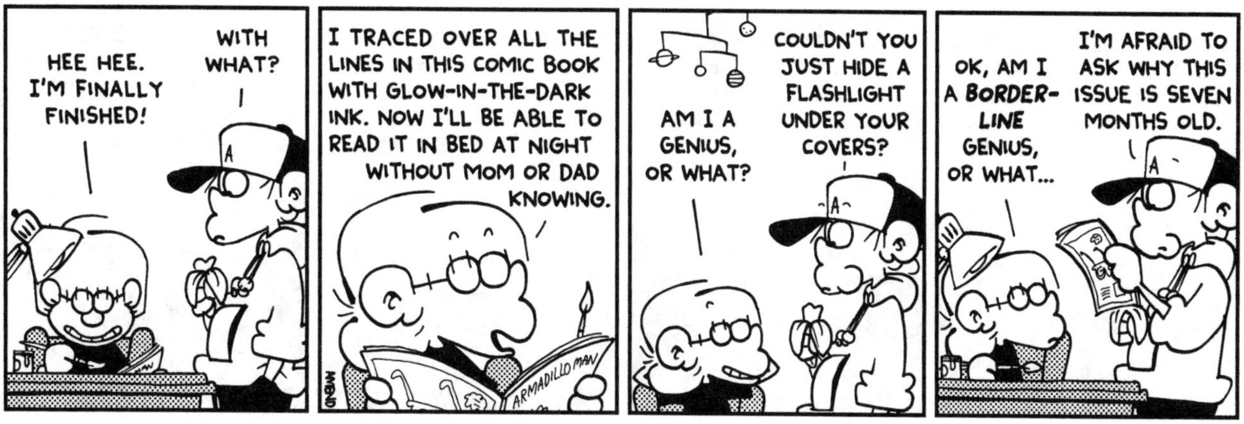
HEE HEE. I'M FINALLY FINISHED!
WITH WHAT?
I TRACED OVER ALL THE LINES IN THIS COMIC BOOK WITH GLOW-IN-THE-DARK INK. NOW I'LL BE ABLE TO READ IT IN BED AT NIGHT WITHOUT MOM OR DAD KNOWING.
ARMADILLO MAN
AM I A GENIUS, OR WHAT?
COULDN'T YOU JUST HIDE A FLASHLIGHT UNDER YOUR COVERS?
OK, AM I A ***BORDER-LINE*** GENIUS, OR WHAT...
I'M AFRAID TO ASK WHY THIS ISSUE IS SEVEN MONTHS OLD.

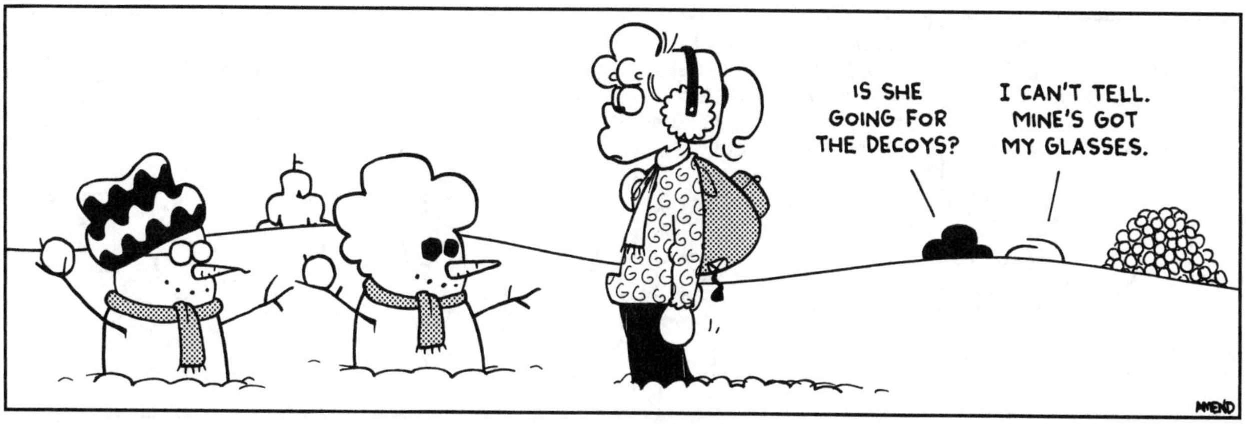
IS SHE GOING FOR THE DECOYS?
I CAN'T TELL. MINE'S GOT MY GLASSES.

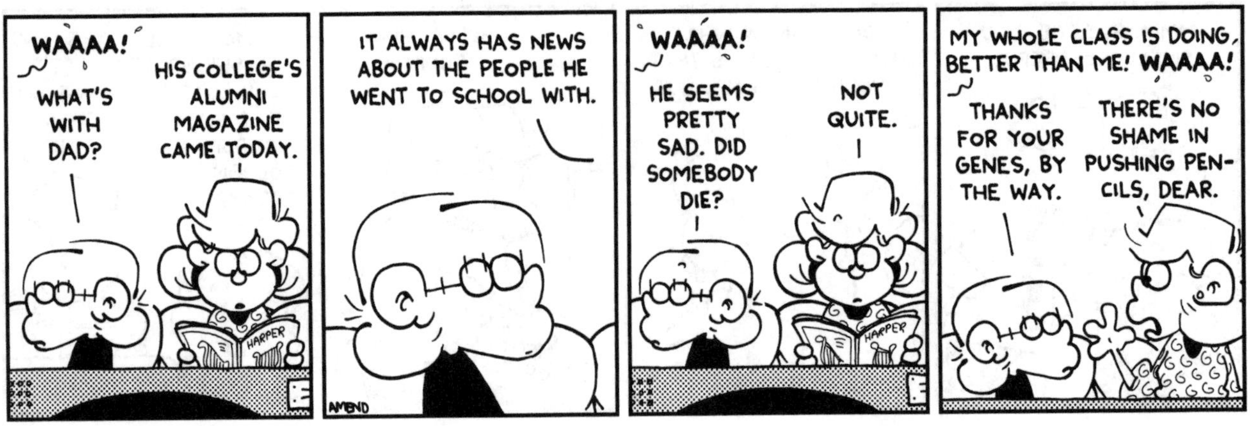
WAAAA!
WHAT'S WITH DAD?
HIS COLLEGE'S ALUMNI MAGAZINE CAME TODAY.
IT ALWAYS HAS NEWS ABOUT THE PEOPLE HE WENT TO SCHOOL WITH.
WAAAA!
HE SEEMS PRETTY SAD. DID SOMEBODY DIE?
NOT QUITE.
MY WHOLE CLASS IS DOING BETTER THAN ME! WAAAA!
THANKS FOR YOUR GENES, BY THE WAY.
THERE'S NO SHAME IN PUSHING PENCILS, DEAR.
HARPER
AMEND

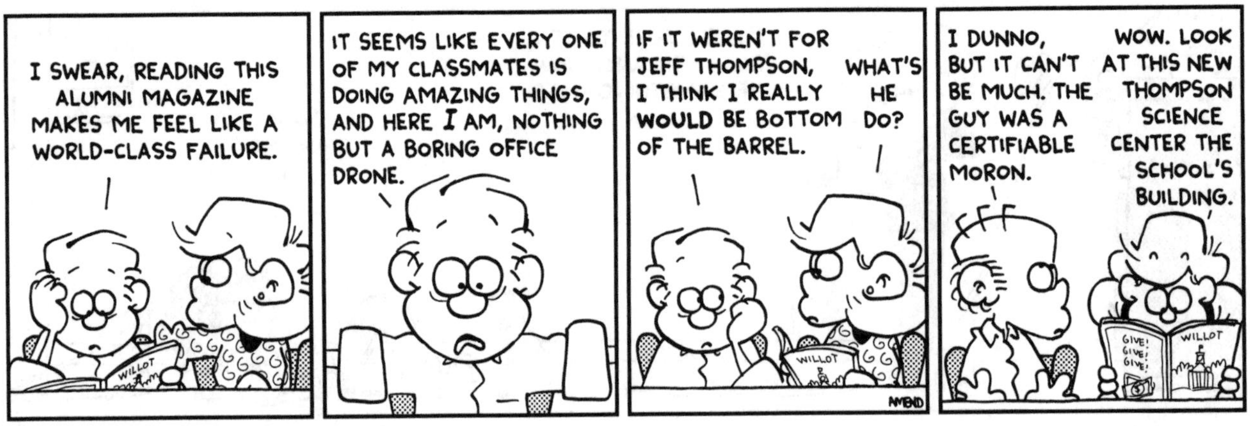
I SWEAR, READING THIS ALUMNI MAGAZINE MAKES ME FEEL LIKE A WORLD-CLASS FAILURE.
IT SEEMS LIKE EVERY ONE OF MY CLASSMATES IS DOING AMAZING THINGS, AND HERE I AM, NOTHING BUT A BORING OFFICE DRONE.
IF IT WEREN'T FOR JEFF THOMPSON, I THINK I REALLY WOULD BE BOTTOM OF THE BARREL.
WHAT'S HE DO?
I DUNNO, BUT IT CAN'T BE MUCH. THE GUY WAS A CERTIFIABLE MORON.
WOW. LOOK AT THIS NEW THOMPSON SCIENCE CENTER THE SCHOOL'S BUILDING.
WILLOT
GIVE! GIVE! GIVE!
AMEND

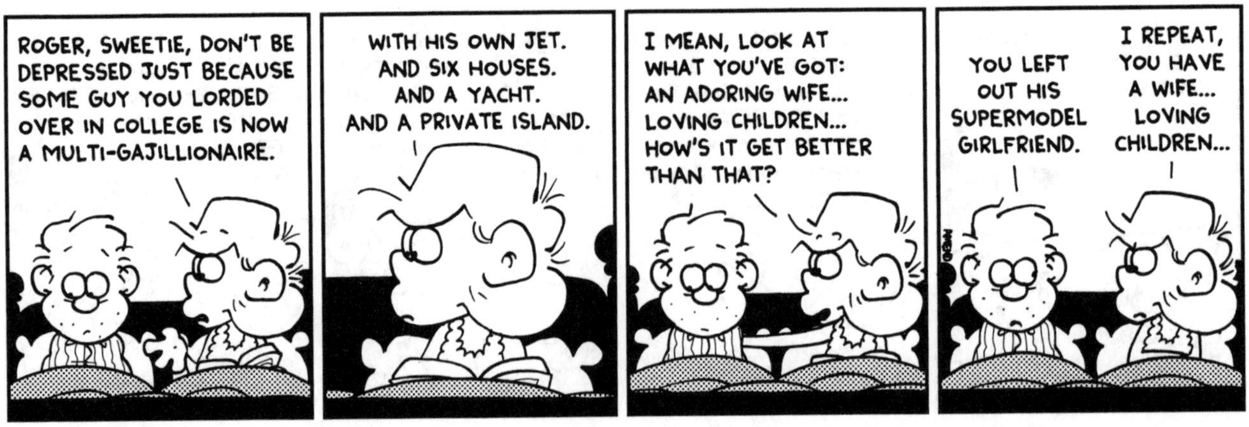
ROGER, SWEETIE, DON'T BE DEPRESSED JUST BECAUSE SOME GUY YOU LORDED OVER IN COLLEGE IS NOW A MULTI-GAJILLIONAIRE.
WITH HIS OWN JET. AND SIX HOUSES. AND A YACHT. AND A PRIVATE ISLAND.
I MEAN, LOOK AT WHAT YOU'VE GOT: AN ADORING WIFE... LOVING CHILDREN... HOW'S IT GET BETTER THAN THAT?
YOU LEFT OUT HIS SUPERMODEL GIRLFRIEND.
I REPEAT, YOU HAVE A WIFE... LOVING CHILDREN...
AMEND

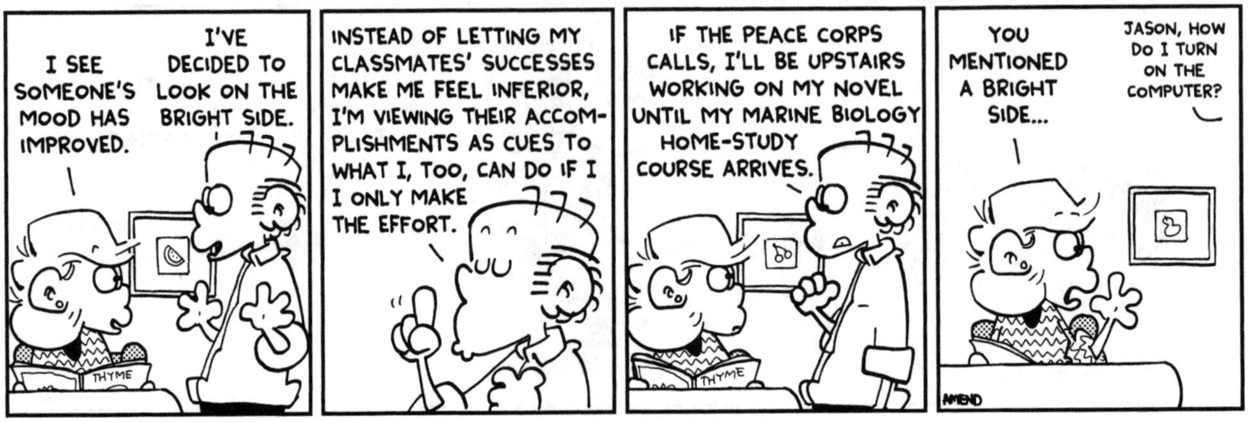
I SEE SOMEONE'S MOOD HAS IMPROVED.
I'VE DECIDED TO LOOK ON THE BRIGHT SIDE.
INSTEAD OF LETTING MY CLASSMATES' SUCCESSES MAKE ME FEEL INFERIOR, I'M VIEWING THEIR ACCOMPLISHMENTS AS CUES TO WHAT I, TOO, CAN DO IF I ONLY MAKE THE EFFORT.
IF THE PEACE CORPS CALLS, I'LL BE UPSTAIRS WORKING ON MY NOVEL UNTIL MY MARINE BIOLOGY HOME-STUDY COURSE ARRIVES.
YOU MENTIONED A BRIGHT SIDE...
JASON, HOW DO I TURN ON THE COMPUTER?
THYME
AMEND

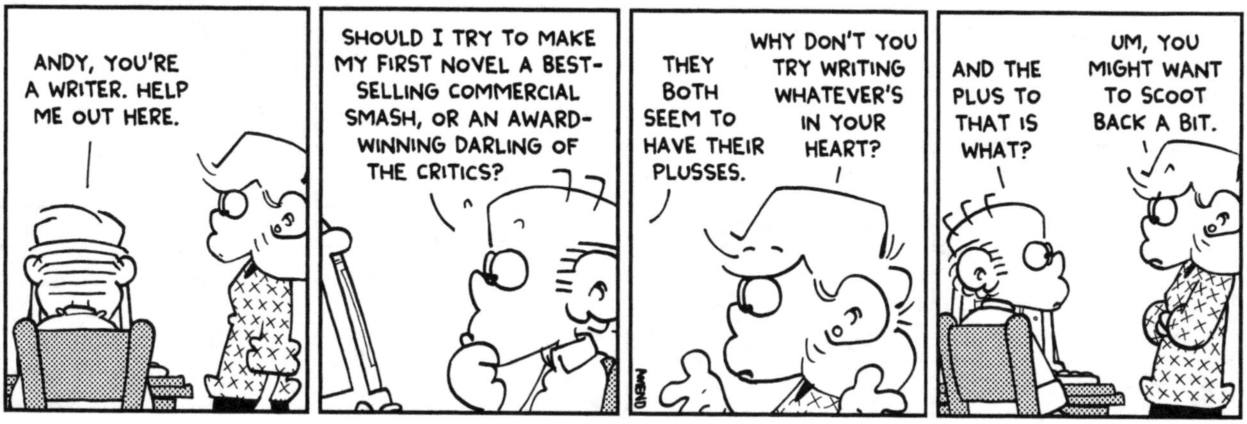
ANDY, YOU'RE A WRITER. HELP ME OUT HERE.
SHOULD I TRY TO MAKE MY FIRST NOVEL A BEST-SELLING COMMERCIAL SMASH, OR AN AWARD-WINNING DARLING OF THE CRITICS?
THEY BOTH SEEM TO HAVE THEIR PLUSSES.
WHY DON'T YOU TRY WRITING WHATEVER'S IN YOUR HEART?
AND THE PLUS TO THAT IS WHAT?
UM, YOU MIGHT WANT TO SCOOT BACK A BIT.
AMEND

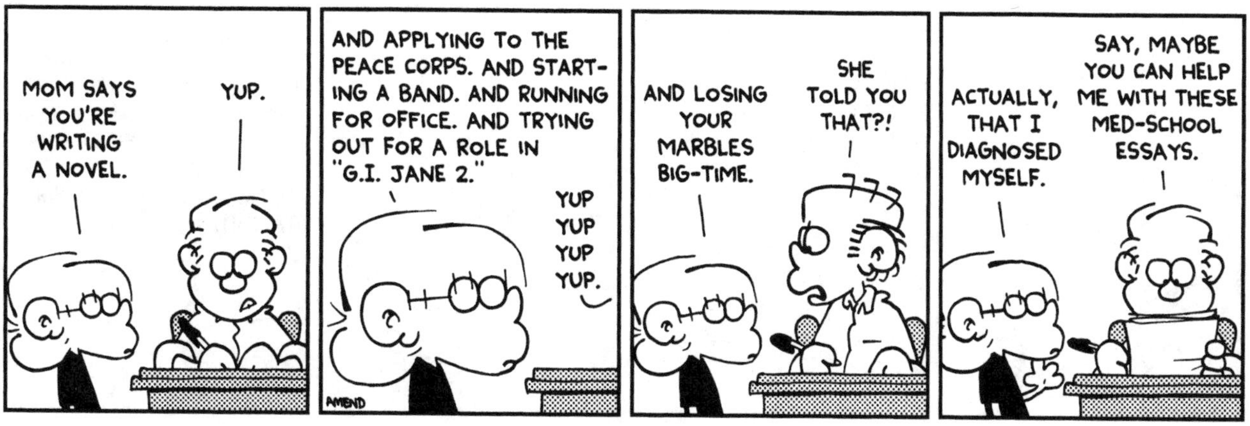
MOM SAYS YOU'RE WRITING A NOVEL.
YUP.
AND APPLYING TO THE PEACE CORPS. AND STARTING A BAND. AND RUNNING FOR OFFICE. AND TRYING OUT FOR A ROLE IN "G.I. JANE 2."
YUP YUP YUP YUP.
AMEND
AND LOSING YOUR MARBLES BIG-TIME.
SHE TOLD YOU THAT?!
ACTUALLY, THAT I DIAGNOSED MYSELF.
SAY, MAYBE YOU CAN HELP ME WITH THESE MED-SCHOOL ESSAYS.

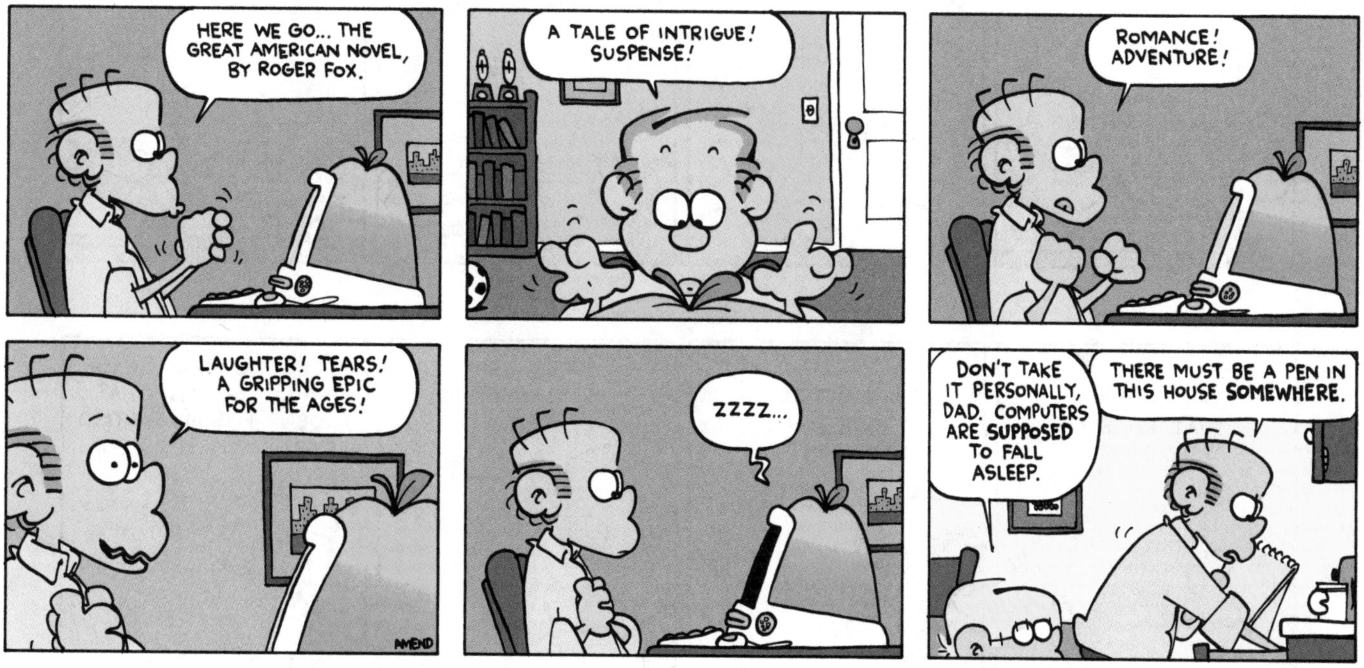
HERE WE GO... THE GREAT AMERICAN NOVEL, BY ROGER FOX.
A TALE OF INTRIGUE! SUSPENSE!
ROMANCE! ADVENTURE!
LAUGHTER! TEARS! A GRIPPING EPIC FOR THE AGES!
AMEND
ZZZZ...
DON'T TAKE IT PERSONALLY, DAD. COMPUTERS ARE SUPPOSED TO FALL ASLEEP.
THERE MUST BE A PEN IN THIS HOUSE SOMEWHERE.

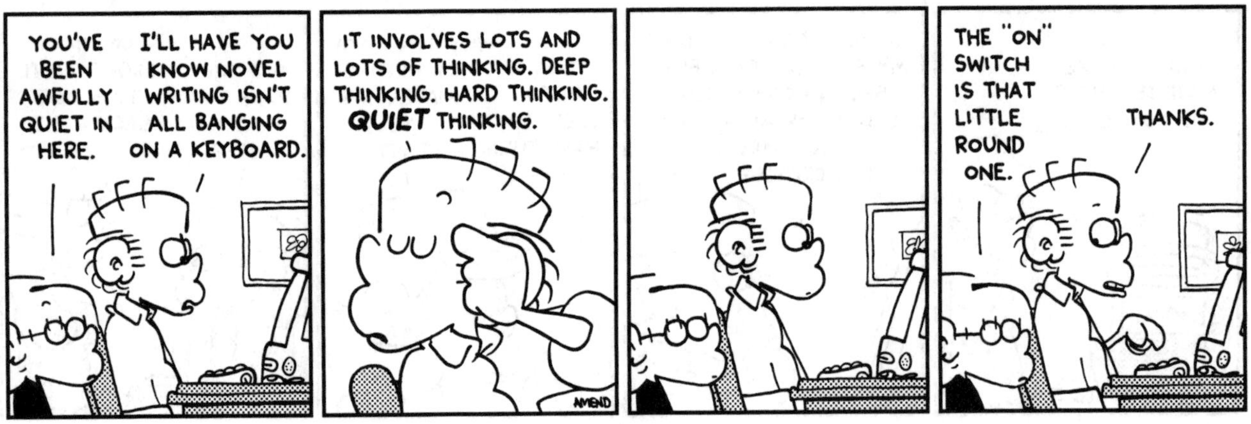

YOU'VE BEEN AWFULLY QUIET IN HERE.
I'LL HAVE YOU KNOW NOVEL WRITING ISN'T ALL BANGING ON A KEYBOARD.
IT INVOLVES LOTS AND LOTS OF THINKING. DEEP THINKING. HARD THINKING. **QUIET** THINKING.
THE "ON" SWITCH IS THAT LITTLE ROUND ONE.
THANKS.


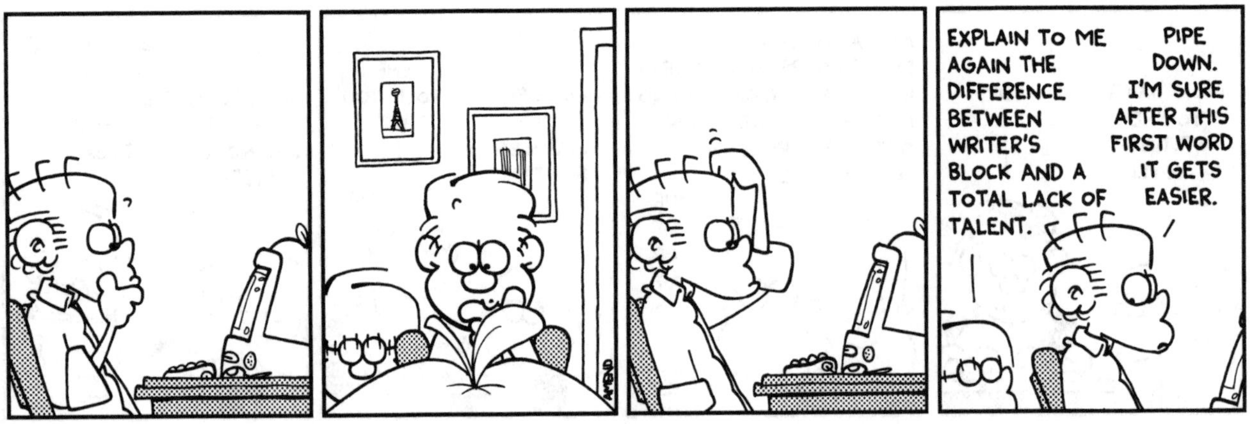

EXPLAIN TO ME AGAIN THE DIFFERENCE BETWEEN WRITER'S BLOCK AND A TOTAL LACK OF TALENT.
PIPE DOWN. I'M SURE AFTER THIS FIRST WORD IT GETS EASIER.


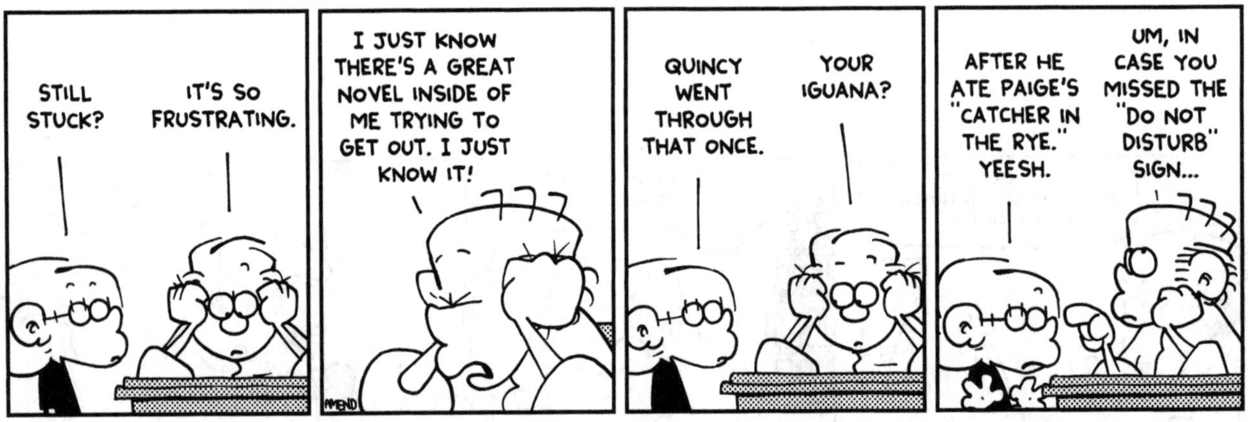

STILL STUCK?
IT'S SO FRUSTRATING.
I JUST KNOW THERE'S A GREAT NOVEL INSIDE OF ME TRYING TO GET OUT. I JUST KNOW IT!
QUINCY WENT THROUGH THAT ONCE.
YOUR IGUANA?
AFTER HE ATE PAIGE'S "CATCHER IN THE RYE." YEESH.
UM, IN CASE YOU MISSED THE "DO NOT DISTURB" SIGN...


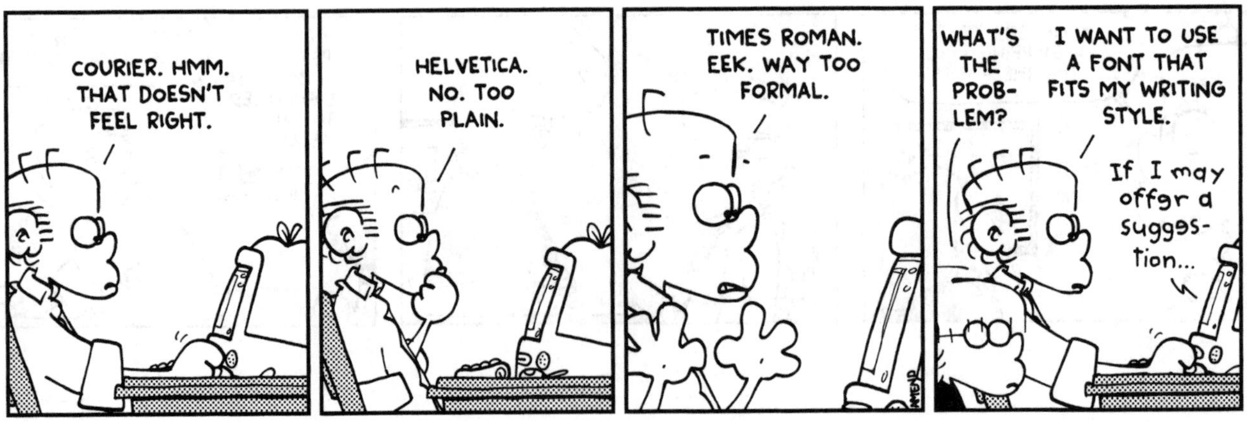

COURIER. HMM. THAT DOESN'T FEEL RIGHT.
HELVETICA. NO. TOO PLAIN.
TIMES ROMAN. EEK. WAY TOO FORMAL.
WHAT'S THE PROB-LEM?
I WANT TO USE A FONT THAT FITS MY WRITING STYLE.
If I may offer a sugges-tion...

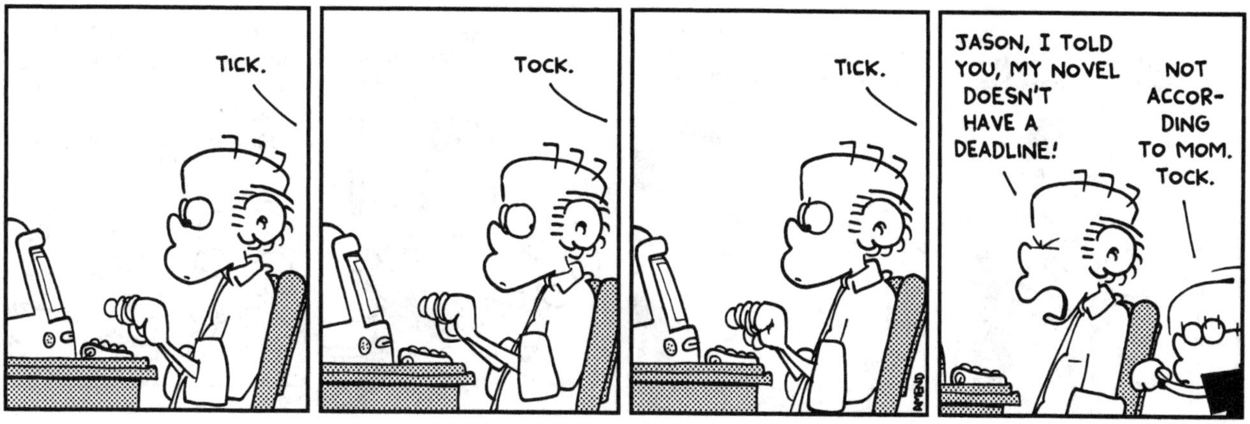
TICK.
TOCK.
TICK.
JASON, I TOLD YOU, MY NOVEL DOESN'T HAVE A DEADLINE!
NOT ACCORDING TO MOM. TOCK.

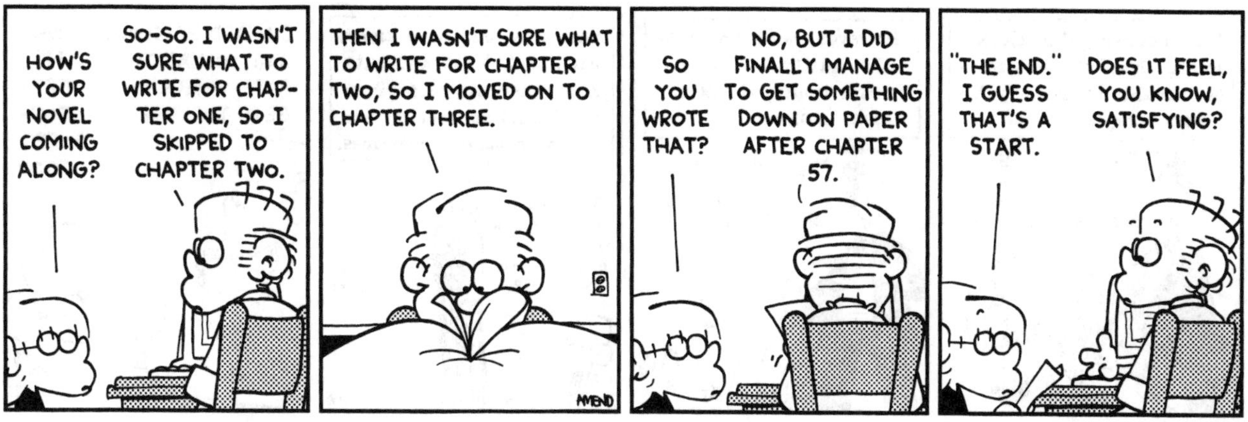
HOW'S YOUR NOVEL COMING ALONG?
SO-SO. I WASN'T SURE WHAT TO WRITE FOR CHAPTER ONE, SO I SKIPPED TO CHAPTER TWO.
THEN I WASN'T SURE WHAT TO WRITE FOR CHAPTER TWO, SO I MOVED ON TO CHAPTER THREE.
SO YOU WROTE THAT?
NO, BUT I DID FINALLY MANAGE TO GET SOMETHING DOWN ON PAPER AFTER CHAPTER 57.
"THE END." I GUESS THAT'S A START.
DOES IT FEEL, YOU KNOW, SATISFYING?

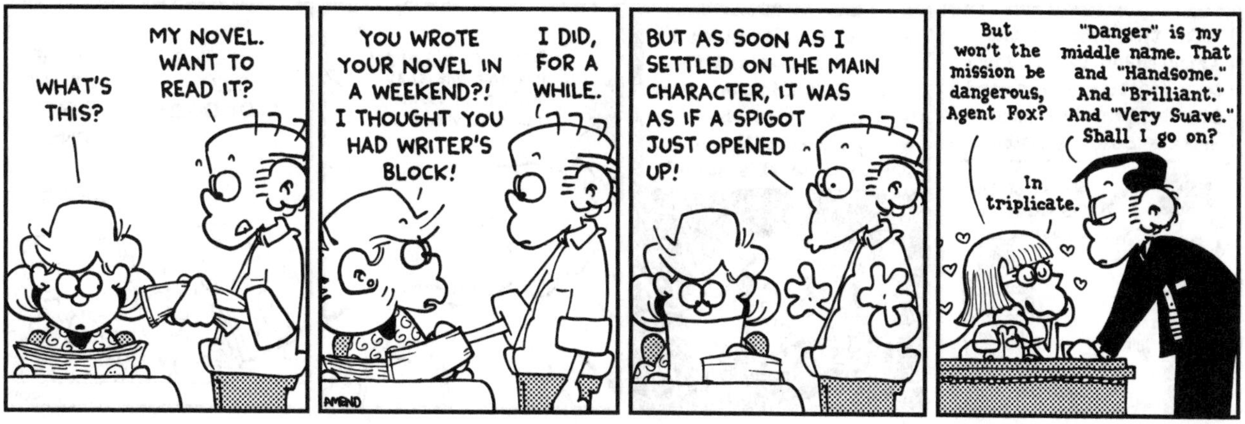
WHAT'S THIS?
MY NOVEL. WANT TO READ IT?
YOU WROTE YOUR NOVEL IN A WEEKEND?! I THOUGHT YOU HAD WRITER'S BLOCK!
I DID, FOR A WHILE.
BUT AS SOON AS I SETTLED ON THE MAIN CHARACTER, IT WAS AS IF A SPIGOT JUST OPENED UP!
But won't the mission be dangerous, Agent Fox?
"Danger" is my middle name. That and "Handsome." And "Brilliant." And "Very Suave." Shall I go on?
In triplicate.

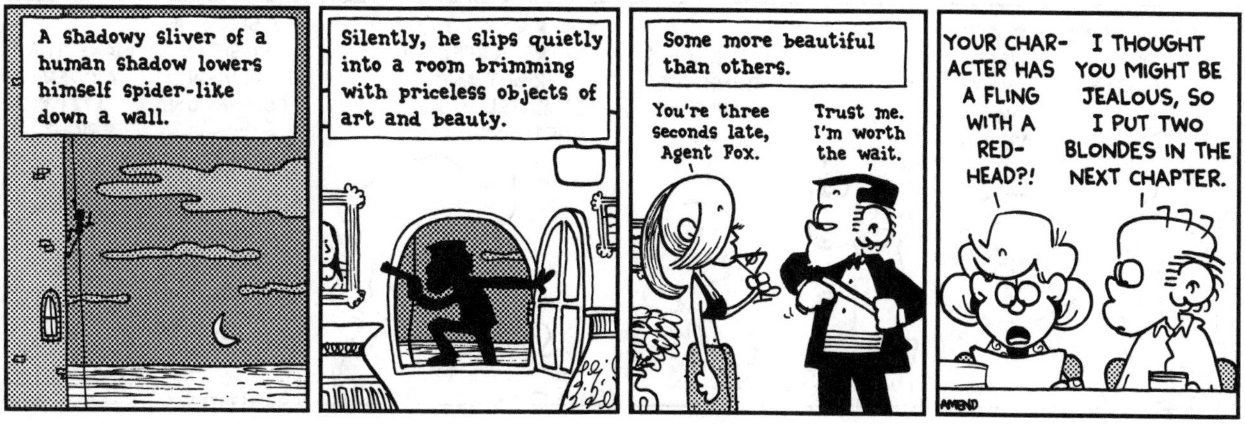
A shadowy sliver of a human shadow lowers himself spider-like down a wall.
Silently, he slips quietly into a room brimming with priceless objects of art and beauty.
Some more beautiful than others.
You're three seconds late, Agent Fox.
Trust me. I'm worth the wait.
YOUR CHARACTER HAS A FLING WITH A RED-HEAD?!
I THOUGHT YOU MIGHT BE JEALOUS, SO I PUT TWO BLONDES IN THE NEXT CHAPTER.

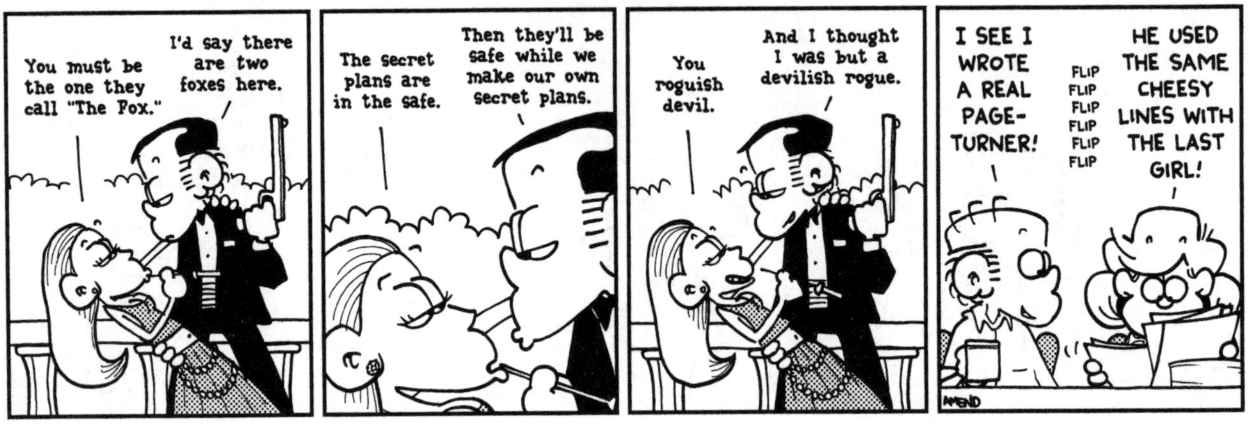
You must be the one they call "The Fox."
I'd say there are two foxes here.
The secret plans are in the safe.
Then they'll be safe while we make our own secret plans.
You roguish devil.
And I thought I was but a devilish rogue.
I SEE I WROTE A REAL PAGE-TURNER!
FLIP FLIP FLIP FLIP FLIP FLIP
HE USED THE SAME CHEESY LINES WITH THE LAST GIRL!

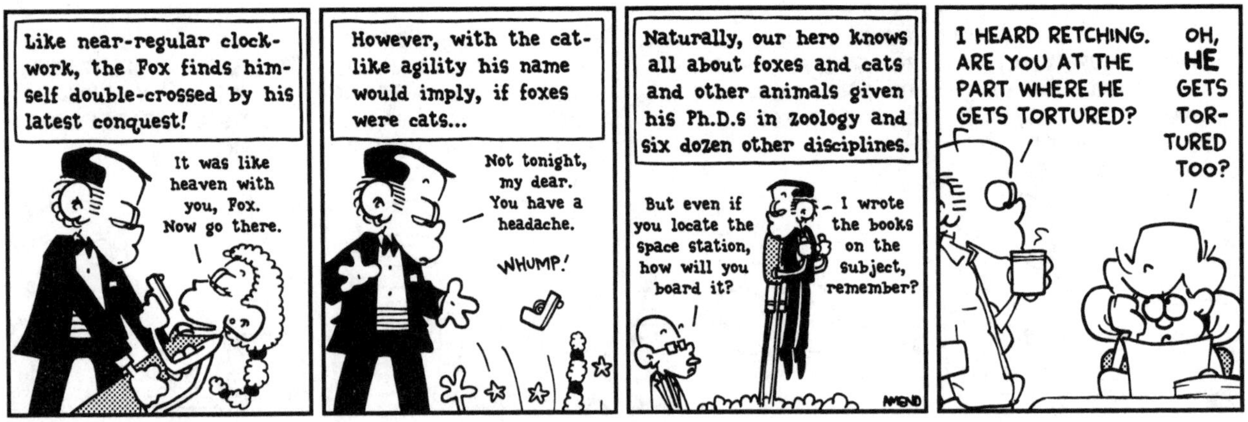
Like near-regular clock-work, the Fox finds him-self double-crossed by his latest conquest!
It was like heaven with you, Fox. Now go there.
However, with the cat-like agility his name would imply, if foxes were cats...
Not tonight, my dear. You have a headache.
WHUMP!
Naturally, our hero knows all about foxes and cats and other animals given his Ph.D.s in zoology and six dozen other disciplines.
But even if you locate the space station, how will you board it?
I wrote the books on the subject, remember?
I HEARD RETCHING. ARE YOU AT THE PART WHERE HE GETS TORTURED?
OH, HE GETS TOR-TURED TOO?

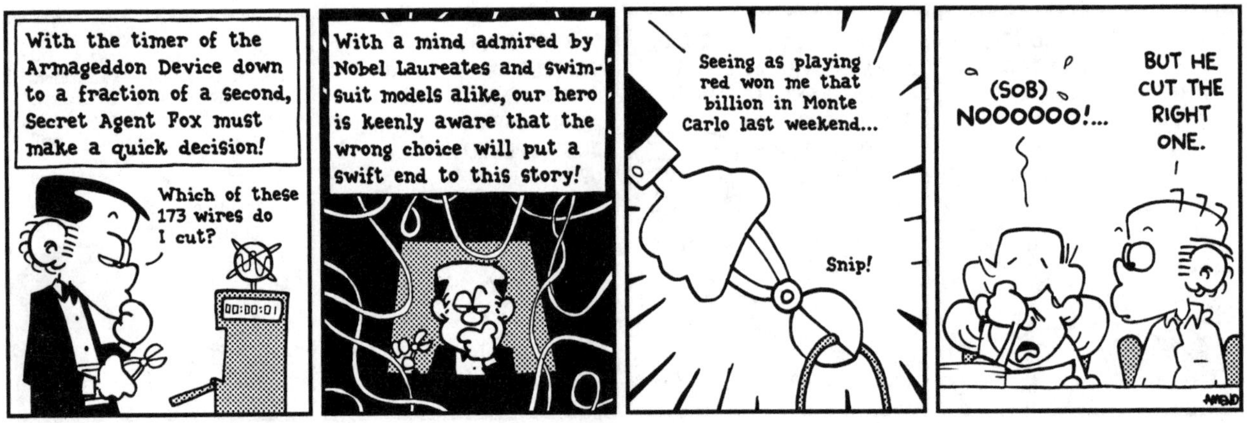
With the timer of the Armageddon Device down to a fraction of a second, Secret Agent Fox must make a quick decision!
Which of these 173 wires do I cut?
00:00:01
With a mind admired by Nobel Laureates and swim-suit models alike, our hero is keenly aware that the wrong choice will put a swift end to this story!
Seeing as playing red won me that billion in Monte Carlo last weekend...
Snip!
(SOB) NOOOOOO!...
BUT HE CUT THE RIGHT ONE.

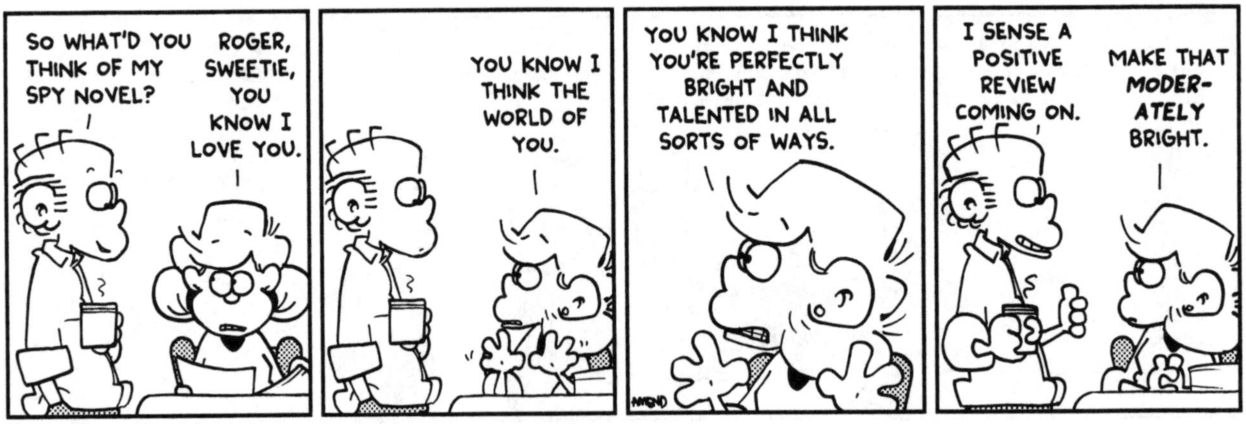
SO WHAT'D YOU THINK OF MY SPY NOVEL?
ROGER, SWEETIE, YOU KNOW I LOVE YOU.
YOU KNOW I THINK THE WORLD OF YOU.
YOU KNOW I THINK YOU'RE PERFECTLY BRIGHT AND TALENTED IN ALL SORTS OF WAYS.
I SENSE A POSITIVE REVIEW COMING ON.
MAKE THAT MODER-ATELY BRIGHT.

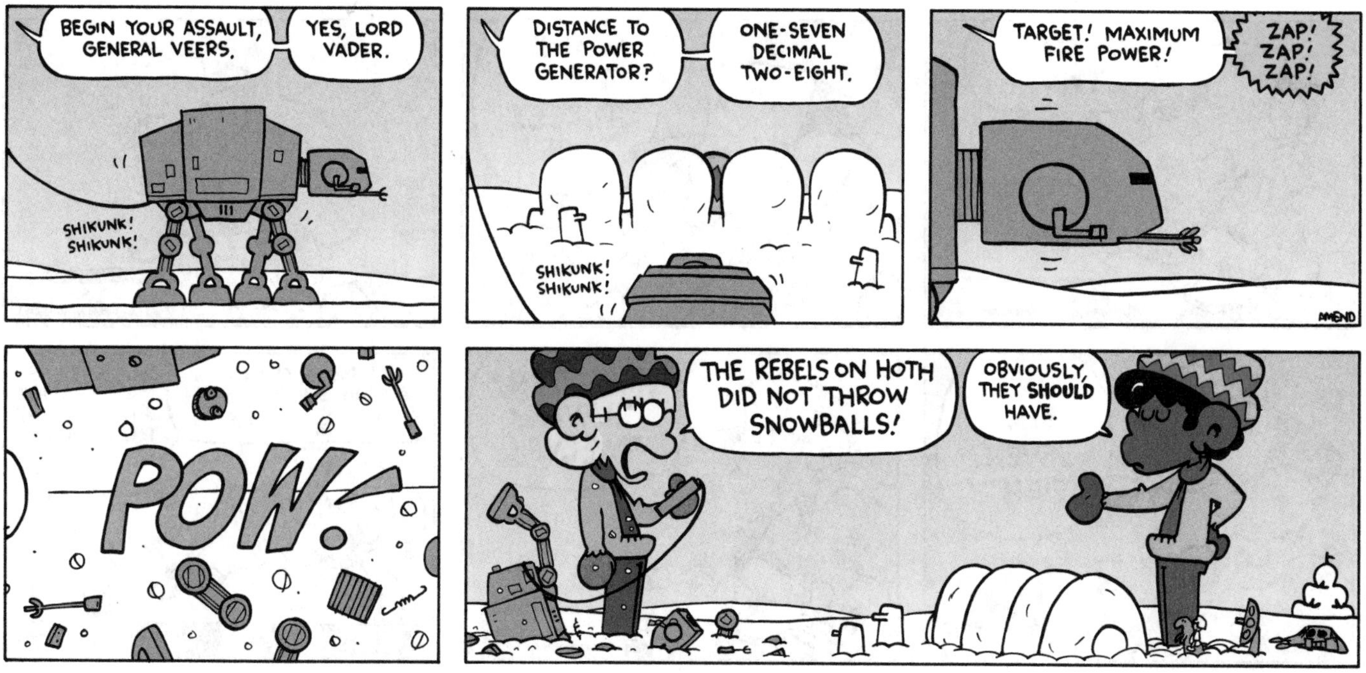
BEGIN YOUR ASSAULT, GENERAL VEERS.
YES, LORD VADER.
SHIKUNK! SHIKUNK!
DISTANCE TO THE POWER GENERATOR?
ONE-SEVEN DECIMAL TWO-EIGHT.
SHIKUNK! SHIKUNK!
TARGET! MAXIMUM FIRE POWER!
ZAP! ZAP! ZAP!
AMEND
POW
THE REBELS ON HOTH DID NOT THROW SNOWBALLS!
OBVIOUSLY, THEY SHOULD HAVE.

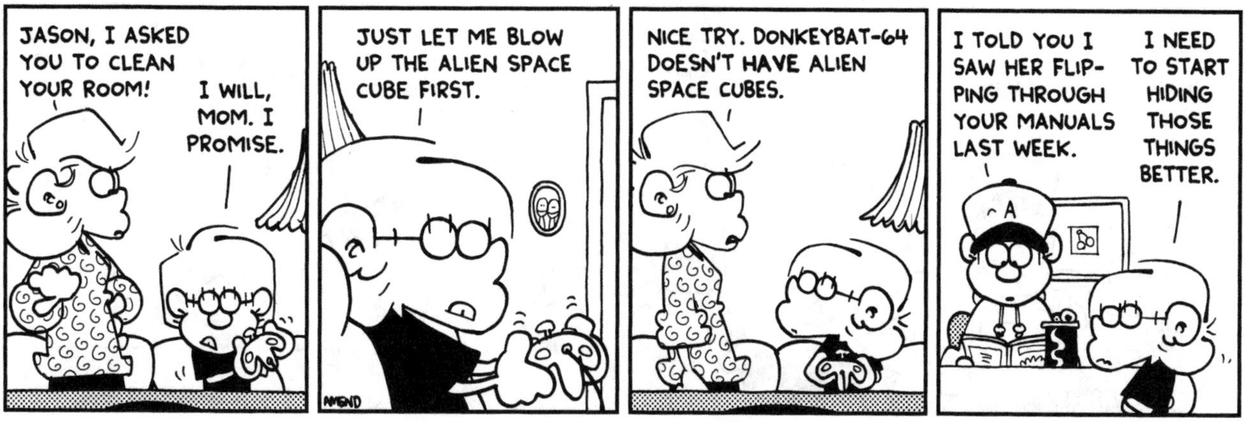
JASON, I ASKED YOU TO CLEAN YOUR ROOM!
I WILL, MOM. I PROMISE.
JUST LET ME BLOW UP THE ALIEN SPACE CUBE FIRST.
AMEND
NICE TRY. DONKEYBAT-64 DOESN'T HAVE ALIEN SPACE CUBES.
I TOLD YOU I SAW HER FLIP-PING THROUGH YOUR MANUALS LAST WEEK.
I NEED TO START HIDING THOSE THINGS BETTER.

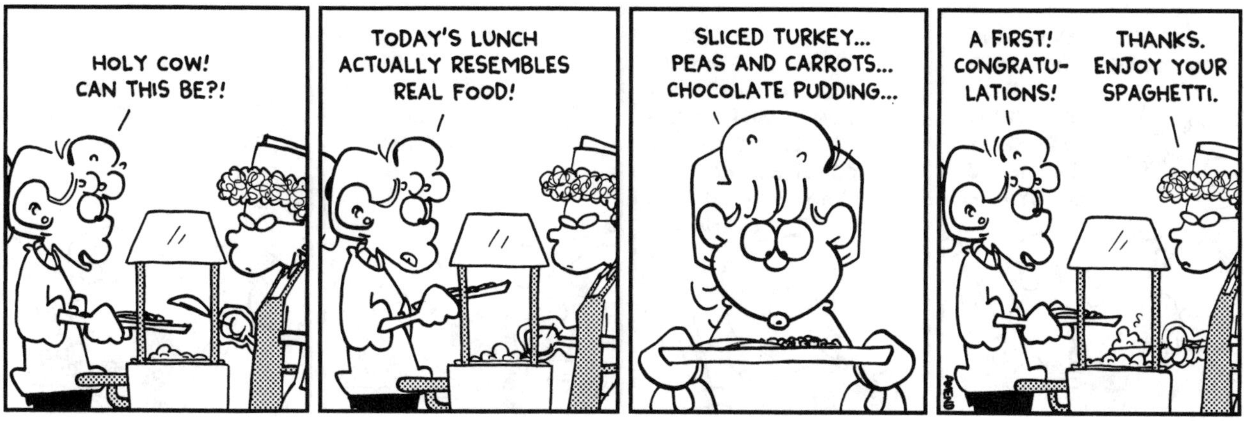
HOLY COW! CAN THIS BE?!
TODAY'S LUNCH ACTUALLY RESEMBLES REAL FOOD!
SLICED TURKEY... PEAS AND CARROTS... CHOCOLATE PUDDING...
A FIRST! CONGRATU-LATIONS!
THANKS. ENJOY YOUR SPAGHETTI.

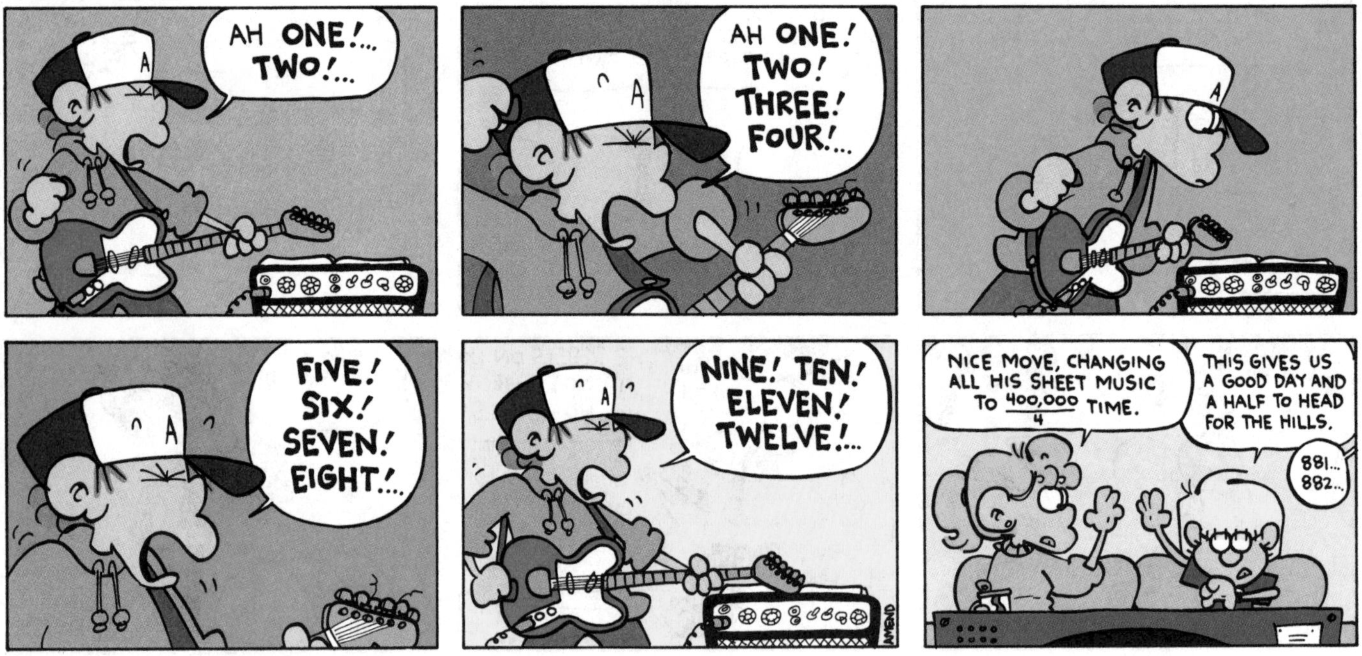
AH ONE!... TWO!...
AH ONE! TWO! THREE! FOUR!...
FIVE! SIX! SEVEN! EIGHT!...
NINE! TEN! ELEVEN! TWELVE!...
AMEND
NICE MOVE, CHANGING ALL HIS SHEET MUSIC TO 400,000/4 TIME.
THIS GIVES US A GOOD DAY AND A HALF TO HEAD FOR THE HILLS.
881... 882...

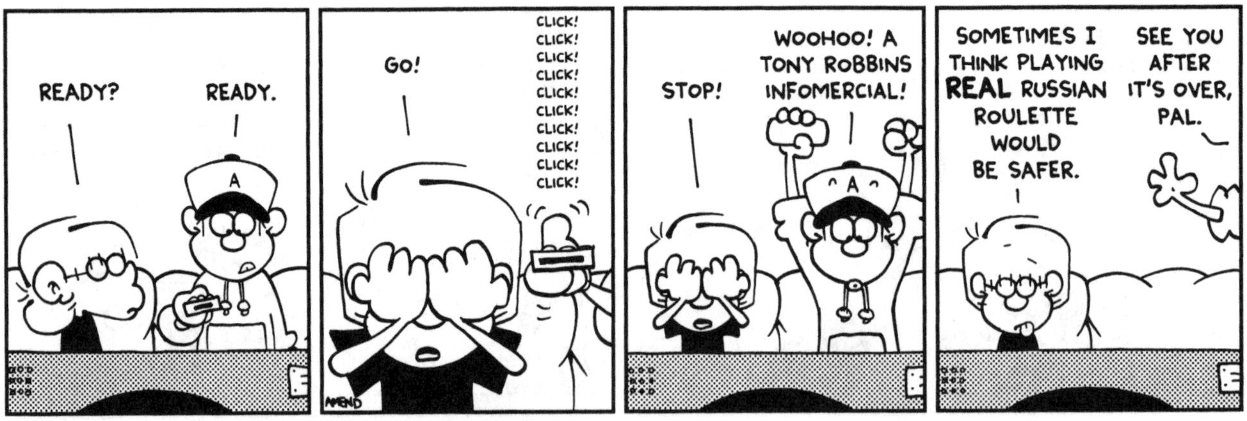
READY?
READY.
GO!
CLICK! CLICK! CLICK! CLICK! CLICK! CLICK! CLICK! CLICK! CLICK! CLICK!
AMEND
STOP!
WOOHOO! A TONY ROBBINS INFOMERCIAL!
SOMETIMES I THINK PLAYING REAL RUSSIAN ROULETTE WOULD BE SAFER.
SEE YOU AFTER IT'S OVER, PAL.

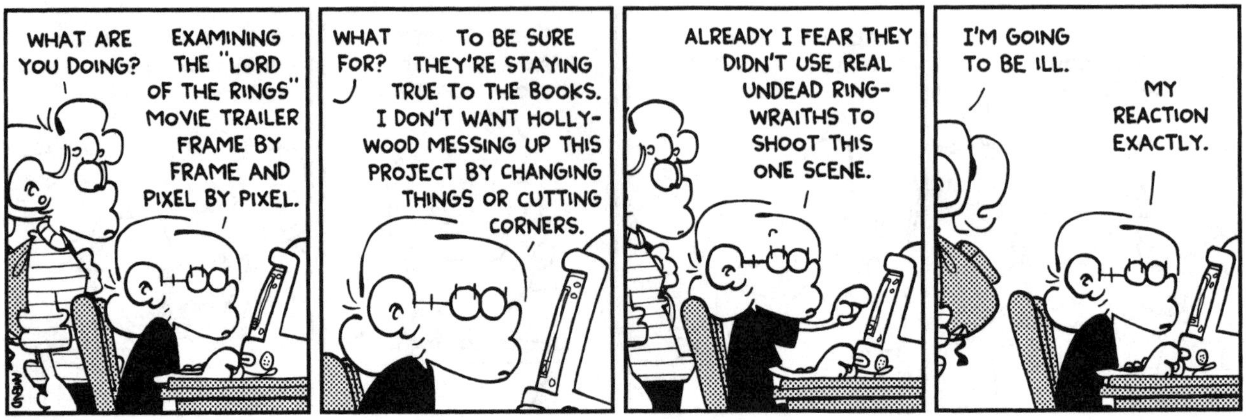
WHAT ARE YOU DOING?
EXAMINING THE "LORD OF THE RINGS" MOVIE TRAILER FRAME BY FRAME AND PIXEL BY PIXEL.
AMEND
WHAT FOR?
TO BE SURE THEY'RE STAYING TRUE TO THE BOOKS. I DON'T WANT HOLLYWOOD MESSING UP THIS PROJECT BY CHANGING THINGS OR CUTTING CORNERS.
ALREADY I FEAR THEY DIDN'T USE REAL UNDEAD RINGWRAITHS TO SHOOT THIS ONE SCENE.
I'M GOING TO BE ILL.
MY REACTION EXACTLY.

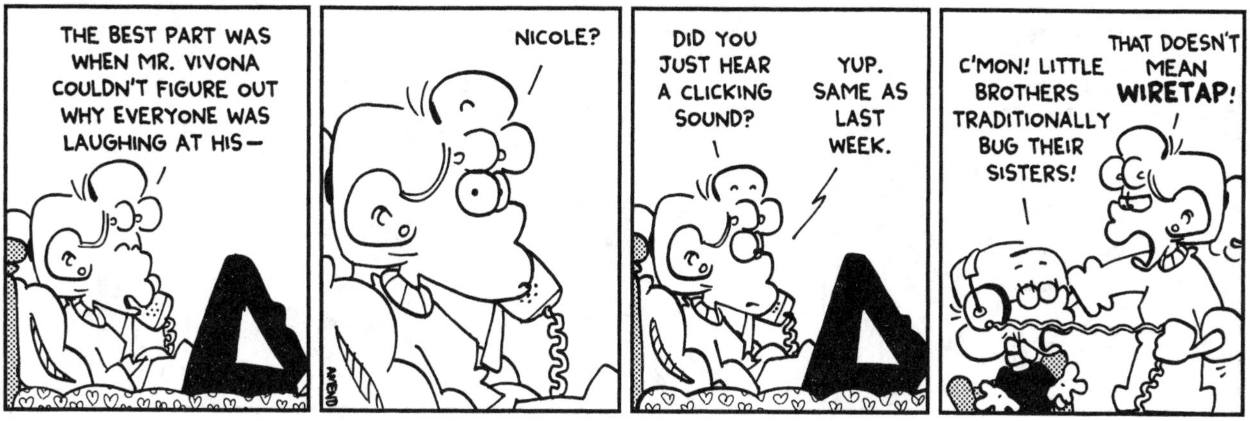
THE BEST PART WAS WHEN MR. VIVONA COULDN'T FIGURE OUT WHY EVERYONE WAS LAUGHING AT HIS—
NICOLE?
DID YOU JUST HEAR A CLICKING SOUND?
YUP. SAME AS LAST WEEK.
C'MON! LITTLE BROTHERS TRADITIONALLY BUG THEIR SISTERS!
THAT DOESN'T MEAN **WIRETAP**!

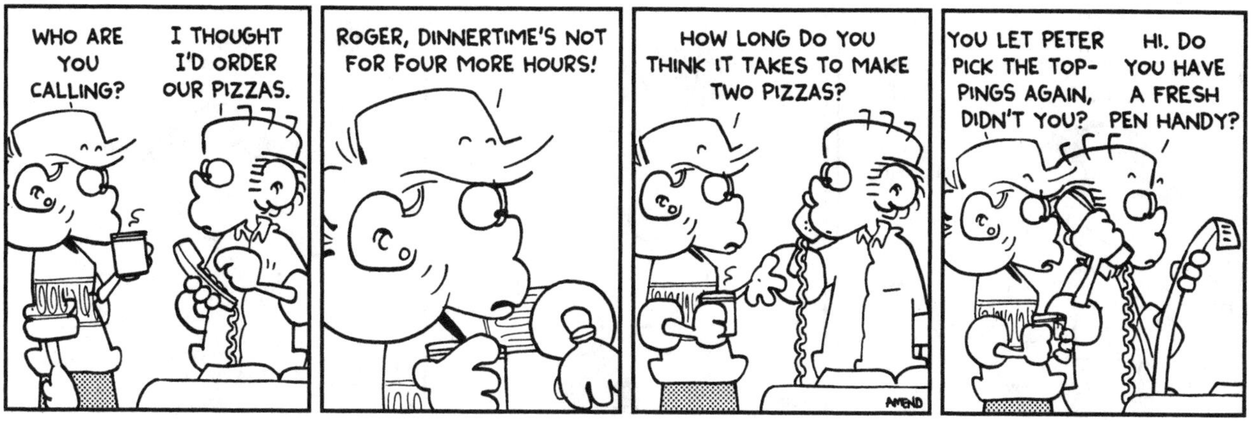
WHO ARE YOU CALLING?
I THOUGHT I'D ORDER OUR PIZZAS.
ROGER, DINNERTIME'S NOT FOR FOUR MORE HOURS!
HOW LONG DO YOU THINK IT TAKES TO MAKE TWO PIZZAS?
YOU LET PETER PICK THE TOP-PINGS AGAIN, DIDN'T YOU?
HI. DO YOU HAVE A FRESH PEN HANDY?

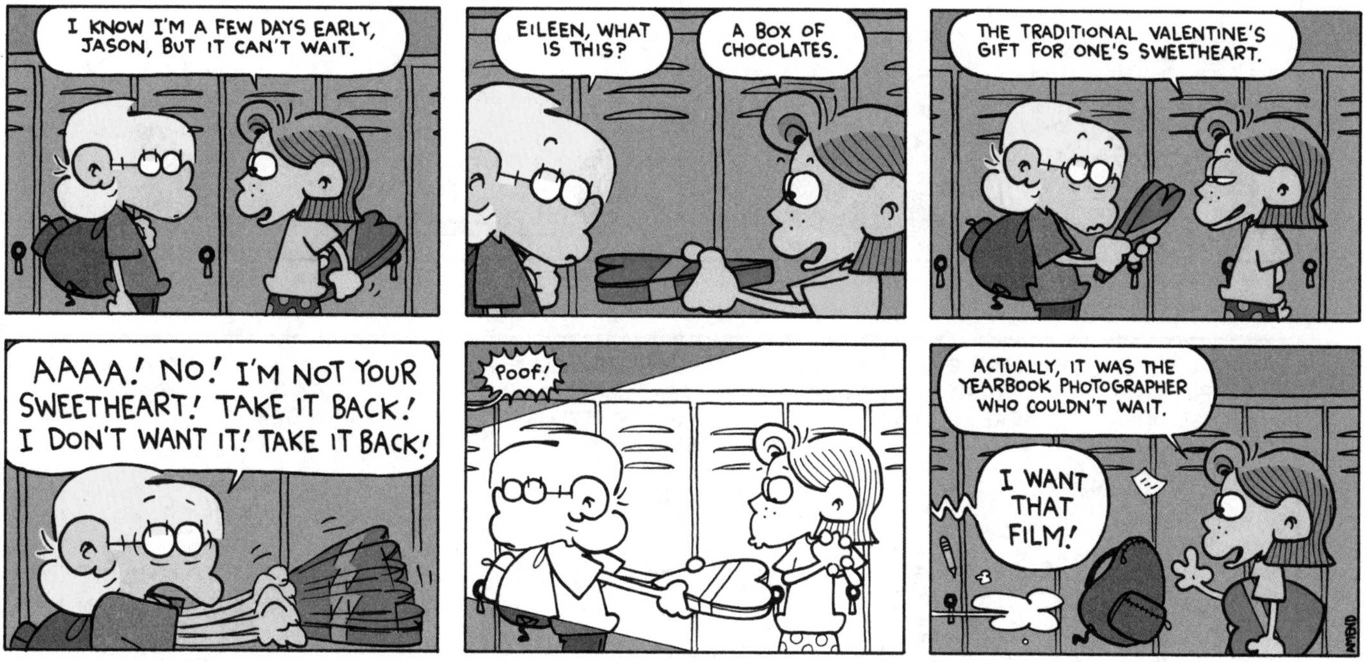
I KNOW I'M A FEW DAYS EARLY, JASON, BUT IT CAN'T WAIT.
EILEEN, WHAT IS THIS?
A BOX OF CHOCOLATES.
THE TRADITIONAL VALENTINE'S GIFT FOR ONE'S SWEETHEART.
AAAA! NO! I'M NOT YOUR SWEETHEART! TAKE IT BACK! I DON'T WANT IT! TAKE IT BACK!
Poof!
ACTUALLY, IT WAS THE YEARBOOK PHOTOGRAPHER WHO COULDN'T WAIT.
I WANT THAT FILM!

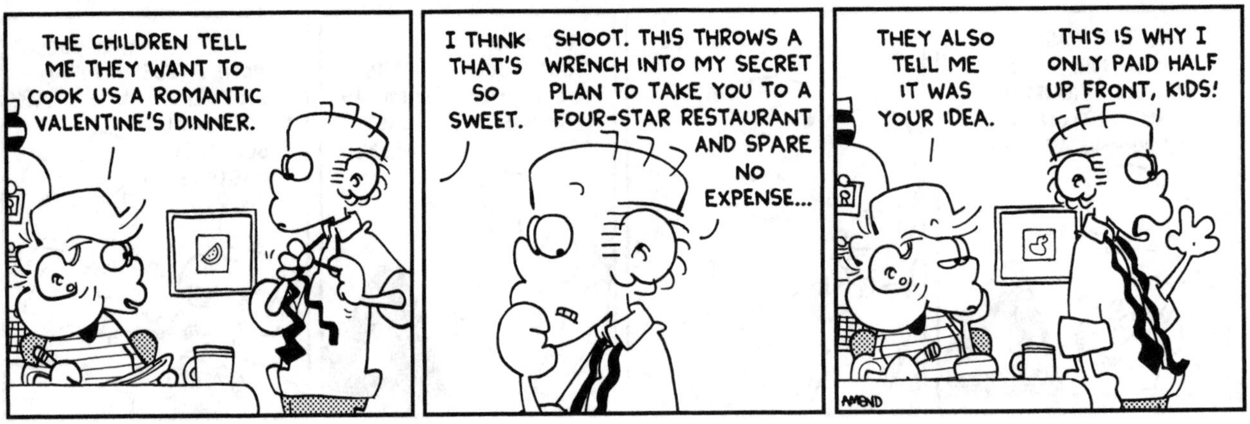
THE CHILDREN TELL ME THEY WANT TO COOK US A ROMANTIC VALENTINE'S DINNER.
I THINK THAT'S SO SWEET.
SHOOT. THIS THROWS A WRENCH INTO MY SECRET PLAN TO TAKE YOU TO A FOUR-STAR RESTAURANT AND SPARE NO EXPENSE...
THEY ALSO TELL ME IT WAS YOUR IDEA.
THIS IS WHY I ONLY PAID HALF UP FRONT, KIDS!
AMEND

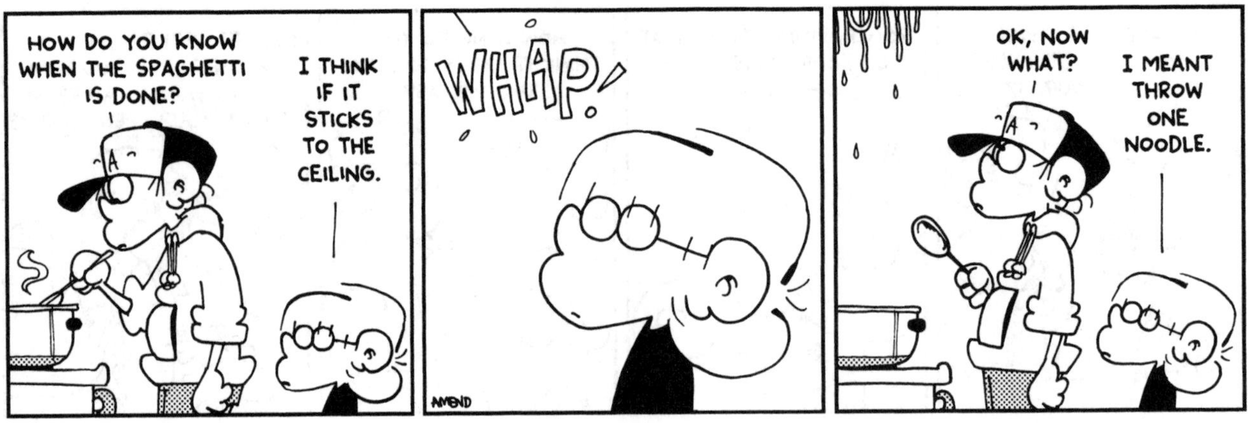
HOW DO YOU KNOW WHEN THE SPAGHETTI IS DONE?
I THINK IF IT STICKS TO THE CEILING.
WHAP!
AMEND
OK, NOW WHAT?
I MEANT THROW ONE NOODLE.

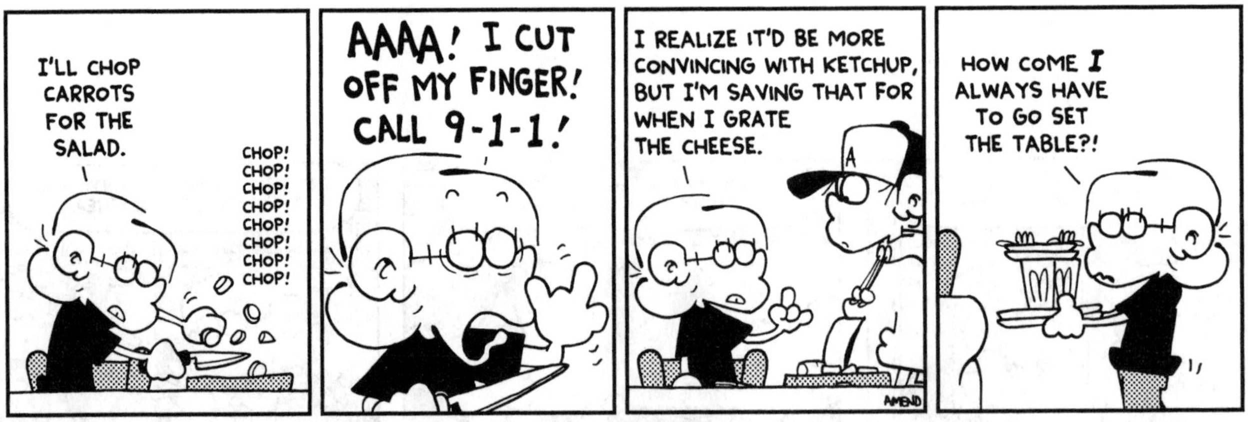
I'LL CHOP CARROTS FOR THE SALAD.
CHOP! CHOP! CHOP! CHOP! CHOP! CHOP! CHOP! CHOP!
AAAA! I CUT OFF MY FINGER! CALL 9-1-1!
I REALIZE IT'D BE MORE CONVINCING WITH KETCHUP, BUT I'M SAVING THAT FOR WHEN I GRATE THE CHEESE.
AMEND
HOW COME I ALWAYS HAVE TO GO SET THE TABLE?!

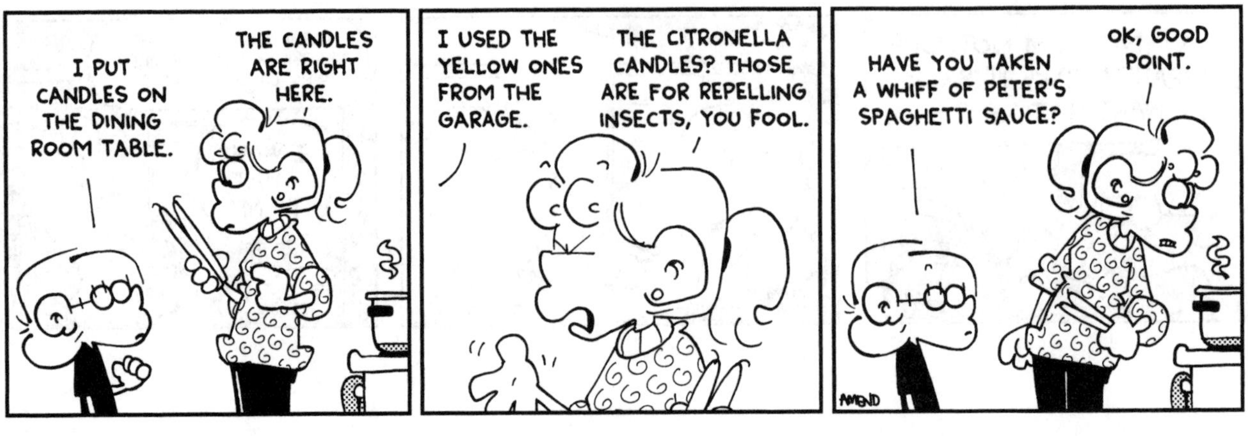
I PUT CANDLES ON THE DINING ROOM TABLE.
THE CANDLES ARE RIGHT HERE.
I USED THE YELLOW ONES FROM THE GARAGE.
THE CITRONELLA CANDLES? THOSE ARE FOR REPELLING INSECTS, YOU FOOL.
HAVE YOU TAKEN A WHIFF OF PETER'S SPAGHETTI SAUCE?
OK, GOOD POINT.
AMEND

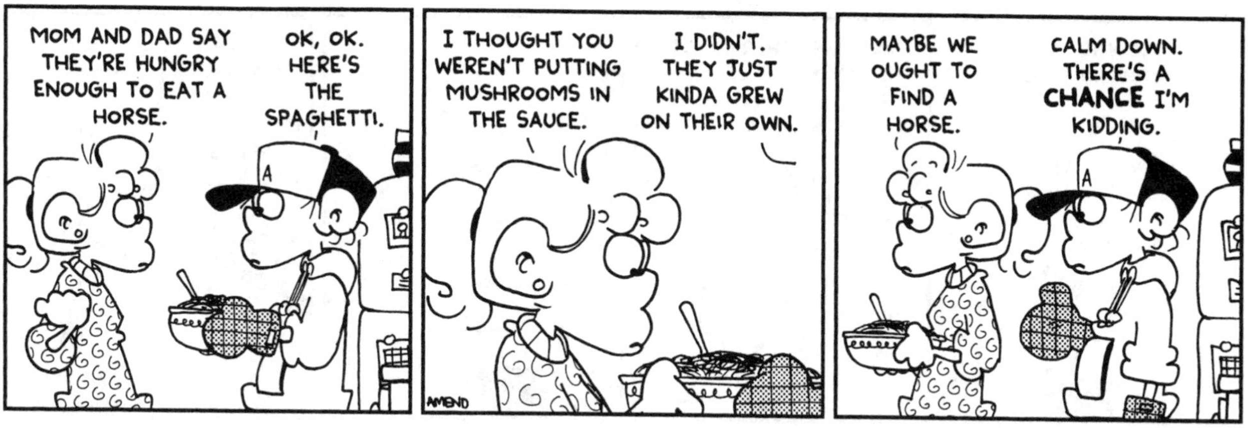
MOM AND DAD SAY THEY'RE HUNGRY ENOUGH TO EAT A HORSE.
OK, OK. HERE'S THE SPAGHETTI.
I THOUGHT YOU WEREN'T PUTTING MUSHROOMS IN THE SAUCE.
I DIDN'T. THEY JUST KINDA GREW ON THEIR OWN.
AMEND
MAYBE WE OUGHT TO FIND A HORSE.
CALM DOWN. THERE'S A **CHANCE** I'M KIDDING.

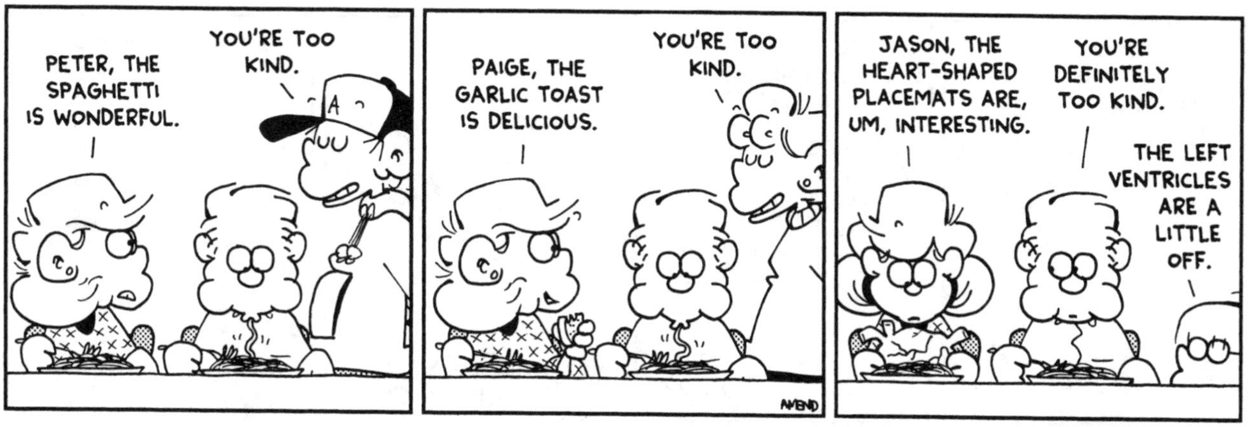
PETER, THE SPAGHETTI IS WONDERFUL.
YOU'RE TOO KIND.
PAIGE, THE GARLIC TOAST IS DELICIOUS.
YOU'RE TOO KIND.
AMEND
JASON, THE HEART-SHAPED PLACEMATS ARE, UM, INTERESTING.
YOU'RE DEFINITELY TOO KIND.
THE LEFT VENTRICLES ARE A LITTLE OFF.

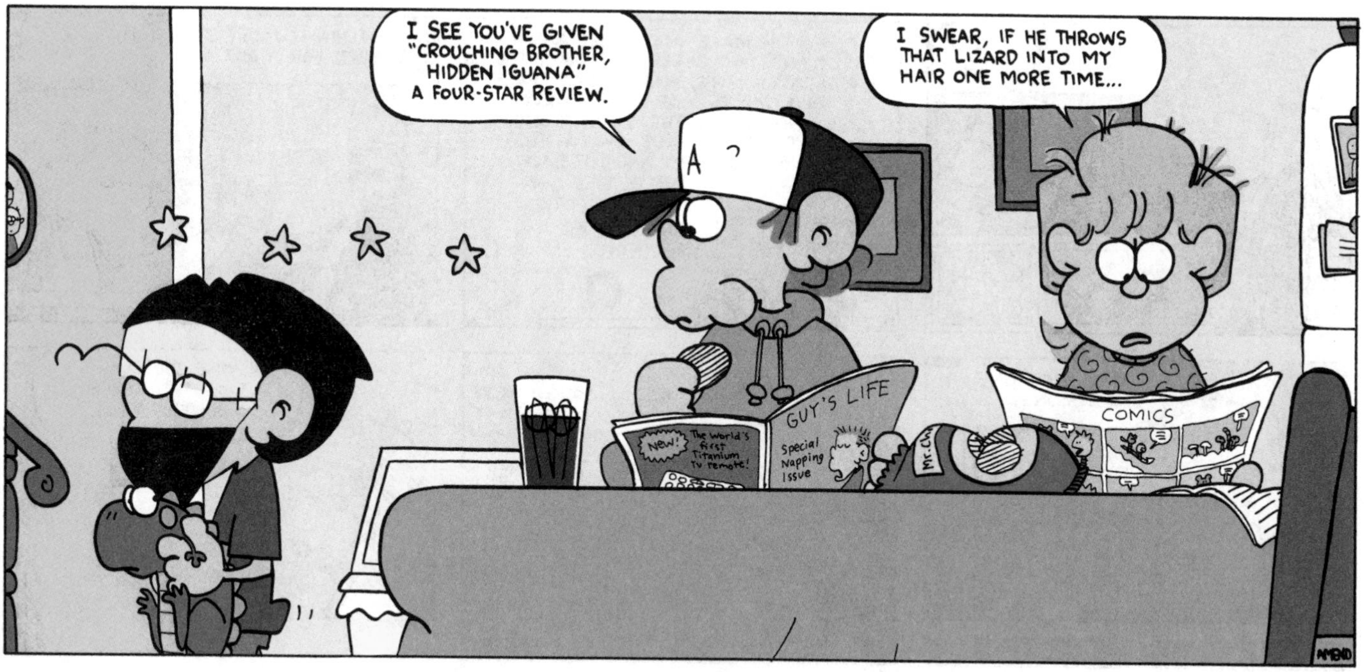
I SEE YOU'VE GIVEN "CROUCHING BROTHER, HIDDEN IGUANA" A FOUR-STAR REVIEW.
I SWEAR, IF HE THROWS THAT LIZARD INTO MY HAIR ONE MORE TIME...
GUY'S LIFE
New!
The World's first Titanium TV remote!
Special Napping Issue
COMICS
AMEND

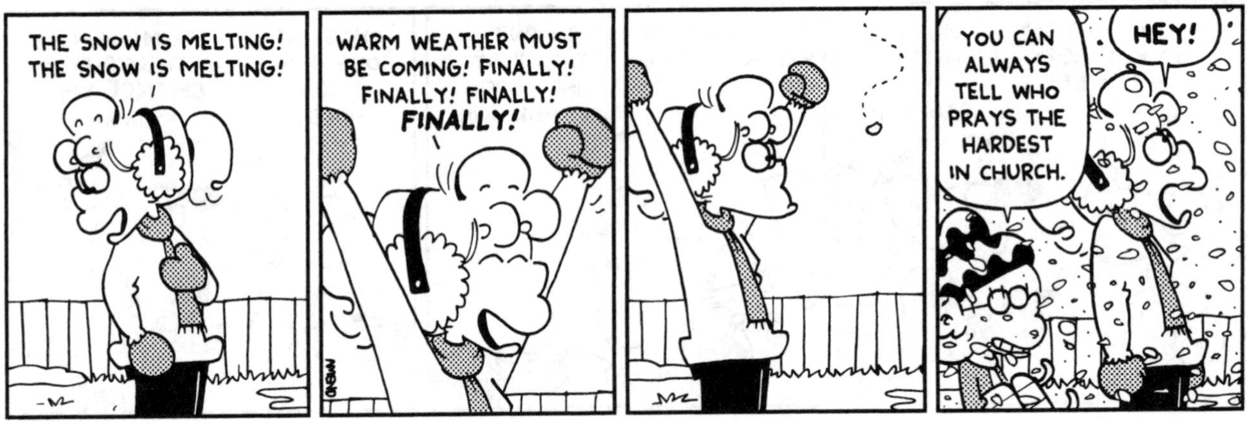
THE SNOW IS MELTING! THE SNOW IS MELTING!
WARM WEATHER MUST BE COMING! FINALLY! FINALLY! FINALLY! FINALLY!
YOU CAN ALWAYS TELL WHO PRAYS THE HARDEST IN CHURCH.
HEY!

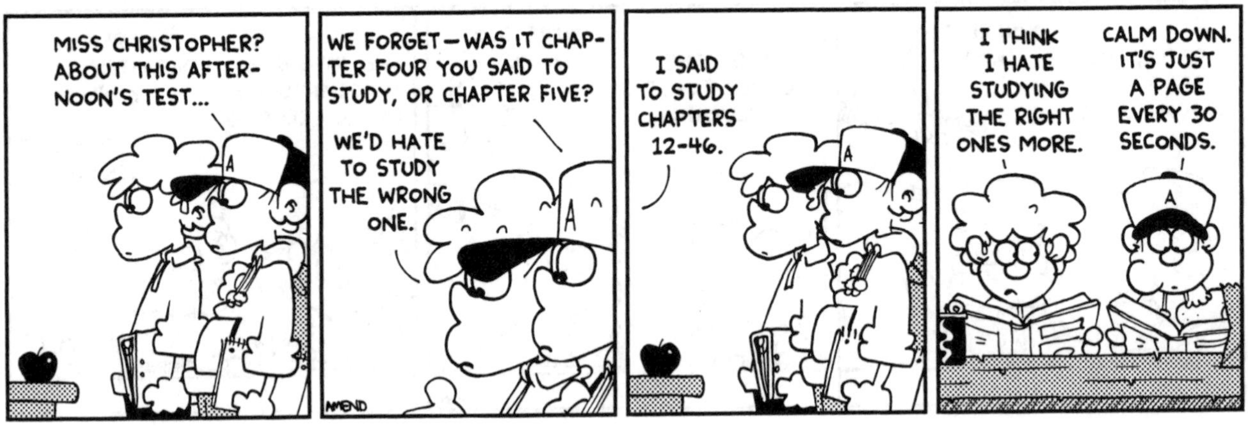
MISS CHRISTOPHER? ABOUT THIS AFTERNOON'S TEST...
WE FORGET—WAS IT CHAPTER FOUR YOU SAID TO STUDY, OR CHAPTER FIVE?
WE'D HATE TO STUDY THE WRONG ONE.
I SAID TO STUDY CHAPTERS 12-46.
I THINK I HATE STUDYING THE RIGHT ONES MORE.
CALM DOWN. IT'S JUST A PAGE EVERY 30 SECONDS.

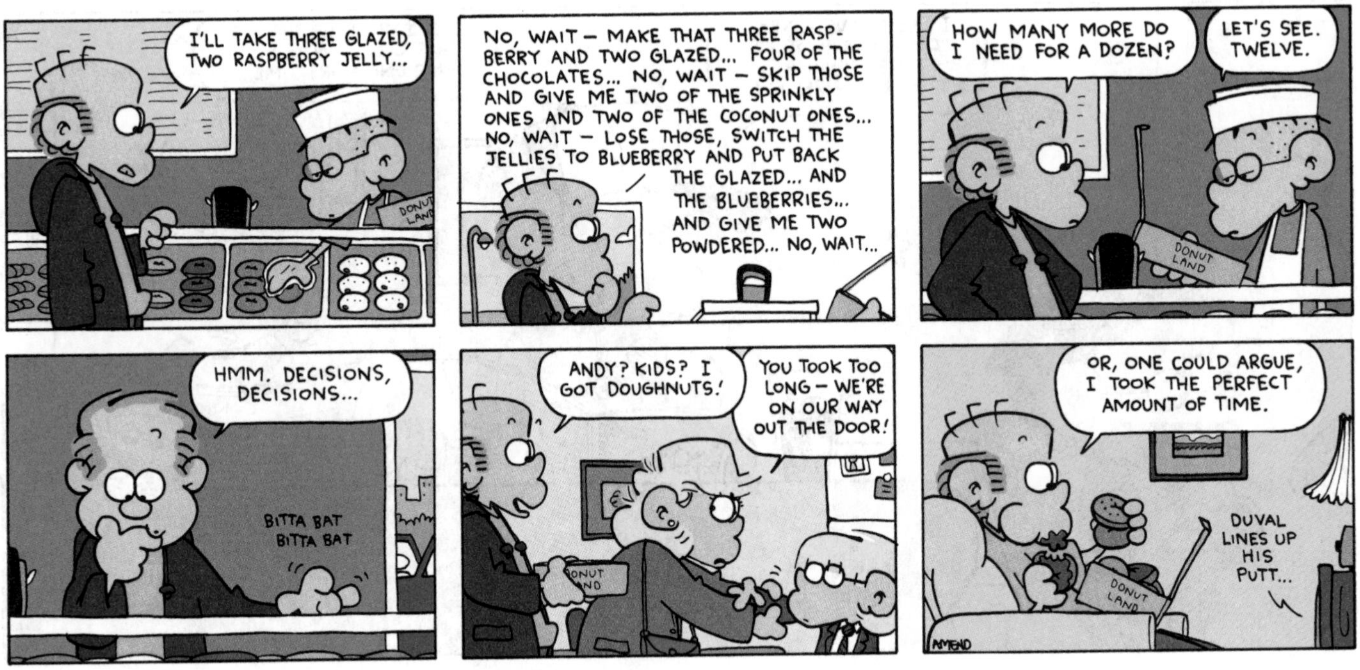
I'LL TAKE THREE GLAZED, TWO RASPBERRY JELLY...
DONUT LAND
NO, WAIT – MAKE THAT THREE RASPBERRY AND TWO GLAZED... FOUR OF THE CHOCOLATES... NO, WAIT – SKIP THOSE AND GIVE ME TWO OF THE SPRINKLY ONES AND TWO OF THE COCONUT ONES... NO, WAIT – LOSE THOSE, SWITCH THE JELLIES TO BLUEBERRY AND PUT BACK THE GLAZED... AND THE BLUEBERRIES... AND GIVE ME TWO POWDERED... NO, WAIT...
HOW MANY MORE DO I NEED FOR A DOZEN?
LET'S SEE. TWELVE.
DONUT LAND
HMM. DECISIONS, DECISIONS...
BITTA BAT BITTA BAT
ANDY? KIDS? I GOT DOUGHNUTS!
YOU TOOK TOO LONG – WE'RE ON OUR WAY OUT THE DOOR!
OR, ONE COULD ARGUE, I TOOK THE PERFECT AMOUNT OF TIME.
DUVAL LINES UP HIS PUTT...
DONUT LAND

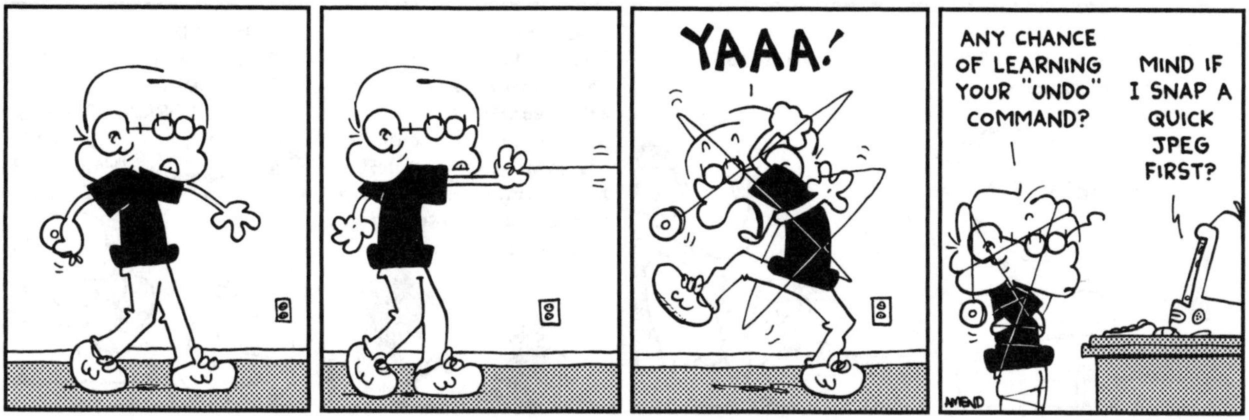
YAAA!
ANY CHANCE OF LEARNING YOUR "UNDO" COMMAND?
MIND IF I SNAP A QUICK JPEG FIRST?

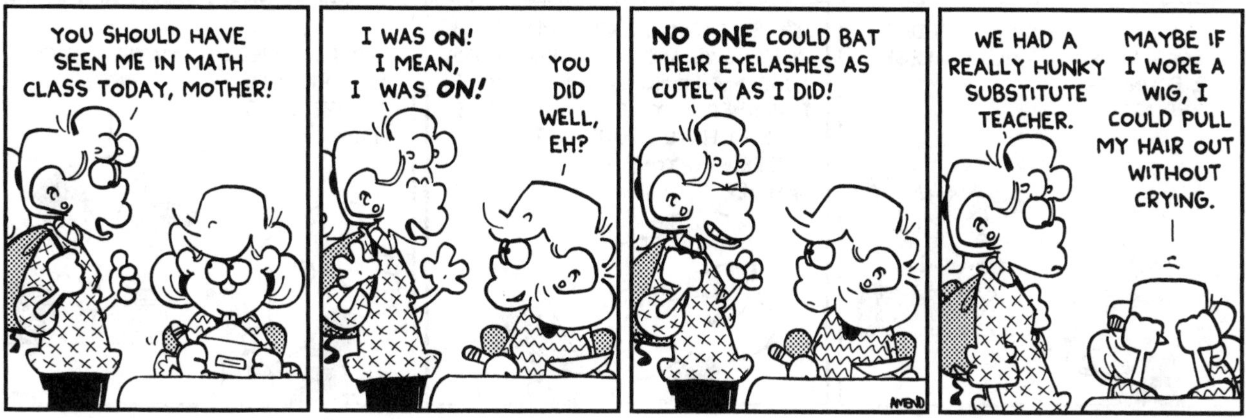
YOU SHOULD HAVE SEEN ME IN MATH CLASS TODAY, MOTHER!
I WAS ON! I MEAN, I WAS ON!
YOU DID WELL, EH?
NO ONE COULD BAT THEIR EYELASHES AS CUTELY AS I DID!
WE HAD A REALLY HUNKY SUBSTITUTE TEACHER.
MAYBE IF I WORE A WIG, I COULD PULL MY HAIR OUT WITHOUT CRYING.

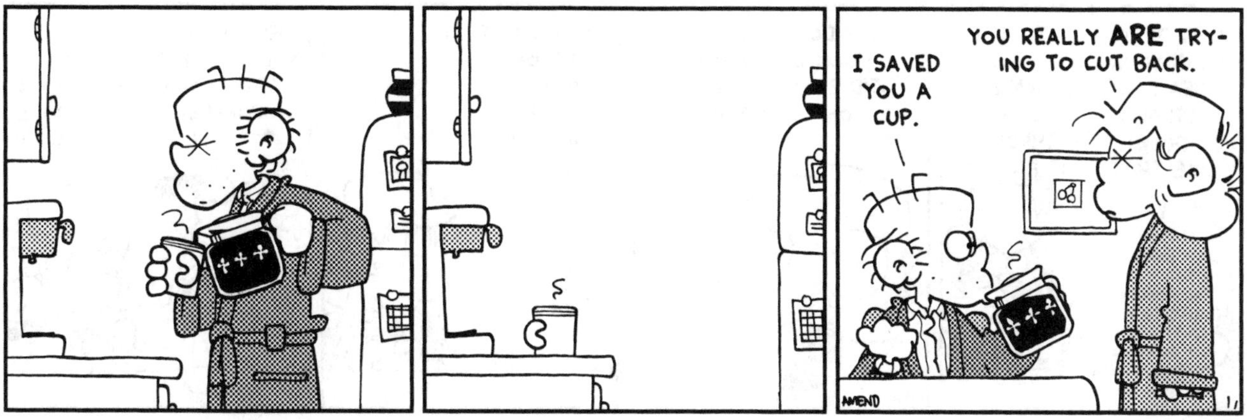
I SAVED YOU A CUP.
YOU REALLY ARE TRYING TO CUT BACK.

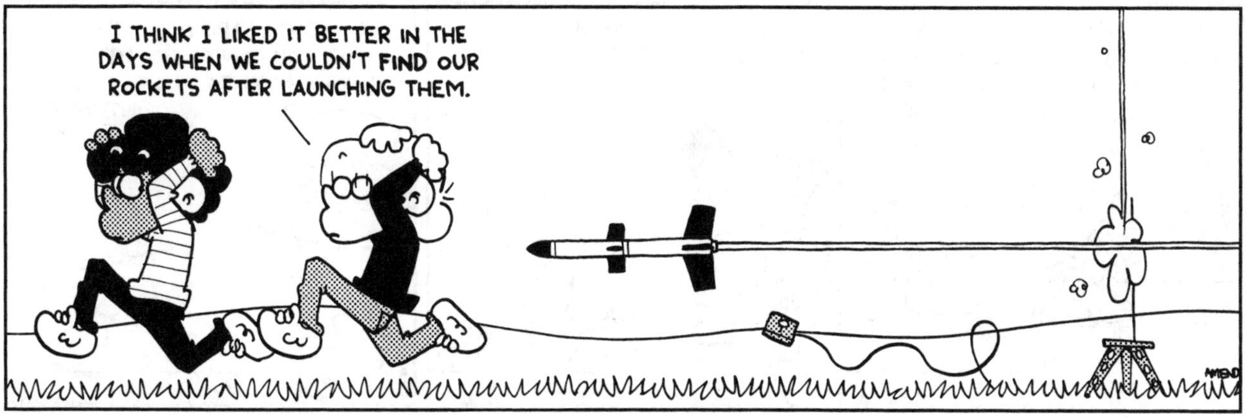
I THINK I LIKED IT BETTER IN THE DAYS WHEN WE COULDN'T FIND OUR ROCKETS AFTER LAUNCHING THEM.

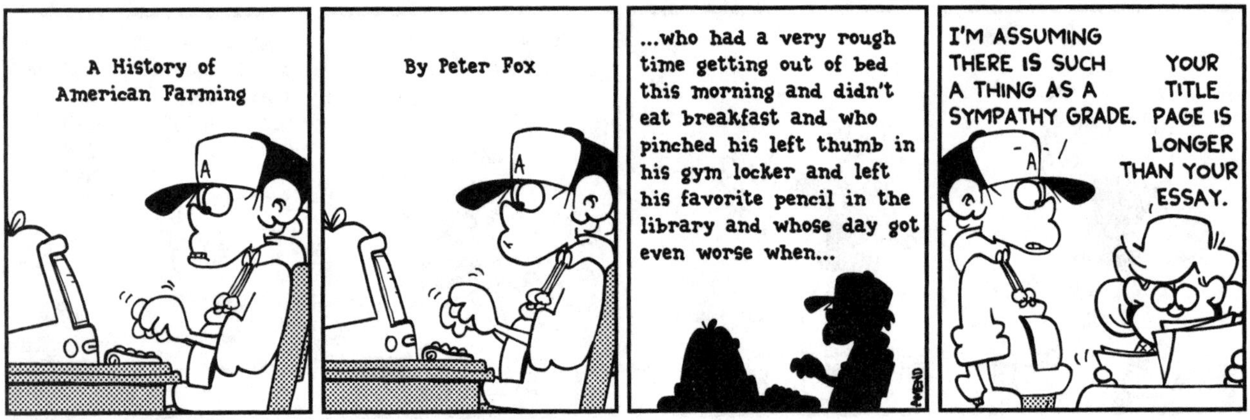
A History of American Farming
By Peter Fox
...who had a very rough time getting out of bed this morning and didn't eat breakfast and who pinched his left thumb in his gym locker and left his favorite pencil in the library and whose day got even worse when...
I'M ASSUMING THERE IS SUCH A THING AS A SYMPATHY GRADE.
YOUR TITLE PAGE IS LONGER THAN YOUR ESSAY.

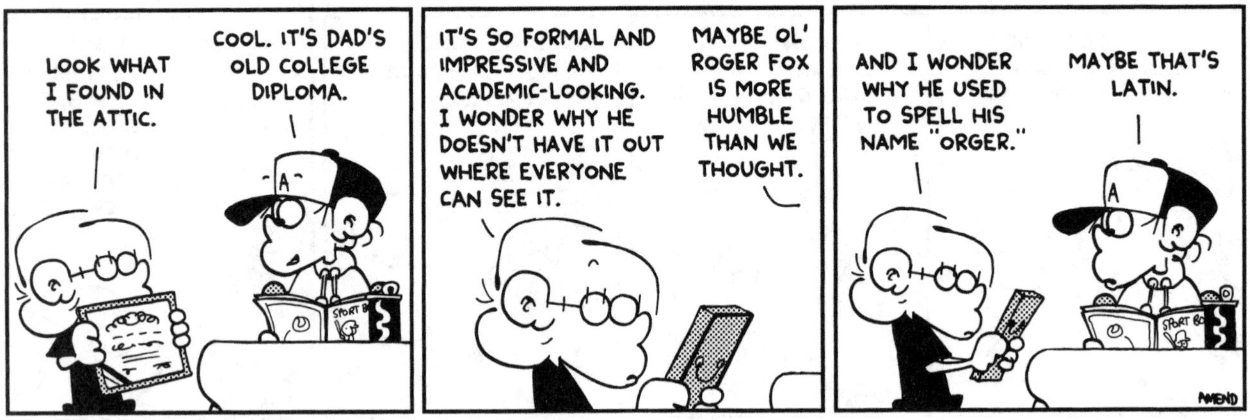
LOOK WHAT I FOUND IN THE ATTIC.
COOL. IT'S DAD'S OLD COLLEGE DIPLOMA.
IT'S SO FORMAL AND IMPRESSIVE AND ACADEMIC-LOOKING. I WONDER WHY HE DOESN'T HAVE IT OUT WHERE EVERYONE CAN SEE IT.
MAYBE OL' ROGER FOX IS MORE HUMBLE THAN WE THOUGHT.
AND I WONDER WHY HE USED TO SPELL HIS NAME "ORGER."
MAYBE THAT'S LATIN.

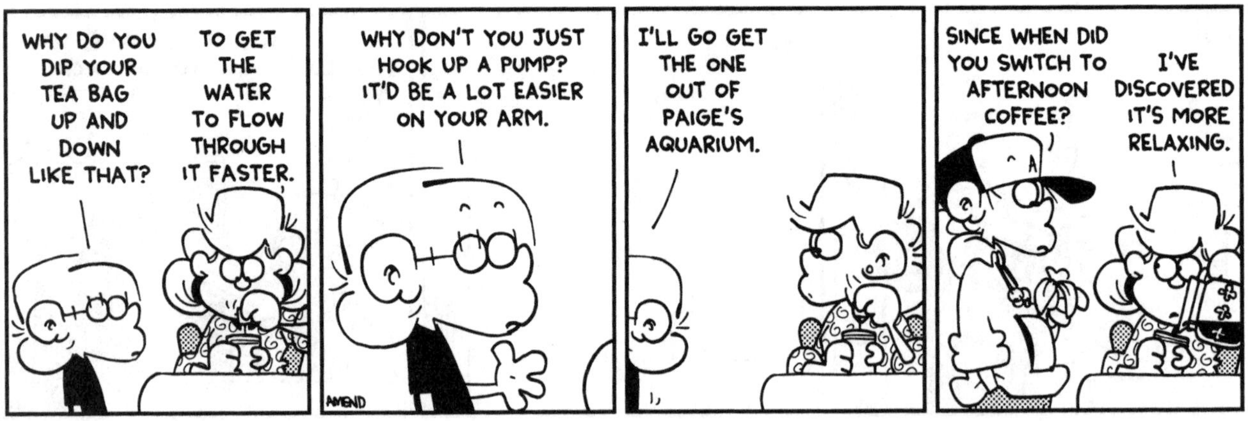
WHY DO YOU DIP YOUR TEA BAG UP AND DOWN LIKE THAT?
TO GET THE WATER TO FLOW THROUGH IT FASTER.
WHY DON'T YOU JUST HOOK UP A PUMP? IT'D BE A LOT EASIER ON YOUR ARM.
I'LL GO GET THE ONE OUT OF PAIGE'S AQUARIUM.
SINCE WHEN DID YOU SWITCH TO AFTERNOON COFFEE?
I'VE DISCOVERED IT'S MORE RELAXING.

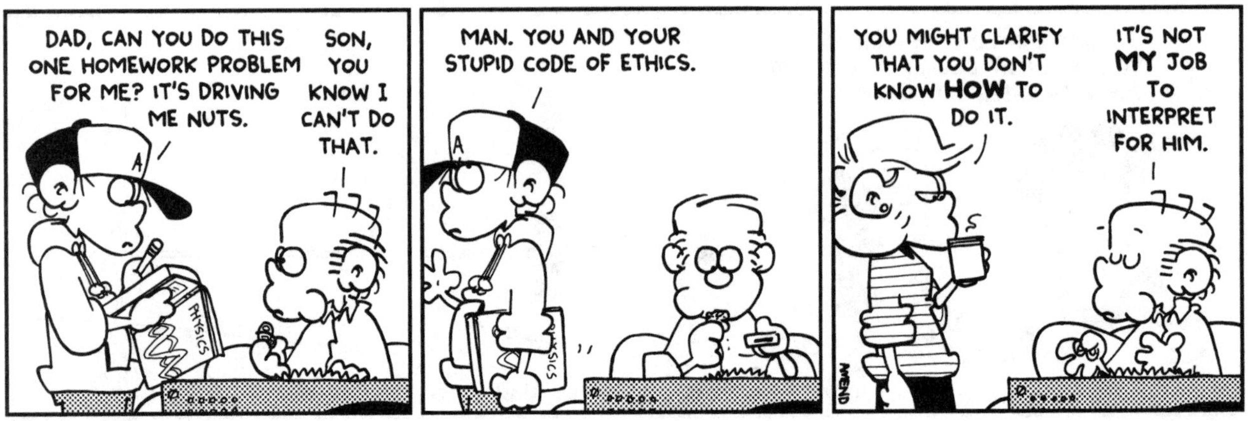
DAD, CAN YOU DO THIS ONE HOMEWORK PROBLEM FOR ME? IT'S DRIVING ME NUTS.
SON, YOU KNOW I CAN'T DO THAT.
MAN. YOU AND YOUR STUPID CODE OF ETHICS.
YOU MIGHT CLARIFY THAT YOU DON'T KNOW HOW TO DO IT.
IT'S NOT MY JOB TO INTERPRET FOR HIM.

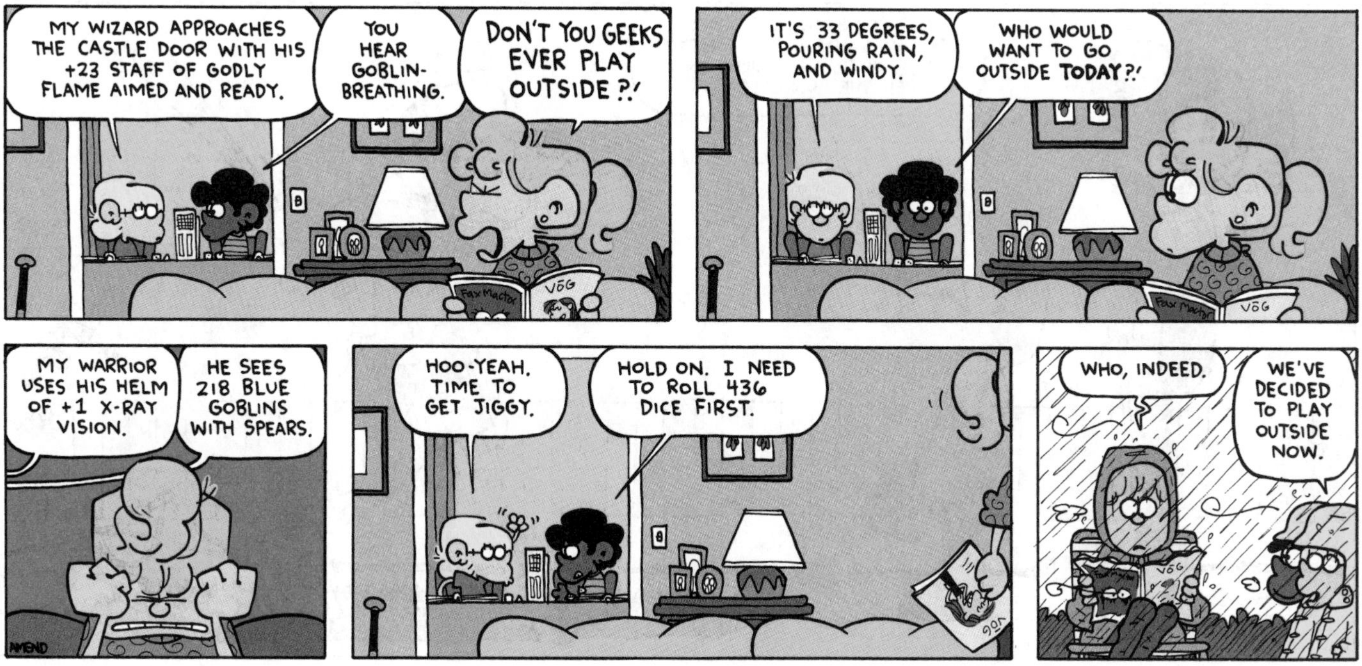
MY WIZARD APPROACHES THE CASTLE DOOR WITH HIS +23 STAFF OF GODLY FLAME AIMED AND READY.
YOU HEAR GOBLIN-BREATHING.
DON'T YOU GEEKS EVER PLAY OUTSIDE ?!
IT'S 33 DEGREES, POURING RAIN, AND WINDY.
WHO WOULD WANT TO GO OUTSIDE TODAY ?!
MY WARRIOR USES HIS HELM OF +1 X-RAY VISION.
HE SEES 218 BLUE GOBLINS WITH SPEARS.
HOO-YEAH. TIME TO GET JIGGY.
HOLD ON. I NEED TO ROLL 436 DICE FIRST.
WHO, INDEED.
WE'VE DECIDED TO PLAY OUTSIDE NOW.
AMEND

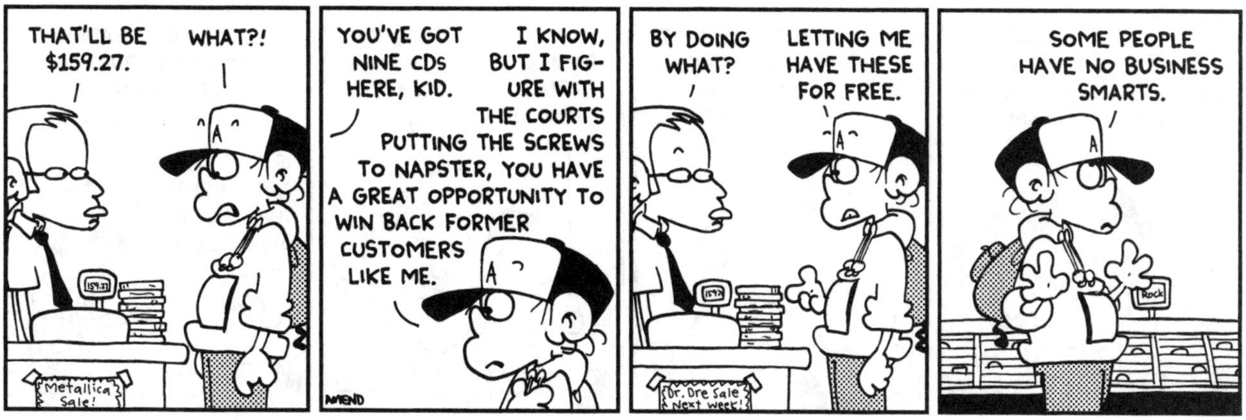
THAT'LL BE $159.27.
WHAT?!
YOU'VE GOT NINE CDs HERE, KID.
I KNOW, BUT I FIGURE WITH THE COURTS PUTTING THE SCREWS TO NAPSTER, YOU HAVE A GREAT OPPORTUNITY TO WIN BACK FORMER CUSTOMERS LIKE ME.
BY DOING WHAT?
LETTING ME HAVE THESE FOR FREE.
SOME PEOPLE HAVE NO BUSINESS SMARTS.
Metallica Sale!
Dr. Dre Sale Next Week!
Rock
AMEND

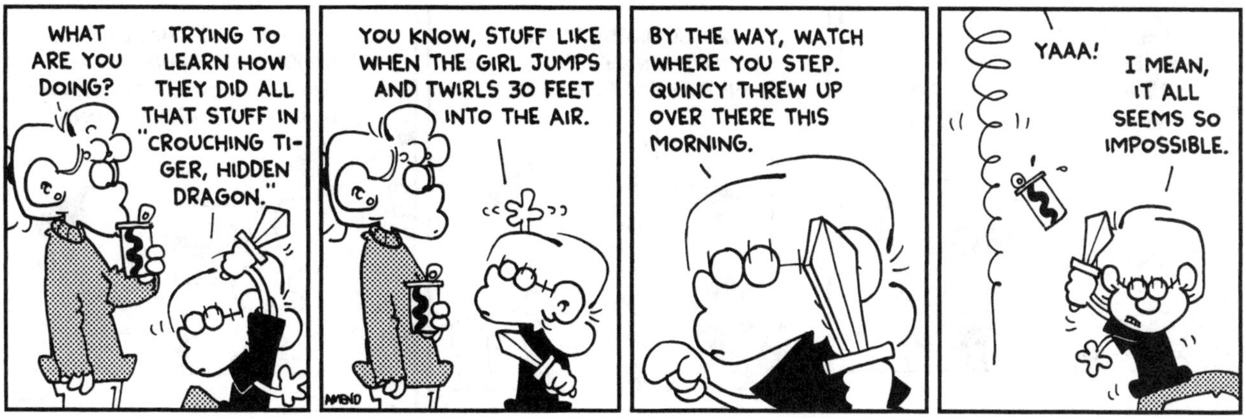
WHAT ARE YOU DOING?
TRYING TO LEARN HOW THEY DID ALL THAT STUFF IN "CROUCHING TIGER, HIDDEN DRAGON."
YOU KNOW, STUFF LIKE WHEN THE GIRL JUMPS AND TWIRLS 30 FEET INTO THE AIR.
BY THE WAY, WATCH WHERE YOU STEP. QUINCY THREW UP OVER THERE THIS MORNING.
YAAA!
I MEAN, IT ALL SEEMS SO IMPOSSIBLE.
AMEND

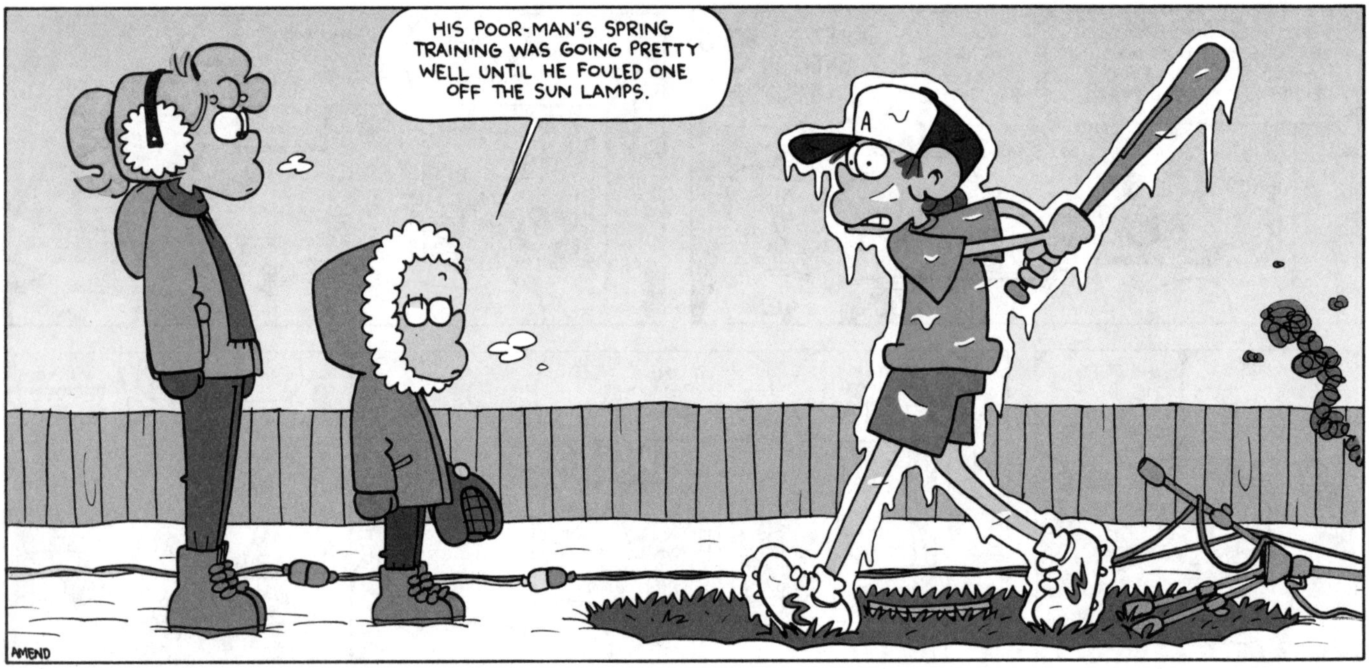
HIS POOR-MAN'S SPRING TRAINING WAS GOING PRETTY WELL UNTIL HE FOULED ONE OFF THE SUN LAMPS.
AMEND

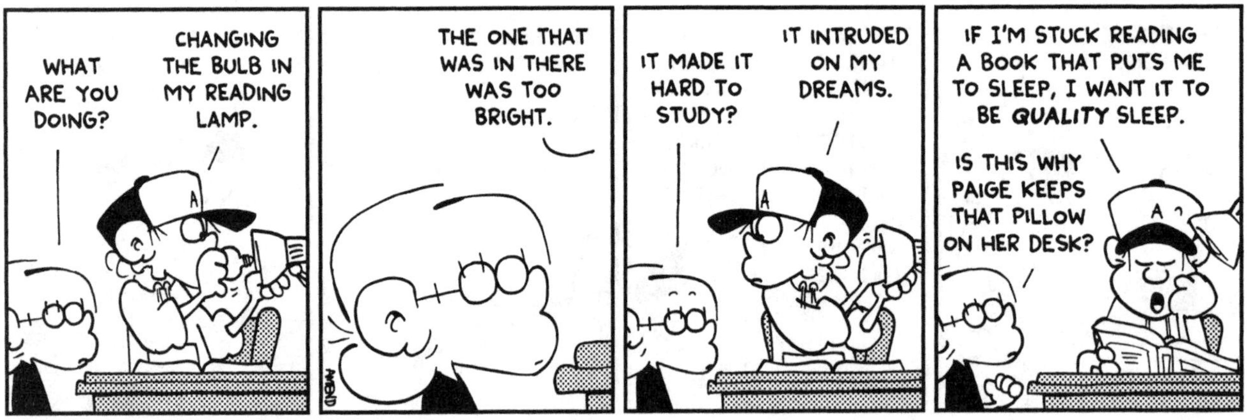
WHAT ARE YOU DOING?
CHANGING THE BULB IN MY READING LAMP.
THE ONE THAT WAS IN THERE WAS TOO BRIGHT.
AMEND
IT MADE IT HARD TO STUDY?
IT INTRUDED ON MY DREAMS.
IF I'M STUCK READING A BOOK THAT PUTS ME TO SLEEP, I WANT IT TO BE QUALITY SLEEP.
IS THIS WHY PAIGE KEEPS THAT PILLOW ON HER DESK?

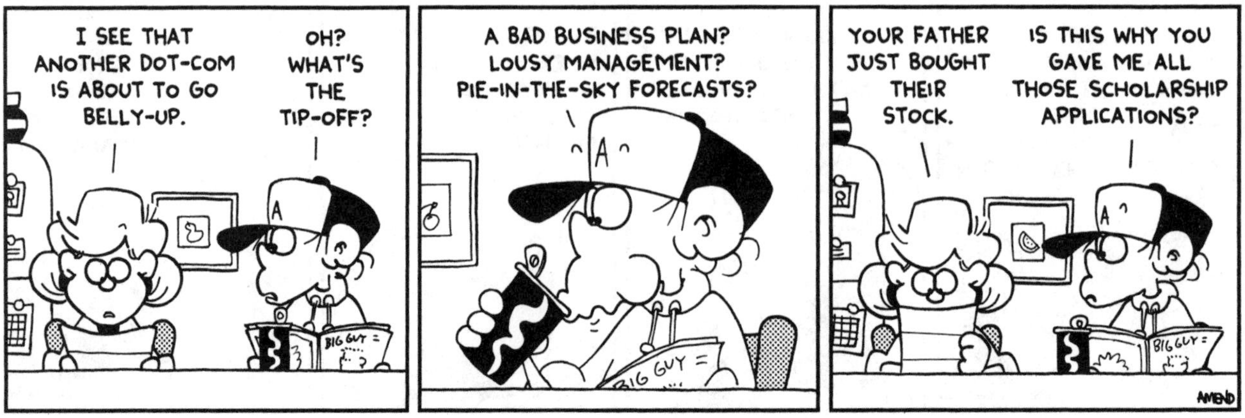
I SEE THAT ANOTHER DOT-COM IS ABOUT TO GO BELLY-UP.
OH? WHAT'S THE TIP-OFF?
BIG GUY
A BAD BUSINESS PLAN? LOUSY MANAGEMENT? PIE-IN-THE-SKY FORECASTS?
BIG GUY
YOUR FATHER JUST BOUGHT THEIR STOCK.
IS THIS WHY YOU GAVE ME ALL THOSE SCHOLARSHIP APPLICATIONS?
BIG GUY
AMEND

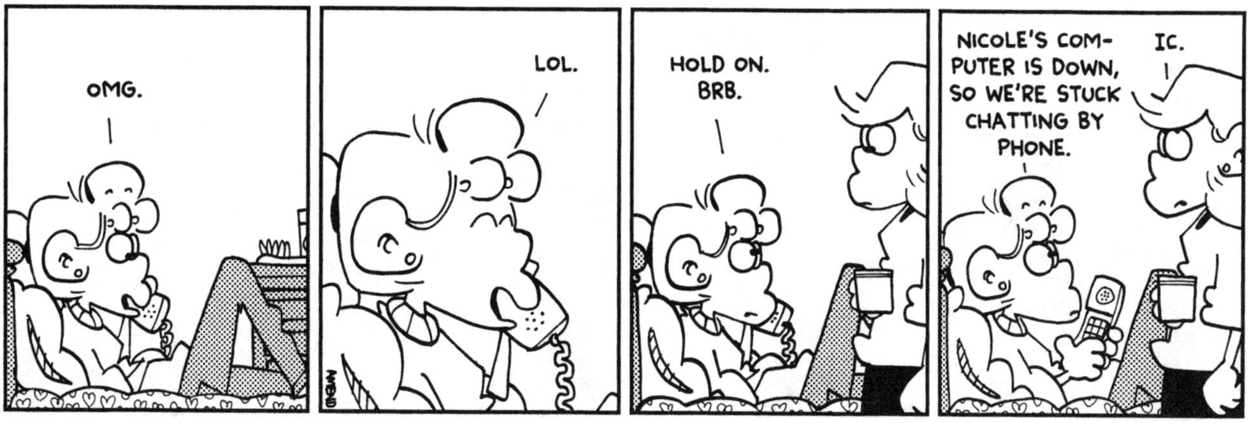
OMG.
LOL.
HOLD ON. BRB.
NICOLE'S COMPUTER IS DOWN, SO WE'RE STUCK CHATTING BY PHONE.
IC.
AMEND

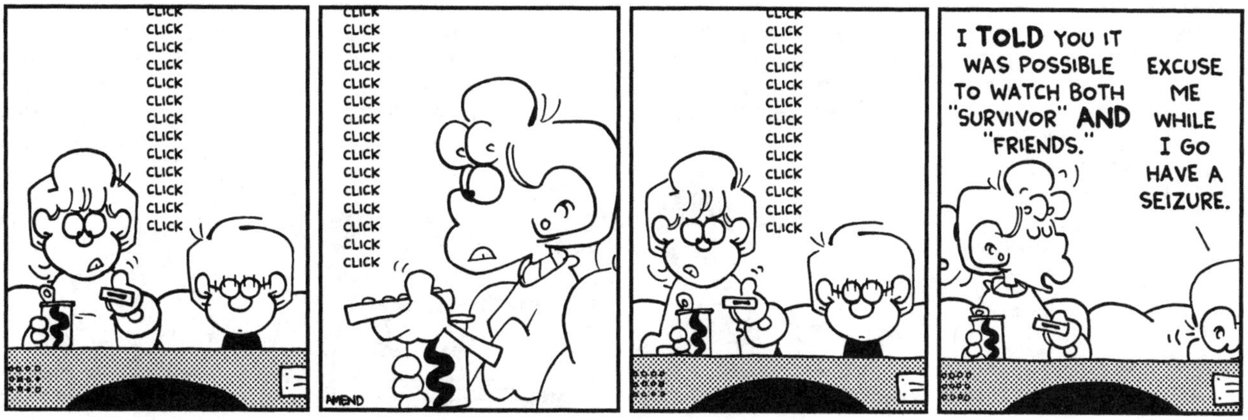
CLICK CLICK CLICK CLICK CLICK CLICK CLICK CLICK CLICK CLICK CLICK CLICK
CLICK CLICK CLICK CLICK CLICK CLICK CLICK CLICK CLICK CLICK CLICK CLICK CLICK CLICK
CLICK CLICK CLICK CLICK CLICK CLICK CLICK CLICK CLICK CLICK CLICK CLICK
I **TOLD** YOU IT WAS POSSIBLE TO WATCH BOTH "SURVIVOR" **AND** "FRIENDS."
EXCUSE ME WHILE I GO HAVE A SEIZURE.
AMEND

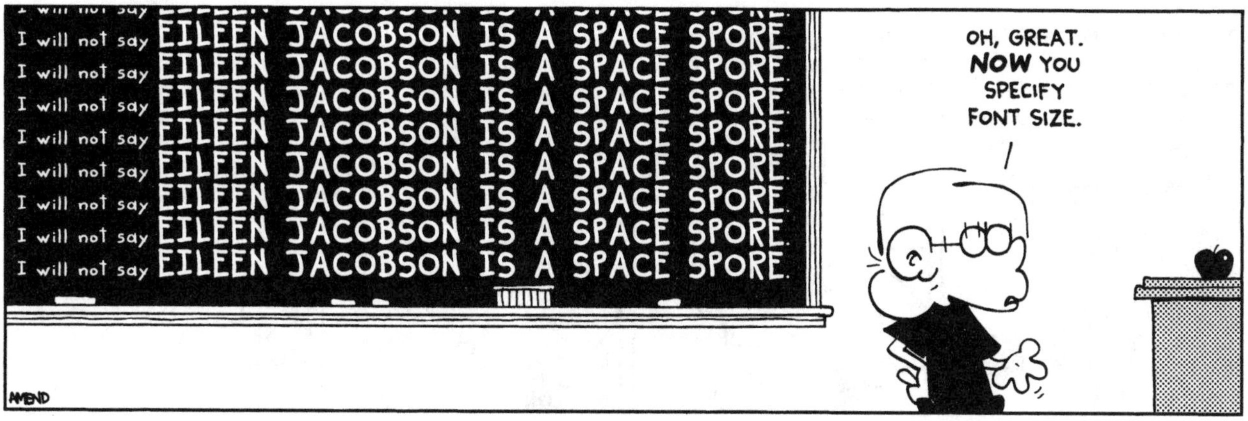
I will not say EILEEN JACOBSON IS A SPACE SPORE.
I will not say EILEEN JACOBSON IS A SPACE SPORE.
I will not say EILEEN JACOBSON IS A SPACE SPORE.
I will not say EILEEN JACOBSON IS A SPACE SPORE.
I will not say EILEEN JACOBSON IS A SPACE SPORE.
I will not say EILEEN JACOBSON IS A SPACE SPORE.
I will not say EILEEN JACOBSON IS A SPACE SPORE.
I will not say EILEEN JACOBSON IS A SPACE SPORE.
OH, GREAT. **NOW** YOU SPECIFY FONT SIZE.
AMEND

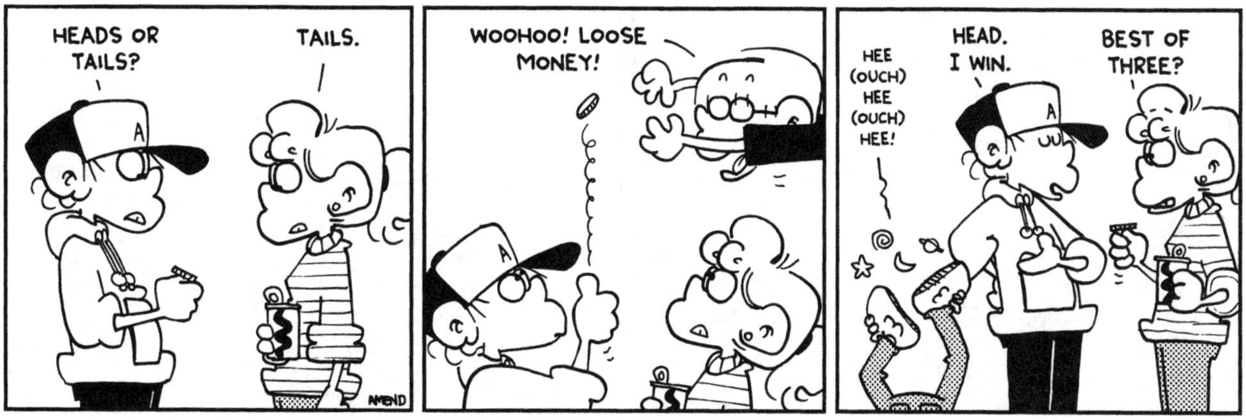
HEADS OR TAILS?
TAILS.
AMEND
WOOHOO! LOOSE MONEY!
HEE (OUCH) HEE (OUCH) HEE!
HEAD. I WIN.
BEST OF THREE?

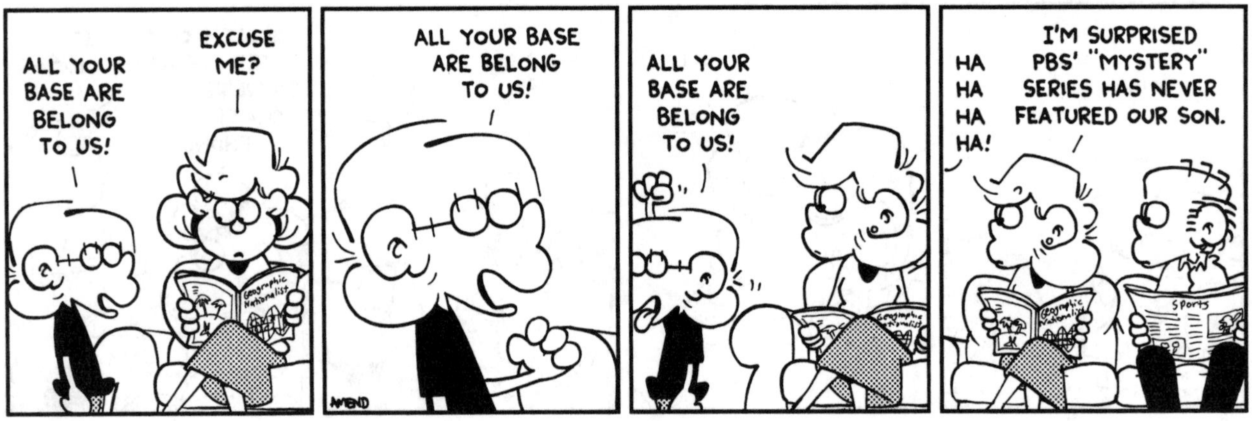
ALL YOUR BASE ARE BELONG TO US!
EXCUSE ME?
ALL YOUR BASE ARE BELONG TO US!
ALL YOUR BASE ARE BELONG TO US!
HA HA HA HA!
I'M SURPRISED PBS' "MYSTERY" SERIES HAS NEVER FEATURED OUR SON.

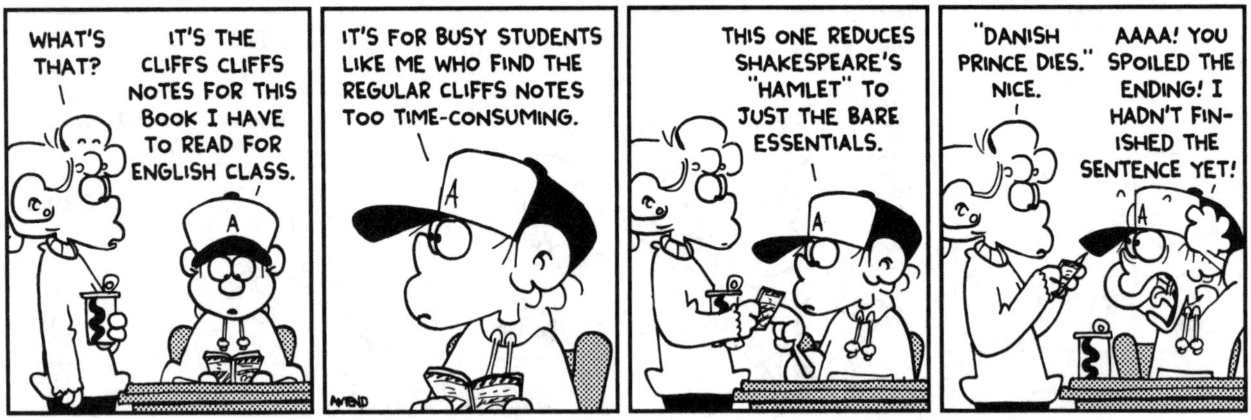
WHAT'S THAT?
IT'S THE CLIFFS CLIFFS NOTES FOR THIS BOOK I HAVE TO READ FOR ENGLISH CLASS.
IT'S FOR BUSY STUDENTS LIKE ME WHO FIND THE REGULAR CLIFFS NOTES TOO TIME-CONSUMING.
THIS ONE REDUCES SHAKESPEARE'S "HAMLET" TO JUST THE BARE ESSENTIALS.
"DANISH PRINCE DIES." NICE.
AAAA! YOU SPOILED THE ENDING! I HADN'T FINISHED THE SENTENCE YET!

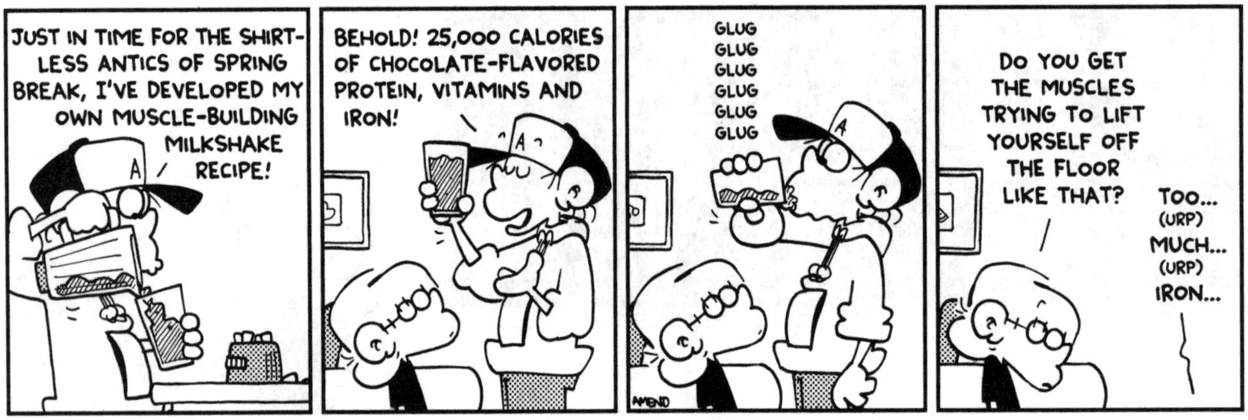
JUST IN TIME FOR THE SHIRTLESS ANTICS OF SPRING BREAK, I'VE DEVELOPED MY OWN MUSCLE-BUILDING MILKSHAKE RECIPE!
BEHOLD! 25,000 CALORIES OF CHOCOLATE-FLAVORED PROTEIN, VITAMINS AND IRON!
GLUG GLUG GLUG GLUG GLUG GLUG
DO YOU GET THE MUSCLES TRYING TO LIFT YOURSELF OFF THE FLOOR LIKE THAT?
TOO... (URP) MUCH... (URP) IRON...

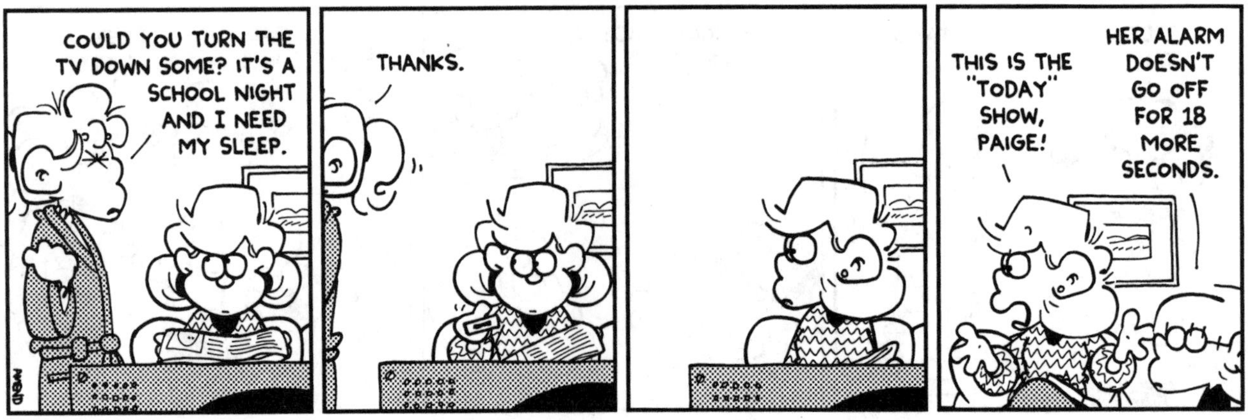
COULD YOU TURN THE TV DOWN SOME? IT'S A SCHOOL NIGHT AND I NEED MY SLEEP.
THANKS.
THIS IS THE "TODAY" SHOW, PAIGE!
HER ALARM DOESN'T GO OFF FOR 18 MORE SECONDS.

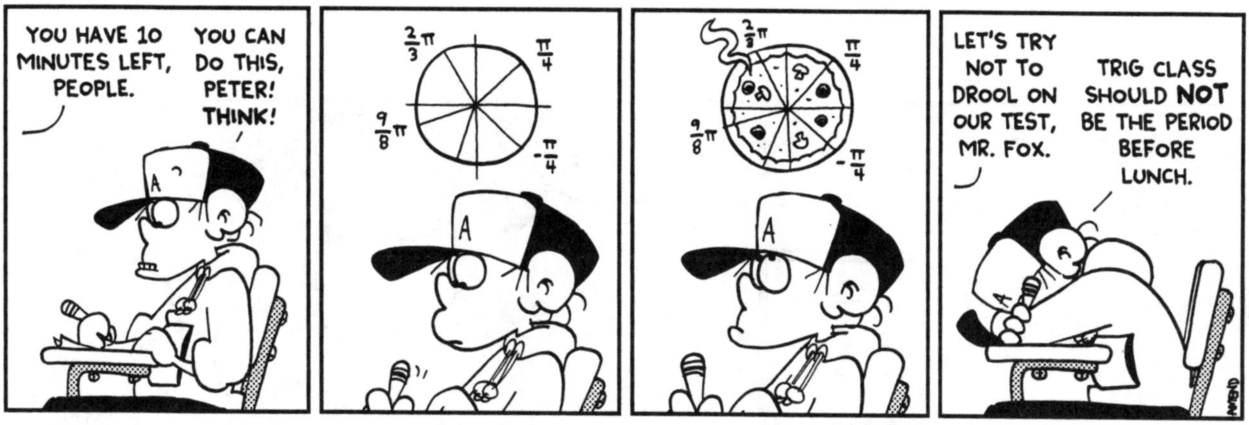
YOU HAVE 10 MINUTES LEFT, PEOPLE.
YOU CAN DO THIS, PETER! **THINK!**
$\frac{2}{3}\pi$
$\frac{\pi}{4}$
$\frac{9}{8}\pi$
$-\frac{\pi}{4}$
$\frac{2}{3}\pi$
$\frac{\pi}{4}$
$\frac{9}{8}\pi$
$-\frac{\pi}{4}$
LET'S TRY NOT TO DROOL ON OUR TEST, MR. FOX.
TRIG CLASS SHOULD **NOT** BE THE PERIOD BEFORE LUNCH.
AMEND

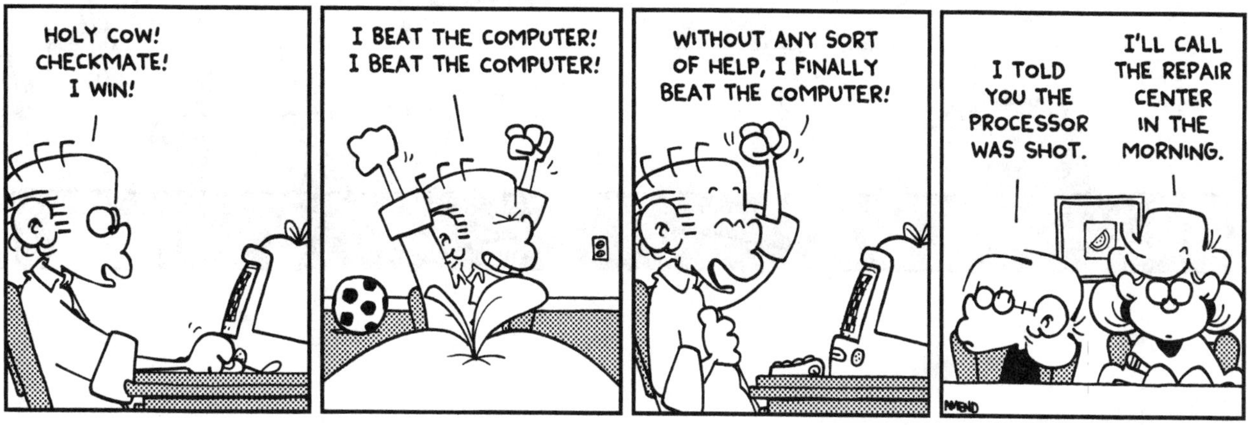
HOLY COW! CHECKMATE! I WIN!
I BEAT THE COMPUTER! I BEAT THE COMPUTER!
WITHOUT ANY SORT OF HELP, I FINALLY BEAT THE COMPUTER!
I TOLD YOU THE PROCESSOR WAS SHOT.
I'LL CALL THE REPAIR CENTER IN THE MORNING.
AMEND

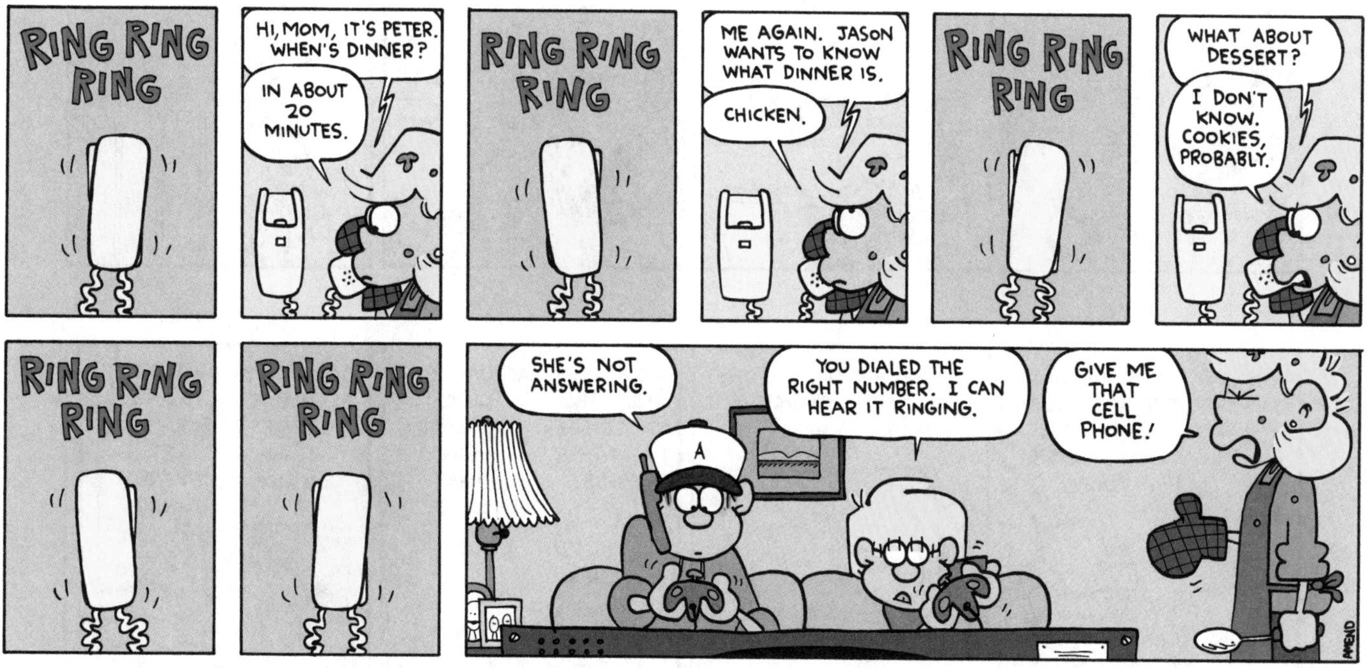
RING RING RING
HI, MOM, IT'S PETER. WHEN'S DINNER?
IN ABOUT 20 MINUTES.
RING RING RING
ME AGAIN. JASON WANTS TO KNOW WHAT DINNER IS.
CHICKEN.
RING RING RING
WHAT ABOUT DESSERT?
I DON'T KNOW. COOKIES, PROBABLY.
RING RING RING
RING RING RING
SHE'S NOT ANSWERING.
YOU DIALED THE RIGHT NUMBER. I CAN HEAR IT RINGING.
GIVE ME THAT CELL PHONE!
AMEND

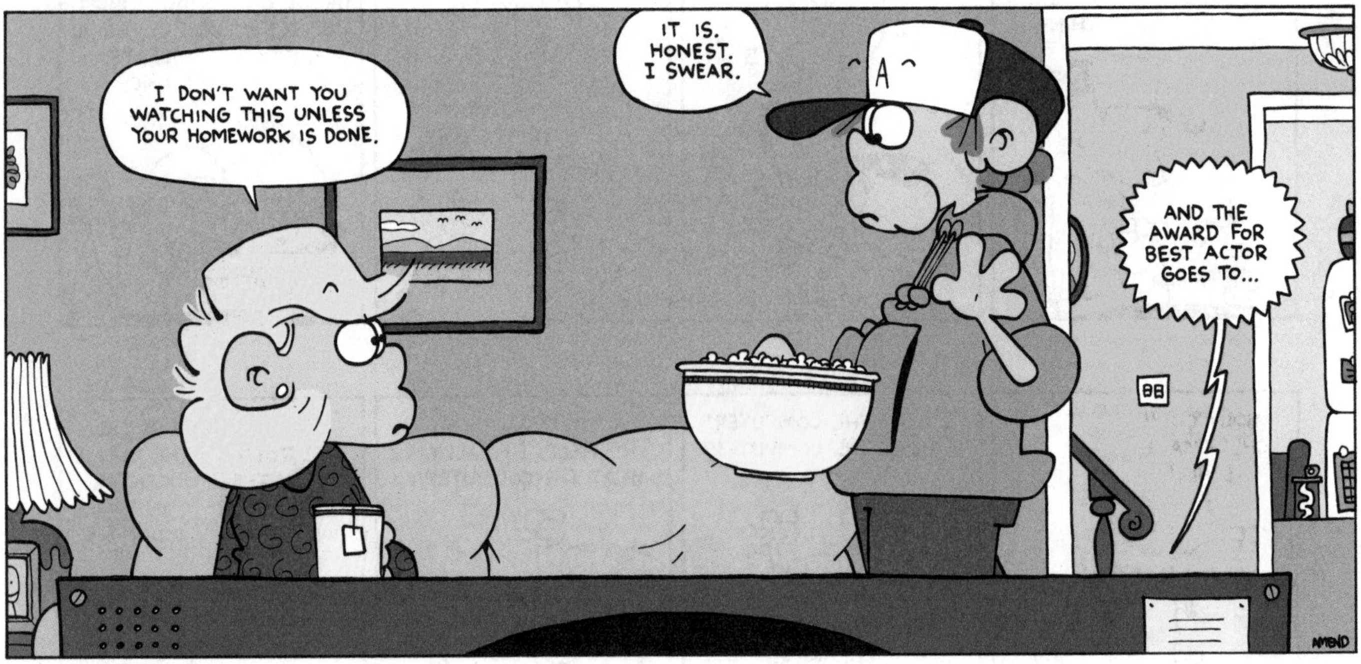
I DON'T WANT YOU WATCHING THIS UNLESS YOUR HOMEWORK IS DONE.
IT IS. HONEST. I SWEAR.
A
AND THE AWARD FOR BEST ACTOR GOES TO...
AMEND

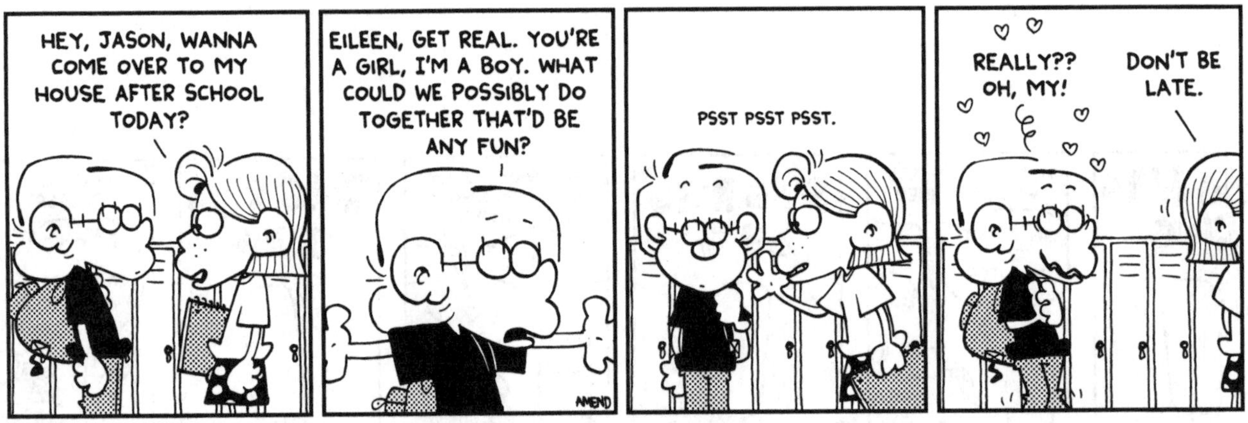
HEY, JASON, WANNA COME OVER TO MY HOUSE AFTER SCHOOL TODAY?
EILEEN, GET REAL. YOU'RE A GIRL, I'M A BOY. WHAT COULD WE POSSIBLY DO TOGETHER THAT'D BE ANY FUN?
AMEND
PSST PSST PSST.
REALLY?? OH, MY!
DON'T BE LATE.

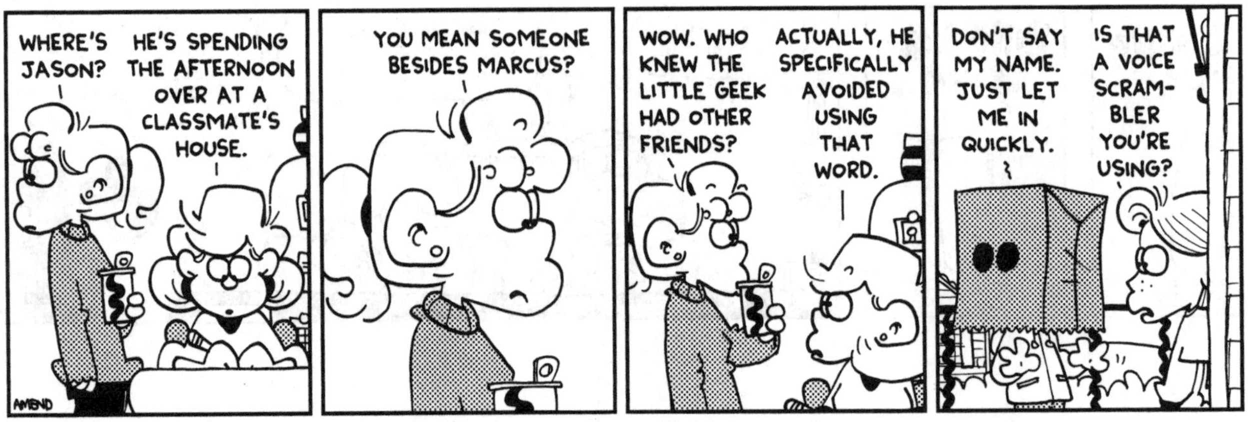
WHERE'S JASON?
HE'S SPENDING THE AFTERNOON OVER AT A CLASSMATE'S HOUSE.
AMEND
YOU MEAN SOMEONE BESIDES MARCUS?
WOW. WHO KNEW THE LITTLE GEEK HAD OTHER FRIENDS?
ACTUALLY, HE SPECIFICALLY AVOIDED USING THAT WORD.
DON'T SAY MY NAME. JUST LET ME IN QUICKLY.
IS THAT A VOICE SCRAMBLER YOU'RE USING?

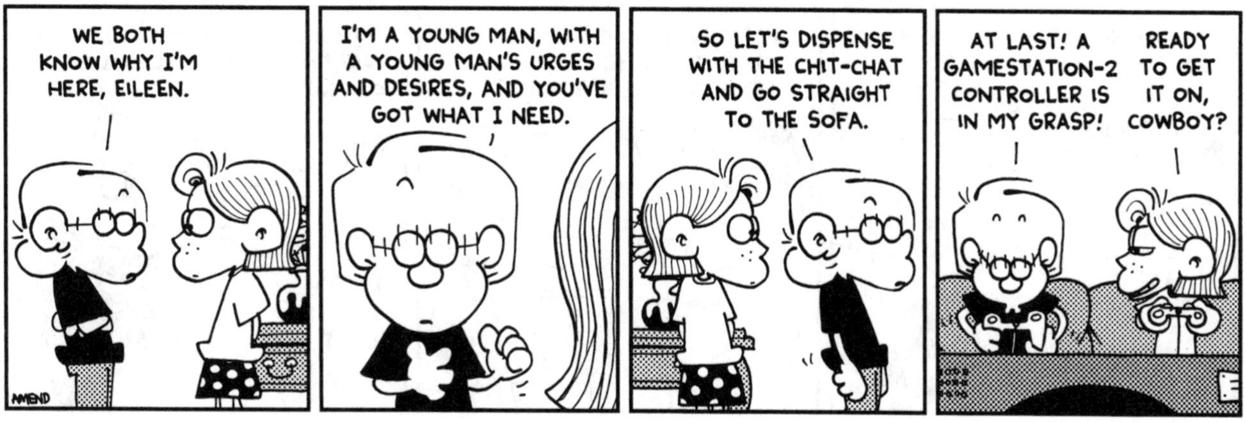
WE BOTH KNOW WHY I'M HERE, EILEEN.
I'M A YOUNG MAN, WITH A YOUNG MAN'S URGES AND DESIRES, AND YOU'VE GOT WHAT I NEED.
SO LET'S DISPENSE WITH THE CHIT-CHAT AND GO STRAIGHT TO THE SOFA.
AT LAST! A GAMESTATION-2 CONTROLLER IS IN MY GRASP!
READY TO GET IT ON, COWBOY?
AMEND

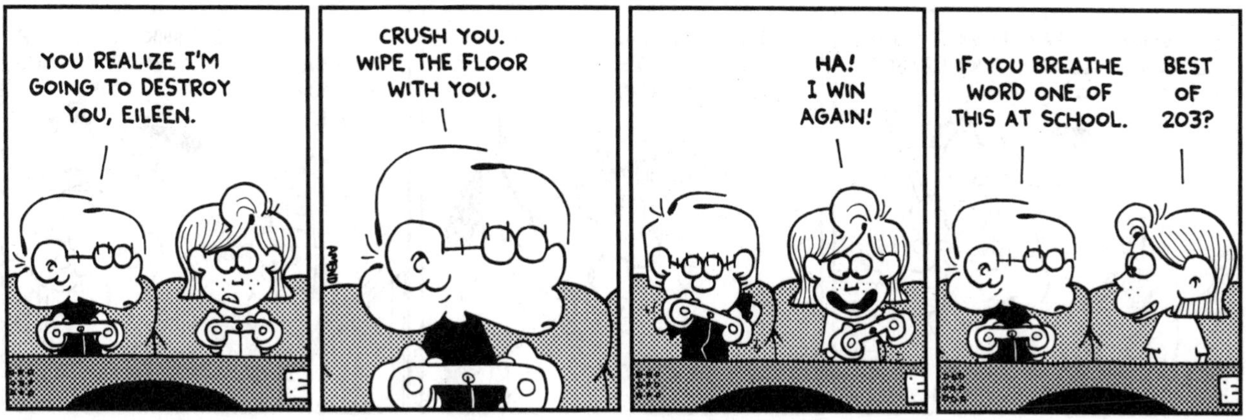
YOU REALIZE I'M GOING TO DESTROY YOU, EILEEN.
CRUSH YOU. WIPE THE FLOOR WITH YOU.
AMEND
HA! I WIN AGAIN!
IF YOU BREATHE WORD ONE OF THIS AT SCHOOL.
BEST OF 203?

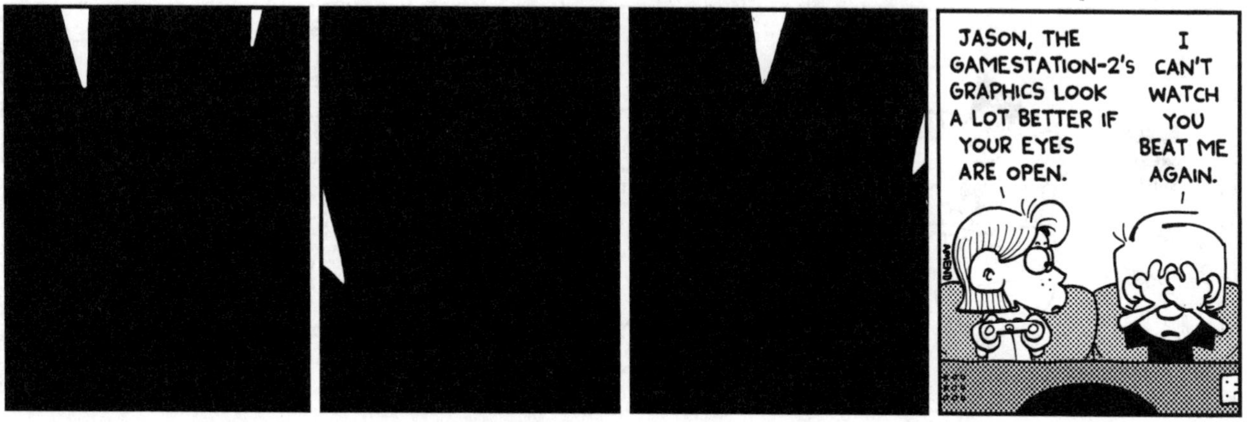
JASON, THE GAMESTATION-2'S GRAPHICS LOOK A LOT BETTER IF YOUR EYES ARE OPEN.
I CAN'T WATCH YOU BEAT ME AGAIN.
AMEND

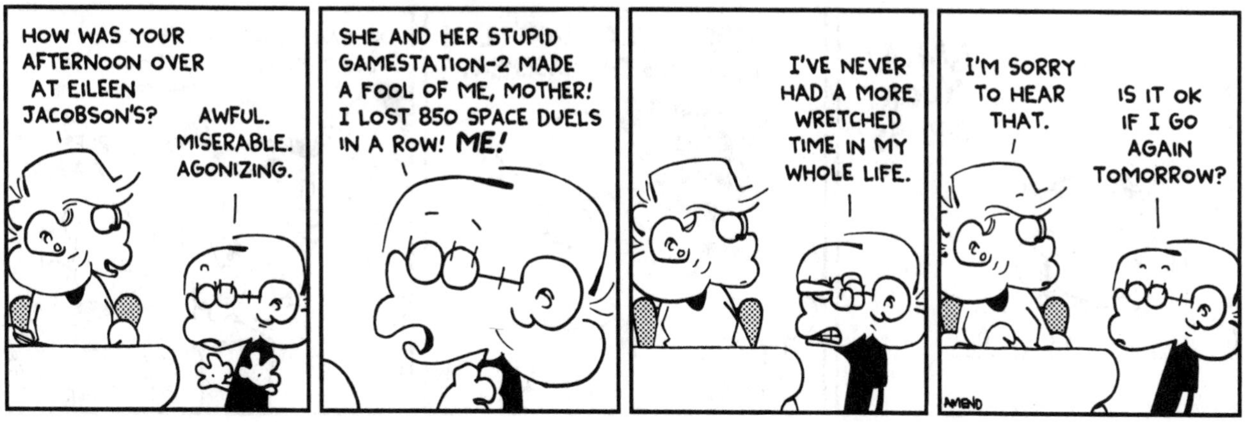
HOW WAS YOUR AFTERNOON OVER AT EILEEN JACOBSON'S?
AWFUL. MISERABLE. AGONIZING.
SHE AND HER STUPID GAMESTATION-2 MADE A FOOL OF ME, MOTHER! I LOST 850 SPACE DUELS IN A ROW! ME!
I'VE NEVER HAD A MORE WRETCHED TIME IN MY WHOLE LIFE.
I'M SORRY TO HEAR THAT.
IS IT OK IF I GO AGAIN TOMORROW?
AMEND

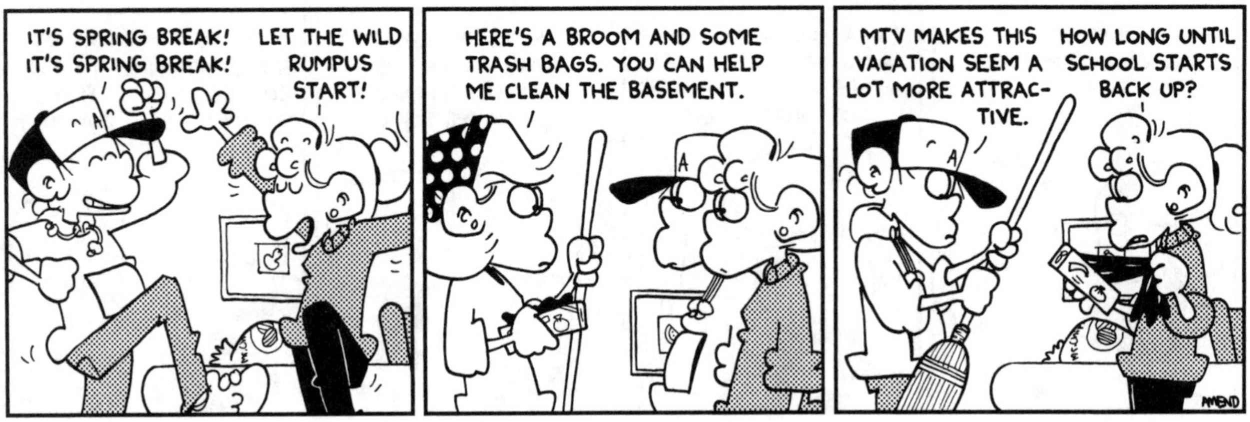
IT'S SPRING BREAK! IT'S SPRING BREAK!
LET THE WILD RUMPUS START!
HERE'S A BROOM AND SOME TRASH BAGS. YOU CAN HELP ME CLEAN THE BASEMENT.
MTV MAKES THIS VACATION SEEM A LOT MORE ATTRACTIVE.
HOW LONG UNTIL SCHOOL STARTS BACK UP?

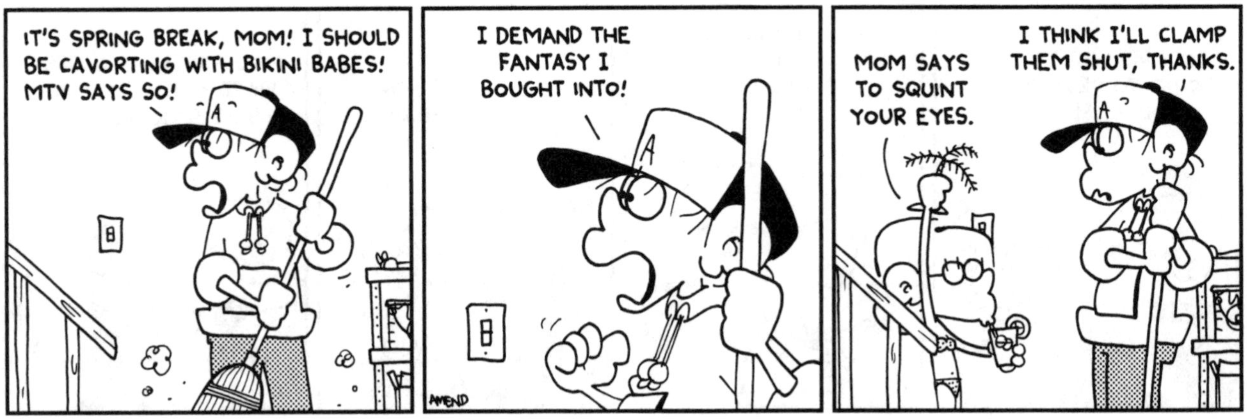
IT'S SPRING BREAK, MOM! I SHOULD BE CAVORTING WITH BIKINI BABES! MTV SAYS SO!
I DEMAND THE FANTASY I BOUGHT INTO!
MOM SAYS TO SQUINT YOUR EYES.
I THINK I'LL CLAMP THEM SHUT, THANKS.

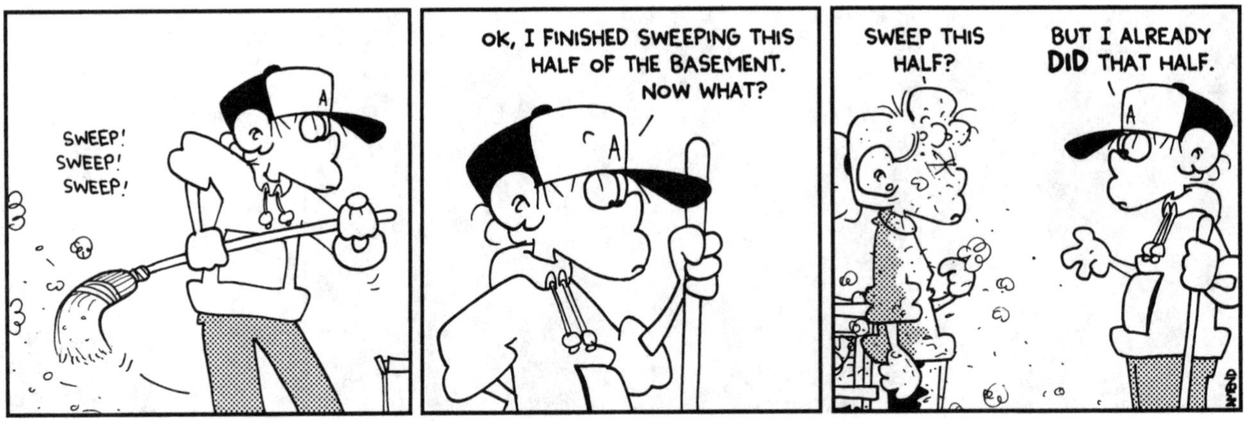
SWEEP! SWEEP! SWEEP!
OK, I FINISHED SWEEPING THIS HALF OF THE BASEMENT. NOW WHAT?
SWEEP THIS HALF?
BUT I ALREADY **DID** THAT HALF.

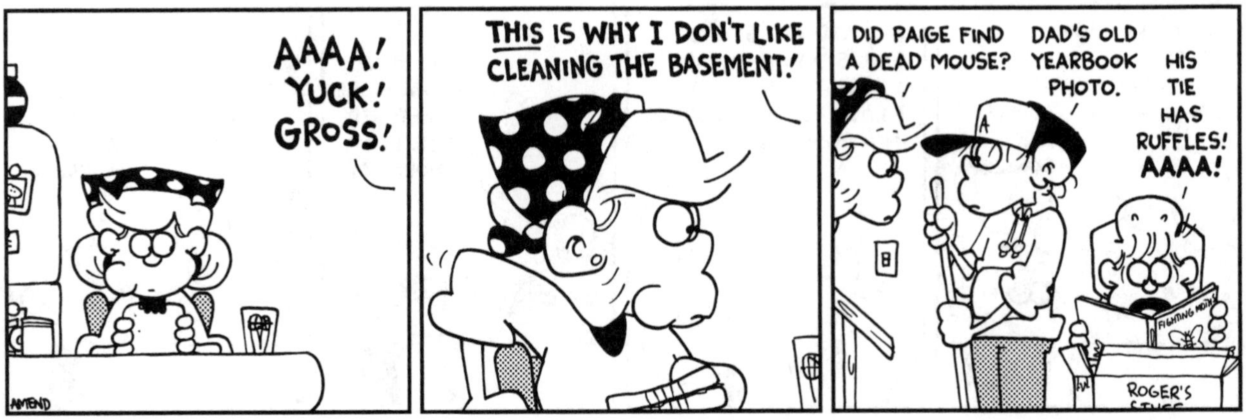
AAAA! YUCK! GROSS!
THIS IS WHY I DON'T LIKE CLEANING THE BASEMENT!
DID PAIGE FIND A DEAD MOUSE?
DAD'S OLD YEARBOOK PHOTO.
HIS TIE HAS RUFFLES! **AAAA!**
ROGER'S

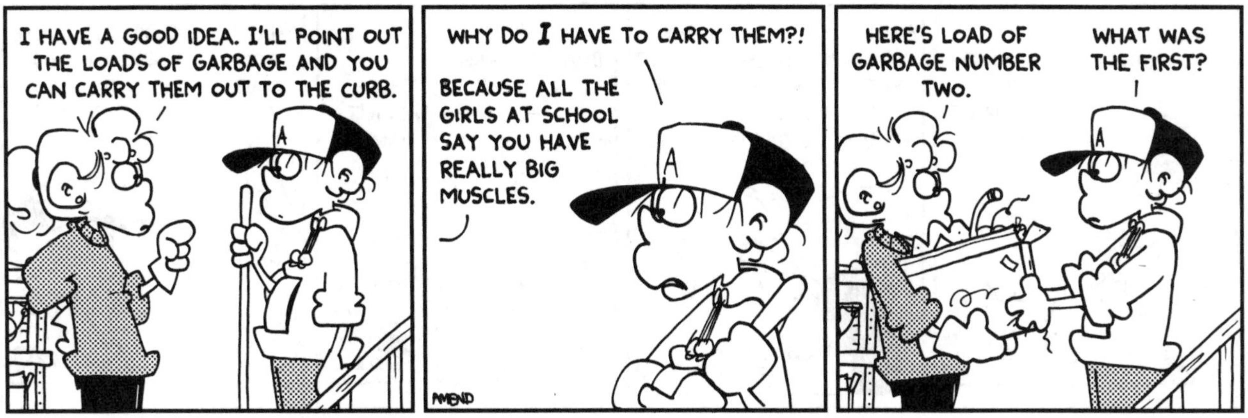
I HAVE A GOOD IDEA. I'LL POINT OUT THE LOADS OF GARBAGE AND YOU CAN CARRY THEM OUT TO THE CURB.
WHY DO I HAVE TO CARRY THEM?!
BECAUSE ALL THE GIRLS AT SCHOOL SAY YOU HAVE REALLY BIG MUSCLES.
AMEND
HERE'S LOAD OF GARBAGE NUMBER TWO.
WHAT WAS THE FIRST?

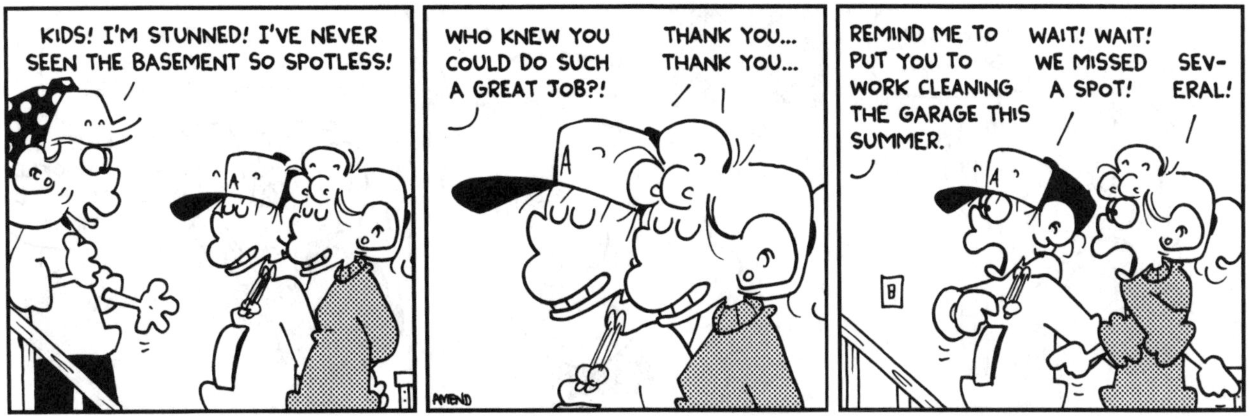
KIDS! I'M STUNNED! I'VE NEVER SEEN THE BASEMENT SO SPOTLESS!
WHO KNEW YOU COULD DO SUCH A GREAT JOB?!
THANK YOU... THANK YOU...
AMEND
REMIND ME TO PUT YOU TO WORK CLEANING THE GARAGE THIS SUMMER.
WAIT! WAIT! WE MISSED A SPOT!
SEV-ERAL!
B

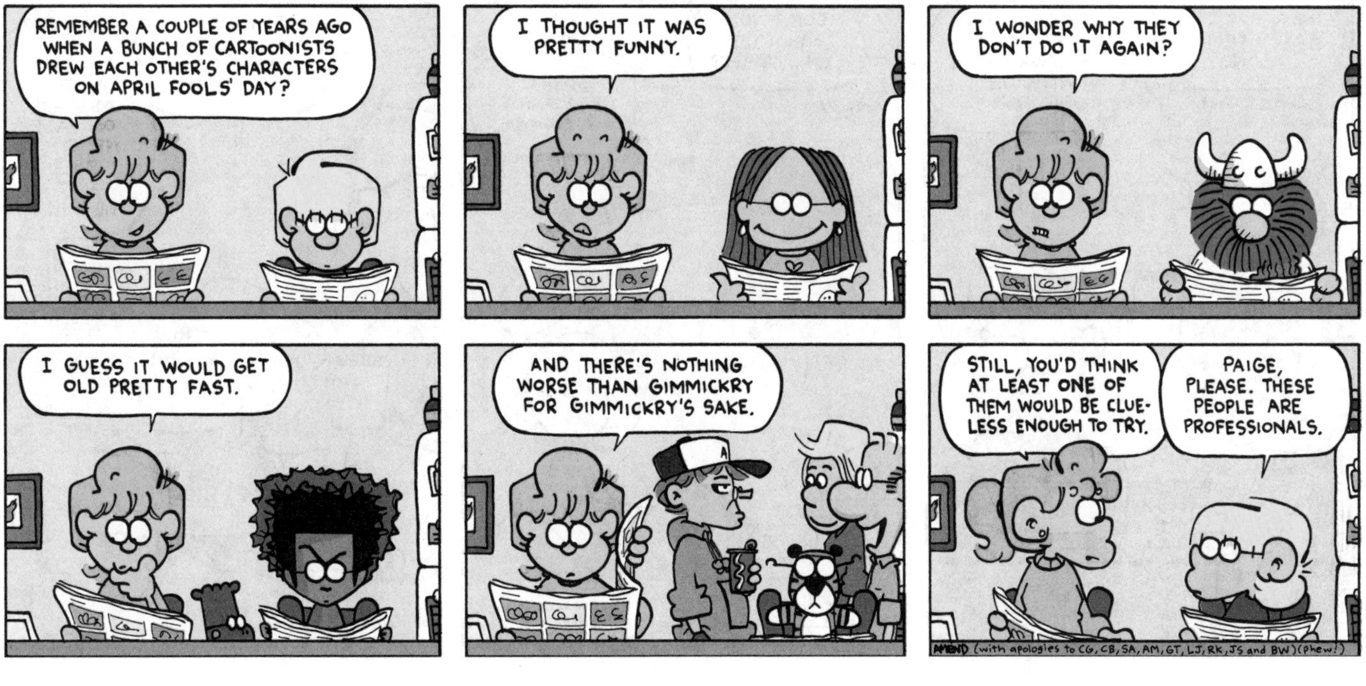
REMEMBER A COUPLE OF YEARS AGO WHEN A BUNCH OF CARTOONISTS DREW EACH OTHER'S CHARACTERS ON APRIL FOOLS' DAY?
I THOUGHT IT WAS PRETTY FUNNY.
I WONDER WHY THEY DON'T DO IT AGAIN?
I GUESS IT WOULD GET OLD PRETTY FAST.
AND THERE'S NOTHING WORSE THAN GIMMICKRY FOR GIMMICKRY'S SAKE.
A
STILL, YOU'D THINK AT LEAST ONE OF THEM WOULD BE CLUE-LESS ENOUGH TO TRY.
PAIGE, PLEASE. THESE PEOPLE ARE PROFESSIONALS.
AMEND (with apologies to CG, CB, SA, AM, GT, LJ, RK, JS and BW) (Phew!)

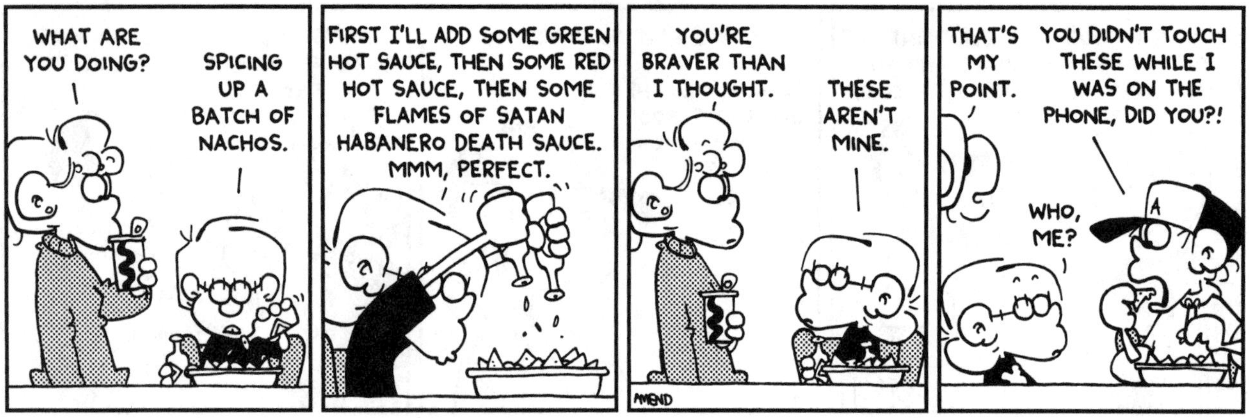
WHAT ARE YOU DOING?
SPICING UP A BATCH OF NACHOS.
FIRST I'LL ADD SOME GREEN HOT SAUCE, THEN SOME RED HOT SAUCE, THEN SOME FLAMES OF SATAN HABANERO DEATH SAUCE. MMM, PERFECT.
YOU'RE BRAVER THAN I THOUGHT.
THESE AREN'T MINE.
AMEND
THAT'S MY POINT.
YOU DIDN'T TOUCH THESE WHILE I WAS ON THE PHONE, DID YOU?!
WHO, ME?

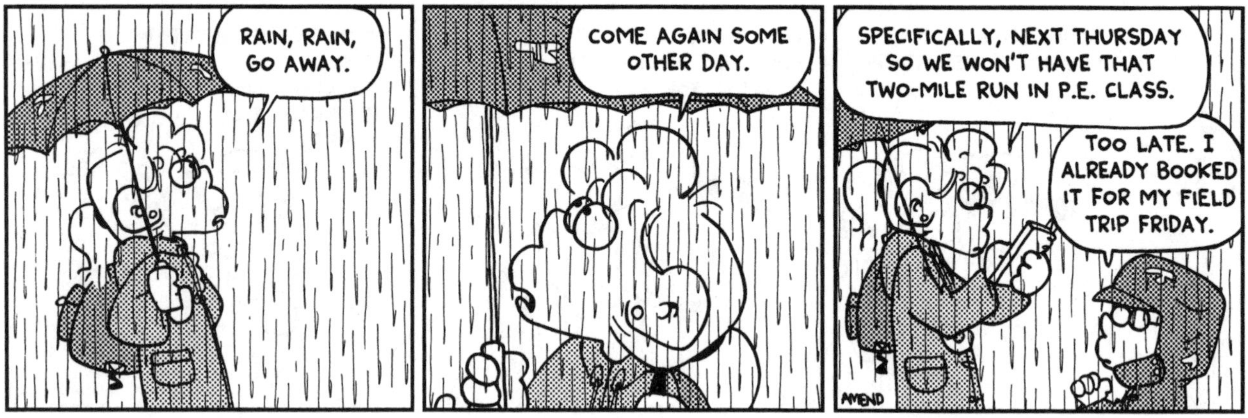
RAIN, RAIN, GO AWAY.
COME AGAIN SOME OTHER DAY.
SPECIFICALLY, NEXT THURSDAY SO WE WON'T HAVE THAT TWO-MILE RUN IN P.E. CLASS.
TOO LATE. I ALREADY BOOKED IT FOR MY FIELD TRIP FRIDAY.
AMEND

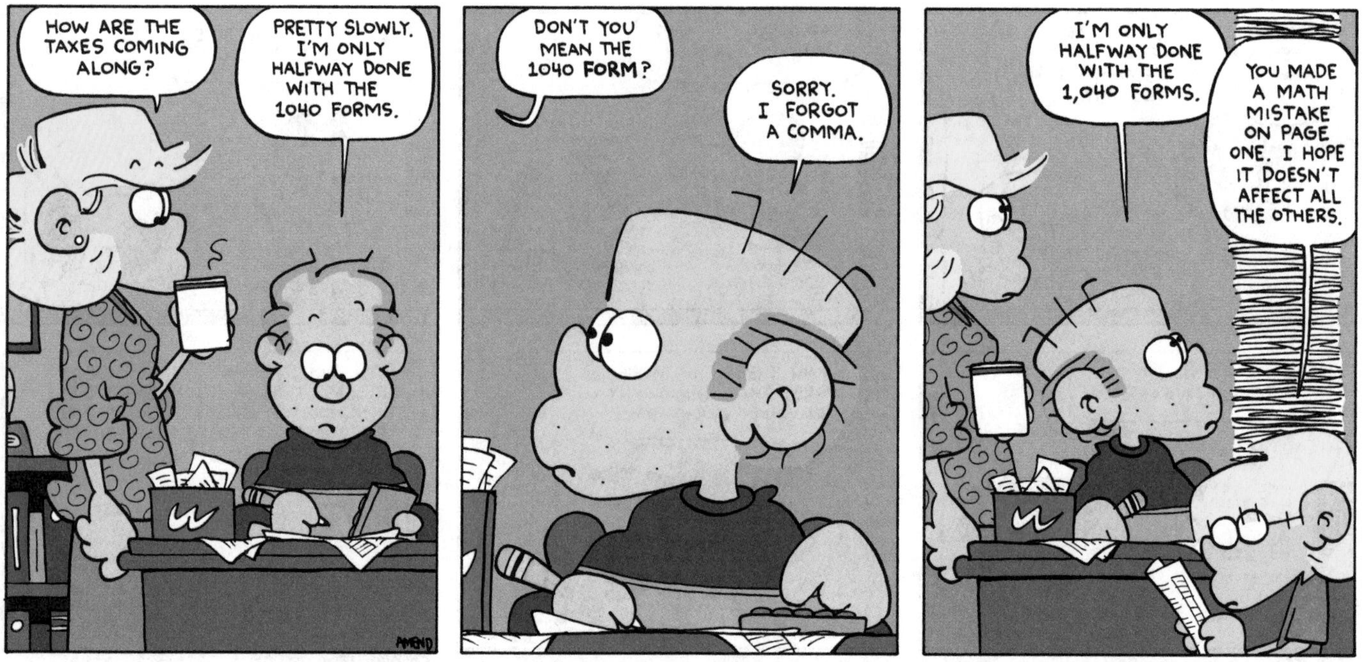
HOW ARE THE TAXES COMING ALONG?
PRETTY SLOWLY. I'M ONLY HALFWAY DONE WITH THE 1040 FORMS.
AMEND
DON'T YOU MEAN THE 1040 FORM?
SORRY. I FORGOT A COMMA.
I'M ONLY HALFWAY DONE WITH THE 1,040 FORMS.
YOU MADE A MATH MISTAKE ON PAGE ONE. I HOPE IT DOESN'T AFFECT ALL THE OTHERS.

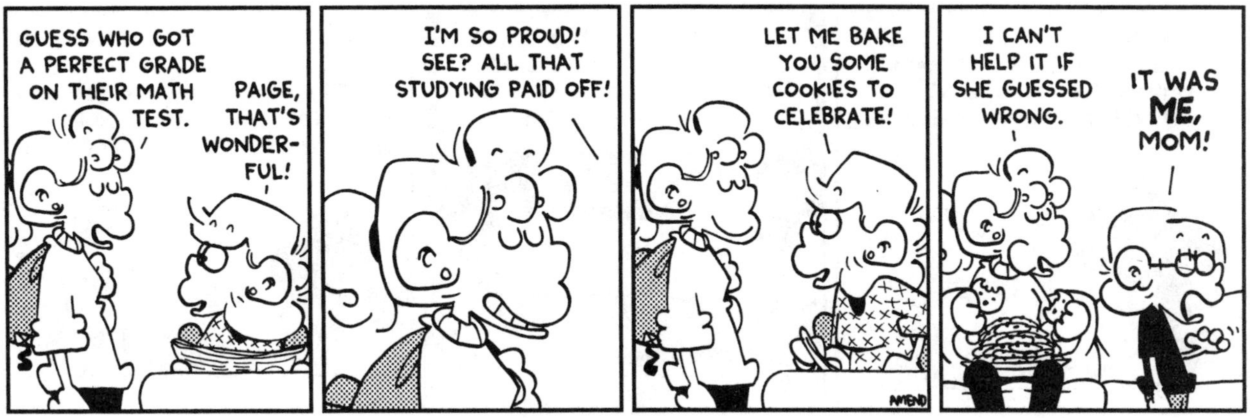
GUESS WHO GOT A PERFECT GRADE ON THEIR MATH TEST.
PAIGE, THAT'S WONDERFUL!
I'M SO PROUD! SEE? ALL THAT STUDYING PAID OFF!
LET ME BAKE YOU SOME COOKIES TO CELEBRATE!
I CAN'T HELP IT IF SHE GUESSED WRONG.
IT WAS **ME,** MOM!

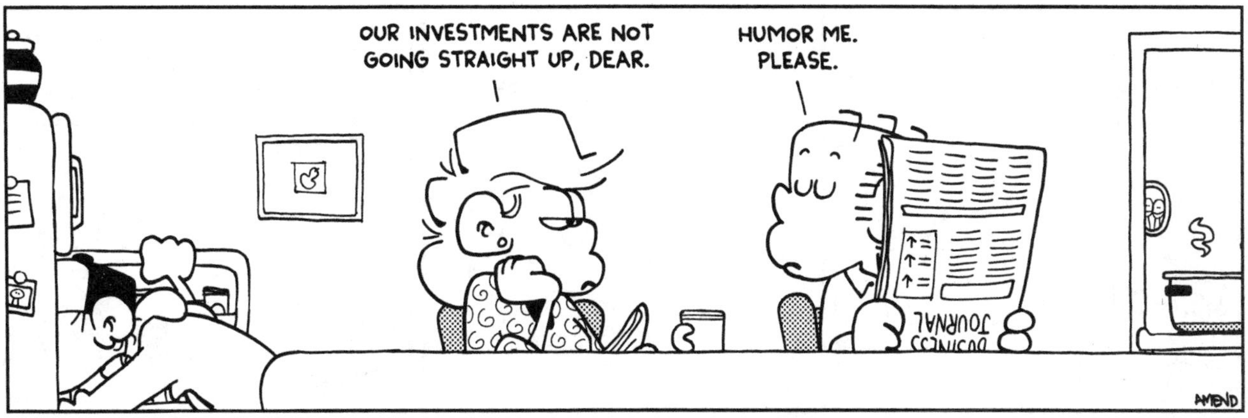
OUR INVESTMENTS ARE NOT GOING STRAIGHT UP, DEAR.
HUMOR ME. PLEASE.

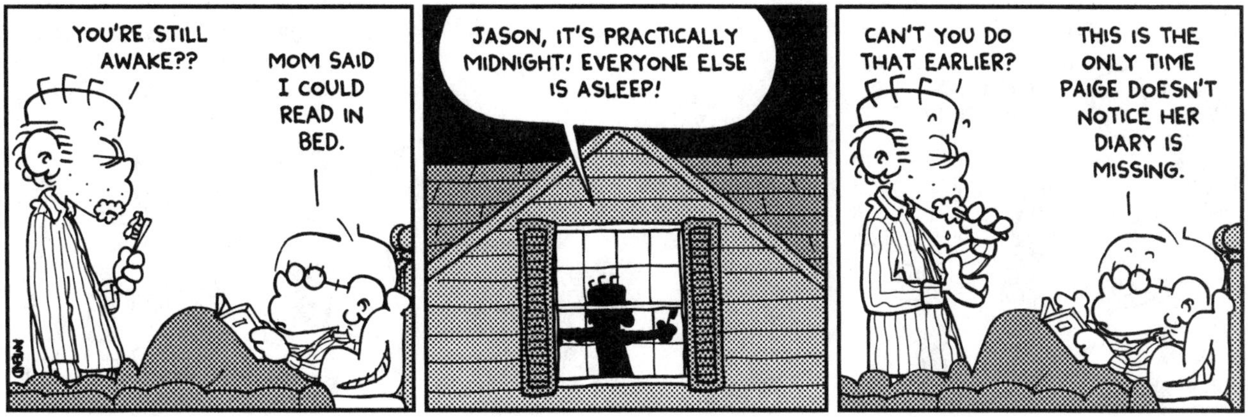
YOU'RE STILL AWAKE??
MOM SAID I COULD READ IN BED.
JASON, IT'S PRACTICALLY MIDNIGHT! EVERYONE ELSE IS ASLEEP!
CAN'T YOU DO THAT EARLIER?
THIS IS THE ONLY TIME PAIGE DOESN'T NOTICE HER DIARY IS MISSING.

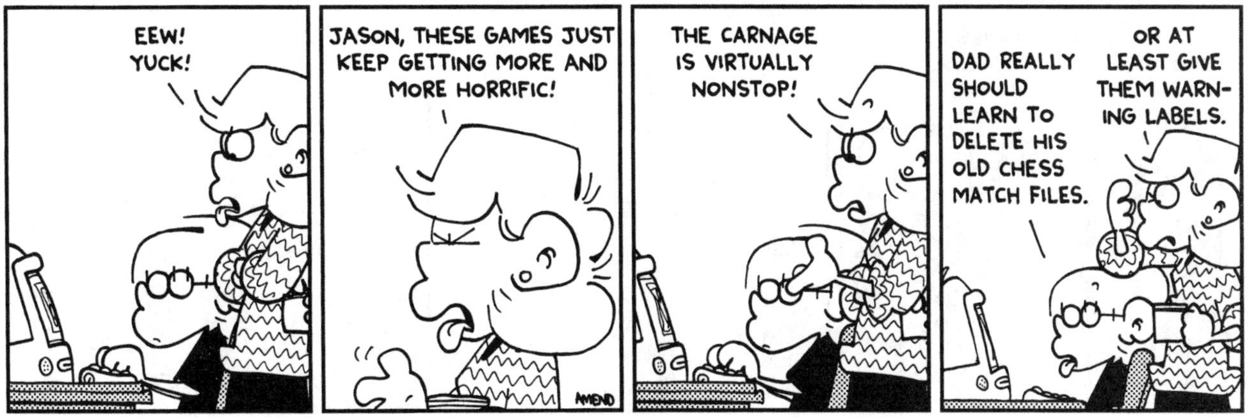
EEW! YUCK!
JASON, THESE GAMES JUST KEEP GETTING MORE AND MORE HORRIFIC!
THE CARNAGE IS VIRTUALLY NONSTOP!
DAD REALLY SHOULD LEARN TO DELETE HIS OLD CHESS MATCH FILES.
OR AT LEAST GIVE THEM WARNING LABELS.

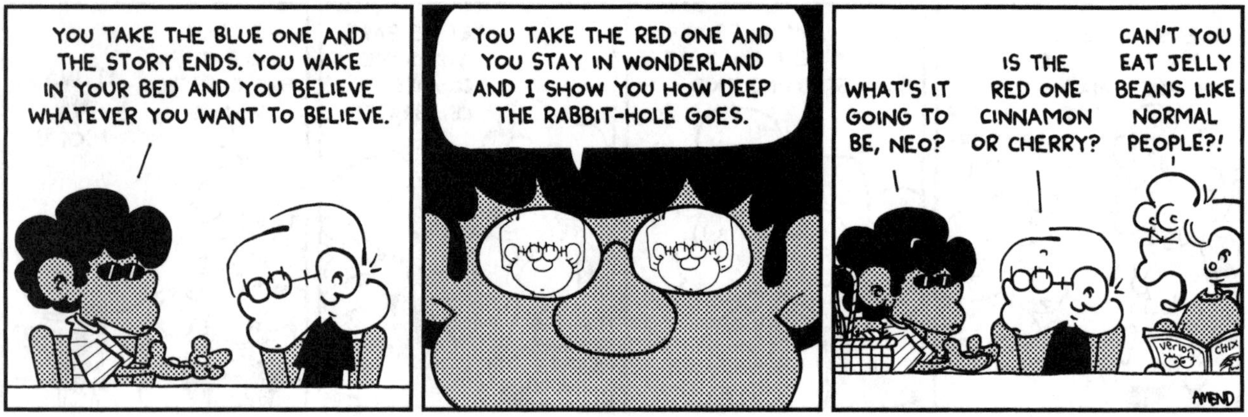
YOU TAKE THE BLUE ONE AND THE STORY ENDS. YOU WAKE IN YOUR BED AND YOU BELIEVE WHATEVER YOU WANT TO BELIEVE.
YOU TAKE THE RED ONE AND YOU STAY IN WONDERLAND AND I SHOW YOU HOW DEEP THE RABBIT-HOLE GOES.
WHAT'S IT GOING TO BE, NEO?
IS THE RED ONE CINNAMON OR CHERRY?
CAN'T YOU EAT JELLY BEANS LIKE NORMAL PEOPLE?!

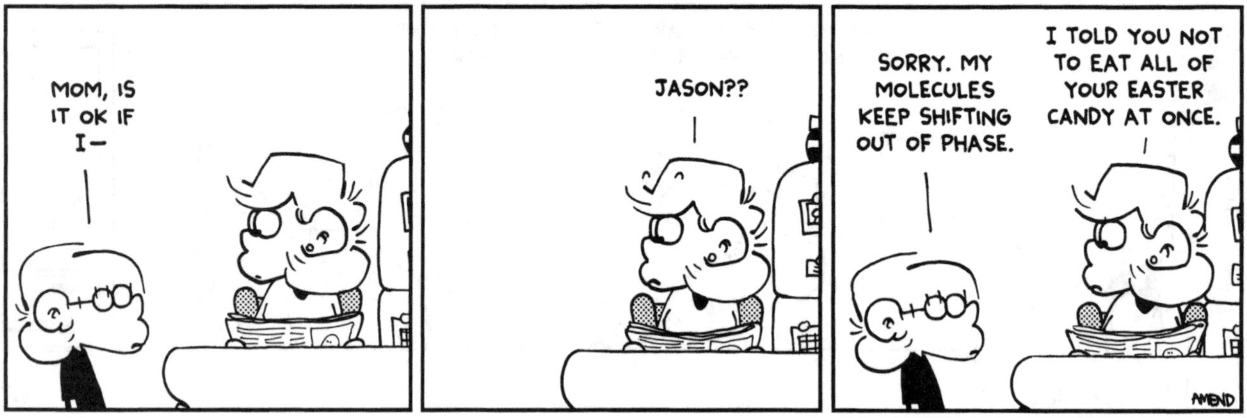
MOM, IS IT OK IF I—
JASON??
SORRY. MY MOLECULES KEEP SHIFTING OUT OF PHASE.
I TOLD YOU NOT TO EAT ALL OF YOUR EASTER CANDY AT ONCE.

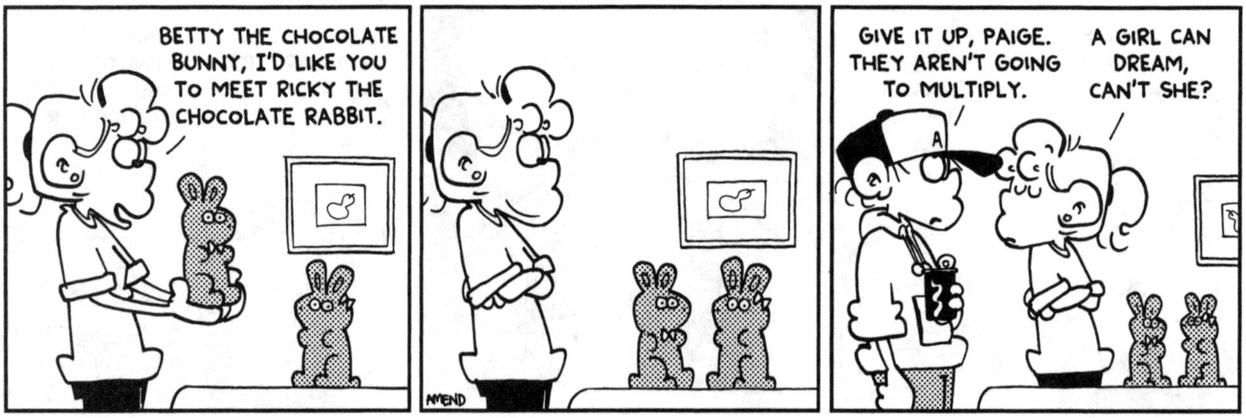
BETTY THE CHOCOLATE BUNNY, I'D LIKE YOU TO MEET RICKY THE CHOCOLATE RABBIT.
GIVE IT UP, PAIGE. THEY AREN'T GOING TO MULTIPLY.
A GIRL CAN DREAM, CAN'T SHE?

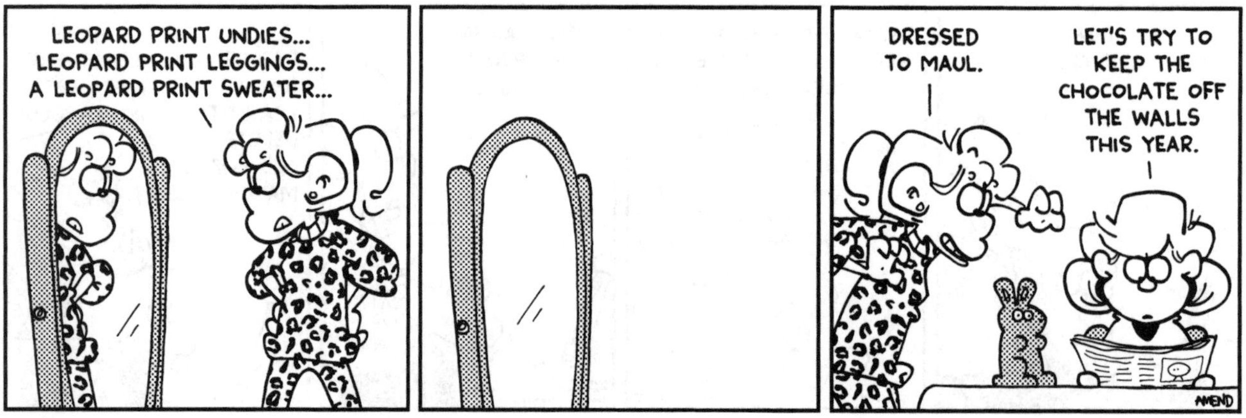
LEOPARD PRINT UNDIES... LEOPARD PRINT LEGGINGS... A LEOPARD PRINT SWEATER...
DRESSED TO MAUL.
LET'S TRY TO KEEP THE CHOCOLATE OFF THE WALLS THIS YEAR.

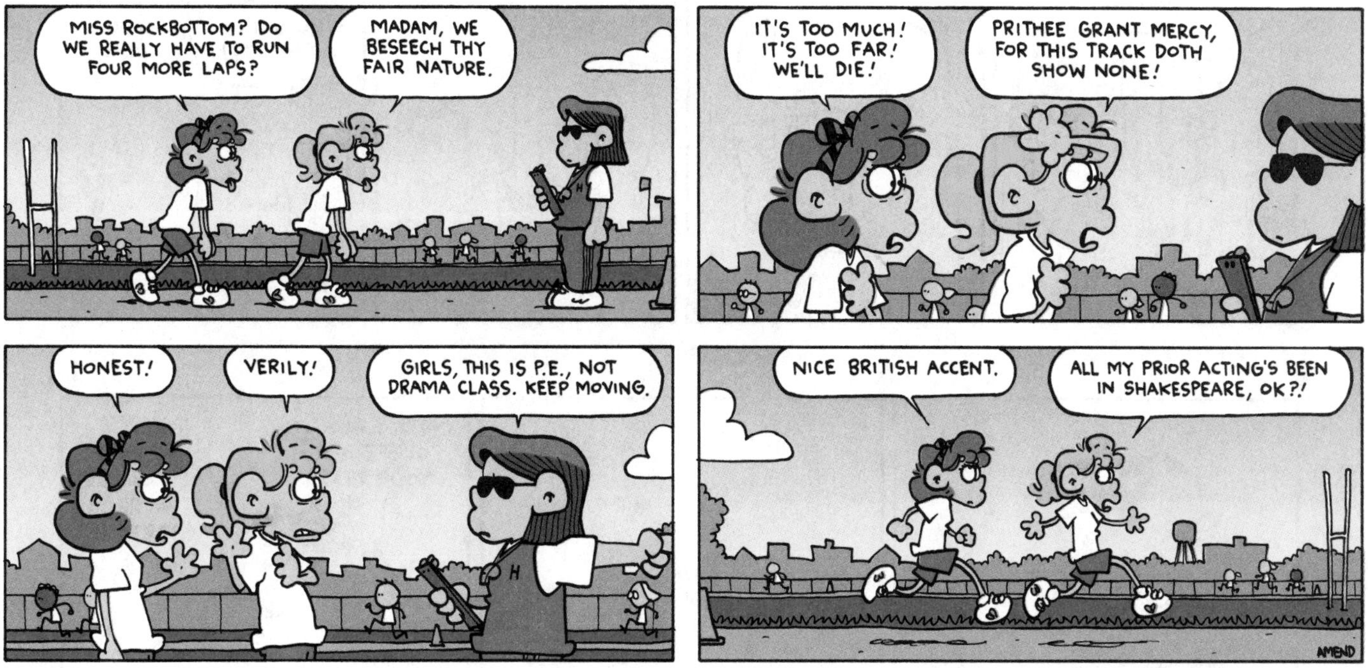
MISS ROCKBOTTOM? DO WE REALLY HAVE TO RUN FOUR MORE LAPS?
MADAM, WE BESEECH THY FAIR NATURE.
IT'S TOO MUCH! IT'S TOO FAR! WE'LL DIE!
PRITHEE GRANT MERCY, FOR THIS TRACK DOTH SHOW NONE!
HONEST!
VERILY!
GIRLS, THIS IS P.E., NOT DRAMA CLASS. KEEP MOVING.
NICE BRITISH ACCENT.
ALL MY PRIOR ACTING'S BEEN IN SHAKESPEARE, OK?!
AMEND

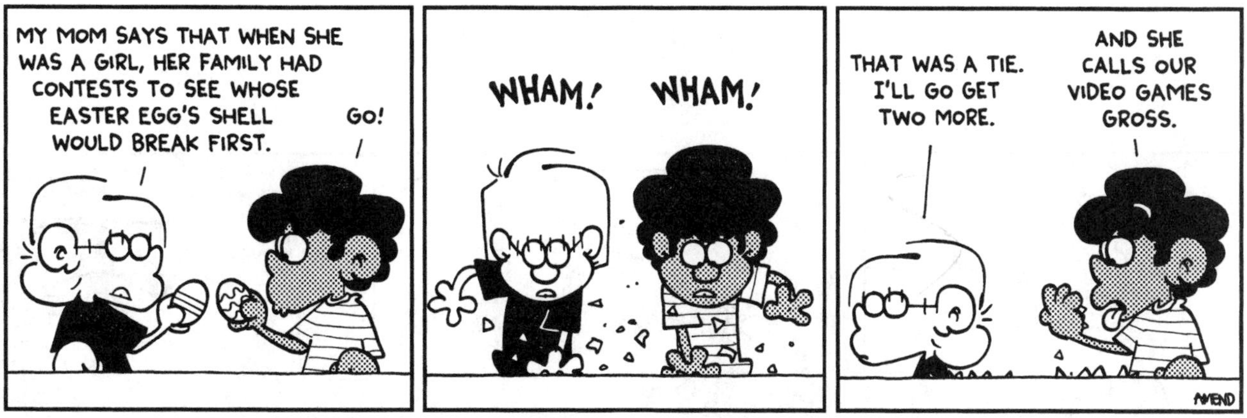
MY MOM SAYS THAT WHEN SHE WAS A GIRL, HER FAMILY HAD CONTESTS TO SEE WHOSE EASTER EGG'S SHELL WOULD BREAK FIRST.
GO!
WHAM! WHAM!
THAT WAS A TIE. I'LL GO GET TWO MORE.
AND SHE CALLS OUR VIDEO GAMES GROSS.
AMEND

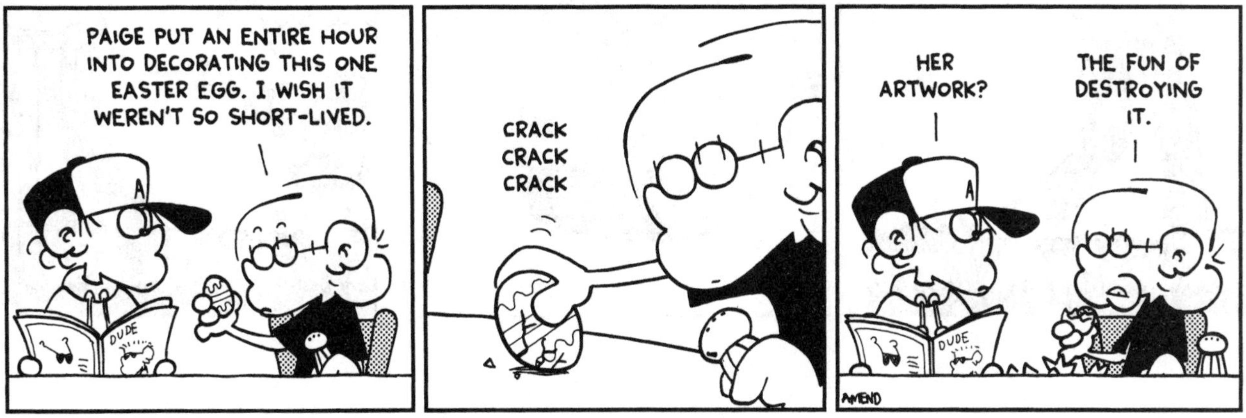
PAIGE PUT AN ENTIRE HOUR INTO DECORATING THIS ONE EASTER EGG. I WISH IT WEREN'T SO SHORT-LIVED.
DUDE
CRACK CRACK CRACK
HER ARTWORK?
THE FUN OF DESTROYING IT.
AMEND

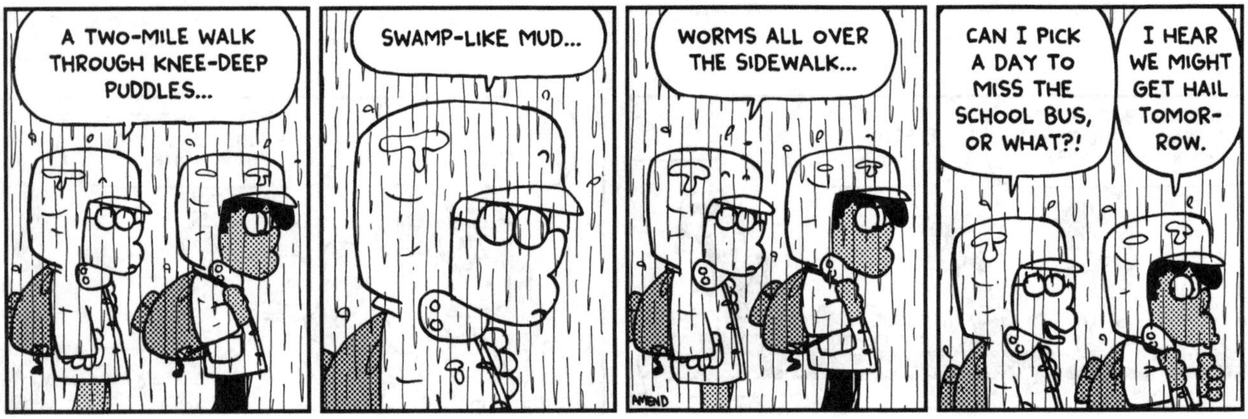
A TWO-MILE WALK THROUGH KNEE-DEEP PUDDLES...
SWAMP-LIKE MUD...
WORMS ALL OVER THE SIDEWALK...
CAN I PICK A DAY TO MISS THE SCHOOL BUS, OR WHAT?!
I HEAR WE MIGHT GET HAIL TOMOR-ROW.
AMEND

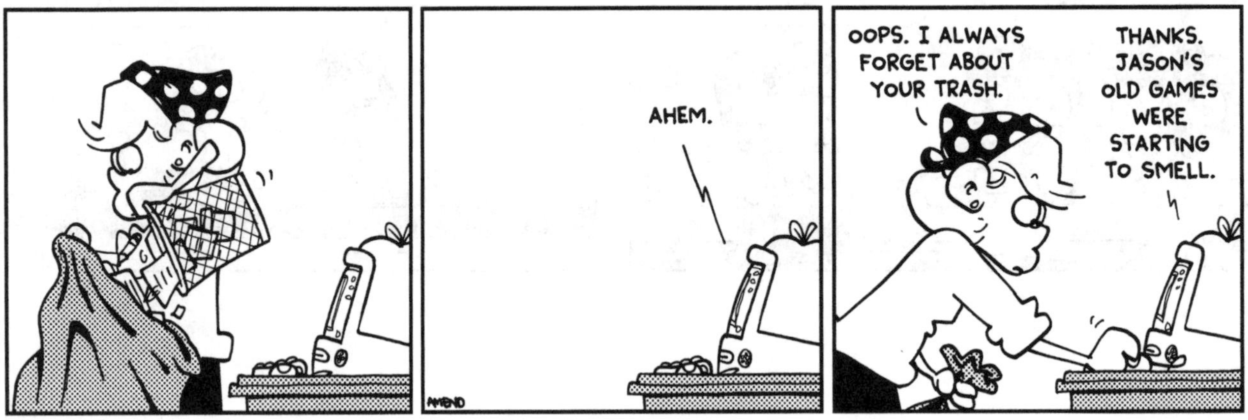
AHEM.
OOPS. I ALWAYS FORGET ABOUT YOUR TRASH.
THANKS. JASON'S OLD GAMES WERE STARTING TO SMELL.
AMEND

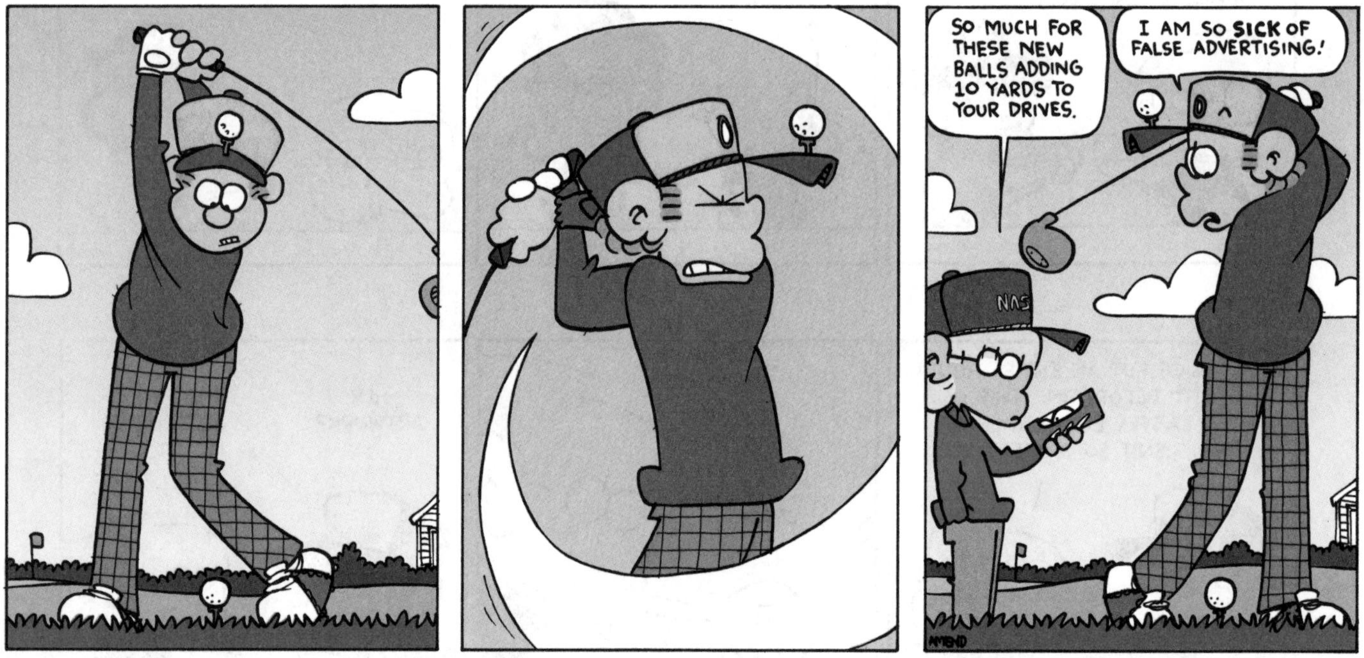
SO MUCH FOR THESE NEW BALLS ADDING 10 YARDS TO YOUR DRIVES.
I AM SO **SICK** OF FALSE ADVERTISING!
AMEND

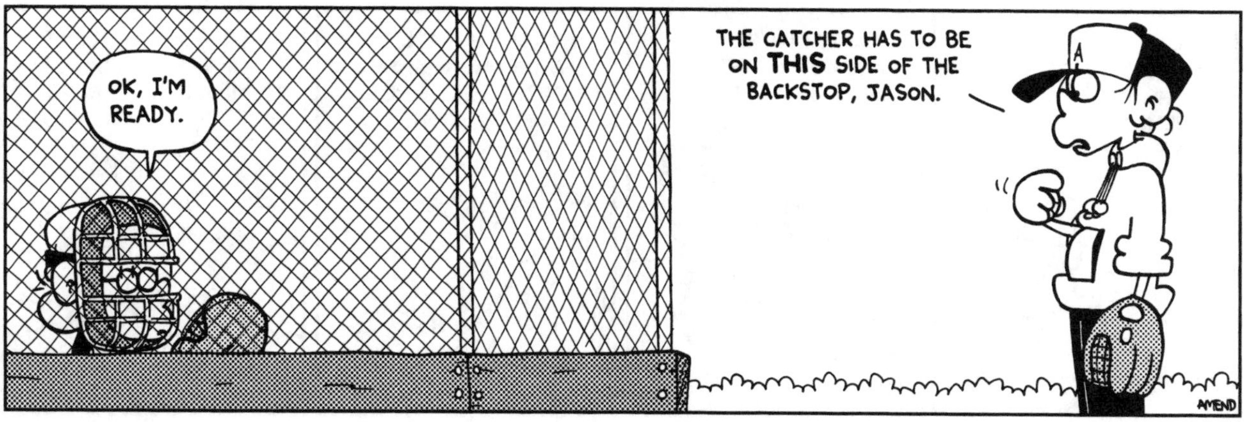
OK, I'M READY.
THE CATCHER HAS TO BE ON **THIS** SIDE OF THE BACKSTOP, JASON.
A
AMEND

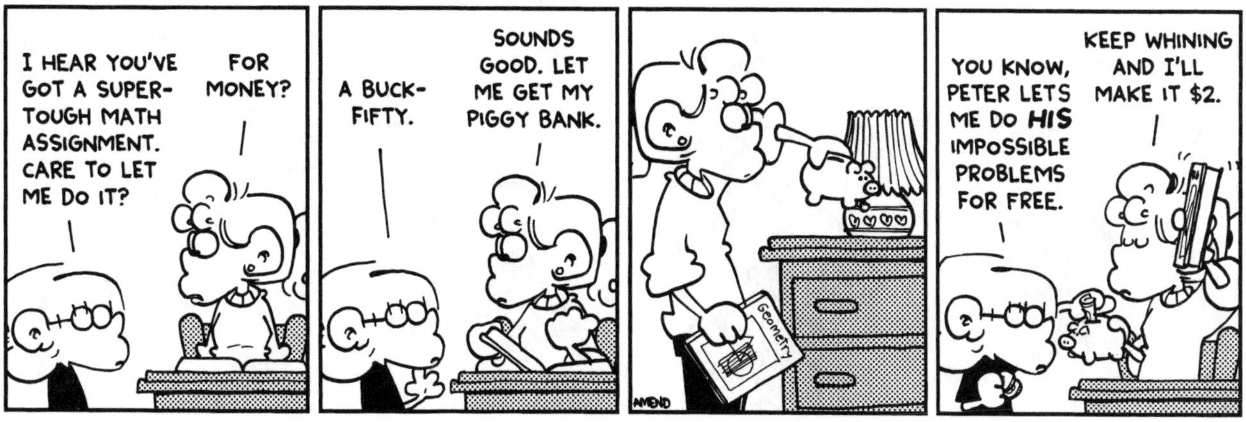
I HEAR YOU'VE GOT A SUPER-TOUGH MATH ASSIGNMENT. CARE TO LET ME DO IT?
FOR MONEY?
A BUCK-FIFTY.
SOUNDS GOOD. LET ME GET MY PIGGY BANK.
Geometry
AMEND
YOU KNOW, PETER LETS ME DO **HIS** IMPOSSIBLE PROBLEMS FOR FREE.
KEEP WHINING AND I'LL MAKE IT $2.

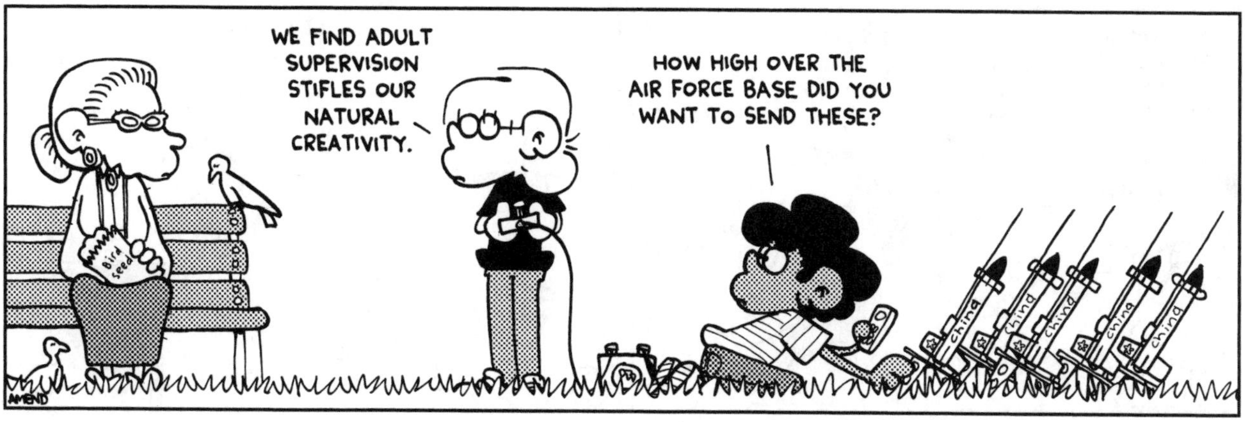
WE FIND ADULT SUPERVISION STIFLES OUR NATURAL CREATIVITY.
HOW HIGH OVER THE AIR FORCE BASE DID YOU WANT TO SEND THESE?
Bird seed
china
china
china
china
china
AMEND

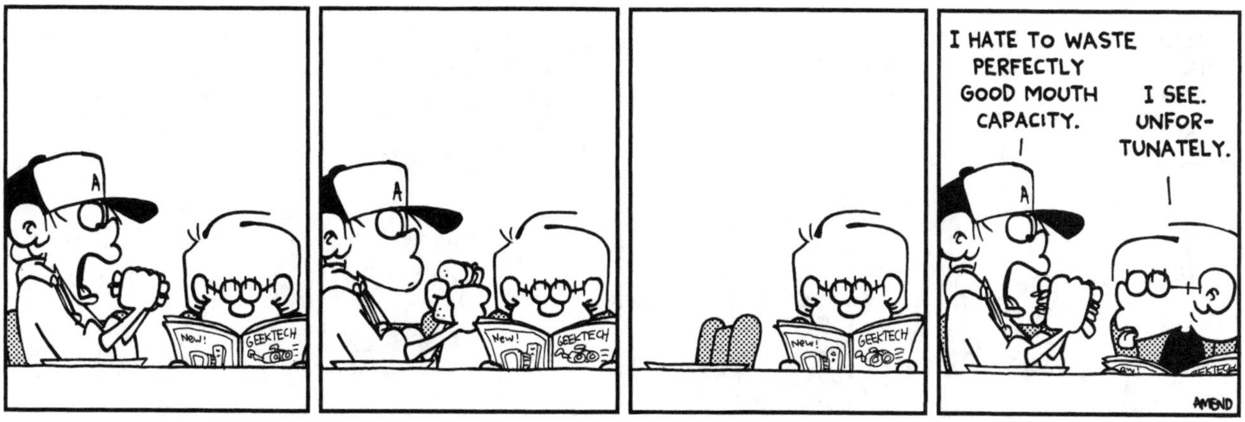
A
New!
GEEKTECH
A
New!
GEEKTECH
New!
GEEKTECH
I HATE TO WASTE PERFECTLY GOOD MOUTH CAPACITY.
I SEE. UNFORTUNATELY.
A
AMEND

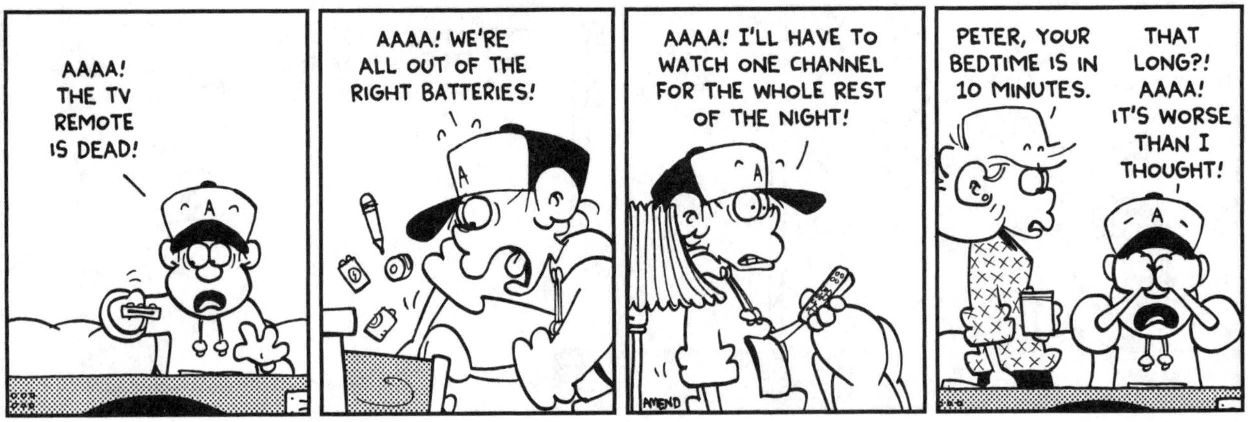
AAAA! THE TV REMOTE IS DEAD!
AAAA! WE'RE ALL OUT OF THE RIGHT BATTERIES!
AAAA! I'LL HAVE TO WATCH ONE CHANNEL FOR THE WHOLE REST OF THE NIGHT!
PETER, YOUR BEDTIME IS IN 10 MINUTES.
THAT LONG?! AAAA! IT'S WORSE THAN I THOUGHT!
AMEND

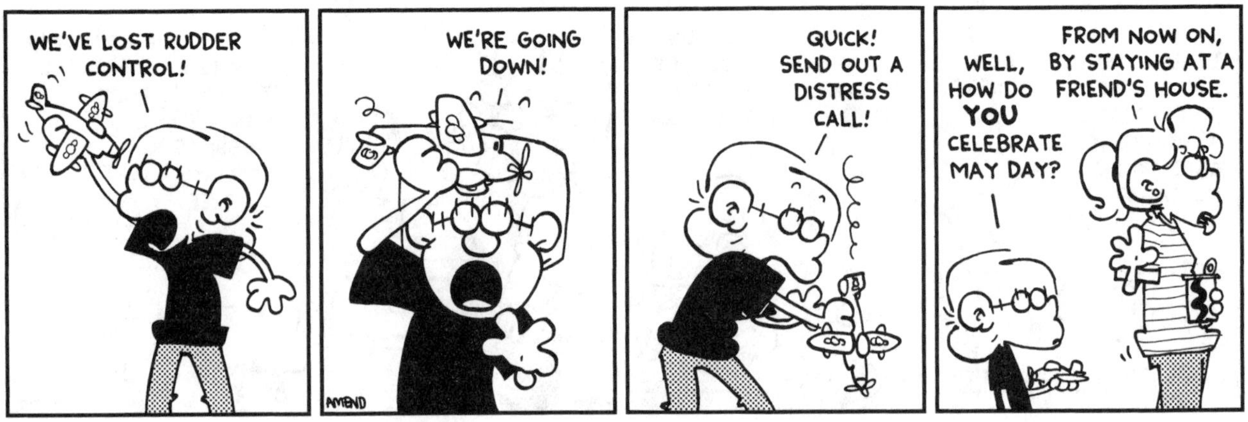
WE'VE LOST RUDDER CONTROL!
WE'RE GOING DOWN!
AMEND
QUICK! SEND OUT A DISTRESS CALL!
WELL, HOW DO YOU CELEBRATE MAY DAY?
FROM NOW ON, BY STAYING AT A FRIEND'S HOUSE.

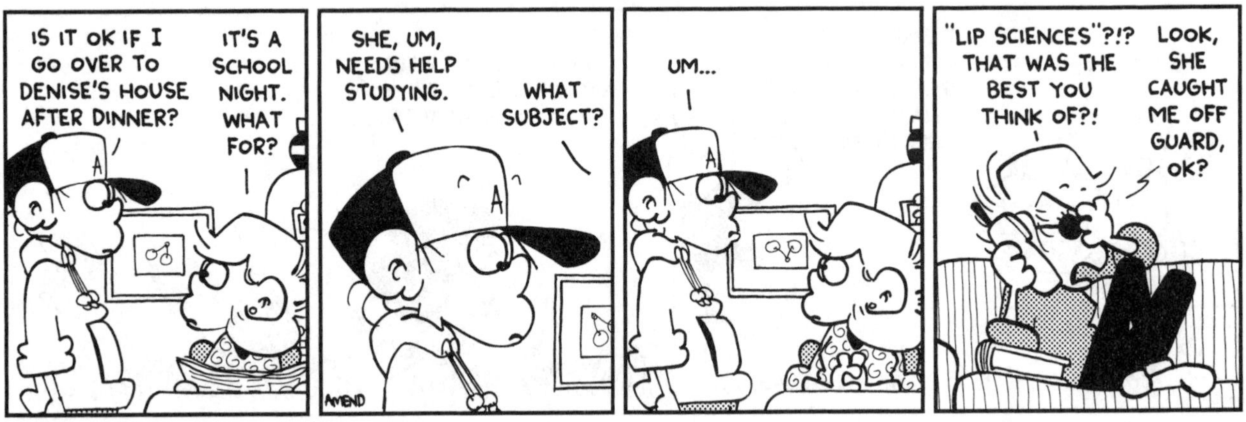
IS IT OK IF I GO OVER TO DENISE'S HOUSE AFTER DINNER?
IT'S A SCHOOL NIGHT. WHAT FOR?
SHE, UM, NEEDS HELP STUDYING.
WHAT SUBJECT?
AMEND
UM...
"LIP SCIENCES"?!? THAT WAS THE BEST YOU THINK OF?!
LOOK, SHE CAUGHT ME OFF GUARD, OK?

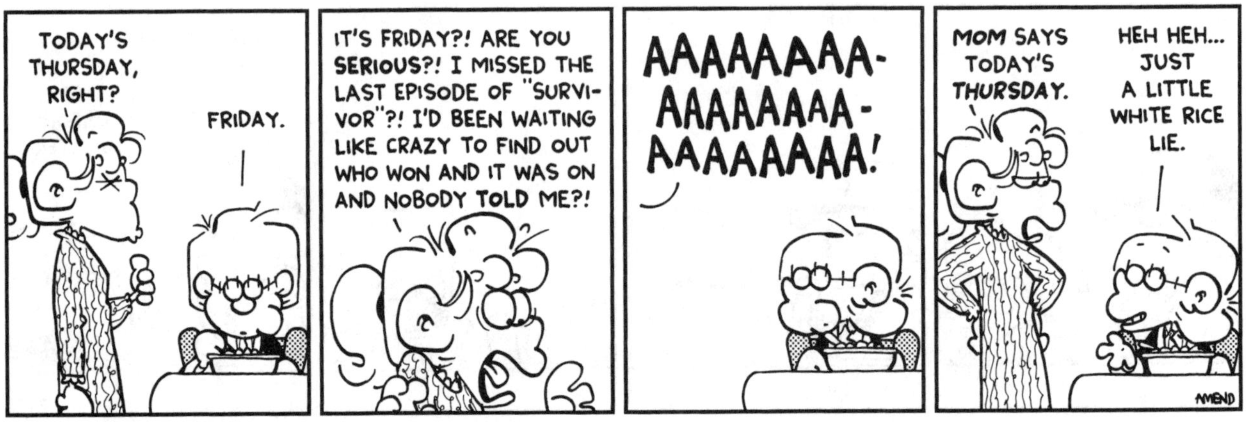
TODAY'S THURSDAY, RIGHT?
FRIDAY.
IT'S FRIDAY?! ARE YOU SERIOUS?! I MISSED THE LAST EPISODE OF "SURVIVOR"?! I'D BEEN WAITING LIKE CRAZY TO FIND OUT WHO WON AND IT WAS ON AND NOBODY TOLD ME?!
AAAAAAAA-AAAAAAAA-AAAAAAAA!
MOM SAYS TODAY'S THURSDAY.
HEH HEH... JUST A LITTLE WHITE RICE LIE.
AMEND

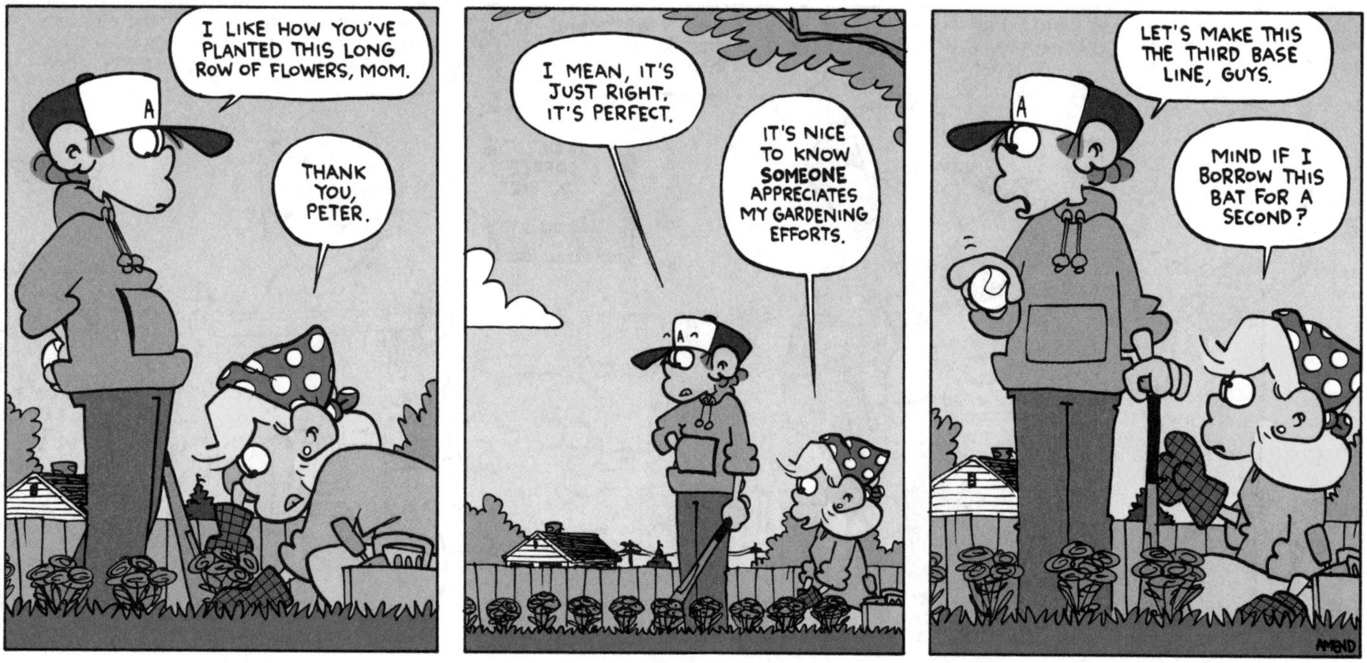
I LIKE HOW YOU'VE PLANTED THIS LONG ROW OF FLOWERS, MOM.
THANK YOU, PETER.
I MEAN, IT'S JUST RIGHT. IT'S PERFECT.
IT'S NICE TO KNOW SOMEONE APPRECIATES MY GARDENING EFFORTS.
LET'S MAKE THIS THE THIRD BASE LINE, GUYS.
MIND IF I BORROW THIS BAT FOR A SECOND?
AMEND

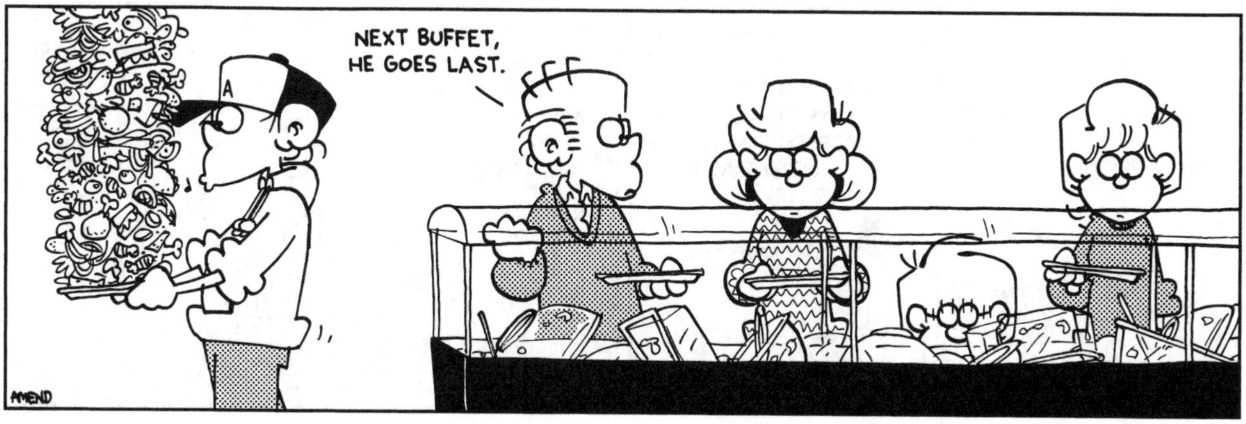
NEXT BUFFET, HE GOES LAST.
AMEND

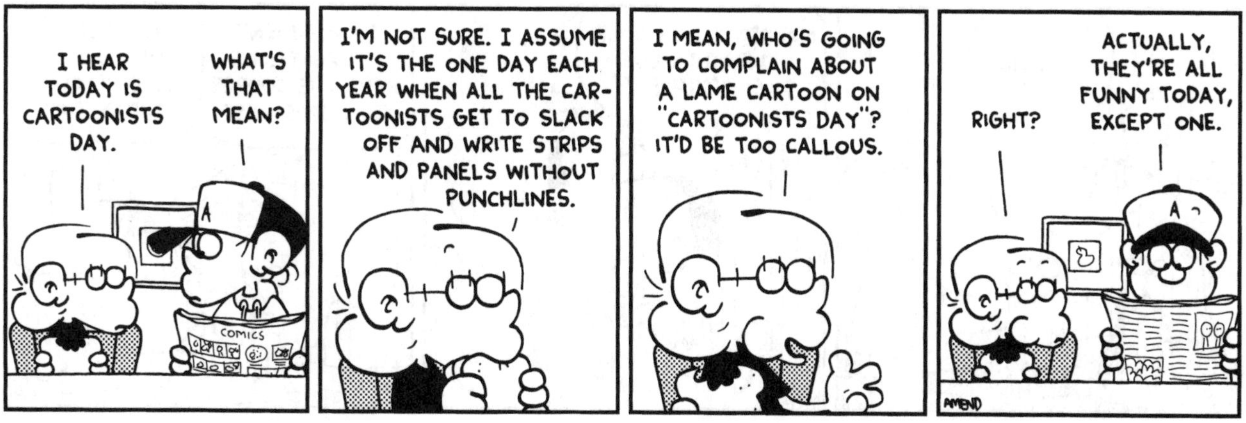
I HEAR TODAY IS CARTOONISTS DAY.
WHAT'S THAT MEAN?
COMICS
I'M NOT SURE. I ASSUME IT'S THE ONE DAY EACH YEAR WHEN ALL THE CARTOONISTS GET TO SLACK OFF AND WRITE STRIPS AND PANELS WITHOUT PUNCHLINES.
I MEAN, WHO'S GOING TO COMPLAIN ABOUT A LAME CARTOON ON "CARTOONISTS DAY"? IT'D BE TOO CALLOUS.
RIGHT?
ACTUALLY, THEY'RE ALL FUNNY TODAY, EXCEPT ONE.
AMEND

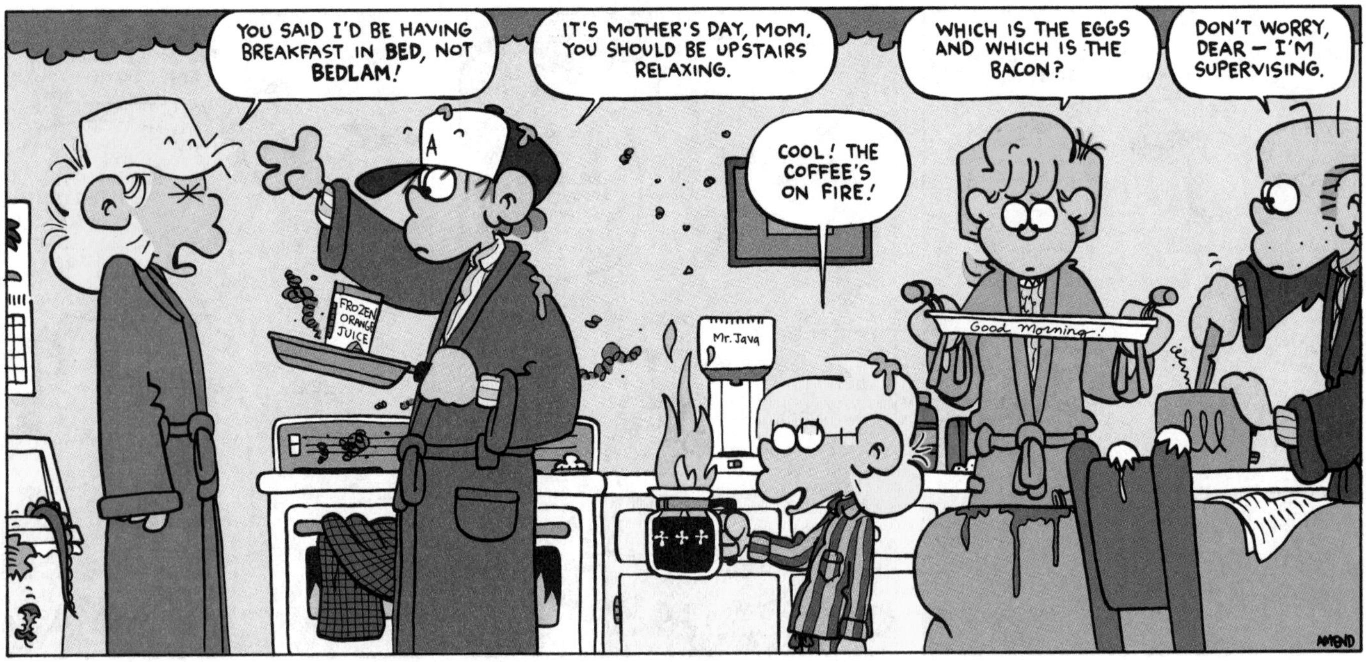
YOU SAID I'D BE HAVING BREAKFAST IN BED, NOT BEDLAM!
IT'S MOTHER'S DAY, MOM. YOU SHOULD BE UPSTAIRS RELAXING.
FROZEN ORANGE JUICE
COOL! THE COFFEE'S ON FIRE!
Mr. Java
WHICH IS THE EGGS AND WHICH IS THE BACON?
Good Morning!
DON'T WORRY, DEAR – I'M SUPERVISING.
AMEND

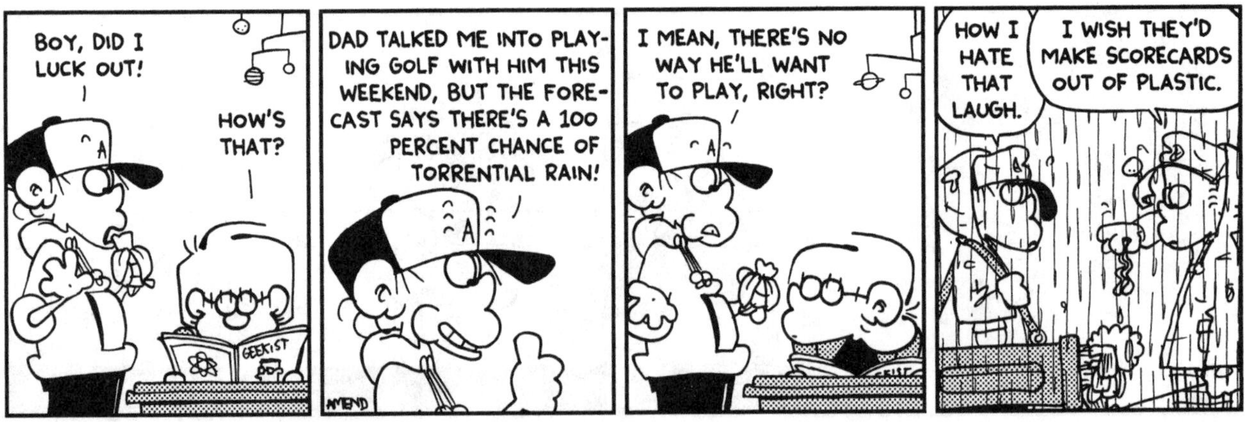
BOY, DID I LUCK OUT!
HOW'S THAT?
GEEKIST
DAD TALKED ME INTO PLAYING GOLF WITH HIM THIS WEEKEND, BUT THE FORECAST SAYS THERE'S A 100 PERCENT CHANCE OF TORRENTIAL RAIN!
AMEND
I MEAN, THERE'S NO WAY HE'LL WANT TO PLAY, RIGHT?
HOW I HATE THAT LAUGH.
I WISH THEY'D MAKE SCORECARDS OUT OF PLASTIC.

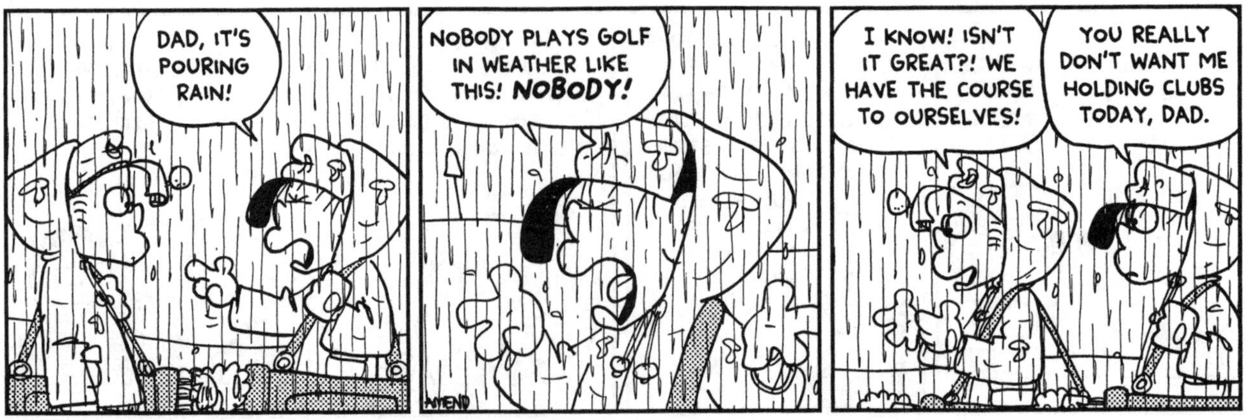
DAD, IT'S POURING RAIN!
NOBODY PLAYS GOLF IN WEATHER LIKE THIS! NOBODY!
AMEND
I KNOW! ISN'T IT GREAT?! WE HAVE THE COURSE TO OURSELVES!
YOU REALLY DON'T WANT ME HOLDING CLUBS TODAY, DAD.

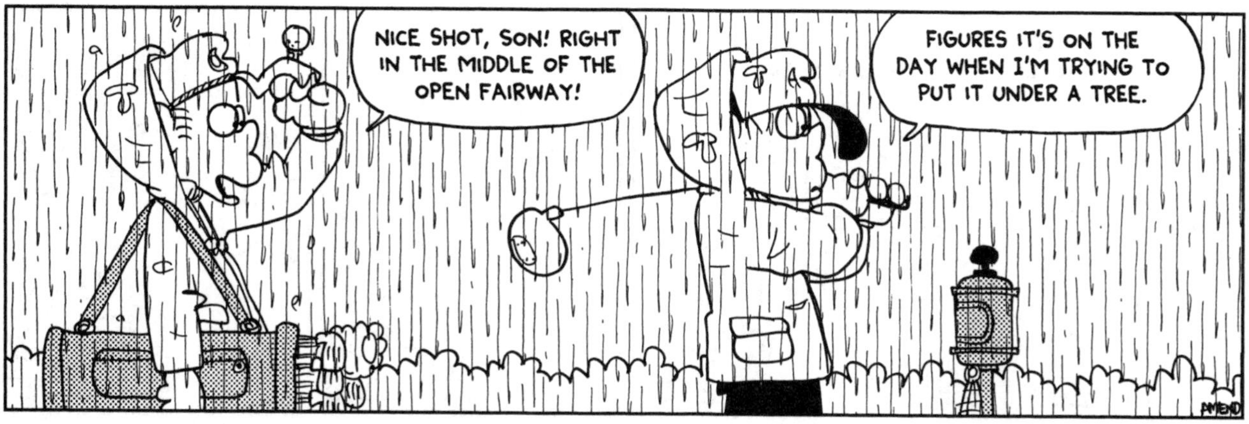
NICE SHOT, SON! RIGHT IN THE MIDDLE OF THE OPEN FAIRWAY!
FIGURES IT'S ON THE DAY WHEN I'M TRYING TO PUT IT UNDER A TREE.
AMEND

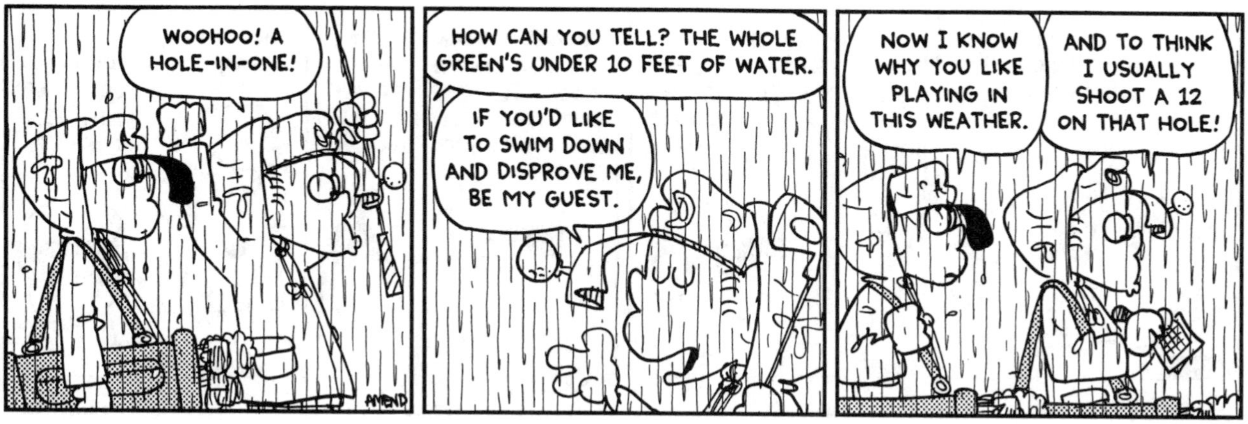
WOOHOO! A HOLE-IN-ONE!
AMEND
HOW CAN YOU TELL? THE WHOLE GREEN'S UNDER 10 FEET OF WATER.
IF YOU'D LIKE TO SWIM DOWN AND DISPROVE ME, BE MY GUEST.
NOW I KNOW WHY YOU LIKE PLAYING IN THIS WEATHER.
AND TO THINK I USUALLY SHOOT A 12 ON THAT HOLE!

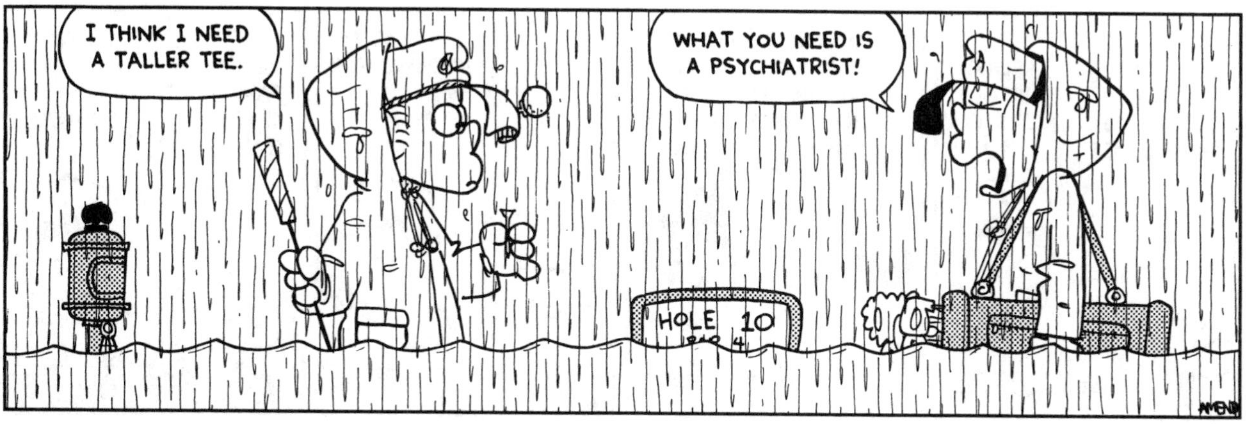
I THINK I NEED A TALLER TEE.
WHAT YOU NEED IS A PSYCHIATRIST!
HOLE 10
AMEND

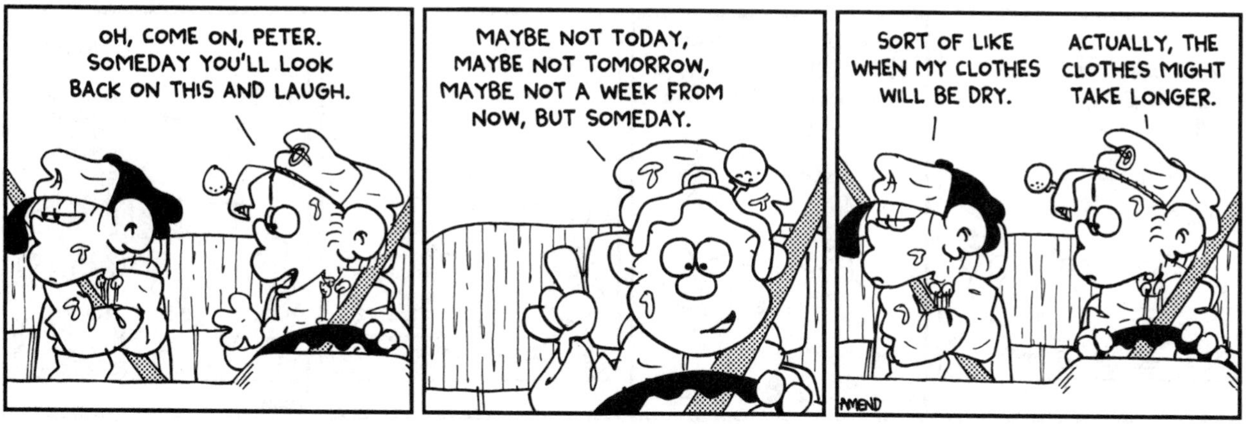
OH, COME ON, PETER. SOMEDAY YOU'LL LOOK BACK ON THIS AND LAUGH.
MAYBE NOT TODAY, MAYBE NOT TOMORROW, MAYBE NOT A WEEK FROM NOW, BUT SOMEDAY.
SORT OF LIKE WHEN MY CLOTHES WILL BE DRY.
ACTUALLY, THE CLOTHES MIGHT TAKE LONGER.
AMEND

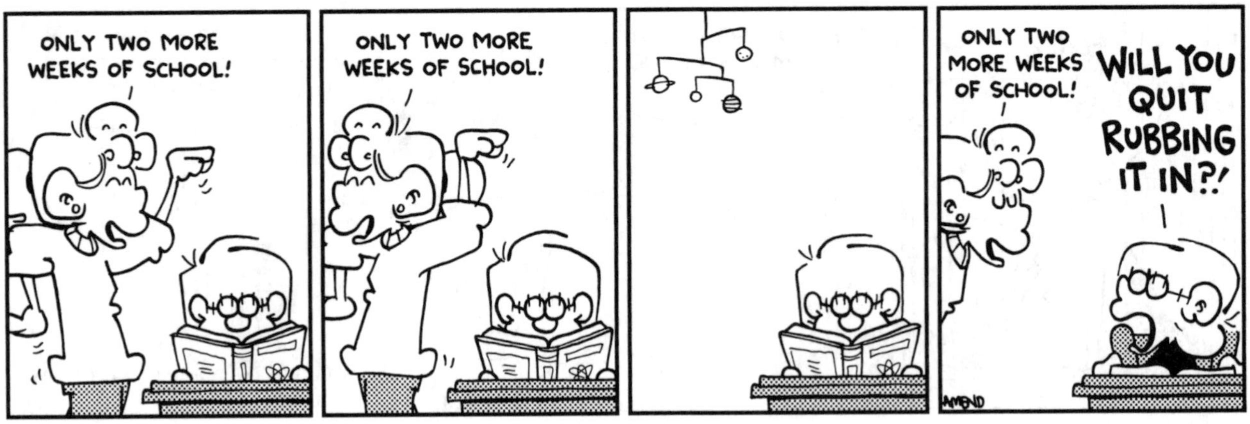
ONLY TWO MORE WEEKS OF SCHOOL!
ONLY TWO MORE WEEKS OF SCHOOL!
ONLY TWO MORE WEEKS OF SCHOOL!
WILL YOU QUIT RUBBING IT IN?!
AMEND

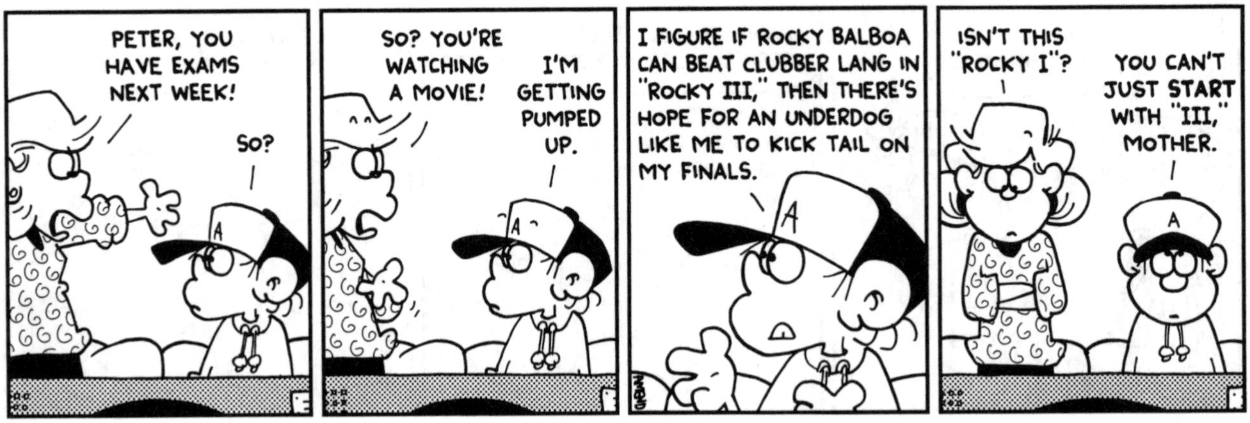
PETER, YOU HAVE EXAMS NEXT WEEK!
SO?
SO? YOU'RE WATCHING A MOVIE!
I'M GETTING PUMPED UP.
I FIGURE IF ROCKY BALBOA CAN BEAT CLUBBER LANG IN "ROCKY III," THEN THERE'S HOPE FOR AN UNDERDOG LIKE ME TO KICK TAIL ON MY FINALS.
AMEND
ISN'T THIS "ROCKY I"?
YOU CAN'T JUST START WITH "III," MOTHER.

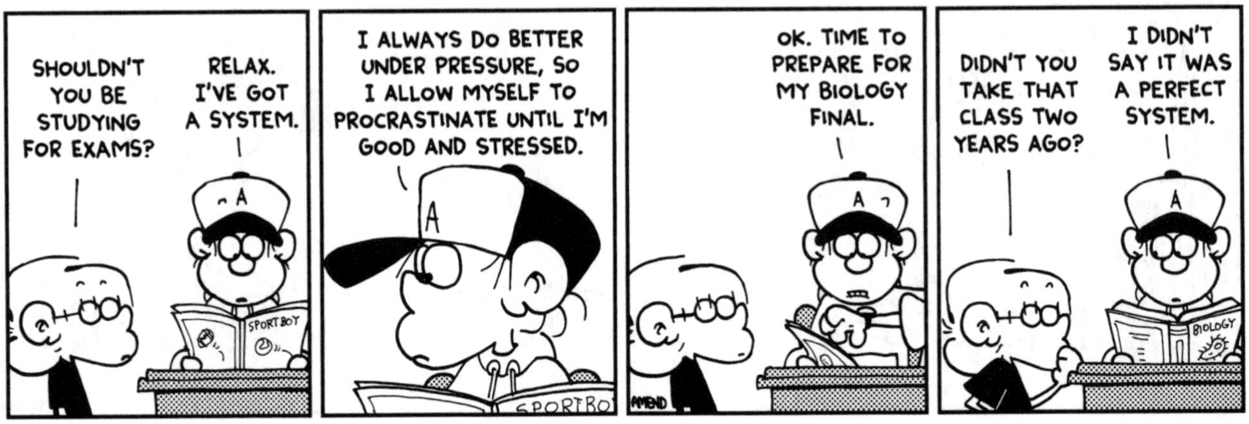
SHOULDN'T YOU BE STUDYING FOR EXAMS?
RELAX. I'VE GOT A SYSTEM.
SPORT BOY
I ALWAYS DO BETTER UNDER PRESSURE, SO I ALLOW MYSELF TO PROCRASTINATE UNTIL I'M GOOD AND STRESSED.
SPORTBO
AMEND
OK. TIME TO PREPARE FOR MY BIOLOGY FINAL.
DIDN'T YOU TAKE THAT CLASS TWO YEARS AGO?
I DIDN'T SAY IT WAS A PERFECT SYSTEM.
BIOLOGY

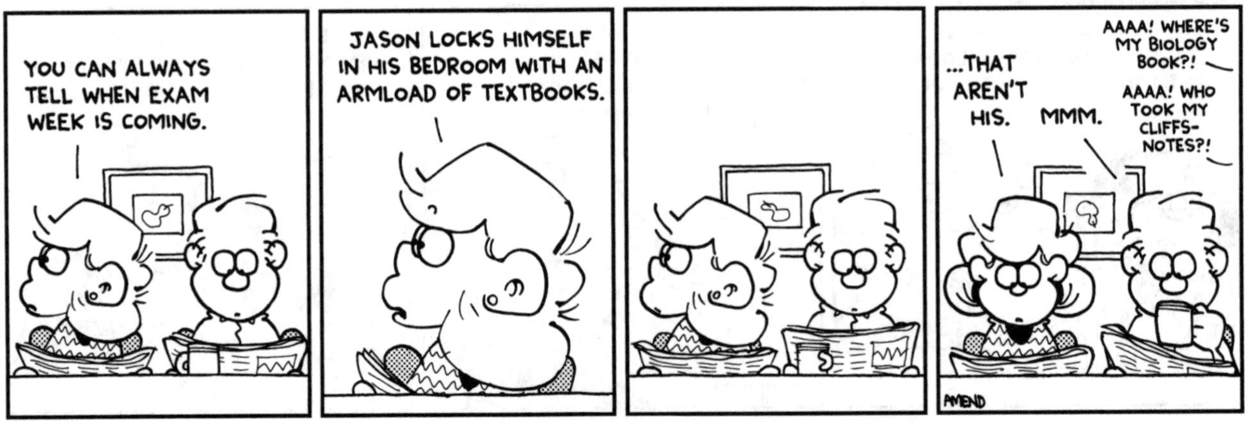
YOU CAN ALWAYS TELL WHEN EXAM WEEK IS COMING.
JASON LOCKS HIMSELF IN HIS BEDROOM WITH AN ARMLOAD OF TEXTBOOKS.
...THAT AREN'T HIS.
MMM.
AAAA! WHERE'S MY BIOLOGY BOOK?!
AAAA! WHO TOOK MY CLIFFS-NOTES?!
AMEND

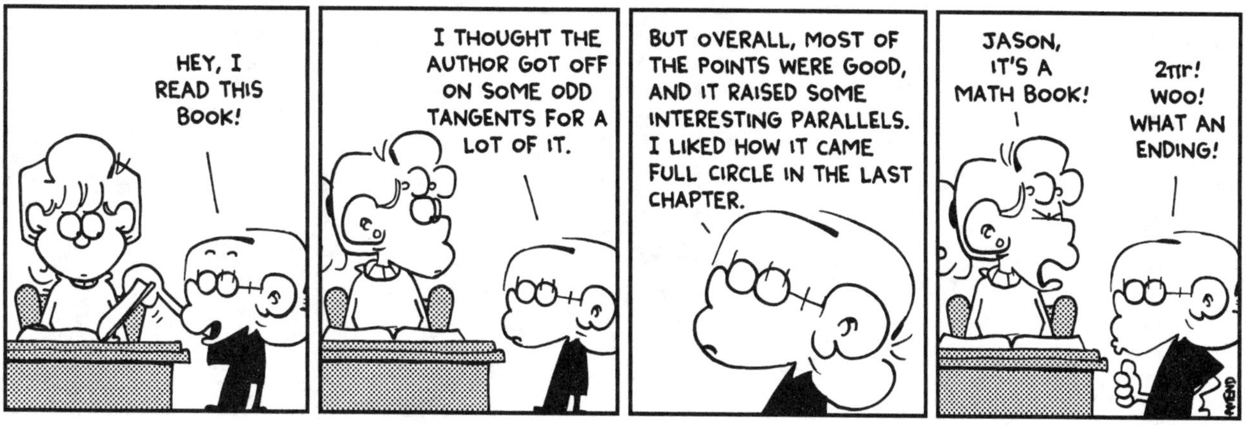
HEY, I READ THIS BOOK!
I THOUGHT THE AUTHOR GOT OFF ON SOME ODD TANGENTS FOR A LOT OF IT.
BUT OVERALL, MOST OF THE POINTS WERE GOOD, AND IT RAISED SOME INTERESTING PARALLELS. I LIKED HOW IT CAME FULL CIRCLE IN THE LAST CHAPTER.
JASON, IT'S A MATH BOOK!
$2\pi r$! WOO! WHAT AN ENDING!
AMEND

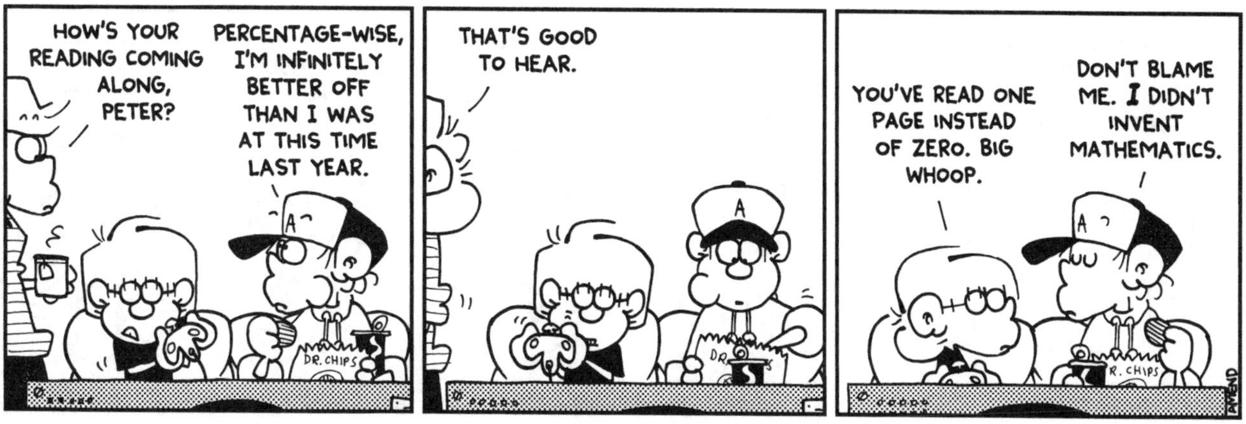
HOW'S YOUR READING COMING ALONG, PETER?
PERCENTAGE-WISE, I'M INFINITELY BETTER OFF THAN I WAS AT THIS TIME LAST YEAR.
DR. CHIPS
THAT'S GOOD TO HEAR.
YOU'VE READ ONE PAGE INSTEAD OF ZERO. BIG WHOOP.
DON'T BLAME ME. I DIDN'T INVENT MATHEMATICS.
AMEND

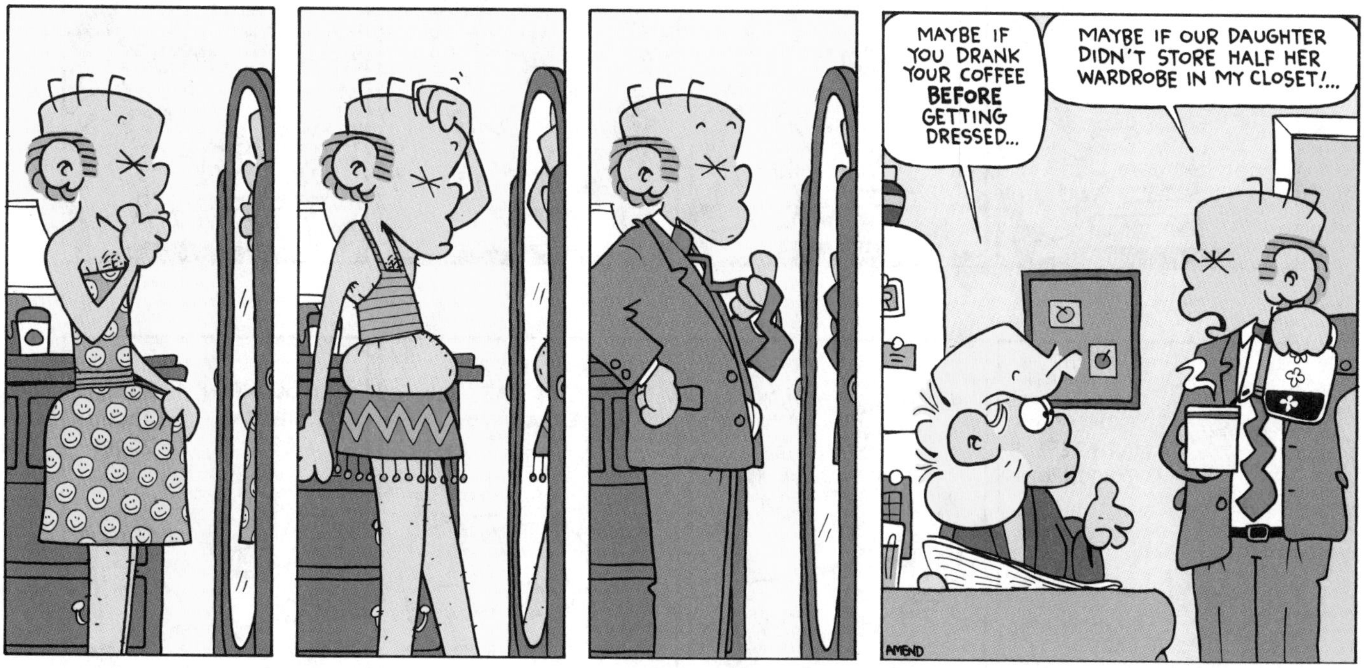
MAYBE IF YOU DRANK YOUR COFFEE BEFORE GETTING DRESSED...
MAYBE IF OUR DAUGHTER DIDN'T STORE HALF HER WARDROBE IN MY CLOSET!...
AMEND

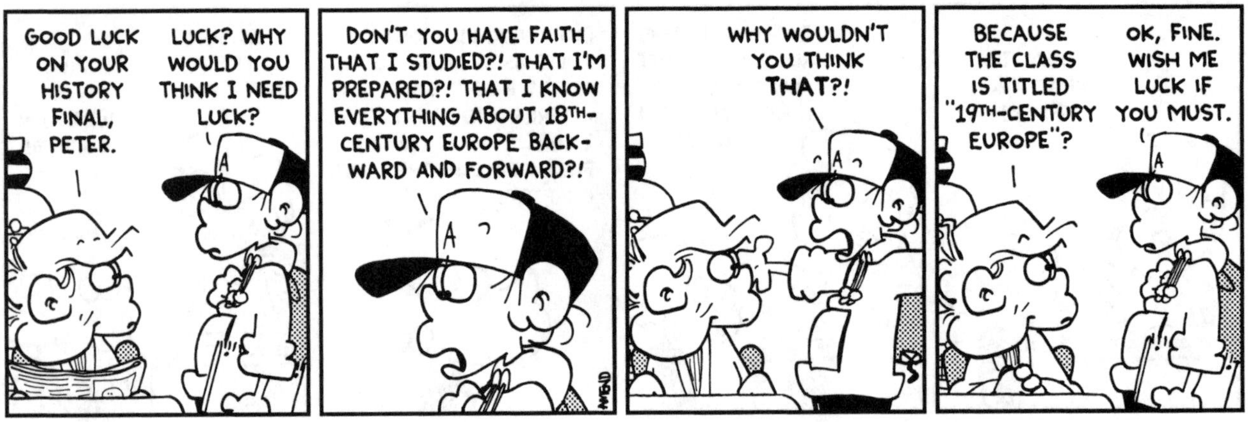
GOOD LUCK ON YOUR HISTORY FINAL, PETER.
LUCK? WHY WOULD YOU THINK I NEED LUCK?
DON'T YOU HAVE FAITH THAT I STUDIED?! THAT I'M PREPARED?! THAT I KNOW EVERYTHING ABOUT 18TH-CENTURY EUROPE BACKWARD AND FORWARD?!
WHY WOULDN'T YOU THINK THAT?!
BECAUSE THE CLASS IS TITLED "19TH-CENTURY EUROPE"?
OK, FINE. WISH ME LUCK IF YOU MUST.

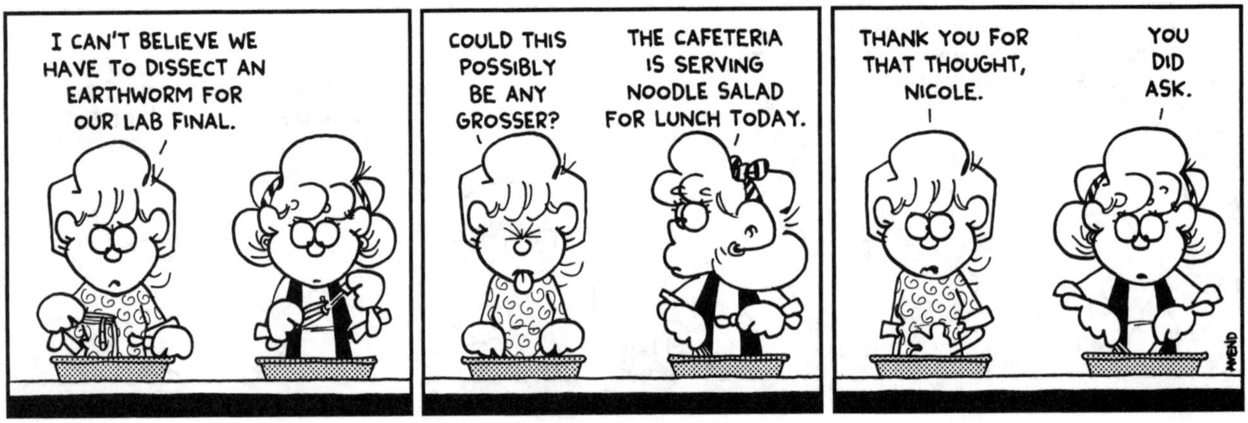
I CAN'T BELIEVE WE HAVE TO DISSECT AN EARTHWORM FOR OUR LAB FINAL.
COULD THIS POSSIBLY BE ANY GROSSER?
THE CAFETERIA IS SERVING NOODLE SALAD FOR LUNCH TODAY.
THANK YOU FOR THAT THOUGHT, NICOLE.
YOU DID ASK.

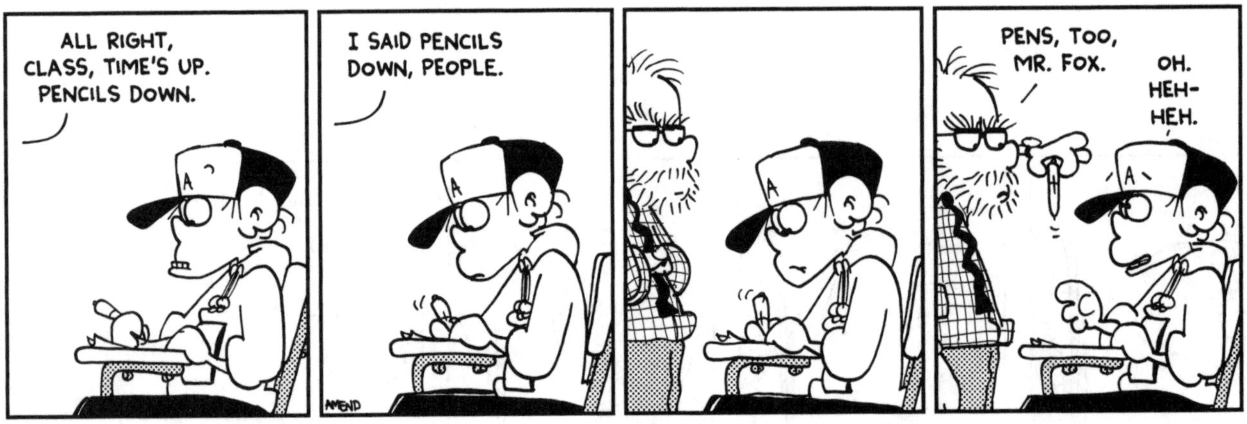
ALL RIGHT, CLASS, TIME'S UP. PENCILS DOWN.
I SAID PENCILS DOWN, PEOPLE.
PENS, TOO, MR. FOX.
OH. HEH-HEH.

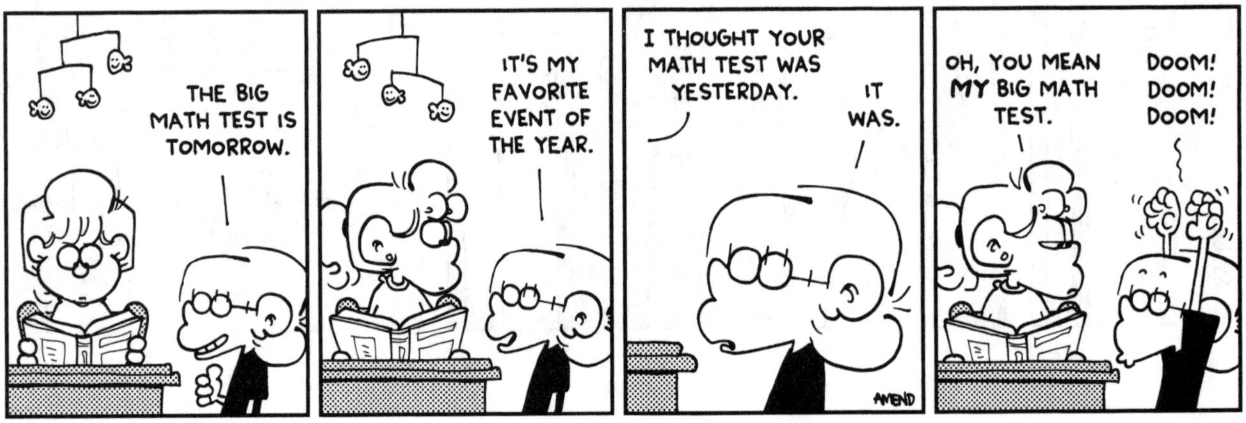
THE BIG MATH TEST IS TOMORROW.
IT'S MY FAVORITE EVENT OF THE YEAR.
I THOUGHT YOUR MATH TEST WAS YESTERDAY.
IT WAS.
OH, YOU MEAN MY BIG MATH TEST.
DOOM! DOOM! DOOM!

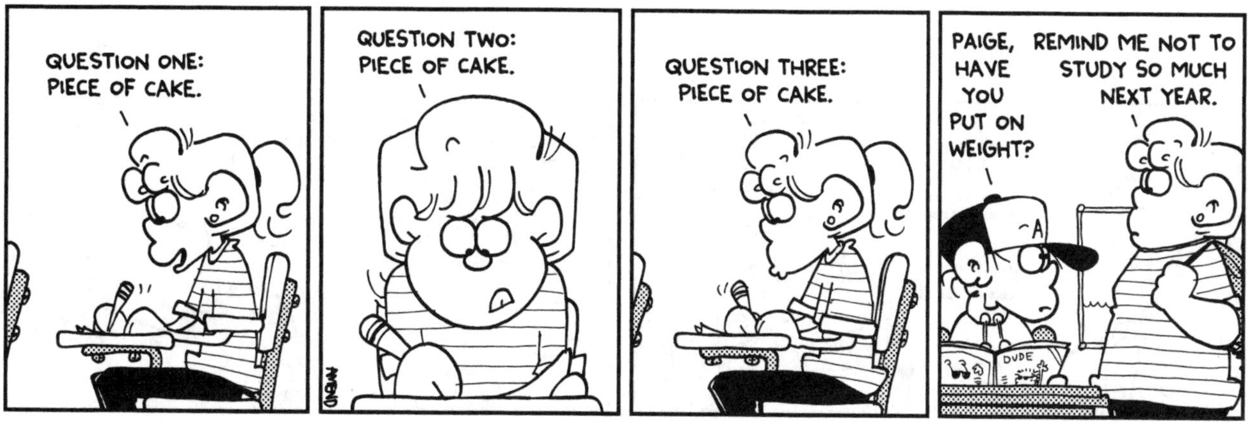
QUESTION ONE: PIECE OF CAKE.
QUESTION TWO: PIECE OF CAKE.
QUESTION THREE: PIECE OF CAKE.
PAIGE, HAVE YOU PUT ON WEIGHT?
REMIND ME NOT TO STUDY SO MUCH NEXT YEAR.
DUDE

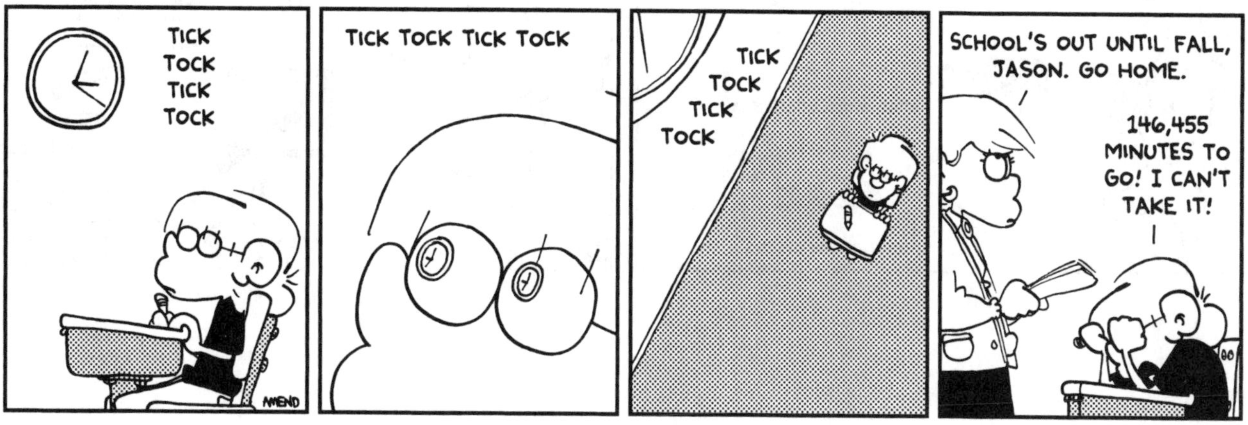
TICK TOCK TICK TOCK
TICK TOCK TICK TOCK
TICK TOCK TICK TOCK
SCHOOL'S OUT UNTIL FALL, JASON. GO HOME.
146,455 MINUTES TO GO! I CAN'T TAKE IT!
AMEND

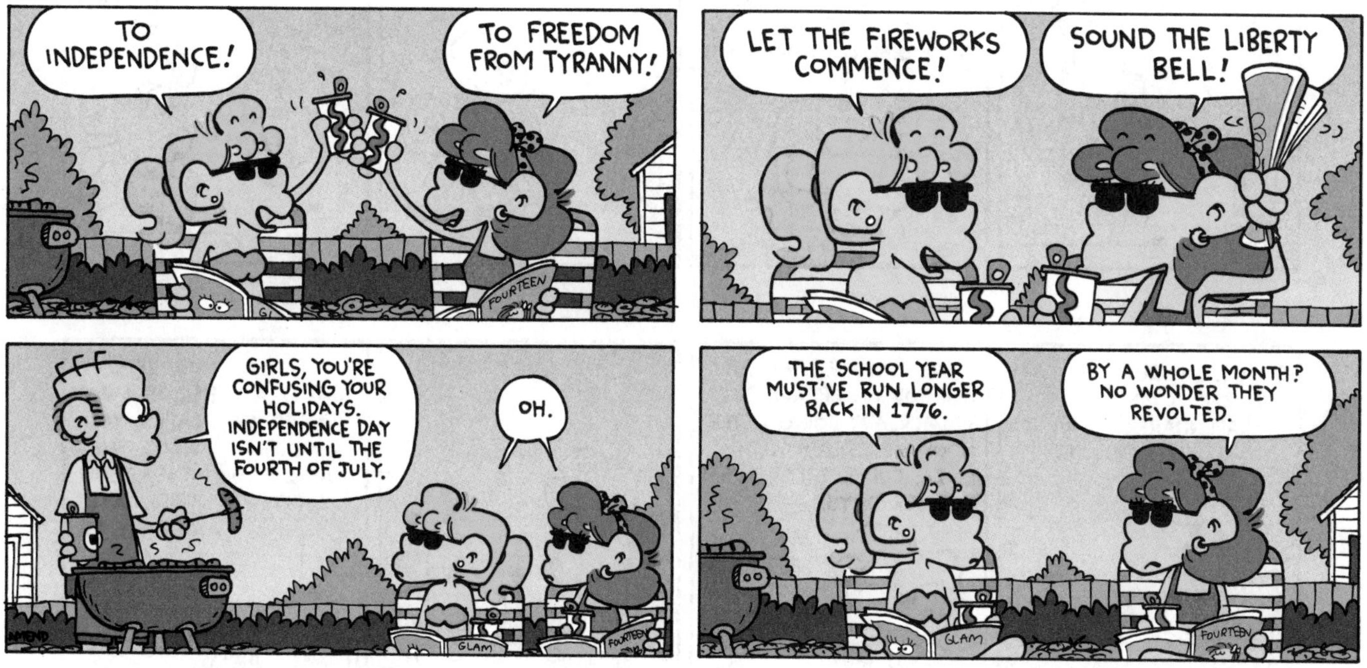
TO INDEPENDENCE!
TO FREEDOM FROM TYRANNY!
FOURTEEN
LET THE FIREWORKS COMMENCE!
SOUND THE LIBERTY BELL!
GIRLS, YOU'RE CONFUSING YOUR HOLIDAYS. INDEPENDENCE DAY ISN'T UNTIL THE FOURTH OF JULY.
OH.
AMEND
GLAM
FOURTEEN
THE SCHOOL YEAR MUST'VE RUN LONGER BACK IN 1776.
BY A WHOLE MONTH? NO WONDER THEY REVOLTED.
GLAM
FOURTEEN

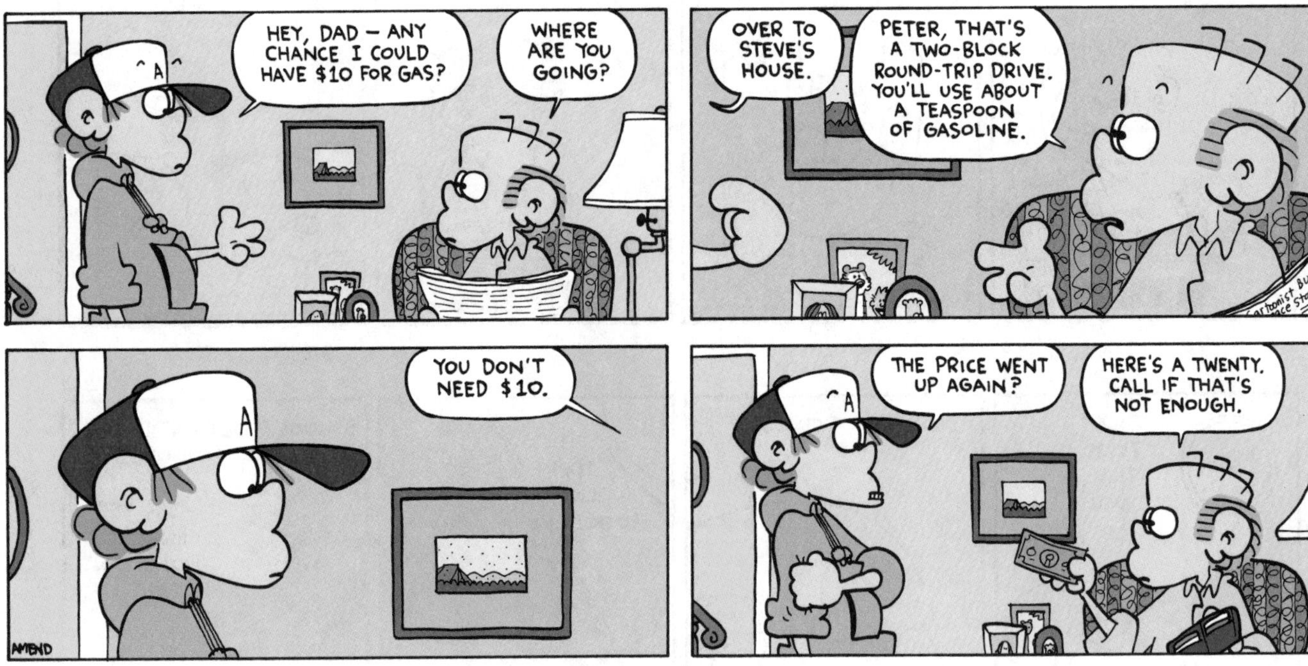
HEY, DAD – ANY CHANCE I COULD HAVE $10 FOR GAS?
WHERE ARE YOU GOING?
OVER TO STEVE'S HOUSE.
PETER, THAT'S A TWO-BLOCK ROUND-TRIP DRIVE. YOU'LL USE ABOUT A TEASPOON OF GASOLINE.
YOU DON'T NEED $10.
THE PRICE WENT UP AGAIN?
HERE'S A TWENTY. CALL IF THAT'S NOT ENOUGH.
AMEND

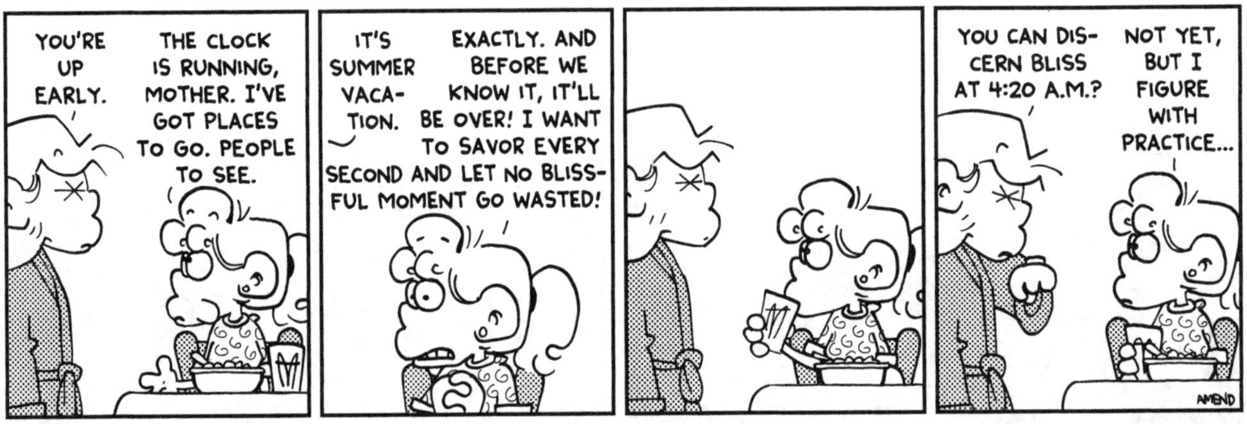
YOU'RE UP EARLY.
THE CLOCK IS RUNNING, MOTHER. I'VE GOT PLACES TO GO. PEOPLE TO SEE.
IT'S SUMMER VACATION.
EXACTLY. AND BEFORE WE KNOW IT, IT'LL BE OVER! I WANT TO SAVOR EVERY SECOND AND LET NO BLISSFUL MOMENT GO WASTED!
YOU CAN DISCERN BLISS AT 4:20 A.M.?
NOT YET, BUT I FIGURE WITH PRACTICE...
AMEND

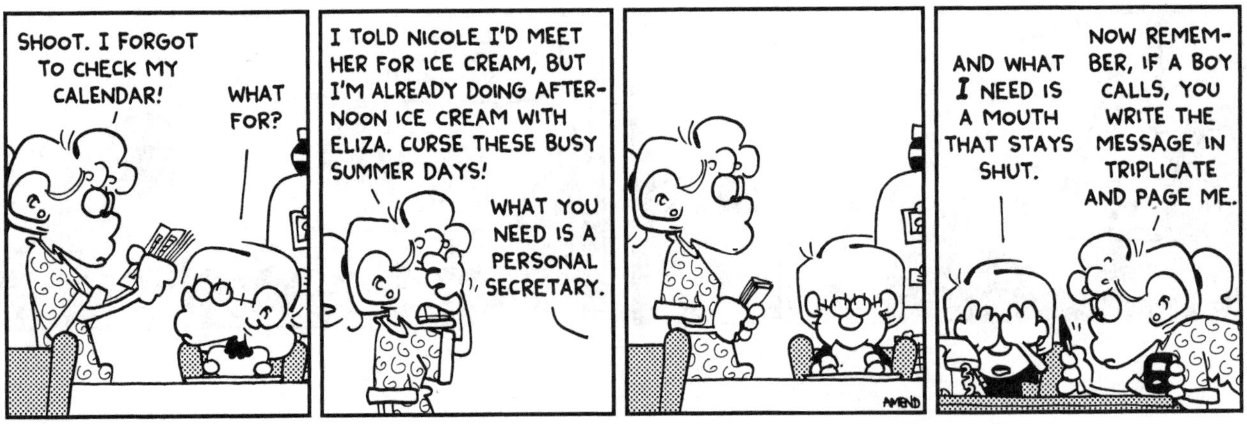
SHOOT. I FORGOT TO CHECK MY CALENDAR!
WHAT FOR?
I TOLD NICOLE I'D MEET HER FOR ICE CREAM, BUT I'M ALREADY DOING AFTERNOON ICE CREAM WITH ELIZA. CURSE THESE BUSY SUMMER DAYS!
WHAT YOU NEED IS A PERSONAL SECRETARY.
AND WHAT I NEED IS A MOUTH THAT STAYS SHUT.
NOW REMEMBER, IF A BOY CALLS, YOU WRITE THE MESSAGE IN TRIPLICATE AND PAGE ME.
AMEND

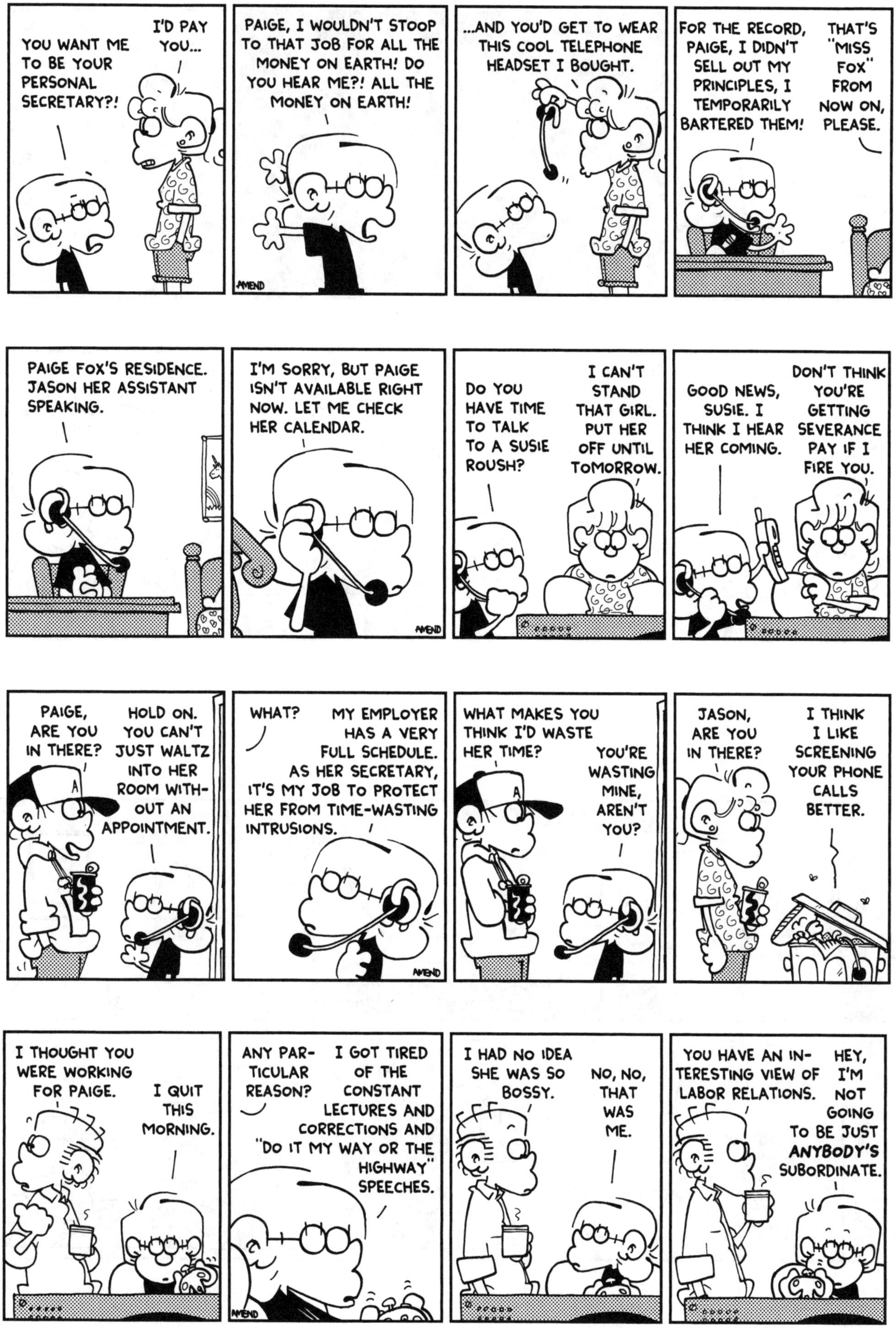
YOU WANT ME TO BE YOUR PERSONAL SECRETARY?!
I'D PAY YOU...
PAIGE, I WOULDN'T STOOP TO THAT JOB FOR ALL THE MONEY ON EARTH! DO YOU HEAR ME?! ALL THE MONEY ON EARTH!
AMEND
...AND YOU'D GET TO WEAR THIS COOL TELEPHONE HEADSET I BOUGHT.
FOR THE RECORD, PAIGE, I DIDN'T SELL OUT MY PRINCIPLES, I TEMPORARILY BARTERED THEM!
THAT'S "MISS FOX" FROM NOW ON, PLEASE.
PAIGE FOX'S RESIDENCE. JASON HER ASSISTANT SPEAKING.
I'M SORRY, BUT PAIGE ISN'T AVAILABLE RIGHT NOW. LET ME CHECK HER CALENDAR.
AMEND
DO YOU HAVE TIME TO TALK TO A SUSIE ROUSH?
I CAN'T STAND THAT GIRL. PUT HER OFF UNTIL TOMORROW.
GOOD NEWS, SUSIE. I THINK I HEAR HER COMING.
DON'T THINK YOU'RE GETTING SEVERANCE PAY IF I FIRE YOU.
PAIGE, ARE YOU IN THERE?
HOLD ON. YOU CAN'T JUST WALTZ INTO HER ROOM WITHOUT AN APPOINTMENT.
WHAT?
MY EMPLOYER HAS A VERY FULL SCHEDULE. AS HER SECRETARY, IT'S MY JOB TO PROTECT HER FROM TIME-WASTING INTRUSIONS.
AMEND
WHAT MAKES YOU THINK I'D WASTE HER TIME?
YOU'RE WASTING MINE, AREN'T YOU?
JASON, ARE YOU IN THERE?
I THINK I LIKE SCREENING YOUR PHONE CALLS BETTER.
I THOUGHT YOU WERE WORKING FOR PAIGE.
I QUIT THIS MORNING.
ANY PARTICULAR REASON?
I GOT TIRED OF THE CONSTANT LECTURES AND CORRECTIONS AND "DO IT MY WAY OR THE HIGHWAY" SPEECHES.
AMEND
I HAD NO IDEA SHE WAS SO BOSSY.
NO, NO, THAT WAS ME.
YOU HAVE AN INTERESTING VIEW OF LABOR RELATIONS.
HEY, I'M NOT GOING TO BE JUST ANYBODY'S SUBORDINATE.

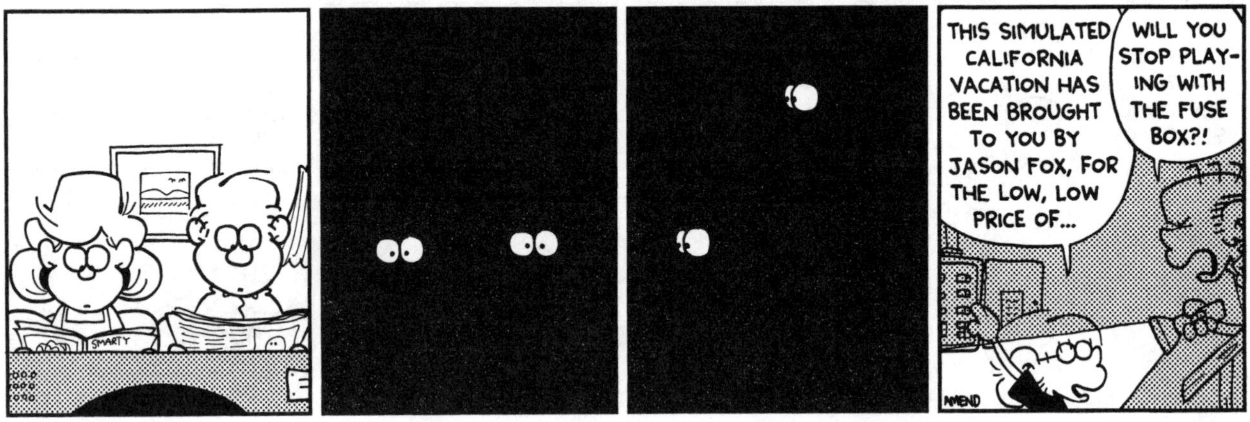
SMARTY
THIS SIMULATED CALIFORNIA VACATION HAS BEEN BROUGHT TO YOU BY JASON FOX, FOR THE LOW, LOW PRICE OF...
WILL YOU STOP PLAYING WITH THE FUSE BOX?!
AMEND

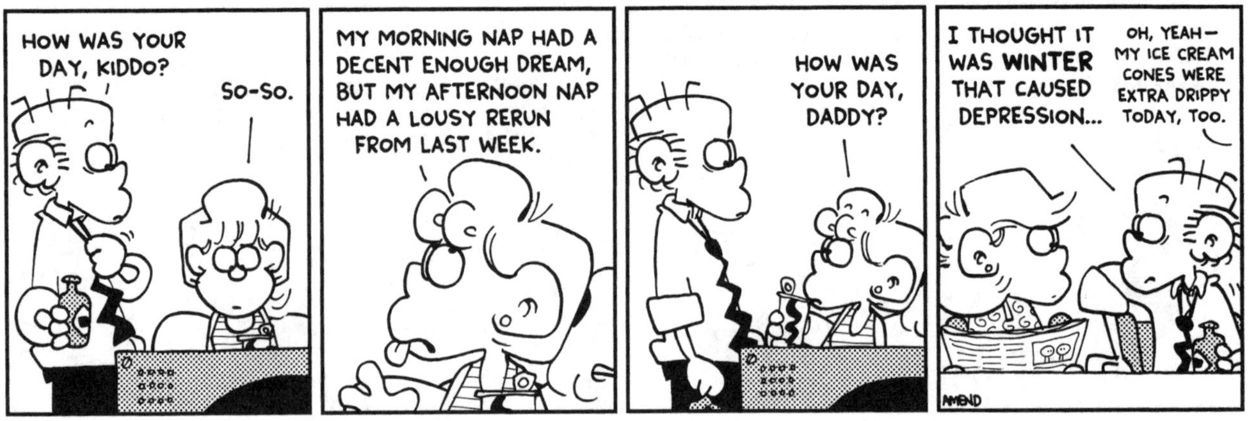
HOW WAS YOUR DAY, KIDDO?
SO-SO.
MY MORNING NAP HAD A DECENT ENOUGH DREAM, BUT MY AFTERNOON NAP HAD A LOUSY RERUN FROM LAST WEEK.
HOW WAS YOUR DAY, DADDY?
I THOUGHT IT WAS **WINTER** THAT CAUSED DEPRESSION...
OH, YEAH— MY ICE CREAM CONES WERE EXTRA DRIPPY TODAY, TOO.
AMEND

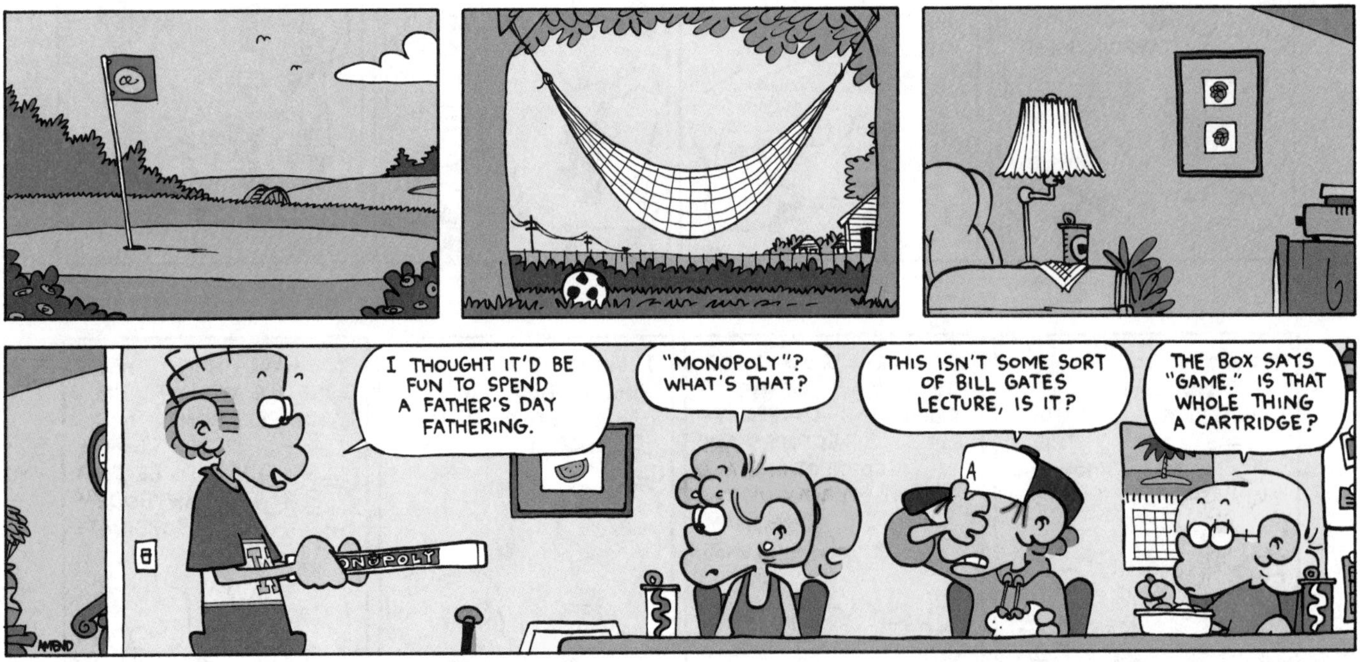
I THOUGHT IT'D BE FUN TO SPEND A FATHER'S DAY FATHERING.
MONOPOLY
"MONOPOLY"? WHAT'S THAT?
THIS ISN'T SOME SORT OF BILL GATES LECTURE, IS IT?
THE BOX SAYS "GAME." IS THAT WHOLE THING A CARTRIDGE?
AMEND

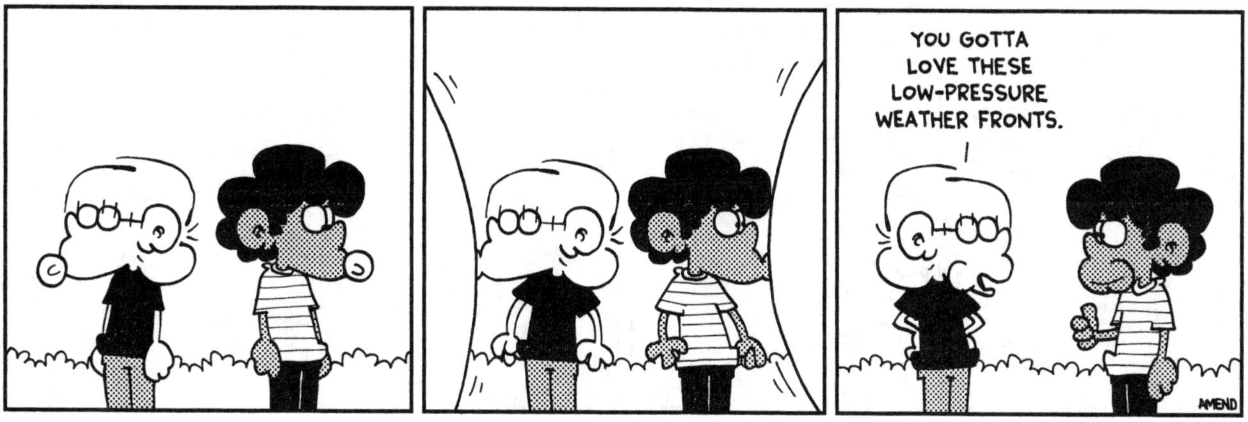
YOU GOTTA LOVE THESE LOW-PRESSURE WEATHER FRONTS.

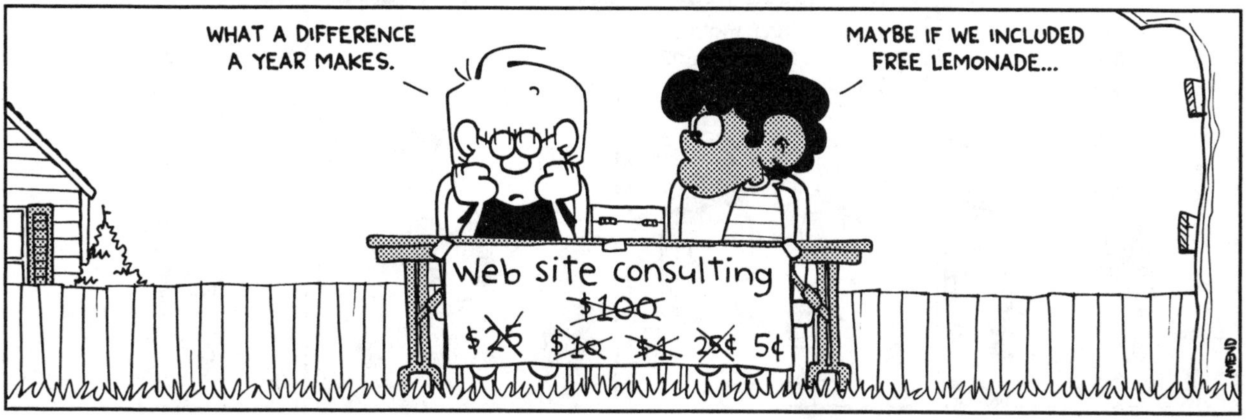
WHAT A DIFFERENCE A YEAR MAKES.
MAYBE IF WE INCLUDED FREE LEMONADE...
Web site consulting
$100
$25 $10 $1 25¢ 5¢

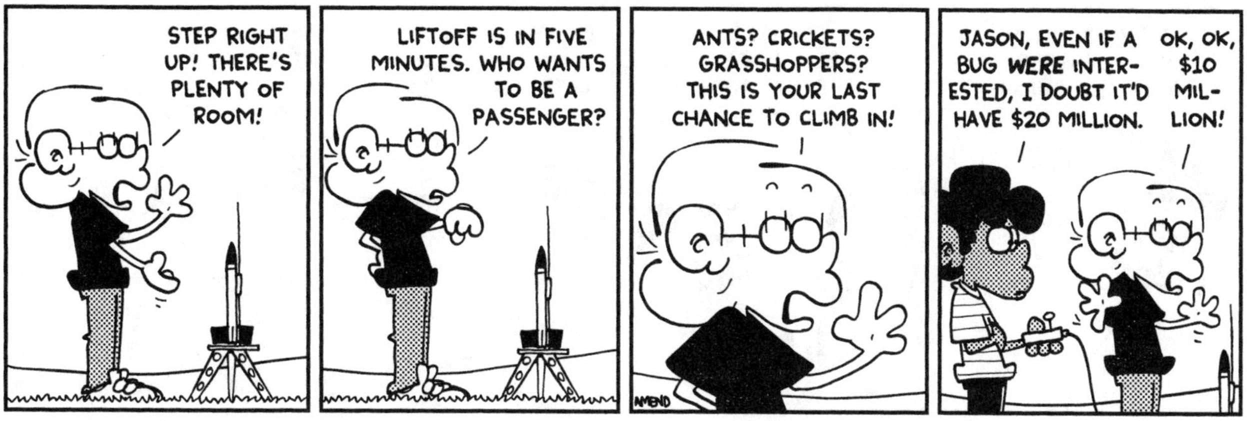
STEP RIGHT UP! THERE'S PLENTY OF ROOM!
LIFTOFF IS IN FIVE MINUTES. WHO WANTS TO BE A PASSENGER?
ANTS? CRICKETS? GRASSHOPPERS? THIS IS YOUR LAST CHANCE TO CLIMB IN!
JASON, EVEN IF A BUG WERE INTERESTED, I DOUBT IT'D HAVE $20 MILLION.
OK, OK, $10 MILLION!

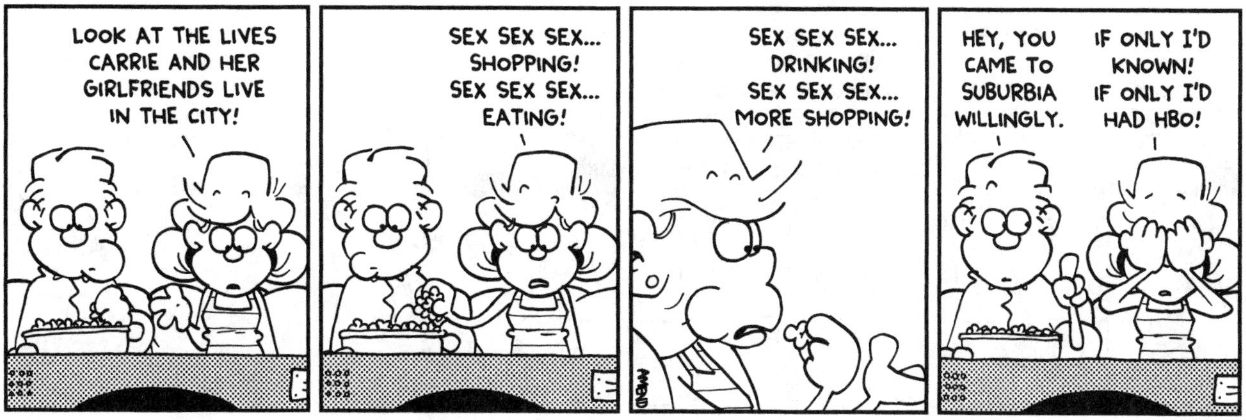
LOOK AT THE LIVES CARRIE AND HER GIRLFRIENDS LIVE IN THE CITY!
SEX SEX SEX... SHOPPING! SEX SEX SEX... EATING!
SEX SEX SEX... DRINKING! SEX SEX SEX... MORE SHOPPING!
HEY, YOU CAME TO SUBURBIA WILLINGLY.
IF ONLY I'D KNOWN! IF ONLY I'D HAD HBO!

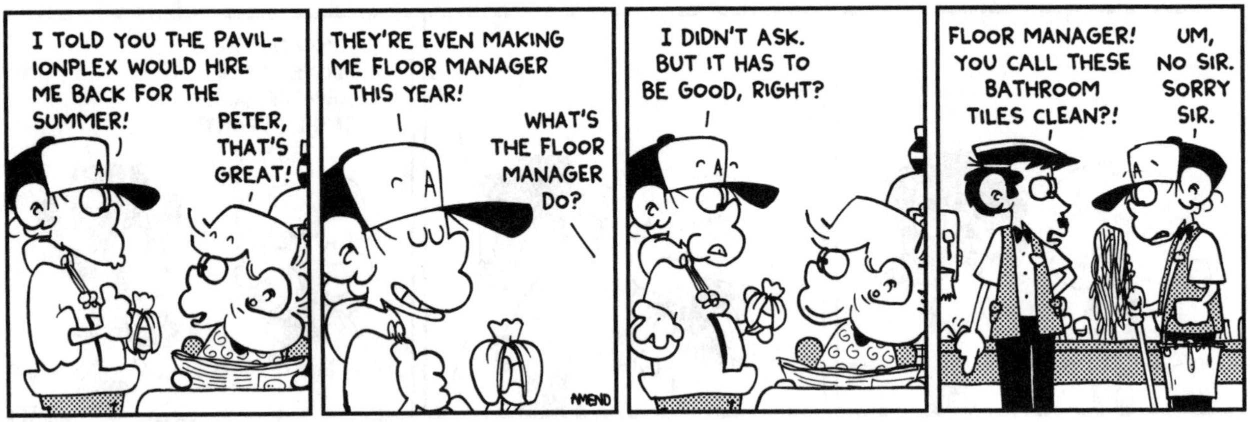
I TOLD YOU THE PAVILIONPLEX WOULD HIRE ME BACK FOR THE SUMMER!
PETER, THAT'S GREAT!
THEY'RE EVEN MAKING ME FLOOR MANAGER THIS YEAR!
WHAT'S THE FLOOR MANAGER DO?
I DIDN'T ASK. BUT IT HAS TO BE GOOD, RIGHT?
FLOOR MANAGER! YOU CALL THESE BATHROOM TILES CLEAN?!
UM, NO SIR. SORRY SIR.
AMEND

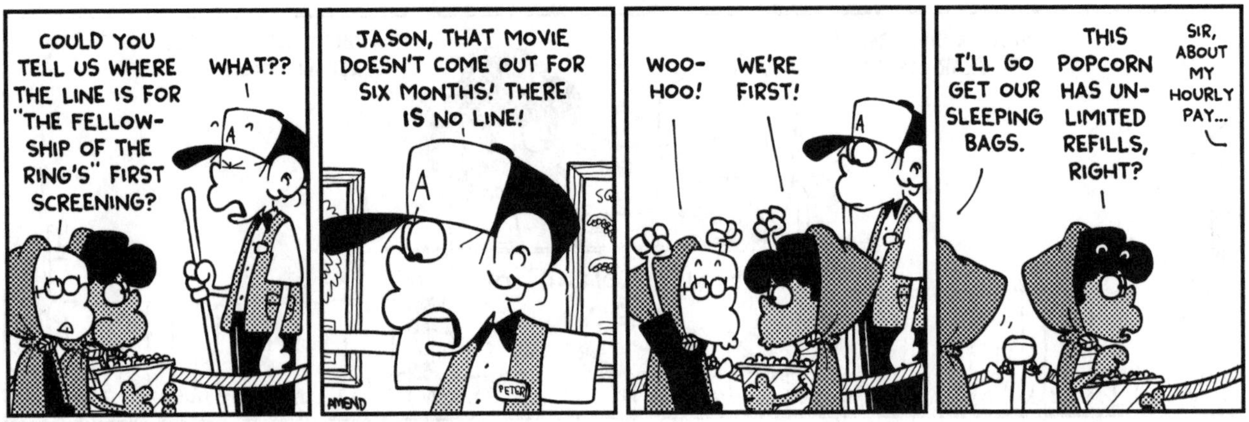
COULD YOU TELL US WHERE THE LINE IS FOR "THE FELLOWSHIP OF THE RING'S" FIRST SCREENING?
WHAT??
JASON, THAT MOVIE DOESN'T COME OUT FOR SIX MONTHS! THERE IS NO LINE!
PETER
AMEND
WOO-HOO!
WE'RE FIRST!
I'LL GO GET OUR SLEEPING BAGS.
THIS POPCORN HAS UNLIMITED REFILLS, RIGHT?
SIR, ABOUT MY HOURLY PAY...

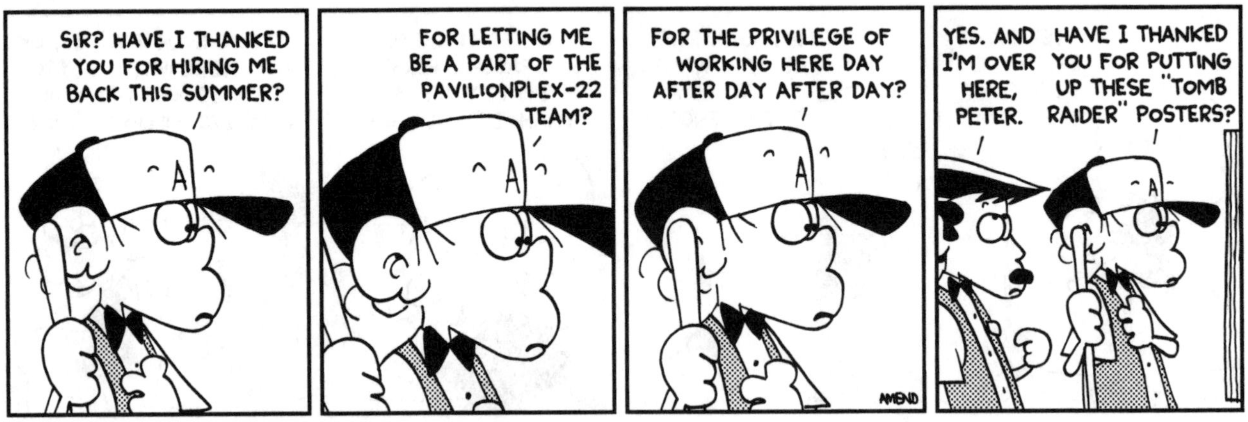
SIR? HAVE I THANKED YOU FOR HIRING ME BACK THIS SUMMER?
FOR LETTING ME BE A PART OF THE PAVILIONPLEX-22 TEAM?
FOR THE PRIVILEGE OF WORKING HERE DAY AFTER DAY AFTER DAY?
AMEND
YES. AND I'M OVER HERE, PETER.
HAVE I THANKED YOU FOR PUTTING UP THESE "TOMB RAIDER" POSTERS?

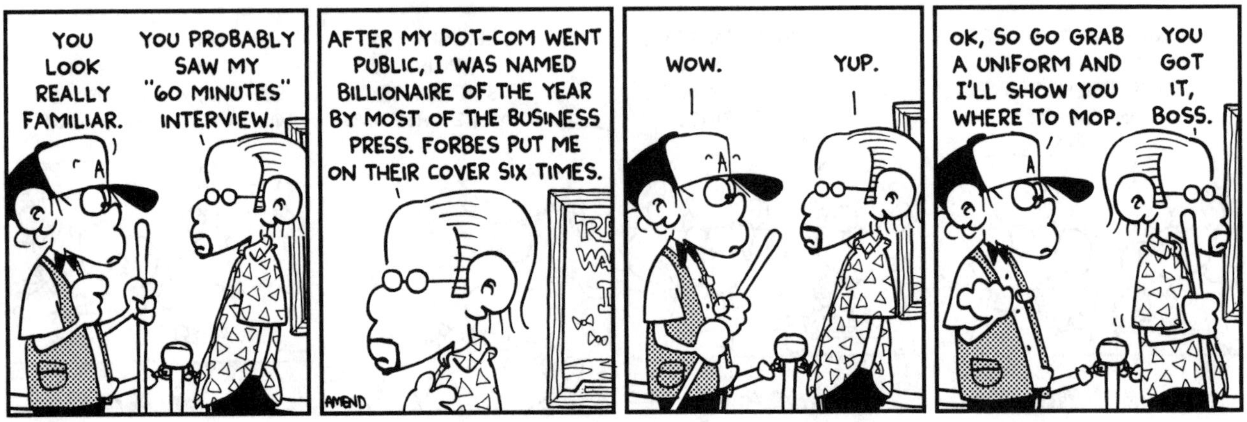
YOU LOOK REALLY FAMILIAR.
YOU PROBABLY SAW MY "60 MINUTES" INTERVIEW.
AFTER MY DOT-COM WENT PUBLIC, I WAS NAMED BILLIONAIRE OF THE YEAR BY MOST OF THE BUSINESS PRESS. FORBES PUT ME ON THEIR COVER SIX TIMES.
AMEND
WOW.
YUP.
OK, SO GO GRAB A UNIFORM AND I'LL SHOW YOU WHERE TO MOP.
YOU GOT IT, BOSS.

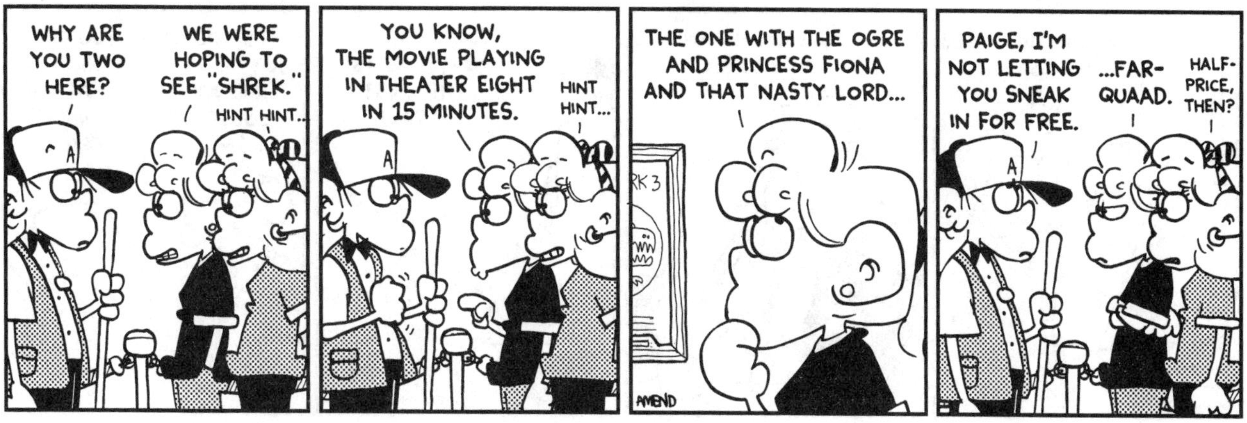
WHY ARE YOU TWO HERE?
WE WERE HOPING TO SEE "SHREK."
HINT HINT...
YOU KNOW, THE MOVIE PLAYING IN THEATER EIGHT IN 15 MINUTES.
HINT HINT...
THE ONE WITH THE OGRE AND PRINCESS FIONA AND THAT NASTY LORD...
PAIGE, I'M NOT LETTING YOU SNEAK IN FOR FREE.
...FAR-QUAAD.
HALF-PRICE, THEN?
AMEND

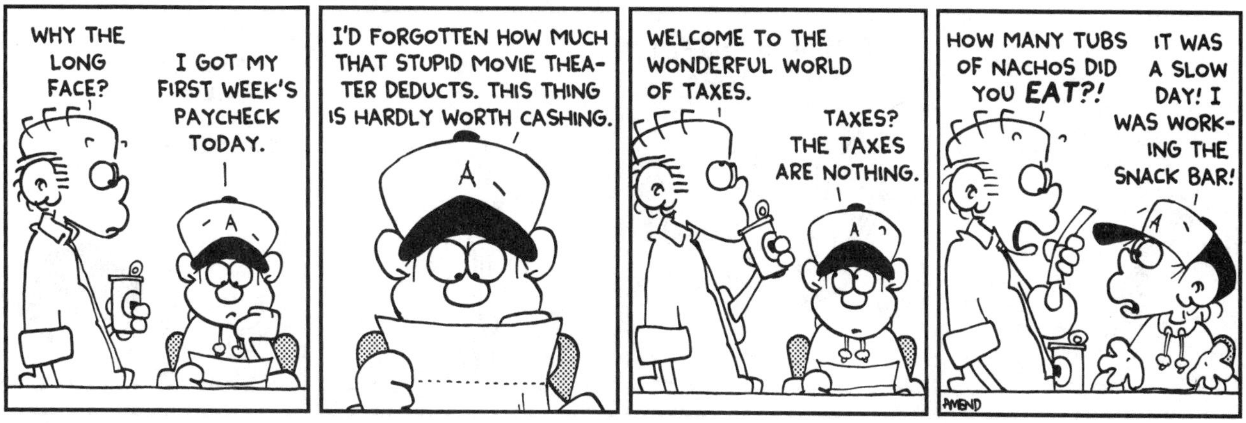
WHY THE LONG FACE?
I GOT MY FIRST WEEK'S PAYCHECK TODAY.
I'D FORGOTTEN HOW MUCH THAT STUPID MOVIE THEATER DEDUCTS. THIS THING IS HARDLY WORTH CASHING.
WELCOME TO THE WONDERFUL WORLD OF TAXES.
TAXES? THE TAXES ARE NOTHING.
HOW MANY TUBS OF NACHOS DID YOU EAT?!
IT WAS A SLOW DAY! I WAS WORKING THE SNACK BAR!
AMEND

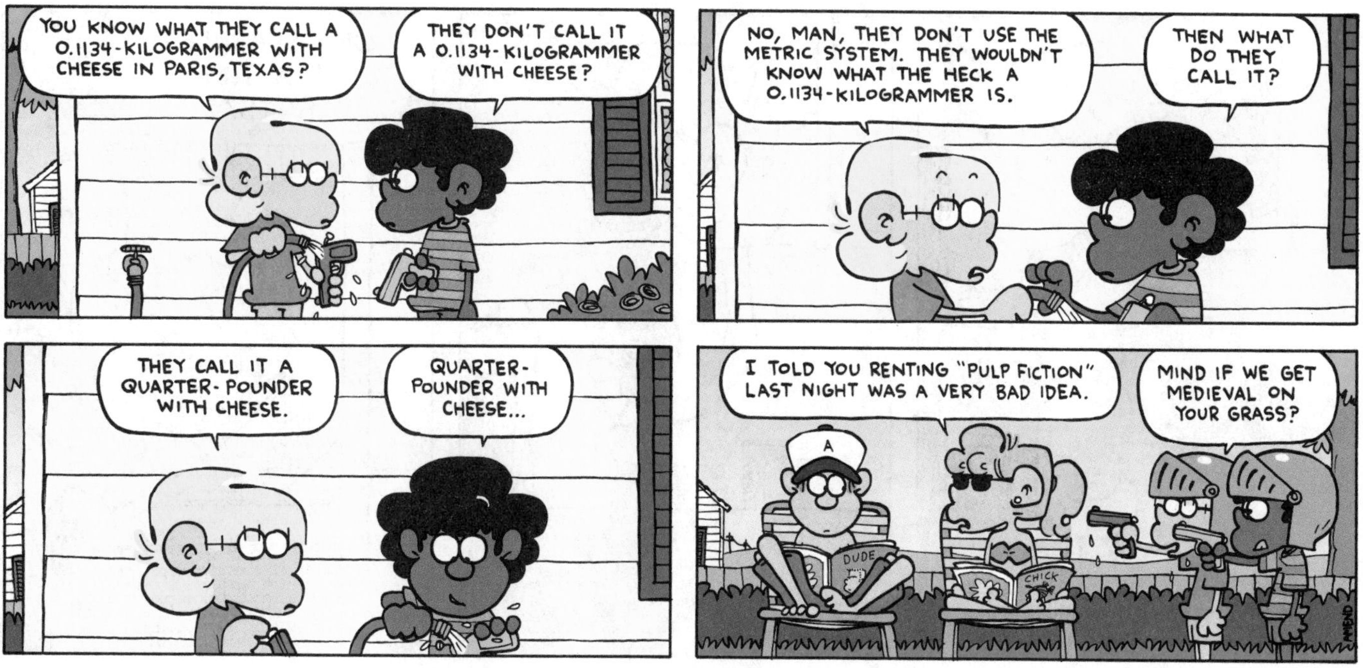
YOU KNOW WHAT THEY CALL A 0.1134-KILOGRAMMER WITH CHEESE IN PARIS, TEXAS?
THEY DON'T CALL IT A 0.1134-KILOGRAMMER WITH CHEESE?
NO, MAN, THEY DON'T USE THE METRIC SYSTEM. THEY WOULDN'T KNOW WHAT THE HECK A 0.1134-KILOGRAMMER IS.
THEN WHAT DO THEY CALL IT?
THEY CALL IT A QUARTER-POUNDER WITH CHEESE.
QUARTER-POUNDER WITH CHEESE...
I TOLD YOU RENTING "PULP FICTION" LAST NIGHT WAS A VERY BAD IDEA.
MIND IF WE GET MEDIEVAL ON YOUR GRASS?
DUDE
CHICK
AMEND

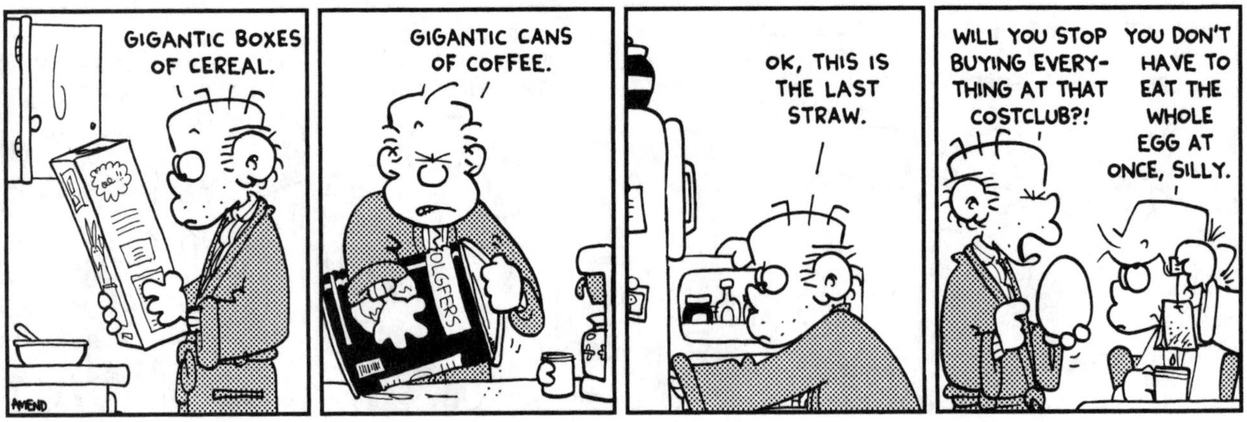
GIGANTIC BOXES OF CEREAL.
GIGANTIC CANS OF COFFEE.
OK, THIS IS THE LAST STRAW.
WILL YOU STOP BUYING EVERY-THING AT THAT COSTCLUB?!
YOU DON'T HAVE TO EAT THE WHOLE EGG AT ONCE, SILLY.
AMEND

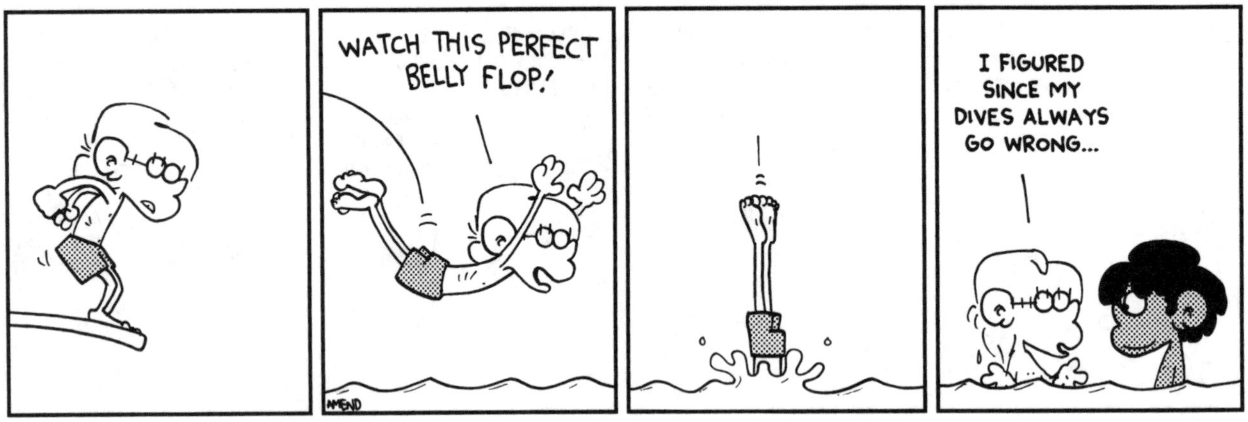
WATCH THIS PERFECT BELLY FLOP!
I FIGURED SINCE MY DIVES ALWAYS GO WRONG...
AMEND

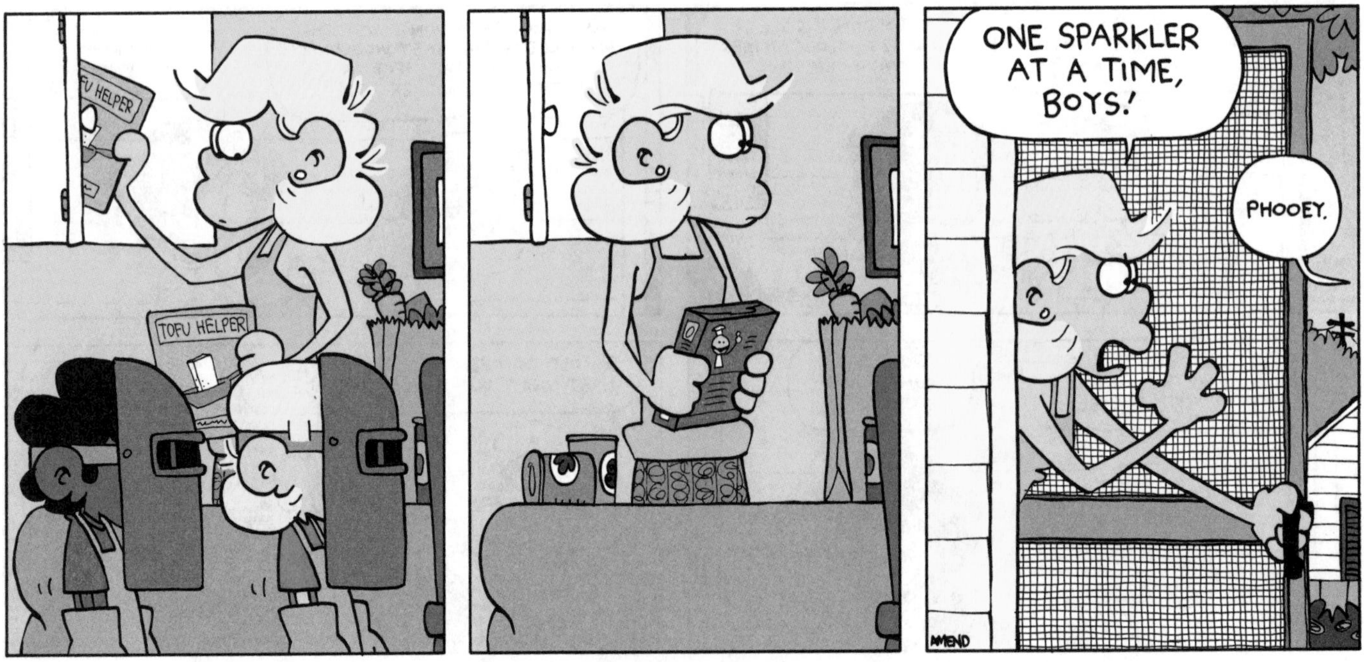
TOFU HELPER
TOFU HELPER
ONE SPARKLER AT A TIME, BOYS!
PHOOEY.
AMEND

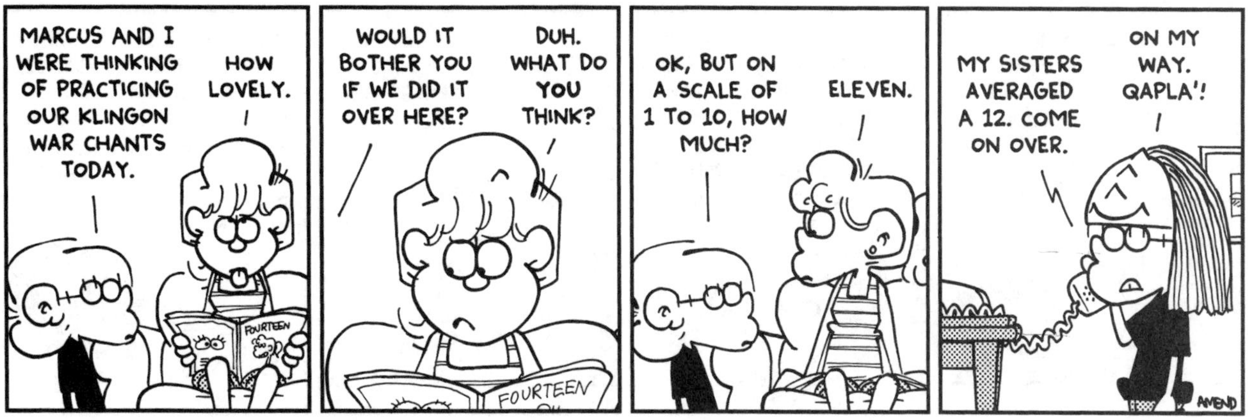
MARCUS AND I WERE THINKING OF PRACTICING OUR KLINGON WAR CHANTS TODAY.
HOW LOVELY.
WOULD IT BOTHER YOU IF WE DID IT OVER HERE?
DUH. WHAT DO YOU THINK?
OK, BUT ON A SCALE OF 1 TO 10, HOW MUCH?
ELEVEN.
MY SISTERS AVERAGED A 12. COME ON OVER.
ON MY WAY. QAPLA'!

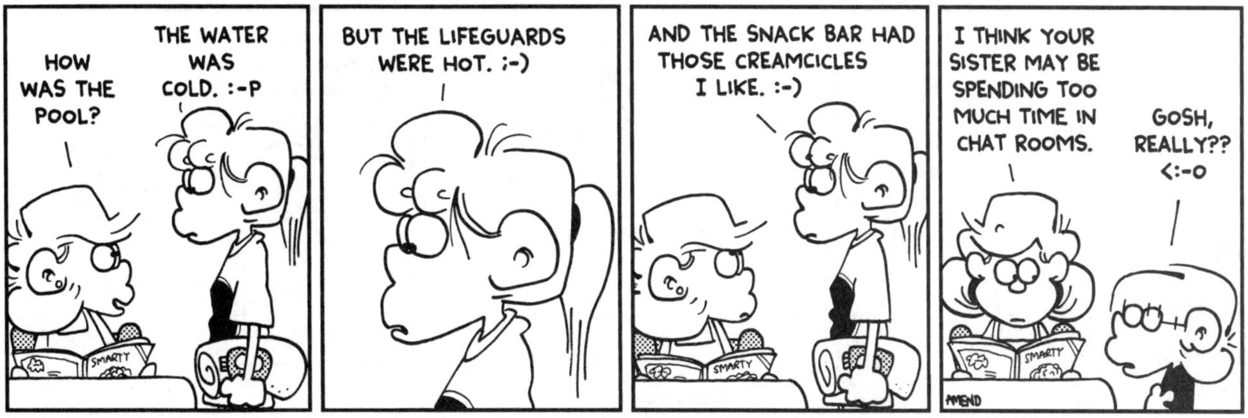
HOW WAS THE POOL?
THE WATER WAS COLD. :-P
BUT THE LIFEGUARDS WERE HOT. ;-)
AND THE SNACK BAR HAD THOSE CREAMCICLES I LIKE. :-)
I THINK YOUR SISTER MAY BE SPENDING TOO MUCH TIME IN CHAT ROOMS.
GOSH, REALLY?? <:-O

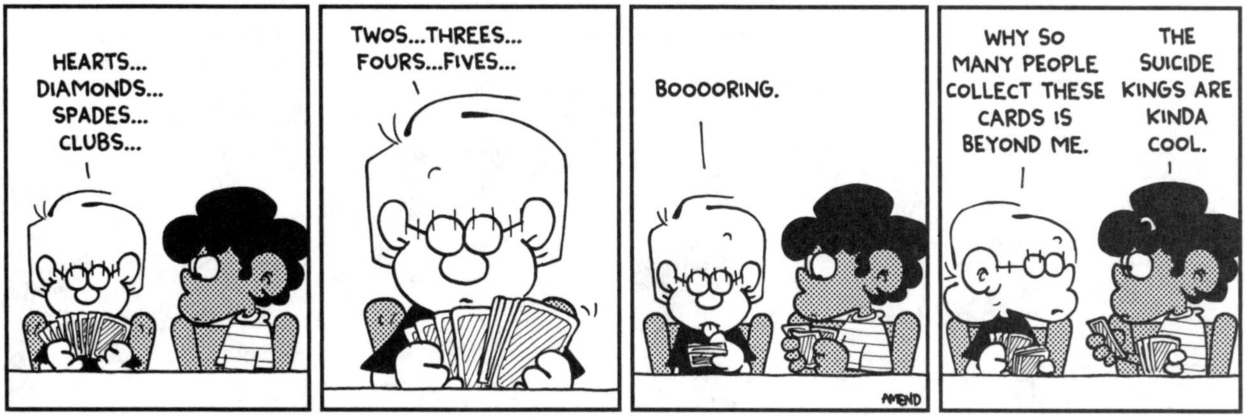
HEARTS... DIAMONDS... SPADES... CLUBS...
TWOS...THREES... FOURS...FIVES...
BOOOORING.
WHY SO MANY PEOPLE COLLECT THESE CARDS IS BEYOND ME.
THE SUICIDE KINGS ARE KINDA COOL.

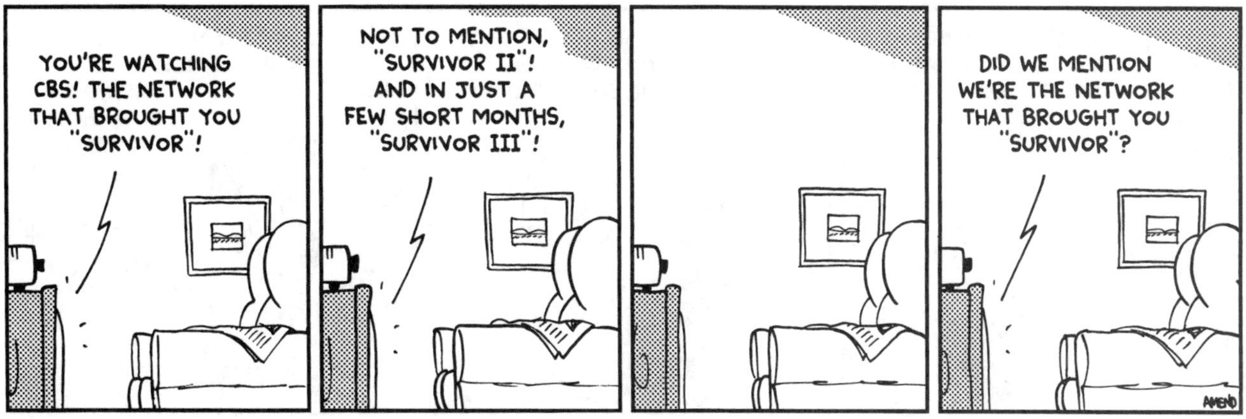
YOU'RE WATCHING CBS! THE NETWORK THAT BROUGHT YOU "SURVIVOR"!
NOT TO MENTION, "SURVIVOR II"! AND IN JUST A FEW SHORT MONTHS, "SURVIVOR III"!
DID WE MENTION WE'RE THE NETWORK THAT BROUGHT YOU "SURVIVOR"?

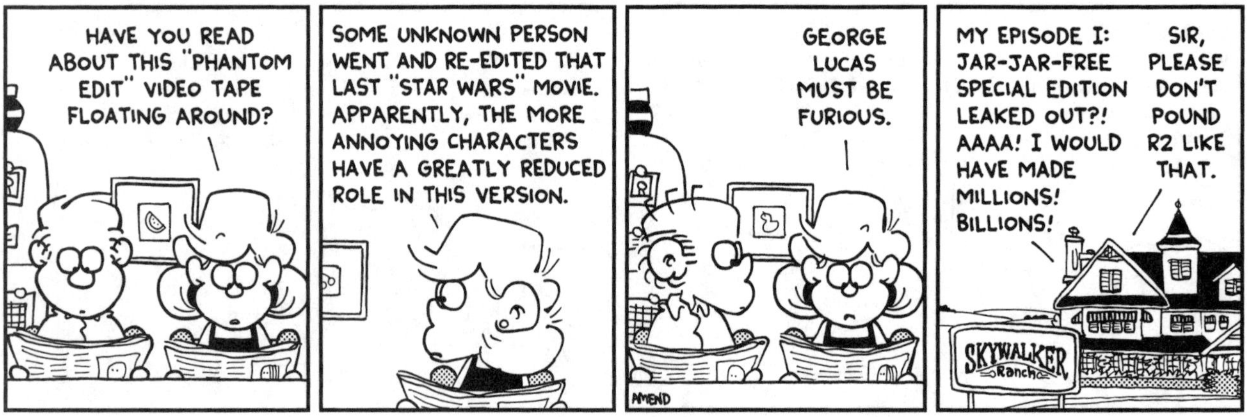
HAVE YOU READ ABOUT THIS "PHANTOM EDIT" VIDEO TAPE FLOATING AROUND?
SOME UNKNOWN PERSON WENT AND RE-EDITED THAT LAST "STAR WARS" MOVIE. APPARENTLY, THE MORE ANNOYING CHARACTERS HAVE A GREATLY REDUCED ROLE IN THIS VERSION.
GEORGE LUCAS MUST BE FURIOUS.
AMEND
MY EPISODE I: JAR-JAR-FREE SPECIAL EDITION LEAKED OUT?! AAAA! I WOULD HAVE MADE MILLIONS! BILLIONS!
SIR, PLEASE DON'T POUND R2 LIKE THAT.
SKYWALKER Ranch

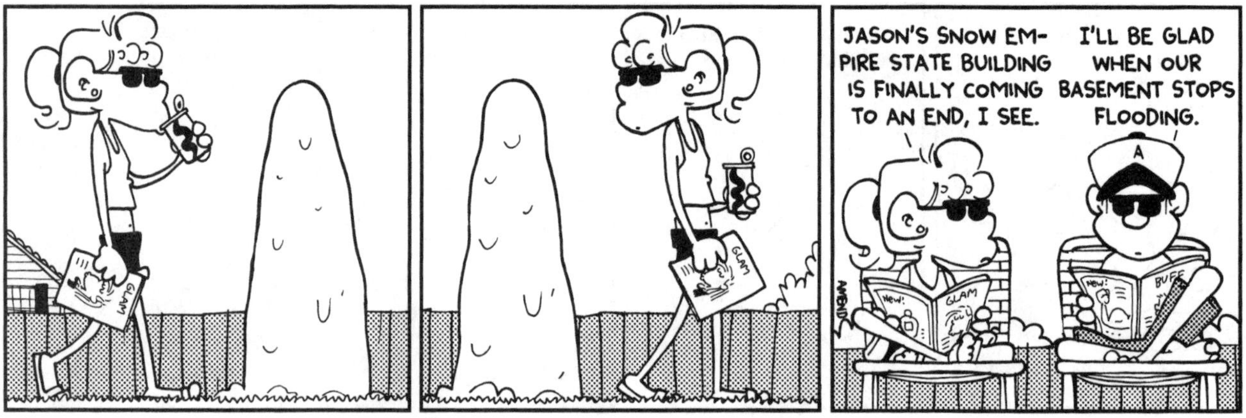
GLAM
GLAM
JASON'S SNOW EMPIRE STATE BUILDING IS FINALLY COMING TO AN END, I SEE.
I'LL BE GLAD WHEN OUR BASEMENT STOPS FLOODING.
AMEND
NEW!
GLAM
NEW!
BUFF

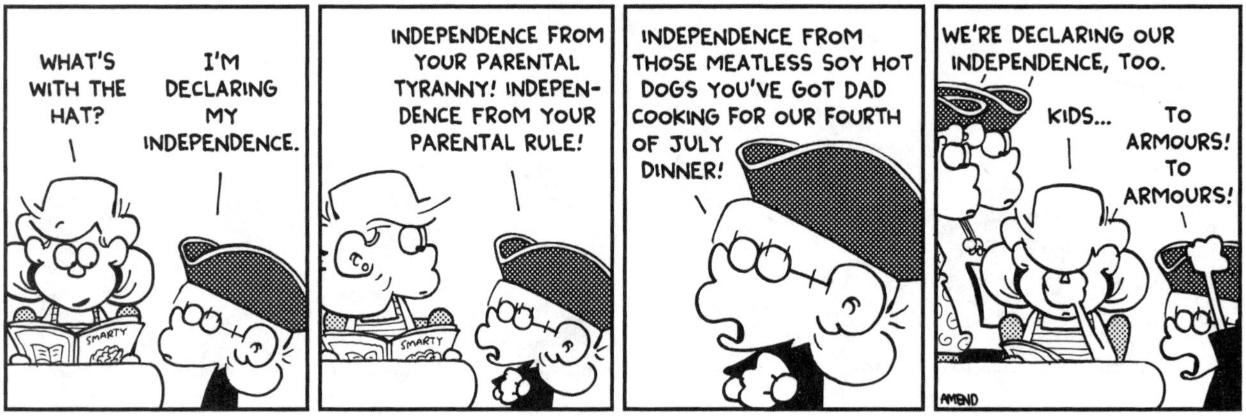
WHAT'S WITH THE HAT?
I'M DECLARING MY INDEPENDENCE.
SMARTY
INDEPENDENCE FROM YOUR PARENTAL TYRANNY! INDEPENDENCE FROM YOUR PARENTAL RULE!
SMARTY
INDEPENDENCE FROM THOSE MEATLESS SOY HOT DOGS YOU'VE GOT DAD COOKING FOR OUR FOURTH OF JULY DINNER!
WE'RE DECLARING OUR INDEPENDENCE, TOO.
KIDS...
TO ARMOURS! TO ARMOURS!
AMEND

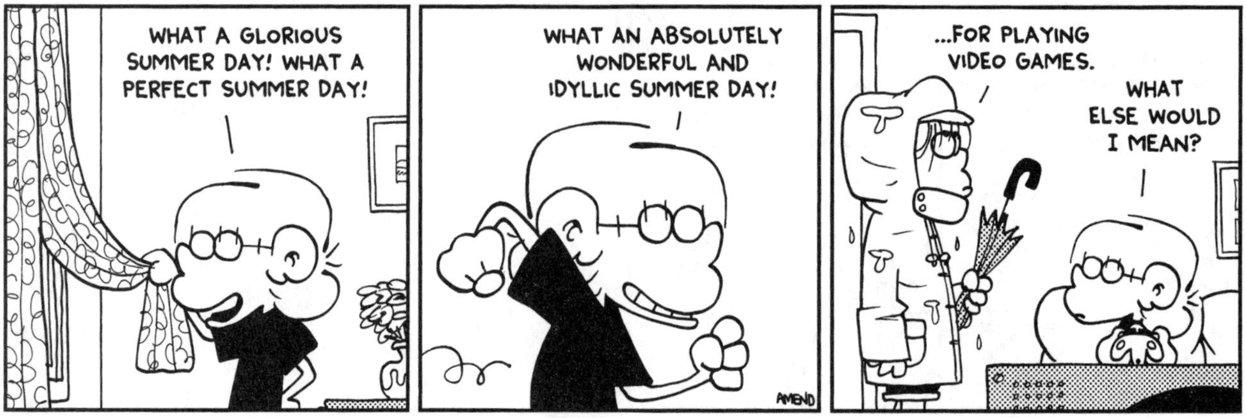
WHAT A GLORIOUS SUMMER DAY! WHAT A PERFECT SUMMER DAY!
WHAT AN ABSOLUTELY WONDERFUL AND IDYLLIC SUMMER DAY!
AMEND
...FOR PLAYING VIDEO GAMES.
WHAT ELSE WOULD I MEAN?

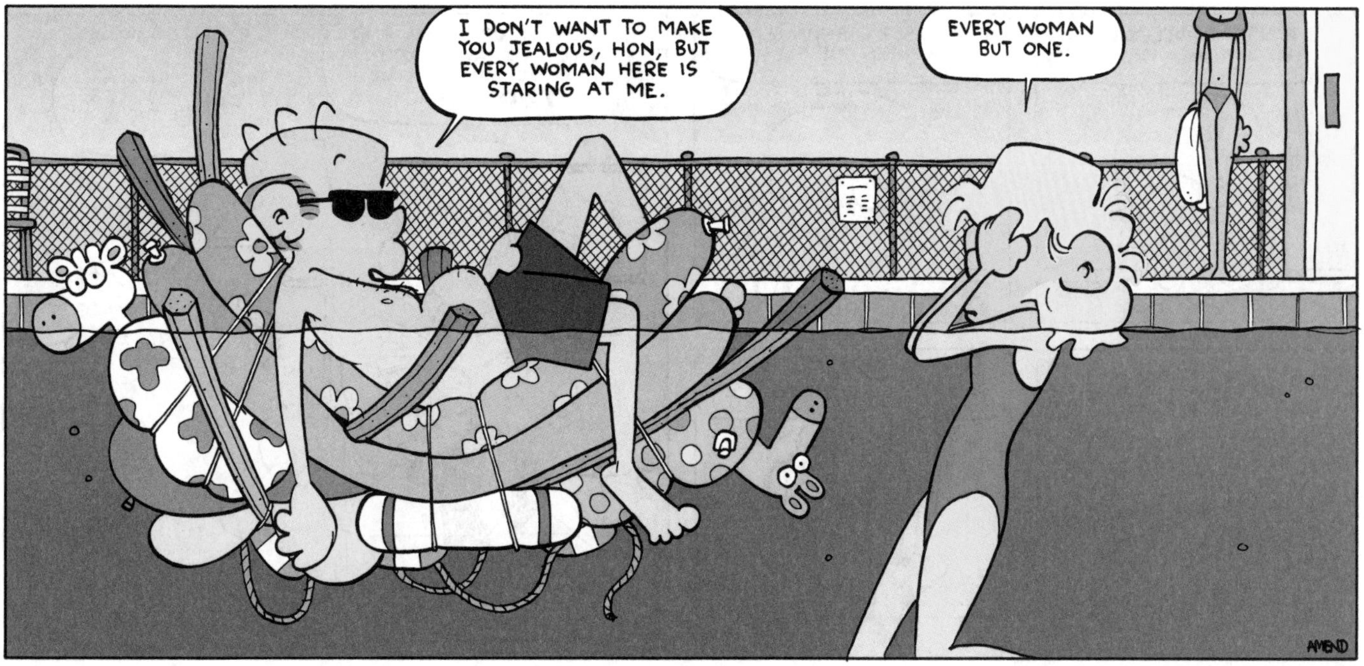
I DON'T WANT TO MAKE YOU JEALOUS, HON, BUT EVERY WOMAN HERE IS STARING AT ME.
EVERY WOMAN BUT ONE.
AMEND

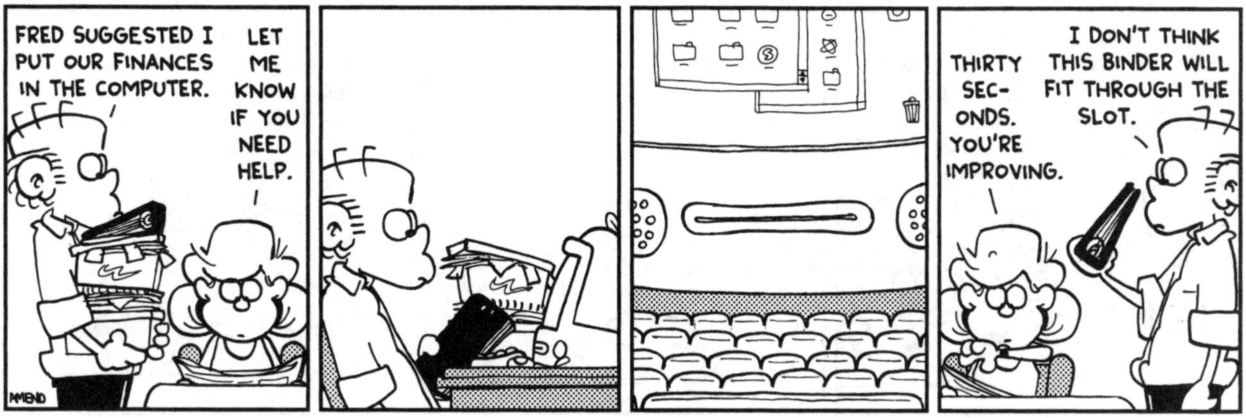
FRED SUGGESTED I PUT OUR FINANCES IN THE COMPUTER.
LET ME KNOW IF YOU NEED HELP.
AMEND
THIRTY SEC-ONDS. YOU'RE IMPROVING.
I DON'T THINK THIS BINDER WILL FIT THROUGH THE SLOT.

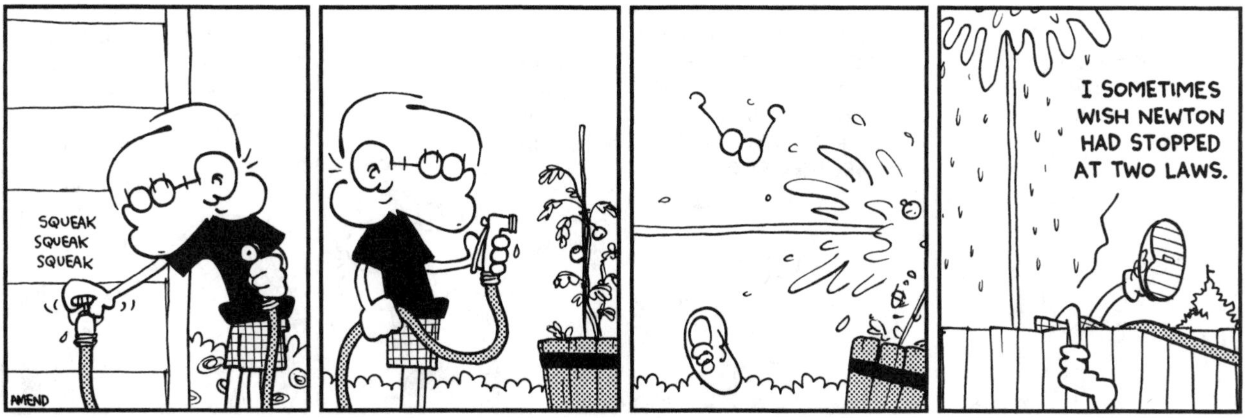
SQUEAK SQUEAK SQUEAK
AMEND
I SOMETIMES WISH NEWTON HAD STOPPED AT TWO LAWS.

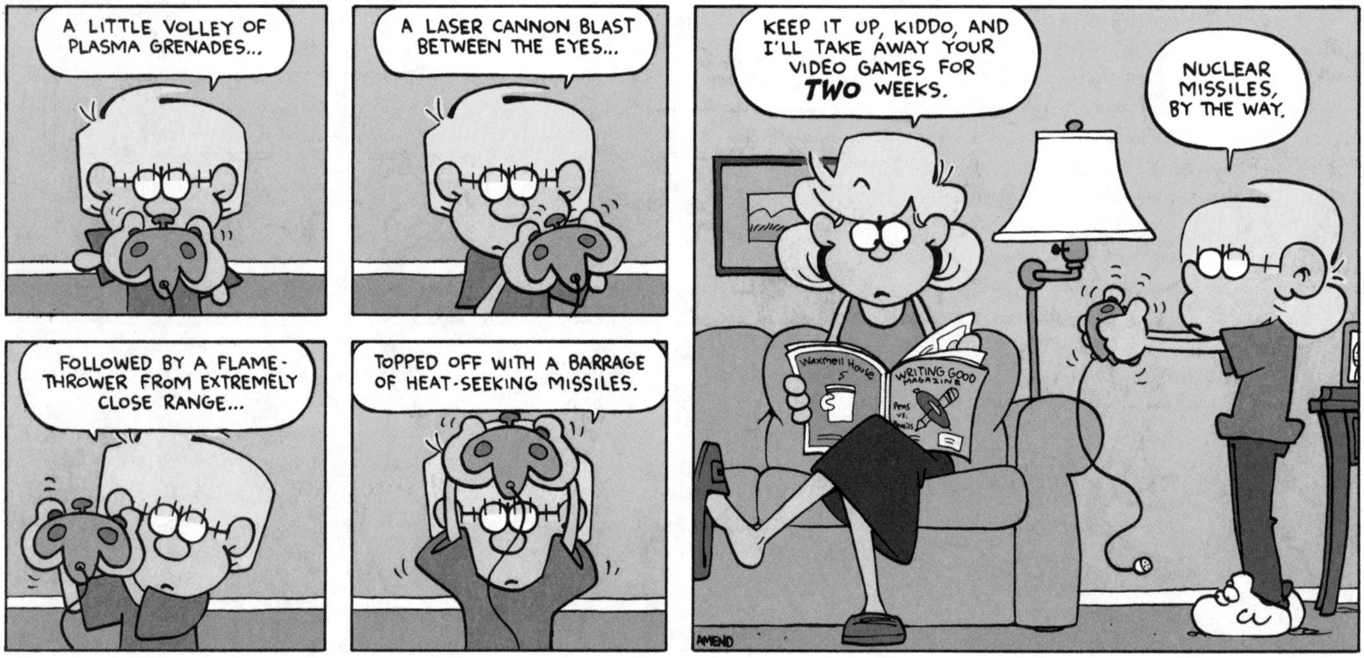
A LITTLE VOLLEY OF PLASMA GRENADES...
A LASER CANNON BLAST BETWEEN THE EYES...
FOLLOWED BY A FLAME-THROWER FROM EXTREMELY CLOSE RANGE...
TOPPED OFF WITH A BARRAGE OF HEAT-SEEKING MISSILES.
KEEP IT UP, KIDDO, AND I'LL TAKE AWAY YOUR VIDEO GAMES FOR **TWO** WEEKS.
NUCLEAR MISSILES, BY THE WAY.

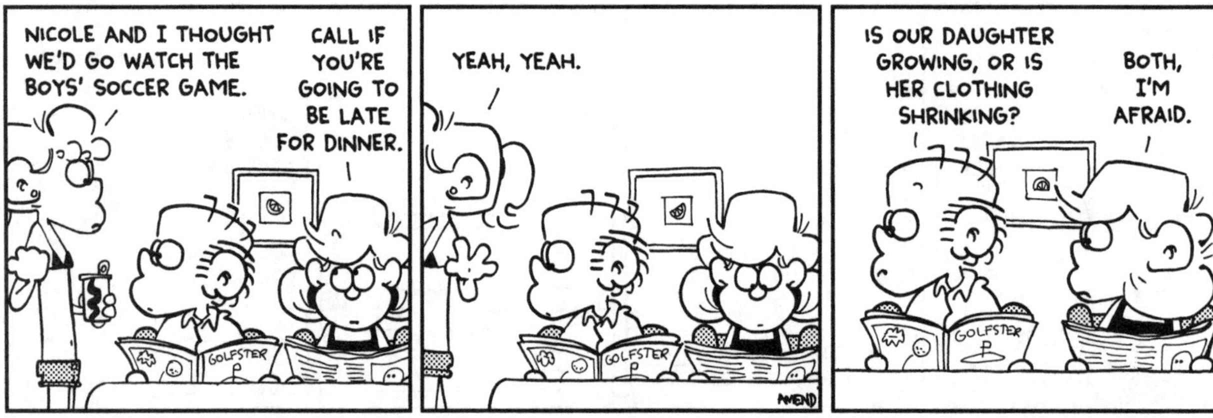
NICOLE AND I THOUGHT WE'D GO WATCH THE BOYS' SOCCER GAME.
CALL IF YOU'RE GOING TO BE LATE FOR DINNER.
YEAH, YEAH.
IS OUR DAUGHTER GROWING, OR IS HER CLOTHING SHRINKING?
BOTH, I'M AFRAID.

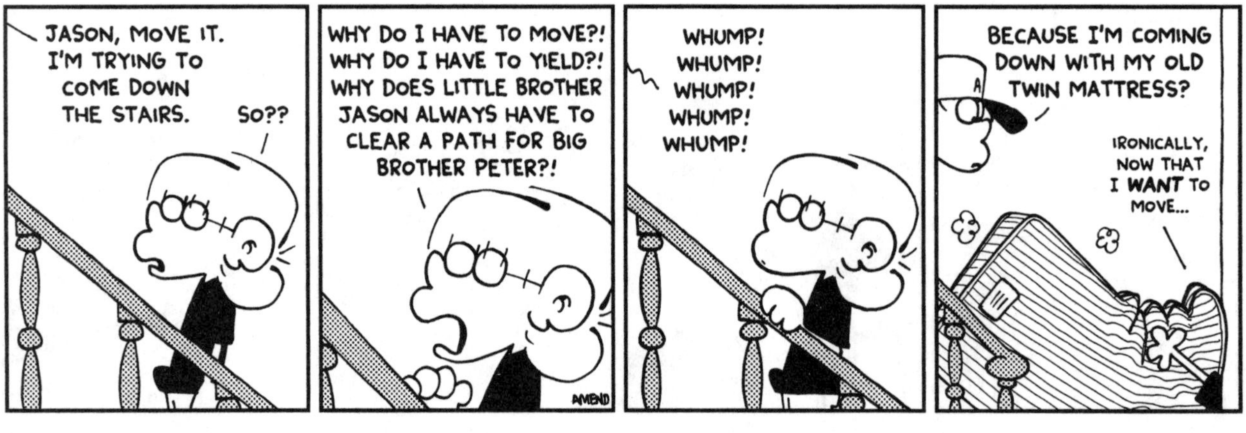
JASON, MOVE IT. I'M TRYING TO COME DOWN THE STAIRS.
SO??
WHY DO I HAVE TO MOVE?! WHY DO I HAVE TO YIELD?! WHY DOES LITTLE BROTHER JASON ALWAYS HAVE TO CLEAR A PATH FOR BIG BROTHER PETER?!
WHUMP! WHUMP! WHUMP! WHUMP! WHUMP!
BECAUSE I'M COMING DOWN WITH MY OLD TWIN MATTRESS?
IRONICALLY, NOW THAT I **WANT** TO MOVE...

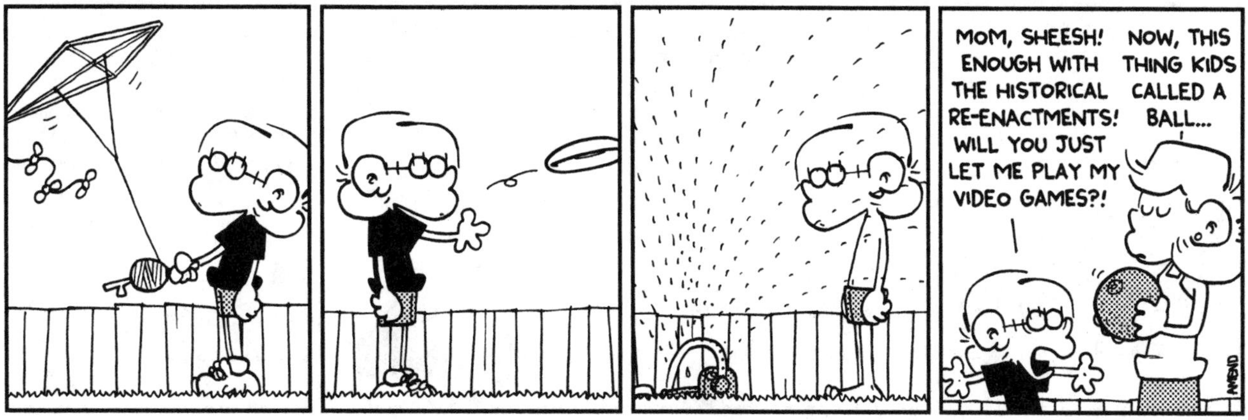
MOM, SHEESH! ENOUGH WITH THE HISTORICAL RE-ENACTMENTS! WILL YOU JUST LET ME PLAY MY VIDEO GAMES?!
NOW, THIS THING KIDS CALLED A BALL...

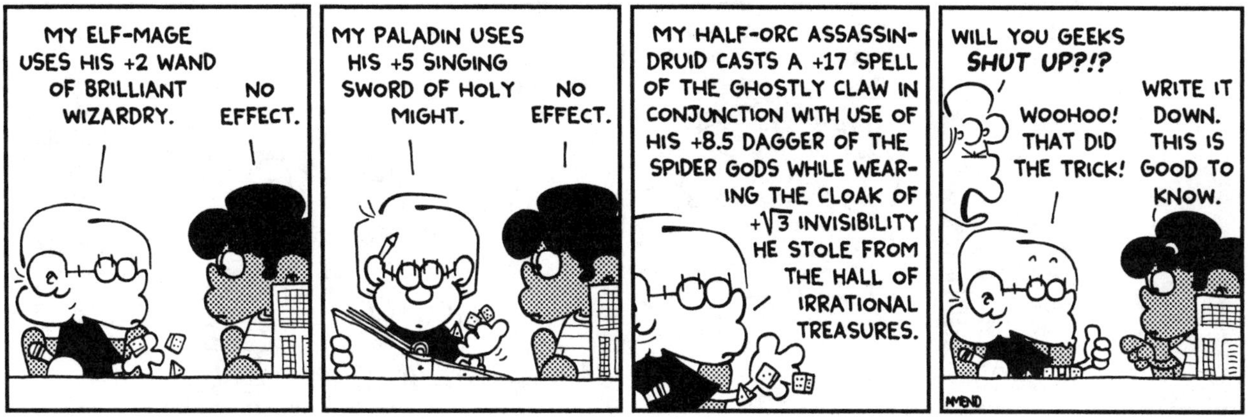
MY ELF-MAGE USES HIS +2 WAND OF BRILLIANT WIZARDRY.
NO EFFECT.
MY PALADIN USES HIS +5 SINGING SWORD OF HOLY MIGHT.
NO EFFECT.
MY HALF-ORC ASSASSIN-DRUID CASTS A +17 SPELL OF THE GHOSTLY CLAW IN CONJUNCTION WITH USE OF HIS +8.5 DAGGER OF THE SPIDER GODS WHILE WEARING THE CLOAK OF $+\sqrt{3}$ INVISIBILITY HE STOLE FROM THE HALL OF IRRATIONAL TREASURES.
WILL YOU GEEKS *SHUT UP?!?*
WOOHOO! THAT DID THE TRICK!
WRITE IT DOWN. THIS IS GOOD TO KNOW.

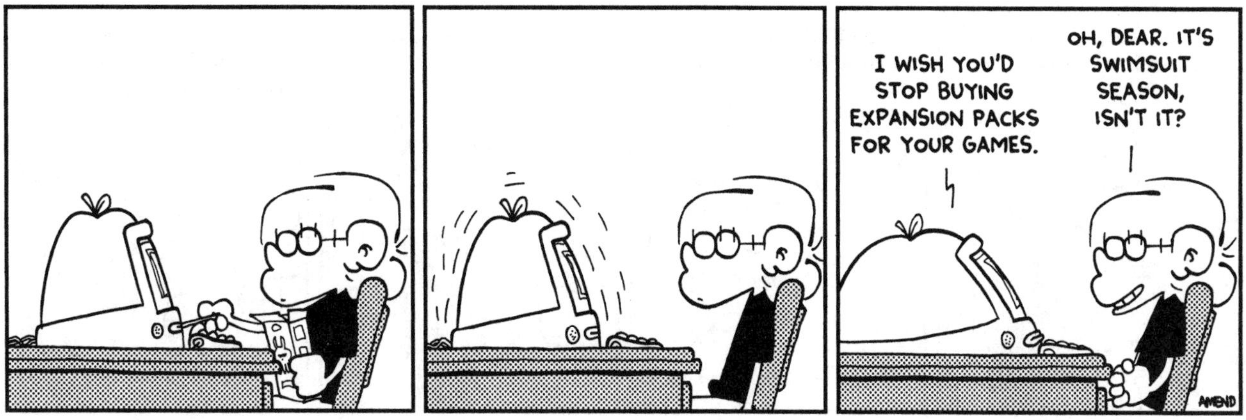
I WISH YOU'D STOP BUYING EXPANSION PACKS FOR YOUR GAMES.
OH, DEAR. IT'S SWIMSUIT SEASON, ISN'T IT?

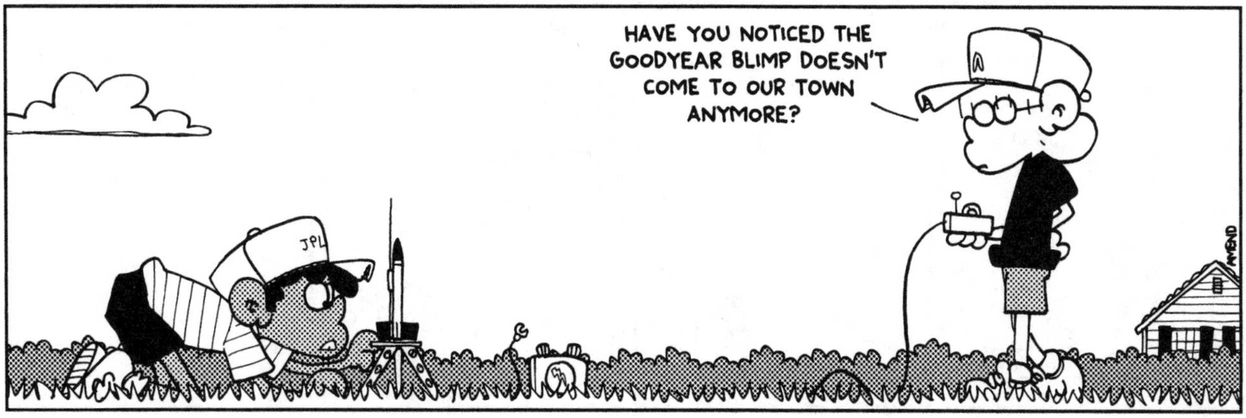
HAVE YOU NOTICED THE GOODYEAR BLIMP DOESN'T COME TO OUR TOWN ANYMORE?
JPL

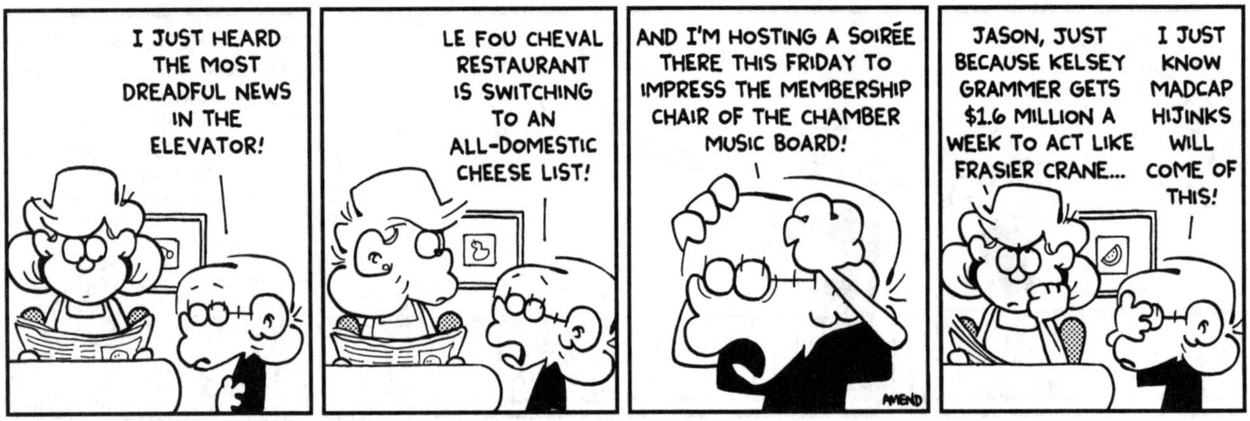
I JUST HEARD THE MOST DREADFUL NEWS IN THE ELEVATOR!
LE FOU CHEVAL RESTAURANT IS SWITCHING TO AN ALL-DOMESTIC CHEESE LIST!
AND I'M HOSTING A SOIRÉE THERE THIS FRIDAY TO IMPRESS THE MEMBERSHIP CHAIR OF THE CHAMBER MUSIC BOARD!
AMEND
JASON, JUST BECAUSE KELSEY GRAMMER GETS $1.6 MILLION A WEEK TO ACT LIKE FRASIER CRANE...
I JUST KNOW MADCAP HIJINKS WILL COME OF THIS!

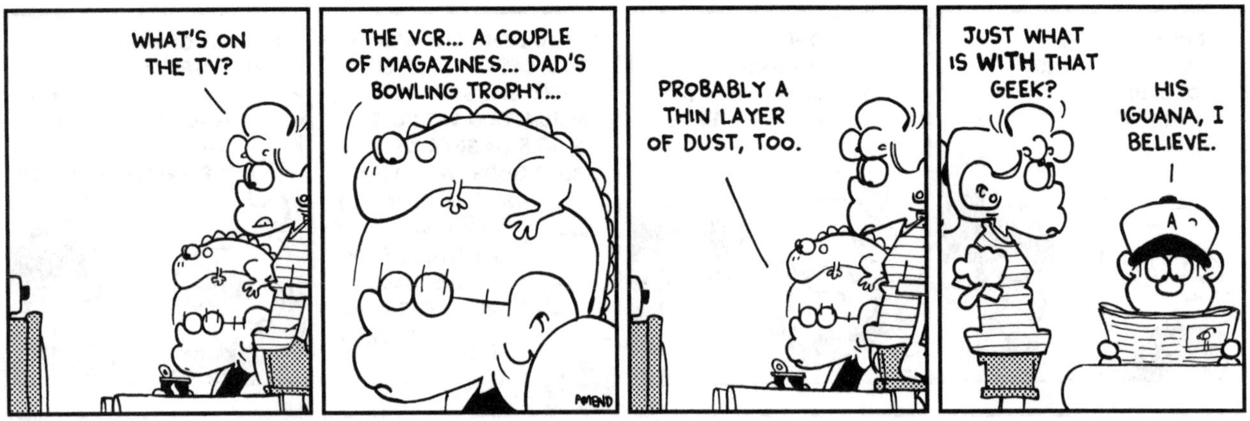
WHAT'S ON THE TV?
THE VCR... A COUPLE OF MAGAZINES... DAD'S BOWLING TROPHY...
AMEND
PROBABLY A THIN LAYER OF DUST, TOO.
JUST WHAT IS WITH THAT GEEK?
HIS IGUANA, I BELIEVE.

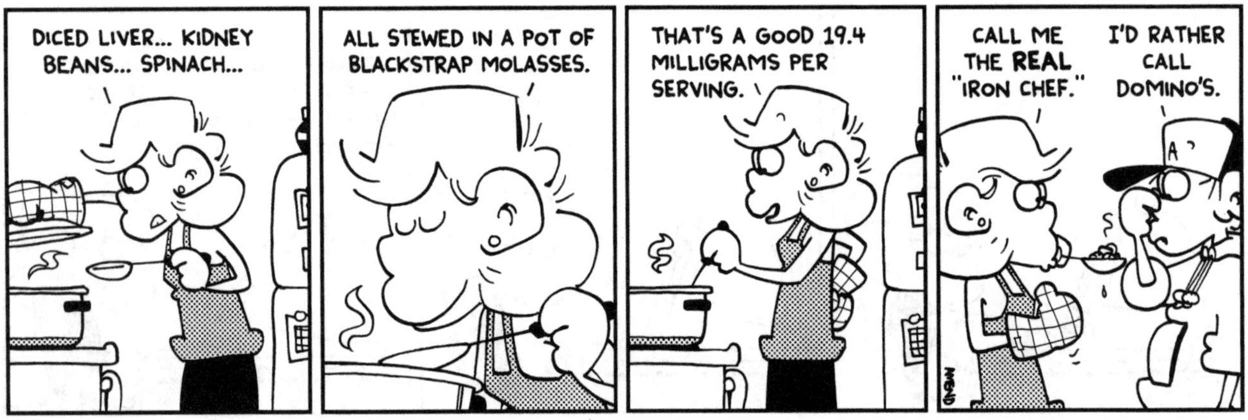
DICED LIVER... KIDNEY BEANS... SPINACH...
ALL STEWED IN A POT OF BLACKSTRAP MOLASSES.
THAT'S A GOOD 19.4 MILLIGRAMS PER SERVING.
CALL ME THE REAL "IRON CHEF."
I'D RATHER CALL DOMINO'S.
AMEND

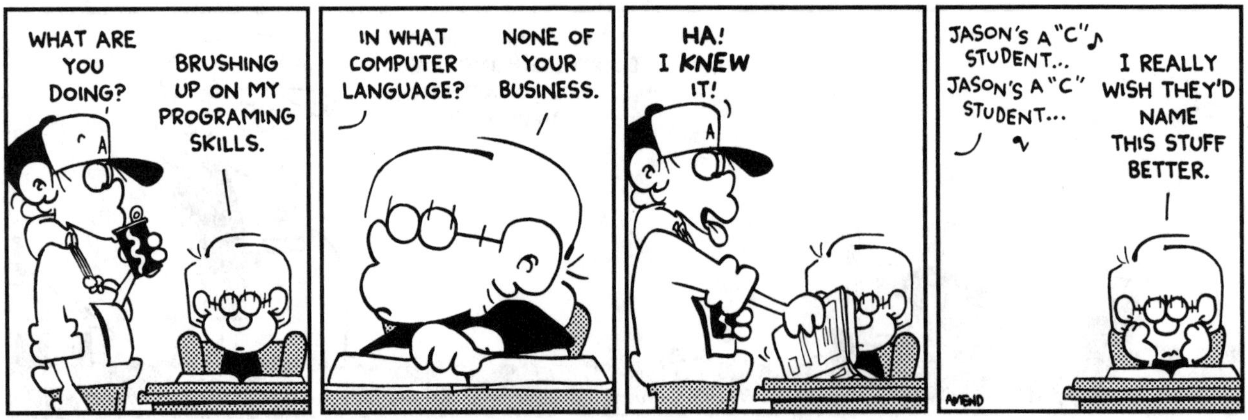
WHAT ARE YOU DOING?
BRUSHING UP ON MY PROGRAMING SKILLS.
IN WHAT COMPUTER LANGUAGE?
NONE OF YOUR BUSINESS.
HA! I KNEW IT!
JASON'S A "C" STUDENT... JASON'S A "C" STUDENT...
I REALLY WISH THEY'D NAME THIS STUFF BETTER.
AMEND

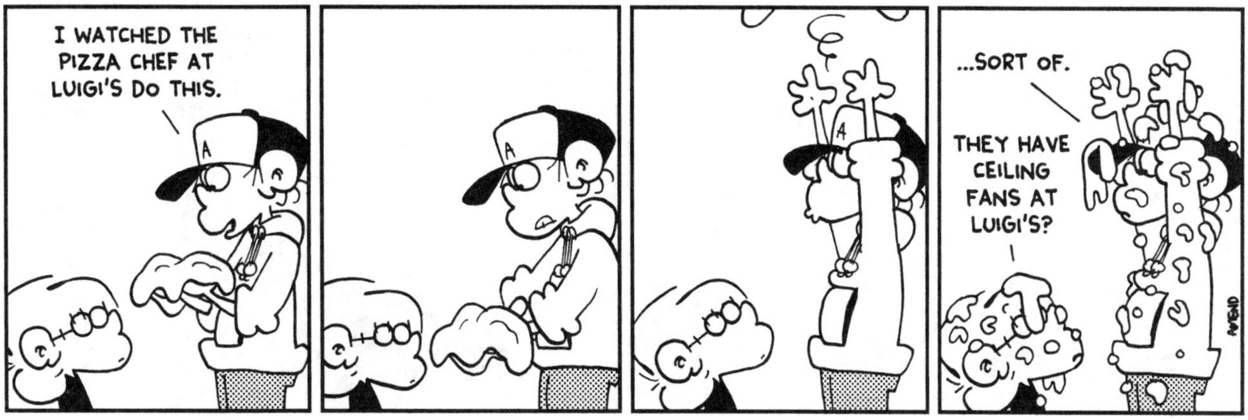
I WATCHED THE PIZZA CHEF AT LUIGI'S DO THIS.
...SORT OF.
THEY HAVE CEILING FANS AT LUIGI'S?
AMEND

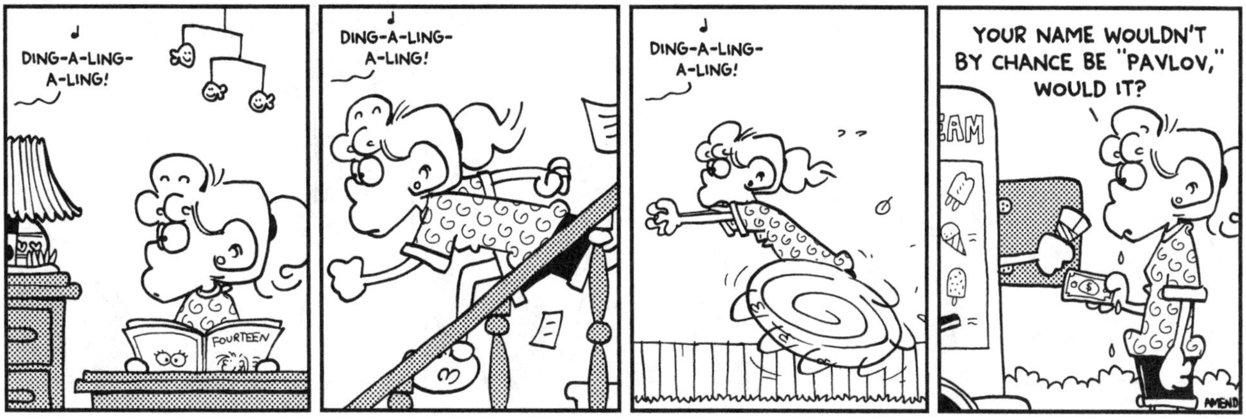
DING-A-LING-A-LING!
FOURTEEN
DING-A-LING-A-LING!
DING-A-LING-A-LING!
YOUR NAME WOULDN'T BY CHANCE BE "PAVLOV," WOULD IT?
AMEND

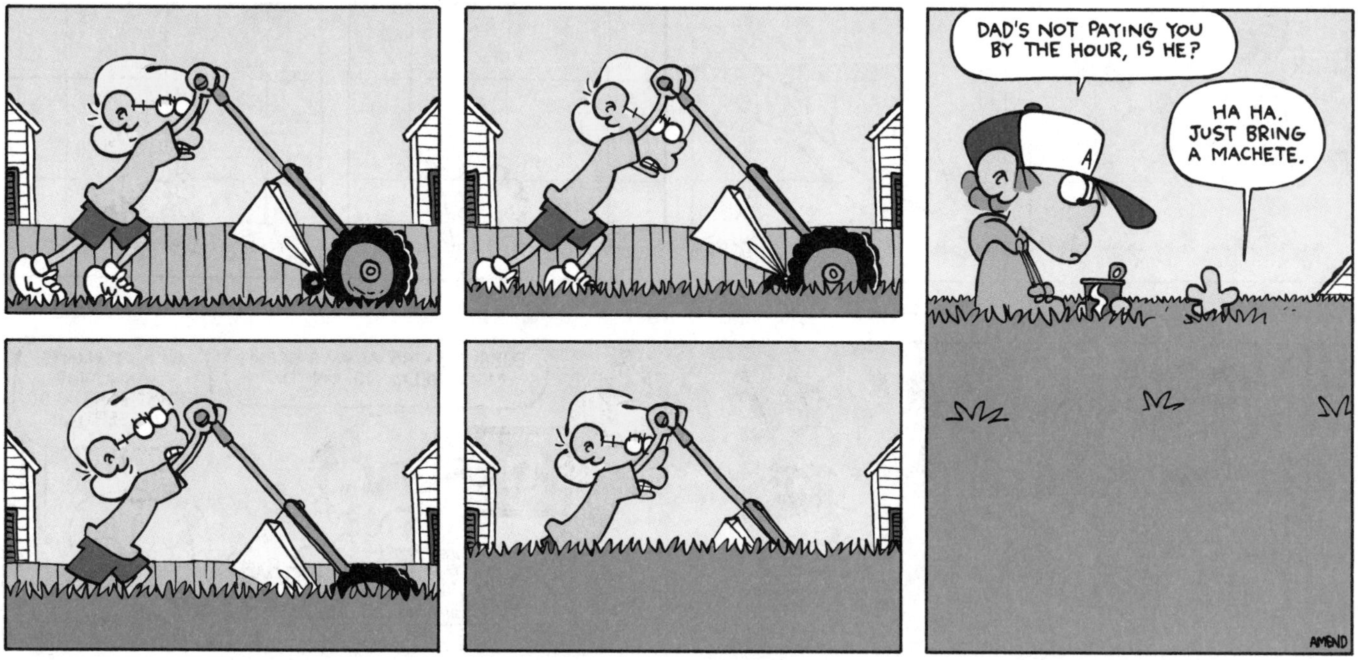
DAD'S NOT PAYING YOU BY THE HOUR, IS HE?
HA HA. JUST BRING A MACHETE.
AMEND

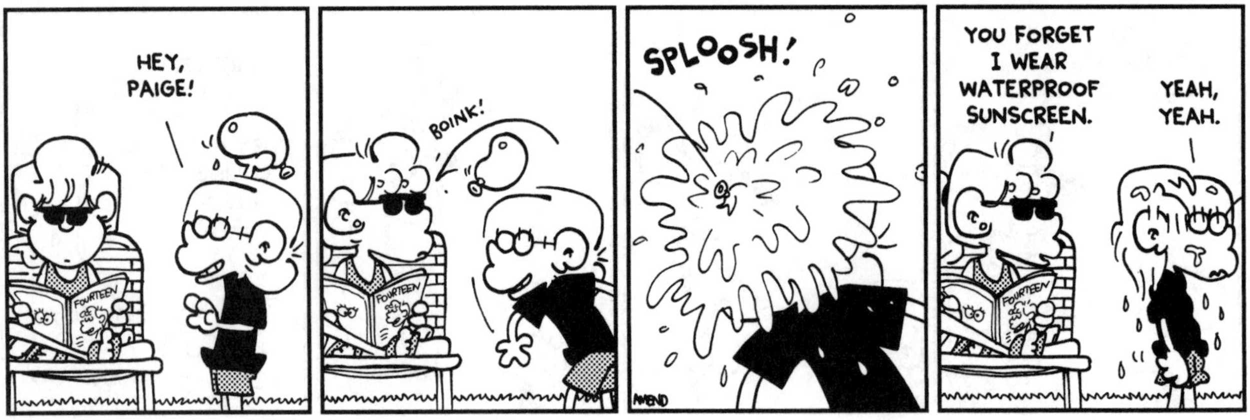
HEY, PAIGE!
FOURTEEN
BOINK!
SPLOOSH!
AMEND
YOU FORGET I WEAR WATERPROOF SUNSCREEN.
YEAH, YEAH.

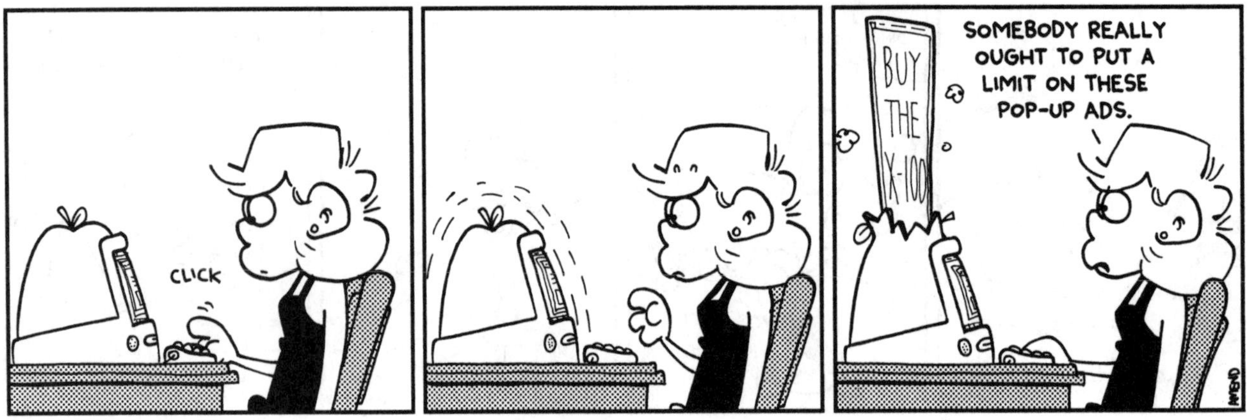
CLICK
BUY THE X-100
SOMEBODY REALLY OUGHT TO PUT A LIMIT ON THESE POP-UP ADS.
AMEND

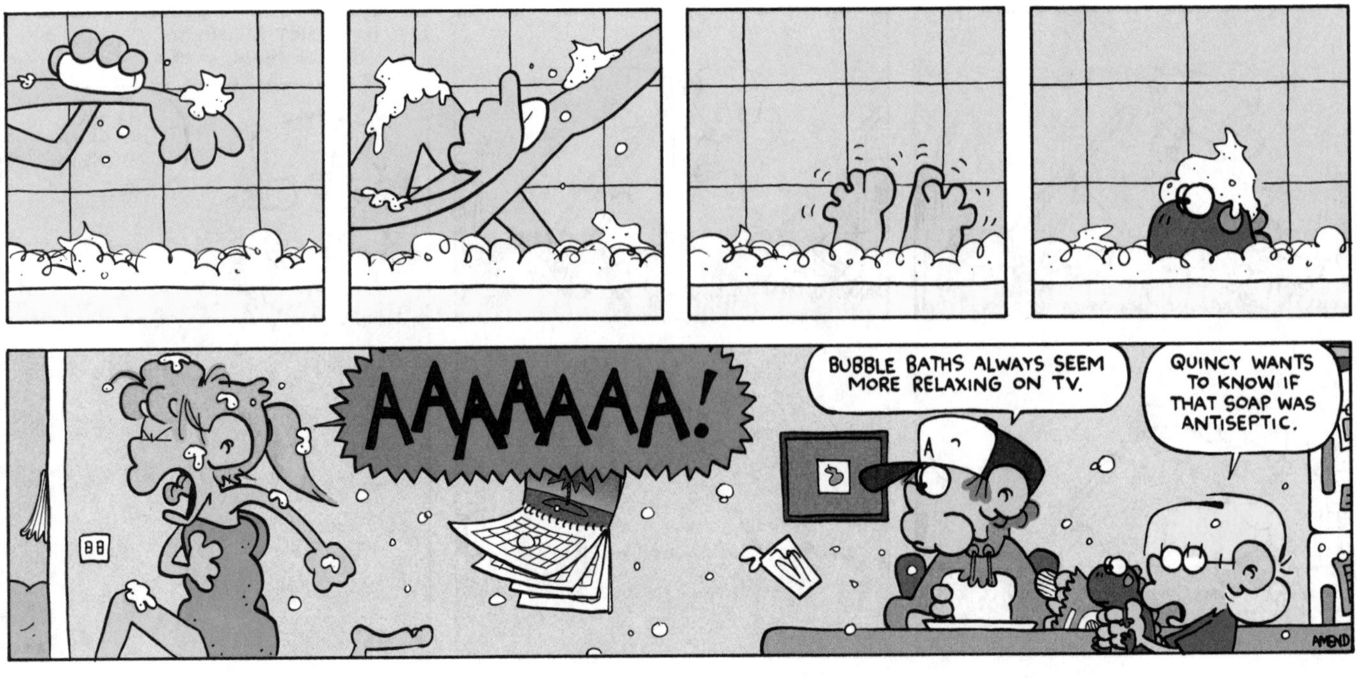
AAAAAAA!
BUBBLE BATHS ALWAYS SEEM MORE RELAXING ON TV.
QUINCY WANTS TO KNOW IF THAT SOAP WAS ANTISEPTIC.
AMEND

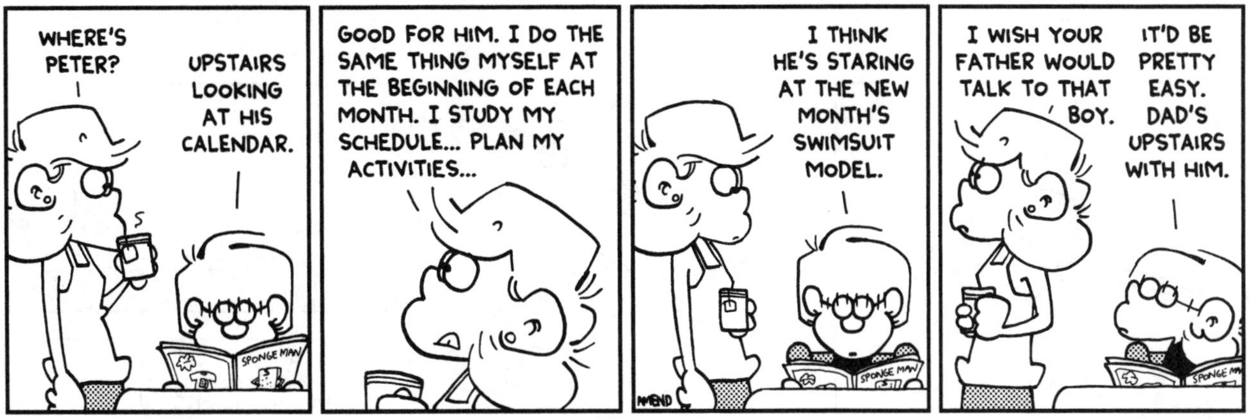
WHERE'S PETER?
UPSTAIRS LOOKING AT HIS CALENDAR.
GOOD FOR HIM. I DO THE SAME THING MYSELF AT THE BEGINNING OF EACH MONTH. I STUDY MY SCHEDULE... PLAN MY ACTIVITIES...
I THINK HE'S STARING AT THE NEW MONTH'S SWIMSUIT MODEL.
I WISH YOUR FATHER WOULD TALK TO THAT BOY.
IT'D BE PRETTY EASY. DAD'S UPSTAIRS WITH HIM.
SPONGE MAN
AMEND

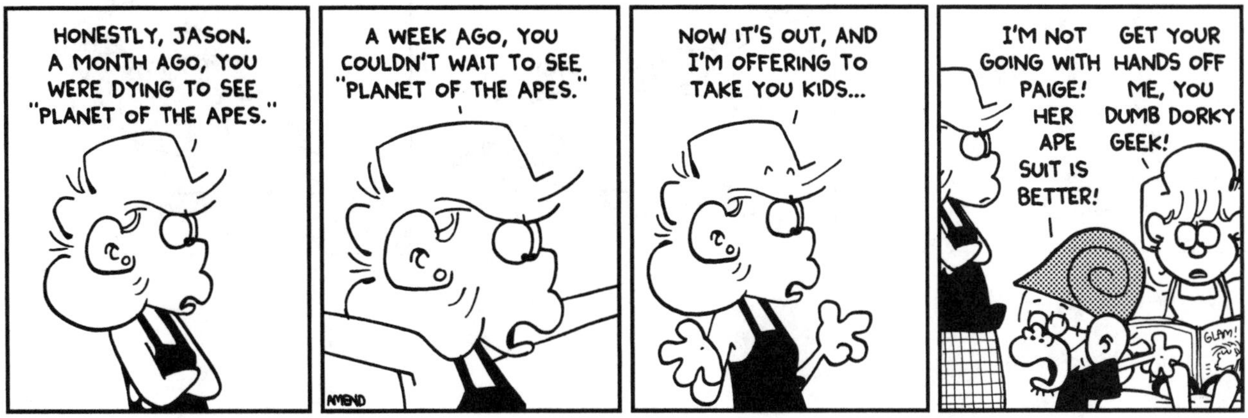
HONESTLY, JASON. A MONTH AGO, YOU WERE DYING TO SEE "PLANET OF THE APES."
A WEEK AGO, YOU COULDN'T WAIT TO SEE "PLANET OF THE APES."
NOW IT'S OUT, AND I'M OFFERING TO TAKE YOU KIDS...
I'M NOT GOING WITH PAIGE! HER APE SUIT IS BETTER!
GET YOUR HANDS OFF ME, YOU DUMB DORKY GEEK!
GLAM!
AMEND

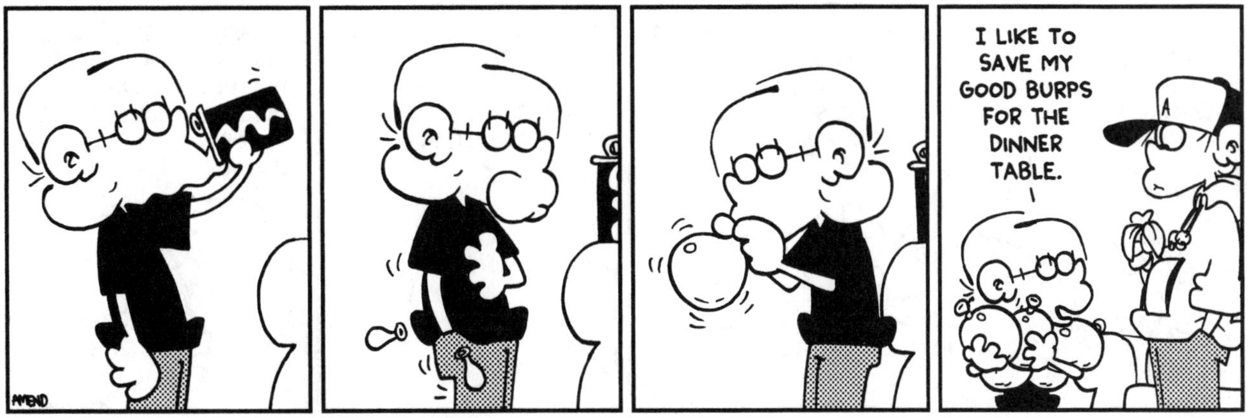
I LIKE TO SAVE MY GOOD BURPS FOR THE DINNER TABLE.
AMEND

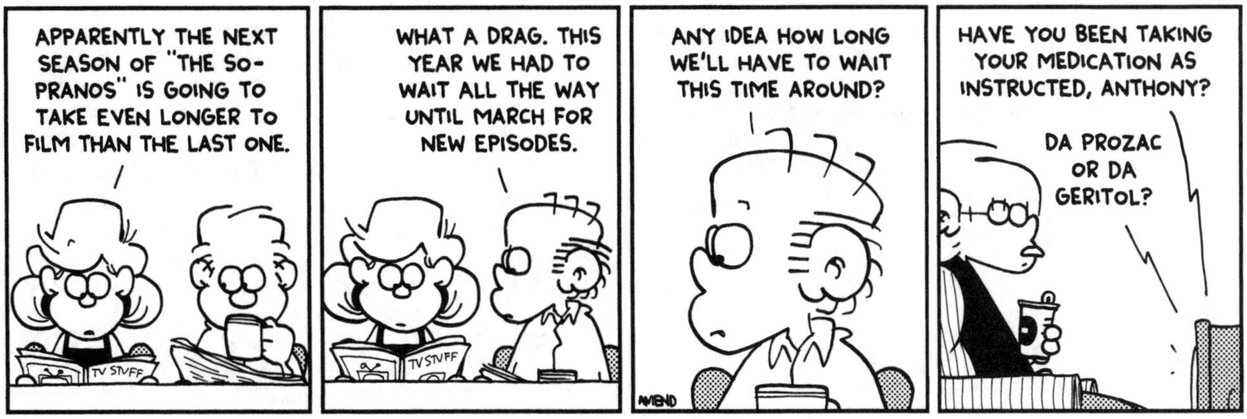
APPARENTLY THE NEXT SEASON OF "THE SOPRANOS" IS GOING TO TAKE EVEN LONGER TO FILM THAN THE LAST ONE.
WHAT A DRAG. THIS YEAR WE HAD TO WAIT ALL THE WAY UNTIL MARCH FOR NEW EPISODES.
ANY IDEA HOW LONG WE'LL HAVE TO WAIT THIS TIME AROUND?
HAVE YOU BEEN TAKING YOUR MEDICATION AS INSTRUCTED, ANTHONY?
DA PROZAC OR DA GERITOL?
TV STUFF
AMEND

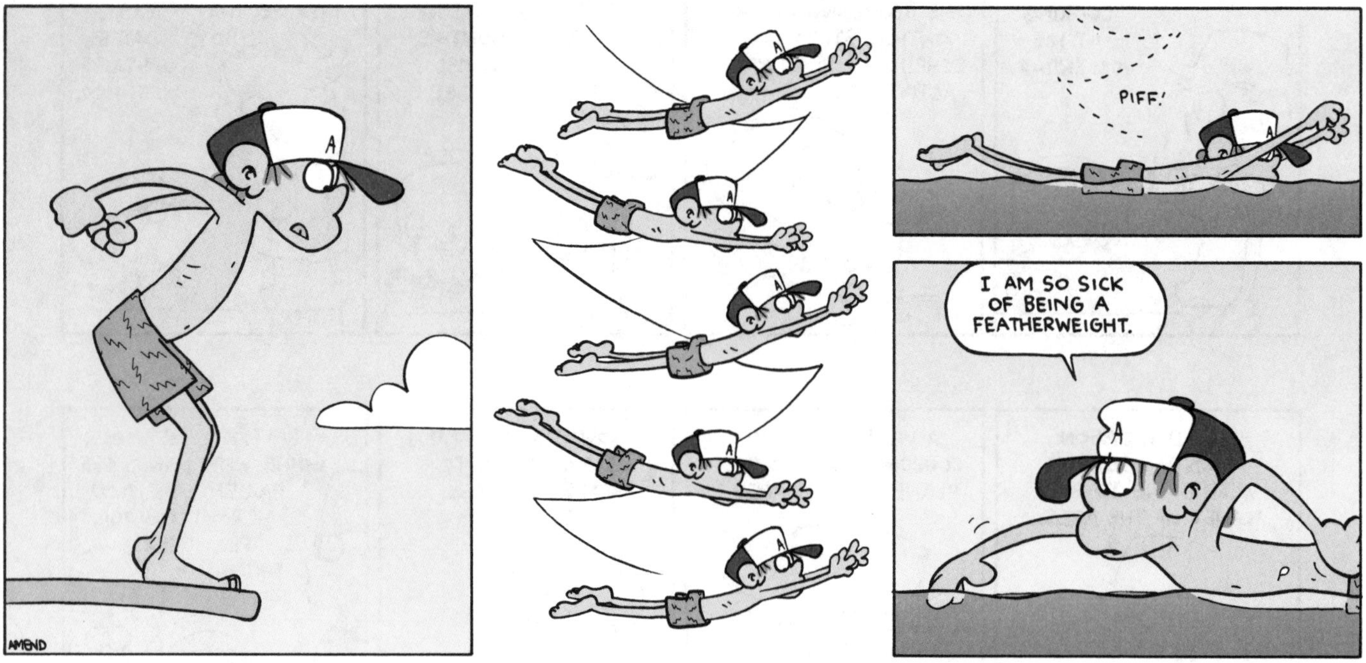
AMEND
PIFF!
I AM SO SICK OF BEING A FEATHERWEIGHT.

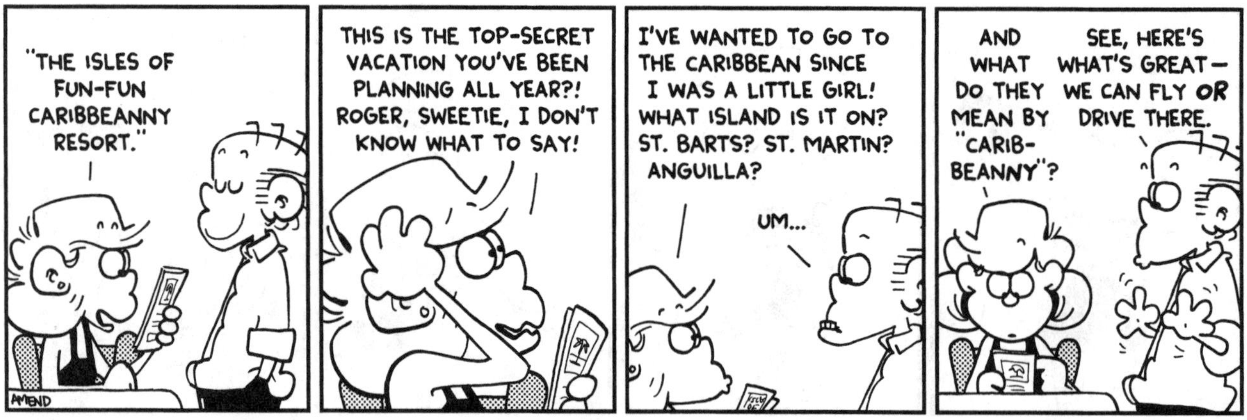
"THE ISLES OF FUN-FUN CARIBBEANNY RESORT."
AMEND
THIS IS THE TOP-SECRET VACATION YOU'VE BEEN PLANNING ALL YEAR?! ROGER, SWEETIE, I DON'T KNOW WHAT TO SAY!
I'VE WANTED TO GO TO THE CARIBBEAN SINCE I WAS A LITTLE GIRL! WHAT ISLAND IS IT ON? ST. BARTS? ST. MARTIN? ANGUILLA?
UM...
AND WHAT DO THEY MEAN BY "CARIB-BEANNY"?
SEE, HERE'S WHAT'S GREAT— WE CAN FLY OR DRIVE THERE.

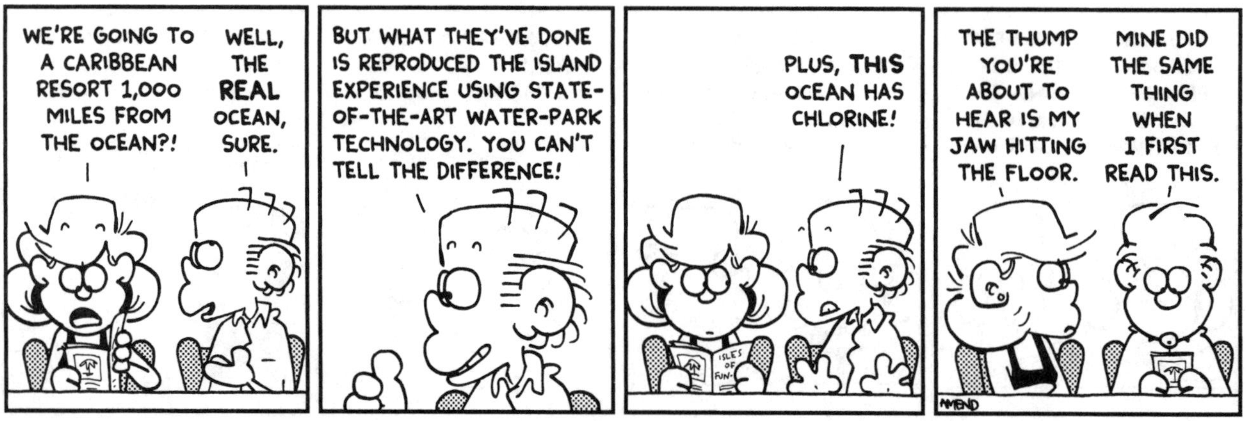
WE'RE GOING TO A CARIBBEAN RESORT 1,000 MILES FROM THE OCEAN?!
WELL, THE REAL OCEAN, SURE.
BUT WHAT THEY'VE DONE IS REPRODUCED THE ISLAND EXPERIENCE USING STATE-OF-THE-ART WATER-PARK TECHNOLOGY. YOU CAN'T TELL THE DIFFERENCE!
PLUS, THIS OCEAN HAS CHLORINE!
ISLES OF FUN-
THE THUMP YOU'RE ABOUT TO HEAR IS MY JAW HITTING THE FLOOR.
MINE DID THE SAME THING WHEN I FIRST READ THIS.
AMEND

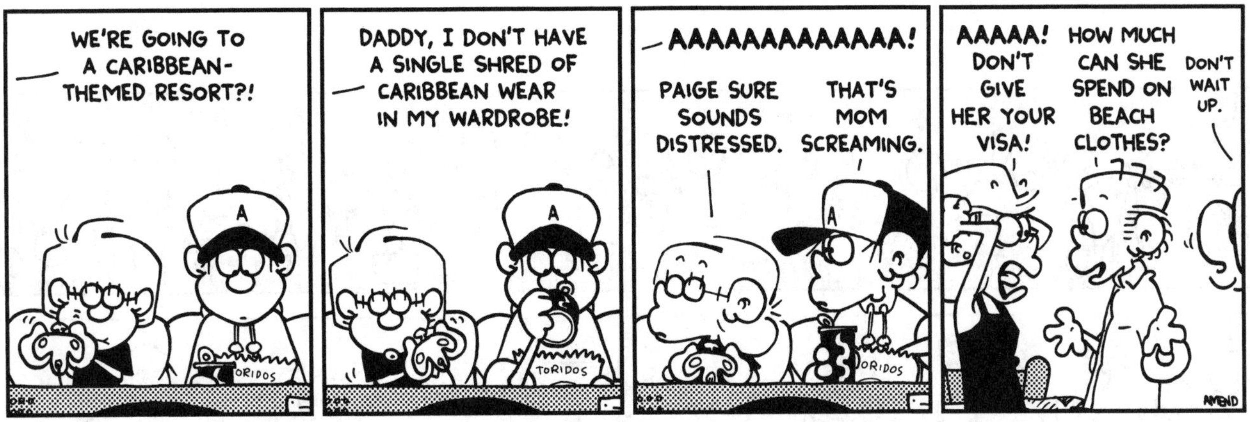
WE'RE GOING TO A CARIBBEAN-THEMED RESORT?!
DADDY, I DON'T HAVE A SINGLE SHRED OF CARIBBEAN WEAR IN MY WARDROBE!
AAAAAAAAAAAAA!
PAIGE SURE SOUNDS DISTRESSED.
THAT'S MOM SCREAMING.
TORIDOS
AAAAA! DON'T GIVE HER YOUR VISA!
HOW MUCH CAN SHE SPEND ON BEACH CLOTHES?
DON'T WAIT UP.
AMEND

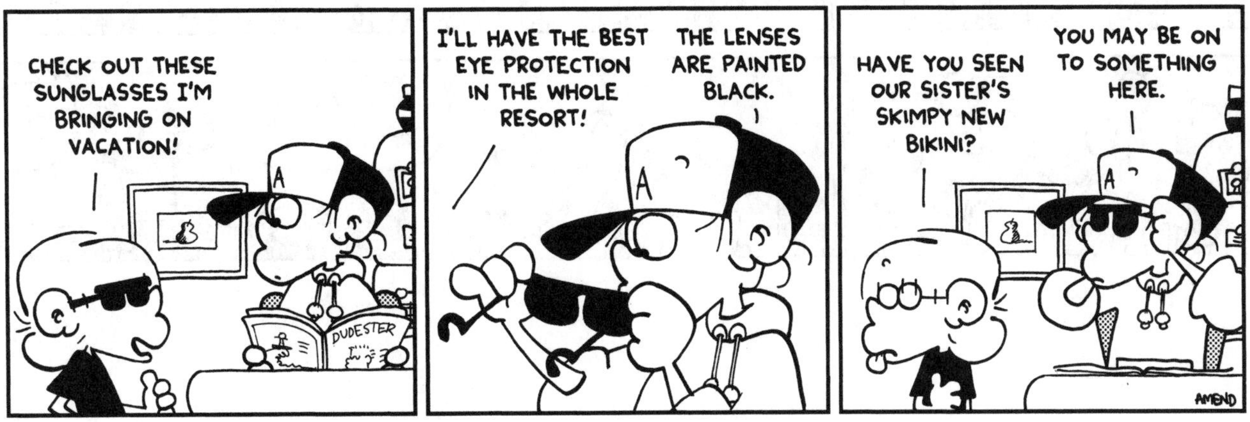
CHECK OUT THESE SUNGLASSES I'M BRINGING ON VACATION!
DUDESTER
I'LL HAVE THE BEST EYE PROTECTION IN THE WHOLE RESORT!
THE LENSES ARE PAINTED BLACK.
HAVE YOU SEEN OUR SISTER'S SKIMPY NEW BIKINI?
YOU MAY BE ON TO SOMETHING HERE.
AMEND

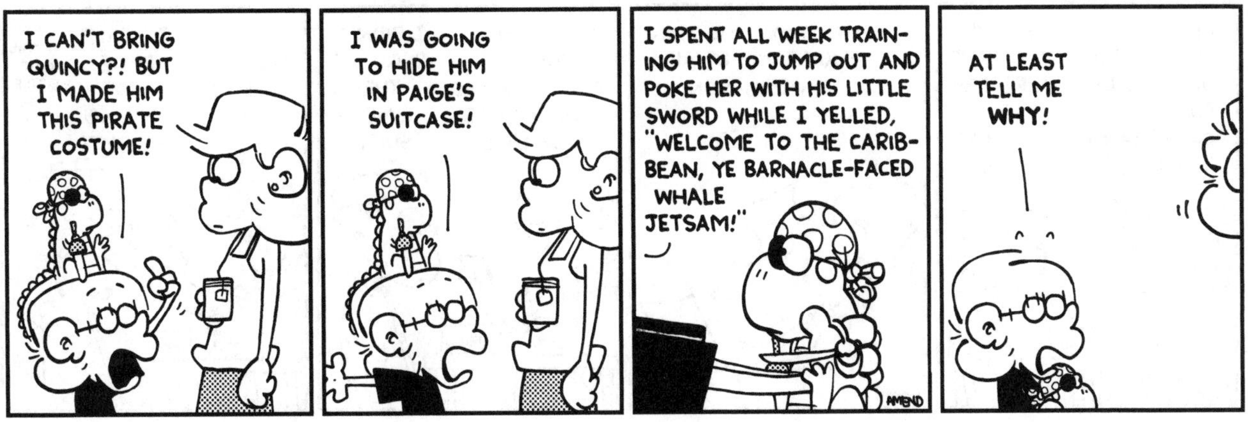
I CAN'T BRING QUINCY?! BUT I MADE HIM THIS PIRATE COSTUME!
I WAS GOING TO HIDE HIM IN PAIGE'S SUITCASE!
I SPENT ALL WEEK TRAINING HIM TO JUMP OUT AND POKE HER WITH HIS LITTLE SWORD WHILE I YELLED, "WELCOME TO THE CARIBBEAN, YE BARNACLE-FACED WHALE JETSAM!"
AMEND
AT LEAST TELL ME WHY!

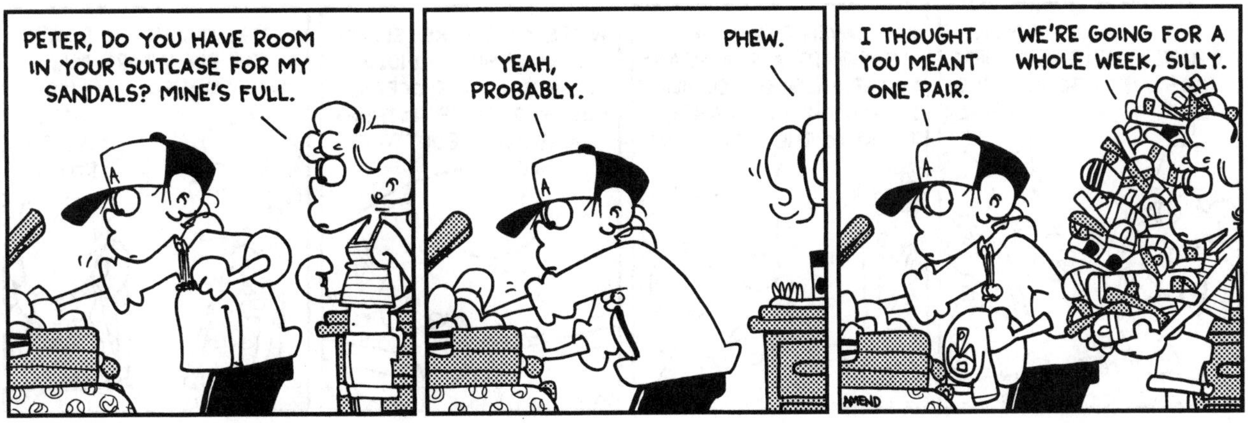
PETER, DO YOU HAVE ROOM IN YOUR SUITCASE FOR MY SANDALS? MINE'S FULL.
YEAH, PROBABLY.
PHEW.
I THOUGHT YOU MEANT ONE PAIR.
WE'RE GOING FOR A WHOLE WEEK, SILLY.
AMEND

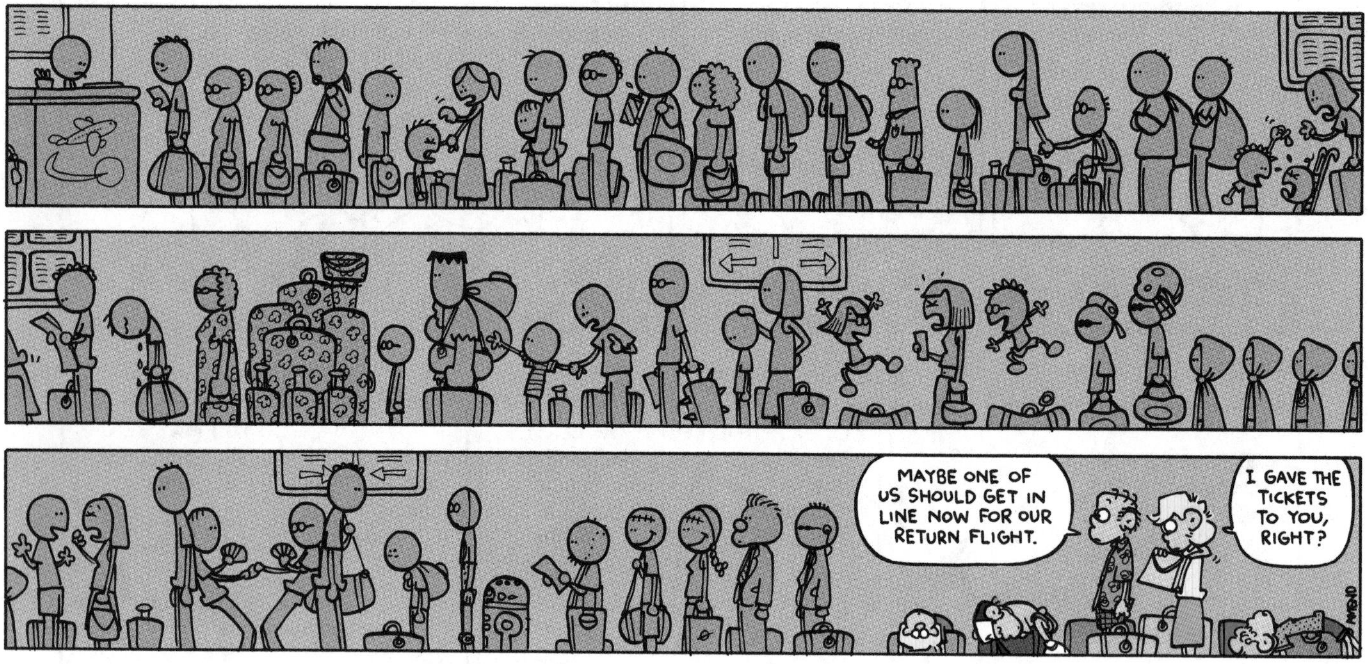
MAYBE ONE OF US SHOULD GET IN LINE NOW FOR OUR RETURN FLIGHT.
I GAVE THE TICKETS TO YOU, RIGHT?
AMEND

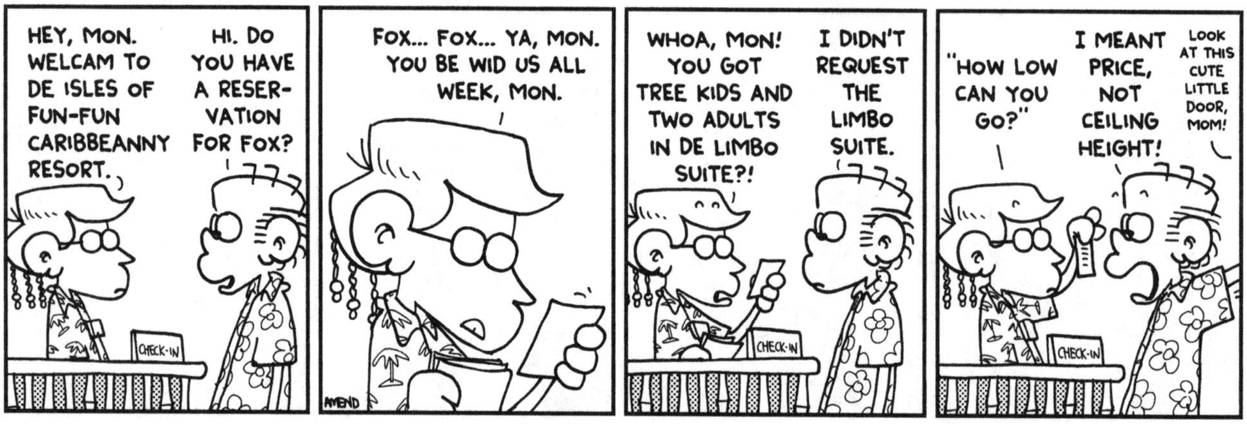
HEY, MON. WELCAM TO DE ISLES OF FUN-FUN CARIBBEANNY RESORT.
HI. DO YOU HAVE A RESERVATION FOR FOX?
CHECK-IN
FOX... FOX... YA, MON. YOU BE WID US ALL WEEK, MON.
AMEND
WHOA, MON! YOU GOT TREE KIDS AND TWO ADULTS IN DE LIMBO SUITE?!
I DIDN'T REQUEST THE LIMBO SUITE.
CHECK-IN
"HOW LOW CAN YOU GO?"
I MEANT PRICE, NOT CEILING HEIGHT!
LOOK AT THIS CUTE LITTLE DOOR, MOM!
CHECK-IN

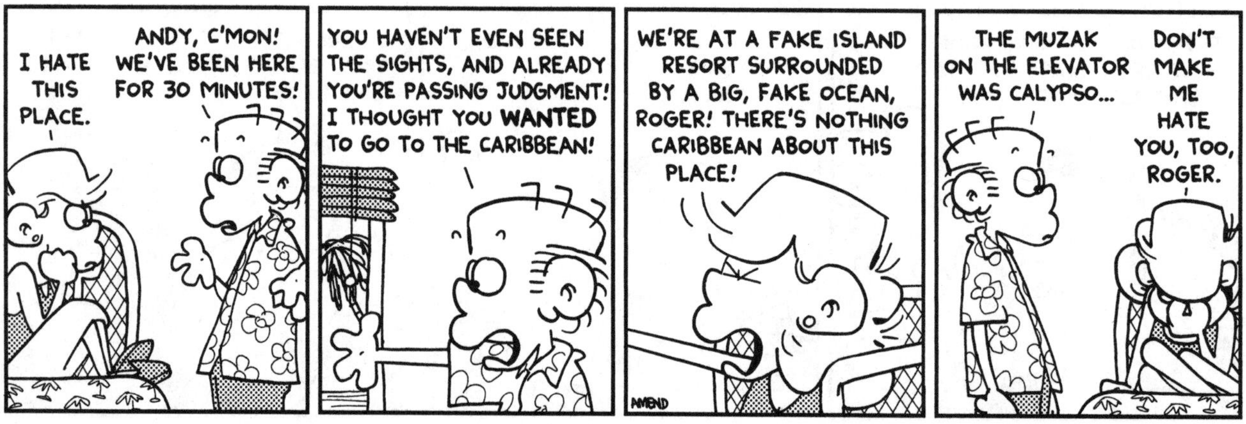
I HATE THIS PLACE.
ANDY, C'MON! WE'VE BEEN HERE FOR 30 MINUTES!
YOU HAVEN'T EVEN SEEN THE SIGHTS, AND ALREADY YOU'RE PASSING JUDGMENT! I THOUGHT YOU WANTED TO GO TO THE CARIBBEAN!
WE'RE AT A FAKE ISLAND RESORT SURROUNDED BY A BIG, FAKE OCEAN, ROGER! THERE'S NOTHING CARIBBEAN ABOUT THIS PLACE!
AMEND
THE MUZAK ON THE ELEVATOR WAS CALYPSO...
DON'T MAKE ME HATE YOU, TOO, ROGER.

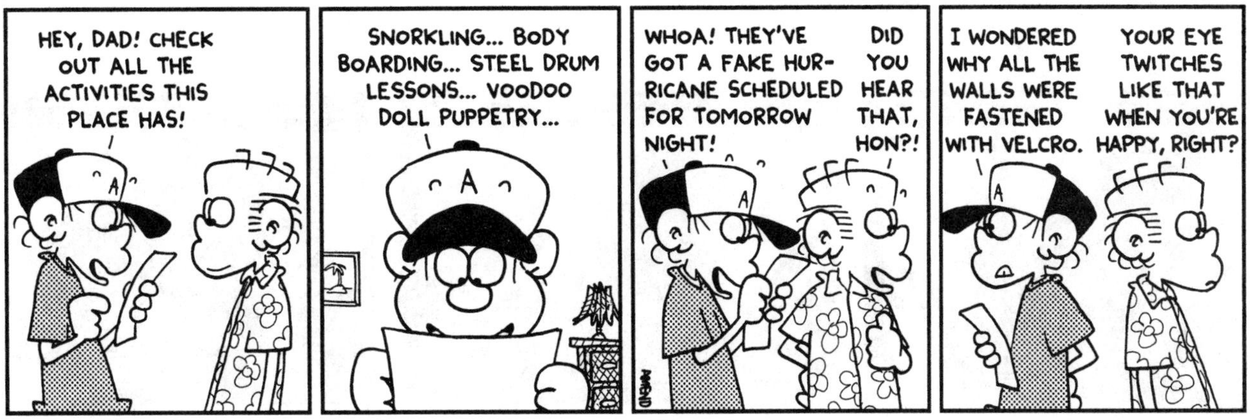
HEY, DAD! CHECK OUT ALL THE ACTIVITIES THIS PLACE HAS!
SNORKLING... BODY BOARDING... STEEL DRUM LESSONS... VOODOO DOLL PUPPETRY...
WHOA! THEY'VE GOT A FAKE HURRICANE SCHEDULED FOR TOMORROW NIGHT!
DID YOU HEAR THAT, HON?!
I WONDERED WHY ALL THE WALLS WERE FASTENED WITH VELCRO.
YOUR EYE TWITCHES LIKE THAT WHEN YOU'RE HAPPY, RIGHT?
AMEND

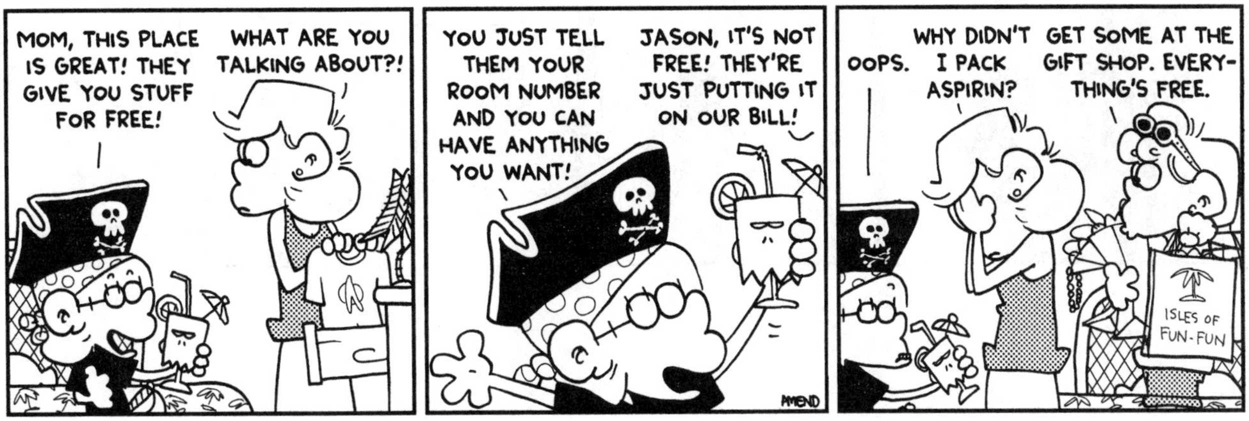
MOM, THIS PLACE IS GREAT! THEY GIVE YOU STUFF FOR FREE!
WHAT ARE YOU TALKING ABOUT?!
YOU JUST TELL THEM YOUR ROOM NUMBER AND YOU CAN HAVE ANYTHING YOU WANT!
JASON, IT'S NOT FREE! THEY'RE JUST PUTTING IT ON OUR BILL!
AMEND
OOPS.
WHY DIDN'T I PACK ASPIRIN?
GET SOME AT THE GIFT SHOP. EVERYTHING'S FREE.
ISLES OF FUN-FUN

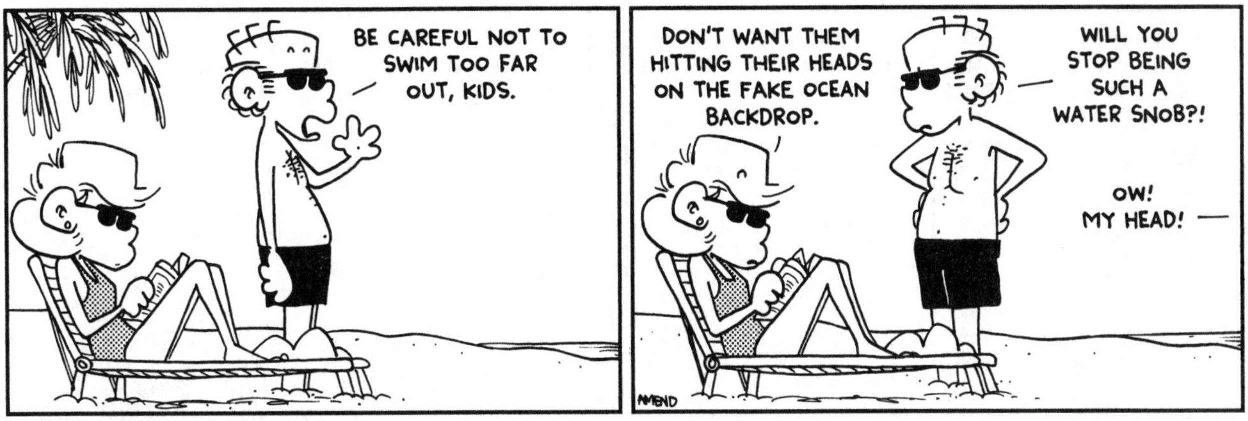
BE CAREFUL NOT TO SWIM TOO FAR OUT, KIDS.
DON'T WANT THEM HITTING THEIR HEADS ON THE FAKE OCEAN BACKDROP.
WILL YOU STOP BEING SUCH A WATER SNOB?!
OW! MY HEAD!
AMEND

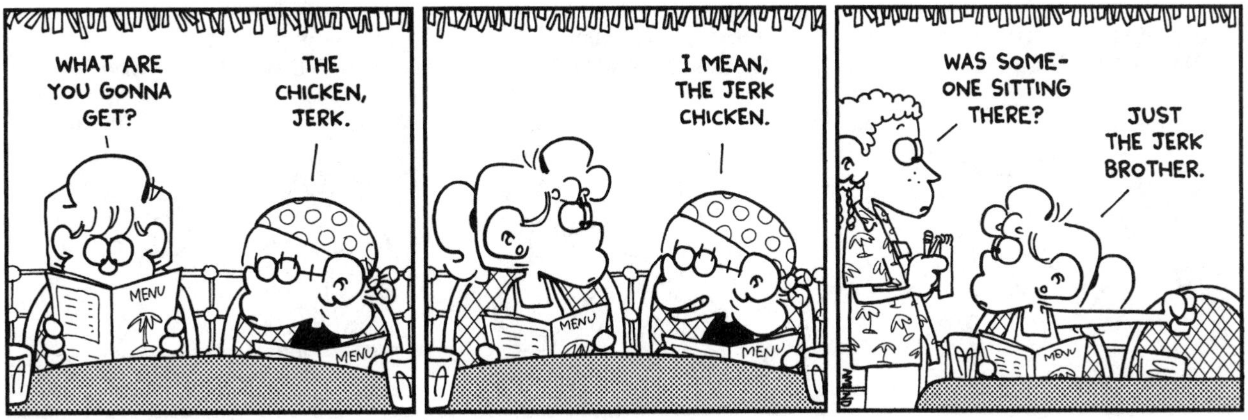
WHAT ARE YOU GONNA GET?
THE CHICKEN, JERK.
MENU
MENU
I MEAN, THE JERK CHICKEN.
MENU
MENU
WAS SOMEONE SITTING THERE?
JUST THE JERK BROTHER.
MENU
AMEND

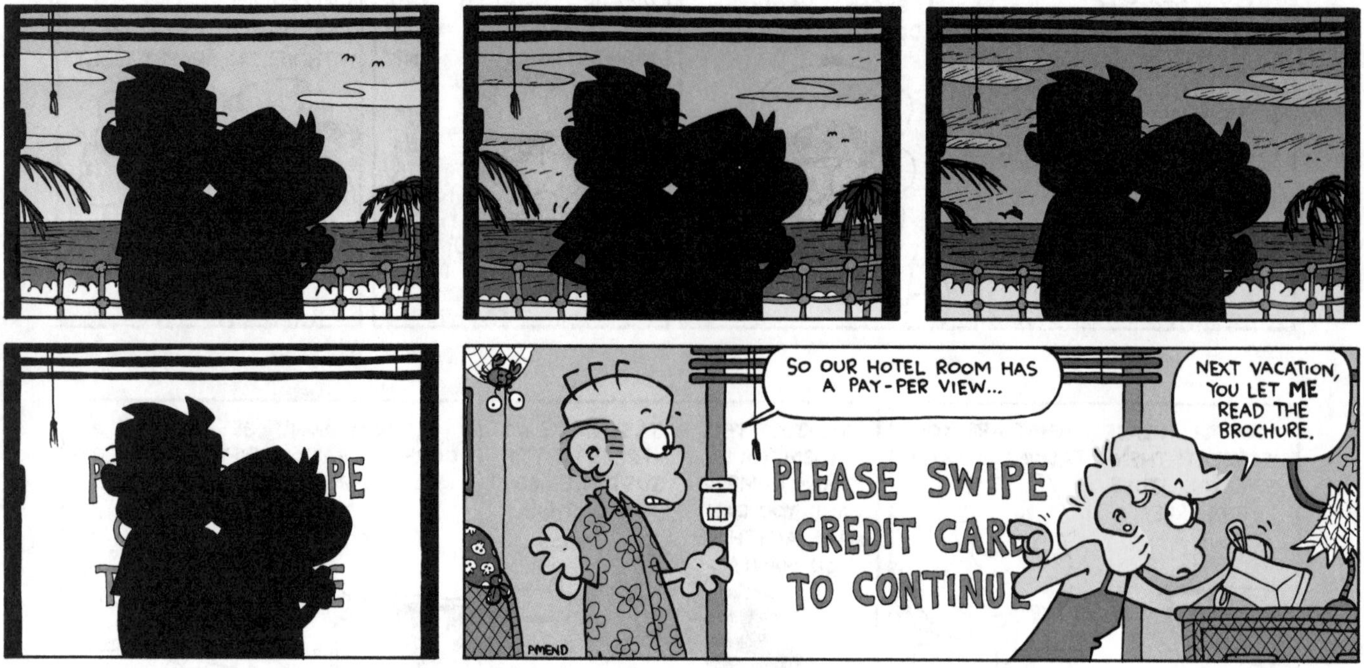
SO OUR HOTEL ROOM HAS A PAY-PER VIEW...
PLEASE SWIPE
CREDIT CAR
TO CONTINU
NEXT VACATION, YOU LET **ME** READ THE BROCHURE.
AMEND

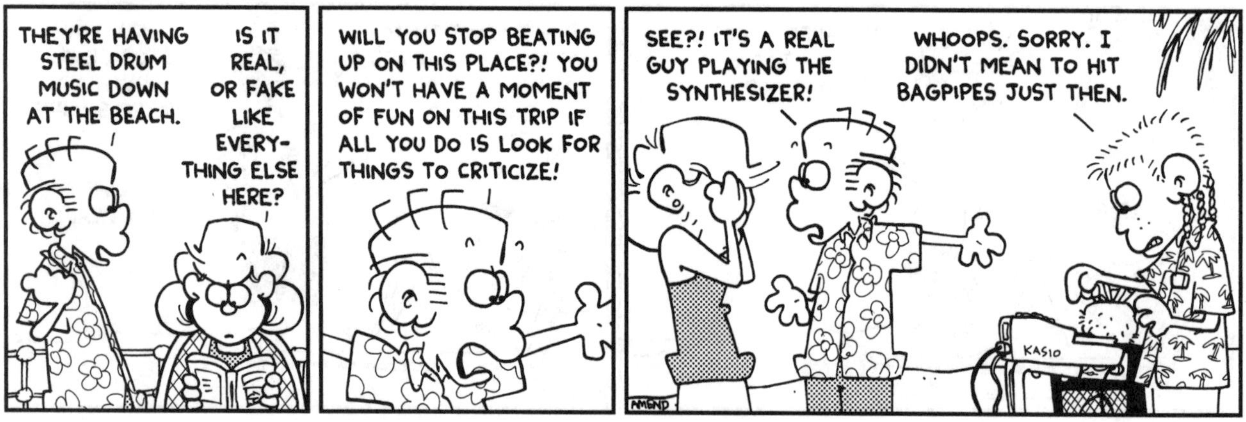
THEY'RE HAVING STEEL DRUM MUSIC DOWN AT THE BEACH.
IS IT REAL, OR FAKE LIKE EVERYTHING ELSE HERE?
WILL YOU STOP BEATING UP ON THIS PLACE?! YOU WON'T HAVE A MOMENT OF FUN ON THIS TRIP IF ALL YOU DO IS LOOK FOR THINGS TO CRITICIZE!
SEE?! IT'S A REAL GUY PLAYING THE SYNTHESIZER!
WHOOPS. SORRY. I DIDN'T MEAN TO HIT BAGPIPES JUST THEN.
KASIO
AMEND

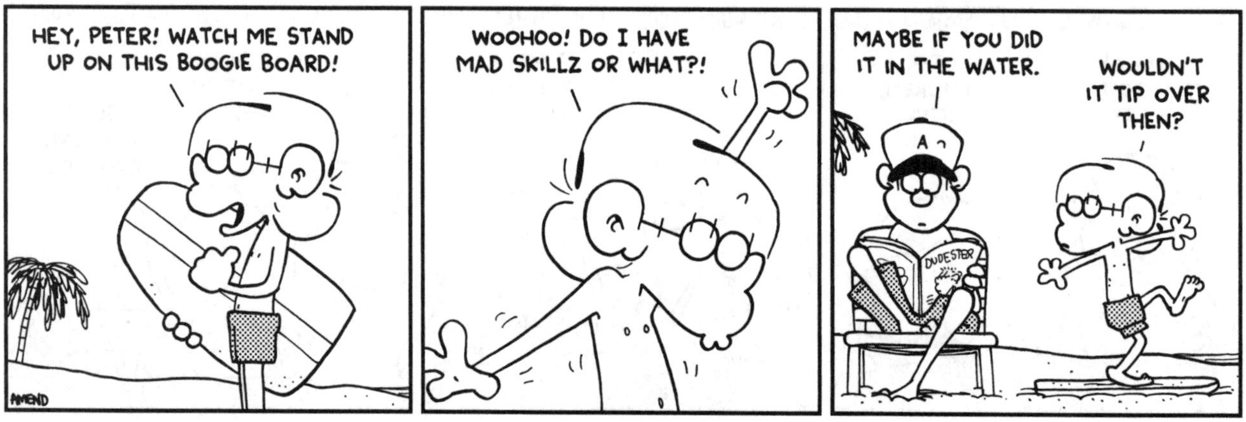
HEY, PETER! WATCH ME STAND UP ON THIS BOOGIE BOARD!
WOOHOO! DO I HAVE MAD SKILLZ OR WHAT?!
MAYBE IF YOU DID IT IN THE WATER.
WOULDN'T IT TIP OVER THEN?
DUDESTER
AMEND

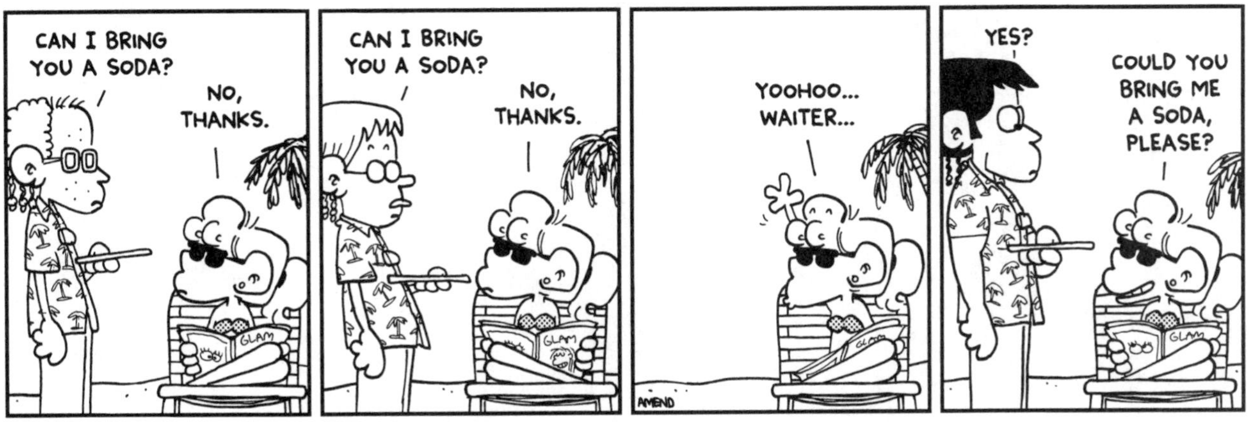
CAN I BRING YOU A SODA?
NO, THANKS.
GLAM
CAN I BRING YOU A SODA?
NO, THANKS.
GLAM
YOOHOO... WAITER...
AMEND
YES?
COULD YOU BRING ME A SODA, PLEASE?
GLAM

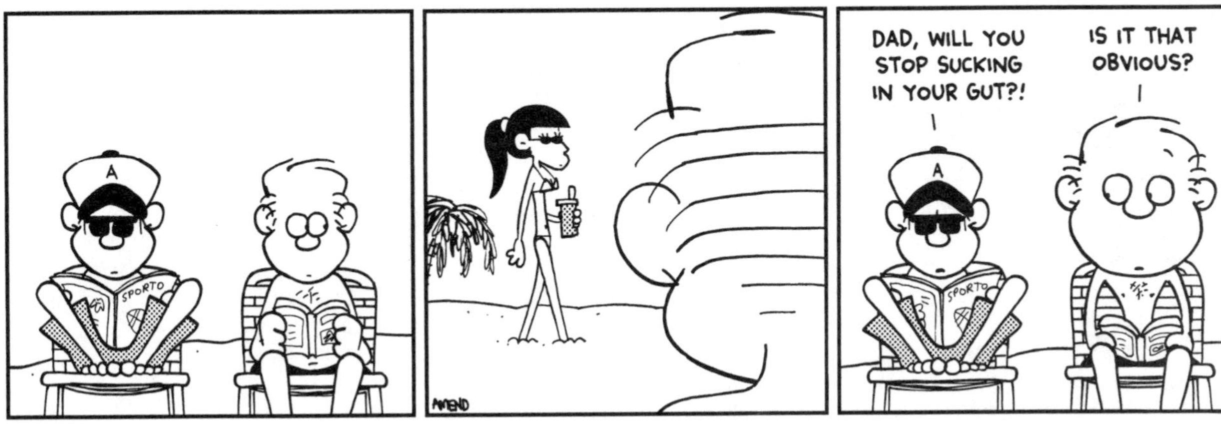
SPORTO
AMEND
DAD, WILL YOU STOP SUCKING IN YOUR GUT?!
IS IT THAT OBVIOUS?
SPORTO

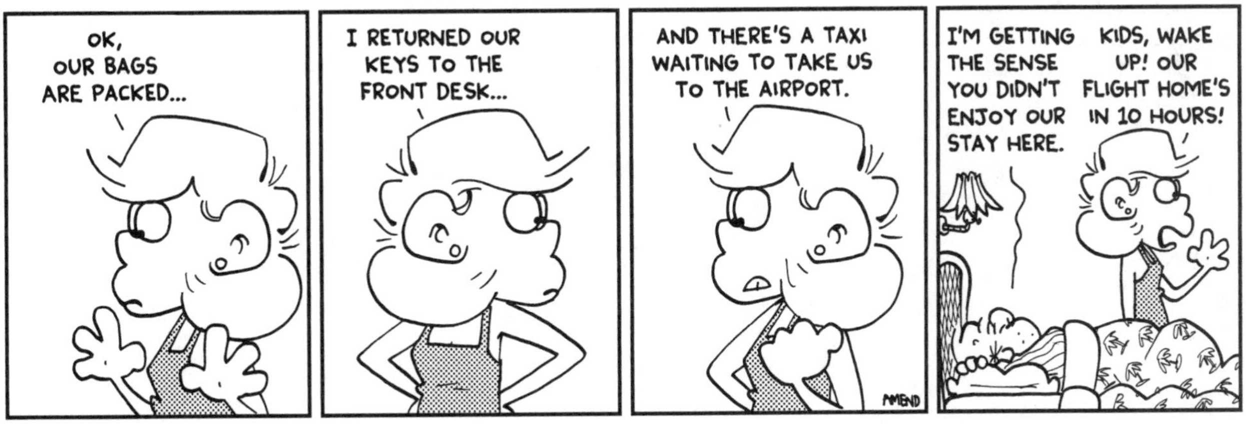
OK, OUR BAGS ARE PACKED...
I RETURNED OUR KEYS TO THE FRONT DESK...
AND THERE'S A TAXI WAITING TO TAKE US TO THE AIRPORT.
AMEND
I'M GETTING THE SENSE YOU DIDN'T ENJOY OUR STAY HERE.
KIDS, WAKE UP! OUR FLIGHT HOME'S IN 10 HOURS!

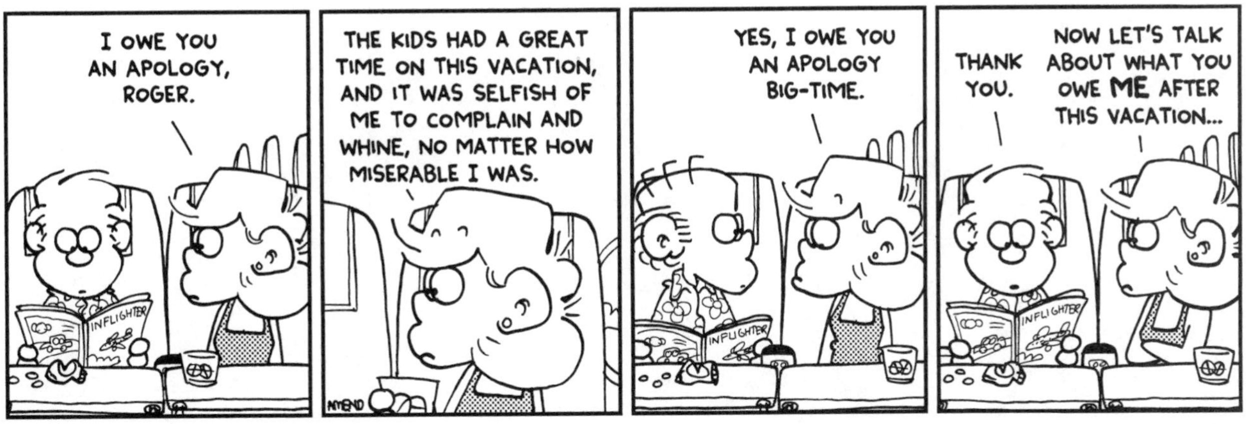
I OWE YOU AN APOLOGY, ROGER.
INFLIGHTER
THE KIDS HAD A GREAT TIME ON THIS VACATION, AND IT WAS SELFISH OF ME TO COMPLAIN AND WHINE, NO MATTER HOW MISERABLE I WAS.
AMEND
YES, I OWE YOU AN APOLOGY BIG-TIME.
INFLIGHTER
THANK YOU.
NOW LET'S TALK ABOUT WHAT YOU OWE ME AFTER THIS VACATION...
INFLIGHTER